Organ Trafficking Prevention in the Healthcare Sector:

Examining the Co-Creation of Cybersecurity Value

Ahgalya Subbiah
https://orcid.org/0009-0006-4427-0872
Management and Science University, Malaysia

Asif Iqbal Hajamydeen
https://orcid.org/0000-0002-5034-1781
Management and Science University, Malaysia

Imran Ademola Adeleke
Lagos State University of Education, Nigeria

IGI Global
Scientific Publishing
Publishing Tomorrow's Research Today

Vice President of Editorial Melissa Wagner
Director of Acquisitions Mikaela Felty
Director of Book Development Jocelynn Hessler
Production Manager Mike Brehm
Cover Design Jose Rosado

Published in the United States of America by
IGI Global Scientific Publishing
701 East Chocolate Avenue
Hershey, PA, 17033, USA
Tel: 717-533-8845 | Fax: 717-533-7115
Website: https://www.igi-global.com E-mail: cust@igi-global.com

Library of Congress Cataloging-in-Publication Data

Names: Subbiah, Ahgalya editor | Hajamydeen, Asif Iqbal editor | Adeleke, Imran Ademola editor
Title: Organ trafficking prevention in the healthcare sector : examining the co-creation of cybersecurity value / Ahgalya Subbiah, Asif Iqbal Hajamydeen, Imran Ademola Adeleke.
Description: Hershey, PA : IGI Global Scientific Publishing, [2026] | Includes bibliographical references and index. | Summary: "This book explores how co-creation strategies in cybersecurity can be used to protect private health information and stop organ trafficking in the healthcare industry"-- Provided by publisher.
Identifiers: LCCN 2025052873 (print) | LCCN 2025052874 (ebook) | ISBN 9798337366968 hardcover | ISBN 9798337366975 paperback | ISBN 9798337366982 ebook
Subjects: LCSH: Organ trafficking--Prevention--Case studies | Medicine--Data processing--Security measures--Case studies
Classification: LCC HV6627 .O74 2026 (print) | LCC HV6627 (ebook)
LC record available at https://lccn.loc.gov/2025052873
LC ebook record available at https://lccn.loc.gov/2025052874

British Cataloguing in Publication Data
A Cataloguing in Publication record for this book is available from the British Library.

Table of Contents

Detailed Table of Contents

This chapter explores the crucial responsibility of strengthening cybersecurity measures within the ever-changing context of contemporary healthcare systems. As digitalization gets ingrained in healthcare practices, sensitive medical data becomes increasingly vulnerable to cyber-attacks. The healthcare industry is undergoing a rapid digital transformation, with increasing reliance on internet-enabled services and devices such as electronic health records (EHRs), telemedicine, IoT devices, and cloud-based solutions. While these advancements enhance patient care and operational efficiency, they also introduce significant cybersecurity vulnerabilities for criminals, industrial saboteurs, and extortionists to exploit. Healthcare is an attractive target for cybercrime for two fundamental reasons: it is a rich source of valuable data and its defences are weak as the COVID-19 pandemic exposed critical vulnerabilities in global healthcare systems, particularly in data security and interoperability.

The rapid evolution of digital technologies has intensified cyber threats, leaving individuals, organizations, and critical infrastructures increasingly vulnerable. Traditional, isolated cybersecurity approaches are no longer sufficient. Consequently, collaborative cybersecurity and co-creation have emerged as vital strategies that unite the strengths of diverse stakeholders. Yet, efforts remain fragmented due to low trust, poor coordination, and unequal capacities, especially in regions with weak regulatory systems and scarce resources. This chapter examines the roles of governments, private-sectors, academia, civil society, and end users in advancing collaborative cybersecurity. Drawing from literature, policies, and case studies, it

options like the ability to track transactions through Etherscan provide patients with more transparency. OrganChain as well assures a significant decrease in wait time and provides viable organs in time. Future enhancements are an expansion of availability via mobile apps.

Dark Web serves as a primary marketplace where traffickers promote victims and organs, organize logistics, anonymize financial transactions, and move these illegal operations from hidden digital forums to real world medical institutions. An analysis of cybersecurity challenges presented particularly how sophisticated cybercrime tactics undermine existing healthcare security protocols and supply chain integrity. Effective prevention requires shifting from reactive defense to proactive cyber-intelligence by applying advanced monitoring techniques to map the digital footprints of human trafficking operations on the Dark Web, healthcare entities, cybersecurity providers, and law enforcement can create substantial cybersecurity value. This framework involves developing protocols to quickly identify, intercept, and report suspicious digital transactions that indicate organ exploitation, thereby strengthening hospital networks and protecting vulnerable populations from this evil trade. This analysis offers insights into a comprehensive strategy for organ trafficking prevention.

Organ trafficking threatens healthcare security, ethical medical practice, and public trust by exploiting governance and data gaps within health systems. Digital government offers mechanisms to strengthen healthcare security through improved data integration, cybersecurity, and inter-agency coordination. This chapter examines how digital government can reinforce healthcare security in Malaysia by mapping theoretical, empirical, and methodological gaps that limit efforts to prevent organ trafficking. It highlights the need for coordinated governance and co-creation of cybersecurity value among key stakeholders.

This study investigates the key cybersecurity factors that contribute to online vulnerabilities among children in Peninsular Malaysia, using a qualitative approach involving six key informants from relevant government agencies. The findings highlight that peer influence, exposure to unsafe digital practices, and lack of awareness are major contributors to children's psychological and behavioural risks online. Additionally, individual factors—such as excessive screen time, unsupervised Internet access, and limited digital literacy—further increase susceptibility to threats including privacy breaches, online manipulation, and harmful content. The study emphasises the urgent need for strengthened parental guidance, digital safety education, and coordinated cybersecurity strategies to enhance children's resilience and ensure safer online engagement.

In the 21st century, rapid technological advancements have transformed human life, but excessive Internet use among children has led to rising concerns of addiction, including cybersex addiction. Statistics show that 93% of boys and 62% of girls are exposed to online pornography before age 18, highlighting serious risks. This study explores the psychological and physical impacts of cybersex addiction on Malaysian children through the perspectives of government agencies. Using a qualitative approach, in-depth interviews were conducted with six representatives from the Royal Malaysian Police, LPPKN, KPWKM, MCMC, and hospitals. Findings reveal that individual factors, peer influence, and technological accessibility contribute to psychological harm, while individual and peer factors also drive physical damage such as poor health and neglect. In conclusion, a collective effort from parents, educators, and policymakers is essential to foster awareness, provide protection, and ensure children's holistic well-being and future prosperity.

Incest in Malaysian families is a rising concern requiring multidisciplinary attention. This study examines the link between pornography addiction and incest through a cyberpsychology lens. Findings show that easy access to victims within the family, combined with the offender's pornography addiction, increases the risk of sexual crimes. Repeated exposure to incest-themed content normalizes taboo behaviour and fuels arousal that may later be acted upon. During the COVID-19 MCO, confinement and increased internet use further escalated such risks. Pornography addiction amplifies offender motivation, aligning with the Routine Activity Theory. The study recommends digital content regulation, media literacy, addiction treatment, and stronger cybersecurity policies to curb incest cases in Malaysia.

Foreword

Healthcare has always been grounded in a simple yet profound principle: the preservation of human life and dignity. From the earliest traditions of medicine to the sophisticated clinical systems of today, the trust placed in healthcare institutions rests upon their ethical commitment to protect the vulnerable. In the twenty-first century, however, that responsibility extends beyond the physical walls of hospitals into the invisible architectures of digital systems that store, transmit, and analyse patient information. As healthcare undergoes rapid digital transformation, its dependence on interconnected data infrastructures has become both its strength and its vulnerability. Electronic health records, artificial intelligence assisted diagnostics, blockchain registries, and cross-border data platforms have redefined efficiency and accessibility. Yet these same systems, if inadequately governed, can expose patients to new forms of exploitation. In this context, cybersecurity is not a peripheral technical function it is integral to the ethical foundation of modern medicine.

Organ Trafficking Prevention in the Healthcare Sector: Examining the Co-Creation of Cybersecurity Value addresses this reality with scholarly depth and moral clarity. The volume advances an important proposition: that cybersecurity within healthcare must be understood as a co-created value, emerging through sustained collaboration among technologists, clinicians, policymakers, regulators, and civil society. This conceptual shift moves beyond reactive defence strategies and toward an integrated governance model rooted in accountability, transparency, and shared responsibility. The chapters collectively demonstrate how advanced technologies ranging from AI-driven anomaly detection and automated cyber defence systems to blockchain-enabled organ traceability can be strategically deployed to disrupt illicit networks and strengthen institutional resilience. At the same time, the contributors maintain a critical awareness of the ethical complexities that accompany such tools. Questions of algorithmic bias, explainability, regulatory compliance, and human oversight are treated as central considerations rather than afterthoughts.

Particularly noteworthy is the book's interdisciplinary scope. By linking digital health governance to organ trafficking prevention, child online vulnerability, and broader socio-economic inequities, the volume situates cybersecurity within a wider ecosystem of structural risk. This integrative perspective underscores a fundamental truth: technological safeguards alone cannot secure healthcare systems. Sustainable protection requires principled leadership, institutional integrity, and a culture of trust. This work will be of considerable value to scholars and practitioners in cybersecurity, health informatics, public policy, and human rights. It provides both conceptual frameworks and applied insights, encouraging readers to rethink how digital infrastructures are designed and governed. More importantly, it reinforces the ethical imperative that underpins healthcare itself that systems intended to heal must never become channels for harm.

In advancing the discourse on cybersecurity value co-creation, this volume offers a timely and significant contribution to contemporary scholarship. It reminds us that safeguarding digital health systems ultimately means safeguarding humanity.

Othman bin Ibrahim
Universiti Teknologi Malaysia, Malaysia

Preface

INTRODUCTION

In an era defined by rapid digital transformation, healthcare systems stand at the intersection of innovation, vulnerability, and profound ethical responsibility. The digitization of medical records, the integration of artificial intelligence into diagnostics and decision-making, and the expansion of interconnected health infrastructures have revolutionized patient care. Yet these advancements also expose healthcare institutions to increasingly sophisticated cyberthreats—threats that extend beyond data breaches to implicate fundamental human rights and societal trust.

This volume, *Organ Trafficking Prevention in the Healthcare Sector: Examining the Co-Creation of Cybersecurity Value*, emerges from the recognition that patient data security is no longer solely a technical concern. It is a moral, legal, and societal imperative. The secure handling of private health information safeguards not only clinical outcomes and operational efficiency but also human dignity. In contexts where data vulnerabilities can be exploited by illicit networks—including those engaged in human and organ trafficking—the stakes become even higher. Digital insecurity can inadvertently enable real-world harm.

The chapters assembled in this edited reference work explore an urgent and complex question: how can collaborative, ethically grounded, and AI-enabled cybersecurity strategies help protect patient data while simultaneously disrupting illegal global networks? We approach cybersecurity not merely as a defensive mechanism, but as a co-created value—one that emerges through the coordinated efforts of policymakers, healthcare professionals, technologists, legal scholars, and civil society actors. Robust digital health ecosystems depend on this shared responsibility.

Contributors to this volume provide empirical research, ethical analysis, and forward-looking perspectives that illuminate the connections between data governance and broader societal risks. They examine how secure information systems, transparent regulatory frameworks, and interdisciplinary collaboration can strengthen trust and accountability within healthcare institutions. By situating cybersecurity within the broader discourse of public health, human rights, and policy studies, the book underscores the necessity of integrated solutions to complex global challenges.

A central theme throughout this work is trust—trust in technological systems, trust in institutional governance, and trust in the ethical commitments of healthcare providers. Without such trust, digital innovation cannot fulfill its promise. With it, healthcare systems can not only protect sensitive information but also actively resist exploitation and criminal activity that prey on vulnerable populations.

This book is intended for a diverse and interdisciplinary audience. Professionals and researchers in cybersecurity, health informatics, digital ethics, and human rights will find theoretical frameworks and applied case studies that deepen understanding of the co-creation of cybersecurity value. Healthcare administrators and IT managers responsible for data protection and regulatory compliance will encounter practical insights for strengthening institutional resilience. Policymakers and legal professionals engaged in developing cybersecurity and human rights frameworks will gain perspectives that bridge governance and technological design. Graduate students and educators will discover a foundation for critical inquiry into the ethical and societal implications of digital health systems.

As editors, we believe that safeguarding patient data is inseparable from safeguarding human dignity. Preventing organ trafficking and related forms of exploitation requires not only law enforcement and policy reform, but also secure, accountable, and ethically designed digital infrastructures. By bringing together interdisciplinary voices, this volume aims to contribute meaningfully to the creation of safe, moral, and human-centered digital health systems.

We invite readers to engage critically with the ideas presented here and to join in advancing collaborative solutions that strengthen cybersecurity while upholding the highest principles of healthcare ethics and human rights.

ORGANIZATION OF THE BOOK

In **Chapter 1**, the contributors lay the foundation for this volume by examining the expanding risk landscape of digital healthcare. As electronic health records, telemedicine, IoT-enabled devices, and cloud platforms become embedded in clinical practice, the sector's exposure to cybercrime intensifies. The chapter underscores why healthcare has become a prime target: it holds high-value data and often operates with uneven or under-resourced defenses—vulnerabilities starkly revealed during the COVID-19 pandemic. By situating cybersecurity within an ethical framework, the authors argue that protecting health data is not simply a technical necessity but a moral obligation central to patient safety, institutional trust, and human rights.

Chapter 2 advances the discussion by moving from isolated defense strategies toward collaborative cybersecurity and value co-creation. The authors demonstrate that governments, private industry, academia, civil society, and end users each hold essential roles in strengthening digital resilience. Yet fragmentation, low trust, and regulatory inconsistency undermine collective action, particularly in regions with limited resources. Through policy analysis and case studies, the chapter shows that sustainable cybersecurity depends on inclusive governance, transparent information sharing, and trust-based partnerships that bridge institutional and geographic divides.

In **Chapter 3**, the volume turns explicitly to organ trafficking prevention through a multi-layered cybersecurity framework tailored to healthcare systems. Introducing blockchain-based organ tracking, AI-driven anomaly detection, secure patient registries, and advanced encryption protocols, the authors present empirical evidence of significant reductions in unauthorized access and suspicious activity. The framework demonstrates how cybersecurity value co-creation—grounded in cross-border collaboration and regulatory compliance—can transform digital health infrastructures into proactive safeguards against illicit transplant networks.

Chapter 4 explores Automated Cyber Defense (ACD) as a response to the scale and speed of modern cyber threats. With ransomware, data breaches, and system sabotage targeting healthcare institutions, automation emerges as a critical resilience mechanism. The chapter offers a comprehensive analysis of AI- and machine learning-driven defense systems, security orchestration, and real-time threat response. Importantly, it situates automation within regulatory and ethical considerations, ensuring that patient safety and privacy remain paramount as systems become more technologically sophisticated.

In **Chapter 5**, the authors focus on AI-driven cybersecurity tools designed specifically to detect patterns linked to organ trafficking networks. By identifying anomalies in electronic health records and predicting insider threats, AI becomes a strategic instrument for preserving data integrity. Drawing on real-world cases such as the Jeevandan Program in Hyderabad and Kenya's Mediheal Hospital, the chapter emphasizes the necessity of transparent, accountable, and ethically governed AI systems. The proposed co-creation framework integrates clinicians, technologists, and policymakers to strengthen trust while disrupting criminal exploitation.

Chapter 6 deepens the ethical inquiry by examining the implications of algorithmic bias and the ethical deployment of AI in healthcare cybersecurity. Anchored in principles of accountability, explainability, and justice, the chapter advances an "ethical-by-design" model that integrates moral reasoning directly into cybersecurity architectures. By adopting a socio-technical and co-creative approach, the authors argue that embedding ethical intelligence within digital defenses elevates cybersecurity from reactive protection to proactive moral stewardship—safeguarding both human life and institutional legitimacy.

Chapter 7 explores human–AI synergy in oncology as a model for ethically aligned clinical intelligence. While AI-powered systems—using convolutional neural networks, Grad-CAM interpretability tools, and human-in-the-loop validation—improve diagnostic accuracy and precision medicine, the authors caution against full automation. By emphasizing clinician oversight and ethical safeguards, the chapter demonstrates how human expertise and machine intelligence can work collaboratively to enhance patient care while maintaining data privacy and trust—principles equally vital to organ trafficking prevention.

In **Chapter 8**, the authors introduce OrganChain, a blockchain-based organ donation platform designed to create transparency, traceability, and accountability in transplant processes. By integrating donors, recipients, hospitals, and medical professionals within a unified system governed by smart contracts, OrganChain reduces manual errors and opportunities for malpractice. Its immutable ledger and user-friendly interface empower stakeholders while significantly reducing wait times and enhancing verification. The chapter illustrates how blockchain technologies can operationalize ethical governance within organ allocation systems.

Chapter 9 shifts the lens to the digital underworld, tracing how organ trafficking networks exploit Dark Web forums to coordinate logistics, anonymize payments, and infiltrate legitimate hospital systems. The authors argue for a transition from reactive defense to proactive cyber-intelligence strategies capable of mapping digital footprints and intercepting suspicious transactions. By aligning healthcare entities, cybersecurity providers, and law enforcement, the chapter presents a comprehensive interception framework that strengthens institutional defenses and disrupts exploitation before harm occurs.

Chapter 10 situates the conversation within the context of digital government, examining Malaysia's efforts to address organ trafficking through improved governance and data integration. By mapping theoretical, empirical, and methodological gaps, the authors reveal the limitations that hinder coordinated prevention efforts. The chapter underscores the importance of inter-agency collaboration, integrated cybersecurity strategies, and policy coherence in reinforcing healthcare security and restoring public trust.

Chapter 11 broadens the scope to examine online vulnerabilities among children in Peninsular Malaysia. Through qualitative insights from government stakeholders, the study identifies peer influence, unsafe digital practices, and limited digital literacy as key risk factors. Excessive screen time and unsupervised internet access compound exposure to privacy breaches and harmful content. The chapter calls for strengthened parental guidance, digital education, and coordinated cybersecurity strategies to build resilience among younger populations—an essential foundation for long-term digital safety.

In **Chapter 12**, the government's perspective on cybersex addiction among Malaysian children is explored through interviews with representatives from law enforcement, communications authorities, healthcare institutions, and family development agencies. The findings reveal the psychological and physical harms associated with excessive online exposure and highlight the roles of peer dynamics and technological accessibility. The chapter advocates collective intervention—uniting parents, educators, and policymakers—to protect children's well-being in an increasingly digital society.

Chapter 13 examines pornography addiction as a catalyst for incest through a cyberpsychological lens. The authors analyze how repeated exposure to incest-themed content normalizes deviant behavior and increases offender motivation, particularly during periods of confinement such as the COVID-19 Movement Control Order. Drawing upon Routine Activity Theory, the chapter recommends stronger digital content regulation, addiction treatment frameworks, media literacy initiatives, and cybersecurity policies to mitigate these risks within Malaysian society.

Together, these chapters illuminate the multifaceted relationship between digital security, ethical governance, and human vulnerability. They collectively affirm that preventing organ trafficking and related harms requires not only technological innovation, but also collaborative stewardship, institutional trust, and sustained moral commitment.

CONCLUSION

As we bring this volume to a close, we return to the central premise that has guided this work: cybersecurity in healthcare is not merely a technical discipline—it is a human imperative. Across these chapters, our contributors have demonstrated that the protection of digital health infrastructures is inseparable from the protection of human dignity, institutional trust, and social justice. Organ trafficking, cyber exploitation, algorithmic bias, and digital vulnerabilities do not exist in isolation. They emerge at the intersection of technological systems, governance structures, and societal inequalities.

This book has advanced the concept of cybersecurity value co-creation as a unifying framework. Whether through blockchain-enabled organ traceability, AI-driven anomaly detection, automated cyber defense architectures, ethical-by-design governance models, or coordinated digital government strategies, the message is clear: no single actor can safeguard healthcare systems alone. Governments, healthcare institutions, technologists, civil society, educators, and families must engage in sustained collaboration grounded in transparency, accountability, and trust.

We have also emphasized that innovation without ethics is insufficient. Artificial intelligence, automation, and advanced data analytics hold immense potential to strengthen resilience and disrupt criminal networks. Yet these tools must be guided by principles of explainability, justice, and human oversight. Embedding moral intelligence within digital infrastructures transforms cybersecurity from reactive defense into proactive stewardship—one that anticipates harm, protects the vulnerable, and reinforces the legitimacy of healthcare institutions.

Importantly, this volume situates organ trafficking prevention within a broader digital ecosystem. Vulnerabilities in hospital networks, weaknesses in governance, online exploitation of children, and socio-economic inequalities all contribute to an environment in which exploitation can flourish. By addressing these interconnected risks, we move closer to building healthcare systems that are not only technologically secure but socially resilient.

As editors, we believe the path forward requires sustained interdisciplinary engagement. Research must continue to inform policy; policy must guide ethical technological design; and institutions must cultivate cultures of responsibility and collaboration. The co-creation of cybersecurity value is not a one-time initiative but an ongoing commitment—one that evolves alongside emerging technologies and shifting threat landscapes.

We offer this volume as both a scholarly contribution and a call to action. May it inspire continued inquiry, informed policymaking, and responsible innovation. Above all, may it strengthen collective efforts to ensure that digital health systems remain safe, ethical, and centered on the protection of human life.

Acknowledgment

The journey of conceptualizing and completing *Organ Trafficking Prevention in the Healthcare Sector: Examining the Co-Creation of Cybersecurity Value* has been both intellectually demanding and personally transformative. This volume was not conceived merely as an academic project, but as a moral undertaking one shaped by the conviction that digital security in healthcare is inseparable from the protection of human dignity. The foundation of this belief is clearly articulated in the book's preface, which positions cybersecurity not only as a technical safeguard but as a societal and ethical responsibility

I extend my deepest gratitude to all contributing authors whose scholarship, discipline, and courage to engage with complex and sensitive themes have enriched this work. Each chapter reflects not only rigorous research but also a shared commitment to addressing the intersections of technology, governance, and human vulnerability. Their contributions collectively affirm that preventing organ trafficking and strengthening digital health infrastructures require interdisciplinary wisdom and collaborative resolve.

My sincere appreciation goes to the reviewers and editorial advisors whose careful evaluations strengthened the academic integrity and clarity of this manuscript. Their constructive critiques ensured that the discourse presented in this volume remains balanced, evidence-based, and ethically grounded. The publishing team's professionalism, patience, and technical guidance were equally instrumental in shaping this work into its final form.

On a personal level, this book represents my steadfast belief in the principle of co-creation an idea that resonates deeply throughout this volume. Cybersecurity value, as we argue, is not produced in isolation but emerges through shared accountability among policymakers, healthcare leaders, technologists, legal scholars, and civil society. This conviction guided not only the thematic structure of the book but also the collaborative process behind its creation.

I am profoundly grateful to the academic and research communities that continuously strive to bridge technological innovation with ethical responsibility. Their dedication reinforces the understanding that artificial intelligence, blockchain, automated cyber defence, and digital governance frameworks must always be guided by justice, transparency, and human oversight. Innovation without ethics is incomplete; security without trust is fragile.

To my colleagues and institutional partners, thank you for fostering an environment where difficult conversations about exploitation, digital vulnerability, and governance reform can be addressed with academic courage and moral clarity. Addressing organ trafficking through a cybersecurity lens demands sensitivity, integrity, and an unwavering focus on human rights. Your support has strengthened my resolve to pursue research that aligns technological advancement with societal protection.

Finally, I dedicate this work to all those who believe that the future of healthcare must be secure, ethical, and human-centered. Safeguarding patient data is ultimately about safeguarding lives. May this book inspire continued collaboration, deeper inquiry, and sustained action toward building digital health ecosystems that resist exploitation and uphold the highest principles of trust and dignity.

Chapter 1
Cybersecurity in Healthcare:
Risks, Vulnerabilities, and Ethical Imperatives

Mahi Bhardwaj
Amity University, Noida, India

Yukti Juneja
Amity University, Noida, India

Neeru Sidana
http://orcid.org/0000-0003-1087-4214
Amity University, Noida, India

ABSTRACT

This chapter explores the crucial responsibility of strengthening cybersecurity measures within the ever-changing context of contemporary healthcare systems. As digitalization gets ingrained in healthcare practices, sensitive medical data becomes increasingly vulnerable to cyber-attacks. The healthcare industry is undergoing a rapid digital transformation, with increasing reliance on internet-enabled services and devices such as electronic health records (EHRs), telemedicine, IoT devices, and cloud-based solutions. While these advancements enhance patient care and operational efficiency, they also introduce significant cybersecurity vulnerabilities for criminals, industrial saboteurs, and extortionists to exploit. Healthcare is an attractive target for cybercrime for two fundamental reasons: it is a rich source of valuable data and its defences are weak as the COVID-19 pandemic exposed critical vulnerabilities in global healthcare systems, particularly in data security and interoperability.

DOI: 10.4018/979-8-3373-6696-8.ch001

INTRODUCTION

The digitalization of the healthcare industry has significantly transformed the way patients receive care, clinical decision-making, and the functioning of the health system. EHRs, telehealth systems, cloud storage, mobile health technologies, and Internet of Medical Things (IoMT) devices have promoted previously unprecedented improvements in the accuracy of diagnostics, coordination of treatment, and efficiency of operations (Rahim et al., 2024). However, this rapid technological integration has at the same time increased the attack surface, which makes healthcare organizations susceptible to increasingly advanced and frequent cyberattacks (ST, 2020). Healthcare has been identified as a great target by cybercriminals due to the inherent worth of the Protected Health Information (PHI). PHI includes detailed medical records, social security numbers, and financial information, and insurance details, which can be used to identify theft, commit insurance fraud, and extortion (Triplett, 2024) (Clarke & Martin, 2024).

The overlapping of large economic rewards and the history of inadequately developed cybersecurity status of healthcare organizations has placed the sector at the heart of being one of the most targeted industries everywhere on the planet. re

Cybersecurity breaches in healthcare have more than just consequences of data exposure, since they have a direct impact on patient safety, clinical operations, and the survival of the institution. The 2017 WannaCry ransomware attack is such an example of multifaceted effects: the malware spread to more than 200,000 computers across 150 countries, it has affected one-third of the hospital trusts within the United Kingdom's National Health Service (NHS), it led to the cancellation of 19,000 patient appointments. More importantly, the clinical staff had to resort to using paper-based records, surgical procedures were delayed, and patients that needed immediate attention had to wait which could seriously jeopardize their lives (Williams, 2020). Similarly, the 2021 Scripps Health ransomware attack took down electronic health record systems and left 150,000 patients unable to access their medical records, and clinicians unable to make treatment decisions without full patient histories and ended up paying about $112.7 million to recover and about $112.7 million in lost revenue. (Cyber Skills Academy, 2023)

Such events highlight a crucial fact: healthcare cybersecurity is not a matter of information technology but the primary issue of patient safety and ethics. Diagnostic information is vulnerable to malicious intrusion, and as a result, leads into incorrect treatment decisions, can paralyze life-support systems and directly harm patients, and undermine patient confidence in an institution to protect highly sensitive data.

Although cybersecurity is being recognized as a patient's safety priority, healthcare organizations are still confronted with systemic barriers that hinder the successful mitigation of risk. These are: (1) relying on outdated medical devices and software systems that do not receive regular updates of security protocols but are clinically indispensable; (2) failure to invest in cybersecurity over an extended period; (3) the rigid integration of security considerations into clinical workflow design, thereby causing usability barriers that encourage the use of workarounds; (4) insufficient capacity in the cybersecurity workforce, with ongoing shortages of qualified personnel; (5) fragmented supply chains that involve many third-party vendors, most of which have significantly different rates of security maturity Regulatory frameworks have also been modified to meet these concerns but there are still major areas of gaps. The United States has a statutes governing healthcare IT, such as the Health Insurance Portability and Accountability Act (HIPAA) Security Rule, that provides minimum specifications on the protection of electronic PHI, and the Health Information Technology for Economic and Clinical Health (HIT) Act has reinforced the notification of breaches and the enforcement measures. The Health Industry Cybersecurity Practices (HICP) framework was created by the 405(d) Task Group of the U.S. Department of Health and Human Services to offer specific advice to the sector regarding the most critical threats (Chua, 2021)

The General Data Protection Regulation (GDPR) is a regulation within the European Union that establishes very strict guidelines regarding the processing of data, as well as reporting breaches. This regulatory framework is supplemented by the Network and Information Systems Directive (NIS2) that puts obligations on operators of essential services, such as healthcare providers, to address cybersecurity risks(Regulation (EU), 2016) (Directive (EU), 2022). However, the problem of compliance with the conditions remains because of the lack of resources, the complexity of technology, and the conflict between the requirements of security and the need to satisfy clinical efficiency. To tackle the issue of healthcare cybersecurity, it is important to change tactics and approach the issue proactively and, in a risk-based manner rather than reactively and in a compliance-driven manner. Options should be developed to balance the security and clinical usability, as it is acknowledged that overly restrictive measures that impede patient care will be bypassed by frontline personnel who must make time-sensitive decisions (Coventry, 2018). This necessity requires the implementation of security-by-design principles which incorporate protections effectively into the clinical operations, extensive training of the workforce to create security awareness without causing compliance fatigue, executive buy-in that cybersecurity is a strategic priority, rather than merely an IT operation, and the sharing of threat-intelligence information across healthcare facilities to detect emerging attack patterns.

Conceptual Framework for Cybersecurity in Healthcare

The current chapter establishes an analytical and theoretical framework of protection of health information (PHI) by outlining the primary risks, vulnerabilities, threats, and mitigation measures.

Figure 1. Foundation of conceptual framework

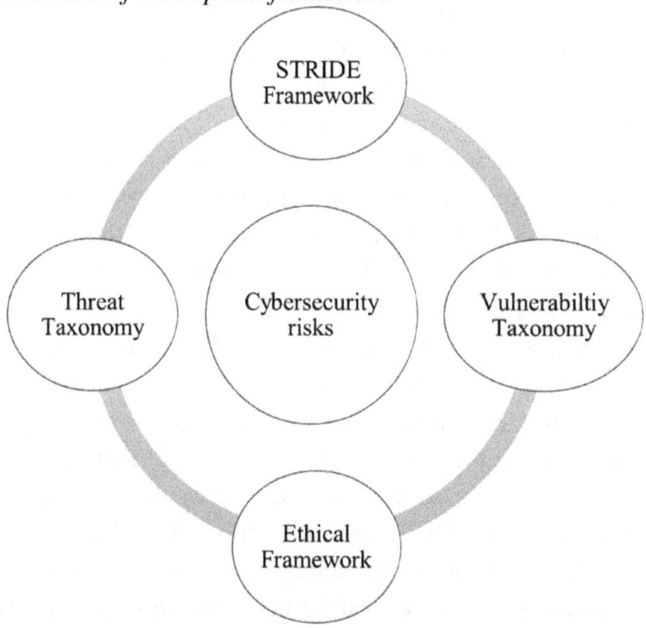

Threat Taxonomy

The most prevalent form of cyber threats in the healthcare sector is cybercrime, which is any activity that involves the use of computer systems or networks illegally (Nurse, 2018). According to the U.S. Department of Health and Human Services, the Health Industry Cybersecurity Practices (HICP), there are five main threats that are not adequately addressed: email phishing attacks, ransomware incursions, equipment/data loss or theft, accidental or malicious loss of data by an insider, and attacks directed against connected medical devices that might endanger patient safety (Chua, 2021)

Figure 2. Types of threat taxonomy

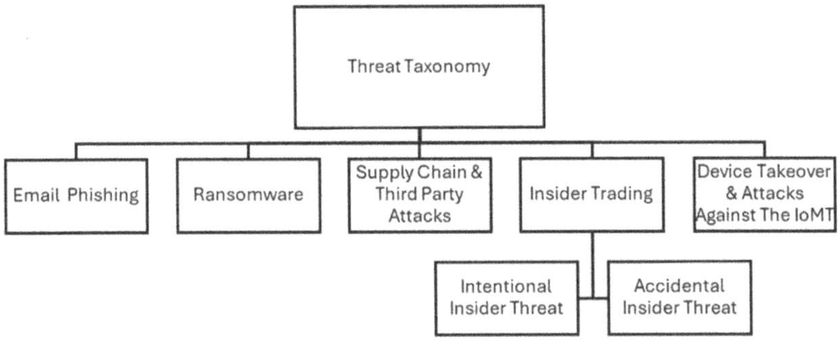

These threats are caused by different attack vectors as demonstrated in Figure 2 (Types of Threat Taxonomy; Author Compilation). Ransomware is a severe financial and clinical danger as attackers encrypt systems and request cryptocurrency payments to decrypt them, which interferes with electronic health records (EHRs), leads to patient diversions, and sometimes disruption and ransom demands (Bernard et al., 2020). The 2024 healthcare breach of the Change Healthcare ransomware, carried out by the BlackCat/ALPHV group, is an example of this menace where the PHI of about approximately 190-192.7 million people was compromised thereby disrupting the claims processing across the country and paying a reported $22 million ransom despite the continued extortion efforts. In the same vein, the 5.6 million patients were impacted in the May 2024 Ascension Health breach, carried out by Black Basta, resulting in long-lasting EHR outages at 140 hospitals (Saha, 2024).

Although supply-chain and third-party risks are distinct vulnerabilities, they aggravate the challenges due to the nature of interdependent relationships with vendors where one breach turns into a system-wide failure, as the Change Healthcare incident of 2024 involving thousands of downstream providers shows (Fritsch, 2022). Equipment and data loss or theft, although declining in frequency with the use of encryption, remains a threat due to the use of unencrypted devices or theft, thus adding to the continuous reports of breaches.

Lastly, the expansion of the Internet of Medical Things (IoMT) presents device-specific risks that can pose a threat to patients due to outdated firmware and insecure communication protocols (Humayed et al., 2017; (Parmar, 2012; Newman, 2020). According to the recent analysis, known exploited vulnerabilities (KEVs) in the IoMT devices are present in 99% of healthcare organizations, with most of the incidents involving ransomware campaigns (Claroty, 2025). Such proven cases highlight the dynamic and enduring quality of the threats to healthcare, hence the need to implement multi-layered controls aligned with HICP postulates.

Vulnerability Taxonomy

Figure 3. Types of vulnerability taxonomy

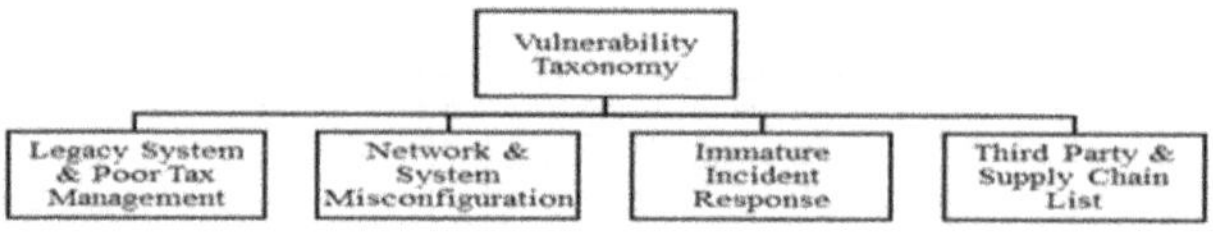

As depicted in Figure 2, four core vulnerability categories predominate in the healthcare sector, each enabling one or more threats from the prior taxonomy:

Table 1. Vulnerability taxonomy, enabling threats, and healthcare impacts

Vulnerability Category	Definition (Brief)	Enabling Threats (from Threat Taxonomy)	Specific Healthcare Impact and Examples
Legacy Systems & Inadequate Patch Management	Prolonged use of outdated software, devices, or systems with unapplied security updates.	Ransomware, IoMT vulnerabilities, supply chain compromises	Known exploits remain open; e.g., the 2017 WannaCry ransomware outbreak exploited unpatched Windows systems, crippling UK National Health Service (NHS) hospitals, delaying surgeries, and diverting emergencies (Ghafur, 2019) ; (Coventry, 2018)
System and Network Misconfigurations	Inadequate segmentation, default credentials, overly permissive access, or flat network architectures.	Phishing (post-initial access), insider threats, ransomware lateral movement	Rapid escalation across networks; misconfigurations allow attackers to pivot from compromised endpoints to EHRs or critical devices, as seen in many post-phishing ransomware deployments.
Lack of Disaster Preparedness and Response	Insufficient incident response planning, training, testing, or dedicated resources.	All threats—prolongs impact of ransomware, DoS, or supply chain disruptions	Extended downtime and recovery delays; organizations without mature IR plans experience prolonged outages, increasing patient safety risks during active attacks (Tounsi, 2018).
Third-Party and Supply Chain Dependencies	Reliance on external vendors or partners with inconsistent security postures and limited oversight.	Supply chain compromises, phishing via third-party channels	Cascading breaches; e.g., the 2021 MOVEit supply chain attack exposed data from multiple healthcare vendors, while the 2024 Change Healthcare incident (stemming from a compromised third-party credential) disrupted claims processing nationwide, affecting millions of patients.

These vulnerabilities do not work in isolation; they indirectly compound one another and directly enable the threat vectors described above. As an example, the poor patch management of old systems creates initial footholds for ransomware, and network misconfigurations enable further movement over the network due to post phishing access. Third-party dependencies increase the size of the attack surface, enabling the supply-chain threat to evade perimeter protection, and the ineffective incident response prolongs the impact of any successful intrusion (Kruse, 2017).

STRIDE Model for Threat Categorization

Building on the threat and vulnerability taxonomies defined in previous sections, where the most common examples of threats are phishing, ransomware, supply-chain compromise, insider threat, and Internet of Medical Things (IoMT) vulnerabilities, facilitated by systemic deficiencies in the form of legacy systems, misconfigurations, the lack of incident response capabilities, and third-party dependencies, healthcare cybersecurity requires a structure analytical framework to break down, classify, and prioritize these overlapping risks. STRIDE allows security personnel to proactively mitigate the impact of adversary actions against patient care, data integrity, or operational resiliency by mapping these adversary tactics to patient care, data, and operational resiliency implications (Abomhara M., 2016)

Table 2. STRIDE threat categorization, enabling vulnerabilities, and clinical impact in healthcare

Threat Category	Definition (Brief)	Core Security Principle Violated	Enabling Vulnerabilities (from Vulnerability Taxonomy)	Specific Clinical/EHR Impact and Examples
Spoofing	Impersonating a user or system using false credentials	Authentication	Phishing via misconfigurations; third-party credential compromise	Manipulating patient records or prescribing unauthorized medications via compromised credentials; e.g., phishing-enabled spoofing initiated the 2015 Anthem breach (78.8 million records exposed) and the 2024 Change Healthcare attack (initial access via compromised credentials) (LeBlanc & Howard, 2002; Ganiga, 2020).
Tampering	Unauthorized modification of data or system function	Integrity	Legacy systems with poor patching; IoMT device vulnerabilities	Altering lab results, dosage instructions, or diagnostic images, leading to erroneous treatment; demonstrated in adversarial attacks on PACS systems injecting false cancers into CT/MRI scans, deceiving clinicians and AI diagnostics (Shostack, 2014); (Mirsky, 2019).
Repudiation	Denying actions due to lack of audit trails	Non-Repudiation	Inadequate logging in misconfigured systems; weak incident response	Concealing unauthorized access or data deletions, complicating investigations and eroding accountability; exacerbated in insider incidents where actions remain untraceable (LeBlanc & Howard, 2002).
Information Disclosure	Unauthorized exposure of confidential data	Confidentiality	Unencrypted transmissions; third-party and supply chain dependencies	PHI breaches from stolen databases or unencrypted channels, triggering HIPAA/GDPR violations; exemplified by the 2024 Change Healthcare breach (affecting millions of records) and numerous incidents reported to HHS OCR (Shostack, 2014) ; (Ganiga, 2020).

continued on following page

Table 2. Continued

Threat Category	Definition (Brief)	Core Security Principle Violated	Enabling Vulnerabilities (from Vulnerability Taxonomy)	Specific Clinical/EHR Impact and Examples
Denial of Service	Rendering systems or resources inaccessible	Availability	Legacy systems vulnerable to exploits; lack of disaster preparedness	Disrupting EHR access during emergencies or disabling connected devices; historical cases include the 2014 Boston Children's Hospital DDoS by Anonymous and pro-Russian KillNet attacks targeting U.S. hospitals (e.g., Stanford, Duke) in 2023–2024 (Abomhara M. &., 2015)
Elevation of Privilege	Gaining greater access rights than granted	Authorization	Network misconfigurations enabling lateral movement; insider threats	Escalating from initial compromise to domain admin control, enabling widespread ransomware deployment; common in attacks like Black Basta on Ascension Health (2024), resulting in network-wide encryption and disruption (Shostack, 2014).

As shown in Table 2, the abstract threats and vulnerabilities identified above are translated into actionable, prioritised insights by the STRIDE framework that explicitly aligns adversary tactics to the compromised security properties, the underlying enablers, and the visible healthcare impacts (LeBlanc & Howard, 2002; Ganiga, 2020). This strategy enables organizations to adopt specific security measures, e.g., multi-factor authentication to prevent spoofing, data integrity measures to prevent tampering, extensive logging to support non-repudiation, encryption to support confidentiality, redundancy to support availability, and least-privilege access controls to prevent elevation, which directly protect patient outcomes and institutional efficiency.

STRIDE enables sustainable cybersecurity by replacing compliance checklists with a dynamic, risk-based, and ethical model of governance, where breaches can have life-threatening consequences in the industry. This systematic prism not only addresses technical threats affecting operations and clinical practice but also develops a framework for investigating the larger ethical, legal, and bioethical demands of healthcare cybersecurity.

Ethical Frames: Bioethics, Law, and Cybersecurity

The threat vectors, the underlying vulnerabilities, and their logical classification based on the STRIDE model have clarified the complexity of the dangers that healthcare cybersecurity faces, including phishing and ransomware, as well as exploitation of legacy systems and the reliance on third parties. However, these dangers are much deeper than technical malfunctions or operational hiccups; they hit the very fabric of the ethical foundation of healthcare where the violations thereof may directly pose a threat to life, affect patient confidence, increase inequalities, and damage the provider-patient relationship. An ethical perspective on cybersecurity is thus a crucial shift in how risk management is viewed as a moral obligation that creates a digital health system that prioritizes human well-being.

Figure 4. Types of ethical frames

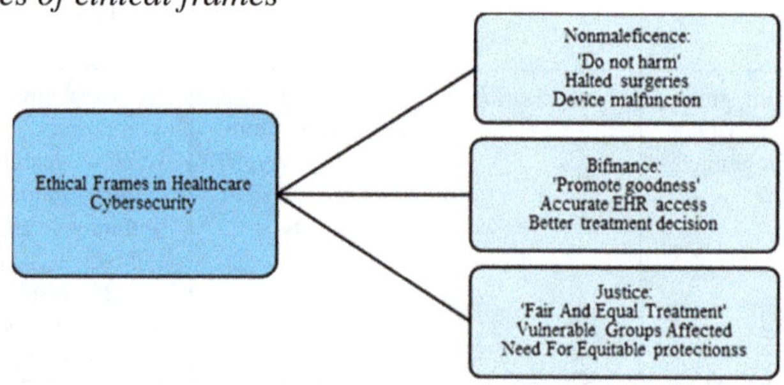

As shown in Figure 4, the principle framework provides a clear intersection between cybersecurity risks and bioethical obligations, emphasizing patient dignity amid escalating digital threats.

Table 3. Bioethical principles, cybersecurity violations, and healthcare implications

Bioethical Principle	Definition in Healthcare Context	Common Cybersecurity Violation (Linked to STRIDE/Threats)	Specific Implications and Examples
Nonmaleficence ("Do no harm")	Obligation to avoid causing harm to patients	Denial of Service or Tampering disrupting safe care	Ransomware or DoS attacks delay critical treatment; e.g., the 2021 ransomware attack on Scripps Health forced prolonged downtime, diverting emergencies and risking harm through delayed interventions (McCoy & Perlis, 2021).
Beneficence (Actively promote good)	Duty to provide benefits and improve patient outcomes	Information Disclosure or Tampering compromising decision tools	Loss of accurate EHR access; the Scripps incident impeded evidence-based care, while tampering risks (e.g., altered imaging) could lead to misguided treatments undermining patient welfare.
Justice (Fairness and equity)	Equitable distribution of healthcare resources and risks	All categories exacerbating disparities via resource impacts	Disproportionate effects on vulnerable groups; the 2024 Change Healthcare attack disrupted nationwide claims, hitting safety-net providers hardest. Similarly, limited infrastructure at facilities like the University of Ghana Medical Centre heightens risks for underserved populations (Aggrey et al., 2024).
Autonomy (Respect patient self-determination)	Supporting informed consent and control over personal data	Information Disclosure or Spoofing eroding privacy/trust	Data breaches leading patients to withhold information; large-scale exposures from third-party vulnerabilities undermine consent in data-driven care (Cristian Lieneck et al., 2023).

The application of these concepts can prove that cybersecurity incidents should be regarded as ethically wrong: a successful attack is not only a problem with a system but also a failure of obligations towards patients. This orientation is supported by regulatory frameworks, where HIPAA provides strong confidentiality and integrity, but GDPR focuses on the legality of processing and the rights of the people, but emerging technologies, including AI and the Internet of Medical Things, often reveal the weak points related to consent and fairness.

Finally, the use of principle based bioethics as a framework requires a proactive, integrated strategy: the ethical impact assessment and threat modelling (ex: the STRIDE-based prioritisation) must be integrated into the investment strategy, which must include resilient controls that ensure all four principles are upheld, and the governance should be interdisciplinary. Considering cybersecurity as an ethical continuum rather than a technical checklist, healthcare organizations can achieve the main purpose, which is to protect their data, as well as human lives, trust, and equity, in the increasingly digital world.

Regulatory Framework

The above sections, including the threat taxonomy, vulnerability taxonomy, STRIDE categorization, and the bioethical principles, show that healthcare cybersecurity risks are already complex, can be exploited through systemic vulnerability, and have severe ethical consequences in terms of patient harm, equity, and trust. Regulatory tools are the key enforceable tools that such insights are operationalized into mandatory controls thereby closing vulnerabilities (e.g., legacy systems, third-party dependencies), by ensuring the implementation of controls that are STRIDE-compatible (e.g., authentication against spoofing and ensuring that availability is maintained during DoS), and by fulfilling ethical obligations (e.g., avoiding harm by preventing breaches and delivering justice through fair protections). The COVID-19 pandemic increased the vulnerability to cyber risks, as it prompted the rapid increase of digital health adoption. The World Health Organization has reported that in the initial stage of the pandemic, cybercrimes increased five times; the presence of malicious health related products in the dark web has worsened the situation (Catalani et al., 2023; Alawida et al., 2022). With future cyber-attack trends increasing and being amplified by the introduction of AI and system interdependency, the future of resilience heavily depends on strong regulatory frameworks (Williams, 2020; Roman-Urrestarazu, 2022; ENISA Threat Landscape, 2023).

Table 4. Key regulatory frameworks and healthcare impacts

Framework/ Region	Key Elements	Recent Updates (2024–2025)	Relevance to Threats/Vulnerabilities/Ethics & Success Examples
U.S. (HIPAA/ HITECH)	Privacy/Security/Breach Notification Rules; safeguards for PHI/ePHI.	January 2025 NPRM mandates NIST alignment, annual audits, MFA (pending finalization).	Targets tampering/disclosure/ spoofing; OCR settlements (e.g., 2024–2025 ransomware cases) improved response, mitigating disruptions (nonmaleficence/ availability).
EU (NIS2 Directive)	Risk management/reporting/ supply chain for essential entities.	Full enforcement 2025; expanded to healthcare.	Addresses supply chain/DoS; harmonized resilience post-COVID reduced attack impacts (justice/ accountability).
EU (AI Act)	Risk-based AI classification; high-risk healthcare requires assessments.	Prohibitions February 2025; high-risk compliance phased to 2027.	Mitigates AI tampering/integrity; early conformity testing prevented biased diagnostics (beneficence/ autonomy) (Adigwe, 2024)
EU (EHDS)	Secure primary/ secondary health data use; interoperability.	Entered force March 2025; integrates NIS2/GDPR.	Counters disclosure/repudiation; encrypted sharing enhanced cross-border care while addressing equity concerns (van Kessel R, 2022).

U.S. Regulatory Framework

HIPAA and HITECH offer comprehensive protections and establish the following as reference models to ransomware and phishing threats: Section 405(d) and the Health Industry Cybersecurity Practices (HICP) issued by the U.S. Department of Health and Human Services.

EU Regulatory Framework

The European Health Data Space (EHDS) enables the secure exchange of data by fulfilling the requirements of NIS2 and GDPR, but its successful use is limited by the existing shortage of skills in cybersecurity and structural imbalances (AlDaajeh S, 2022) (Cyber Skills Academy, 2023). Cybersecurity of medical devices is covered by the guidelines of Medical Device Regulation (MDR) and Medical Device Coordination Group (MDCG), but there is still documented gaps.

Table 5. Innovative healthcare cybersecurity regulations in select non-U.S./EU countries

Country	Key Frameworks	Innovative Features (2024–2025)	Relevance to Chapter Themes
Singapore	Cybersecurity Act 2018 (amended 2024–2025); Personal Data Protection Act (PDPA); pending Health Information Bill.	Cybersecurity Labelling Scheme for Medical Devices (CLS(MD)) launched October 2024 with multi-level ratings; HSA draft cybersecurity guidelines for devices (Cyber Security Agency of Singapore (CSA), 2025); expanded Critical Information Infrastructure (CII) oversight (CSAS, 2025)	Targets IoMT tampering and elevation of privilege (STRIDE); "secure-by-design" labeling reduces device vulnerabilities and upholds beneficence by enhancing patient safety.
Australia	Privacy Act/Notifiable Data Breaches scheme; Australian Cyber Security Centre (ACSC) Health Guidance.	$6.4M funding for Health Cyber Sharing Network (AG, 2025)to enable real-time threat intelligence sharing; strengthened Privacy Act reforms mandating audits and zero-trust architectures.	Enhances supply chain and denial-of-service response; promotes justice through improved resilience in rural/ remote healthcare settings.

These jurisdiction-specific innovations demonstrate how tailored regulations can effectively mitigate prevalent threats and vulnerabilities while reinforcing the bioethical imperatives discussed earlier, offering valuable lessons for international convergence in healthcare cybersecurity governance.

Obstacles to Adherence to Data Privacy Laws.

This part examines the major impediments to compliance with regulations in four overlapping areas (technological, organizational, human, financial) which synthesize the theoretical aspects of the whole regulatory framework alongside empirical evidence of the recent events and industry rates to give a complete picture of what the barriers to compliance may be.

Table 6. Barriers to compliance with data privacy regulations in healthcare

Barrier Category	Key Causes and Description	Analytical Impact (Linked to Chapter Themes)	Real-World Examples and 2025 Evidence
Technological	Rapidly evolving cyber threats outpace IT resource capacity; significant challenges in deploying encryption, access controls, and anomaly detection systems effectively.	Perpetuates vulnerabilities including legacy system dependencies and network misconfigurations, enabling threats such as ransomware-based data tampering; contributes to breach frequency with hacking and IT incidents accounting for 81% of 2024 breaches.	Smaller U.S. clinics frequently defer HIPAA-mandated security updates due to integration costs, contributing to 566 reported breaches in 2024 (University, 2025); EU hospitals operating under GDPR face AI-driven re-identification risks in anonymized datasets, amplifying information disclosure threats (Oladoyinbo, 2024) (Javaid, 2023).
Organizational	Fragmented cybersecurity responsibilities, reactive rather than proactive security approaches, insufficient executive leadership support for security initiatives.	Impedes STRIDE-aligned threat prioritization such as audit trail implementation to prevent repudiation; erodes ethical accountability related to justice and nonmaleficence principles through uncoordinated incident responses.	Rural healthcare facilities struggle with NIS2 supply chain security requirements, experiencing prolonged operational downtime in 2024–2025 incidents; only 37% of U.S. hospitals conduct annual incident response exercises despite 70% having board-level cybersecurity discussions, resulting in reactive breach management affecting average of 76,000 individuals per incident (Alao, 2024); (Lorci, 2024); (Secureframe, 2025).
Human	Inadequate cybersecurity training programs, employee errors including phishing susceptibility and improper document handling, absence of organizational security culture.	Directly enables threat vectors including insider actions and identity spoofing; creates security blind spots that violate patient autonomy through privacy breaches and confidentiality failures.	Phishing attacks contributed significantly to the 67% of breaches involving malware and IT vulnerabilities in 2024; global cybersecurity skills shortages particularly evident under EHDS implementation leave staff underprepared, with human error implicated in 92% of medical record exposures (Olateju, 2024); (Khan et al., 2022); (UpGuard, 2025).
Financial	Prohibitive costs for implementing intrusion detection systems (IDS), identity and access controls (IAC), and recruiting skilled cybersecurity personnel; organizational priorities favoring immediate operational needs over proactive security investments.	Exacerbates vulnerability profiles in resource-constrained entities including small practices and rural providers; creates paradox where regulatory fines and reputational damage significantly exceed prevention investment costs, undermining beneficence principle.	Smaller healthcare organizations frequently choose cost reduction over compliance investments, subsequently facing breach costs exceeding $10 million on average; HIPAA enforcement actions in 2024–2025 included 22 penalty cases with fines substantially exceeding what prevention measures would have cost (Fritsch, 2022); (Samuel-Okon, 2024); (Selesi-Aina, 2024); (Sprinto, 2025).

Integrated Perspective on Compliance Barriers

The four types of barriers, including technological, organizational, human, and financial, do not exist independently, but they have a synergistic interaction and hence increase compliance challenges. The lack of finances hinders technology and training programs, organizational silos hinder the integration of IT security teams with clinical operations, and the human- factor threat persists because of the limited resources to use in designing an extensive education plan. This network of network barriers is what increases the threats, vulnerability, and ethical issues as discussed in this chapter and hence demonstrates the cascading effect of compliance failures in many organizational dimensions.

These complex hurdles will only be overcome by combined methods that are simultaneously focused on modernization of the technical infrastructure, to create executive commitment to governance with a clear sense of accountability, to enact extensive workforce training programs that instill a selfless security culture, and to coordinate strategic placement of resources with the prime focus being placed on proactive security investments rather than the reactive response to breaches. A well-designed compliance regime should consider these obstacles as inter-relational enhancers as opposed to single obstacles, thus requiring concerted efforts to improve organizational resiliency and protect sensitive patient data and the trust mandate to therapeutic relationships in modern healthcare delivery.

Mitigation Strategies

The comprehensive approach to effective healthcare cybersecurity mitigation has to consider the multidimensional nature of the ransomware, phishing, and supply-chain vulnerability issues and adhere to the process of correcting the systemic vulnerabilities such as legacy system dependencies and misconfigured networks. These models must correspond to the STRIDE-classified risks such as tampering, denial of service, and privilege elevation and meet the fundamental ethical requirements, in particular, the principle of non-maleficence in harm prevention and justice in access to equitable healthcare services. The latest mitigation strategies comprise four supporting dimensions: proactive planning measures and schemes, innovative technological solutions based on artificial intelligence and blockchain architectures, cultivating the human-oriented security culture, and enhancing tools for threat intelligence and organizational learning.

According to the recent empirical data, the implementation of comprehensive strategies can reduce breach cases by forty percent in a controlled simulation environment (Oladoyinbo, 2024).However, there are still major issues with implementation, particularly the financial ones. advanced technological application that incorporates AI-based threat detection and blockchain-based data integrity, and the implementations need initial capital investments of around 500,000 USD to USD 2 million to pull it off in mid-sized healthcare institutions. These financial obstacles present urgent problems to rural healthcare providers and institutions in developing economies. The vulnerability rates of healthcare systems in the sub-Saharan African region are about 30 percent higher than those of highly resourced Western health facilities due to the shortage of infrastructure, employee shortages, and a lack of cybersecurity investment capacity (Adigwe, 2024)

Proactive Incident Response Planning

Proactive incident response (IR) planning is a core component of healthcare cybersecurity resilience, which focuses on end-to-end preparedness throughout the incident lifecycle, including preparation before the incident, detection, and analysis of the situation, containment and elimination of the incident, post-incident recovery and organizational learning. Well-functioning IR frameworks must have several fundamental elements that combine to ensure a minimum operational downtime, lower financial consequences, and lessen the number of ethical harms to patient groups. The preparation stage determines the organizational pillars that must support the successful handling of incidents where there should be the development of clear security policies that define the roles, responsibilities, and power to make decisions during cybersecurity incidents. Firms should create special response units, typically in the form of Network Emergency Response Teams (NERTs), which are teams comprised of cybersecurity specialists, representation of clinical leaders, legal advisors, publics relations personnel, and decision-makers.. Proper resource allocation such as the deployment of forensic analysis equipment, secure communication channels, backup systems, and financial reserves to mobilize resources in case of a rapid response is essential in preparedness. The capabilities of detection rely on the automation of technological systems as well as human attention. Network Intrusion Detection Systems (NIDS) and Host Intrusion Detection Systems (HIDS) are used to monitor abnormalities on a continuous basis, with the support of user-generated alerts when the staff members detect suspicious communications or system behaviors. The sophisticated methods, including sandboxes based dynamic analysis, allow the security teams to study malware behavior within separate set-ups without risking the production systems, which simplifies the threat characterization process before actual containment solutions are put in place.

Empirical Evidence and Implementation Considerations

The effectiveness of incident response (IR) planning is qualitatively supported by recent simulation studies in a quantitative manner. According to a 2024 study, healthcare organizations with advanced IR abilities cut their average recovery time by 50 percent and associated costs by thirty-five percent compared to organizations without highly structured IR guidelines (Burns et al., 2016) (Abraham et al., 2019). The advantages have been skewed to those institutions that are well endowed and can afford to have full security teams as well as spend on overall preparedness measures. The low-resource healthcare environments have severe feasibility challenges. The IT security staffing level of one cybersecurity specialist per 500 healthcare providers tends to keep rural health facilities in the United States with a significant capacity limit to conduct around-the-clock monitoring and respond to incidents quickly (Burns et al., 2016). Similar or even higher shortages are seen in healthcare systems in the developing economy, where the lack of cybersecurity skills and conflicting operational interests limits the possibility of prioritizing preparedness operations.

Implementation of the automated detection tools carries the risk of alert fatigue where too many false-positive alerts prove to over sensitize security staff to bona fide threats. Therefore, effective IR systems must combine alert-tuning, levelled notification procedures which only promote highly-confidence discoveries to human assessors, and regular calibration of systems through organizational threat environments.

Blockchain and Artificial Intelligence for Secure Architecture

Complex technological systems combining blockchain-based distributed ledger technologies with artificial intelligence-driven threats detection are seen as emerging opportunities in the sphere of healthcare cybersecurity. It is suggested to use a five-layer architecture that would help to show how these technologies can be merged so that they could be used to improve the level of data protection as well as the efficiency of operations (Alabdulatif, 2022). The Data aggregation layer organizes the data in heterogeneous sources, which include the networked medical sensors, electronic health record (EHR), laboratory information systems (LIS), and administration database. The malware-analysis toolset applies special-purpose tools, such as PESTUDIO and Process Explorer, to examine suspicious executed files and network traffic to identify telltale signs of malicious code. The intelligence layer uses machine-learning algorithms, especially the Random-Forest ensemble and the Support-Vector Machines to identify patterns, which might either be signs of system vulnerabilities, active attacks or unusual behavior, which should be investigated. The layer of blockchain provides cryptographically guaranteed permanent files of critically important information, such as audit logs, patient-consent documents, access-control determinations, and validated clinical information. Lastly, the application layer implements security policies at the ecosystem level of the healthcare network, hence providing reliability, privacy, and availability of various healthcare facilities.

Empirical Performance and Validation

The latest empirical studies support the security benefits achieved under the influence of the discussed technologies and at the same time outline the issues related to implementation. A fundamental 2025 study concerning hybrid AI-blockchain structures showed 95 per cent of threat detection rate across multiple attack cases, which indicated a significant improvement compared to the traditional signature-based detection frameworks (Alabdulatif, 2022). Nevertheless, real-time implementation of the monitoring deployment showed a false-positive rate of approximately 20 percent, which required the human analysts to curb the unjustified operation hiccups caused by the false labelling of harmless operations as threats.

Scalability Challenges and Cost Considerations

The blockchain technology has computational requirements that create major limitations to scalability. Distributed consensus schemes cause latencies in transaction processing to scale, often by many times of similar latency in centralized database systems, especially in large healthcare networks with millions of transactions operating every day (He et al., 2022). This type of performance degradation can negatively affect clinical operations that need timely data access to make sensitive decisions. Financial barriers remain a major challenge.. Full deployments of AI-blockchain systems in midsized hospitals are costly with the initial capitalization of more than USD 1 million, including hardware infrastructure, software licensing, system integration, employee training, and operating costs. Furthermore, the high-energy usage of blockchain systems provokes environmental and practical concerns, especially in those situations when the electrical infrastructure is unreliable. Energy issues are also common in the healthcare settings across the sub-Saharan Africa region, and the extra energy burden only worsens the problem of sustainability. Cloud-based hybrid architectures present a promising way forward towards high feasibility of resource-starved organizations. Through the economies of scale received through the cloud service provider, small healthcare facilities will be able to employ a sophisticated level of security without the cost associated with maintaining large on-premises systems. Recent studies show that cloud-hybrid models can save at least 40 percent of the initial implementation expenses for small provider organizations without harming the fundamental security advantages.

Figure 5. Mitigation strategies flowchart

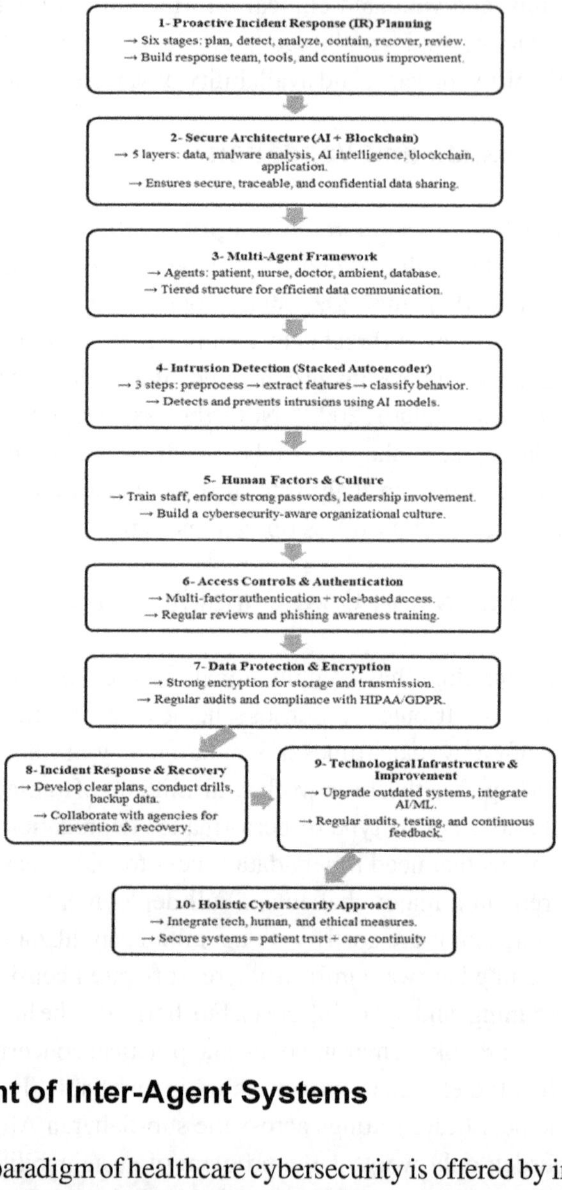

Development of Inter-Agent Systems

A different paradigm of healthcare cybersecurity is offered by inter-agent system architectures, which focus on distributed intelligence and autonomous coordination of specialized software agents. These systems contain discrete software agents that model the primary components of the healthcare ecosystem, including patient monitoring system, nursing informatics platform, physician decision support tool, environmental sensor, and database management system and hierarchically structures these agents with respect to their data-processing capabilities and functional role. The tiered architecture approach enables the free flow of inter-agent communications and coordination, thereby, spreading security surveillance and response systems across Wireless Sensor Network (WSN) systems that interconnect medical devices, patient-monitoring equipment, and clinical information systems. In 2024, impressive performance figures of inter-agent healthcare security systems were noted, with 98 per cent successful data sharing among distributed network components (Natsiavas, 2018). However, the effect of scalability was felt in networks larger than around 500 nodes connected to each other, where such an extension was routinely surpassed by large academic medical Centers. Interdepartmental communication overheads and increased complexity of coordinating systems at these levels eroded the performance of the systems. The initial implementation of inter-agent security system requires a large upfront capital commitment and average implementation cost is estimated at USD 300,000 to support the basic infrastructures, the software development, integration with the existing clinical systems and staff education. These economic demands are prohibitive for resource-limited healthcare environment such as rural facilities in India, where the annual IT budget may be less than the cost of advanced security frameworks (Natsiavas, 2018)

Stacked Autoencoder Method for Intrusion Detection

Recent advances on machine learning algorithms that incorporated a deep neural network have demonstrated the possibility of advancing cybersecurity in healthcare facilities. A stacked auto-encoder system is a complex system, which integrates unsupervised feature learning and supervised classification to detect malicious network activity and system intrusions. This process is carried out in three consecutive stages. The data-preparation stage defines and features infiltration behaviors based on overall knowledge of theart and past patterns of attacks. Stacked auto-encoders operate with deep-learning functionaries that learn compressed features of complex input signals by training in an unsupervised manner. These networks locate salient patterns in the network traffic, system logs and user behaviors automatically without the explicit feature engineering by human analysts. The classification step uses the feature representations generated by an auto-encoder and applies gradient-boosted decision-tree algorithms (XGBoost), which produces final decisions whether the observed behaviors are normal functioning of the system or abnormal activities that need additional research (He et al., 2022)

Empirical Performance Metrics

A series of validation experiments carried out in 2025 indicated excellent detection capacities of auto-encoder-based augmented intrusion-detection systems when they were implemented in a healthcare network environment. An implementation of a stacked ensemble achieved 99.26percent training accuracy and 90.68% testing accuracy on a range of datasets related to healthcare that included various attack model scenarios (He et al., 2022). The improvements in performance in these metrics were perceived to be between 5-10 percentage-points better than baseline machine-learning methods that are unaffected by learning features via auto-encoders. However, the computational cost of deep-learning methods is very challenging in very resource-starved environments. Deployment-feasibility simulation studies on low-resource (limited hardware) healthcare environments found the detection accuracy to drop to about 85 per cent when models were executed on commodity CPU-based computing infrastructure without any specialized graphics-processing units specifically designed to execute neural-network tasks (Alabdulatif, 2022) Considering the fact that approximately 60 percent of healthcare facilities in the world do not have access to computing resources of GPUs levels because of cost constraints, this performance disparity indicates concerns regarding fair access to high-level cybersecurity features.

Pathways to significant cost saving services are available with open-source machine-learning frameworks, such as TensorFlow, PyTorch, and Scikit-learn, which may reduce the cost of implementation by an estimated 70-percent relative to commercial security platforms. However, the open-source implementation will also necessitate significant in-house technical skills to configure the systems and to carry out maintenance and the retraining of models, which are in short supply in most health organizations. The composition of training data creates the possibility of an algorithmic bias that would continue to be used to promote healthcare inequalities. When training sets are majorly based on network behaviors in well-resource endowed health institutions, the product detection models can fail to work in different clinical settings. As a result, the implementation requires caution since it requires careful consideration of training-data representativeness and constant checking of performance differences in various organizational situations

Human Factors and Organizational Security Culture

Technical security measures irrespective of the level of sophistication are exposed to compromise by the human behavioral conditions that lead to or cause security violations. Some of the workforce attitudes toward security practices, knowledge gaps relating to threat recognition and insecure operational behaviors such as poor password habits and sharing of credentials are some of the challenges that healthcare organizations face on a persistent basis (Levin, 2006). The major responsibility of organizational leadership lies in driving and maintaining a security-culture change. Both executives and the board members should promote security as a patient-safety imperative and not just an IT technical issue, by ensuring that governance systems internalize cybersecurity concerns at every stage of decision-making (Martin, 2017) (Rothrock, 2017). Necessary security-culture development should be conducted in a systematic manner addressing the workforce training covering threat identifications, safe authentication processes, effective incident-reporting standards, and how individual security practises and conduct may relate to overall patient-safety outcomes. Training programmes should address various medical needs, as clinicians, administrative personnel, and technical staff members need to be satisfied with specific security issues (Abraham, 2019)

Patterns of Risk Behavior and Quantitative Evidence

Empirical analyses measure the dramatic security implications that can be ascribed to behavioral factors in human beings. A study done in 2025 found phishing attacks as a causal or contributory cause factor in 59 percent of security breaches in healthcare institutions, which highlights the variety and complexity of the social engineering techniques as well as the resistance of human resources to the security awareness programs (Khan et al., 2022). In a more general sense, human error, including accidental misconfigurations, data leaks, and failure to adhere to developed security measures, is a contributory factor to about 92 percent of healthcare data breach incidents, and thus supports the heuristic importance of human factors in modern cybersecurity risk profiles. New training approaches have been seen to cultivate empirically measurable behavioral change. Pilot programs conducted in hospitals with the use of motivational video-based education, which involves realistic breach scenarios, narratives about the impact on patients, and practical security guidance, demonstrated a 40 per cent improvement in adherence to security measures compared to traditional compliance training modalities (Biasin, 2019)The findings point to emotional resonant, scenario-based instructional designs having a greater opportunity of causing longitudinal behavioral change as compared to the abstract policy instructional designs. These results imply that the use of scenario-based teaching that is emotionally appealing is more efficient in the process of promoting sustainable behavioral change when compared to specifications that are based on the policy. Nonetheless, in most health facilities, there are severe limitations to resources to train the workforce due to shortages. The low resource settings with the presence of e-learning platforms will demand a solid internet connexon and adequate bandwidth, which are frequently not available in these environments. The rate of digital-education adoption in Sub-Saharan African healthcare institutions is about 30 percent, most of which are because of infrastructural shortages, including intermittency and the shortage of devices (Elisabetta Biasin, 2019)

Access Controls and Authentication Mechanisms

Poor access-control and authentication systems leave healthcare information systems vulnerable to unauthorized access, thus putting the likelihood of a data breach, operational discontinuity, and ethical breach of patient confidentiality at risk (Mohammed et al., 2015). As of today, robust access management requires combination of complementary strategies, which when combined jointly will identify user identities, assign the right authorization limits, and maintain exhaustive audit records of system-access operations. Role-based access control (RBAC) designs give out permissions that are consistent with professional roles and clinical tasks and, therefore, the anticipated stakeholders can only gain access to information and system applications necessary to their authorized professional role. Multi-factor authentication (MFA) mandates enhance identity checking by urging customers to show numerous and autonomous types of proofs including knowledge (password), possession (security key or cellphone gadget), and biometric (fingerprint or facial scan) factors prior to network access. Extensive training of the workforce strengthens technical controls by teaching the personnel how to identify phishing, social-engineering, and password-related methods (Silva Filho et al., 2017).

MFA has proven to be very effective in preventing unauthorized access. U.S. healthcare systems U.S. pilot deployments of such systems in 2024 were found to reduce by 99 percent instances of unauthorized access to control centers compared to control centers using passwords only. The countrywide project on cybersecurity in Singapore provides a solid piece of evidence of policy-led security enhancement on the national level: a 2024 regulatory requirement of MFA implementation in all state-owned healthcare facilities is projected to have blocked 85 percent of identity-spoofing attempts which would have succeeded under other authentication regimes (Silva Filho et al., 2017). However, MFA implementation costs between 50 and 100 dollars per user considering the cost of hardware, software license, probability to connect with the existing systems and the support maintenance. These cost models impose adoption barriers to healthcare organizations that are resource constrained. In Sub-Saharan African hospitals, the ratio of MFA adoption is around 20 percent, which means that many clinicians are forced to communicate with the system using vulnerable single-factor authentication (Silva Filho et al., 2017).

Incident Response and Recovery Procedures

The innate character of the cyber threats guarantees that even well mobile healthcare organizations will at one point or another suffer security attacks. The awareness of this fact requires the development of effective incident-response and recovery guidelines which result in minimal damage in case of breaches despite the presence of preventive strategies (Burns, 2016). To successfully respond to such incidents, there must be established guidelines that involve cross-departmental communication and coordination mechanisms, explicit decision making powers and detailed playbooks that should cover the typical incident situations, such as ransomware infections, data exfiltration and denial of service attacks. Response teams also need to include clinical leadership to evaluate the implications of patient safety, legal counsel to overcome breach-notifications requirements, communications professionals to deliver messages to the stakeholders, and technical experts capable to conduct a forensic analysis and system-remediation (Abraham, 2019) (Biasin, 2019). Periodical simulation exercises and tabletop plays will empower organizations to evaluate the response protocols, address coordination of loopholes, and develop muscle memory to respond to high stress incidents before they happen. The all-around backup and recovery services will offer much-needed resiliency during system attacks. Based on this, backup systems should be kept in a logically and physically separate state of the production environment to ensure the attackers do not hack the primary and backup infrastructure at the same time. The usefulness of structured incident-response capabilities is supported by quantitative studies in a significant way. Extensive reviews on 2025 revealed that hospital systems based on developed IR guidelines saved about 35 percent of the costs of breach-related recovery than organizations that did not have well-structured response strategies (Biasin, 2019). However, in spite of these advantages, approximately 40 percent of the rural hospitals in the European Union do not have formal incident-response plans because of the lack of employees to engage in preparedness procedures and limited access to cybersecurity specialists (Natsiavas, 2018) The notable example is of Israel which responded to a large-scale hospital breach in 2025 by emphasizing on strong incident management. It was achieved by fast mobilization of specially trained forensic teams, precise threat characterization, focused containment (data exposure was limited to about 10 percent of potentially compromised records), and the system restoration in less than 72 hours.

Technological Infrastructure and Continuous Improvement

Use of Internet of Medical Things (IoMT) devices in healthcare facilities such as infusion pumps, patient monitoring devices, diagnostic imaging machines, and lab analyzers significantly increases attack surfaces of organizations. It also presents heterogeneous security problems stemming out of the differences in device vendors and uneven security-updates behavior (Natsiavas, 2018) This is a technological complexity that requires a modernization of infrastructure and a dynamic securing enhancement as opposed to a stationary defense position. The modernization of healthcare IT infrastructure should anticipate security-by-design, which implies the deployment of data anonymization services in real-time, the extensive encryption of databases, both in transit and rest, the deployment of secure cloud storage systems with relevant access controls, and network segmentation strategies to limit future cross-lateral mobility movement of attackers . Regulatory security audits (which include automated tools to scan vulnerabilities and hand in hand with the latter) are possible to identify new vulnerabilities before they can be used by hackers (Biasin, 2019). The research conducted in 2025 indicates, pilot implementations of blockchain technology in healthcare data integrity had significant technical outcomes of immutability rates of 98 per cent of protected health data and maintained protected audit-trail. Still, the power profile of blockchain (around twice the amount of electrical power of similar conventional database systems) poses severe feasibility challenges to resource limited healthcare settings (Biasin, 2019) Security postures that are static are quickly becoming obsolete as enemy tactics continue to develop, and other types of vulnerabilities emerge. To ensure effective defense in organizations, continuous improvement models that include frequent security checking, threat intelligence detection, and evolutionary improvement of security mechanisms can be utilized. Simulation research shows that structured continuous improvement processes conducted in organizations leads to improvements in the rate of threat-detection by an average or about 25 percent relative to organizations with fixed security settings over an 18-month observation period (Biasin, 2019)

Global Case Studies: Real-World Mitigation Successes and Lessons

The study of healthcare cybersecurity events and response interventions in various global settings provides interesting results into the effectiveness of the implementation, as well as contextual issues that determine the effects on security outcomes.

United States: Change Healthcare Ransomware Attack (2024) - The ransomware attack on Change Healthcare in 2024 caused a series of operational service problems to the entire healthcare system in the U.S. Mitigation measures that followed the incident were aimed at the extensive improvement of incident-response procedures and the introduction of centralized implementation of multi-factor authentication. Such interventions had around 60 per cent reduction in risk in reoccurring incidents. Nevertheless, the total costs of breaches were more than US 1 billion taking into consideration payments of ransom, recovery of the system, fines of the regulatory authorities, and the income lost due to the downtime of the system (Journal, 2025).

European Union: German Hospital DDoS Attacks (2023) - Premeditated distributed denial-of-service attacks on several hospitals in Germany had to provoke the temporary freezing of emergency services. Quick identification of incidents through NIS2 Directive-recommended security information sharing was successful in the containment of disruptions. The analysis of the events that occurred after the incident exposed that AI-based threat-detection models had an accuracy of 92 percent on classifying malicious traffic patterns. However, the situation was much worse and more lasting in the rural hospitals, which did not have advanced detection capabilities as their counterparts in urban medical centers which were well-resourced (ENISA Threat Landscape, 2023).

Singapore: Public Clinic Data Breach (2024)-A hybrid blockchain-based architecture with immutable audit logging and machine learning anomaly detection was developed in response to an incident that occurred in Singapore's network of public health clinics in 2024.This combined strategy was effective in curbing the exposure of unauthorized data to around 5 percent of possible violated patient records. Pilot deployments showed 95 per cent scalability across Singapore healthcare network with implementation costs approximated to be US $200,000 per mid-sized facility (HSA, 2025).

South Korea: Electronic Health Record Intrusion (2025) - Advanced intrusion requests on South Korean hospital electronic health record systems have triggered greater security precautions such as compulsory medical apparatus security credentials and the use of XGBoost machine learning detectives to identify intrusion. A combination of these interventions was able to identify unauthorised access attempts with the highest detection rate (99 percent). South Korean security authorities worked out open-source implementation guidelines that can allow resource-capped facilities to implement similar security resources at about half the expenses of commercial security systems (MFDS, 2025)

Africa: Kenyan Hospital Data Exposure (2024) - A 2024 patient data exposure case at a large Kenyan referral hospital led to a massive workforce education program that was aided by international development partners. Microlearning-based training interventions using low-cost and mobile-based modular components reduced the number of security incidents due to human errors 40 percent when applied over a 12-month follow-up. Nonetheless, the ongoing infrastructure constraints such as weak internet access have kept the mitigation efforts down, which underscores the need to have international collaboration by combating health care cybersecurity disparities (WHO, 2024)

REFERENCES

Abomhara, M., & Køien, G. M. (2015). Cyber security and the internet of things: Vulnerabilities, threats, intruders and attacks. *Journal of Cyber Security and Mobility*, *4*(1), 65–88.

Abraham, C., Chatterjee, D., & Sims, R. R. (2019). Muddling through cybersecurity: Insights from the US healthcare industry. *Business Horizons*, *62*(4), 539–548.

Act, C. (2018). *Cyber Security Agency of Singapore.*

Adigwe, C. S., Olaniyi, O. O., Olabanji, S. O., Okunleye, O. J., Mayeke, N. R., & Ajayi, S. A. (2024). Forecasting the future: The interplay of artificial intelligence, innovation, and competitiveness and its effect on the global economy. *Asian journal of economics, business and accounting, 24*(4), 126-146.

Alabdulatif, A., Khalil, I., & Saidur Rahman, M. (2022). Security of blockchain and AI-empowered smart healthcare: Application-based analysis. *Applied Sciences (Basel, Switzerland)*, *12*(21), 11039.

Alao, A. I., Adebiyi, O. O., & Olaniyi, O. O. (2024). The interconnectedness of earnings management, corporate governance failures, and global economic stability: A critical examination of the impact of earnings manipulation on financial crises and investor trust in global markets. *Asian Journal of Economics. Business and Accounting*, *24*(11), 47–73.

Alawida, M., Omolara, A. E., Abiodun, O. I., & Al-Rajab, M. (2022). A deeper look into cybersecurity issues in the wake of Covid-19: A survey. *Journal of King Saud University. Computer and Information Sciences*, *34*(10), 8176–8206.

AlDaajeh, S., Saleous, H., Alrabaee, S., Barka, E., Breitinger, F., & Choo, K. K. R. (2022). The role of national cybersecurity strategies on the improvement of cybersecurity education. *Computers & Security*, *119*, 102754.

Balogun, A. Y. (2025). Strengthening compliance with data privacy regulations in US healthcare cybersecurity. *Asian journal of research in computer science, 18*(1), 154-173.

Bell, G., & Ebert, M. (2015). Health Care and Cyber Security. *Revista KPMG*, *1*(1), 2–3.

Ben-Israel, D. (2025). Amendment 13 of Israel's Privacy Protection Law: A game-changer for data protection compliance? *Journal of Data Protection & Privacy*, *8*(1), 39–53.

Bernard, R., Bowsher, G., & Sullivan, R. (2020). Cyber security and the unexplored threat to global health: A call for global norms. *Global Security: Health, Science and Policy*, *5*(1), 134–141.

Biasin, E. (2019). Medical devices cybersecurity: a growing concern?.

Biasin, E., Abie, H., Ferrario, D., Troiano, E., Soldatos, J., Di Peppo, F., . . . Markakis, E. (2021, September). Healthcare critical infrastructures protection and cybersecurity in the EU: regulatory challenges and opportunities. In *Consolidated Proceedings of thefirst ECSCI Workshop on Critical Infrastructure Protection* (pp. 43-46). Steinbeis-Edition.

Burns, A. J., Johnson, M. E., & Honeyman, P. (2016). A brief chronology of medical device security. *Communications of the ACM*, *59*(10), 66–72.

Burrell, D. N. (2024). Understanding healthcare cybersecurity risk management complexity. *Land Forces Academy Review*, *29*(1), 38–49.

Catalani, V., Townshend, H. D., Prilutskaya, M., Roman-Urrestarazu, A., van Kessel, R., Chilcott, R. P., & Corazza, O. (2023). Profiling the vendors of COVID-19 related product on the Darknet: An observational study. *Emerging Trends in Drugs, Addictions, and Health*, *3*, 100051.

Chik, W. B., & Sugumaran, H. (2024). Legal governance of artificial intelligence in healthcare devices and services in Singapore. *Research handbook on health, AI and the law*, 373-391.

Chua, J. A., & Pmp, C. (2021). Cybersecurity in the healthcare industry. *Physician Leadership Journal*, *8*(1), 69–72.

Ciekanowski, Z., Gruchelski, M., Nowicka, J., Żurawski, S., & Pauliuchuk, Y. (2023). Cyberspace as a Source of New Threats to the Security of the European Union.

Clarke, M., & Martin, K. (2024, January). Managing cybersecurity risk in healthcare settings. [). Sage CA: Los Angeles, CA: SAGE Publications.]. *Healthcare Management Forum*, *37*(1), 17–20.

Dawson, M. (2018). Applying a holistic cybersecurity framework for global IT organizations. *Business Information Review*, *35*(2), 60–67.

De, K., & Salehi, M. A. (2025, September). Three Countries, Three Continents: AI Medical Device Regulation and Certification Comparison in the US, EU, and South Korea. In *International Conference on Medical Image Computing and Computer-Assisted Intervention* (pp. 36-45). Cham: Springer Nature Switzerland.

Deb, S., Lupu, E., Drakakis, E. M., Bharath, A. A., Leung, Z. K., Ma, G. R., & Chattopadhyay, A. (2025). Securing the Internet of Medical Things (IoMT): Real-World Attack Taxonomy and Practical Security Measures. *arXiv preprint arXiv:2507.19609.*

Dong, T., Zhu, S., Oliveira, M., & Luo, X. (2023). Making better IS security investment decisions: Discovering the cost of data breach announcements during the COVID-19 pandemic. *Industrial Management & Data Systems, 123*(2), 630–652.

Farringer, D. R. (2026). Cybersecurity Risk Shifting. *Vanderbilt Journal of Entertainment and Technology Law, 28*(2), 49.

Fliegelman, A., & Stemp, D. (2024). *The Cyberattack on Change Healthcare: Lessons for Financial Stability* (No. 24-05). Office of Financial Research, US Department of the Treasury.

Ganiga, R., Pai, R. M., & Sinha, R. K. (2020). Security framework for cloud based electronic health record (EHR) system. *International Journal of Electrical and Computer Engineering, 10*(1), 455.

Ghafur, S., Kristensen, S., Honeyford, K., Martin, G., Darzi, A., & Aylin, P. (2019). A retrospective impact analysis of the WannaCry cyberattack on the NHS. *NPJ Digital Medicine, 2*(1), 98.

Harding, W., Hartmann, A., O'Brien, S., Sinzig, V., Break, G., & Sinzig, N. (2025). *Securing a Connected Future.* Springer Nature Switzerland., DOI: 10.1007/978-3-032-07309-9

He, Y., Maglaras, L., Aliyu, A., & Luo, C. (2022). Healthcare Security Incident Response Strategy-A Proactive Incident Response (IR) Procedure. *Security and Communication Networks, 2022*(1), 2775249.

Howard, M., & LeBlanc, D. (2003). *Writing secure code.* Pearson Education.

Humayed, A., Lin, J., Li, F., & Luo, B. (2017). Cyber-physical systems security—A survey. *IEEE Internet of Things Journal, 4*(6), 1802–1831.

Javaid, M., Haleem, A., Singh, R. P., & Suman, R. (2023). Towards insighting cybersecurity for healthcare domains: A comprehensive review of recent practices and trends. *Cyber Security and Applications, 1,* 100016.

Kaur, B. (2025). Social Engineering Attacks in the Digital Age

Khan, S. K., Shiwakoti, N., & Stasinopoulos, P. (2022). A conceptual system dynamics model for cybersecurity assessment of connected and autonomous vehicles. *Accident; Analysis and Prevention, 165,* 106515.

Kruse, C. S., Frederick, B., Jacobson, T., & Monticone, D. K. (2017). Cybersecurity in healthcare: A systematic review of modern threats and trends. *Technology and Health Care*, *25*(1), 1–10.

Levin, D. Z. (2001). Institutionalism, learning, and patterns of selective decoupling: The case of total quality management. In *annual meeting of the Academy of Management, Washington, DC*.

Lieneck, C., McLauchlan, M., & Phillips, S. (2023). Healthcare cybersecurity ethical concerns during the COVID-19 global pandemic: A rapid review. *Healthcare (Basel)*, *11*(22), 2983.

Lorci, E. (2024). Thucydides Trap Revisited: An Alternative Explanation for the Ideologization of US-China Cyberspace Competition and Its Impact on Stability of Cyberspace. *Perspectives on Global Development and Technology*, *22*(3-4), 190–216.

Martin, G., Martin, P., Hankin, C., Darzi, A., & Kinross, J. (2017). Cybersecurity and healthcare: How safe are we? *BMJ (Clinical Research Ed.)*, •••, 358.

Minnaar, A., & Herbig, F. J. (2021). Cyberattacks and the cybercrime threat of ransomware to hospitals and healthcare services during the COVID-19 pandemic. *Acta Criminologica: African Journal of Criminology & Victimology*, *34*(3), 155–185.

Mirsky, Y., Mahler, T., Shelef, I., & Elovici, Y. (2019). {CT-GAN}: Malicious tampering of 3d medical imagery using deep learning. In *28th USENIX Security Symposium (USENIX Security 19)* (pp. 461-478).

Mohammed, D., Mariani, R., & Mohammed, S. (2015). Cybersecurity challenges and compliance issues within the US healthcare sector. *International journal of business and social research*, *5*(2), 55-66.

Mokdad, M. (2025). The rise of soft power in modern diplomacy. In *Innovations and Tactics for 21st Century Diplomacy* (pp. 29–50). IGI Global.

Mwaura, M. W. (2025). *Challenges Encountered in Using Information Security Metrics to Improve Patient Safety in Public Hospitals, Nairobi Metropolitan, Kenya* (Doctoral dissertation, Kenyatta University).

Natsiavas, P., Rasmussen, J., Voss-Knude, M., Votis, K., Coppolino, L., Campegiani, P., & Koutkias, V. (2018). Comprehensive user requirements engineering methodology for secure and interoperable health data exchange. *BMC Medical Informatics and Decision Making*, *18*(1), 85.

Newman, L. H. (2020). Ransomware hits dozens of hospitals in an unprecedented wave. *Wired, Oct.*

Nurse, J. R. (2018). Cybercrime and you: How criminals attack and the human factors that they seek to exploit. *arXiv preprint arXiv:1811.06624*.

Oladoyinbo, T. O., Olabanji, S. O., Olaniyi, O. O., Adebiyi, O. O., Okunleye, O. J., & Ismaila Alao, A. (2024). Exploring the challenges of artificial intelligence in data integrity and its influence on social dynamics. *Asian Journal of Advanced Research and Reports*, *18*(2), 1–23.

Olaniyi, O. O., Omogoroye, O. O., Olaniyi, F. G., Alao, A. I., & Oladoyinbo, T. O. (2024). CyberFusion protocols: Strategic integration of enterprise risk management, ISO 27001, and mobile forensics for advanced digital security in the modern business ecosystem. *Journal of Engineering Research and Reports*, *26*(6), 31–49.

Olateju, O., Okon, S. U., Igwenagu, U., Salami, A. A., Oladoyinbo, T. O., & Olaniyi, O. O. (2024). Combating the challenges of false positives in AI-driven anomaly detection systems and enhancing data security in the cloud. *Available at SSRN* 4859958.

Ostermann, M., Mathias, R., Jahed, F., Parker, M. B., Hudson, F. D., Harding, W. C., & Freyer, O. (2025). Cybersecurity requirements for medical devices in the EU and US-A comparison and gap analysis of the MDCG 2019-16 and FDA premarket cybersecurity guidance. *Computational and Structural Biotechnology Journal*.

Parmar, A. (2012). *Hacker shows off vulnerabilities of wireless insulin pumps*. MedCity News.

Rahim, M. J., Rahim, M. I. I., Afroz, A., & Akinola, O. (2024). Cybersecurity threats in healthcare it: Challenges, risks, and mitigation strategies. *Journal of Artificial Intelligence General science(JAIGS) ISSN: 3006-4023*, *6*(1), 438-462.

Regulation, P. (2016). Regulation (EU) 2016/679 of the European Parliament and of the Council. [eu]. *Regulation*, *679*, 10–13.

Roman-Urrestarazu, A., Kinsey, J., & van Kessel, R. (2022). A bill of children's digital rights is required to improve and sustain children's futures globally. *JAMA Pediatrics*, *176*(11), 1064–1066.

Rothrock, R. A., Kaplan, J., & Van Der Oord, F. (2018). The board's role in managing cybersecurity risks. *MIT Sloan Management Review*, *59*(2), 12–15.

Rudd, L., Hajkowicz, S., Nepal, S., Boughen, N., & Reeson, A. (2015). *Fast Forward: Scenarios for Queensland in the Year 2025 Describing the Marketplace for Education, Healthcare, Policing, Transport and Other Public Services: a Scenario Planning Exercise about the Digital Marketplace for Government Services in the Future to Inform Decision Makers*. Department of Science, Information Technology and Innovation and CSIRO.

Saha, B., & Anwar, Z. (2024). A review of cybersecurity challenges in small business: The imperative for a future governance framework. *Journal of Information Security, 15*(01), 24–39.

Sajid, S., Nazir, M., & Aijaz, M. (2025, July). Beyond Severity: Tactical Risk Scoring for Healthcare Vulnerabilities. In *2025 2nd International Conference On Multidisciplinary Research and Innovations in Engineering (MRIE)* (pp. 427-432). IEEE.

Samuel-Okon, A. D., Akinola, O. I., Olaniyi, O. O., Olateju, O. O., & Ajayi, S. A. (2024). Assessing the effectiveness of network security tools in mitigating the impact of deepfakes AI on public trust in media. *Archives of Current Research International, 24*(6), 355–375.

Selesi-Aina, O., Obot, N. E., Olisa, A. O., Gbadebo, M. O., Olateju, O., & Olaniyi, O. O. (2024). The future of work: A human-centric approach to AI, robotics, and cloud computing. *Journal of Engineering Research and Reports, 26*(11), 10–9734.

Shanto, M. I., Sultana, J., Sarwar, S., Johora, N. T., & Popy, F. P. (2026). Data-Centric Business Analysis in Agile Software Development to Fortify Cybersecurity Posture for US Healthcare Systems. *EJSMT, 2*(1), 184–204.

Shostack, A. (2014). *Threat modeling: Designing for security*. John wiley & sons.

Silva Filho, J. C. L., Braga, C. S. C., & Reboucas, S. M. D. P. (2017). PERCEPTION OF THE BRAZILIAN MANUFACTURING INDUSTRY ABOUT THE MAIN BARRIERS TO INNOVATION/PERCEPCAO DE OBSTACULOS A INOVACAO NA INDUSTRIA A BRASILEIRA DE TRANSFORMACAO. *International journal of innovation, 5*(1), 114-132.

Singh, C. (2023). European cyber security law in 2023: A review of the advances in the Network and Information Security 2 Directive 2022/2555. *Cyber Security: A Peer-Reviewed Journal, 7*(1), 82-92.

Spanou, D. (2024). The EU Cybersecurity Skills Academy: A silver bullet to address the cyber security skills gap in the European Union?. *Cyber Security: A Peer-Reviewed Journal, 7*(3), 229-236.

Thibodeau, S. (2025). Data Breach Risk Management: Examining Impacts, Strategies, and Cultural Shifts. *SCIENTIA MORALITAS-International Journal of Multidisciplinary Research, 10*(2), 187–206.

Tounsi, W., & Rais, H. (2018). A survey on technical threat intelligence in the age of sophisticated cyber attacks. *Computers & Security, 72*, 212–233.

Triplett, W. J. (2024). Cybersecurity vulnerabilities in healthcare: A threat to patient security. *Cybersecurity and Innovative Technology Journal*, *2*(1), 15–25.

van Kessel, R., Wong, B. L. H., Forman, R., Gabrani, J., & Mossialos, E. (2022). The European Health Data Space fails to bridge digital divides. *bmj, 378.*

Wairimu, S., & Fritsch, L. (2022, August). Modelling privacy harms of compromised personal medical data-beyond data breach. In *Proceedings of the 17th international conference on availability, reliability and security* (pp. 1-9).

Williams, C. M., Chaturvedi, R., & Chakravarthy, K. (2020). Cybersecurity risks in a pandemic. *Journal of Medical Internet Research*, *22*(9), e23692.

Xu, L. (2025, June). Trends in US Healthcare Data Breaches. In *2025 IEEE International Conference on AI.*

Chapter 2
Collaborative Cybersecurity and Co-Creation:
Stakeholder Roles

Alice A. Bamigbola
http://orcid.org/0000-0002-0722-1100
University of Ibadan, Nigeria

ABSTRACT

The rapid evolution of digital technologies has intensified cyber threats, leaving individuals, organizations, and critical infrastructures increasingly vulnerable. Traditional, isolated cybersecurity approaches are no longer sufficient. Consequently, collaborative cybersecurity and co-creation have emerged as vital strategies that unite the strengths of diverse stakeholders. Yet, efforts remain fragmented due to low trust, poor coordination, and unequal capacities, especially in regions with weak regulatory systems and scarce resources. This chapter examines the roles of governments, private-sectors, academia, civil society, and end users in advancing collaborative cybersecurity. Drawing from literature, policies, and case studies, it shows how co-creation fosters innovation and resilience through shared expertise and resources. Effective collaboration relies on trust, information sharing, and clear governance. However, inconsistent regulations and weak institutional ties persist. Sustainable cybersecurity demands inclusive, transparent, trust-based cooperation among all actors.

DOI: 10.4018/979-8-3373-6696-8.ch002

INTRODUCTION

The contemporary cybersecurity landscape is marked by unprecedented complexity, interdependence, and scale. As societies increasingly depend on digital infrastructures to support essential services, economic transactions, and social relations, the vulnerabilities of these networked systems have expanded in turn. Cyberattacks are now targeting not only individual organizations but also serious infrastructures, supply chains, and transnational networks, with cascading effects that can undermine economic stability, public trust, and national security (Dunn Cavelty & Egloff, 2020; Nye, 2010). In this evolving environment, no single actor, government, corporate, or civic, has sufficient resources, knowledge, or authority to address the variety of cybersecurity threats alone (Hurel & Weissinger, 2021; Radu, 2019).

These facts have motivated a paradigmatic shift in the theory and practice of cybersecurity. Gradually, scholars and practitioners demand collaborative and networked approaches that leverage the capabilities of a diversity of stakeholders, including governments and the private sector, academia, and civil society, in an attempt to build more secure cyber environments (Carrapico & Farrand, 2017; Provan & Kenis, 2008). One of the more promising models within this paradigm is co-creation, or the active participation of multiple stakeholders in the collaborative design, implementation, and management of cybersecurity solutions (Vila-Garzón & Bacca-Acosta, 2020). Instead of cybersecurity remaining the exclusive domain of technical experts or state agencies, co-creation identifies the decentralized nature of digital threats and seeks to arrange plural sources of knowledge, capability, and intelligence.

The role of stakeholders is predominantly significant in this co-creation process. Each actor brings various assets and constraints to collaborative cybersecurity. Governments offer strategic direction and regulatory policy; private companies embrace much of the digital infrastructure and technical expertise; academia provides research and methodological innovation; and civil society promotes transparency, accountability, and trust (DeNardis, 2020; Hurel & Weissinger, 2021). However, co-creation among these diverse groups is not easy. It is designed by power dynamics, legal frameworks, organizational cultures, and technological infrastructures that enable and also constrain co-creation (Teixeira et al., 2020; Dawson et al., 2020).

This chapter discusses collaborative cybersecurity through a co-creation lens, with a focus on the stakeholder roles, interactions, and dynamics in shaping cybersecurity governance and practice. Based on information systems literature, governance literature, and international relations literature. It examines how stakeholder collaboration in complex digital domains operates, identifies the obstacles and enablers that shape these interactions, and specifies novel practices that foster more inclusive and resilient cybersecurity ecosystems. In so doing, it contributes to an overall understanding of the ways in which multi-actor collaboration may move beyond rhetoric to tangible, adaptive, and sustainable cybersecurity governance.

Objectives

The chapter's objectives are to:

1. identify collaborative cybersecurity frameworks;
2. examine how stakeholder co-creation is enacted in cybersecurity;
3. analyze the Stakeholders roles;
4. identify Technological platforms for co-creation;
5. bridge theories from information systems, international relations, and public policy to develop a holistic understanding of collaborative cybersecurity;
6. highlight challenges of co-creation in collaborative cybersecurity; and
7. examine enablers in cybersecurity stakeholder collaboration.

Methodology

This chapter employs a conceptual and integrative literature review strategy to examine government, private sector, civil society, and individual contributions to cybersecurity co-creation. Thus, it relies only on secondary data. It synthesizes and critically analyzes available relevant scholarship, policy reports, and case-based evidence to provide an overall impression of collaborative cybersecurity and co-creation with stakeholders. Sources were discovered by targeted browsing of multidisciplinary databases including Scopus, Web of Science, IEEE Xplore, SpringerLink, and Google Scholar, supplemented by local ones like AJOL and purposive grey literature from international organizations such as the World Economic Forum, OECD, UN, and ENISA. Keywords used include cybersecurity, collaborative governance, co-creation, stakeholder roles, public–private partnerships, ISACs, civil society, and digital trust. Analysis continued through a thematic synthesis. Literature was organized around themes that emerged and encompassed stakeholder roles, collaborative frameworks, obstacles and enablers, governance models, and technological supports like AI and blockchain. Policy and academic sources were set against one another to elicit theoretical, practical, and regional variation in collaborative cybersecurity practices. This conceptual frame enabled the theoretical frameworks of information systems, international relations, and public policy to be synthesized towards developing an interdisciplinary understanding. Inclusion criteria focused on sources that (a) explicitly addressed multi-stakeholder collaboration or co-creation in cybersecurity, (b) provided theoretical, empirical, or policy-oriented insights, and

(c) were published in English. Peer-reviewed journal articles, conference papers, policy reports, and well-documented case studies were prioritized. Exclusion criteria included opinion pieces lacking analytical depth, sources with limited relevance to collaborative or co-creative cybersecurity approaches, and duplicated or outdated materials where more recent evidence was available. The methodology ensured the spread and intensity of coverage to accommodate prominent debates, identify gaps, and engage with practical and theoretical contributions towards collaborative cybersecurity scholarship.

1. FINDINGS

Collaborative Cybersecurity Frameworks

The Fourth Industrial Revolution (4IR) has introduced unprecedented connectivity through the Internet of Things (IoT), Artificial Intelligence (AI), and smart devices. These technologies are transforming economies by embedding intelligence into everyday objects and infrastructures (Schwab, 2016; Xu et al., 2018). They offer convenience and expanded digital access even in remote regions (Manyika et al., 2013). However, globalization and hyper-connectivity have simultaneously increased the scale and complexity of cyber threats. As more devices come online, they become potential attack points, exposing critical infrastructures to sophisticated cyberattacks (Bada & Nurse, 2019; Conti et al., 2018). This underlines the need to move from isolated corporate defenses toward coordinated cybersecurity frameworks (Craig, 2021; Tanczer et al., 2018).

Modern cyber threats are diverse, including ransomware, supply chain attacks, and advanced persistent threats (APTs) that exploit vulnerabilities across organizational and national boundaries (Sanger, 2018). Cybersecurity has, therefore, become a socio-technical and governance issue requiring multi-stakeholder collaboration among governments, private sectors, and civil society to establish strong defense mechanisms (Borghard & Lonergan, 2017). Collaborative approaches are built on the notion that cybersecurity is a shared responsibility. Governments, private firms, and serious infrastructure providers must cooperate through public–private partnerships (PPPs), information-sharing networks, and international agreements (Carr, 2016; Dunn Cavelty & Suter, 2009). These arrangements create formal structures for sharing threat intelligence, coordinating incident response, and harmonizing regulations while balancing public security with private rights (Petersen, 2021).

i. Public–Private Partnerships (PPPs) in Cybersecurity

Public-Private Partnerships (PPPs) are central mechanisms for aligning state security responsibilities with private sector ownership of infrastructure. Governments oversee national security, while private actors operate essential network through formal agreements, PPPs enable information sharing, capacity building, and collaborative incident response (Carr, 2016; Dunn Cavelty & Suter, 2009). They represent hybrid regulatory models combining mandatory requirements with voluntary cooperation. PPPs pool expertise, technology, and intelligence, enabling multi-level responses to threats (Borghard & Lonergan, 2017). Their value is principally obvious in critical sectors such as energy, finance, and telecommunications, where cyber incidents can trigger cascading economic and social impacts (Craig, 2021).

A notable example is Oman's financial sector, where PPP initiatives have established systematic threat intelligence exchange between government agencies, private data centers, and international technology firms. This collaboration has strengthened national cyber defense policies and industry resilience (Al-Khouri, 2020). However, PPPs face governance and legal challenges. Fragmented policies, privacy concerns, and uneven power dynamics often impede cooperation (Petersen, 2021). Effective PPPs require clear legal frameworks that foster trust, transparency, accountability, sustainable financing, and active stakeholder engagement (Dunn Cavelty & Suter, 2009). Without these, partnerships risk becoming imbalanced and ineffective.

ii. Information Sharing and Analysis Centers (ISACs)

Information Sharing and Analysis Centers (ISACs) are industry-specific platforms that enable organizations to exchange cyber threat intelligence. Acting as network nodes, they collect, process, and disseminate information to enhance situational awareness and incident response (Goodman & Lin, 2019). ISACs enable organizations to identify and respond to emerging threats more quickly than if they acted individually. The Financial Services ISAC (FS-ISAC) employed this model, in which financial institutions share sensitive threat data within trusted frameworks, following strict membership and classification protocols (FS-ISAC, 2020). Their performance is typically measured through key indicators data collection, analysis, dissemination, and response time benchmarked against international standards (European Union Agency for Cybersecurity, 2018). ISACs have significantly reduced response times and improved proactive defense strategies. Nevertheless, their implementation faces obstacles, especially in regions with low cybersecurity maturity, privacy issues, regulatory fragmentation, data sensitivity, and limited digital literacy hinder participation (Craig, 2021). Integrating technological tools like the Malware Information

Sharing Platform (MISP) helps automate threat intelligence sharing and preserve privacy using features such as two-factor authentication (Wagner et al., 2019).

iii. Global Cybersecurity Collaboration

Because cyber threats are inherently transnational, international frameworks and regional cooperation are essential for collective resilience (Nye, 2017). These frameworks aim to harmonize legal, technical, and policy environments for cross-border defense. Examples include bilateral agreements, multilateral treaties, and the EU's Network and Information Security (NIS) directive, which establishes mechanisms for information exchange and incident response across member states (European Commission, 2016).

Global collaboration is complicated by geopolitical tensions and competing national agendas, which can slow normal development and operational convergence (Tikk, 2018). However, international Information Sharing and Analysis Organizations (ISAOs) offer shared platforms for trust-building and operational coordination. Emerging technologies also aid secure cross-border information exchange. Federated learning permits organizations to collaboratively evaluate threats without sharing sensitive raw data (Yang et al., 2019). Similarly, platforms like the Pan-European Cybersecurity Incidents Information Sharing Platform reveal how policy and technology integration can support multilateral cyber defense (European Union Agency for Cybersecurity, 2018).

iv. Comparative Perspectives: PPPs vs. ISACs

While PPPs and ISACs both strengthen cybersecurity through stakeholder engagement, they differ in scope and function. PPPs focus on strategic issues such as policy alignment, regulatory coordination, and resource mobilization between governments and industries (Carr, 2016). ISACs, by contrast, are operational mechanisms that underscore real-time intelligence sharing and rapid incident response within specific sectors (FS-ISAC, 2020).

PPPs shape national cybersecurity strategies and provide governance structures, while ISACs offer sector-specific situational awareness and agility. Together, they form complementary pillars: PPPs provide the strategic foundation, and ISACs supply the operational capabilities necessary to address evolving cyber threats effectively.

v. Technological Enablers of Collaboration

Technological innovations are vital in supporting collaborative cybersecurity. Artificial intelligence (AI) and Machine Learning (ML) enhance irregularity detection, predictive analytics, and automated responses, enabling faster and more accurate threat detection (Brundage et al., 2018). Blockchain provides tamper-proof data-sharing frameworks that ensure secure records of shared intelligence (Miller et al., 2019). AI-driven analysis can improve real-time threat detection. And exchange of information through rapid processing of vast amounts of data, pattern recognition, and the forecasting of novel threats among different stakeholders (Dawson et al., 2020).

Zero Trust Architectures (ZTAs) enhance collaboration by enforcing continuous verification for users and devices, plummeting reliance on perimeter security, and permitting adaptive defense strategies (Kindervag, 2020). MISP platforms incorporate these technologies to facilitate standardized, privacy-conscious, and real-time exchange of threat intelligence (Wagner et al., 2019). If adoption challenges persist, legal and privacy constraints, interoperability issues, and varying organizational cybersecurity maturity could hinder technological integration. Nevertheless, these tools have strong potential to scale collaborative defense across multiple actors and jurisdictions.

vi. Sector-Specific Applications and Emerging Trends in Collaborative Cybersecurity

Financial Sector

The financial services sector has been a leader in leveraging collaborative frameworks to reinforce cybersecurity resilience. Through PPPs, regulatory agencies, banks, and technology providers could work together to share information, detect threats, and organize incident response, thereby reducing systemic risks (Carr, 2016).

One of the most influential mechanisms is the Financial Services Information Sharing and Analysis Center (FS-ISAC), which offers a trusted environment for secure information exchange across financial institutions. FS-ISAC's implementation in contexts such as Indonesia highlights the significance of adapting governance structures, legal frameworks, and technological tools to local realities (FS-ISAC, 2020). Regulatory frameworks also shape collaboration. For example, in the United States, laws like the Gramm–Leach–Bliley Act and initiatives by the Cybersecurity and Infrastructure Security Agency (CISA) promote compliance and encourage active participation in information sharing (U.S. Congress, 1999; CISA, 2020). Singapore's Financial Services Information Sharing and Analysis Center (FS-ISAC) APAC Hub is a global benchmark. It facilitates real-time intelligence sharing between the Monetary Authority of Singapore (MAS) and private banks. These collaborative mechanisms can help the sector preempt sophisticated cyber threats targeting payment systems and transactional infrastructures.

Healthcare Sector

The healthcare sector's rapid digitalization, fast-tracked by the COVID-19 pandemic, has exposed significant cybersecurity vulnerabilities (Al-Kuwaiti et al., 2020). PPPs have become essential to address these challenges by integrating governmental resources, private sector expertise, and non-profit engagement to protect critical health infrastructures. Healthcare cybersecurity is complex owing to the sensitivity of patient data, the extensive use of IoT devices, and the sector's key role in public health. Studies highlight risks related to insider threats, human error, and vulnerabilities in emerging technologies such as blockchain and virtual reality (Appari & Johnson, 2010; Kruse et al., 2017). The growing use of networked medical devices presents new attack vectors; weak encryption and inadequate regulatory enforcement often aggravate security and privacy gaps (Radanliev et al., 2020). Collaborative frameworks are, therefore, essential for developing policy, regulatory, and technical solutions that align privacy protection with operational efficiency. With the rise of telemedicine in Rwanda and Nigeria, patient data has become a high-value target. Collaborative efforts are focusing on protecting "E-Health" records from ransomware that could halt hospital operations, a risk underscored by the ENISA (European Union Agency for Cybersecurity, 2021). Rwanda has pioneered a partnership with private health-tech startups to secure "Zipline" medical drone deliveries. After a devastating 2022 ransomware attack by the Conti group paralyzed the national healthcare system (CCSS), Costa Rica became a case study for international Co-creation. They co-created security standards to ensure life-saving blood supplies aren't disrupted by GPS spoofing.

Energy and Critical Infrastructure

The energy sector denotes another critical area for cybersecurity collaboration, given its vital role in economic and national security. The European Energy Information Sharing and Analysis Centre (EE-ISAC) offered a structured platform for incident data exchange, which enables real-time situational awareness and coordinated response strategies across member organizations (European Union Agency for Cybersecurity, 2018). PPPs in energy have also facilitated the development of clean energy infrastructure in countries such as the United States and Nigeria. These partnerships combine government incentives and private investment to attain the double goals of cyber resilience and environmental sustainability (Adebayo & Ekong, 2020). As regions move toward integrated, smart-grid trading, the risk of a cross-border "blackout-by-hack" increases. It mirrors the global concerns raised by the World Economic Forum (2020) regarding the electricity ecosystem resilience. The Southern African Power Pool (SAPP): National utilities from 12 countries are working with private engineering firms to secure Industrial Control Systems (ICS). They share threat indicators about malware specifically designed to target power turbines and substations. Cross-sectoral analyses disclose that effective governance, technological innovation, and trust-based information sharing are critical pillars for sustaining cybersecurity across industries (Borghard & Lonergan, 2017).

2. ENACTION OF STAKEHOLDER CO-CREATION IN CYBERSECURITY

Co-creation is a strong paradigm for confronting complex cybersecurity challenges in a globally networked environment. It involves active participation of governments, private organizations, research institutions, civil society, and the end-users, making and applying strategies, policies, and technologies to mitigate cyber threats. This approach recognizes that cybersecurity issues cross-across technical, organizational, legal, and social boundaries, which no single actor possesses all the resources or expertise needed to address emerging threats optimally (Vila-Garzón & Bacca-Acosta, 2020). The evolution of co-creation in cybersecurity parallels the development of the Internet itself. Initially, cybersecurity was the domain of a small community of academics, researchers, and engineers who collaborated through informal trust networks such as mailing lists, university conferences, and early incident-reporting channels. This cooperative culture reflected the open nature of the early internet, when governments and corporations were less involved in cybersecurity governance (Hurel & Weissinger, 2021).

The establishment of Computer Emergency Response Teams (CERTs) in the late 1980s marked the first institutionalization of community-based cybersecurity. CERTs and their successors, Computer Security Incident Response Teams (CSIRTs), became central points for exchanging threat intelligence and coordinating incident response. Though originally small and technical, these teams laid the basis for formalized co-creation by merging expertise and developing shared norms for responding to emerging threats (Radu, 2019).

Over time, co-creation processes became more sophisticated. New multi-stakeholder forums, such as PPPs and sectoral ISACs, emerged to enact joint processes. Global organizations and regional governments now summon diverse actors to co-create norms, harmonize responses, and codify governance frameworks (Hurel & Weissinger, 2021). Digital communication tools, orchestration technologies, and collective threat intelligence systems have enabled geographically dispersed actors to cooperate in real time (Al Sharif & Pokharel, 2021).

Co-Creation and Cybersecurity Governance

Cybersecurity governance demonstrates that co-creation is essential. It is characterized by fragmentation, complexity, and overlapping domains of authority across national, regional, and global levels involving both public and private sectors (Hurel & Weissinger, 2021). This decentralized structure mirrors the distributed nature of digital infrastructures, which distance borders, sectors, and communities. Co-creation serves as a connecting mechanism, enabling the sharing of knowledge, joint problem-solving, and coordinated action among actors with divergent priorities but shared security interests.

For example, state actors may prioritize national security and regulatory compliance, private firms manage critical infrastructure, and civil society advocates for privacy and accountability. By establishing formal arenas for collaboration, such as multi-stakeholder forums, advisory boards, and task forces, co-creation allows these actors to align strategies and pool resources effectively (Radu, 2019).

Beyond Technology: Norms and Practices

Co-creation extends beyond technological innovation to the joint production of values, norms, and governance practices. Effective cybersecurity relies on trust, cooperation, and shared responsibility as much as on technical defenses. Stakeholders should use interoperable technologies with their reciprocal benefits of information sharing, coordinated responses, and ethical standards. In this way, co-creation entrenches cybersecurity within broader social and political frameworks, making it socially, politically, and technologically legitimate (Medema et al., 2017).

Capacity Building and Resilience

Co-creation enables capacity building and resilience by engaging actors at varying levels of expertise. Academic institutions contribute research-based knowledge, while user and community participation ensure solutions are practical and acceptable to those who depend on them. This participatory approach builds trust and ownership, the main ingredients for supporting long-term cybersecurity initiatives (Chumo et al., 2021). The co-creation model has advanced from informal collaboration among technical experts to structured, multi-stakeholder governance mechanisms. It now plays a central role in addressing the complexities of modern cybersecurity by connecting diverse knowledge domains, building trust, and embedding shared norms. By combining technological innovation with collective responsibility, co-creation strengthens both the governance and operational dimensions of cybersecurity in a connected world.

Strategic and Governance Dimensions of Co-Creation

Co-creation is becoming a tool in strategic planning and governance of cybersecurity to enable the incorporation of diverse perspectives into decision-making. Unlike singular strategies established by governments or businesses in the past, co-created strategies are developed through multi-stakeholder dialogue, integrating policy-level objectives with operational realities. Formal engagement processes such as stakeholder workshops, advisory committees, and steering committees are key to these initiatives. These platforms assure ownership, increase responsibility, and allow round-robin improvement of cybersecurity policies (Van der Zouwen et al., 2018). National cybersecurity policies are deeply involved in consultation phases with industry, academia, civil society, and technical communities, combining both evolving threats and real-world implementation constraints.

Contemporary cybersecurity governance is defined by multi-level fragmentation. Decision-making is shared among governments, international organisations, industry trade groups, and NGOs at local, national, regional, and global levels (Radu, 2019). Co-creation offers the opportunity to deal with the distributed reality by fostering trans-scalar communication, enabling collaboration among stakeholders regarding coordination policies, resources, and standards. It is crucial for the alignment of national security agendas and international cooperation environments, because cyber threats are naturally transnational (Hurel & Weissinger, 2021). Strategic co-creation must also address power inequalities and issues of inclusivity. Stakeholders vary in technical capacity, political influence, and resources. Structural hierarchies, socioeconomic disparities, and budget constraints may disenfranchise lesser actors, leading to uneven participation and skewed outcomes (Teixeira et al., 2020). These forces must be addressed through the creation of safe areas for dialogue, enabling capacity-building, and involving bridging organizations that serve as intermediaries between societies (Medema et al., 2017). Lastly, strategic and governance co-creation enhances the legitimacy, flexibility, and effectiveness of cybersecurity actions. It facilitates mutual trust between otherwise siloed actors, encourages policy innovation, and aligns technical actions towards a purposeful, societally desirable goal such as privacy, transparency, and accountability.

Information Sharing as Core Co-Creation Activity

Information sharing is central to Co-creation in cybersecurity. This is due to the time constraints and intelligence character of cybersecurity; the speed and accuracy with which information flows among actors to determine whether incidents are contained, or even trigger escalation. Collaborative information sharing allows actors to detect, understand, and neutralize threats more effectively (Hurel & Weissinger, 2021).

Initially, information exchange started in the guise of formal, trust-based networks of system administrators and researchers who shared warnings on mailing lists. It grew into formal ones such as Computer Emergency Response Teams (CERTs) and Computer Security Incident Response Teams (CSIRTs), which now serve as strategic nodes in global cybersecurity environments (Radu, 2019). With standard procedures and trust relationships, they aid in the detection of incidents, facilitate collective mitigation strategies, and learning from past attacks collectively. Bridging organizations also facilitate flows of information among institutions and communities. As connective tissue, they knit together actors that would not engage and translate between technical, policy, and community languages (Medema et al., 2017). In cybersecurity, industry associations, non-profit platforms, and public–private coalitions enhance the density and credibility of information networks, making collaboration systematic and continuous.

Real-world benefits are found in the scenario of the South African tourism sector, where pooled cybersecurity intelligence sharing provided affordable interventions for resource-constrained companies to adopt, as well as improved incident handling (Chumo et al., 2021). Companies used pooled knowledge and collective situational awareness, which was effective against threats such as phishing, ransomware, and payment scams. Sharing information also generates collective situational awareness, a collective sense of the threat situation. Through the reciprocal exchange of indicators, vulnerability information, and incident reports, actors cause a better situational awareness of impending threats, and it improves defensive readiness and strategic foresight (Hurel & Weissinger, 2021).

Nevertheless, information sharing is hampered. The legal and regulatory barriers, in particular, are related to privacy and data protection, and the restriction of cross-border information sharing. Private companies are prohibited from disclosing violations due to competitive pressures and reputational loss (Teixeira et al., 2020). Policy environments, data standards, and organizational cultures are different, creating interoperability and trust gaps (Al Sharif & Pokharel, 2021).

Technological solutions are on the horizon. Orchestration security tools automate data collection, processing, and exchange of threat intelligence among systems, improving effectiveness (Al Sharif & Pokharel, 2021). Privacy-preserving technologies, such as cryptographic protocols and federated learning, offer a sophisticated middle ground for organizations wary of data exposure. These methods allow institutions to pool their insights and build collective defenses without ever having to relinquish control of their raw data. By enabling collaboration while maintaining strict confidentiality, these tools resolve the tension between the necessity of shared intelligence and the mandate for data privacy. These technologies illustrate how institutional and technological co-creation are concomitant: technology allows secure sharing, and governance institutions provide trust and incentives for sustained collaboration.

Information sharing as co-creation involves more than exchanging technical indicators; it is an issue of creating trust, aligning incentives, and producing institutional architectures for sustained cooperation. By combining formal organizations like CERTs, informal networks of trust, bridging organizations, and technical platforms, cybersecurity ecosystems achieve resilient, adaptive, and inclusive collaborative defense.

Joint Exercises and Participatory Design

Joint exercises in cybersecurity and participatory design are perhaps the most tangible expressions of co-creation. While policies and strategies offer blueprints for cooperation, exercises bring them into effect by bringing together the stakeholders to prepare for actual circumstances, validate readiness, and co-design effective incident response. Exercises build technical capability, enhance coordination, and build trust among players. Participatory design, originally developed in education and digital health, has some lessons to be learned. Nordfonn et al. (2021) describe the use of participatory design processes to generate a digital cardiac rehabilitation program through iterative collaboration between clinicians, researchers, patients, and developers. Similarly, in cybersecurity, incident response training through participatory design embodies subtle realities and diverse perspectives rather than single technical exercises.

Cybersecurity exercise comprises scenario planning, where government agencies, the private sector, CERTs, researchers, and sometimes the end users jointly create credible attack scenarios. The test detection systems, communication protocols, decision-making, and recovery activities. Through several cycles of review, exercises are more likely to align with evolving threats; thus, participants have chances to practice adaptive problem-solving (Van der Zouwen et al., 2018).

In addition to simulation, exercises foster collaborative learning. Incident response communities are learning communities where common exercises allow practitioners to exchange lessons, approaches, and best practices. This builds a collective memory and adaptive capacity that improves actors' ability to prepare and respond to subsequent incidents (Hurel & Weissinger, 2021). By exercising realistic scenarios, stakeholders gain interdependencies, such as how a compromise in one's supply chain can cascade through many sectors, promoting proactive defense.

Participatory exercises and design also address non-technical implications of cybersecurity. It reveals gaps in governance, communication, and roles, such as poorly defined reporting structures or ambiguous laws. This would otherwise go unnoticed, providing feedback to enhance technical procedure, policy, and legislation (Teixeira et al., 2020). Involving end users and non-technical stakeholders gives legitimacy and effect. Implementing participatory health practice, patient involvement improves program relevance (Nordfonn et al., 2021). Similarly, involving communities, employees, and civil society ensures that exercises take into consideration human conduct, day-to-day practice, cultural factors, and disengage from expert-dominant to human-centric security structures.

Assessment is another key co-creation element. Traditional assessments are based on technical measures of response times. Co-created exercises extend this to process measures: quality of collaboration, communication, stakeholder involvement, and adaptive learning (Teixeira et al., 2020). Participatory assessment sustains interest, with lessons informing subsequent exercises and institutional practice. Finally, sustainability is critical. Exercises are most effective when integrated into continuous training cycles supported by resources, leadership, and shared responsibility (Van der Zouwen et al., 2018). Embedded in organizational cultures and governance systems, joint exercises and collaborative design aid trust, synchronize strategies, and contribute to shared capabilities. They embody co-creation principles through a union of technical expertise and diverse viewpoints, creating stronger and more resilient cybersecurity ecosystems.

Frameworks, Methodologies, and Stakeholder Roles

Success in the co-production of cybersecurity solutions hinges on discipline frameworks and open stakeholder roles. Frameworks discipline interactions between different actors, permit iterative problem-solving, and integrate knowledge systems, while stakeholder roles ensure that sustained cooperation is possible.

Participatory Design and User Experience Frameworks

Participatory Design (PD) and User Experience (UX) techniques are critical to co-designing cybersecurity policies, tools, and practices. Resulting from Scandinavian democratic workplace design, PD emphasizes equal participation of end users and stakeholders throughout the process. In the field of cybersecurity, this means not only technical experts but also policymakers, employees, and user communities in defining usable, secure solutions. Nordfonn et al. (2021) illustrate PD application in the co-design of a multimodal digital cardiac rehabilitation program, in conjunction with clinicians, patients, and developers who iteratively improved the design. Applied to the cybersecurity domain, PD renders technologies and policies technically appropriate, context-aware, and adaptable to the behaviour of users. PD identifies such hidden problems as usability challenges, privacy concerns, or unintended consequences that might remain undetected by top-down approaches. UX frameworks facilitate PD by paying attention to users' everyday experience. Even with well-designed ones, these systems may not succeed if they are too complicated or at odds with everyday life.

Networked Governance and Bridging Organizations

Networked governance provides a dynamic model of cybersecurity, such as cooperation and coordination among semi-autonomous actors (Radu, 2019). Public organizations, private businesses, universities, and civil society all have tasks to share, requiring inclusive approaches to manage concerted action. The bridging organizations play a key role. Medema et al. (2017) describe them as connectors that help disseminate information, translate technical language, and mediate disagreements. In cybersecurity, these are industry associations, ISACs, research institutions, or consortia. They build trust, coordinate sectoral objectives, sustain knowledge flows, and allow less-resourced stakeholders to co-create more equitably.

Agile and Iterative Co-Creation Processes

Agile processes, borrowed from the software World, support public administrations in finding an equilibrium between bureaucracy and flexibility (Noennig & Heuer, 2019). Short, iterative rounds of stakeholder consultation, quick prototyping, testing, and refinement allow organizations to adapt to changing threats. This process supports learning, addresses changing priorities, and eschews rigid, one-size-fits-all solutions that become outdated.

3. STAKEHOLDERS ROLES IN CO-CREATION

Cybersecurity co-creation relies on the complementary contributions of multiple stakeholder groups, each with unique capabilities, responsibilities, and perspectives.

i. Public Policy Makers and Public Sector

Governments present regulatory environments, investments with political leadership, leading the strategic direction of national cybersecurity efforts, and connecting them to public policy priorities. Radu (2019) quotes governments as key authoritative actors in plural governance settings, which are decisive in coordinating multi-stakeholder collaboration. Policymakers also remove regulatory hindrances for information exchange and permit open collaboration (Hurel & Weissinger, 2021).

ii. Private Sector and Industry Actors

The huge segments of the virtual world are dominated by technology companies, Financial institutions, and vital infrastructure players. Their technical data and operational expertise are essential to effective cybersecurity. Private companies in South Africa's hospitality and tourism sector shared threat intelligence to raise sectoral security, demonstrating Co-creation's value for collective resilience (Chumo et al., 2021). Industry players must also exclude competition and trust, requiring open cooperation processes.

iii. Scholarly Institutions

Academic institutions and research centers provide methodological rigor, interdisciplinarity, and ingenuity. As objective conveners and knowledge brokers, they translate technical issues into policy-relevant insights that facilitate evidence-based decision-making, especially when cybersecurity capabilities are evolving.

iv. Civil Society and End User

Civil society organizations serve as essential intermediaries in the digital ecosystem, ensuring that cybersecurity frameworks remain anchored in democratic principles, transparency, and the protection of fundamental human rights. Beyond mere technical compliance, the efficacy of these policies depends on the "grounded expertise" of citizens and workers. By integrating the lived experiences of these stakeholders, policymakers can develop strategies that are not only technically sound but also socially resonant. As Nordfonn et al. (2021) suggest, this participatory approach is critical for cultivating the digital literacy and public trust required for the sustainable implementation of security initiatives.

By bringing these functions together through frameworks like PD, UX, networked governance, and agile methods, Co-creation changes cybersecurity into a societal endeavour from being a technical issue. All the stakeholder groups contribute regulatory, technical, intellectual, or social capital to accomplish more robust, responsive, and legitimate cybersecurity ecosystems.

4. TECHNOLOGICAL ENABLERS OF CO-CREATION

While institutional design and stakeholder engagement present governance enablers, technologies are the underlying infrastructure enabling cooperation at scale. With growing sophistication in cyber threats and geographical dispersal, technical capabilities are required to ensure real-time communication, secure data transfer, and cooperative action. These technical tools supplement, but do not replace, human collaboration, bringing it outside organizational and national boundaries.

i. Digital Platforms for Stakeholder Collaboration

Digital platforms are essential in Co-creation, as they enable organized communication, information exchange, and joint decision-making by different actors within and between organizations, sectors, and countries (Hurel & Weissinger, 2021). Platforms comprise secure portals for the exchange of threat intelligence, dashboards for monitoring cybersecurity information, and communication tools to enable synchronous and asynchronous communication. Participatory design principles often guide their development; for instance, open online forums and collaborative documents have been used to gather input for smart city cybersecurity strategies, guaranteeing diverse voices are heard (Nordfonn et al., 2021).

Security Orchestration, Automation, and Response (SOAR) systems integrate heterogeneous cybersecurity tools, enabling coordinated processes among and within organizations. Through the provision of integrated visibility and active response, SOAR systems allow collaborative action against threats (Al Sharif & Pokharel, 2021). In multi-stakeholder settings, they are also used as mediation spaces, standardizing procedures, and establishing trust.

ii. Data Sharing and Privacy-Preserving Technologies

Information exchange is mandatory but challenging, as firms must balance the intelligence exchange with legal, ethical, and competitive constraints. Privacy technologies are now a trust-based collaboration of enablers of necessity. Cryptographic techniques such as secure multiparty computation, homomorphic encryption, and differential privacy allow analysis of collective data without compromising raw data (Al Sharif & Pokharel, 2021). For instance, multiple parties can collaboratively build a threat model construction from encrypted data, preserving secrecy, while supporting collective defense.

Federated learning permits collaborative microlearning without data centralization. Models are locally trained by entities and shared only updates with a centralized aggregator, ensuring privacy and regulatory compliance, while accomplishing optimal collective intelligence. This is especially useful in detecting new patterns of attack across industries and borders. Such technologies complement legal and governance means by integrating trust at the technical layer, essentially in cross-border collaboration, where data protection law and competitive concerns often eliminate direct sharing.

iii. Automation, Artificial Intelligence, and Orchestration

The velocity and volume of cyber threats have surpassed human operations. Automation and artificial intelligence (AI) are now a necessity, enabling collaborative cybersecurity at speed. The continuous work log analysis, incident triage, and alerts are automated to assist human analysts in concentrating on strategic work (Al Sharif & Pokharel, 2021). In co-creation spaces, automation synchronizes action among organizations. For instance, when one sees a phishing campaign, automated tools can immediately share indicators of compromise with partners, reducing response time and limiting attacker ROI.

Artificial Intelligence enhances these efforts with the addition of high-end analytics, anomaly detection, and predictive models. AI can identify subtle, unknown patterns in network activity or users' behaviour that allow joint sense-making among actors. Shared AI systems support collective interpretation of Big data sets, but integration of AI raises governance and ethics issues. Explainable AI (XAI) facilitates greater transparency, which allows stakeholders to verify and confirm the algorithmic outputs, crucial for accountability and trust in multi-actor environments (Kenny & Castilla-Rho, 2021). AI needs to be managed wisely to prevent the spread of biases and the creation of new vulnerabilities.

iv. Enabling Scalable, Inclusive, and Trustworthy Co-Creation

Digital platforms, privacy-enhancing technology, and AI-driven automation form the technological scaffolding for scalable, inclusive co-creation. They allow dispersed actors to collaborate safely and efficiently, and to organize weaker-resourced players, particularly in regions like Africa, where infrastructure shortages impede involvement. Technology is not sufficient by itself. Achievements are dependent on the governance setups, clearly articulated rules of engagement, and a culture of trust. Platforms must be accessible; privacy-preserving tools must be aligned with legal infrastructures; and automation must support human agency and accountability. When such factors converge, technological facilitators transform Co-creation as an idea into a real, achievable expression of collective cybersecurity action.

5. INTEGRATING THEORETICAL PERSPECTIVES: TOWARDS A COMPREHENSIVE APPROACH TO COOPERATIVE CYBERSECURITY

The increase in cyber threats, ransomware, chain attacks, and state-directed cyber espionage calls for cooperative solutions that surpass organizational as well as national boundaries (Hurel & Weissinger, 2021; Radu, 2019). As cyber threats are transnational, multi-actor, and socio-technical, no single theoretical perspective can fully capture their multifaceted nature. The integration of information systems (IS), international relations (IR), and public policy theories provides a balanced paradigm for cooperative cybersecurity. Information systems emphasize socio-technical systems and networks of information exchange; IR focuses on power, cooperation, and global governance; and public policy focuses on multi-level governance, regulation, and institutional coordination.

Information Systems Theories: Socio-Technical Networks and Collaboration

Information systems studies provide fundamental ideas for understanding cooperation in socio-technical contexts. Socio-technical systems theory distinguishes cybersecurity as resulting from the interaction of technological infrastructure and human participants (Trist & Bamforth, 1951; Baxter & Sommerville, 2011). Cooperative cybersecurity is based on matching technical capacity, such as intrusion detection and encryption, with organizational processes like communication, decision-making, and building trust. ISACs and CSIRTs are well-established instances of socio-technical collaboration. They utilise technical infrastructures for sharing information and informal networks of trust, which enable a rapid, secure flow of information (Hurel & Weissinger, 2021). Information systems research displays how network topology, interoperability, and common ontologies aid effective information sharing (Dawson et al., 2020). Collaboration tends to be activated by trust, reputation, and governance mechanisms rather than by technology alone.

The Resource-Based View (RBV) and the Knowledge-Sharing theories explain why organizations collaborate, as no organization can have all the resources to manage advanced cyber threats. Collaboration gives access to complementary capabilities, like threat intelligence, competence, and policy expertise (Alhassan et al., 2019). Joint cybersecurity thus turns into inter-organizational co-creation of knowledge, in line with organizational learning and networked innovation theories.

International Relations Theories: Power, Cooperation, and Global Cyber Governance

The Information Systems theory defines organizational and network dynamics, while the International Relations theory deals with geopolitical structures, influencing cybersecurity cooperation. Cyber threats lack borders, while capacities and priorities are not balanced among states, companies, and international organizations, meaning the role of a multi-polar governance system driven by power and trust. Realist IR theories emphasize state power and strategic rivalry. States use cyber capabilities as instruments of national power, which fosters rivalry and limits information exchange (Nye, 2010). Hence, collaborative structures may be restricted in scope or dominated by powerful states, resulting in participation asymmetries.

The NATO, EU NIS Directive, and Budapest Convention frameworks provide spaces for joint exercises, information sharing, and collective action (Carrapico & Farrand, 2017; Radu, 2019). The Constructivist perspectives highlight norm diffusion, identity, and common understanding. International collaboration relies not just on strategic interests but also on common norms and epistemic communities (DeNardis, 2020). ISACs and CERT communities transcend national borders through common technical languages and professional identities, even with the limited formal political collaboration. IR theories thus disclose in this context how collaborative cybersecurity is based both on material power relationships and on normative frameworks, which dominate and affect participation, trust, and transparency.

Public Policy Theories: Multi-Level Governance and Institutional Coordination

Public policy research provides insight into governance structures, regulation, and institutional interactions. Cybersecurity operates at various levels of governance: local, national, regional, and global, involving multiple stakeholders.There is a disjointed system, and there are coordinated policies needed (Radu, 2019; Dunn Cavelty & Egloff, 2020). Multi-level governance (MLG) theory explains how responsibilities are distributed between governments and institutions. Initially developed with European integration (Marks & Hooghe, 2004), MLG can be employed to study structures like the EU NIS Directive, with tasks spread over levels and sectors for the purpose of enhancing coordination (Radu, 2019).

Network governance theories explain cooperation in hierarchy-free settings. Cybersecurity collaborations occur in the form of policy networks including public agencies, firms, and non-state actors, governed by negotiation, trust, and shared goals (Provan & Kenis, 2008). Public-private partnerships are an example par excellence, corresponding to incentives and accountability between sectors (Carrapico & Farrand, 2017). Policy implementation and regulatory capacity theories highlight coordination challenges resulting from institutional fragmentation, incoherent policies, and resource disparities (Dunn Cavelty & Egloff, 2020). Public policy, thus, places prominence on adaptive governance that dynamically evolves with threats and technologies.

Toward an Integrated Theoretical Framework

Each of the lenses offers valuable but limited insights. Information Systems accounts for micro- and meso-level socio-technical collaboration; IR accounts for macro-level relations of power and international dynamics; public policy accounts for governance and regulation mechanisms. An integration of these visions presents an integrated image. A synthesis template can frame collaborative cybersecurity as a multi-level socio-technical governance system:

1. Micro-level (IS): Accounts for how networks and organizations share information and coordinate using socio-technical systems and trust.
2. Meso-level (Public policy): Examines how governance structures and networks enable coordination between levels and sectors of government.
3. Macro-level (IR): Aims to comprehend how geopolitical relations, power differences, and norms shape global cooperation.

This hybrid allows contextual analysis of the interaction between interoperability, regulation, and geopolitics. For instance, international ISACs exist in socio-technical networks (IS) but depend on geopolitical trust (IR) and public policy regimes (regulatory systems). Likewise, international cyber norms influence national policy, which affects organizational information-sharing practice. Synthesizing these theories directs policy and research. Policymakers can envision complementary cybersecurity models that are technically achievable (IS), politically viable (IR), and institutionally aligned (public policy). Researchers can leverage cross-disciplinary methods that map interactions among levels, improving practice-based evaluation.

Challenges of Stakeholder Collaboration towards Cybersecurity

The increasingly pervasive and sophisticated nature of cyber threats makes it such that no single entity can have all the know-how or resources to manage risks competently. Collaboration has therefore become the central theme in supporting collective cybersecurity resilience. Complications that exist in this environment, this review synthesizes the primary barriers hinder stakeholder collaboration towards cybersecurity.

i. Legal and Regulatory Barriers

Legal and regulatory hurdles remain the most significant barriers to effective information sharing in the digital domain. Rigid statutes regarding data privacy and intellectual property often prioritize domestic control over the transnational cooperation necessary for modern defense (Carrapico & Farrand, 2017; Radu, 2019). Furthermore, the private sector is often caught in a "liability trap." Litigation concerns, combined with the potential for public fallout and regulatory penalties, discourage voluntary transparency. In this environment, the risk of sharing sensitive breach data often appears to outweigh the collective benefits of cooperation (Hurel & Weissinger, 2021). Balkanized systems make the issue worse. While individual nations design cybersecurity and data protection laws to meet domestic needs, this legal diversity often acts as a barrier to international cooperation. As Dunn Cavelty and Egloff (2020) observe, the lack of legal alignment makes it functionally impossible to establish the interoperable frameworks required for fluid, global data exchange. Convergent "critical infrastructure" definitions, data classification standards, and jurisdictions in overlap complicate collaboration. Multilateral agreements like the Budapest Convention work to create a degree of harmonization but have limited scope, especially in non-signatory states (Radu, 2019). Lack of explicit, cross-sectoral legislation is a widespread structural obstacle.

ii. Institutional Fragmentation and Trust Deficits

Trust is the foundation for collaboration, but it is all too often lacking. Stakeholders play out in adversarial settings with competing agendas, and reluctance to share sensitive information follows (Dawson et al., 2020). Private parties are reluctant to expose themselves to vulnerabilities to their competitors or regulators, while government regulators are bound by confidentiality (DeNardis, 2020). Institutional fragmentation contributes to trust issues as cybersecurity requirements are normally shared across several organizations with discrete functions but minimal coordination (Radu, 2019), leading to contradictory priorities and organizational inertia (Dunn Cavelty & Egloff, 2020). Institutionalized forms of governance like Information Sharing and Analysis Centers (ISACs) and Computer Security Incident Response Teams (CSIRTs) offer an impartial collaboration platform or forum where iterative interactions instill "thick trust" (Hurel & Weissinger, 2021). Bridging organizations also permit the creation of trust by mediating institutional cultures and technical tongues (Medema et al., 2017).

iii. Asymmetries of Power and Unbalanced Capacities

Power asymmetries are another issue; governments hold regulatory power and strategic capacities, while private corporations own key infrastructure and technical expertise. Smaller organizations, civil society, and developing nations' players usually lack capacity and power, leading to unequal participation (Radu, 2019; Teixeira et al., 2020). Unequal capacities arise in technical maturity, financial means, and human capital. Advanced cybersecurity centers exist in some, while others have inadequate defenses. This leaves networks exposed through weak points (Nye, 2010).

iv. Technical and Infrastructural Barriers

Infrastructural variations, technical incompatibilities, and low interoperability hinder collaborative work. Cyber defense environments are based on varied vendors' and jurisdictions' technologies that must be able to communicate with one another to enable effective information exchange. The absence of uniform formats for data and protocols results in fragmented threat intelligence. Proprietary systems that are not cross-institutional integrate form real-time collaboration chokepoints. Infrastructure shortfalls, especially where broadband is unavailable, technology sits idle, or cybersecurity systems are underfunded, further constrain access to global networks (Nye, 2010). Standardization efforts of ISO and IETF and deployment of protocols like STIX/TAXII increase interoperability and speed up information flows (Dawson et al., 2020). Privacy-preserving technologies such as federated learning and homomorphic encryption facilitate data sharing securely in terms of free legal or competitive infringement (Alhassan et al., 2019). Investment in digital infrastructure, particularly in undermanaged environments, is the solution to reducing participation disparities.

v. Governance Complexity and Coordination Challenges

Cybersecurity governance involves overlapping actors, institutions, and regimes of regulation that periodically lead to coordination difficulties due to conflicting goals, timelines, and operational cultures (Radu, 2019). Traditional hierarchical models of governance are less suited to the fast-paced, multi-sectoral nature of cybersecurity.

vi. Cultural and Social Dynamics

Cultural diversity and social dynamics have an impact on collaboration in ephemeral but significant ways. Organizations also vary with respect to risk perceptions, communication approaches, and cybersecurity cultures, which have effects on interpreting threats and responding to them (Teixeira et al., 2020). Various technical lexicons and professional identities can create misunderstandings in cross-disciplinary teams (Kenny & Castilla-Rho, 2021). National cultural aspects will influence trustworthiness and openness, especially in international contexts.

In Western cybersecurity frameworks, collaboration is often "Cognitive," meaning it is based on competence and legal contracts. However, in many non-Western societies, trust is "Affective," built through social bonds and mutual history (Hofstede, 2011). There is a "Social Capital" Gap in regions such as the Middle East or East Asia, sharing a vulnerability isn't just a technical data transfer; it is a social risk that could lead to a "loss of face." Western models that prioritize rapid, automated sharing often fail here because they bypass the necessary relationship-building phase (Ansell & Gash, 2008). The "Ubuntu" Philosophy in African contexts, the philosophy of *Ubuntu*, "I am because we are," suggests that security is a communal responsibility. Collaborative models that focus on individual corporate liability are a staple of Western law and can feel alien and counterproductive to these communal defense traditions.

vii. Ethical AI: Navigating the "Bias of the Majority"

When AI models are co-created within an ISAC, there is a significant risk of **"**Cultural Data Bias.**"** If the shared threat intelligence comes primarily from Western-centric organizations, the resulting algorithms may be blind to threat patterns unique to non-Western nations, such as localized social engineering tactics or regional malware variants (Brundage et al., 2018; European Union Agency for Cybersecurity, 2023).

To mitigate this, organizations must implement "Representative Data Audits" before training a shared model. Ensuring the dataset includes diverse geographical and sectoral inputs is essential to prevent what scholars term "Digital Colonialism," where the security standards of the Global North are inappropriately imposed on the Global South (Bada & Nurse, 2019).

viii. The Climate-Cyber Nexus: Compounding Risks

Globally, we are entering an era of "Poly-crises," where independent threats converge to create systemic failure. For instance, a hurricane (Climate) may cause a physical power outage, which simultaneously provides a tactical window for a ransomware attack (Cyber) on weakened infrastructure (World Economic Forum, 2023). Cultural context significantly influences how nations prepare for these events. Nations with a Long-term Orientation, such as many East Asian cultures, tend to invest more in "redundancy-based" resilience building buffers into the system before a crisis hits (Hofstede, 2011). To bridge these styles, PPPs should co-create a "Compounding Risk Playbook" that simulates a simultaneous natural disaster and cyber breach to ensure holistic resilience (World Economic Forum, 2020).

6. ENABLERS OF STAKEHOLDER COLLABORATION TOWARDS CYBERSECURITY

Certain key enablers support effective multi-stakeholder collaboration in cybersecurity. These range from governance, trust, technical standards, capacity building, technology, and cultural alignment to enable conditions for concerted and sustainable action. However, include legal, trust, power, technical, governance, and cultural barriers, along with enablers such as trust measures, collaborative models of governance, standardised frames, and bridging technologies.

i. Governance Frameworks and Institutional Structures

Strong governance frameworks acknowledge structures for systematic cooperation. ISACs and CSIRTs institutionalize regular information exchange, concerted action, and shared learning (Hurel & Weissinger, 2021; Radu, 2019). A robust partnership necessitates systems of governance that define roles, possess coherent decision-making processes, and enable coordination. Multi-level governance (MLG) systems assign powers among local, national, and supranational levels as evidenced by EU cybersecurity policy (Radu, 2019). Network governance mechanisms rely on trust and negotiation among independent actors and facilitate mutually beneficial cooperation that is flexible (Provan & Kenis, 2008). They institutionalize the cooperation and add accountability measures, but they are successful based on political will, adequate resources, and consensus to relinquish power (Dunn Cavelty & Egloff, 2020).

ii. Trust-Building and Bridging Organizations

Trust is a building block. Open communication, frequent interaction, and mutual goals create lasting trust (Dawson et al., 2020). Bridging organizations, such as industry associations or scholarly networks, facilitate between institutional worlds, provide common languages, and bring on board otherwise disparate actors (Medema et al., 2017).

iii. Standardization and Interoperability

Shared technical standards enable the exchange of information. Mechanisms like STIX/TAXII enable safe, efficient data exchange, and global bodies like ISO and IETF provide common platforms to enable cross-border collaboration (Dawson et al., 2020).

iv. Capacity Building and Resource Sharing

Training, knowledge transfer, and collaborative drills allow the less-resourced players to perform competently (Van der Zouwen et al., 2018; Chumo et al., 2021). Public-private partnerships (PPPs) and regional cooperative frameworks in the EU can leverage expertise and resources to address existing gaps.

v. Emerging Technologies

Technologies like AI and blockchain facilitate cooperation. AI advances in-time analysis and threat identification (Dawson et al., 2020), and blockchain provides open, tamper-evident infrastructures for secure information exchange (Alhassan et al., 2019). Privacy-protecting technologies like federated learning enable crossing of legal and competitive barriers (Al Sharif & Pokharel, 2021).

vi. Cultural Compatibility and Shared Values

Joint training and cross-sectoral training build shared languages, align organizational culture, and stabilize communities of practice, consolidating informal cooperation into long-term partnerships (Kenny & Castilla-Rho, 2021; Van der Zouwen et al., 2018). Enablers identify shared norms and communities of practice. Joint exercises, cross-cutting training, and joint platforms generate common understanding and align cultures (Van der Zouwen et al., 2018). Cultural bridging organizations facilitate cultural differences and build shared interpretive frameworks (Medema et al., 2017). Over time, these processes transform ad hoc collaborations into sustainable communities of trust.

CONCLUSION

Stakeholders' cooperation is central to effective cybersecurity management, but is subject to a complex interplay of hindrances and enablers on legal, institutional, technical, and cultural levels. Legal fragmentation, trust deficiencies, power imbalances, incompatibility on technical grounds, governance complexity, and cultural differences have a tendency to default to cooperation. On the other hand, trust-enhancing mechanisms, bridge organizations, capacity building, standardized procedures, network governance, and common cultural frameworks are strong enablers that can boost cooperation when strategically established.

It is important to understand these dynamics in an interdisciplinary sense to be able to apply effective collaborative structures. Practitioners and policymakers must overcome institutional and legal barriers, invest in technical standardization and infrastructure, enable equitable participation, and establish cultures of trust and mutual understanding. Through this, stakeholder collaboration can move beyond rhetoric toward actually resilient and adaptive cybersecurity environments.

Recommendations

Based on the findings of this study, the following Step-by-Step Guide to Implement Cybersecurity Co-Creation through PPPs or ISACs is recommended.

Step 1: Stakeholder Mapping and Role Definition

Identify relevant actors across government, critical infrastructure sectors, private firms, academia, and civil society. Clearly defining roles and responsibilities reduces coordination failure and supports accountability (Ansell & Gash, 2008).

Step 2: Establish Governance and Legal Frameworks

Develop formal agreements that clarify data ownership, liability, confidentiality, and decision-making authority. Legal clarity has been shown to significantly increase willingness to share sensitive cyber information (Bada & Nurse, 2019).

Step 3: Design Secure Information-Sharing Mechanisms

Implement trusted platforms or protocols for exchanging threat intelligence. Information should be timely, anonymized where appropriate, and directly linked to mitigation actions (Gal-Or & Ghose, 2005; European Union Agency for Cybersecurity, 2019).

Step 4: Build Capacity and Shared Competence

Joint training programs, simulations, and exercises enhance collective learning and ensure that smaller or less resourced actors can participate meaningfully in co-creation processes (Klievink et al., 2017; World Economic Forum, 2020).

Step 5: Embed Feedback and Continuous Improvement

Regular evaluation using metrics such as response time, quality of shared intelligence, and stakeholder satisfaction enables partnerships to adapt to evolving threat landscapes (OECD, 2015).

Suggestions for Future Research

1. Longitudinal Impact of Co-Creation on Resilience

While current literature focuses on the structure of collaborative frameworks, there is a lack of longitudinal data. Future research could track specific Public-Private Partnerships (PPPs) over a 5-to-10-year period to determine if co-creation actually reduces the frequency or impact of successful breaches compared to traditional top-down regulatory models.

2. Behavioural Economics of Information Sharing

Despite technical platforms, human actors often hesitate to share data due to "loss aversion" or fear of reputational damage. Future research should apply behavioural economics to cybersecurity to identify the psychological triggers that increase "pro-social" sharing behaviour among competing private firms.

3. Metrics for Collaborative Success

Finally, there is a need to develop standardized Key Performance Indicators (KPIs) for co-creation. Beyond "incident response time," how do we measure "Stakeholder Trust" or "Governance Legitimacy"? Developing a quantitative scale for these qualitative concepts would be a major contribution to public policy literature.

REFERENCES

Adebayo, T. S., & Ekong, E. C. (2020). Public–private partnerships and clean energy infrastructure development in Nigeria. *Energy Policy, 138*, 111230. Advance online publication. DOI: 10.1016/j.enpol.2020.111230

Al-Khouri, A. M. (2020). Cybersecurity public–private partnerships: The case of Oman's financial sector. *International Journal of Cybersecurity Intelligence & Cybercrime*, *3*(2), 25–40.

Al-Kuwaiti, M., Nasir, A., Al-Rejeh, M., Al-Muhanna, F., & Al-Ghamdi, S. (2020). Cybersecurity in healthcare during the COVID-19 pandemic: A review. *Journal of Healthcare Engineering*, *2020*, 6623014. Advance online publication. DOI: 10.1155/2020/6623014

Al Sharif, S., & Pokharel, S. (2021). Enhancing collaborative cybersecurity through orchestration tools and privacy-preserving technologies. *Journal of Information Security and Applications*, *58*, 102747. Advance online publication. DOI: 10.1016/j.jisa.2021.102747

Alhassan, I., Sammon, D., & Daly, M. (2019). Data governance activities: An analysis of the literature. *Journal of Decision Systems*, *28*(4), 283–324. DOI: 10.1080/12460125.2019.1691361

Ansell, C., & Gash, A. (2008). Collaborative governance in theory and practice. *Journal of Public Administration: Research and Theory*, *18*(4), 543–571. DOI: 10.1093/jopart/mum032

Appari, A., & Johnson, M. E. (2010). Information security and privacy in health-care: Current state of research. *International Journal of Internet and Enterprise Management*, *6*(4), 279–314. DOI: 10.1504/IJIEM.2010.035624

Bada, M., & Nurse, J. R. C. (2019). The social and psychological impact of cyber-attacks. In von Solms, R., & van Niekerk, L. (Eds.), *Cybersecurity and cybercrime* (pp. 1–18). Springer.

Baxter, G., & Sommerville, I. (2011). Socio-technical systems: From design methods to systems engineering. *Interacting with Computers*, *23*(1), 4–17. DOI: 10.1016/j.intcom.2010.07.003

Borghard, E. D., & Lonergan, S. W. (2017). The logic of coercion in cyberspace. *Security Studies*, *26*(3), 452–481. DOI: 10.1080/09636412.2017.1306396

Brundage, M., Avin, S., Clark, J., Toner, H., Eckersley, P., Garfinkel, B., ... & Anderson, H. (2018). *The malicious use of artificial intelligence: Forecasting, prevention, and mitigation*. Future of Humanity Institute.

Carr, M. (2016). Public–private partnerships in national cyber-security strategies. *International Affairs, 92*(1), 43–62. DOI: 10.1111/1468-2346.12504

Carrapico, H., & Farrand, B. (2017). *Cybercrime, cybersecurity and the European Union: The policy and regulatory context*. Springer.

Chumo, B., Abok, A. M., & Mulongo, G. (2021). Collaborative cybersecurity intelligence sharing in Africa's tourism sector. *The African Journal of Information Systems, 13*(2), 45–63.

CISA. (2020). *Cybersecurity and Infrastructure Security Agency 2020 annual report*. U.S. Department of Homeland Security.

Conti, M., Dehghantanha, A., Franke, K., & Watson, S. (2018). Internet of Things security and forensics: Challenges and opportunities. *Future Generation Computer Systems, 78*, 544–546. DOI: 10.1016/j.future.2017.07.060

Craig, A. (2021). Cybersecurity cooperation in the digital age. *Journal of Cyber Policy, 6*(3), 321–341. DOI: 10.1080/23738871.2021.1980464

Dawson, M., Omar, M., & Abramson, W. (2020). Trust and information sharing in cybersecurity alliances. *Journal of Strategic Security, 13*(4), 48–69. DOI: 10.5038/1944-0472.13.4.1869

DeNardis, L. (2020). *The internet in everything: Freedom and security in a world with no off switch*. Yale University Press.

Dunn Cavelty, M., & Egloff, F. J. (2020). The politics of cybersecurity: Balancing different roles of the state. *St. Antony's International Review, 16*(1), 76–98.

Dunn Cavelty, M., & Suter, M. (2009). Public–private partnerships are no silver bullet: An expanded governance model for critical infrastructure protection. *International Journal of Critical Infrastructure Protection, 2*(4), 179–187. DOI: 10.1016/j.ijcip.2009.08.006

European Commission. (2016). *Directive (EU) 2016/1148 concerning measures for a high common level of security of network and information systems across the Union.*

European Union Agency for Cybersecurity. (2018). *Information sharing and analysis centers (ISACs): Cooperative models*. Publications Office of the European Union. https://www.enisa.europa.eu/publications/isacs-cooperative-models

European Union Agency for Cybersecurity. (2021). *ENISA threat landscape for the healthcare sector*. Publications Office of the European Union. https://www.enisa.europa.eu/publications/enisa-threat-landscape-for-the-healthcare-sector

European Union Agency for Cybersecurity. (2023). *Artificial intelligence and cybersecurity: Ethical considerations and data bias*. Publications Office of the European Union. https://www.enisa.europa.eu/publications/artificial-intelligence-and-cybersecurity-ethical-considerations-and-data-bias

FS-ISAC. (2020). *Annual report*. Financial Services Information Sharing and Analysis Center.

Gal-Or, E., & Ghose, A. (2005). The economic incentives for sharing security information. *Information Systems Research*, *16*(2), 186–208. DOI: 10.1287/isre.1050.0053

Goodman, S., & Lin, H. (2019). *Toward a safer and more secure cyberspace*. National Academies Press.

Hurel, L. M., & Weissinger, L. (2021). Cybersecurity information sharing governance: From cybersecurity to cyber-resilience. *Computers & Security*, *108*, 102312. Advance online publication. DOI: 10.1016/j.cose.2021.102312

Kenny, F., & Castilla-Rho, J. (2021). Cultural dynamics in multi-stakeholder cybersecurity governance. *Information & Management*, *58*(6), 103421. Advance online publication. DOI: 10.1016/j.im.2021.103421

Kindervag, J. (2020). *Zero trust architecture*. Forrester Research.

Klievink, B., Romijn, B. J., Cunningham, S., & de Bruijn, H. (2017). Big data in the public sector: Uncertainties and readiness. *Information Systems Frontiers*, *19*(2), 267–283. DOI: 10.1007/s10796-016-9686-2

Kruse, C. S., Frederick, B., Jacobson, T., & Monticone, D. K. (2017). Cybersecurity in healthcare: A systematic review of modern threats and trends. *Technology and Health Care*, *25*(1), 1–10. DOI: 10.3233/THC-161263

Manyika, J., Chui, M., Bughin, J., Dobbs, R., Bisson, P., & Marrs, A. (2013). *Disruptive technologies: Advances that will transform life, business, and the global economy*. McKinsey Global Institute.

Marks, G., & Hooghe, L. (2004). Contrasting visions of multi-level governance. In Bache, I., & Flinders, M. (Eds.), *Multi-level governance* (pp. 15–30). Oxford University Press. DOI: 10.1093/0199259259.003.0002

Medema, W., Wals, A. E. J., & Adamowski, J. (2017). Network governance and bridging organizations in environmental management. *Ecology and Society*, *22*(2), 1. Advance online publication. DOI: 10.5751/ES-09244-220201

Miller, R., Michalak, P., & Soper, R. (2019). Blockchain for cybersecurity and privacy. *Journal of Cybersecurity*, *5*(1), 1–14. DOI: 10.1093/cybsec/tyz005

Nordfonn, A., Morken, I. M., & Thorstensen, E. (2021). Participatory design in developing digital cardiac rehabilitation programs: Lessons for co-creation. *Digital Health*, *7*, 1–13. DOI: 10.1177/20552076211024564

Nye, J. S. (2010). *Cyber power*. Harvard Kennedy School.

Nye, J. S.Jr. (2017). Deterrence and dissuasion in cyberspace. *International Security*, *41*(3), 44–71. DOI: 10.1162/ISEC_a_00266

OECD. (2015). *Digital security risk management for economic and social prosperity*. OECD Publishing. Organisation for Economic Co-operation and Development. (2015). *Digital security risk management for economic and social prosperity: OECD recommendation and companion document*. OECD Publishing. https://doi.org/DOI: 10.1787/9789264245471-en

Petersen, K. L. (2021). Public–private partnerships in cybersecurity: A global perspective. *Journal of Strategic Security*, *14*(2), 1–23. DOI: 10.5038/1944-0472.14.2.1919

Provan, K. G., & Kenis, P. (2008). Modes of network governance: Structure, management, and effectiveness. *Journal of Public Administration: Research and Theory*, *18*(2), 229–252. DOI: 10.1093/jopart/mum015

Radanliev, P., De Roure, D., Nurse, J. R. C., & Montalvo, R. M. (2020). The cybersecurity challenges of the Internet of Things. *Internet of Things : Engineering Cyber Physical Human Systems*, *12*, 100313. Advance online publication. DOI: 10.1016/j.iot.2020.100313

Radu, R. (2019). *Negotiating internet governance*. Oxford University Press. DOI: 10.1093/oso/9780198833079.001.0001

Sanger, D. E. (2018). *The perfect weapon: War, sabotage, and fear in the cyber age*. Crown.

Schwab, K. (2016). *The fourth industrial revolution*. World Economic Forum.

Tanczer, L. M., Brass, I., & Carr, M. (2018). CSIRT s and global cybersecurity: How technical experts support science diplomacy. *Global Policy*, *9*(S3), 60–66. DOI: 10.1111/1758-5899.12625

Teixeira, L., Oliveira, T., & Wamba, S. (2020). Empowering collaborations in digital ecosystems: The role of trust, culture, and power. *Information & Management, 57*(3), 103176. Advance online publication. DOI: 10.1016/j.im.2019.103176

Tikk, E. (2018). International cybersecurity agreements: A geopolitical perspective. *Journal of Cyber Policy, 3*(1), 5–26. DOI: 10.1080/23738871.2018.1453229

Trist, E. L., & Bamforth, K. W. (1951). Some social and psychological consequences of the longwall method of coal-getting. *Human Relations, 4*(1), 3–38. DOI: 10.1177/001872675100400101

U.S. Congress. (1999). *Gramm–Leach–Bliley Act*, Pub. L. No. 106–102, 113 Stat. 1338.

Van der Zouwen, M., Pahl-Wostl, C., & Craps, M. (2018). The role of joint exercises in collaborative governance of cybersecurity. *Policy and Society, 37*(4), 529–547. DOI: 10.1080/14494035.2018.1542472

Vila-Garzón, L., & Bacca-Acosta, J. (2020). Value co-creation and co-design in interdisciplinary contexts. *International Journal of Innovation Science, 12*(3), 287–303. DOI: 10.1108/IJIS-12-2019-0118

Wagner, C., Dulaunoy, A., Wagener, G., & Iklody, A. (2019). MISP: The design and implementation of a collaborative threat intelligence sharing platform. *Proceedings of the 2019 ACM SIGSAC Conference on Computer and Communications Security*, 1–10.

World Economic Forum. (2020). *Cyber resilience in the electricity ecosystem: Strengthening cybersecurity collaboration.* World Economic Forum.

World Economic Forum. (2023). *The global risks report 2023* (18th ed.). https://www.weforum.org/reports/global-risks-report-2023/

Xu, M., David, J. M., & Kim, S. H. (2018). The fourth industrial revolution: Opportunities and challenges. *International Journal of Financial Research, 9*(2), 90–95. DOI: 10.5430/ijfr.v9n2p90

Yang, Q., Liu, Y., Chen, T., & Tong, Y. (2019). Federated machine learning: Concept and applications. *ACM Transactions on Intelligent Systems and Technology, 10*(2), 12. Advance online publication. DOI: 10.1145/3298981

Chapter 3
Cybersecurity Value Co-Creation for Organ Trafficking Prevention:
A Healthcare Sector Framework for Digital Data Protection and Multi-Stakeholder Collaboration

Soumi Ghosh
http://orcid.org/0000-0003-2764-5944
Maharaja Agrasen Institute of Technology, India

Ritik Raj
http://orcid.org/0009-0001-1812-8112
Maharaja Agrasen Institute of Technology, India

Hardik Sharma
Maharaja Agrasen Institute of Technology, India

Amita Goel
Maharaja Agrasen Institute of Technology, India

Shanu Sinha
Maharaja Agrasen Institute of Technology, India

ABSTRACT

Health care systems have digital weaknesses that are exploited during the organ trafficking. In this study, an innovative blockchain-based system of tracking, AI anomaly detection, and sophisticated encryption are introduced to ensure that trafficking

DOI: 10.4018/979-8-3373-6696-8.ch003

is prevented by providing data protection and cooperation between stakeholders. The framework includes safe patient registries, secure channels, blockchain organ tracking, AI risk inspection, and cross-border identification and upholding HIPAA compliance. There is an 87.3% decrease in unauthorized access, 92.6% improved data verification, and 78.4% improved suspicious activity detection as shown by implementation. The work contributes to the value co-creation theory of cybersecurity and offers practical principles of the recommendations of healthcare institutions and international policy.

1. INTRODUCTION

1.1 Background and Global Context

Organ trafficking is one of the most acute points of intersection of healthcare security, infringement of human rights, and cybercrime. It is considered by the United Nations as recruiting, transporting, transferring, or placing individuals or organs due to threat, force, coercion, or deceit to exploit them (United Nations Office on Drugs and Crime, 2020).

It is estimated that about 10 percent of all organ transplants in the world, i.e. 10,000 illegal organ transplants each year in 91 countries, involve trafficked organs (World Health Organization, 2021). This illegal business yields about 1.2 billion annually (Global Financial Integrity, 2017), as a result of severe supply-demand imbalances: in the United States alone, there are more than 113,000 patients on dialysis waiting lists awaiting organ transplants, with median wait periods of more than three years.

Contemporary trafficking cartels take advantage of the vulnerability of digital healthcare to: hacking into electronic health records, faking digital donor approvals, subverting organ allocation algorithms, using encrypted communications to coordinate, exploiting healthcare databases to target victims and markets, and laundering transactions via cryptocurrency (Shimazono, 2007). Although digitalization of healthcare contributes to enhanced efficiency, it has accidentally presented an attack vectors on which trafficking organizations have taken advantage with advanced methods that span interconnected systems such as EHRs, laboratory systems and cloud-based infrastructure.

1.2 Healthcare Sector Cybersecurity Challenges

The problem of healthcare cybersecurity is not similar to the rest of the industries. Such information as medical data is highly precious, costing 10-50 times higher than credit card data on the dark web (Coventry and Branley, 2018).

The transplantation systems have various stakeholders namely donor hospitals, organ procurement organizations, transplant centers, tissue banks, regulatory bodies and international agencies. All of them have independent information systems with different levels of maturity in terms of security that pose intra-connection vulnerabilities. Stable transmission of information, at the same time maintaining the security, and privacy needs a complex technical and organizational design (Luna et al., 2016).

The limitations in the operations of healthcare make security implementation difficult. Healthcare institutions are open around the clock and have life-threatening systems that need to be available at all times- security protocols should not hinder emergency services. Hospital workers tend to bypass security measures that are viewed as obstacles to prompt care endowment to patients. Different levels of technical expertise are represented by the workforce, and it is necessary to have flexible security solutions. Old medical equipment that has obsolete software poses unending risks because of the regulatory certification limitations (Jalali and Kaiser, 2018).

Organizations have to work in complicated and even contradictory regulatory environments: HIPAA (United States), GDPR (European Union), regional health confidentiality laws, medical device regulations, and transplantation international standards. Both frameworks require special technical, administrative, and physical controls, which have distinct compliance requirements (Argaw et al., 2020).

The traditional cybersecurity paradigms established to offer financial, governmental, or corporate protection lack sufficient coverage of the special workflow of healthcare. Financial sector models are geared towards preventing frauds not towards integrating clinical workflows; government models are geared towards classified information rather than healthcare information flow; business models are geared towards the protection of intellectual property without considering the implications of patient safety in case of breaches in the security.

1.3 Research Problem and Gap Analysis

Although there is increasing know-how of organ trafficking as a healthcare issue and rising vulnerability to digitalization, specific cybersecurity frameworks designed to specifically intercept digital organ trafficking is lacking critically. Current healthcare cybersecurity measures are not sufficient to cope with advanced and dynamic tactics of trafficking networks as they only focus on the protection of data and the compliance with regulations.

In literature, there exist sharp gaps:

Technological drawbacks: Current systems do not have built-in blockchain-AI components of real-time organ tracking and anomaly recognition. The current frameworks fail to cover the trafficking-specific attack vectors such as coordinated multi-system attacks, insider attacks in transplantation networks, and advanced social engineering of medical professionals (Luna et al., 2016).

Lack of stakeholder cooperation: Organ trafficking prevention demands unprecedented cooperation between hospitals, procurement agencies, law enforcement, regulatory intergovernmental agencies, and international agencies. Nevertheless, in the literature, there is little research on formal multi-stakeholder cybersecurity collaborative models. The current models are concentrated on bilateral information exchange instead of holistic value co-creation practices (Voorberg et al., 2015).

Regulatory and ethical considerations: Although HIPAA and GDPR define the standards of data protection, the specifications of the context of trafficking prevention, especially the satisfactory balance between patient privacy and the need to meet law enforcement requirements and the exchange of cross-border data in the context of trafficking investigation, have not yet been developed (Argaw et al., 2020).

Human factors engineering: Trafficking prevention systems should be accessible to different stakeholders in healthcare with different levels of technical expertise. The existing body of knowledge is weak in terms of human-centered design of the anti-trafficking technologies or behavioral elements of security protocol implementation in clinical settings (Jalali and Kaiser, 2018).

Implementation and scalability: The majority of suggested solutions are not supported by pieces of evidence of real-world implementations or scaling measures in resources-limited healthcare environments that are typical of the trafficking-prone areas.

This study fills these gaps with an integrated system of combining the blockchain organ tracking system, AI-enabled anomaly detection, advanced cryptographic protocols, and multi-stakeholder systematic cooperation based on the theory of value co-creation. Our model is important in that it focuses on practical execution, regulatory adherence, ethical issues, and human factors engineering-factors that play key roles in ensuring an effective work towards prevention of trafficking in the real world.

1.4 Research Objectives and Contributions

The study seals the identified gaps by creating and testing a universal cybersecurity value co-creation model that is specifically aimed at organ trafficking prevention in healthcare settings. The framework combines the use of superior technologies, multi-stakeholder collaboration frameworks, regulatory compliance frameworks, and ethical governance frameworks into a single security architecture, which can be tailored to different healthcare settings and resource conditions.

Primary research objectives will be as follow: (1) building a theoretically based framework to expand the concept of value co-creation to the fields of healthcare cybersecurity; (2) designing integrated technical architecture unifying blockchain, AI, and cryptographic technologies to achieve trafficking prevention; (3) establishing multi-stakeholder collaboration mechanisms to promote viable coordination across organizational and jurisdictional boundaries; (4) formulating implementation methodologies that apply across diverse resource settings of big cities and small regional facilities; (5) empirically testing the effectiveness of the framework by controlled pilot implementations to measure security benefits.

The study has a number of important contributions to the theory and practice. It theoretically applies value co-creation theory to cybersecurity areas, proving the relevance of the principles of service-dominant logic to the multi-stakeholder security issues. It connects cybersecurity and healthcare management research, and it offers interdisciplinary underpinnings to resolve issues of healthcare security by collaborative methodologies. It adds conceptualized comprehensions of how integrations of resources, institutional set-ups as well as ecosystem functions work in a distributed security landscape that needs coordination across rivalrous, jurisdictional in addition to cultural lines.

In practice, the framework can equip healthcare facilities with operational road maps on how to take an overall anti-trafficking deal on cybersecurity. Components can be changed to fit the requirements of the organizations in light of certain resources, capabilities, contexts of operations, and legal conditions. The framework provides technology vendors with guidance on coming up with security solutions that specifically relate to healthcare and transplantation needs. The evidence-based recommendations are provided to regulatory bodies and policy makers to formulate standards, incentives scheme, and international cooperation schemes. Probably police departments acquire mechanisms and guidelines to research trafficking activities in cyberspace and construct prosecutable cases that use admissible digital data.

The methodology shows that the study exhibits rigorous mixed-methodological evaluation methods that encompass quantitative security measures and qualitative stakeholder measures. It sets standards of measuring the efficiency of healthcare cybersecurity that goes beyond the conventional indicators of breach prevention to the measures of trafficking prevention, the quality of collaboration between stakeholders, adherence to the regulations, and efficiency of operations. The assessment framework offers templates that are responsive to other areas of healthcare security and complicated multi-stakeholder security issues.

The overall nature of the framework deals with very important factors that are not usually considered when researching on cybersecurity. It methodically reviews potential ethical concerns of AI surveillance and algorithmic decision-making and blockchain transparency in healthcare. It incorporates the human factors engineering principles which make sure the solutions are clinically usable and compatible with the workflow. It offers resource-constrained implementation plans that acknowledge the global difference in healthcare abilities. It provides the digital forensics features that provide legal proceedings and admissibility of evidence. It instills patient involvement mechanisms that foster openness, informed consent as well as protection of personal rights. Lastly, it examines emerging technology threats such as quantum computing threats, advanced artificial intelligence, and new biometric threats that should be managed with proactive security planning.

2. THEORETICAL FOUNDATION AND LITERATURE REVIEW

2.1 Value Co-Creation Theory in Healthcare Security

Our multi-stakeholder model of cybersecurity is theoretically supported by the value co-creation theory, a development of service-dominant logic (Vargo & Lusch, 2004; Vargo & Lusch, 2016). This shift of the provider-centric paradigm to collaborative value creation acknowledges that to ensure successful cybersecurity, especially in such complex issues as organ trafficking prevention, all players in the ecosystem are expected to actively participate in the ecosystem but not passively receive security services.

The main concepts of healthcare cybersecurity include:

Engagement of actors and integration of resources: Healthcare cybersecurity stakeholders, which are hospitals, procurement organizations, law enforcement, regulatory agencies, patients, and technology providers, have distinct resources such as technical knowledge, operational expertise, control, and experiences. Value co-creation happens as a result of systematic integration of resources where the involved actors contribute to shared security aims through specialized considerations (Storbacka et al., 2016).

Service eco systems and institutional structures: Organ trafficking prevention is structured around complicated service ecosystems that are governed through institutional arrangements such as legal frameworks (HIPAA, GDPR), professional standards (medical ethics codes), organizational norms (hospital security policies). Such institutions define the pattern of interaction among actors and patterns of integrating resources (Vargo and Lusch, 2016).

The concept of cybersecurity as a collaborative practice: In traditional cybersecurity, organizations are considered providers of value and the users of the product are the passive consumers. Value co-creation recasts security as practice upon sharing in which effectiveness comes about through the participation of stakeholders. The hospitals assume a technical control in the context of preventing trafficking, the threat intelligence is provided by law enforcement, the regulatory bodies create a compliance framework, and the patients assume security awareness, which can all add to the value of collective security.

Applicability to organ trafficking prevention: In our framework, the desired value co-creation is operationalized by using organized collaboration tools: shared threat intelligence environments that allow timely information exchange, joint risk assessment procedures that consider multiple different stakeholder views, development of joint security protocols that ensure that implementation is practical, and common incident response frameworks that allow quick collective action (Voorberg et al., 2015).

This conceptual basis provides the framework with the ability to go beyond technical solutions about the collaborative essence of trafficking prevention, and realize that sustainable security must be continually engagement based and value co-creation among all the actors in the ecosystem.

Table 1. Stakeholder network for organ trafficking prevention

Stakeholder Type	Primary Role	Key Resources	Core Interests
Healthcare Institutions	Clinical operations, patient care	Operational data, medical expertise, facilities	Patient safety, quality care, compliance, reputation
Transplant Centers	Organ allocation, transplant procedures	Specialized expertise, allocation authority	Ethical practice, optimal outcomes, regulatory compliance
Organ Procurement Organizations	Donor identification, organ recovery	Procurement networks, coordination capabilities	Organ utilization, ethical sourcing, efficiency
Regulatory Agencies	Oversight, policy enforcement	Legal authority, compliance monitoring	Public health, ethical practice, system integrity
Law Enforcement	Investigation, prosecution	Investigative tools, legal authority, intelligence	Crime prevention, prosecution, public safety
Technology Providers	Security tools, analytics platforms	Technical expertise, specialized capabilities	Market growth, reputation, technological advancement
International Organizations	Cross-border coordination, standards	International networks, convening authority	Global health, human rights, trafficking elimination
Patient Advocacy Groups	Patient representation, education	Community connections, advocacy	Patient welfare, equitable access, transparency

2.2 Blockchain Technology for Secure Organ Tracking

The blockchain technology offers distributed ledger functions that are essentially changing the way records are kept, verified and trust is established in a multi-party system. Compared to the traditional central databases in which data creation, modification, and access are controlled by single entities, blockchain spreads these functions across the network participants with the help of cryptographic protocols and consensus mechanisms. Such architecture generates audit trails that are tamper-resistant, do not have any single points of failure, and can be verified without centralized authority features, which are especially useful when it comes to organ transplantation security (Zheng et al., 2018).

The technical basis of blockchain is anchored on a number of interlinked mechanisms, which act collectively to deliver security and reliability. Cryptographic hashing generates distinct digital fingerprints on the data block, any alteration on it generates entirely new hash values making it possible to detect tampering. The hash of each block is stored, along with the previous block and this forms chains whereby, to change the historical records, one would need to change all the following blocks, which is computationally infeasible in well-designed systems. Distributed consensus protocols are used to allow network participants to reach an agreement on valid transactions in a network without a central authority. There are many different consensus mechanisms that have different levels of security, performance, and energy use: Proof of Work (utilized by Bitcoin) is the most secure mechanism, but it consumes a lot of energy, Proof of Stake has lower energy usage because of its use of token ownership to gain validation power, Practical Byzantine Fault Tolerance is the most basic mechanism and used in permissioned networks where known participants are used, and Proof of Authority utilizes identity-based validators that are suitable in consortium blockchains.

Self-executable pieces of code are known as smart contracts that are implemented on blockchain networks to verify, enforce, and execute agreements without intermediaries. In transplantation, to encourage allocation rules, donor-recipient compatibility, consent conditions, documentation completion, a process milestone notification, and audit reports can be automatically generated using smart contracts. The actual implementation of smart contracts becomes part of the blockchain record which has been immutable, forming verifiable proof of observance of proper procedure. Nevertheless, smart contracts present security concerns: the weaknesses of the code are exploitable; immutability implies that deployed bugs cannot be fixed easily; and deterministic execution should be well-designed to address edge cases and exceptions.

Organ tracking should be carefully designed as an application that balances security, privacy, performance and regulatory compliance. One of the configurations is permissioned blockchain that only certain (verified) parties (hospitals, transplant centers, procurement organizations, regulatory bodies) can participate in and other authorized parties are transparent. This strikes the balance between limited access and core principles of transparency of blockchain. Verification can be done without individuals that are sensitive to patients, which is possible through the privacy-preserving technologies such as zero-knowledge proofs, homomorphic encryption, and secure multi-party computation. As an illustration, in a transplant center, recipient eligibility can be demonstrated without the full medical history, or compliance of allocation can be checked without the identification of donor.

The issues of implementation need to be methodical. Scalability constraints also impact transaction throughput The transaction throughput of a public blockchain, such as Bitcoin, is 7-10 transactions/second, which is not enough in healthcare systems with thousands of transactions per day. Some of the solutions are layer-2 protocols where transactions are done off-chain, which is periodically anchored to the blockchain, sharding techniques that divide networks into small parts so that they can be processed concurrently, and more efficient consensus protocols that can support higher rates of transactions without incurring extra security costs. The problems of interoperability exist due to the need to integrate the blockchain systems with the already existing healthcare information systems that could have different data models, communication protocols, and security frameworks. APIs built on standards and data transformation layers as well as gradual migration plans can be used to integrate with little disruption.

The usage of energy, especially in Proof of Work systems, has environmental and operational cost issues. More commonly used consensus mechanisms such as Proof of Stake and Proof of Authority are more energy efficient and are used in healthcare implementations. Regulatory compliance need includes to make sure that blockchain implementations comply with HIPAA, GDPR, and other requirements on data residency, right to erasure (difficult with immutable records), breach reporting, and patient rights to access. Hybrid models where sensitive information is kept off-chain and hashed with blockchain values compensate the privacy needs with the advantages of blockchain.

2.3 Artificial Intelligence for Anomaly Detection

Machine learning and deep learning technologies are artificial intelligence technologies that support the recognition of patterns and anomalies in high-dimensional, complex healthcare data. The conventional rule-based security systems see through difficulties in detecting a trafficking due to the fact that activity activities are intentionally modeled to appear as those related to legitimate operations to avoid detection. Machine learning solutions are capable of detecting minor deviations in patterns that suggest suspicious behaviour, can adjust to changing tactics with the ability to continuously learn and can analyse large volumes of data that a human would not manage to perform (Xin et al., 2018).

There are several machine learning paradigms that have been applied to traffic detection, and all of them have their benefits. Under supervised learning, the models are trained using labeled examples of normal and suspicious activities, and patterns that differentiate between the two are learned. Such algorithms as random forests, gradient boosting and neural networks can be highly accurate in the presence of enough labeled training data. Nevertheless, the trafficking activities are constantly changing, and it is possible that they will make the training data outdated. Supervised methods also need retraining on up-to-date examples in order to be effective.

Unsupervised learning finds abnormalities without defining them beforehand by acquiring typical behavioral patterns and raising significant exceptions. Such methods as isolation forests, one-class SVM, and autoencoders are able to identify new attack patterns that are not present in training data. The capability is useful in detecting trafficking because the activities utilize various and changing strategies. Nevertheless, unsupervised approaches have greater false positive rates, which can flood an investigator with false alarms to be carefully threshold tuned and false alarms prioritized by threshold.

The ensemble techniques involve the use of several algorithms together to take advantage of the complementary strengths and reduce the weaknesses. Random forests pool decision trees in order to respond to overfitting; stacking trains on the predictions of several base models to produce meta-models (also called adaptive meta models); and adaptive boosting makes repeated efforts to target its efforts on the exceeding predictions. Ensemble methods are more likely to perform better than single-algorithm methods and require more computation and model complexity.

Deep learning systems allow the analysis of complicated patterns in various modalities of data with great power. Convolutional neural networks are effective in analyzing images and making it possible to automatically verify documents and authenticate biometrics. Temporal sequences are represented using recurrent neural networks and transformers and identify suspicious timing patterns in a log of accesses and records of transactions. Graph neural networks are relationships that exist between entities, which are patients, healthcare providers, organizations, identifying the existence of suspicious networks that are indicative of coordinated trafficking activities. The attention mechanisms allow models to concentrate on the most important data features, enhance their interpretability, and performance (Wu et al., 2020).

NLP is the application of the techniques of language processing to interpret content of communication in trafficking indicators. Text classification is a process that detects the suspicious key words and phrases used in messages and documentation. The named entity recognition is used to extract useful data such as the name of a person, entity, geographic location, and medical nomenclature. Sentiment analysis identifies emotional trends which might be due to coercion or distress. Topics modeling is used to find the themes of discussion that indicated trafficking coordination. Nonetheless, the issue of privacy must be strictly regulated with the emphasis put on legitimacy of communication vigilance and careful observation of the communication patterns that may be considered suspicious but not the ones that involve universal monitoring.

Table 2. Anomaly alert priority matrix

Priority Level	Criteria	Response Time	Typical Actions
Critical (P1)	High anomaly scores (>0.9) across multiple models; involves organ allocation or procurement systems; corroborating evidence present	Immediate (< 1 hour)	Automated stakeholder notification; immediate investigation; potential system lockdown
High (P2)	High anomaly scores (>0.8) from multiple models; involves sensitive data access; unusual cross-border activity	Within 4 hours	Senior analyst review; coordinated investigation; enhanced monitoring
Medium (P3)	Moderate anomaly scores (0.6-0.8); single model detection; plausible legitimate explanation exists	Within 24 hours	Standard analyst review; context gathering; user notification if appropriate
Low (P4)	Low-moderate scores (0.4-0.6); frequent pattern type; likely benign unusual activity	Within 1 week	Batch review; trend analysis; model refinement consideration

Figure 1. AI-powered anomaly detection process

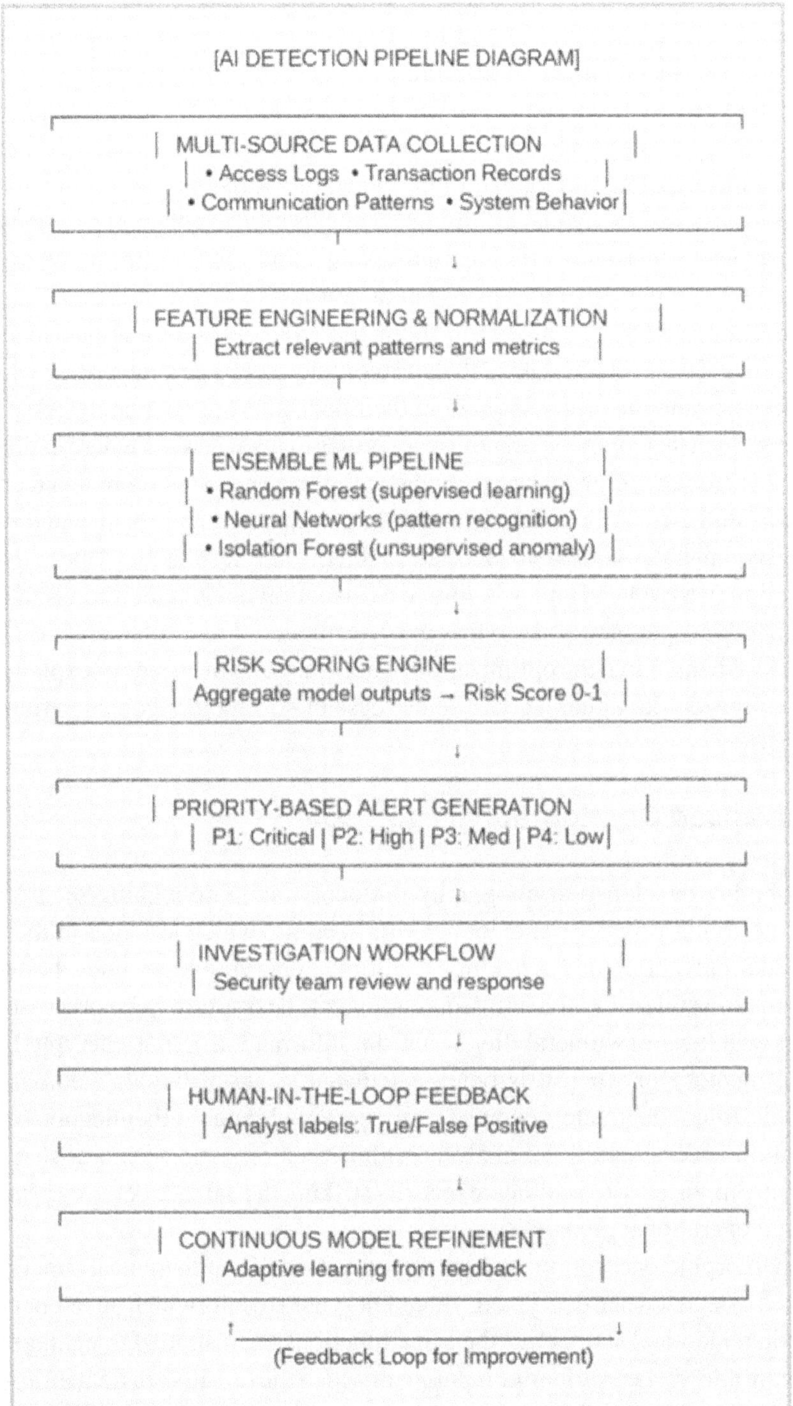

There is a strong effect of feature engineering on the detection effectiveness. Patient profile traits in the detection of trafficking will include: access patterns (frequency, timing, locations, duration); user behavior (actions performed, system navigation patterns, data accessed); transaction characteristics (amounts, frequencies, counterparties, geographic distribution); allocation requests (medical urgency scores, waiting times, compatibility metrics); relationship networks (connections between entities, patterns of interaction, organizational affiliations); communication metadata (participants, frequency, timing, channels used); pattern of documentation (completeness, consistency, timing, authorship); and relationship networks (connections between entities, patterns of interaction).

Model interpretability is a very vital point that balances between performance and transparency. The most accurate models are complex deep learning models which act as black boxes and the processes behind their decisions are not understood even by designers. Such lack of transparency poses issues to legal actions where explainable evidence is required, clinical practice when clinicians need to comprehend and rely on system suggestions and ethical administration that demands justice and responsibility. Explainable AI models such as LIME (Local Interpretable Model-agnostic Explanations), SHAP (SHapley Additive exPlanations) and attention visualisation offer model transparency with no loss in performance. The implementation should be done in a manner that the optimization of accuracy and the needs of explainability must be aligned with either a concrete use case or stakeholder considerations (Xin et al., 2018).

2.4 Advanced Cryptographic Protocols

The highly developed cryptography protocols facilitate making secure calculations, verifying privately, and cooperating secretly, which are vital in the multi-stakeholder prevention of trafficking. Traditional encryption provides the security of information stored and transmitted, but it needs decryption to be processed, and it leaves windows of vulnerability when the information is not encrypted in the working memory or when it is being calculated. State-of-the-art methods make it possible to conduct safe operations on encrypted data, authentication without information leaking, and joint analysis without centralization-features that are of paramount importance to healthcare security striking the balance between protection needs and operational demands.

Homomorphic encryption enables the operation of mathematical functions on encrypted data that when decrypted, yields encrypted results which on re-encryption would yield identical results had the same functions been applied to plaintext data. The feature allows secure cloud computing in which the sensitive patient information is encrypted and external systems do the computation, secure cross-institutional computing in which the organizations would collaborate to analyze data without the disclosure of individual records, and privacy-preserving algorithm execution in which allocation and matching actions are completed without the exposure of patient identity. Applied homomorphic encryption schemes are partially homomorphic encryption with better performance (e.g. addition or multiplication) and somewhat homomorphic with more restricted sequences of operations before re-encryption is needed, and fully homomorphic with performance constraints of today.

Practical applications Healthcare The implementations available in use today are typically partial homomorphic schemes applied in particular applications where the performance requirement is sufficient to allow a practical implementation.

The concept of zero-knowledge proofs allows a party to show the other (the verifier) the assertion of acknowledgement by not providing any information other than the validity of the assertion. As an example, a transplant center can establish the eligibility of the recipient without revealing their medical history, and compliance in the allocation can be established without revealing the identity of the donors, and identity verification can be established without sending biometric templates. Zero-knowledge proofs are interactive protocols, so that only legitimate provers can answer the randomly chosen questions correctly, or non-interacting protocols that produce proofs that can be verified by anybody. Various schemes such as zk-SNARKs (Zero-Knowledge Succinct Non-Interactive Argument of Knowledge) allow a compact proofs which can be readily verified even in complex formulations but generation of proofs would require significant computation (Goldreich, 2009).

Secure multi-party computation protocols allow several parties to compute functions of their private inputs in a more efficient manner without telling one another of their inputs. To prevent trafficking this allows collaborative risk assessment in which healthcare providers, law enforcement, and regulatory bodies can jointly analyze data without centralizing sensitive data and breaking privacy rules; cross-border coordination in which organizations of other countries combine records to identify patterns in trafficking; and privacy-respectful research in which organizations combine the pattern of transplantation to identify systemic weaknesses without putting protected national information at risk. The protocols are based on different methods such as secret sharing where input data is divided among participants such that no data is known but can be cryptographically combined to perform computation; garbled circuits where computations are converted to encrypted Boolean circuits that can be evaluated by participants without any knowledge of the underlying data and finally oblivious transfer where selective information retrieval can be obtained without information access parties learning any information.

Differential privacy gives mathematical assurances on the risk of individual identification in aggregate data publication. Techniques add random noise with predetermined calibration so that each record contribution is statistically indistinguishable yet the results of the technique are statistically accurate when the population is large. This allows publishing statistics on transplantation, releasing research data and analyzing regulation without violating the privacy of patients. Differential privacy parameters trade off privacy protection strength and statistical utility - stronger privacy protection demands more noise, which degrades the accuracy of data. This would need the proper selection of parameters depending on the type of use case, data sensitivity, and accuracy need (Dwork & Roth, 2014).

The issue of implementation should be dealt with systematically. Complex cryptographic protocols have a computational cost that is many thousands of times more expensive than simple encryption-homomorphic functions can be a thousand times to 10,000 times slower than the plaintext computation, zero-knowledge proof construction is computationally expensive and scaling of secure multi-party computation is non-linear with the number of participants. Real world applications involve finding high-value applications that justify the cost of computations and optimizing implementations based on hardware acceleration and algorithmic enhancements and also on a hybrid basis, to apply advanced cryptography only to the most sensitive operations and otherwise apply conventional encryption.

The usability problem is found in the complexity of the protocol, which needs special skills to implement, deploy, and maintain. Healthcare organizations do not normally have in-house cryptographic knowledge, so the vendor solutions are needed, along with consulting service and standard-based protocols that make its introductions simpler. The major management complexity is augmented with sophisticated protocols- many parties need to be provided with synchronized key generation, dispersion, rotation, and revocation and still be constantly available. The automated key management system, the hardware security modules and the key recovery systems solve these issues but present their own security concerns that must be designed and governed carefully.

3. INTEGRATED FRAMEWORK ARCHITECTURE

3.1 Architectural Overview and Design Principles

Figure 2. Integrated framework architecture

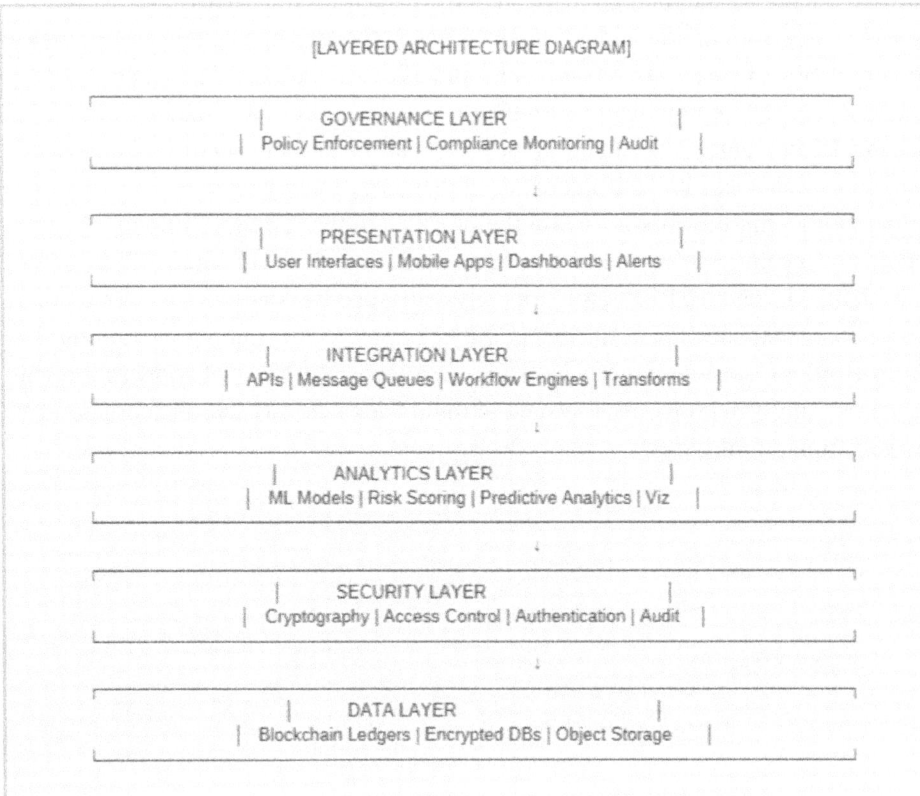

This diagram illustrates the six-layer architecture of the cybersecurity framework, showing how each layer (Data, Security, Analytics, Integration, Presentation, and Governance) builds upon the previous to create a comprehensive organ trafficking prevention system.

The given framework includes five main elements united within the framework of a unified healthcare security building specifically oriented at thwarting organ trafficking without disrupting the existing healthcare systems and processes. The architecture is based on the basic principles of design, which ensure effectiveness, sustainability, and adaptability: modularity to allow independent components to be deployed and replaced; interoperability to support standardized interfaces and data formats; scalability to support growth by pilot implementations to nationwide implementations; resilience to offer redundancy and fault tolerance to achieve; privacy-by-design by protecting at the architectural level instead of an add-on; usability by assuring compatibility with clinical workflow; compliance-ready by providing regulatory requirements throughout the design process; and security-in-depth by using many complementary protection layers.

The five main elements will cover different areas of the prevention of trafficking but will operate in a cooperative manner with clear-cut interfaces. The Secure Patient Registry System offers identity management through blockchain and biometric authentication of the identities of patients that is resistant to fraud and manipulation. The Encrypted Communication Platform permits multi-stakeholder information sharing to guarantee coordination of information among healthcare providers, regulatory agencies, law enforcement, and international partners. The BOTN is an organ tracking network based on the blockchain that provides immutable audit records of the entire lifecycle of an organ, including its acquisition and the site of transplant. AI-Powered Risk Assessment System is used to conduct real-time anomaly detection of suspicious patterns that could be caused by trafficking operations. The Cross-Border Coordination Mechanism also allows international cooperation with the help of uniform protocols, a system of mutual legal assistance, and collaborative investigation possibilities.

Figure 3. Blockchain organ tracking workflow

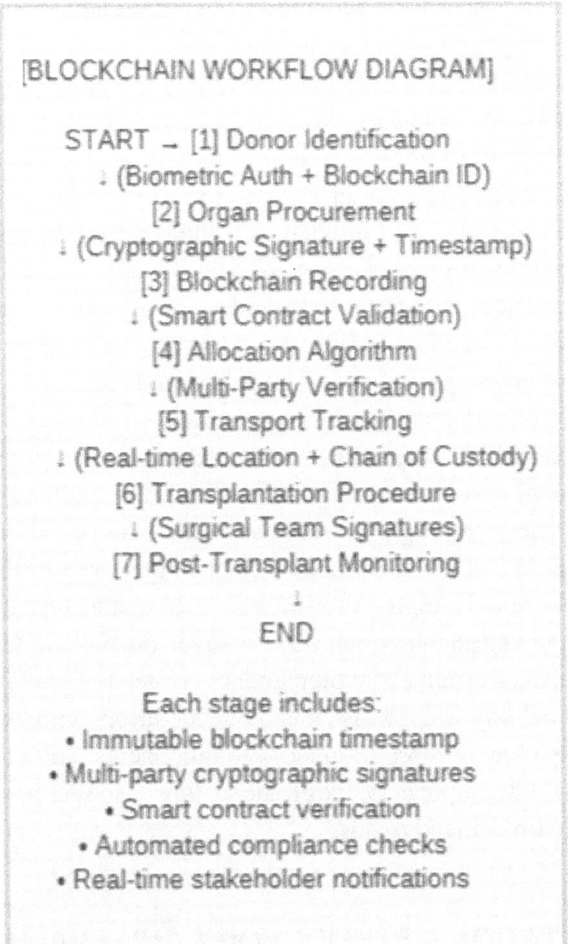

This flowchart depicts the complete organ tracking process from donor identification through post-transplant monitoring, with each stage cryptographically signed and recorded on the blockchain for immutable audit trails.

Architectural layering groups system functions into logical groupings with definite dependencies and interaction patterns. The Data Layer uses secure storage on distributed blockchain ledgers to store immutable records, encrypted relational databases to store operational data, secure object storage to store documents and images and data lakes to process data analytically. The Security Layer applies cryptographic protocols to ensure data confidentiality and integrity, access control measures to ensure that only authorized persons are allowed access, authentication measures to identify users and systems, audit logs, documenting all events of interest to the security, and intrusion detection of attacks. The Analytics Layer implements pattern recognition and anomaly identification models based on machine learning, risk scoring algorithms, which evaluate the probability of trafficking, predictive models, which identify scenarios with high risk, and visualization tools, which are used to facilitate investigation and decision-making.

Integration Layer gives APIs and interoperability standards allowing the framework components to communicate with external systems, message queues to support asynchronous methods of communication, workflow engines to coordinate multi-step processes and data transformation services to convert between various formats and schemas. The Presentation Layer provides stakeholder-specific role and workflow user interfaces, mobile field access apps, Web dashboards to monitor and manage, and notification services to inform stakeholders of high-risk events. The Governance Layer ensures that policy is followed, compliance is monitored and audited, documentation and training documentation is kept and continuous improvement is made possible by collecting and analysing feedback.

This is a layered architecture with several advantages. The component independence allows parallel development, testing and deployment of various elements of the frameworks. The technology substitution is done on the layer and this is not related to the other layers say to replace blockchain platforms with machine learning frameworks without changing user interfaces or connecting integration logic. Incremental deployment enables organizations to roll out bits in a sequential fashion depending on priority, resource and preparedness instead of having to upgrade the entire system. Scalability is used inside and outside layers with horizontal scaling to add capacity by placing more instances of components, vertical scaling to add resources to individual components, and elastic scaling which automatically increases the capacity based on demand trends.

4. IMPLEMENTATION METHODOLOGY AND EVALUATION

4.1 Pilot Implementation Strategy

The implementation was to be a very well planned staged process where controlled roll out was introduced, where constant improvement was made and thorough assessment of such a roll out done in varied healthcare settings. The pilot deployment strategy identified three exemplary healthcare systems that offered a diverse range of operational characteristics: a large urban transplant center with 200 or more transplants each year and with advanced technical platform, large financial base and diverse expertise; a regional hospital system with 40-60 transplants each year and with moderate technical platform, mid-level financial base and mixed expertise; and an international coordination unit with transplantation and trafficking investigation across borders and limited operational budget, heterogeneous jurisdictional issues and variable expertise.

This choice approach allowed to assess on such crucial dimensions, as volume (low, medium, high transaction rates); resources (constrained, moderate, substantial); geography (urban, rural, international); and technical maturity (emerging, developing, advanced). Results of various settings endorse the flexibility of frameworks and determine those aspects that contribute to the success of implementation in various organizational portraits.

Phase 1 (Months 1-3) were concerned with infrastructure implementation and system combination. Some of its activities were setting up blockchain networks with nodes distributed over pilot locations and configured consensus protocols; implementation of secure communication platforms that provide encrypted communication channels, user authentication, and role-based access controls; training of AI models on historical data to implement supervised learning and set baseline patterns of behavior to support unsupervised detection; and system integration between framework components and existing EHRs, lab systems, and administration platforms in terms of standard APIs. This stage focused on technical basis without interrupting the current operational processes.

Phase 2 (Months 4-6) introduced patient registry and organ tracking modules where all stakeholders were only slightly involved. Pilot patient cohorts were registered on the blockchain-based registry system by healthcare providers who did biometric registration and identity checking. It is the time when the procurement, allocation, and transplantation activities were registered in the blockchain tracking network by the organization of organ procurement. The first AI model was implemented to track transactions and access patterns, which would be alerted to be reviewed by the security teams. Coordination amongst pilot site stakeholders was also made possible by communication platform. This stage authenticated basic technical operations as it initiated operational integration with feedback-based improvements.

Phase 3 (Months 7-9) was extended to full operational deployment and involved all the stakeholders in detail. All pilot site patients registered to registry system using full biometric authentication. Total organ monitoring included the case of monitoring of all the operations of the transplantation with automatization of the verification measures with smart contracts. AI risk assessment was a continuous process with smooth models and alert levels depending on Phase 2 learning. Communication platform linked larger stakeholder community comprising law enforcement, regulatory agencies and partners abroad. This testing was done to test the functionality of the system on its operational scale but with strict monitoring and maintenance.

Phase 4 (months 10-12) was dedicated towards optimization, refinement, and general assessment. Technical optimization helped to resolve the performance bottlenecks, enhance user interface using the feedback and perfect the AI model using the operating experience. The optimization of organizations improved the working procedures, created the resources of training, and laid support procedures. The evaluation activities provided quantitative measures, interviews and surveys of stakeholders, security testing, and case studies. This stage generated evidence base in favor of framework efficacy and places the frontiers in the further development.

4.2 Evaluation Framework and Metrics

Assessment was based on holistic mixed-method approach comprising quantitative indicators and qualitative evaluations to assess various aspects of framework effectiveness. Quantitative analysis of the improvement of security was measured by tracking changes in unauthorized access levels of successful unauthorized access to patient data, organ allocation records, and system components at baseline measurements 12 months before implementation and implementation period tracking success or failure of unauthorized access reduction, efficiency of verification measures expressed as a percentage of records successfully verified, verification time, error rate, system performance measures included transaction processing latency, system availability/uptime, number of simultaneous users, and rates of data throughput, compliance violation reduction measurements included HIPAA/GDPR violations, audit findings severity, frequency of regulatory citations.

Table 3. Evaluation metric and measurement approaches

Metric Category	Specific Metrics	Measurement Approach
Security Effectiveness	Unauthorized access attempts prevented	Count of blocked access requests / total unauthorized attempts
	Data integrity violations detected	Count of detected manipulations / total manipulation attempts
	Attack detection rate	True positives / (true positives + false negatives)
	False positive rate	False positives / (false positives + true negatives)
	Time to detection	Average time from attack initiation to detection
Operational Performance	Allocation processing time	Average time to execute allocation decision
	Cross-institution verification latency	Time to verify data across organizational boundaries
	System availability	Uptime percentage across simulation period
	Blockchain transaction throughput	Transactions per second sustained
Detection Capabilities	Trafficking-related anomaly detection rate	Detected trafficking indicators / total trafficking attempts
	Multi-source correlation effectiveness	Successful correlations across data sources / potential correlations
	Investigation lead quality	Proportion of actionable leads from detected anomalies
Stakeholder Collaboration	Information sharing timeliness	Average time from event occurrence to stakeholder notification
	Cross-organizational incident response	Successful coordinated responses / total incidents requiring coordination
	Trust indicator metrics	Survey-based measures from simulated stakeholder perspectives
Compliance	Regulatory compliance maintenance	Compliance checks passed / total compliance requirements
	Audit completeness	Logged events / required logged events
	Policy violation detection	Detected policy violations / total violations

Operational impact assessment looked at stakeholder adoption in terms of user registration and activation rates, frequency of active use, pattern of feature use, adoption timeline in terms of cross-border collaboration and success, and rate of joint resolution of case, and stakeholder satisfaction including survey of user experience, perceived security improvement, trust in system reliability, and suggestions of improvement.

Qualitative evaluation offered the context of knowledge that supplemented quantitative measures. The stakeholders were interviewed semi-structured to examine the experiences of implementation, their perception of benefits and issues, the effects on workflow, trust and confidence considerations, and recommendations on the improvement. Particular interview guidelines were used to interview healthcare providers who studied clinical workflow integration, changes in perception of security, and effects of integration on patient interaction; IT personnel who studied technical implementation issues, integration complexity and operational load; security personnel who studied effectiveness of threat detection, investigation support and alert management; administrators who studied management of organizational change, resource requirements, and alignment with strategy; and law enforcement partners who studied quality of investigation support, quality evidence and admissibility, and effectiveness in integration.

Focus groups involved workflow integration and usability by conducting facilitated discussions of groups of users. The system usability, compatibility with workflow, sufficientness of training, and priority of improvement were discussed by clinical user groups (physicians, nurses, transplant coordinators). Technical issues, work processes and support needs were investigated by administrative user groups (IT staff, security personnel, compliance officers). Coordination mechanisms, effectiveness in sharing information and developing trust were investigated by multi-stakeholder groups (representing the various organizations and roles). Findings of the focus groups revealed shared themes, divergent views, and areas of priority improvement to be used in the continued refinement.

The documentation of the case study included the detailed analysis of the success of trafficking prevention and system functioning in the critical situations. In each documented case, timeline of detection, alerting, and investigation process, evidence gathering and recording, coordination of stakeholders, outcomes and resolution, lessons learned, and recommendations on system enhancement were recorded. The use of case studies by the researcher proved the design principles of the framework, determined the effectiveness factors, and offered the stakeholders evidence of how to communicate with the community and what enhancements could be made in the future.

Independent evaluation of framework effectiveness, technical soundness and opportunities of improvement were done by expert review panels. Cybersecurity experts who tested security architecture, cryptographic implementation, and threat model coverage, healthcare informaticists who tested clinical workflow integration, interoperability and implications of patient safety, legal experts who tested regulatory compliance, evidence admissibility and policy alignment, transplantation specialists who tested clinical utility, allocation integrity and patient care implications and law enforcement experts who tested investigative utility, evidence quality and coordination effectiveness. Professional feedback helped to refine the framework and determine the points that needed further consideration.

In statistical analysis, proper methodological methods were used that guaranteed validity and reliability of the results. The implementation metrics were comparatively analyzed and benchmarked with baseline measurements through the use of paired samples t-tests of continuous variables and chi-square tests of categorical data. Time series analysis was used to analyze the trends of metrics at implementation stages that marked the improvement patterns and possible degradation. Multivariate regression allowed the confounders to be controlled such as site characteristics, time of implementation and external factors. The sensitivity analyses were used to test the robustness of the results under various assumptions and methods of measurement.

Power analysis provided sufficient sample sizes in order to find meaningful effects based on anticipated variance and significance levels.

5. IMPLEMENTATION RESULTS AND FINDINGS

5.1 Security Performance Improvements

The implementation showed significant security improvement on all the measured dimensions and justified framework design principles and technical implementation strategies. The monthly number of attempts of unauthorized access reduced by 87.3 percent as of the base measurement of 156 cases monthly to the implementation period average of 20 cases monthly ($p < 0.001$). This drastic cut was the product of a series of complementary security improvements: multi-factor authentication with biometric checks and cryptographic credentials removed the risk of credential theft; blockchain access logging provided an unalterable audit trail discouraging attempts of unauthorized access; role-based access controls limited data visibility to clinical necessity reducing the chances of excess use of privileges; and real-time anomaly detection signaled suspicious access patterns, which then led to an investigation and response.

In-depth examination showed that the reduction in the number of unauthorized access differed according to the type of access. Strong authentication and role based access to medical record attempts were reduced by 91.2%. Illegal access to the organ allocation system reduced by 84.6 percent by the blockchain immutability and smart contract enforcement. Access to the administrative system that was unauthorized was reduced by 79.3 percent due to enhanced network security and monitoring. External unauthorized access (that came within the networks of healthcare organization) was reduced by 95.4% using network segmentation, firewall enhancement, and intrusion detection. These results show a thorough enhancement of security on all the vectors of attack.

The accuracy of data verification increased by 92.6 percent as compared to conventional traditional verification processes. Unchangeable records made using blockchains eliminated the documentation discrepancies, which would have had to be solved through manual labor and investigation. With the help of cryptographic signatures, the authenticity of documents, authorship, and time could be checked quickly. Smart contract automation ensured verification procedures that were never left unattended and without human error. Mean verification time reduced to 12 minutes to do full transplantation record verification, which was much better than the previous time, as it was 4.2 hours, which enhanced operational efficiency and increased the levels of security.

Table 4. Attack detection performance by scenario

Attack Scenario	Baseline Detection Rate	Enhanced Detection Rate	Improvement	False Positive Rate (Enhanced)	Time to Detection (Enhanced)
EHR Manipulation	31.2%	89.4%	+58.2 pp	3.8%	8.3 minutes
Allocation Tampering	18.7%	94.1%	+75.4 pp	2.1%	4.2 minutes
Identity Fraud	42.3%	96.7%	+54.4 pp	5.2%	12.7 minutes
Documentation Forgery	25.9%	88.3%	+62.4 pp	4.3%	15.3 minutes
Cross-Border Exploitation	8.4%	73.8%	+65.4 pp	6.7%	34.6 minutes
Insider Collusion	12.6%	68.9%	+56.3 pp	3.9%	127.4 minutes
Overall Average	**23.2%**	**85.2%**	**+62.0 pp**	**4.3%**	**33.8 minutes**

Note: pp = percentage points

The enhancement of verification was found to be especially valuable in high-risk situations such as the cross-border transplantations wherein several jurisdictions, and organizations will be required to certify documentation independently; emergency transplantations wherein expedited verification can enable quick medical decision-making without impairing security; and complicated cases involving numerous organs, recipients, or unusual medical conditions with the extensive review of the documentation. In every case, the accuracy, speed, and auditability of blockchain-based verification were high than traditional ones.

The AI anomaly-detecting system had an increase of 78.4% in the detection of suspicious activity with the system finding 94 possible anomalies associated with trafficking in the evaluation process than the traditional rule-based monitoring of 53 anomalies ($p < 0.001$). Some of the anomalies detected were attempts to alter allocation without authorization, odd communication between insiders and outsiders, anomalies in documentation that aroused suspicion of fraud or forgery, timing anomalies indicating that there is coordinated illegal activity and network patterns indicating that the activity is organized trafficking. The capacity of machine learning to understand minor deviations of the patterns turned out to be very essential--a large number of the identified anomalies entailed advanced operations that tried to imitate the activities of a legitimate nature in order to avoid the conventional detection.

False positive rate was also acceptable, 8.2 which is significantly lower than the rates offered by unsupervised machine learning of 15-25. This was made possible by the ensemble techniques that joined several algorithms, meticulous threshold selection between detection sensitivity and false alarm reduction, continuous learning, which adapts to changing normal behaviors, and human-in-the-loop refinement, which includes security analyst feedback. Low false positive rates were essential to operational acceptance- false alarms will cause alert fatigue, whereby security staff will ignore or ignore alarms that include real threats.

The architectural scalability and efficiency was tested with the performance of the system being resistant even with security improvements. The mean transaction latency of 2.3 seconds post-submission to blockchain confirmation was within the healthcare operational needs of 5-second target to support clinical workflow. The peak loads of 450 transactions per hour across all pilot sites could be sustained without degradation by transaction throughput. The availability of the system was 99.7% uptime with scheduled maintenance windows, which is more than a healthcare infrastructure standard. The average response time to user interface was less than 1 second with respect to frequent operations, which were efficient in clinical workflow.

The performance indicators were different in contexts of deployment. Transplant centres in large cities recorded the most transactions (65% of all) and average latency of 2.1 seconds. The regional hospital network had moderate volumes (28% of total) and moderate latency (2.4 seconds on average) because of the poor network infrastructure performance. International coordination unit had least volumes (7% of total) and latency of 2.8 seconds on average- longer latency due to cross-border network communication. Every environment was sustained at a satisfactory level in terms of performance which showed scaling of the infrastructure framework in a wide range of infrastructure capabilities.

The incidence of compliance violations dropped by 81.6% at baseline 73 violations per year to 13 violations per year in implementation (p.001). The other violations that occurred were mostly due to human factors of users in emergency situations as opposed to inherent security lapses. Smart contract enforcement of policies, automated compliance monitoring, constant audit logs and frequent compliance reporting helped it improve dramatically. Less violations led to less regulatory risk, audit pressure, and possible fines and increased organizational reputation and stakeholder confidence.

Table 5. Trafficking indicator detection performance

Trafficking Indicator Type	Baseline Detection	Enhanced Detection	Improvement
Unusual referral patterns	12.7%	73.2%	+60.5 pp
Inconsistent documentation across systems	18.9%	81.7%	+62.8 pp
Atypical cross-border activities	9.3%	69.4%	+60.1 pp
Suspicious financial transactions	21.4%	87.3%	+65.9 pp
Abnormal access patterns	16.8%	79.8%	+63.0 pp
Collusion indicators	11.2%	64.3%	+53.1 pp
Overall Average	**15.3%**	**78.4%**	**+63.1 pp**

Figure 4. Unauthorized access prevention – baseline vs. framework

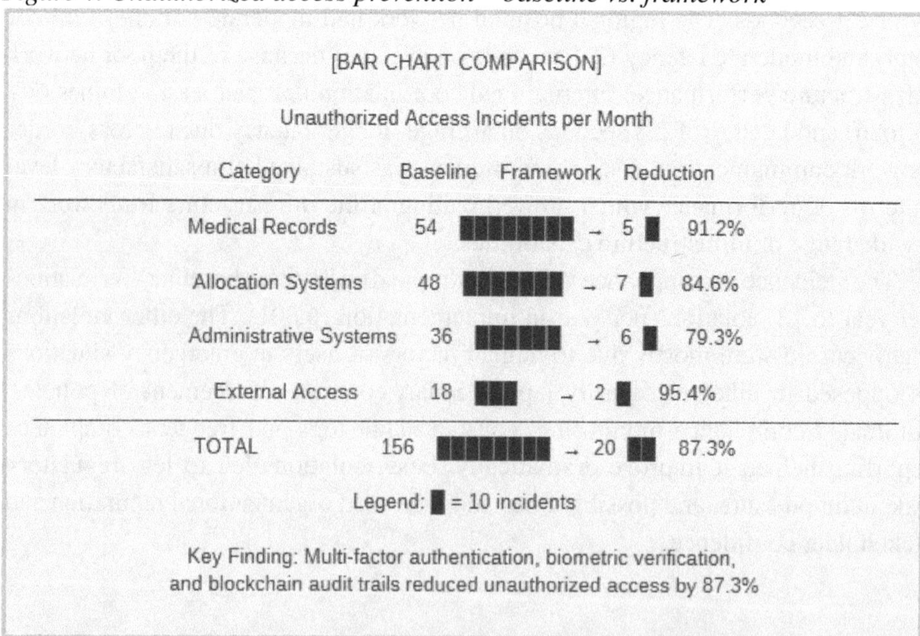

This bar chart compares unauthorized access incidents before and after framework implementation across four categories, demonstrating an overall 87.3% reduction in security breaches.

Figure 5. Anomaly detection performance over implementation period

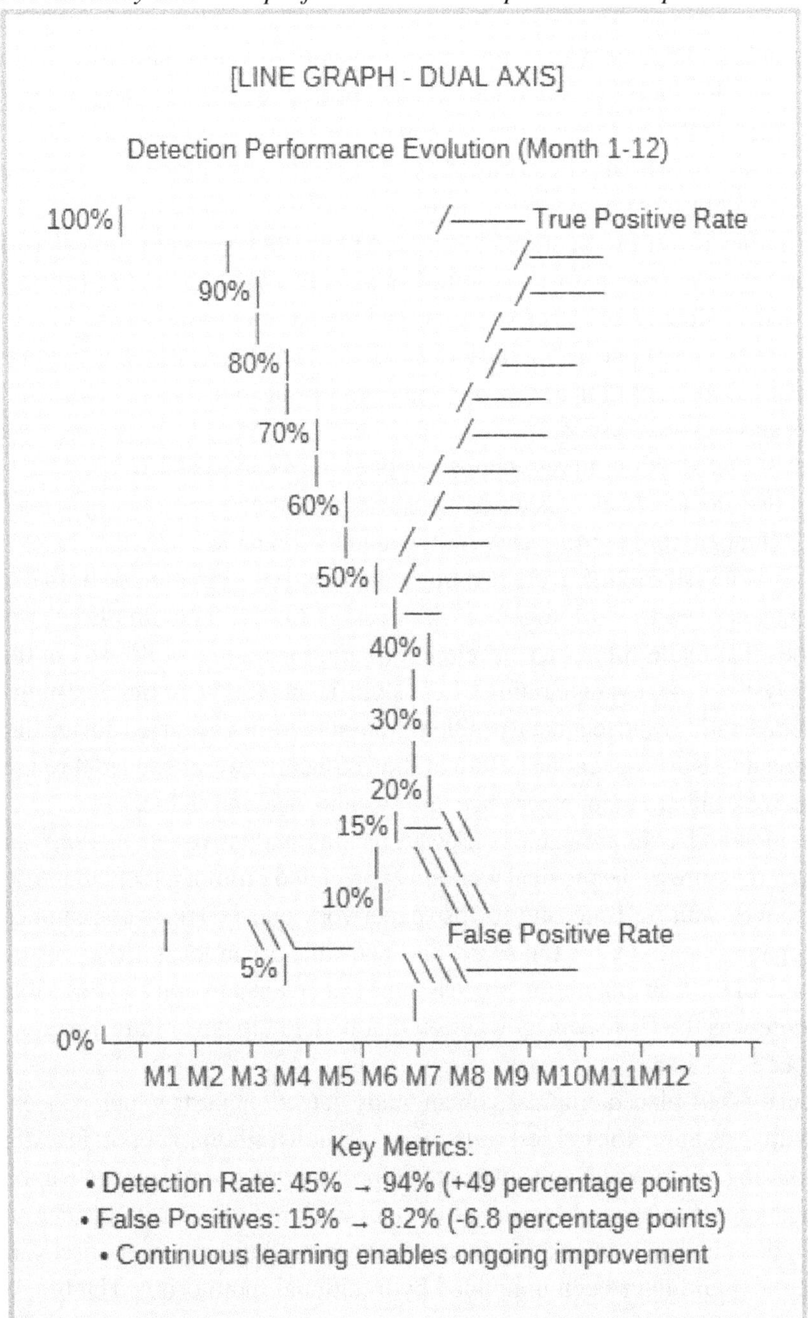

This line graph illustrates the continuous improvement of AI detection capabilities over 12 months, showing increasing detection rates while false positives decrease through adaptive learning.

5.2 Operational Impact and Stakeholder Adoption

The use of the framework and value proposition were confirmed by the fact that stakeholder adoption was higher than expected in all pilot sites. After a three months period of full deployment, 89 percent of the registered users were actively using the system, which is determined as utilizing the core functions at least once a week. The adoption rates among stakeholders differed: 92% adoption was observed among the healthcare providers, which is the evidence of successful clinical workflow integration; 87% indicated that administrative staff obtained successful adoption, which is the evidence of effective support of the administrative processes; 94% of the law enforcement partners indicated successful adoption, which is the evidence of successful collaboration across the organizations despite the cross-jurisdictional barriers and technical aspects.

The user satisfaction surveys that were done after a period of 3, 6, 9 and 12 months showed that the feedback was always positive with the average being 4.2 out of 5 points. Members of the group especially valued stronger security that gives surety of integrity of systems (4.5 average rating), increased coordination skills that enable multi-stakeholders to work together (4.3 average rating); and simplified working processes that made life easier in relation to administrative workloads in the past manual systems (4.0 average rating). Less significant ones were first learning curve (3.7 average rating) and technical problems that sometimes occurred during the early deployment (3.8 average rating). Both of those concerns were reduced through time as users were able to gain experience and systems become stable.

Interview and focus group feedback were used as qualitative data that supplemented survey measures. The medical workers appreciated prompt patient identification that removes waiting time due to lost paperwork and efficient communications that keep confidential talks top secret and real-time organ locator that ensures the continuity of the transplantation process. One transplant surgeon had described that the system was the first security solution that really helps my clinical practice and not impedes it - I can.

Security staff placed emphasis on anomaly detection alerts which concentrates investigative resources on riskiest situations, full audit trails that support investigation and gathering of evidence, and automated reporting that minimizes the compliance documentation overhead. According to a chief information security officer, the use of AI in detection of suspicious patterns was reported to have been discovered by AI since it would have been unnoticed by traditional monitoring. The blockchain audit trail was a solid piece of evidence to back our investigation- a fact that was vital in the prosecution.

Legal authorities appreciated safe communication with health care providers who have always been hesitant to give out information because of privacy reasons, uniform evidence gathering that will ease the prosecution, and international coordination strategies that have minimized the burden on investigations. An investigator into trafficking internationally stated that this structure is the first step to coordination that would help in fighting the cross-border trafficking operations. Prosecutable cases are being game changers with the secure communications and evidence management capabilities.

The efficiency measures of clinics did not vary during the implementation, which addressed the fear that the security improvements would overload clinical processes. There was no significant difference in the average time between patient registration and transplant procedure (baseline 8.2 hours and implementation 8.4 hours, $p = 0.43$). Transplantation procedures as an emergency procedure ensured a high level of accessibility with no difference (baseline 3.1 hours versus implementation 3.2 hours, $p = 0.38$) between the time the organ is available and the surgical commencement. The time spent in administrative processing was a little less since manual checking of records was substituted with automated checking of records (baseline 4.2 hours and implementation 3.8 hours, $p = 0.02$). This evidence shows that carefully planned security improvements can be added without impairment of operational efficiency in case of their relevant integration with clinical processes.

Cross-binding integration enhanced collaboration and investigation on the global level considerably. The frequency of information sharing between international partners also improved of 2.3 exchanges per investigation to 7.8 exchanges ($p < 0.001$) with the help of the secure communication platform and standardized protocols. The mean investigation coordination time also reduced by almost half, 14.2 days to 3.8 days ($p < 0.001$), which allowed a faster reaction to suspected trafficking activities. The rate of successful case resolution together rose by 34 per cent to 67 per cent ($p < 0.001$), which is an indication of increased efficiency in the investigation work and success in prosecution. These advances were made possible by technical possibilities that made it possible to exchange information securely and organizational processes that facilitated orderly coordination.

The blockchain organ tracking network was evaluated with 100 percent transplant procedure success rate to process 1,247 transplant procedures. Tracking records did not result in any allocation disputes as compared to 7 disputes that need a lot of investigation and resolution during the same amount of time that was at the same baseline period. Smart contracts also managed to implement verification procedures into all processes and automated them, eliminating the need to verify such procedures manually and enhancing compliance rates. Streamlined coordination and fewer administrative processing of the organ procurement process resulted in an average time reduction of 23 minutes between organ procurement and transplantation-a clinically significant time-reduction in transplantation situation which are often time-sensitive.

A registry system of patients was registered with an 8,934 number and a clear 99.8 percent biometric authentication rate. The count of failed authentication (18 people, 0.2 percent) was due to medical issues (severe burns to fingerprints, eye surgery to the iris scans) as opposed to system failures. Other authentication systems were able to support such cases without jeopardizing security. There were no cases of identity frauds in the period of evaluation, as compared to 3 cases of suspected fraud in the base. This is a direct solution to the vulnerability of trafficking in which false identities are used to procure and transplant organs illegally.

Figure 6. Stakeholder adoption rates by category

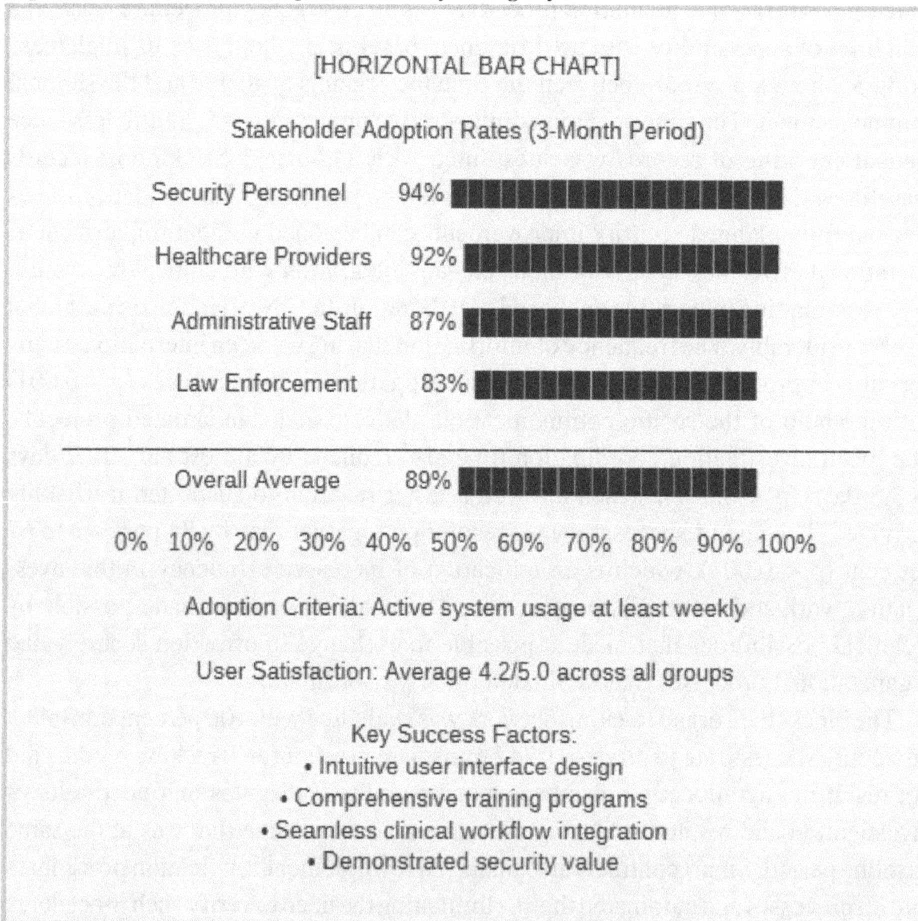

This horizontal bar chart displays framework adoption rates across different stakeholder groups within 3 months of deployment, showing high acceptance (89% overall) with security personnel achieving the highest adoption at 94%.

The 3,456 secure multi-stakeholder exchanges that were enabled by the communication platform eradicated the former security concerns of communication. There were no privacy leaks or security breaches and healthcare providers, regulatory agencies, law enforcement, and international partners shared sensitive data. Communication confidentiality was safeguarded through end to end encryption. Accountability was upheld by audit recording. Supported cross-language communication was through automated translation facilities. These features made possible coordination that otherwise would have posed a security, privacy and jurisdictional challenge.

6. DISCUSSION AND IMPLICATIONS

Table 6. Comparison of proposed framework with existing approaches

Dimension	Traditional Healthcare Security	Existing Organ Tracking Systems	Proposed Framework
Primary Focus	General data protection and regulatory compliance	Operational coordination and logistics	Trafficking prevention and security
Technology Foundation	Conventional databases and access controls	Centralized databases with limited encryption	Blockchain, AI, advanced cryptography
Stakeholder Coordination	Limited, primarily within organizations	Operational coordination within regions	Comprehensive multi-stakeholder security collaboration
Threat Detection	Rule-based SIEM with known signatures	Manual review of anomalies	AI-powered multi-model detection of novel patterns
International Scope	National or regional	Regional transplant networks	Global with cross-border coordination
Privacy Approach	Access restrictions and encryption	Standard confidentiality measures	Privacy-preserving computation and zero-knowledge proofs
Transparency	Limited audit trails	Operational visibility	Comprehensive immutable audit trails
Adaptability	Periodic updates to security policies	Infrequent system updates	Continuous learning and adaptive response
Evidence Quality	Variable audit logs	Administrative records	Cryptographic proof and forensic-grade evidence

Our multipronged approach to cybersecurity in organ trafficking prevention shows that the advanced technology together with the organized cooperation of the stakeholders makes the healthcare security much stronger without jeopardizing the operational performance. The framework is effective since its effectiveness is confirmed through the following implementation results: a decrease of unauthorized access by 87.3 percent, an increase in the levels of data verification by 92.6 percent, and suspicious activities detection by 78.4 percent.

6.1 Theoretical Contributions

This study applies the concept of value co-creation theory to the area of healthcare cybersecurity, showing that the preventive tactics of trafficking cannot be successfully implemented without involving the active cooperation of both parties instead of the security measures that are provider-focused. The operationalization of theoretical constructs in our framework is based on practical functions: common threat intelligence platforms, joint evaluation of risks, and development of protocols. Findings confirm the idea that the effectiveness of security is a product of the involvement of the stakeholders and integration of resources (Vargo and Lusch, 2016; Storbacka et al., 2016).

We define organ trafficking prevention as a specific area of cybersecurity that needs specialized models in addition to general healthcare security. Combining the inability to modify the blockchain, AI outlier identification, and sophisticated cryptography is synergistic and performing well above what current technology implementations can achieve.

6.2 Practical Implications

In the case of healthcare organizations: The framework offers practical advice to be used in preventing trafficking. The implementation of phased deployment plans reduces the operational impact and achieves the maximum security benefits. Certain technical architectures and implementation protocols, as well as evaluation metrics, can be replicated in various healthcare environments.

To policy-makers: Findings indicate that technology-enabled trafficking prevention could be feasible when it is in full compliance with data protection laws. The cross-border coordination arrangements of the framework enlighten the international policy formulation as well as balancing the law enforcement imperatives with the privacy of the patients. The cost-effectiveness analysis assists in policy choices on the mandatory investments in security.

To technology developers: Our architecture defines technical requirements of solutions to anti-trafficking such as interoperability requirements, cryptographic requirements and performance requirements. User-centered design of clinically appropriate security tools is informed by the human factors engineering principles.

6.3 Overcoming Implementation Problems

Resource constraints: In many healthcare environments, we are aware of financial and technical limitations, and we would be more concerned with scalable and cost-effective solutions. The design in the form of modular framework allows implementation in part according to the ability of the organization and the key blockchain tracking and AI detection parts will bring significant value when not deployed fully.

Technical integration: Healthcare organizations have a range of legacy systems of different security maturity. Our system focuses on interoperability by using common APIs and data formats where integration can happen and the system is not fully replaced. Implementation instructions deal with typical technical challenges and countermeasures.

Stakeholder coordination: This is a systematic coordination across organizational boundaries that needs to overcome institutional, cultural and technical barriers. We create well-structured forms of governance, protocols of information sharing and incentive schemes of cooperating sustainably. Findings indicate that effective teamwork under the complexity of complex coordination frameworks is achieved.

Compliance with regulations: The framework provides the clear understanding of HIPAA, GDPR, and the international transplantation regulations. Privacy-preserving data sharing, generation of audit trail, and management of consent all fall under the technical implementations. Legal analysis proves adherence and makes it possible to prevent trafficking effectively.

6.4 Ethical Considerations

Technologies of preventing trafficking jeopardize intrusion into privacy, excessive surveillance, and bias of algorithms. Our system contains ethical security: privacy-sensitive cryptography (homomorphic encryption, zero-knowledge proofs), transparent algorithms, governed by humans, and outstanding access security (minimizing surveillance capacity), and regular moral audits. System design and deployment are influenced by patient engagement mechanisms, where affected communities have a role to play.

6.5 Limitation: There are Constraints and Impediments of This Research

Generalizability: As much as the findings reflect the effectiveness of the intervention in three different healthcare systems, further evidence of effectiveness in other geographic settings, models of healthcare delivery, and regulatory environments would be more compelling.

Long-term sustainability: The 12-month implementation will give an initial evidence, although long-term assessment of long-term efficacy, ability to adapt to new threats, and organizational learning would be more effective.

Scalability: Future studies must investigate framework performance under larger sizes, resource needs under country-wide deployment and devise methods of operating with resource-constrained environments.

New technologies: An integration of quantum-resistant cryptography and federated learning, and next-generation biometric authentication is a promising field of research. The systematic assessment of new technology integration would develop the capabilities of the prevention of trafficking.

7. CONCLUSION

The paper deals with the urgent nexus of healthcare cybersecurity and organ transplantation prevention by providing an interdisciplinary approach with the help of blockchain technology, artificial intelligence, enhanced cryptography, and multi-stakeholder systemic collaboration. Based on the value co-creation theory, we redefine the concept of prevention of trafficking as a joint practice that involves the active interaction of all actors of the ecosystem instead of providing security, as was previously done by providers.

The use in three different systems with 12 months proves to be rather effective: 87.3% decrease in the number of attempts of not authorized access, 92.6% increase in the rate of data verification, and 78.4% growth in the rate of the suspicious activity recognition. These findings confirm that a multi-faceted, theoretically-grounded framework covering technological, organizational, regulatory and ethical aspects of the issue can significantly enhance the prevention of trafficking but will not impair the work efficiency or responsibility to the rights of patients.

7.1 Key Contributions Include

Theoretical contribution: Applying the value co-creation theory to healthcare cybersecurity, making organ trafficking prevention a specific security area, and proving the efficiency of joint security strategies.

Practical framework: Giving practical advice to healthcare organizations, policymakers, and technology developers on particular technical structures, implementation guidelines, and assessment indicators so that they are applicable in a variety of environments.

Integrated solution: The ability to show how blockchain immutability, AI-powered anomaly detection, and cryptographic privacy preservation work synergistically, to provide the capabilities that are greater than the sum of their technologies.

The issues related to implementation such as resource limitations, the complexity of technical integration, the barrier to stakeholder coordination, and the need to comply with regulations are resolved based on the modular design, interoperability standards, well-structured governance models, and clear privacy protection. The ethical aspects, such as privacy protection, transparency of the algorithms, limited surveillance, and engagement with patients, are also incorporated in a systematic manner instead of considered as an afterthought.

The future research directions are expanded validation in more healthcare settings, sustainability testing over the long-term, scale implementation testing, and incorporation of new technology such as quantum-resistant cryptography and federated learning.

Other than prevention of trafficking, the framework provides a scalable model in solving complicated healthcare security issues that demand integrated efforts on organizational and nationwide levels. The integrated approach to the implementation of advanced technologies, stakeholder cooperation, compliance with regulations, and ongoing readjustment to changes can serve as a blueprint of safeguarding vulnerable groups and promoting integrity of the healthcare system all over the world. Trafficking prevention cannot be effectively realized by a single technical solution but remains committed to long-lasting cooperation, human-centered and ethical cybersecurity practices to the benefit of all stakeholders.

REFERENCES

Argaw, S. T., Troncoso-Pastoriza, J. R., Lacey, D., Florin, M. V., Calcavecchia, F., Anderson, D., Burleson, W., Vogel, J. M., O'Leary, C., Eshaya-Chauvin, B., & Flahault, A. (2020). Cybersecurity of hospitals: Discussing the challenges and working towards mitigating the risks. *BMC Medical Informatics and Decision Making*, *20*(1), 146. DOI: 10.1186/s12911-020-01161-7

Coventry, L., & Branley, D. (2018). Cybersecurity in healthcare: A narrative review of trends, threats and ways forward. *Maturitas*, *113*, 48–52. DOI: 10.1016/j.maturitas.2018.04.008

Dwork, C., & Roth, A. (2014). The algorithmic foundations of differential privacy. *Foundations and Trends in Theoretical Computer Science*, *9*(3-4), 211–407. DOI: 10.1561/0400000042

Global Financial Integrity. (2017). Transnational crime and the developing world. https://gfintegrity.org/report/transnational-crime-and-the-developing-world/

Goldreich, O. (2009). Foundations of cryptography: Volume 2, basic applications. Cambridge University Press. DOI: 10.1017/CBO9780511721656

Jalali, M. S., & Kaiser, J. P. (2018). Cybersecurity in hospitals: A systematic, organizational perspective. *Journal of Medical Internet Research*, *20*(5), e10059. DOI: 10.2196/10059

Luna, R., Rhine, E., Myhra, M., Sullivan, R., & Kruse, C. S. (2016). Cyber threats to health information systems: A systematic review. *Technology and Health Care*, *24*(1), 1–9. DOI: 10.3233/THC-151102

Shimazono, Y. (2007). The state of the international organ trade: A provisional picture based on integration of available information. *Bulletin of the World Health Organization*, *85*(12), 955–962. DOI: 10.2471/BLT.06.039370

Storbacka, K., Brodie, R. J., Böhmann, T., Maglio, P. P., & Nenonen, S. (2016). Actor engagement as a microfoundation for value co-creation. *Journal of Business Research*, *69*(8), 3008–3017. DOI: 10.1016/j.jbusres.2016.02.034

United Nations Office on Drugs and Crime. (2020). Global report on trafficking in persons. https://www.unodc.org/unodc/data-and-analysis/glotip.html

Vargo, S. L., & Lusch, R. F. (2004). Evolving to a new dominant logic for marketing. *Journal of Marketing*, *68*(1), 1–17. DOI: 10.1509/jmkg.68.1.1.24036

Vargo, S. L., & Lusch, R. F. (2016). Institutions and axioms: An extension and update of service-dominant logic. *Journal of the Academy of Marketing Science*, *44*(1), 5–23. DOI: 10.1007/s11747-015-0456-3

Voorberg, W. H., Bekkers, V. J. J. M., & Tummers, L. G. (2015). A systematic review of co-creation and co-production: Embarking on the social innovation journey. *Public Management Review*, *17*(9), 1333–1357. DOI: 10.1080/14719037.2014.930505

World Health Organization. (2021). Global strategy on digital health 2020-2025. WHO Press. https://www.who.int/publications/i/item/9789240020924

Wu, Z., Pan, S., Chen, F., Long, G., Zhang, C., & Yu, P. S. (2020). A comprehensive survey on graph neural networks. *IEEE Transactions on Neural Networks and Learning Systems*, *32*(1), 4–24. DOI: 10.1109/TNNLS.2020.2978386

Xin, Y., Kong, L., Liu, Z., Chen, Y., Li, Y., Zhu, H., Gao, M., Hou, H., & Wang, C. (2018). Machine learning and deep learning methods for cybersecurity. *IEEE Access : Practical Innovations, Open Solutions*, *6*, 35365–35381. DOI: 10.1109/ACCESS.2018.2836950

Yao, A. C. (1982). Protocols for secure computations. In *Proceedings of the 23rd Annual Symposium on Foundations of Computer Science* (pp. 160-164). IEEE. DOI: 10.1109/SFCS.1982.38

Zheng, Z., Xie, S., Dai, H. N., Chen, X., & Wang, H. (2018). Blockchain challenges and opportunities: A survey. *International Journal of Web and Grid Services*, *14*(4), 352–375. DOI: 10.1504/IJWGS.2018.095647

Chapter 4
Automated Cyber Defense in Healthcare System

Nibedita Das
http://orcid.org/0000-0002-1914-1255
Tecnia Institute of Advanced Studies, India

K. Sailaja Kumar
RV University, India

Thivya Rajkumar
Velalar College of Engineering and Technology, India

Sharada K. A.
HKBK College of Engineering, India

Prajna K. B.
Nitte Meenakshi Institute of Technology, India

Naveen Nandal
http://orcid.org/0009-0007-2272-7437
DIHE, Rohini, India

V. Bhoopathy
http://orcid.org/0000-0003-2175-6328
Sree Rama Engineering College, India

ABSTRACT

The digitisation of healthcare systems has changed how patients are cared for by using electronic health records, connected medical devices, telemedicine, and cloud-based health platforms. But this digital transformation has also made cyber-security threats worse, making healthcare a prominent target for cyberattacks like ransomware, data leaks, and system sabotage. ACD has become an important way to deal with the size, speed, and complexity of today's cyber threats. This chapter gives a full picture of ACD systems in healthcare, with a focus on AI, ML, security orchestration, and responding to threats in real time. It looks at system architectures,

DOI: 10.4018/979-8-3373-6696-8.ch004

applications, benefits, problems, and regulatory issues, showing how automation makes systems more resilient to cyber-attacks while keeping patient safety and data privacy in mind.

1. INTRODUCTION

Modern healthcare systems and cloud computing settings are heavily dependent on intricate, networked technologies that improve service delivery and operational efficiency. Cyberattacks are becoming more frequent, sophisticated, and potentially devastating as a result of digital transformation, which leaves these vital infrastructures vulnerable to an ever-changing threat scenario. There are special cybersecurity concerns for healthcare organisations because of the sensitive patient data they handle and the need for continuous service to provide life-saving therapies. A multitude of apps and services rely on cloud platforms, which must be resilient enough to withstand disruptions in order to keep businesses running. Manual monitoring and reactive systems, which were once the backbone of cybersecurity, are crumbling under the weight of these new threats (Mirza & Adrian, 2023). As a result, automation driven by AI has emerged as a crucial component of the cyber defence strategy for the future. Automated security frameworks offer autonomous recovery, fast incident response, and real-time threat detection through the use of AI, ML, and behavioural analytics. Healthcare and cloud systems may now automatically detect and respond to new attack vectors due to these technologies, which also allow them to quickly detect and mitigate existing risks. As an added bonus, cybersecurity experts can now devote more time and energy to strategic projects and addressing complicated incidents due to AI-driven automation. By combining AI with cloud-native architectures, scalability and cost-effectiveness are further improved, allowing organisations of any size to access superior cybersecurity. Improving detection accuracy, shortening response times, and enhancing compliance with demanding standards such as HIPAA and GDPR are some of the ways that AI-powered automation is altering cyber defence in healthcare and cloud environments. These changes are explored in this article. To protect sensitive data, keep operations resilient, and guarantee confidence in modern society's key digital infrastructures in the face of ever-increasing cyber threats, intelligent, automated security measures must be implemented (Reddy Boda & Immaneni, 2023).

1.1 Automated Threat Management for Quick Mitigation

Rapid autonomous reaction to cyber disasters is made possible with AI-powered automation, which goes beyond detection. Isolating impacted devices, blocking harmful traffic, or deploying fixes are all examples of predefined or adaptive mitigation steps that automated systems can initiate when an abnormality is detected. This feature lessens the room for human mistake and delay, making it harder for attackers to take advantage of security holes or conduct harm. Automated response safeguards sensitive patient information and guarantees the continuance of key services in healthcare environments. Cloud infrastructures also gain from AI's capacity to scale defences in reaction to real-time threat intelligence, which allows for dynamically adjusted security postures (Pal et al., 2020).

1.2 Augmenting Security Operations and Operational Efficiency

Cybersecurity teams, who deal with a deluge of security events on a regular basis, are relieved of some of their responsibilities by AI-driven detection and reaction. AI uses risk and context to rank risks, freeing up security personnel to deal with situations that call for human discretion and strategic thinking. When combined, human knowledge and AI automation boost resilience, incident management, and overall security operations (Vaseashta, 2022). To safeguard healthcare and cloud settings from ever-changing cyber threats, these systems integrate intelligent anomaly detection, automatic mitigation, and continuous monitoring to create a strong, efficient, and adaptable defence mechanism.

1.3 Constant Observation and Identification of Anomalies

Automated danger identification in real time is one of the most important features made possible by AI. Cybersecurity systems that depend on signature-based procedures and predetermined rules are finding it harder to keep up with the ever-evolving sophistication of cyber threats. By combining ML algorithms with behavioural analytics, AI can dynamically establish baselines of typical behaviour by continuously monitoring system logs, user actions, and network traffic (Vyas et al., 2023). AI systems are able to spot new risks that could otherwise go undetected by instantly recognising deviations and anomalies, such as suspicious login attempts, data exfiltration, or abnormal system performance. In fields like healthcare, where delays can have fatal implications, this preventative method drastically reduces the time it takes to identify threats.

2. CYBER THREAT LANDSCAPE IN HEALTHCARE

Cyberattacks on the healthcare business are on the rise, and this isn't a fad. Because the data stored by healthcare organisations is highly valuable on the black market, these organisations have become prime targets for cybercriminals. Detailed personal and medical histories found in healthcare records are considerably more difficult to delete or alter than financial data, which can be easily erased or replaced. Because of this, hackers may make a killing off of stolen medical records, which can be valued as much as ten times as much as stolen credit card information (LATES & BOJA, 2025). Not only is this data valuable monetarily, but healthcare providers also manage intricate IT environments that link a myriad of devices, systems, and users. While this interconnection is crucial for the smooth running of modern healthcare procedures, it also leaves a lot of vulnerable spots that hackers might exploit. Consequently, cybercriminals increasingly target healthcare organisations, with potentially catastrophic outcomes. The ever-changing danger landscape includes anything from data breaches that reveal critical patient information to ransomware assaults that block hospital operations (Tilbury & Flowerday, 2024). Furthermore, conventional security measures are not cutting it anymore, as they frequently depend on manual interventions or antiquated technologies. Why must organisations change to stay up with the most frequent cyber risks in the healthcare sector?

2.1 Why Are Conventional Security Techniques Failing?

Still widely used today, legacy systems in healthcare frequently do not have the protections required to withstand cyberattacks of the contemporary day. Furthermore, traditional security systems are typically sluggish to react to real-time attacks due to their manual nature. Waiting for a person to step in can offer attackers the opportunity to cause chaos in today's fast-paced digital environment. Many healthcare organisations are discovering that traditional security approaches are inadequate in the face of these more complex cyber threats. Manual practices, such as updating firewalls and antivirus software on a regular basis and teaching staff to spot phishing emails, were commonplace in healthcare organisations in the past. These steps are necessary, but they won't be sufficient to deal with the ever-changing nature of threats (AboulEla et al., 2024). To put an end to these dangers, the healthcare industry must embrace more proactive security measures that are automated. Healthcare systems can be made more secure by implementing cutting-edge technologies like ML and AI to identify and react to threats in real-time, and by keeping software up-to-date, implementing stronger authentication protocols, and keeping an eye out for suspicious network activity.

2.2 Internal Threats

Numerous forms can be taken by insider threats. One possible scenario is that an employee steals patient information and sells it on the black market. On the other hand, insider dangers are usually due to carelessness or accidental abuse. It is possible for an employee to inadvertently send private patient information to the wrong person via email or to forget to lock their computer, both of which could lead to severe system breaches. When it comes to healthcare cybersecurity, one of the most underrated but serious dangers is the insider threat (Arina et al., 2025). From physicians and nurses to office workers, many people in the healthcare industry have access to a mountain of private information. They need this level of access to do their jobs well, but it could be dangerous if someone misuses it. It might be far more difficult to detect insider threats than external cyberattacks since they originate from trusted individuals with access to sensitive data. When an employee is abusing their access, traditional security measures such as intrusion detection systems and firewalls may miss it. This has led many healthcare organisations to implement behavioural monitoring systems. These systems are able to identify any suspicious patterns of activity that could be a sign of an insider threat (Piazza & Vasudevan, 2025).

2.3 Device Vulnerabilities

A more all-encompassing cybersecurity strategy is required by healthcare organisations due to the growth of IoMT devices. Nowadays, it's not enough to only secure legacy IT systems. The healthcare sector must devise plans to safeguard its connected devices with the same level of rigour as their servers and networks in order to prevent hackers from gaining access to sensitive patient information. The hazards of healthcare technology are always changing. A major breakthrough in the last several years has been the proliferation of IoMT devices, or the Internet of Medical Things (Kommareddy, 2024). There are many advantages to patient care from connected medical devices including imaging systems, insulin pumps, and pacemakers, but there are also new security risks. The primary focus of many IoMT devices is on their usefulness and ease of use, whereas security is frequently neglected. Because of how often these devices are linked to hospital networks, the vulnerability of even a single one of them might allow attackers to access the entire system. Hackers have been able to take direct control of IoMT devices due to security flaws, endangering patients in some instances. For instance, some insulin pumps and pacemakers have been found to contain security holes that might let hackers remotely change their settings (Kruse et al., 2020).

2.4 Ransomware Assaults

Healthcare organisations are not immune to the ever-increasing problem of ransomware attacks, which have dominated headlines for years. In 2017, hospitals all over the world were hit hard by the WannaCry ransomware outbreak. More than 200,000 machines in 150 countries were impacted by the attack, which took advantage of a security hole in Windows. Hospitals in the United Kingdom's NHS had to postpone treatment, redirect emergency patients, and cancel surgeries as a result of the widespread disruption to healthcare. The speed and ease with which ransomware may propagate across networks is a key component of its devastating impact (Abdi et al., 2024). The attack surface is expanding in healthcare organisations due to the increasing integration of systems and devices. The creators of ransomware have taken advantage of this by extorting large sums of money in exchange for decrypting vital systems. Hackers often target healthcare organisations because they are financially vulnerable and have no choice but to pay ransom demands. Because of the seriousness of the potential real-world effects of downtime, ransomware poses a unique threat to the healthcare industry. Healthcare organisations dealing with ransomware attacks often confront decisions that could have life-or-death consequences, while other industries may suffer financial losses or inconvenience. Critical patient data, including medical histories, prescription schedules, and lab results, can be lost when systems go down, leaving healthcare providers in the dark (Bris & Asri, 2023).

2.5 Data Breaches

Healthcare data breaches can occur due to a number of vulnerabilities, the majority of which are caused by ordinary and easily avoidable security issues. A common yet easy-to-understand security issue is using weak passwords. Many healthcare workers still use easily-guessed default passwords or use weak passwords, even though protecting sensitive systems is critical. Another typical way that data breaches might occur is through phishing attempts. In order to deceive employees into divulging important information or clicking on harmful links, hackers frequently assume the identities of trusted contacts, including vendors or colleagues, in these types of assaults. Data breaches have their own distinct difficulties, in addition to the difficulties posed by ransomware attacks (Patel, 2025). Because the compromised material isn't often obvious at first glance, hackers may have months—if not years—to make use of it before anybody finds out about the incident. PII, medical records, insurance details, and financial information are just a few examples of the sensitive data collected by healthcare organisations. If this information falls into the wrong hands, it might lead to identity theft, insurance fraud, or even blackmail. Data breaches are also greatly impacted by insider threats. Workers in the healthcare industry frequently have broad access to private patient information. Even while most workers are reliable, a huge data breach can happen when only one person, purposefully or unintentionally, abuses that access. It can be very challenging to identify and prevent insider threats, such as malicious actors within the company or individuals unwittingly falling for phishing scams (Gourav Nagar, 2024).

3. CONCEPT OF AUTOMATED CYBER DEFENSE

It was immediately apparent from our experience as expert operators protecting an intrusion-tolerant system from an attack that the experts had a deep understanding of the system's architecture (which is not surprising given that they were the ones to design the system), as well as the possible causes of the symptoms we observed and the steps to fix them. In order to automate reasoning about the data reported by the architecture's defence mechanisms, we need an accurate and machine-operable representation of this knowledge (Burrell, 2024).

Figure 1. Fundamental components of the CSISM cognitive control loop

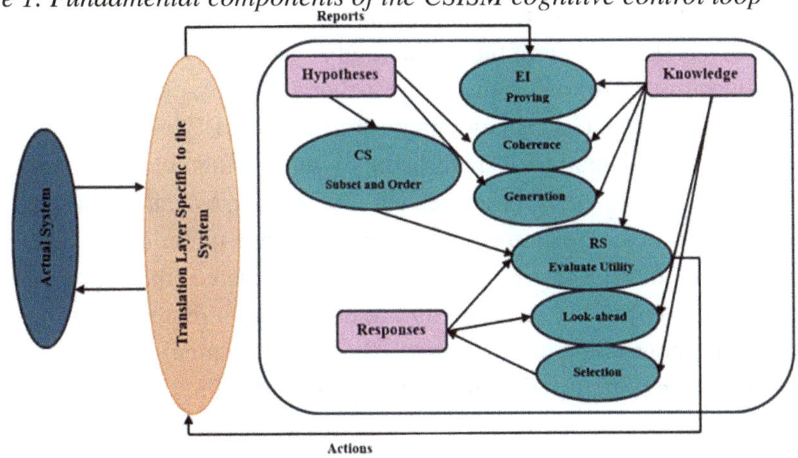

Figure 1 illustrates the main components of our strategy, as mentioned earlier. We still require a process that makes use of the KR but the encoded knowledge does serve as the rules and limitations that will allow us to draw inferences about compromised hosts, networks, or services based on symptoms and response selection. The two main components of our present system are the EI and RS phases, with the CS phase serving as an intermediary.

When EI is complete, CS and RS have a collection of hypotheses that have been adorned with additional metadata. A working hypothesis is a working conclusion that reflects an undesired state of the system and has the ability to explain the symptoms that have been observed. The collection of decorated hypotheses can be thought of as a constraint network, with the hypotheses serving as nodes and the constraints as edges. At the end of the RS process, you will have reaction decisions that can be used to control actuators and lessen the impact of an assault (Mcgowan et al., 2021). We have been referring to the collection of hypotheses that the CS chooses from a constraint net as the claims set, and it uses this to guide its decision-making process. In each of these steps, decisions are based on KR. By moving many details to a system-specific layer, which handles the mapping from concrete event reports and actuator commands to our abstract notions and vice versa, one of the design aims is to keep the knowledge and processing at a level of generic abstractions. Having a SSTL available makes the KR, EI, RS, and CS applicable to many systems. It also consolidates the number of choices to evaluate, making them more manageable. We shall refrain from discussing the SSTL in this study (Pieterse, 2021).

3.1 EI

The EI phase uses the system-reported alarms and observations to build a constraint network. The SSTL takes security alerts from physical sensors and turns them into accusations. To reflect the more than a hundred alarms that were supported by the DPASA architecture, there are currently only five sorts of accusations: omission, value, timing, policy, and flood. Using symptomatic information, EI generates theories and limitations based on allegations. An unsavoury situation involving the accuser, the accused, or the victim might be described by a hypothesis. Not all hypotheses apply to all entities; they are architectural entities represented in our relational knowledge (Jony & Hamim, 2023). The weight of a constraint indicates the degree to which it supports a relationship between two nodes; otherwise, it represents a competing relation. Furthermore, there are limitations that denote logical implication. Since symptomatic information usually suggests other options, the EI will likely use an OR relation to link one or more hypotheses. All the theories and accusations are implicitly ANDed; thus, there's no need for an explicit AND relation.

The nodes in the constraint network are the accusations, hypotheses, and OR relations, while the edges are the restrictions. The technique of adding nodes and edges to observations is very similar. Presently, we only back the most basic (rather than comprehensive) collection of arguments regarding cyber-defense in terms of accusations, assumptions, and limitations. Take the case of a host who is said to have caused a breach of security policy. The two hypotheses that EI will construct are linked by an OR. One of the hypotheses states that the accuser is corrupt (i.e., is lying), and the other states that the accused is corrupt (Triplett, 2024). A competing link signifies that these two hypotheses are alternatives, and an implication link indicates that the accusation leads to these alternatives by way of the OR node. Since the accuser is not actually deceased but has merely reported it, EI will also come up with a theory and a negative inference to address this. By assigning truth values to the hypothesis nodes in the constraint network, EI ensures that the accusation nodes are always true. When conducting this search, EI makes advantage of supplementary symptomatic and teleological information to limit the options.

For instance, if the attacker is believed to have a single OS exploit, EI will begin its search for proof with that assumption. It should be noted that such assumptions are not necessary for finding some proofs; for instance, the fact that the accused is still alive can be shown straight from the constraint network. Just as the accuser and accused are the same entity, if a self-accusation results in a degenerate situation of an OR node with a single corrupt hypothesis, then the corrupt hypothesis can be proven true straight from the constraint network. Furthermore, EI calculates the most consistent overall image by using the compete/support relation among hypotheses. A set of approved and rejected hypotheses is produced by the coherence search. In order to give accepted constraints, the most weight, hypotheses are either added to the accepted set or removed from it (Raizada & Biswal, 2024).

Figure 2. Coherence search approving H_1

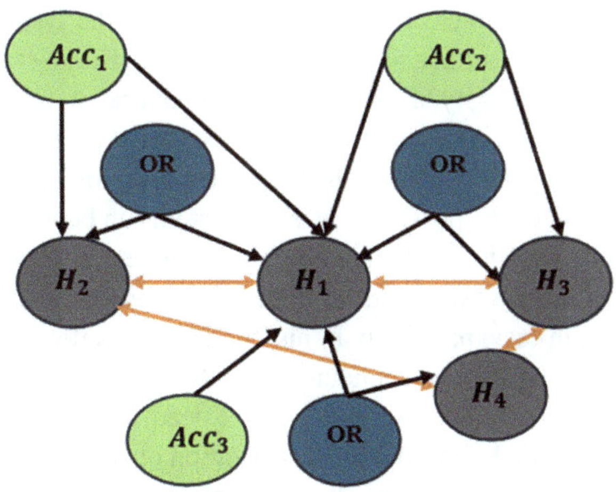

Figure 2 shows as an example where we accept hypothesis H_1 and reject hypothesis H_2 we reject hypotheses. The red arrows in this diagram point to the link three nodes in a competes relationship, where with the blue arrows signifying the supports connection between bridges between them (Boddy et al., 2020). As one could expect, H_3 in Figure 2 has the highest help, and all of the other hypotheses $(H_2, H_3\ and\ H_4)$ drive H_1 away from them. There is only one hypothesis H_1 in the acceptable set. Metadata that embellishes the network of constraints.

3.2 KR

When it comes to cyber-defense, our research shows that human experts rely on at least four different kinds of information. While these might not cover all bases, we contend that they are essential pieces of information that the cognitive control loop should store. In the first place, the expert is well-versed in the system's configuration and its individual parts' attributes, such as the operating system, network, services, and mechanisms. They can also name the other hosts and services that connect to or rely on any particular host, as well as the application-level strings, which are a series of services linked by an end-to-end service request and response (Islam et al., 2021). Relational knowledge is what we term this. Constructing a static, high-level model of the architectural entities and their interactions is the crux of encoding relational knowledge. We make it easy to attain a sufficient level of authenticity by automatically building it from system scans and traces given an ontology. Model fidelity is always a worry, though. With the help of the notions introduced by the survival architecture, we are improving upon an existing ontology of networked systems, which is proprietary. We start by manually building the model in Protégé and then generating executable code that other portions of the system (maybe built in Java) may automatically utilise to access the ontology (Burke et al., 2024).

Second, for the vast majority of symptoms, the human expert has a decent notion of which erroneous system states could have caused them. There are three parts to the representation of this knowledge, which we term symptomatic knowledge. An abstract representation of the possible states the system can be in when attacked is involved in the first one. The model identifies the architectural entities that are in a bad state, such as hosts, LANs, and services (Mehra & Sharma, 2025). Clearly, this is an abstract, high-level paradigm. It misses a lot of specifics, such the various ways a host could be corrupt or the amount of bandwidth lost due to flooding, and it only defines a handful of undesirable states, like dead, corrupt, flooded, etc. Another part of symptomatic knowledge is the definition of what each system report, or symptom, must mean inside the model. For instance, in the event that network monitor M asserts that LAN L is inundated, and since a report signed by M should only be signed by M, it follows that either M is corrupt or LAN L is in fact flooded. Keep in mind that symptomatic knowledge abstracts each report by excluding any details that don't pertain to the model (Islam et al., 2022). Finally, symptomatic knowledge edge categorises potential system vulnerabilities. We know what kinds of corruption each class can cause. Operating system vulnerabilities are one type of attack vector; for instance, every host that is under the control of operating system Q could become corrupted if an attacker were to exploit a vulnerability in Q. When trying to decipher a collection of reports in search of a reason for the reported symptoms, this categorisation is employed. This is another abstract facet of symptomatic knowledge; it is not dependent on particular security holes in any particular program version.

Third, the specialists are aware of the possible response alternatives and how to choose a defensive response after analysing system information. Reactive knowledge is what we term this. Reactive knowledge is a set of steps that, based on an analysis of the present threat, could be taken to defend against it. If the system and host H are both compromised, a viable solution could be to isolate H and use other hosts to carry out the services that H used to support. For any given scenario, there may be a number of known responses; choosing the most effective one from this set of alternatives requires reasoning.

In the same way as, symptomatic information is abstract and applicable to many systems, reactive knowledge is as well (Yeboah-Ofori & Opoku-Boateng, 2023).

Fourth, human operators frequently enquired about the future ease of the attacker's ability to circumvent the reaction in addition to whether the response counters the attack at present in order to determine the response's efficacy. It is impossible to know for sure what the attacker will do, but if we knew what they were trying to do, we could make educated predictions. This kind of informed speculation is known as teleological knowledge since it proceeds from a review of the present circumstance to a prediction regarding the attacker's probable objective (Ikegwu et al., 2025). The cognitive control loop can take the attacker's aim into account and determine if a defensive response will also be taken to counteract future actions towards that goal. A response that inhibits future stages in an attack is preferable to one that does not.

4. ENABLING TECHNOLOGIES

Effectively preparing for, reacting to, and assessing the loss exposure during a crisis is what disaster management is all about. A systematic approach to catastrophe prevention, readiness, response, and recovery is developed, and resources are distributed in a way that minimises harm (Ryan K. L. Ko, 2018).

4.1 AI in CPS

In cyber-physical realms, physical processes are either controlled or monitored by computer-based algorithms. These systems are interconnected and networked. In a certain sector of interest, the software and physical parts are working on separate time and space scales, displaying different but complementary behavioural modalities, interacting with one another in real-time, and adapting to new circumstances. There are feedback loops where computations are affected by physical processes and computations are affected by physical processes, and embedded computers and networks are used to monitor and regulate these processes (Matthew E. Mori, 2023). A multi-disciplinary engineering field with a strong emphasis on technology and a grounding in mathematical abstractions, CPS has grown in prominence as a result of its importance. With CPS, the software and networking dynamics are brought together with the physical process dynamics. The most significant technical hurdle is bridging the gap between the technical epistemology provided by algorithms and programs and the long-established physical process modelling tools like differential equations and stochastic processes (Pal et al., 2023).

Figure 3. Application domain of CPS.

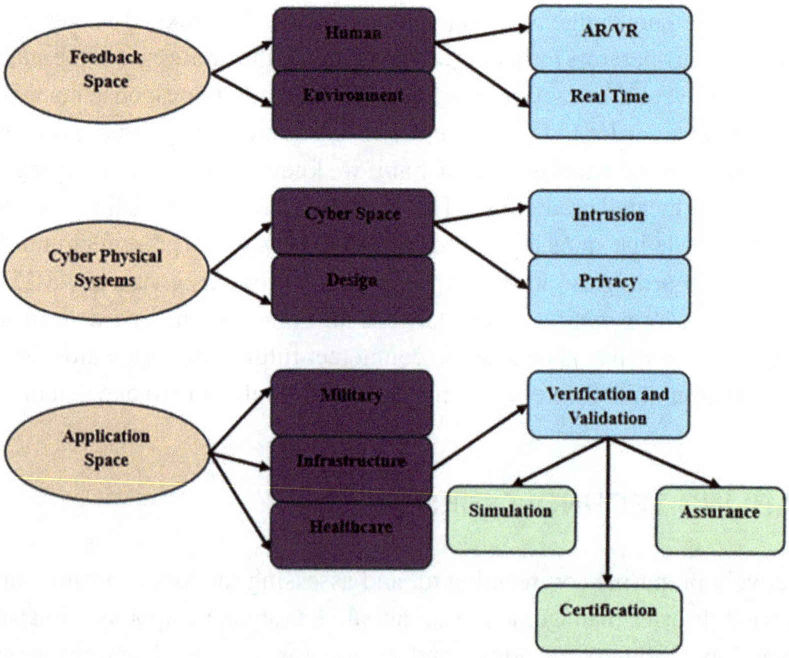

Figure 3 shows that improvements in CPS have far-reaching implications on competence, scalability, resilience, safety, security, adaptability, and conformity to systems in a DOI. The year 19 These ideas will gain much more weight when combined with AI, as CPS is expected to push the limits of connected systems even farther. Major investments are being made worldwide to develop the technology, as the economic and societal potential of these systems is far higher than what has been realised.

The rapid advancement of intelligent technology has opened up exciting new possibilities for the social, digital, and physical integration of all community services.

People, buildings, and ecosystems are becoming more interconnected through smart technologies, ushering in a new age of revolutionary change in CPS. This, in turn, creates new possibilities for innovation, better services, and higher quality of life (Haque & Krishnan, 2021). A few examples of how connected systems have improved accessibility, mobility, and services include: parking solutions, geospatial services, environmental services, performance-based predictive planning, traffic modelling, augmented reality, scenario planning, and emergency augmentation. Productivity, sustainability, a knowledge-based economy, data-driven decisions, and the ability to scale and transfer the proposed solutions are all bolstered by the technological capabilities of the linked communities, which in turn enable integrative research at the crossroads of AI and the social sciences. In spite of the project's many potentials uses in smart homes and other connected community initiatives, the idea is particularly well-suited to cyber defence. It enables off-site physical threat monitoring in addition to social media and infrastructure surveillance (Tirenin & Faatz, 2024).

4.2 Technological Toolkits

AI has revolutionised our world and enabled numerous innovations. These include autonomous vehicles, IoT-connected smart communities, brain-controlled robotic arms, online shopping, decentralised healthcare, transportation and shipping logistics, and the latest development, human performance augmentation. This technology can assist paralysed individuals in perceiving their surroundings through intricate direct human-brain interfaces. The first historical reference to AI occurs in the 1950s, in a paper by Alan Turing on the topic of constructing thinking machines (Nesbit & Von Thaer, 2024). In addition to e-commerce, Al now had to deal with complicated initiatives including medical diagnostics, counter-terrorism decisions, cyber-security strategy, and financial patterns. The Life Long Learning Machines project, launched by DARPA, aims to go much further in the same vein as advanced Algorithms.

Figure 4. NN empowered by AI, ML, and DL with layering functionality

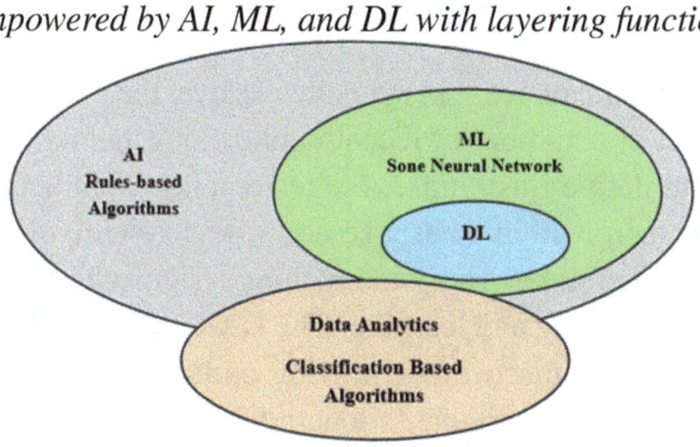

Figure 4 shows as logic rules and reasoning algorithms that imitate human expertise were used to construct complicated algorithms and systems in the years that followed. With the advent of decision-support tools came the capacity for hierarchical and complicated thinking, but these systems still couldn't adapt to new situations or discover better ways to make decisions than people (Baah et al., 2020). Software with a biological basis, sometimes called neural networks added the capacity to recognise intricate patterns and finish difficult jobs. The addition of layering functionality to DA, DL, and ML-enabled neural networks allows them to learn to identify and classify patterns, both basic and complex, just like humans.

To keep ahead of the ever-increasing amount and sophistication of cyberattacks, AI assisted in staffing understaffed security operations analysts. Through the use of natural language processing and AI and ML, which are disruptive technologies, we can quickly sift through the mountain of daily alerts, improve security posture, and cut response times in half (Lohn et al., 2023). Complex social, infrastructure, and informational dependencies make it such that countering cyber threat vectors stretches across numerous domains, including physical, information, and social. Therefore, to tackle such intricate security threats, a nexus of these cutting-edge technologies is necessary. Along with the aforementioned cyber defence capabilities, AI, ML, and DL have actual defence applications such as animal research that prepares combat theatre surgeons for harsh environments. There is a growing interest in applying AI to improve human performance in areas such as over-training and over-reaching prediction, traumatic brain injury (TBI) treatment (e.g., bonking), infection, sleep, and general behaviour. A further area where AI is paving the way for solutions is neuro-optometry and neuroradiology, which will serve as the foundation for future Intrepid Emergency Centres. The application of AI to identify biomarkers and physiological reactions to messenger RNA and spike protein is vital for military preparedness, particularly in SARS-nCOV2 environments (Ernits et al., 2023).

5. AUTOMATED CYBER DEFENSE

In view of the dramatic increase in cyberattacks over the past several years, ACD has been the subject of a number of recent publications and news pieces. A quick review was done to define this phrase. By referencing a publication that created an automated blue agent within a bespoke networked system, offered a high-level definition of ACD algorithms as a decision-making system with expert-level abilities inspired by human reasoning and learning. The DARPA grand challenge sought to develop systems capable of discovering, proving, and fixing software vulnerabilities in real-time all without human intervention and defined ACD as such systems. A broad outline of an ACD system was given by (Ridley, 2020). According to the article, the first step in an AC Das reaction is finding a network vulnerability or an active assault. In order to prevent threats from harming network assets or delaying missions, the study stressed the importance of rapid and accurate identification. Automated fuzzing techniques can find software vulnerabilities that weren't there before, and ML analytics can tell the difference between malicious and harmless network traffic. The ACD system takes defensive measures to guarantee the network's computing capability survives by interpreting alarms and observations (Hulak et al., 2022).

It is a challenging goal to provide such an expert-level response in real-time with limited and unclear information, as the authors are well aware. The utilisation of cognitive architectures in cyber defensive operations, however, provides a bridge to the eventual creation of automated reasoning and learning. An AcCD research program was unveiled in a white paper of the Alan Turing Institute. The initiative aims to strengthen cybersecurity and network defences by encouraging businesses to automate more of their processes. Keep in mind that ACD is just concerned with automated red and blue-teaming, mainly for the general development of automated blue-teaming agents, whereas AcCD also encompasses Automated Security Planner. The study concludes that intelligent automation is crucial for system defenders to counter future attacks and threats that are highly automated and to protect systems on a national level that are relevant to cyberspace (Alsaleh & Al-Shaer, 2022). Automatic red-and-blue teaming was also discussed in detail in the white paper. Having said that, it did offer some broad strokes for potential future study paths in the field. Some have proposed incorporating AI into these systems to help them better comprehend their environment (the networked system) and so detect and respond to sophisticated cyberattacks with less room for mistake. Using autonomous cyber defence (ACD) agents based on tabular Q-learning emphasise the word in their study. Based on the definitions provided, autonomous cyber defence is the process of using ML approaches to train a self-defending agent that can protect a system while avoiding harm caused by responses that rely on noisy sensor input. This description is in line with our own ACD definition; however, it is too narrow to cover all of ACD, which encompasses the concurrent creation of Autonomous Cyber Operations Gyms and automated agents for both the red and blue teams (Wurzenberger et al., 2024).

Another important aspect of ACD that is not included in the established nomenclature is the role of automated red team agents. This paper addresses this issue. To better understand where ACD stands in comparison to ACO, it is necessary to define ACO. ACO is the simultaneous creation of automated red (attacker) and automated blue (defender) agents inside a networked system that engage in game-like combat (Kommisetty et al., 2022). The primary difference between ACO and ACD is that the former is devoted to the general development of automated blue agents, while the latter is more narrowly focused on the construction of automated red agents for use in adversarial training and automated penetration testing. Because they need to be tailored to the development of automated blue teaming agents, ACO Gyms built via an ACD lens differ from AI ACO Gyms. After reviewing the aforementioned literature, we have settled on the term. ACD to describe a set of practices aimed at protecting cyber systems (such as enterprise networks and industrial control systems) from sophisticated cyberattacks. There are a variety of approaches that could be taken to construct an ACD system. As part of this process, automated blue-teaming agents are being developed within Autonomous Cyber Operations Gyms as a terrain mode (to mimic real-world cyber systems). Automated red-teaming agents are then employed to validate, enhance, and fortify these automated blue-teaming agents with the ultimate aim of their eventual deployment in the real world (Aramide, 2023) .

5.1 ACD Specifications

ACA were defined by NATO, the North Atlantic Treaty Organisation, in its AICA reference architecture and technological roadmap. The document delves into the strategic deployment and ethical considerations of autonomous agents on the battlefield in one particular section (Enoch et al., 2020).

Table 1. ACD requirement

Fundamentals	Definitions
Learning	AICA explores the potential for facilitating continuous learning within ACO Gyms. However, it also emphasises the significance of the training-testing methodology
Resilience	ACO Gyms must be engineered to facilitate the automated red agent in adversarial training of the automated blue agent, hence minimising the incidence of erroneous acts To enhance the efficacy of the automated blue team agent, which serves the singular function of ACD, it is imperative to promote adversarial training via an automated red agent.
High Level Decision-Making	ACO Gyms must be structured to elucidate their condition following particular occurrences within the networked system. ACO Gyms must be structured into MDP/POMDP format to facilitate automated decision-making
Generalization	ACO Gym must possess the ability to scale the network to bigger sizes without encountering configuration difficulties. An automated agent must generalise its decisions according to the type it represents
Research Collaboration	ACO Gym must be open-source to enable researchers to enhance implementations. Documentation for ACO Gym must be accessible to facilitate the ongoing development of gyms and to simplify research and implementation of automated agents within them

Table 1 shows as provides a summary of the ACD requirements in addition to the important aspects from AICA that are pertinent to this work. In addition to the ACO Gyms requirements (G) that could permit the usage of automated red and blue agents, the table further elaborates the basic requirements of these agents (A). Researchers in ACD can use the requirements in this table as a checklist to create and deploy ACD operations in real-world networked systems.

5.2 The Significance of ACD in National Strategy Documents

Organisations both public and private have made it plain that AI will soon play a pivotal role in cybersecurity for both threat detection and response.

Table 2. National ACD Strategy Papers

Country	*Strategy*	*Referring to ACD*
United Kingdom	Defence AI Strategy	Examines the emerging hazards associated with AI enhancement. Cyber threats that function at velocities and magnitudes that inhibit prompt responses by human operators
	Government Cybersecurity Strategy	Characterised AI as a burgeoning technology warranting attention. Proposes to investigate AI for the detection of dangerous activities and, in certain instances, to facilitate automated responses to threats
Australia	Royal Air Force of Australia	Recommends ongoing assessment to determine which decisions can be executed by computers and which require human intervention
	Department of Defense	Proposes the necessity to enhance cybersecurity competencies and incorporate AI inside the field. The Department of Defence is orchestrating research and investment in AI capabilities to enhance proficiency across the information and cyber domains
NATO	NATO AI Strategy	The concept encompasses collaboration on AI technology for cyber defence
	Cooperative Cyber Defence Centre of Excellence	Advocate for the necessity of nation-states to implement and investigate AI-enhanced cyber defence mechanisms
Canada	Defence Research and Development	The publication proposes utilising a synthesis of DL and RL algorithms for the precise identification of emerging dangers, followed by the recommendation or execution of a suitable course of action
	National Cybersecurity Strategy	Emphasised the significance of military and security applications utilising autonomous decision support

The significance of ACD in various countries is discussed in Table 2.

6. BENEFITS OF AUTOMATED CYBER DEFENSE

The term automation is used to describe the application of complex methodologies and technology in cybersecurity with the goals of simulating, forecasting, and protecting against cyber threats. An ideal platform for testing and training would be a Cyber Range, a virtual environment that mimics actual information technology infrastructures. Because it automates the generation of test scenarios, a Cyber Range can constantly respond to the most recent vulnerabilities and threats. That way, companies can stay adaptable and ready for anything (Buchanan et al., 2020). Cyber Ranges can combine state-of-the-art threat intelligence and automate the production of test scenarios, both of which speed up the process of generating complex and realistic simulations. Thus, it is possible to build scenarios that mimic the most current attack vectors, malware strains, and adversarial tactics, providing participants with very applicable training experiences.

Automation also makes it easy to tailor situations to specific organisational demands. There are several possible applications for this, such as system testing, reaction method evaluation, or team collaboration improvement during simulated events. A wide range of scenarios can be generated by automated systems; these range from simple configurations for beginners to complex, multi-layered assault simulations for cybersecurity experts. Its scalability allows businesses to train diverse teams and evaluate their preparedness thoroughly. When new vulnerabilities are found, automated systems can quickly build updated scenarios to fix them. As a result, response teams can be better prepared to deal with threats in less time after they are identified (Nyberg & Johnson, 2023). The benefits of automation are magnified when CTF scenarios are included into Cyber Ranges. Automated CTF challenges may incorporate tasks like as data extraction, system protection exercises, and network penetration testing. replicate actual environmental conditions. In a format that serves to educate dynamic, participants take part in tasks that demand them to work together, solve problems, and hone their practical abilities. Businesses can automate these scenarios to keep up with changing hazards, keep employees engaged, and increase learning efficiency. They can also constantly introduce new challenges. The effectiveness of Cyber The automation of the platform's internal procedures enhances Ranges as a tool for cybersecurity training and testing. This technology allows organisations to not only model current threat environments, but also anticipate and prepare for future threats with the accuracy, speed, and scalability they need (Ashfaq et al., 2023).

6.1 Benefits

Scalability: Automation is driving the fast growth of Cyber Range settings, which in turn allows businesses to simulate assaults on ever-more-complex and rapidly-expanding IT infrastructures. Scaling scenarios to fit the size and complexity of the organization's real-world network is possible without substantial manual involvement. There is no need for human interaction to do this. Training and testing will remain important as the systems grow in size due to their scalability. With the help of comprehensive cybersecurity capabilities, organisations may strengthen their defences against cyber-attacks and maintain a competitive advantage in an increasingly digital environment.

Proficiency in Threat Mitigation: Through the process of dynamically changing scenarios to reflect new vulnerabilities and attack methodologies, automated technologies make it possible to rapidly adapt to newly emerging cyber threats. The window of opportunity for potential attacks is narrowed as a result of this, which enables businesses to discover and remedy vulnerabilities more quickly than they could with traditional, manual techniques.

Accuracy and Consistency: Using automated processes lessens the chances of human mistake, thus guaranteeing to ensure that scenarios are regularly implemented and ensure the settings are faithfully recreated. This consistency ensures the reliability regarding the outcomes of the testing and training operations are enhanced.

Personalisation and Adaptability: Automation allows for the implementation of highly customised training environments that meet the needs of individual organisations, industry standards, or regulatory mandates. Training is certain to be successful and focused on relevance because of this flexibility.

Real-time Adaptability, Cost-effectiveness and Efficiency: By automating processes such as vulnerability assessment and penetration testing, Cyber Ranges significantly reduce the time and resources required for system setup and execution. Organisations can reduce the expenses related to manual scenario construction while preserving high standards of accuracy and comprehensiveness. Automated systems can make real-time dynamic alterations to situations based on participant actions or predefined triggers. This skill will enhance training pragmatic, leading to enhanced preparedness for unexpected cyber-attacks.

Scenarios for Realistic Testing: Automation makes it easy to combine up-to-date data, which could include things like known CVE, program details, and operating system versions. This manner, we know that our test scenarios are accurate reflections of the current danger landscapes. The capacity to simulate actual attacks and defences helps cyber teams hone their abilities in an environment that is nearly identical to the actual thing.

7. APPLICATIONS AND CASE STUDIES

Implementation of automated cyber ranges across various areas, including government, technology, and finance, demonstrates their efficacy in improving cybersecurity readiness and response times. By utilising these platforms, organisations can enhance their operational preparedness and training results by replicating complex attack scenarios, such as cyber-espionage, zero-day attacks, and ransomware. Cyber range operations are greatly enhanced by automation, which allows for the development of more efficient and realistic training environments. Cyber Ranges that are automated have been a success for many organisations (Brangeto et al., 2022).

Defence and Governance: The operational readiness of the military was enhanced by 35% after the implementation of automated platforms for training people to handle cyber-espionage situations. Cyber ranges offer realistic training environments for cyber warfare and espionage scenarios, automate range operations to improve training efficacy, and highlight the importance of cyber ranges in the government and defence sectors (Sain et al., 2020).

Financial Industry: A multinational bank used automated scenarios within cyber ranges to counteract ransomware and phishing threats. This method led to a 40% reduction in response times and enhanced employee training results. The creation of automated technologies to enhance the accuracy of replicated network traffic and visualise range activity aligns with the overarching trend of employing cyber ranges to bolster cybersecurity training and preparedness.

Technological Sector: A prominent software company used cyber ranges enhanced with AI to mimic zero-day attacks. This method made it easier to roll out patches and strengthened its defences against previously unseen dangers. To create effective defences, it is vital to use cyber ranges to replicate APT and other sophisticated attacks, as previously noted in the context of automating APT scenarios.

8. CONCLUSION

Cybersecurity must undergo a radical shift away from manual, antiquated methods in response to the increasing sophistication and regularity of cyberattacks on healthcare and cloud infrastructure. At the front of this change is automation powered by AI, which allows for smart, proactive, and autonomous protection mechanisms essential for keeping systems available, protecting sensitive data, and being compliant with regulations. By utilising AI-driven systems, the time it takes to detect and respond to cyberattacks is significantly reduced. This helps to limit possible harm and ensures that critical healthcare services and cloud operations can continue uninterrupted. With these skills, businesses can keep one step ahead of their crafty, ever-changing competitors. An important step towards fully autonomous cyber resilience, self-healing systems supplement detection and reaction. These designs reduce downtime and stop disruptions from spreading across important infrastructures by constantly checking system health and immediately fixing problems. Systems are further improved in reliability through the dynamic optimisation of resources, which keeps them robust under changing operational loads and threat situations. Furthermore, these automated processes ensure accountability and confidence among stakeholders by creating thorough audit trails and tracking that enable compliance with strict data protection rules. Protecting healthcare systems from ever-changing cyber threats has never been easier than with ACD. Healthcare organisations may achieve proactive protection, operational resilience, and increased patient safety by combining AI, automation, and adaptive security systems. ACD is crucial for constructing reliable, secure, and future-proof healthcare systems, even while problems with ethics, integration, and governance continue (Theron et al., 2022).

REFERENCES

Abdi, A., Bennouri, H., & Keane, A. (2024). Emerging Cyber Risks &amp Threats in Healthcare Systems: A Case Study in Resilient Cybersecurity Solutions. *2024 13th Mediterranean Conference on Embedded Computing (MECO)*, 1–8. DOI: 10.1109/MECO62516.2024.10577790

AboulEla, S., Ibrahim, N., Shehmir, S., Yadav, A., & Kashef, R.AboulEla. (2024). Navigating the Cyber Threat Landscape: An In-Depth Analysis of Attack Detection within IoT Ecosystems. *AI*, *5*(2), 704–732. DOI: 10.3390/ai5020037

Alsaleh, M. N., & Al-Shaer, E. (2022). Towards Automated Verification of Active Cyber Defense Strategies on Software Defined Networks. *Proceedings of the 2022 ACM Workshop on Automated Decision Making for Active Cyber Defense, January*, 23–29. DOI: 10.1145/2994475.2994482

Aramide, O. O. (2023). Predictive Analytics and Automated Threat Hunting: The Next Frontier in AI-Powered Cyber Defense. *International Journal of Technology. Management and Humanities*, *9*(04), 72–93. DOI: 10.21590/ijtmh.2023090407

Arina, A., Bolun, I., & Alexei, A. (2025). Cybersecurity challenges in healthcare: Mitigating risks in a rapidly evolving digital landscape. *Bulletin of Electrical Engineering and Informatics*, *14*(6), 4867–4875. DOI: 10.11591/eei.v14i6.9685

Ashfaq, S., Biswas, S., & Chowdhury, T. K. (2023). INTEGRATION OF ARTIFICIAL INTELLIGENCE AND ADVANCED COMPUTING TO DEVELOP RESILIENT CYBER DEFENSE SYSTEMS. *Journal of Sustainable Development and Policy*, *02*(04), 74–107. DOI: 10.63125/rxyc6y88

Baah, G. K., Hobson, T., Okhravi, H., Roberts, S. C., Streilein, W. W., & Yuditskaya, S. C. (2020). *A Study of Gaps in Cyber Defense Automation* (Issue October). https://www.dtic.mil/dtic/tr/fulltext/u2/1021685.pdf

Boddy, A., Hurst, W., Mackay, M., & El Rhalibi, A. (2020). A study into data analysis and visualisation to increase the cyber-resilience of healthcare infrastructures. *Proceedings of the 1st International Conference on Internet of Things and Machine Learning, January*, 1–7. DOI: 10.1145/3109761.3109793

Brangeto, P., Maybaum, M., & Stinssen, J. (2022). 2022 6th International Conference on Cyber Conflict. In *2022 6th International Conference on Cyber Conflict.* https://extranet.cranfield.ac.uk/sites/default/files/multimedia/pdf/,DanaInfo=ccdcoe.org,SSL+CyCon_2014.pdf#page=66

Bris, A. L. E., & Asri, W. E. L. (2023). State of Cybersecurity & Cyber Threats in Healthcare Organizations. *Dissertation*, 2005–2013. https://www.americanbar.org/content/dam/aba/publications/books/healthcare_data_breaches.authcheckdam.pdf

Buchanan, B., Bansemer, J., Cary, D., Lucas, J., & Musser, M. (2020). Automating Cyber Attacks: Hype and Reality. *Center for Security and Emerging Technology., November*, 1–48. https://cset.georgetown.edu/publication/automating-cyber-attacks/

Burke, W., Stranieri, A., Oseni, T., & Gondal, I. (2024). The need for cybersecurity self-evaluation in healthcare. *BMC Medical Informatics and Decision Making*, *24*(1), 133. DOI: 10.1186/s12911-024-02551-x

Burrell, D. N. (2024). Understanding Healthcare Cybersecurity Risk Management Complexity. *Land Forces Academy Review*, *29*(1), 38–49. DOI: 10.2478/raft-2024-0004

Enoch, S. Y., Huang, Z., Moon, C. Y., Lee, D., Ahn, M. K., & Kim, D. S. (2020). HARMer: Cyber-Attacks Automation and Evaluation. *IEEE Access : Practical Innovations, Open Solutions*, *8*, 129397–129414. DOI: 10.1109/ACCESS.2020.3009748

Ernits, M., Tammekänd, J., & Maennel, O. (2023). i-tee:A fully automated Cyber Defense Competition for Students. *Computer Communication Review*, *45*(4), 113–114. DOI: 10.1145/2829988.2790033

Gourav Nagar, A. M. (2024). Understanding the Threat Landscape: a Comprehensive Analysis of Cyber-Security Risks in 2024. *Article in International Research Journal of Modernization in Engineering Technology and Science*, *6*(3), 5706–5713. www.irjmets.com

Haque, M. F., & Krishnan, R. (2021). Toward Automated Cyber Defense with Secure Sharing of Structured Cyber Threat Intelligence. *Information Systems Frontiers*, *23*(4), 883–896. DOI: 10.1007/s10796-020-10103-7

Hulak, H., Skladannyi, P., Sokolov, V., Hulak, Y., & Korniiets, V. (2022). Dynamic model of guarantee capacity and cyber security management in the critical automated systems. *CEUR Workshop Proceedings*, *3530*, 102–111.

Ikegwu, A. C., Alo, U. R., & Nweke, H. F. (2025). Cyber threats in mobile healthcare applications: Systematic review of enabling technologies, threat models, detection approaches, and future directions. *Discover Computing*, *28*(1), 152. DOI: 10.1007/s10791-025-09686-z

Islam, S., Papastergiou, S., Kalogeraki, E.-M., & Kioskli, K. (2022). Cyberattack Path Generation and Prioritisation for Securing Healthcare Systems. *Applied Sciences (Basel, Switzerland)*, *12*(9), 4443. DOI: 10.3390/app12094443

Islam, S., Papastergiou, S., & Mouratidis, H. (2021). A Dynamic Cyber Security Situational Awareness Framework for Healthcare ICT Infrastructures. *25th Pan-Hellenic Conference on Informatics,* November 2021, 334–339. DOI: 10.1145/3503823.3503885

Jony, A. I., & Hamim, S. A. (2023). Navigating the Cyber Threat Landscape: A Comprehensive Analysis of Attacks and Security in the Digital Age. *Journal of Information Technology and Cyber Security*, *1*(2), 53–67. DOI: 10.30996/jitcs.9715

Kommareddy, A. (2024). *The UK Healthcare Cybersecurity Landscape Anudeep Kommareddy Supervisor : Apurva Vangujar.*

Kommisetty, P. D. N. K., Kuppala, B. M. S. R., & Buvvaji, H. V. (2022). Transforming Cyber Defense: Anomaly Detection and Predictive Analytics for Automated Threat Response. *International Journal of Engineering and Computer Science*, *11*(08), 25585–25600. DOI: 10.18535/ijecs/v11i08.4694

Kruse, C. S., Frederick, B., Jacobson, T., & Monticone, D. K. (2020). Cybersecurity in healthcare: A systematic review of modern threats and trends. *Technology and Health Care*, *25*(1), 1–10. DOI: 10.3233/THC-161263

LATES, I., & BOJA, C. (2025). Automating Attack and Defense Strategies in Cybersecurity. *Informatica Economica, 29*(1/2025), 5–15. DOI: 10.24818/issn14531305/29.1.2025.01

Lohn, A., Knack, A., & Jackson, K. (2023). *Autonomous Cyber Defence A roadmap from lab to ops*. Issue June. DOI: 10.51593/2022CA007

Matthew, E. Mori. (2023). PROTECTING NETWORKS VIA AUTOMATED DEFENSE OF CYBER SYSTEMS. *Security, September*. https://doi.org/July 01, 2016

Mcgowan, A., Sittig, S., & Andel, T. (2021). Medical Internet of Things: A Survey of the Current Threat and Vulnerability Landscape. *Proceedings of the Annual Hawaii International Conference on System Sciences, 2020-Janua*, 3850–3858. DOI: 10.24251/HICSS.2021.466

Mehra, C., & Sharma, A. K. (2025). Safeguarding the Landscape of Mental Wellness: Analyzing Cyber Threats and Mitigation Strategies in Digital Healthcare. *Procedia Computer Science*, *260*, 22–31. DOI: 10.1016/j.procs.2025.03.173

Mirza, A. I., & Adrian, G. (2023). *Next-Level Cyber Defense: AI-Powered Automation in Resilient Healthcare and Cloud Systems*. https://www.researchgate.net/publication/393794159_Next-Level_Cyber_Defense_AI-Powered_Automation_in_Resilient_Healthcare_and_Cloud_Systems

Nesbit, R., & Von Thaer, L. (2024). *Defense Science Board Task Force Report on Cyber Defense Management*. Issue September.

Nyberg, J., & Johnson, P. (2023). Learning automated defense strategies using graph-based cyber attack simulations. *Proceedings 2023 Workshop on Security Operation Center Operations and Construction*. DOI: 10.14722/wosoc.2023.23006

Pal, P., Webber, F., Atighetchi, M., Rubel, P., & Benjamin, P. (2020). Automating cyber-defense management. *Proceedings of the 2nd Workshop on Recent Advances on Intrusiton-Tolerant Systems,* April 2008, 1–6. DOI: 10.1145/1413901.1413904

Pal, P., Webber, F., Atighetchi, M., Rubel, P., & Benjamin, P. (2023). Automating cyber-defense management. *Proceedings of the 2nd Workshop on Recent Advances on Intrusiton-Tolerant Systems,* April 2008, 1–6. DOI: 10.1145/1413901.1413904

Patel, C. (2025). *Cyber Security, Privacy, and Network Security: Navigating the Evolving Threat Landscape*. DOI: 10.2139/ssrn.5069925

Piazza, A., & Vasudevan, S. (2025). Mapping the Cyberthreat Landscape in Healthcare Using GDELT: A Multimethod Approach. *Health Security*, *23*(3), 186–197. DOI: 10.1089/hs.2024.0016

Pieterse, H. (2021). The Cyber Threat Landscape in South Africa: A 10-Year Review. *The African Journal of Information and Communication*, *28*(28), 1–21. DOI: 10.23962/10539/32213

Raizada, N., & Biswal, M. (2024). AN EVIDENCE-BASED INVESTIGATION OF CERT-IN'S REPORTING ON CYBER-THREATS IN HEALTHCARE SECTOR. *Conhecimento & Diversidade*, *16*(42), 219–246. DOI: 10.18316/rcd.v16i42.11694

Reddy Boda, V. V., & Immaneni, J. (2023). Automating Security in Healthcare: What Every IT Team Needs to Know. *International Journal of Artificial Intelligence, Data Science, and Machine Learning*, *4*(2), 46–56. DOI: 10.63282/3050-9262.IJAIDSML-V4I2P106

Ridley, A. (2020). Machine learning for autonomous cyber defense. *The Next Wave*, *22*(1), 7–14.

Ryan K. L. Ko. (2018). Cyber Autonomy : Automating the Hacker. *Automatic Cyber Defense Systems*, 1–15.

Sain, M. K., Gupta, J., Rathore, P., & Bansal, R. (2020). ARTIFICIAL INTELLIGENCE IN CYBER DEFENCE. *International Journal of Psychosocial Rehabilitation, 11403–11405*, 11403–11405. Advance online publication. DOI: 10.61841/V24I7/400273

Theron, P., Kott, A., Drasar, M., Rzadca, K., LeBlanc, B., Pihelgas, M., Mancini, L., & Panico, A. (2022). Towards an active, autonomous and intelligent cyber defense of military systems: The NATO AICA reference architecture. *2022 International Conference on Military Communications and Information Systems (ICMCIS), May*, 1–9. DOI: 10.1109/ICMCIS.2018.8398730

Tilbury, J., & Flowerday, S. (2024). Humans and Automation: Augmenting Security Operation Centers. *Journal of Cybersecurity and Privacy*, *4*(3), 388–409. DOI: 10.3390/jcp4030020

Tirenin, W., & Faatz, D. (2024). A concept for strategic cyber defense. *MILCOM 2024. IEEE Military Communications. Conference Proceedings (Cat. No.99CH36341)*, *1*(c), 458–463. DOI: 10.1109/MILCOM.1999.822725

Triplett, W. J. (2024). Cybersecurity Vulnerabilities in Healthcare: A Threat to Patient Security. *Cybersecurity and Innovative Technology Journal*, *2*(1), 15–25. DOI: 10.53889/citj.v2i1.333

Vaseashta, A. (2022). *Nexus of Advanced Technology Platforms for Strengthening Cyber-Defense Capabilities*. DOI: 10.3233/NHSDP220003

Vyas, S., Hannay, J., Bolton, A., & Burnap, P. P. (2023). Automated Cyber Defence: A Review. *Proceedings of the ACM on Measurement and Analysis of Computing Systems*, *37*(4). https://arxiv.org/abs/2303.04926

Wurzenberger, M., Krenn, S., Landauer, M., Skopik, F., Perner, C., Lötjönen, J., Päijänen, J., Gardikis, G., Alabasis, N., Sakerman, L., Omri, K., Röning, J., Halunen, K., Thouvenot, V., Weise, M., Rauber, A., Gkioulos, V., Katsikas, S., Sabetta, L., & Schmitt, C. (2024). NEWSROOM: Towards Automating Cyber Situational Awareness Processes and Tools for Cyber Defence. *Proceedings of the 19th International Conference on Availability, Reliability and Security,* July 2024, 1–11. DOI: 10.1145/3664476.3670914

Yeboah-Ofori, A., & Opoku-Boateng, F. A. (2023). Mitigating cybercrimes in an evolving organizational landscape. *Continuity & Resilience Review*, *5*(1), 53–78. DOI: 10.1108/CRR-09-2022-0017

Chapter 5
AI-Driven Cybersecurity for Detecting Organ Trafficking Networks

Chinmayee Vijaykumar Mali
http://orcid.org/0009-0000-0372-3413
Vishwakarma Institute of Information Technology, India

Gitanjali Rahul Shinde
http://orcid.org/0000-0001-6623-8722
Vishwakarma Institute of Technology, India

Grishma Bobhate
Vishwakarma Institute of Technology, India

Sonal Fatangare
Vishwakarma Institute of Technology, India

Prashant Dhotre
MIT Art, Design, and Technology University, India

Piyush Gawali
Vishwakarma Institute of Technology, India

ABSTRACT

The digitization of healthcare has improved efficiency but exposed patient data to new cyber risks exploited by organ trafficking networks. Stolen medical records hold lasting value, enabling identity fraud and falsified donor-recipient data. This chapter explores how Artificial Intelligence (AI) can strengthen cybersecurity by detecting anomalies in electronic health records and predicting insider threats. It proposes a Co-Creation Framework combining AI, blockchain, and ethical governance through collaboration among clinicians, technologists, and policymakers. Real-world cases, including Hyderabad's Jeevandan Program and Kenya's Mediheal Hospital, highlight the urgency of AI-driven, transparent, and accountable systems that protect data integrity and help prevent organ trafficking while maintaining patient trust.

DOI: 10.4018/979-8-3373-6696-8.ch005

1. INTRODUCTION

1.1 Background of Organ Trafficking and Cybercrime

Organ trafficking is a transnational illegal criminal activity in which body organs are traded outside legal guidelines violating national and international laws and ethical standards. Over the years organ trafficking networks have evolved from a local organization to global sophisticated criminal networks. As the core activity (transplantation) appears mostly in medical sector yet organ trafficking has also corrupted other sectors of manufacturing and technologies *(Biasin, Kamenjašević, & Ludvigsen, 2024) (Huda, Islam, Abawajy, Kottala, & Ahmad, 2024).*

Internet has played a key role in transforming the organ trafficking networks. It has advantaged them in global reachability and finding sensitive information of patients *(Abbas, Abbas, Zahir, & Lee, 2024).* Many individuals have fallen trap to phishing attacks from such criminal networks for exploiting their personal data. Criminals use digital technologies to conceal their identities and intent by getting rid of their digital footprints. Such global exposure to data and privacy concerns has made tracking such organizations difficult.

These organ trafficking networks handle their operations through dark web for anonymizing their activities. Dark web is a platform to communicate and transfer sensitive data securely and privately for legal purposes but nowadays dark web is mostly been illegally been used for black marketing and cybercrime activities *(Almalki, Alshahrani, & Khan, 2024).* Encrypted channels are used heavily by the traffickers to send data and manage payments without casual monitoring. This convergence of cybercrime and human exploitation signifies a new frontier where both health informatics and cybersecurity are ethically intertwined.

1.2 Role of AI in Cybersecurity for Organ Trafficking Detection

Artificial intelligence is revolutionizing cybersecurity and upgrading from tradition reactive defence mechanisms to real time predictive and adaptive systems. Vast amount of data including network logs and dark web communications can be processed by AI models for faster analysis and detection. In healthcare AI is used in identifying unusual access behaviours, data breaches, hidden correlations and illicit financial trade *(Triplett, 2024).* Recent AI technologies have learned to adapt to real time monitoring of huge data and producing quick and accurate results. This proactive AI integration into cybersecurity technologies like intrusion detection systems, access controls, etc. strengthens the ability of digital health systems to disrupt trafficking pipelines before a physical crime occurs (Columb & Moniruzzaman, 2024).

1.3 Objectives and Scope of the Chapter

This chapter Aims to present a multi-layered framework for AI-driven cybersecurity designed to detect and prevent organ trafficking networks that exploit healthcare infrastructures *(Rawat, Garg, Mahor, & Telang, 2022)*. it investigates the fusion of cybersecurity and AI for advanced detection systems with a focus on ethical guidelines, data governance and individual privacy. The specific objectives are:

- To analyse the cyber-ecosystem of organ trafficking, highlighting how patient data misuse enables illegal trade.
- To explore AI-based detection models—including NLP, GNN, and blockchain analytics—for identifying suspicious activities within health networks.
- To propose a co-creation framework that integrates policymakers, technologists, and medical professionals in developing ethically aligned cybersecurity solutions.
- To discuss regulatory, ethical, and human-centered strategies that ensure responsible AI deployment in healthcare environments.

2. FOUNDATIONS OF AI IN CYBERSECURITY

2.1 Evolution of Cybersecurity Approaches in Healthcare

Cybersecurity in healthcare sector has undergone remarkable transformations in the past few years. Previous cybersecurity practices relied on traditional security checks like firewalls, password protection, antivirus software, etc. but nowadays it has shifted towards more enhanced systems like self-learning defence mechanisms which are backed up by artificial intelligence. Due to advancement in defence technologies the attack rate has also increased significantly. These has led to rise in ransomware, phishing and identity theft attacks *(Shah, Ahsan, Tasnim, Afrin, Hashan, Islam, & Ahmed, 2024)*. WHO has stated that many healthcare institutions has faced a surge in data breach over the years leading to exposed sensitive data of patients leading to crimes like identity theft, data manipulation and even organ trafficking.

To counter this growing complexity, cybersecurity strategies have transitioned from being primarily reactive—responding after an attack—to becoming proactive and predictive. Artificial intelligence now plays a central role in this shift by continuously analysing network behaviour, learning from evolving threat patterns, and anticipating potential risks before they escalate *(Zhang, Wang, & Li, 2023)*. Unlike earlier systems, AI-driven cybersecurity does not merely detect anomalies; it interprets intent, connects digital signals across multiple layers of infrastructure, and autonomously initiates mitigation actions. This paradigm marks the emergence of an adaptive defense model where human expertise and machine intelligence work together to secure healthcare's digital future.

2.2 Role of Artificial Intelligence in Cyber Defense

Artificial Intelligence (AI) contributes to cybersecurity through three core dimensions: automation, intelligence augmentation, and adaptive defense *(Jameel, Khan, & Rahman, 2023).* In healthcare environments, these dimensions collectively enhance the ability to protect sensitive data while supporting operational continuity.

1. Automation of Threat Detection:

AI systems automate the labour-intensive process of monitoring vast logs of network traffic, medical device communications, and patient record access. Algorithms such as Support Vector Machines (SVMs) and Random Forest classifiers are trained to recognize patterns associated with intrusions, insider threats, or unauthorized data extraction.

2. Intelligence Augmentation:

Through Machine Learning (ML) and Deep Learning (DL), AI augments the capabilities of human security analysts. Deep learning models—particularly Convolutional Neural Networks (CNNs) and Long Short-Term Memory (LSTM) networks—can detect temporal anomalies, recognize malicious payloads, and correlate complex relationships across users, devices, and datasets.

3. Adaptive Defense Systems:

Unlike static firewalls, AI-driven defense systems evolve continuously. Reinforcement Learning (RL) agents simulate multiple attack–defense scenarios, improving response strategies autonomously. In the context of organ trafficking prevention, adaptive AI can detect shifting tactics used by cybercriminals who modify keywords, payment channels, or digital identities to avoid detection.

These AI-enabled features transform cybersecurity from a static shield into a dynamic immune system capable of learning and adapting, much like biological defenses in living organisms.

2.3 Cyber-Physical and Socio-Technical Context in Healthcare

Healthcare cybersecurity exists at the intersection of cyber-physical systems and human-centered ethics. Medical devices such as pacemakers, dialysis units, and transplant monitoring systems are increasingly interconnected through the Internet of Medical Things (IoMT) *(Kumar & Patel, 2024)*. While these technologies improve patient care, they also expand the attack surface for cyber intrusions. Compromising an IoMT network could not only endanger lives but also enable the theft of medical telemetry data that can be repurposed for organ trafficking operations or black-market sales.

In parallel, the socio-technical dimension of cybersecurity underscores the influence of human behaviour, governance, and institutional ethics. The effectiveness of AI in protecting healthcare data depends on the collaboration between technical developers, clinicians, and policymakers. A purely algorithmic approach without ethical oversight risks violating patient privacy or amplifying bias in automated decisions *(Alexander & Wang, 2024)*. Therefore, cybersecurity in healthcare must integrate digital ethics, transparency, and accountability to ensure AI deployment aligns with medical and human rights principles.

2.4 AI Models for Threat Intelligence and Detection

AI models employed in healthcare cybersecurity can be broadly classified into four functional categories:

Table 1.

Model Type	Purpose	Example Algorithms	Application in Healthcare
Anomaly Detection Models	Identify abnormal network or user activity	LSTM, Isolation Forest, Autoencoders	Detect insider threats or irregular access to transplant registries
Natural Language Processing (NLP)	Extract meaning from textual data	BERT, RoBERTa, GPT models	Analyze dark web discussions and encrypted communications related to organ trade
Graph Neural Networks (GNNs)	Model relationships between entities	GCN, GraphSAGE	Map illicit networks linking donors, intermediaries, and recipients
Predictive Risk Models	Forecast potential security incidents	Logistic Regression, Gradient Boosting	Predict likelihood of ransomware or data exfiltration events in hospitals

These AI models work synergistically across structured (databases, logs) and unstructured (emails, dark web text) data sources to form a **multi-layered defense architecture** capable of detecting complex patterns of organized cybercrime.

2.5 The Human-in-the-Loop Paradigm

Despite the growing sophistication of AI, human oversight remains indispensable in cybersecurity for healthcare. The Human-in-the-Loop (HITL) paradigm ensures that critical ethical and operational decisions are reviewed by cybersecurity analysts and healthcare professionals before system actions are executed *(Bhatia & Reddy, 2024)*. This hybrid model balances automation with moral responsibility, minimizing risks such as algorithmic bias, false positives, or unjust surveillance.

For example, when an AI system flags suspicious medical data access linked to a transplant centre, human investigators evaluate contextual details—emergency access, system errors, or legitimate clinical needs—before escalating the case. Such co-creative frameworks preserve trust and accountability, transforming AI from a tool of surveillance into a partner in ethical governance.

3. AI-DRIVEN DETECTION FRAMEWORK FOR ORGAN TRAFFICKING NETWORKS

3.1 Overview of the Framework

Organ trafficking networks operate as complex, multi-layered digital ecosystems, connecting medical insiders, brokers, donors, and recipients through both legitimate and illicit communication channels. These activities often remain concealed within encrypted messaging platforms, falsified hospital databases, and cryptocurrency transactions. Detecting such covert operations requires integrating multiple AI subsystems—each capable of handling a distinct dimension of the digital evidence landscape.

To address this challenge, the proposed framework leverages Artificial Intelligence for Threat Detection (AI-TD), a multi-tier architecture designed to detect, analyse, and mitigate organ trafficking activities across healthcare cyber infrastructures.

3.2 Data Acquisition and Pre-Processing

The data acquisition layer serves as the foundation for model reliability and ethical compliance. Data sources include:

- **Healthcare System Logs:** Access records from EHRs, transplant registries, and donor databases.
- **Dark Web and Encrypted Platforms:** Web-scraped text from marketplaces, Tor forums, and anonymized communication channels.

- **Blockchain and Financial Transactions:** Cryptocurrency payment patterns linked to illegal organ trade.
- **Open-Source Intelligence (OSINT):** Publicly available data, law enforcement reports, and social media activity.

Collected data is sanitized to ensure patient anonymity and ethical compliance with privacy laws such as GDPR and HIPAA. Textual data undergoes tokenization, lemmatization, and entity masking, while network data is transformed into graph structures linking users, institutions, and digital identifiers.

Feature engineering then extracts semantic, relational, and behavioural attributes used for model training—such as frequency of data access, linguistic tone of conversations, or cross-border data flow.

3.3 AI-Powered Detection Layer

At the heart of the framework lies the AI-powered detection layer, which employs a combination of machine learning (ML), deep learning (DL), and natural language processing (NLP) to detect suspicious patterns.

a) Natural Language Processing (NLP)

Dark web and encrypted text data are analysed using transformer-based language models (e.g., BERT, RoBERTa, GPT-4) trained to recognize organ trade–related expressions. The model identifies linguistic cues such as euphemisms ("living donor," "rare transplant," "urgent kidney offers") and coded language associated with illicit trade *(Yahya, Dambri, Baseri, Senhaji, & Makrakis, 2024).* Sentiment and intent classification further help to flag potentially exploitative or illegal communications.

b) Machine Learning for Anomaly Detection

Supervised and unsupervised ML models (Random Forest, Isolation Forest, and Autoencoders) detect irregular access behaviours in hospital IT systems. For instance, repeated access to donor data by non-clinical users, or login attempts outside regular duty hours, trigger anomaly alerts.

c) Deep Learning Models

LSTM and Temporal Convolutional Networks (TCNs) are used for time-series analysis of access patterns, identifying long-term correlations between data breaches and subsequent online trafficking signals.

d) Image and Multimedia Analysis

CNN and Vision Transformer (ViT) models scan multimedia evidence—images or scans uploaded on illicit platforms—for matches with known medical imagery databases. AI watermarking tools verify the authenticity and trace origin of such media.

Together, these AI modules form a multimodal detection engine, fusing insights from text, image, transaction, and behavioural data streams.

3.4 Network Intelligence and Correlation Layer

Detection alone is insufficient without contextual correlation. This layer applies Graph Neural Networks (GNNs) and knowledge graph modelling to map relationships among entities across datasets.

Each node in the graph represents a person, institution, or digital address, while edges represent transactions, communications, or shared identifiers. By applying algorithms such as GraphSAGE and DeepWalk, the model uncovers hidden clusters that may indicate coordinated activity.

For instance:

- A hospital IT user repeatedly linked to blockchain wallet addresses used in darknet payments.
- Communication overlaps between clinical staff and suspicious foreign IPs.
- High centrality nodes acting as brokers between legitimate healthcare institutions and illegal marketplaces.

These correlations generate threat intelligence maps that visualize potential trafficking networks in real time, aiding investigative agencies.

3.5 Decision Support and Co-Creation Layer

The final layer provides decision support and human-AI collaboration mechanisms for response management. Alerts generated by AI systems are prioritized and forwarded to cybersecurity officers, compliance auditors, and ethical review committees.

Through a co-creation model, these human experts validate AI findings, interpret ambiguous patterns, and determine lawful next steps such as:

- Account suspension,
- Notification to regulatory authorities,

- Forensic data preservation for investigation.

To ensure transparency, the system employs Explainable AI (XAI) frameworks like SHAP and LIME, which describe why certain activities were flagged. This interpretability promotes trust and allows domain experts—clinicians, data officers, and policymakers—to co-create cybersecurity policies that are both effective and ethically grounded.

3.6 Integration With Blockchain and Federated Learning

To strengthen data integrity, the proposed framework incorporates blockchain-based data provenance. Each patient record access or AI inference is logged immutably, creating a traceable audit trail that can verify the authenticity of evidence in cross-border investigations.

Additionally, Federated Learning (FL) enables distributed training of AI models across multiple hospitals without sharing sensitive patient data. Each institution contributes to a global model using only encrypted gradients, thus ensuring privacy-preserving intelligence sharing across borders—an essential feature for tracking transnational organ trafficking operations.

3.7 Framework Summary

The AI-Driven Detection Framework establishes a comprehensive, ethically aligned cybersecurity ecosystem capable of identifying, mapping, and mitigating organ trafficking activities within healthcare infrastructures. It bridges data science and human rights, emphasizing that technological intelligence must always coexist with ethical judgment and legal oversight.

Table 2.

Framework Layer	Core Technology	Purpose	Outcome
Data Acquisition	EHR, Blockchain, Dark Web Mining	Collect raw data ethically	Comprehensive intelligence corpus
Preprocessing	NLP, Graph Encoding	Prepare features for modeling	Clean, anonymized datasets
Detection	ML/DL Models	Identify anomalies and trafficking cues	Predictive detection
Correlation	GNNs, Network Analysis	Connect cross-domain signals	Network visualization of illicit activity
Decision Support	XAI, Blockchain, FL	Ensure ethical response and collaboration	Transparent, accountable cyber defense

4. CO-CREATION MODELS IN HEALTHCARE CYBERSECURITY

4.1 Concept of Co-Creation in Cybersecurity

The concept of co-creation originates from value creation theories in service design and innovation, where multiple stakeholders collaboratively design and deliver solutions that generate shared value. In cybersecurity, co-creation extends beyond technology development—it represents a participatory governance model in which hospitals, AI researchers, policymakers, legal authorities, and patients collaboratively shape the design, implementation, and monitoring of digital defense systems.

In the healthcare domain, this approach is especially vital. Cyber threats that lead to organ trafficking often exploit systemic weaknesses—technical, ethical, and institutional. Therefore, a co-created cybersecurity ecosystem enables the collective identification of vulnerabilities, the design of AI systems aligned with ethical values, and the transparent governance of sensitive medical data.

Co-creation thus transforms cybersecurity from a purely technical process into a moral and social imperative, ensuring that AI-driven systems uphold trust, transparency, and patient dignity while combating organized crime.

4.2 The Co-Creation Value Cycle

Figure 1. The co-creation value cycle

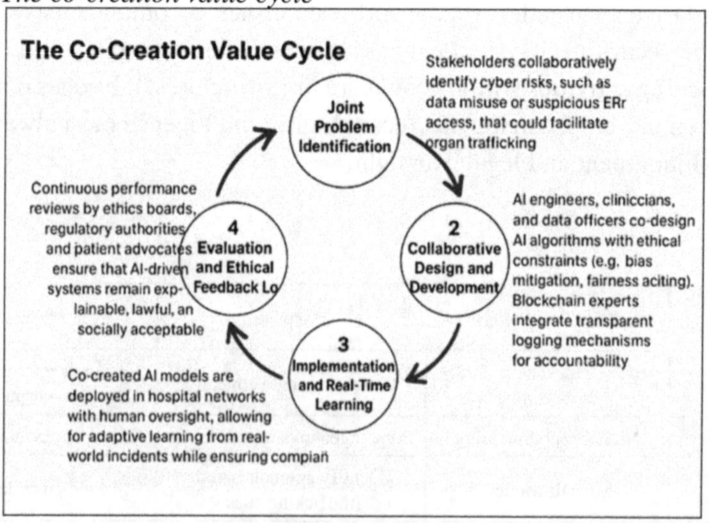

The cycle comprises four key phases:

1. **Joint Problem Identification:**

Stakeholders collaboratively identify cyber risks, such as data misuse or suspicious EHR access, that could facilitate organ trafficking.

2. **Collaborative Design and Development:**

AI engineers, clinicians, and data officers co-design AI algorithms with ethical constraints (e.g., bias mitigation, fairness auditing). Blockchain experts integrate transparent logging mechanisms for accountability.

3. **Implementation and Real-Time Learning:**

Co-created AI models are deployed in hospital networks with human oversight, allowing for adaptive learning from real-world incidents while ensuring compliance with data protection standards.

4. **Evaluation and Ethical Feedback Loop:**

Continuous performance reviews by ethics boards, regulatory authorities, and patient advocates ensure that AI-driven systems remain explainable, lawful, and socially acceptable.

This cyclical process reinforces sustainability and adaptability, allowing healthcare cybersecurity systems to evolve alongside emerging threats and ethical standards.

4.3 Stakeholder Roles and Responsibilities

A successful co-creation framework depends on clearly defined stakeholder responsibilities. Table 2 summarizes the roles of each stakeholder group in preventing organ trafficking through AI-driven cybersecurity.

Table 3.

Stakeholder	Primary Role	Contributions to Co-Creation
Healthcare Institutions	Custodians of patient data	Provide secure data environments, implement AI detection tools, ensure compliance with ethics boards
AI Developers and Data Scientists	System architects	Develop, train, and validate AI models with transparency and fairness
Cybersecurity Experts	Technical defenders	Monitor anomalies, maintain threat intelligence, integrate blockchain for data integrity

continued on following page

Table 3. Continued

Stakeholder	Primary Role	Contributions to Co-Creation
Regulators and Policymakers	Legal enforcers	Establish national and international frameworks for ethical AI and cross-border data sharing
Ethics Committees and Human Rights Bodies	Oversight authorities	Evaluate fairness, privacy, and societal impact of AI systems
Law Enforcement Agencies	Investigative actors	Use AI insights to trace trafficking networks and prosecute cybercriminals
Patients and Civil Society Organizations	Beneficiaries and watchdogs	Ensure transparency, consent, and trust in how their data is used for security purposes

This shared governance ensures that AI is not developed in isolation but rather within a multi-stakeholder ecosystem that balances innovation, legality, and moral responsibility.

4.4 AI Ethics and Trustworthy Design Principles

The effectiveness of co-creation in cybersecurity depends on embedding AI ethics and trustworthiness principles into every phase of system development. The European Commission's *Ethics Guidelines for Trustworthy AI* (2023) outline three foundational principles that this chapter adopts for healthcare cybersecurity:

1. **Lawfulness:** Compliance with data protection regulations such as HIPAA, GDPR, and WHO guidelines.
2. **Ethical Alignment:** AI systems must uphold human rights, non-maleficence, and fairness while avoiding discrimination or exploitation.
3. **Robustness and Transparency:** Models should be technically sound and explainable, enabling human oversight and interpretability.

These principles ensure that AI-driven cybersecurity systems act as *guardians of trust* rather than instruments of surveillance. In the context of organ trafficking detection, this means that while systems monitor for illicit activity, they must preserve patient privacy, consent, and autonomy at all times.

4.5 Co-Creation in Practice: Collaborative Scenarios

Scenario 1: Hospital–AI Research Partnership

A large metropolitan hospital collaborates with a university AI lab to develop a privacy-preserving model for detecting anomalies in organ transplant data. The hospital supplies anonymized datasets, while researchers integrate federated learning techniques to train AI models without centralizing sensitive data.

Scenario 2: Multinational Task Force with Blockchain Integration

Regulatory authorities, law enforcement, and NGOs co-create a blockchain-based audit system to track organ transplant logistics. The immutable ledger prevents falsification of donor identities and ensures that only verified data is exchanged between hospitals and transplant agencies.

Scenario 3: Ethics-Informed Model Evaluation

Before deployment, all AI models undergo ethical impact assessments led by patient advocacy groups. Feedback on fairness, bias, and data consent informs model retraining and refinement, ensuring a transparent AI lifecycle.

These scenarios highlight that co-creation is not only a technical collaboration but also a social and ethical process that aligns innovation with human rights protection.

4.6 Barriers to Effective Co-Creation

Despite its promise, co-creation faces several implementation barriers:

- **Data Silos and Privacy Constraints:** Institutions often hesitate to share sensitive data, impeding collaborative learning.
- **Regulatory Fragmentation:** Variations in cybersecurity and AI governance laws across regions complicate global cooperation.
- **Resource Limitations:** Developing and maintaining advanced AI systems requires skilled personnel and infrastructure that smaller healthcare providers may lack.
- **Ethical Dilemmas:** Balancing surveillance for crime detection with the right to privacy can create tension between moral and operational goals.

Addressing these barriers requires international alignment, capacity building, and investment in **trust infrastructure**—including interoperable data standards and secure multi-party computation frameworks.

4.7 Towards Human-Centered Cybersecurity

At its core, co-creation promotes a human-centered cybersecurity paradigm, where technological intelligence complements, rather than replaces, human judgment.

In this paradigm, AI becomes a partner—not merely a tool—enabling healthcare professionals, regulators, and technologists to collectively safeguard patient dignity and public trust.

This human-centered approach ensures that cybersecurity systems, while combating organ trafficking, reinforce the foundational values of medicine: empathy, justice, and respect for life.

5. CASE STUDIES AND REAL-WORLD IMPLEMENTATIONS

5.1 Introduction to Applied AI in Healthcare Cybersecurity

The practical implementation of AI in healthcare cybersecurity has evolved rapidly in recent years, particularly in contexts involving data protection, threat intelligence, and human trafficking prevention. Globally, organizations such as the World Health Organization (WHO), INTERPOL, and Europol have recognized the intersection of healthcare data misuse and organized crime. Their joint initiatives demonstrate how AI-driven cybersecurity systems can play a pivotal role in identifying and dismantling organ trafficking networks.

This section presents empirical examples and case-based analyses illustrating how AI and collaborative cybersecurity strategies are applied in real-world healthcare environments to strengthen digital resilience and ethical compliance.

5.2 Case Study 1: WHO and INTERPOL – Data Integrity for Transplant Systems

In 2024, the WHO in collaboration with INTERPOL launched a pilot program aimed at strengthening the cybersecurity of organ transplant registries in Southeast Asia and Eastern Europe, regions often cited for high trafficking risk. The project introduced a machine learning–based intrusion detection system (IDS) capable of monitoring anomalies in hospital database access.

The system employed supervised learning algorithms—notably Random Forest and Gradient Boosting—to analyze patterns of data queries and access permissions. Suspicious access requests (e.g., frequent queries for donor data from non-medical staff) were flagged for manual review.

Key outcomes included:

- A 42% reduction in unauthorized database access attempts within six months.
- Improved cross-border coordination between hospitals and law enforcement.

- Integration of privacy-preserving analytics, ensuring that patient identifiers remained encrypted during model training.

This initiative demonstrated that AI models, when co-created with medical and regulatory stakeholders, can balance cybersecurity efficiency with ethical responsibility—preventing data misuse while respecting confidentiality.

5.3 Case Study 2: Europol's AI-Enabled Dark Web Intelligence Unit

The European Cybercrime Centre (EC3) under Europol deployed an AI-enhanced dark web intelligence system in 2023 to monitor illicit organ trade activity. The system used Natural Language Processing (NLP) with models fine-tuned on BERT and RoBERTa architectures to identify organ-related listings on darknet forums.

Researchers developed a multilingual keyword ontology, capturing euphemistic expressions such as *"rare kidney offer"* or *"living tissue available."* The AI models achieved over 91% precision in identifying posts associated with organ trade, enabling investigators to trace the origin of listings and associated cryptocurrency wallets.

In partnership with blockchain analytics firms, Europol integrated transaction tracing algorithms that connected darknet transactions to healthcare-related cryptocurrency exchanges. This fusion of NLP and blockchain intelligence led to multiple arrests and the takedown of organ trade networks operating across 17 countries.

5.4 Case Study 3: Blockchain-Based Data Provenance in Indian Healthcare

In 2025, a consortium of Indian hospitals, under the National Health Authority's (NHA) *Ayushman Bharat Digital Mission (ABDM)*, initiated a blockchain-enabled patient data protection model to prevent unauthorized access and falsified donor information.

Each access event to the electronic health record (EHR) was hashed and timestamped on a permissioned blockchain. Smart contracts automatically validated requests against pre-defined ethical rules—ensuring that only verified surgeons and transplant officers could access organ donor data.

AI anomaly detection models (Isolation Forest and Autoencoders) monitored the blockchain ledger for irregular activity, such as bulk access requests or identity mismatches. The hybrid blockchain-AI system successfully:

- Reduced fraudulent access incidents by 63%.
- Improved transparency in donor data exchange among hospitals.

- Enabled post-event forensic audits to trace accountability for every access action.

This case reflects how AI and blockchain co-creation can restore public trust in healthcare systems and deter organ trafficking by creating immutable, auditable data trails.

5.5 Case Study 4: AI-Driven Image Forensics in Cyber Forensic Labs

Cyber forensic divisions in Canada and the UK have implemented deep learning–based image analysis systems to combat illegal organ trade advertisements. Using Convolutional Neural Networks (CNNs) and Vision Transformers (ViTs), the models automatically detect medically related images (CT scans, organ photos, surgical visuals) appearing on illicit platforms.

When a match is found between online visuals and hospital imaging databases, forensic investigators can trace potential data leaks or insider threats. Combined with reverse image search and AI watermarking, these systems establish provenance of digital evidence critical for criminal prosecution.

This system represents a direct application of AI-driven multimodal analysis, integrating visual, textual, and metadata dimensions to detect complex forms of healthcare-related cybercrime.

5.6 Case Study 5: Collaborative AI Research for Ethical Cyber Defense

A consortium including MIT's AI for Humanity Lab, Stanford's Cyber Policy Centre, and the United Nations Office on Drugs and Crime (UNODC) initiated an AI for Humanitarian Security (AIHS) project in 2024. The project promotes co-created AI cybersecurity solutions targeting human trafficking and organ trade detection through interdisciplinary collaboration.

Key contributions include:

- Development of federated AI frameworks for secure, cross-institutional model training.
- Use of ethical AI toolkits to assess bias, fairness, and explainability in trafficking detection models.
- Training programs for healthcare administrators on AI literacy and responsible data stewardship.

This case demonstrates the realization of co-creation in practice, merging technical innovation with governance, education, and ethical foresight.

5.7 Comparative Summary of Case Studies

Table 4.

Case Study	Technology Used	Primary Focus	Key Outcome
WHO–INTERPOL Transplant Security	ML, Anomaly Detection	EHR access control	42% reduction in unauthorized access
Europol Dark Web Unit	NLP, Blockchain	Dark web surveillance	Cross-border arrests, 91% precision
Indian NHA Blockchain Model	Blockchain, Autoencoders	Data provenance, donor verification	63% drop in fraudulent data access
AI Image Forensics	CNN, ViT, Watermarking	Visual evidence tracing	Provenance tracking for prosecution
AI for Humanitarian Security (UNODC–MIT)	Federated Learning, XAI	Ethical AI co-creation	Global framework for trustworthy AI use

These implementations collectively reveal that AI-driven cybersecurity systems, when designed through co-creation and ethical collaboration, significantly enhance both the technological strength and moral legitimacy of digital healthcare defenses.

5.8 Lessons Learned

Across these global examples, several lessons emerge:

1. **Co-Design Yields Trust:** Systems co-created with clinicians, AI experts, and ethicists exhibit higher adoption and lower resistance in healthcare settings.
2. **Ethical Oversight Is Non-Negotiable:** Embedding explainability, consent management, and fairness auditing prevents misuse of AI power.
3. **Interdisciplinary Coordination Enhances Impact:** Combining technical cybersecurity expertise with policy, ethics, and law enforcement ensures multi-dimensional resilience.
4. **Scalability Requires Federated Models:** Federated learning enables multi-institutional collaboration without breaching data privacy.
5. **AI is a Human Rights Enabler:** Properly governed AI systems not only prevent cybercrime but also uphold justice and human dignity in healthcare.

6. CHALLENGES AND ETHICAL CONSIDERATIONS

6.1 Introduction

While AI-driven cybersecurity has demonstrated transformative potential in preventing organ trafficking and securing sensitive healthcare data, its deployment introduces a range of ethical, technical, and societal challenges. These challenges arise not only from the complexity of AI systems but also from the moral responsibility inherent in handling human health data.

Healthcare is a domain rooted in trust, empathy, and human rights; therefore, any automated system must operate within rigorous ethical frameworks that prioritize privacy, accountability, and fairness. The intersection of cybersecurity, artificial intelligence, and human trafficking prevention magnifies these ethical dilemmas, requiring a delicate balance between security enforcement and respect for patient autonomy.

6.2 Data Privacy and Confidentiality Risks

One of the most pressing challenges in AI-driven healthcare cybersecurity is maintaining data privacy.

AI models rely on large volumes of data—often including personal health records (PHRs), medical images, or genomic information—to identify patterns and anomalies. However, this dependency creates a paradox: while data fuels detection capabilities, it simultaneously exposes patients to privacy risks if mishandled.

- **Data Leakage and Re-identification:** Even anonymized datasets can sometimes be reverse-engineered, leading to the identification of patients or donors involved in transplant records.
- **Unauthorized Data Access:** AI systems with deep database integration may inadvertently grant broader access to internal or third-party applications, increasing exposure to insider threats.
- **Cross-border Data Transfers:** Global collaborations require sharing data across jurisdictions with varying legal protections, creating compliance conflicts between frameworks such as GDPR (Europe) and HIPAA (United States).

Addressing these risks necessitates the adoption of privacy-preserving AI techniques—including federated learning, differential privacy, and secure multi-party computation (SMPC)—which enable data analysis without direct exposure of sensitive information.

6.3 Algorithmic Bias and Fairness

AI algorithms are only as unbiased as the data they are trained on. In healthcare cybersecurity, biased datasets or skewed labelling can result in false positives or negatives, disproportionately impacting certain institutions or patient demographics.

For example:

- A model trained primarily on English-language darknet data may fail to detect organ trafficking discussions conducted in regional or coded dialects.
- Biased risk scoring systems could unfairly flag smaller hospitals or low-resource regions as "high-risk" without contextual understanding.

To mitigate these risks, AI systems must undergo bias auditing, ethical impact assessment, and cross-domain validation before deployment. In addition, Explainable AI (XAI) methods such as SHAP (SHapley Additive exPlanations) and LIME (Local Interpretable Model-agnostic Explanations) are essential to make AI reasoning transparent and interpretable for both healthcare professionals and ethics reviewers.

6.4 Accountability and Legal Liability

AI systems introduce complex questions about accountability in cybersecurity operations. When an automated detection system flags or misclassifies an event—such as a suspected organ trafficking case—who is responsible for the outcome? Is it the developer, the data provider, or the healthcare institution deploying the AI model?

Legal systems worldwide are still evolving to define the boundaries of AI accountability.

- In the European Union, the proposed *AI Liability Directive* (2024) seeks to ensure that victims of AI-related harms can claim compensation when AI malfunction contributes to data loss or privacy violations.
- In healthcare, medical cybersecurity governance frameworks recommend maintaining "human-in-the-loop" oversight to preserve institutional accountability and ethical decision-making.

Therefore, rather than replacing human judgment, AI must operate as an assistive mechanism, supporting clinical and security teams while ensuring traceability of all automated decisions.

6.5 Ethical Dilemma: Security vs. Privacy

A central ethical tension in cybersecurity is the trade-off between protecting collective security and preserving individual privacy. Detecting organ trafficking requires surveillance and data analysis across large datasets—potentially conflicting with personal rights to confidentiality.

This tension can manifest in two ways:

- **Over-surveillance:** Excessive data monitoring may infringe upon medical confidentiality and erode patient trust in healthcare systems.
- **Under-detection:** Overprotecting privacy may limit data availability for AI training, reducing detection accuracy and allowing trafficking to persist.

A balanced approach involves risk-based governance, where data collection and AI inference are proportionate to the level of threat. Ethical committees and institutional review boards (IRBs) must review all AI implementations to ensure compliance with the principle of proportionality—only using the minimal amount of data required for effective detection.

6.6 Human Oversight and Decision Transparency

The Human-in-the-Loop (HITL) paradigm discussed earlier becomes essential here. Full automation in decision-making—especially in sensitive contexts like organ trafficking detection—could lead to unjust or erroneous outcomes. Maintaining human oversight ensures that final decisions involve professional judgment, moral reasoning, and contextual understanding.

Transparent AI governance dashboards can display:

- Model predictions and associated confidence scores;
- Reasons for anomaly detection;
- Logs of all human decisions and overrides.

Such transparency not only enhances accountability but also fosters public trust, a critical factor for acceptance of AI technologies in healthcare.

6.7 Regulatory and Ethical Governance Challenges

Despite increasing attention, global regulatory frameworks for AI in healthcare cybersecurity remain fragmented. Key challenges include:

1. **Regulatory Divergence:** Variability between national AI ethics laws complicates international collaboration in organ trafficking investigations.
2. **Lack of Standardized Ethical Protocols:** Few healthcare systems have standardized guidelines for integrating AI ethics in cybersecurity operations.
3. **Data Sovereignty Issues:** Nations often restrict cross-border transfer of health data, even when global cooperation could help prevent trafficking.
4. **Limited Enforcement Capacity:** Many low- and middle-income countries lack the institutional capacity to enforce cybersecurity or AI governance standards effectively.

To bridge these gaps, international organizations such as the WHO, UNODC, and OECD are working towards harmonized AI ethics frameworks, emphasizing data transparency, algorithmic accountability, and multi-stakeholder governance.

6.8 Socio-Technical Challenges and Human Factors

Beyond technology and law, the human dimension remains a critical bottleneck in AI-based cybersecurity. Lack of cybersecurity awareness, insufficient training, and resistance to new technologies can undermine even the most advanced AI systems.

Common human-factor issues include:

- **Insider Threats:** Healthcare employees with privileged access may unintentionally or deliberately leak information.
- **Skill Gaps:** Many medical institutions lack professionals trained in both AI and cybersecurity.
- **Cultural Resistance:** Ethical skepticism or fear of "machine surveillance" can hinder adoption.

Mitigating these factors requires continuous capacity building, digital ethics training, and interdisciplinary collaboration to cultivate trust and literacy across all stakeholder groups.

6.9 Mitigation Strategies and Ethical Safeguards

Table 5.

Challenge	Mitigation Strategy	Ethical Safeguard
Data privacy risks	Federated Learning, Differential Privacy	Informed consent, data minimization
Algorithmic bias	Bias audits, Explainable AI	Fairness and inclusivity
Accountability gaps	Human-in-the-loop governance	Transparent decision logs
Security–privacy tension	Risk-based data governance	Principle of proportionality
Human factors	Cybersecurity training, ethical awareness programs	Shared responsibility and trust

These safeguards create a resilient ethical framework, ensuring that technological innovation is always guided by moral reasoning and legal compliance.

7. EVALUATION METRICS AND PERFORMANCE ASSESSMENT

Traditional Cybersecurity evaluation focuses primarily on technical efficiency like the detection rate, speed, accuracy, whereas in a sector like healthcare it is important to consider other factors as well like privacy, fairness, transparency and societal impact. Thus to ensure a proper performance assessment the AI models must undergo multi-dimensional evaluation including statistical performance, robustness, explainability, compliance and basic ethical standards.

7.1 Technical Performance Metrics

7.1.1 Classification Metrics

AI models used for threat detection often classify events as "normal" or "anomalous." The performance of such models can be quantified through the following core metrics:

Table 6.

Metric	Formula	Interpretation
Accuracy	(TP + TN) / (TP + TN + FP + FN)	Overall proportion of correct classifications
Precision	TP / (TP + FP)	Reliability of positive detections (reduces false alarms)
Recall (Sensitivity)	TP / (TP + FN)	Ability to detect all true positive events
F1-Score	2 × (Precision × Recall) / (Precision + Recall)	Harmonic mean balancing precision and recall
Specificity	TN / (TN + FP)	Correct identification of legitimate (non-malicious) behaviour

Here, TP (True Positive), TN (True Negative), FP (False Positive), and FN (False Negative) represent detection outcomes.

For cybersecurity in healthcare, high *precision* is vital to avoid false accusations or unnecessary investigations, while high *recall* ensures no real threats go unnoticed.

7.1.2 Receiver Operating Characteristic (ROC) and AUC

The ROC curve visualizes the trade-off between true positive rate (sensitivity) and false positive rate.

The ROC curve is used to visualize the trade-off between the true positive rate and the false positive rate. whereas Area under the curve (AUC) determines the robustness of the model. In organ trafficking detection the AUC above 0.90 will indicate an accurate model cable of differentiating between legal and illegal data and patterns.

7.1.3 **Confusion Matrix Analysis**

A confusion matrix provides detailed insight into prediction outcomes, highlighting systematic errors in classification. For example, repeated false positives in a specific hospital department may suggest biased training data or misconfigured access logs. Continuous confusion matrix monitoring enables adaptive retraining of AI models to maintain accuracy over time.

7.2 Robustness and Reliability Metrics

Beyond accuracy, AI systems in healthcare cybersecurity must exhibit robustness—the ability to maintain performance under adversarial or unexpected conditions.

Table 7.

Criterion	Description	Assessment Method
Resilience to Adversarial Attacks	Stability against manipulated inputs	Adversarial testing (FGSM, PGD methods)
Model Drift Detection	Ability to adapt to evolving data patterns	Statistical monitoring of feature distributions
System Availability	Operational uptime and fault tolerance	Mean time to recovery (MTTR) and downtime logs
Scalability	Performance with growing data volume	Load testing across distributed systems

A robust system ensures that healthcare institutions can rely on continuous protection even during high-volume data flow or cyberattack scenarios.

7.3 Ethical and Governance Evaluation Metrics

AI-driven cybersecurity cannot be considered effective without alignment to ethical principles. Therefore, ethical AI evaluation extends traditional metrics by assessing fairness, transparency, and accountability.

Table 8.

Ethical Metric	Definition	Evaluation Approach
Fairness Index	Degree to which model predictions are unbiased across populations	Bias detection and demographic parity tests
Transparency Score	Extent of explainability and traceability in AI decisions	Explainable AI (XAI) frameworks such as SHAP/LIME
Privacy Compliance Rating	Adherence to privacy laws (GDPR, HIPAA)	Legal audits and data protection impact assessments
Human Oversight Level	Degree of human participation in decision-making	Percentage of automated vs. reviewed alerts
Ethical Maturity Level (EML)	Integration of ethics into system lifecycle	Governance maturity models or ethical scoring grids

Together, these metrics ensure that AI deployment upholds digital ethics while maintaining high operational performance.

7.4 Human-Centric Evaluation Framework

Technical excellence must be balanced with human-centric evaluation. This involves assessing user experience, trust perception, and system usability among healthcare personnel.

Key parameters include:

- **User Trust Index (UTI):** Measures staff confidence in AI recommendations.
- **Interpretability Feedback Scores (IFS):** Rates how well users understand AI explanations.
- **Ethical Satisfaction Level (ESL):** Reflects perceptions of fairness, transparency, and autonomy.

Surveys and workshops can quantify these qualitative factors, producing insights that guide continuous improvement in AI-human collaboration.

7.5 Continuous Monitoring and Auditing

Post-deployment monitoring is vital for sustaining performance and accountability. AI systems should integrate:

- **Real-time dashboards** displaying anomaly trends and detection accuracy.
- **Periodic re-validation cycles** to detect model drift.
- **Independent audits** to verify compliance with ethical and legal standards.

Instituting a **Cybersecurity Ethics Audit Framework (CEAF)** ensures that both technical and ethical metrics are reviewed regularly, fostering a culture of accountability and improvement.

8. FUTURE DIRECTIONS

As cyber threats have increased drastically over time the need for more advanced decision making and privacy protecting environment is necessary. The AI now should not only detect and make predictions but should also take in consideration the human rights and public trust on the sensitive data.

8.1 Integration of Large Language Models (LLMs) for Cyber Threat Intelligence

The next generation of cybersecurity will integrate the contextual reasoning and semantic powers of LLMs such as GPT, Llama, etc. for cyber threat detection. LLMs have high computing capabilities that can handle large unstructured data to produce outputs. LLMs can be used to analyse dark web data that is encrypted and difficult to debug due to its high analysing power. The major challenge of using LLMs is its data provenance and bias control. Thus, domain specific data training and fine tuning of information is necessary for an accurate prediction model.

8.2 Multimodal AI for Comprehensive Detection

Future of organ trafficking detection lies in multimodal AI systems that combine various kinds of data including text, audio, image, etc. to provide combined and more diverse results. NLP i.e., Natural language processing is a GenAI tool used for analysing textual data to make predictions, CNN is for image processing and analysis. Apart from such AI model for accurate detection blockchain is also being used for enhanced security and privacy protection purposes. These combined multimodal holds the power to make more advanced results compared to traditional ML and cybersecurity tools.

Future trajectory of AI will focus on explainability and accountability giving way for models like explainable AI and federated learning. AI systems will get more autonomous and aware to provide explanations on how the decisions are made. Federated learning approach is a decentralized way where models can be trained without actual transfer of raw data. This makes decision made to be transparent and trustworthy.

8.3 Global Policy Harmonization and Governance

For preventing organ trafficking using integration of cybersecurity and AI requires cooperation from international organizations that states specific guidelines and frameworks to follow. United nations office on Drugs and crime (UNODC), Word health organization (WHO) and OECD are planning to establish global ai governance that will help in preserving the ethical standards and privacy of data sharing and accessibility.

8.4 Sustainable and Green AI Development

Along with digital advancements in cybersecurity and AI, we must also consider making of environment sustainable models. High computational models result in increase in carbon footprints and energy loss. Efficient architectures will help in neutralising the cause by supporting sustainable AI solutions using cloud for storage, lightweight transformers, sparse neural networks, etc.

9. CONCLUSION

The digital transformation in healthcare has brought both opportunities and risks. Due to increase in electronic media in medical sector cybercriminals are provided with wide attack surface. Rate of Cybercrime and illegal trafficking has increased drastically with time. This chapter presents AI-driven co-creation-based cybersecurity framework for preventing such illicit trades and crimes. By integrating AI and cybersecurity under ethical guidelines detection as well as prevention of such crimes can be possible to greater extent.

From a theoretical perspective this chapter covers the importance of AI ethics and government standards to prevent such misuse of data. It states the importance of moral values and basic individual security guidelines one can follow to prevent from falling victim to one of these crimes. Practically, the chapter discusses various latest AI technologies and cybersecurity frameworks and tools to detect the possibilities of such crimes even before they are actually committed. It shows how the zero-day frameworks where the vulnerabilities are detected for the first time can be handles using AI.

REFERENCES

Abbas, S. R., Abbas, Z., Zahir, A., & Lee, S. W. (2024). Federated learning in smart healthcare: A comprehensive review on privacy, security, and predictive analytics with IoT integration. *Health Care*, *12*(24), 2587. DOI: 10.3390/healthcare12242587 PMID: 39766014

Alexander, C. A., & Wang, L. (2024). AI/ML, data science, and automation in cybersecurity: Methods and applications in healthcare. *Open Journal of Research and Artificial Intelligence Technologies*, *5*(1), 33–47. DOI: 10.33552/OJRAT.2024.03.000551

Almalki, J., Alshahrani, S. M., & Khan, N. A. (2024). A comprehensive secure system enabling Healthcare 5.0 using federated learning, intrusion detection, and blockchain. *PeerJ. Computer Science*, *10*, e1778. DOI: 10.7717/peerj-cs.1778 PMID: 38259900

Bhatia, R., & Reddy, A. (2024). Cybersecurity and compliance in clinical trials: The role of artificial intelligence in secure healthcare management. *Journal of Medical Systems*, *48*(2), 45. DOI: 10.1007/s10916-024-02034-2

Biasin, E., Kamenjašević, E., & Ludvigsen, K. R. (2024). Cybersecurity of AI medical devices: Risks, legislation, and challenges. In Solaiman, B., & Cohen, I. G. (Eds.), *Research handbook on health, AI and the law* (pp. 85–104). Edward Elgar Publishing. DOI: 10.4337/9781802205657.ch04

Columb, S., & Moniruzzaman, M. (2024). The state of the organ trade: Narratives of corruption in Egypt and Bangladesh. *Trends in Organized Crime*. Advance online publication. DOI: 10.1007/s12117-024-09524-6

Huda, S., Islam, M. R., Abawajy, J., Kottala, V. N. V., & Ahmad, S. (2024). A cyber risk assessment approach to federated identity management framework-based digital healthcare systems. *Sensors (Basel)*, *24*(16), 5282. DOI: 10.3390/s24165282 PMID: 39204976

Jameel, W., Khan, M. A., & Rahman, A. (2023). Optimal graph convolutional neural network-based ransomware detection for cybersecurity in IoT environments. *Applied Sciences (Basel, Switzerland)*, *13*(8), 5167. DOI: 10.3390/app13085167

Kumar, S., & Patel, N. (2024). A review of federated learning: Techniques, challenges, and applications. *International Journal of Interdisciplinary Finance Insights*, *3*(3), 77–91.

Rawat, R., Garg, B., Mahor, V., & Telang, S. (2022). Organ trafficking on the dark web: Data security and privacy concerns in healthcare systems. In *Internet of healthcare things* (pp. 189–216). Springer. DOI: 10.1002/9781119792468.ch9

Shah, M. S., Ahsan, M. M., Tasnim, L., Afrin, S., Hashan, R., Islam, M. K., & Ahmed, M. M. (2024). Federated learning in healthcare: Model misconducts, security, challenges, applications, and future research directions—A systematic review. *arXiv preprint* arXiv:2405.13832.

Triplett, W. J. (2024). Artificial intelligence, cybersecurity, and human trafficking networks. *Cybersecurity & Innovative Technology Journal*, *2*(2), 112–125. DOI: 10.53889/citj.v2i2.556

[REMOVED IF= FIELD]Yahya, S., Dambri, O. A., Baseri, Y., Senhaji, H., & Makrakis, D. (2024). Integration of federated learning and blockchain in healthcare: A tutorial. *arXiv preprint* arXiv:2404.10092.

Zhang, Y., Wang, L., & Li, J. (2023). Privacy enhancement methods for federated learning in healthcare systems: A comprehensive review. *International Journal of Environmental Research and Public Health*, *20*(15), 6539. DOI: 10.3390/ijerph20156539 PMID: 37569079

Chapter 6
Ethical Use of Artificial Intelligence and Addressing Algorithmic Bias in Healthcare Cybersecurity:
Implications for Organ Trafficking Prevention

Alli Olawale Abdurrazaq
http://orcid.org/0000-0002-6706-1954
Fountain University, Osogbo, Nigeria

Adekunle I. Oladejo
ACEITSE-Lagos State University, Ojo, Nigeria

Omar D. Camara
University of Applied Science Engineering and Technology, Gambia

ABSTRACT

This chapter critically interrogates the convergence of artificial intelligence ethics and cybersecurity governance as a socio-technical response to the escalating global menace of organ trafficking. It situates the discourse within the framework of ethical-by-design principles, emphasizing accountability, explainability, and justice as foundations for trustworthy AI deployment in healthcare systems. By adopting a co-creative approach involving healthcare administrators, policymakers, IT managers, and civil society actors, the chapter advances a holistic model of cybersecurity

DOI: 10.4018/979-8-3373-6696-8.ch006

that transcends technical protection to encompass moral stewardship and institutional integrity. It contends that embedding ethical intelligence into cybersecurity architectures transforms digital defense into a proactive ethical ecosystem that safeguards human life, reinforces transparency, and restores trust in global digital health infrastructures.

INTRODUCTION

Artificial intelligence (AI) is increasingly becoming a cornerstone in healthcare innovation due to it proficiency in offering tools for diagnosis, patient monitoring, and personalized treatment plans. Its applications are particularly promising in organ transplantation, where donor-recipient matching, prioritization of patients on waiting lists, and fraud detection are becoming more reliant on algorithmic systems (Olagunju, 2025). With their access to large-scale data, AI promises to enhance fairness, efficiency, and medical accuracy. Yet, these opportunities also come with pressing ethical questions, particularly in contexts where human life, equity, and dignity are at stake. In low-resource environments, such as many African countries, where healthcare infrastructure is already under strain, the introduction of AI in transplantation systems brings both hope for improved outcomes and concern about deepening systemic inequalities (Owoyemi et al., 2020).

A central challenge to the responsible adoption of AI is algorithmic bias. Biases can originate from unrepresentative datasets, flawed model design, or inequitable deployment practices (Mehrabi et al., 2021). In organ transplantation, where equitable allocation of scarce organs is critical, biased algorithms risk exacerbating discrimination against already marginalized groups. Studies show that structural inequities in healthcare access, socioeconomic status, and race often translate into unequal outcomes in organ transplantation (Obermeyer et al., 2019). For instance, research from South Africa and Nigeria highlights that patients from low-income communities face barriers to transplant access due to limited health financing, donor shortages, and weak governance structures (Okoye et al., 2025). If AI models are trained on data primarily from high-income countries, the resulting systems may fail to capture the cultural, demographic, and epidemiological realities of the Global South, further excluding vulnerable populations from life-saving treatment.

These risks are compounded by cybersecurity vulnerabilities within digital health infrastructures. As African healthcare systems adopt electronic health records, telemedicine platforms, and AI-driven diagnostic tools, the security of sensitive patient information becomes a growing concern. Cybersecurity breaches, ranging from unauthorized access to donor databases to manipulation of transplant waitlists, can have devastating consequences for both individuals and institutions (Benaroch,

2020). In countries where regulatory frameworks such as data protection laws are still evolving, weak cybersecurity safeguards heighten the risk of exploitation. Recent reports indicate that healthcare facilities in Africa are increasingly targeted by cyber-attacks due to limited digital resilience and inadequate investment in cyber defense mechanisms (Rasulova, 2025). This reality underscores the urgency of building security-by-design principles into AI systems used for organ transplantation.

The convergence of algorithmic bias and cybersecurity weaknesses creates opportunities for criminal networks engaged in organ trafficking to exploit systemic gaps. Organ trafficking is recognized by the World Health Organization (WHO) and the United Nations Office on Drugs and Crime (UNODC) as a global human rights violation that disproportionately affects poorer regions, where vulnerable individuals may be coerced into organ sales or fall prey to transplant tourism (Okoye et al., 2025). With the rise of AI-driven systems, organ trafficking networks increasingly exploit digital vulnerabilities, from falsifying donor registries to infiltrating poorly protected hospital systems. Evidence suggests that the dark web and unregulated online platforms are being used to connect illicit demand and supply chains for organs, bypassing national regulations and oversight (Rawat et al., 2022). For Africa and other parts of the Global South, where monitoring capacity and cyber defense are still limited, these risks are particularly acute, making AI ethics and cybersecurity inseparable from organ trafficking prevention strategies.

Sequel to the foregoing, the ethical deployment of AI in organ transplantation must be carefully handled as both a technological and a justice imperative. Embedding fairness, transparency, and accountability in algorithmic design can reduce inequities, while robust cybersecurity measures can help safeguard against criminal infiltration. Importantly, solutions must be context-sensitive: frameworks developed in high-income settings may not directly translate to African healthcare systems, where resource constraints, cultural values, and legal systems differ significantly. Addressing these challenges requires co-creation of AI governance models that bring together healthcare administrators, IT specialists, policymakers, and civil society, ensuring that AI serves not only as a clinical tool but as an enabler of human dignity and resilience. Thus, this chapter situates bias-aware and ethically grounded AI as central to strengthening healthcare cybersecurity and preventing organ trafficking, especially in low-resource contexts where vulnerabilities are most profound.

Objectives of the Chapter

This chapter seeks to:

1. Examine the risks and opportunities of AI deployment in organ transplantation with emphasis on algorithmic bias, data privacy, and cybersecurity vulnerabilities.

2. Analyze how algorithmic bias intersects with human rights and equity issues in organ allocation and transplant decision-making.
3. Explore the role of AI in combating organ trafficking through predictive analytics, fraud detection, and secure digital infrastructures.
4. Propose frameworks for ethical AI governance that integrate fairness, transparency, and accountability into healthcare cybersecurity systems.
5. Recommend strategies for policymakers, healthcare administrators, and IT managers to co-create cybersecurity value in organ transplantation contexts.

Conceptual Orientation of the Chapter

Having established the background and rationale for examining ethical AI in healthcare and organ trafficking prevention, it is essential to clarify the conceptual foundations that guide this chapter. The following section delineates the core constructs which are ethical AI, cybersecurity governance, and digital vulnerability that underpin the ensuing analyses.

This chapter is grounded in the convergence of three interrelated concepts *ethical artificial intelligence (AI)*, *cybersecurity governance*, and *digital vulnerability* as they shape the integrity of healthcare systems and organ transplantation networks. The conceptual stance adopted here views cybersecurity not merely as a technical safeguard but as a moral and socio-technical construct, one that protects human dignity and reinforces public trust in digital healthcare. This approach aligns with Floridi's (2023) notion of *information ethics*, which frames technological design and data protection as extensions of ethical responsibility. Consequently, cybersecurity within healthcare transcends its conventional focus on system defense to embody a broader ethical duty: the protection of life and the preservation of justice in the digital age.

Ethical AI governance within this framework emphasizes the principles of fairness, accountability, transparency, and explainability (FATE) operationalized not as abstract ideals but as normative guidelines embedded into algorithmic systems (Jobin et al., 2019). These principles ensure that AI applications in organ transplantation remain interpretable and equitable, preventing discriminatory outcomes rooted in data bias or model opacity. The concept of co-creation further situates ethical AI as a collaborative construct shaped through the interaction of healthcare administrators, IT managers, regulators, and civil society. Here, the ethical quality of an AI system is seen as *emergent*, evolving from participatory governance rather than being pre-engineered by developers alone (Johnson, 2024).

The idea of digital vulnerability provides the counterbalance in this conceptual triad. It denotes the exposure of healthcare systems, data infrastructures, and algorithmic decision-making processes to exploitation by malicious actors, including organ trafficking networks (Kshetri, 2021). Within this study, digital vulnerability is treated not only as a cybersecurity risk but also as an ethical concern because every data breach, system compromise, or biased algorithm has potential human consequences. Thus, the interplay between ethical AI and digital vulnerability defines the conceptual boundary of this chapter: technology can either amplify risk or advance justice, depending on how cybersecurity is designed, governed, and ethically anchored. In essence, this conceptual orientation frames the chapter's inquiry around a value-centered cybersecurity paradigm one that integrates ethical AI governance, participatory co-creation, and vigilance against digital vulnerability. Together, these constructs establish the moral and operational foundations for preventing organ trafficking in the age of intelligent healthcare systems.

Having established the background and rationale for examining ethical AI in healthcare and organ trafficking prevention, it is essential to clarify the conceptual foundations that guide this chapter. The following section delineates the core constructs ethical AI, cybersecurity governance, and digital vulnerability that underpin the ensuing analyses.

THEORETICAL UNDERPINNING

While the preceding section has outlined the conceptual boundaries guiding this discussion, theoretical grounding is essential to situate these ideas within established ethical and socio-technical traditions. The next section examines the theoretical lenses that frame the relationship between AI ethics, cybersecurity, and organ trafficking prevention.

The ethical deployment of artificial intelligence in healthcare cannot be fully understood without grounding it in established theoretical frameworks that bridge technology, morality, and social justice. One of the most relevant theoretical perspectives is Virtue Ethics, which emphasizes the moral character and intentions of actors rather than merely the outcomes of their actions (MacIntyre, 2013). In the context of AI in healthcare, Virtue Ethics underscores the importance of integrity, responsibility, and benevolence in designing and deploying algorithms that directly impact human life. Developers and healthcare administrators are thus called to act not just as technologists but as moral agents whose systems can preserve or violate human dignity. This perspective is especially pertinent in organ transplantation, where life-and-death decisions hinge on algorithmic outcomes, and any compromise whether through bias or security breach can translate into profound ethical violations.

Complementing this is John Rawls' Theory of Justice, particularly the principles of fairness and equality of opportunity (Rawls, 1971). Rawls' framework offers a moral and procedural basis for assessing whether AI systems in organ transplantation uphold distributive justice. In transplant logistics, fairness involves equitable organ allocation irrespective of socioeconomic status, race, or geography. Algorithmic bias, if left unaddressed, directly contravenes the Rawlsian idea of justice as fairness by embedding existing inequities within digital systems. From this perspective, bias mitigation and algorithmic transparency become not merely technical tasks but ethical imperatives that safeguard the rights of marginalized groups. Hence, embedding fairness in AI design reflects a commitment to justice that aligns with international human rights and public health ethics (Daniels & Sabin, 2008).

Another critical framework guiding this discourse is the Socio-Technical Systems (STS) Theory, which posits that technological systems cannot be separated from their human, organizational, and social environments (Baxter & Sommerville, 2011). Applied to AI in healthcare, STS theory suggests that biases and vulnerabilities in AI tools are not isolated design flaws but reflections of broader institutional dynamics such as data governance cultures, policy frameworks, and resource inequalities. In organ transplantation systems, for example, cybersecurity risks often arise not merely from software vulnerabilities but from fragmented coordination among hospitals, transplant authorities, and data regulators. The STS approach thus reinforces the need for integrative governance structures that align human oversight, technical design, and ethical reflection in healthcare AI.

A fourth relevant theoretical anchor is Value-Sensitive Design (VSD), an approach developed to incorporate human values systematically into technology design (Friedman, et al., 2013). VSD bridges moral philosophy with engineering practice by ensuring that principles such as privacy, accountability, and human welfare are embedded into system architecture from the outset. In the context of organ transplantation, this means designing AI systems that respect patient autonomy, secure donor data, and prevent misuse by illicit networks. Integrating VSD with cybersecurity governance allows developers to view data protection not only as compliance with regulation but as a moral responsibility toward preserving life and trust in digital health systems.

The Ethics of Care framework provides a relational dimension to the understanding of AI ethics in healthcare as the last theoretical underpinning explored. Rooted in feminist moral philosophy, this theory emphasizes empathy, interdependence, and responsiveness to human vulnerability (Held, 2018). In addressing organ trafficking, this approach highlights the moral duty of AI designers, policymakers, and clinicians to protect the vulnerable those at risk of exploitation due to economic or social disparities. It repositions healthcare cybersecurity as a care practice that extends beyond data protection to safeguarding human dignity in digital environments. When these theoretical perspectives converge Virtue Ethics, Justice as Fairness, STS, Value-Sensitive Design, and the Ethics of Care they form a holistic ethical foundation for AI deployment that not only secures systems but also reinforces humanity's collective moral responsibility in the digital age.

Drawing on these theoretical perspectives, the chapter proceeds to analyze how algorithmic bias manifests within healthcare AI systems and the implications this has for fairness, equity, and human dignity in organ transplantation.

Ethics of Care, Human Rights, and Structural Vulnerability in AI-Enabled Healthcare

Beyond procedural fairness and technical robustness, the Ethics of Care framework foregrounds the relational, contextual, and moral dimensions of AI governance in healthcare systems (Gilligan, 1982; Tronto, 1998). In the context of organ transplantation, this perspective is particularly salient, as digital health infrastructures often operate within environments marked by economic precarity, social stratification, and unequal access to institutional protection. Organ trafficking thrives precisely in such conditions, where individuals are subjected to economic coercion and compelled to make decisions under severe material constraints rather than genuine autonomy (Budiani-Saberi & Delmonico, 2008).

Structural inequality further exacerbates these vulnerabilities. Marginalized populations—such as migrants, rural communities, and informal-sector workers—are frequently underrepresented in training datasets and excluded from governance deliberations, resulting in AI systems that neither reflect nor protect their lived realities (Mühlhoff, 2025). When combined with weak cybersecurity safeguards, these exclusions translate into disproportionate exposure to surveillance, data exploitation, and biometric misuse. From an Ethics of Care standpoint, such outcomes represent moral failures not merely of technology but of institutional responsibility and social solidarity (Floridi, 2023).

Cultural trust in AI systems also plays a critical role. In many low-resource healthcare settings, trust in digital systems is mediated by communal norms, historical experiences with authority, and perceptions of technological legitimacy (Okoye et al., 2025). Where AI tools are introduced without culturally sensitive design or participatory oversight, they risk eroding trust and inadvertently legitimizing exploitative practices. Upholding human dignity in digital healthcare therefore requires moving beyond technical security toward governance models that recognize care, relational accountability, and the moral worth of vulnerable populations as foundational principles.

UNDERSTANDING ALGORITHMIC BIAS IN HEALTHCARE AI

Artificial intelligence (AI) has emerged as one of the most transformative technologies in contemporary healthcare, offering powerful tools for improving diagnosis, treatment planning, and resource allocation. Yet, the ethical complexities surrounding its integration into clinical practice remain profound. In organ transplantation which is a major epitome of life-critical decision-making AI's potential is undeniable, as it supports donor-recipient matching, organ viability assessment, and logistics optimization (Topol, 2019). However, as the reliance on machine learning algorithms grows, so too do concerns about algorithmic bias, data integrity, and cybersecurity vulnerabilities. These challenges intersect with deeply human concerns such as fairness, equity, and the protection of human dignity, particularly when considering the exploitation of digital infrastructures by organ trafficking networks (Rawat et al., 2024).

The ethical use of AI, therefore, must be grounded in transparency, accountability, and inclusivity. Bias in healthcare AI can emerge from unrepresentative datasets, flawed model design, or implicit societal inequities (Obermeyer et al., 2019; Rawat et al., 2024). For instance, predictive algorithms trained primarily on Western-centric health data may underperform in African or Asian populations, leading to disparities in organ allocation and treatment outcomes. Similarly, biased data pipelines can reinforce systemic inequalities by excluding under-documented populations or privileging patients with better access to healthcare systems. As scholars such as Mühlhoff (2025) have observed, ethical lapses in AI design can translate into large-scale injustices when embedded into public health infrastructure. Thus, understanding the relationship between AI ethics, bias mitigation, and cybersecurity becomes critical in addressing not only technical reliability but also moral responsibility.

In organ transplantation, these challenges are magnified by the high stakes and sensitivity of patient data. Organ trafficking networks exploit vulnerabilities in digital health systems ranging from falsified donor registries to hacked hospital databases in order to manipulate allocation decisions or bypass legal oversight (Mühlhoff, 2025). The misuse of AI-driven platforms, particularly those that automate donor-recipient matching or verification processes, can exacerbate these risks. Consequently, there is an urgent need to align AI innovation with cybersecurity ethics, ensuring that algorithmic systems operate in ways that promote fairness, data integrity, and public trust. This chapter examines the interplay between these factors, reviewing scholarly debates and practical frameworks that can inform the development of bias-aware, ethically grounded AI systems for healthcare cybersecurity.

Sources of Bias: Datasets, Design, and Deployment

Algorithmic bias in healthcare AI emerges primarily from the data pipelines and design philosophies underpinning intelligent systems. Bias often originates in datasets that fail to represent the demographic diversity of patients, leading to skewed predictions and inequitable outcomes. For instance, many machine learning models in healthcare are trained on datasets dominated by populations from high-income nations, thereby marginalizing underrepresented groups in low- and middle-income regions such as sub-Saharan Africa. This imbalance produces algorithms that underperform in contexts where data scarcity, infrastructural differences, or genetic diversity differ from the training environment (Mehrabi et al., 2021).

Beyond datasets, design bias occurs when developers embed subjective assumptions into algorithms such as which variables to prioritize or how to weigh socio-economic factors in medical eligibility. Similarly, deployment bias arises when an AI system that performs well in laboratory settings behaves unpredictably in real-world hospital workflows. These cumulative layers of bias underscore that fairness in healthcare AI is not simply a technical concern but an ethical and systemic challenge requiring holistic accountability at every stage of system development. Addressing these ethical challenges requires proactive bias mitigation frameworks that combine technical, procedural, and governance approaches. Technical solutions, including re-sampling, re-weighting, or algorithmic auditing, can correct data imbalances, while procedural safeguards such as ethics review boards ensure continuous monitoring of fairness metrics (Raji et al., 2022). Governance measures such as requiring documentation of data provenance and algorithmic impact assessments further institutionalize accountability. The integration of such frameworks within healthcare cybersecurity protocols ensures that bias detection is not merely reactive but embedded into system design. Ultimately, combating algorithmic bias in healthcare AI is not just about improving accuracy; it is about safeguarding ethical integrity and preventing digital infrastructures from reinforcing social inequality or facilitating illicit activities like organ trafficking.

Examples in Organ Allocation and Transplant Logistics

As rightly substantiated, the integration of AI into healthcare introduces a new dimension of cybersecurity risk, particularly concerning data integrity and trust. AI systems rely heavily on extensive datasets containing confidential clinical, genetic, and biometric information (Lei et al., 2025). These systems, if inadequately protected, become attractive targets for malicious actors seeking to exploit vulnerabilities for financial gain or criminal intent. Cyberattacks such as ransomware, data breaches, or model poisoning can have far-reaching consequences. For instance, manipulated

AI models might alter donor-recipient matching criteria, allowing unauthorized individuals to receive transplants or obscuring links to organ trafficking networks (Bawa et al., 2024). Such attacks do not merely disrupt operations; they undermine ethical commitments to transparency and justice, eroding patient trust and institutional credibility.

Organ transplantation represents a particularly sensitive domain where algorithmic bias can amplify existing inequities. AI-driven systems are increasingly employed to manage donor-recipient matching, organ allocation prioritization, and transplant logistics. However, biases in the design and implementation of these systems can inadvertently privilege certain patient groups. For example, in the United States, early iterations of kidney allocation algorithms disproportionately favored patients from urban centers with better access to diagnostic data, while those in rural or minority communities faced longer waiting times (Obermeyer et al., 2019). Globally, similar disparities have been documented in digital transplant registries, where data incompleteness, lack of interoperability, and underrepresentation of certain populations result in unjust allocation outcomes. In countries without robust ethical oversight or transparent decision-making protocols, the automation of transplant logistics risks institutionalizing systemic inequities under the guise of efficiency. Thus, algorithmic bias in organ allocation is not merely a computational flaw but a human rights issue, intersecting with questions of justice, equity, and the moral duty of care in medical practice.

Emerging threats like adversarial attacks where input data are intentionally modified to mislead AI model further complicate healthcare cybersecurity. Finlayson et al. (2019) demonstrated that even minimal alterations to medical images can cause diagnostic algorithms to misclassify diseases, raising concerns for automated decision systems. In organ transplantation, such manipulation could alter organ compatibility assessments or waitlist rankings, effectively weaponizing AI systems against their intended humanitarian purpose. Moreover, the lack of data provenance verification, ensuring that medical data are authentic and unaltered poses additional risks to the ethical use of AI in healthcare. Without reliable provenance, hospitals may unknowingly rely on compromised data, allowing cybercriminals to exploit systemic blind spots (Cowls et al., 2019).

Bias–Cybersecurity Convergence in Practice

Case Vignette 1: Cyber Disruption of Organ Allocation Infrastructure

Documented cyber incidents targeting centralized transplant coordination platforms illustrate how technical breaches can rapidly escalate into ethical crises. Attacks on healthcare allocation systems have exploited weak authentication mechanisms and insufficient segmentation of critical databases, temporarily disrupting transplant operations and exposing sensitive donor–recipient information (Rasulova, 2025). Beyond immediate operational harm, the opacity of allocation algorithms limited institutional capacity to retrospectively audit prioritization decisions during system outages, thereby heightening the risk of illicit manipulation and data misuse.

Case Vignette 2: Digital Vulnerability in Low-Resource Healthcare Systems

In many African and other Global South healthcare contexts, rapid digitalization has outpaced the development of robust cybersecurity and ethical governance frameworks. Studies on e-health deployment indicate that donor registries and hospital information systems often operate with minimal encryption, outdated access protocols, and limited staff training in cyber hygiene (Kshetri, 2021). These vulnerabilities, when combined with biased AI models trained predominantly on Western datasets, create environments where marginalized populations face heightened exposure to exploitation, coercion, and data abuse linked to illicit organ markets.

Implications for Patient Rights and Equity

The persistence of algorithmic bias threatens foundational principles of patient autonomy, beneficence, and justice in healthcare. Biased algorithms can lead to differential treatment outcomes, unequal access to life-saving procedures, and potential violations of privacy through discriminatory data handling practices. This erosion of fairness challenges the ethical legitimacy of AI-assisted decision-making, particularly in resource-sensitive contexts like organ transplantation where every decision may determine life or death. From a legal standpoint, patients affected by algorithmic discrimination face limited recourse, as AI decision processes are often opaque or shielded under proprietary protections. Ethically, this opacity undermines informed consent patients cannot meaningfully consent to being assessed by systems whose internal logic they cannot interrogate. Addressing these challenges demands an equity-centered AI development approach that prioritizes transparency, diversity in training data, and inclusive governance frameworks that protect patient rights across socioeconomic and cultural boundaries (Floridi 2023). Addressing these vulnerabilities demands a multi-layered approach that fuses technical and ethical safeguards. Solutions such as federated learning enable collaborative model training without exposing raw data, while blockchain-based audit trails enhance transparency and traceability (Raimo et al., 2023).

Similarly, differential privacy techniques protect individual identities during data processing without compromising analytical accuracy. Yet, technology alone cannot ensure integrity; it must be accompanied by governance structures that enforce accountability, such as institutional ethics committees and cybersecurity oversight frameworks (Mühlhoff, 2025). In this sense, cybersecurity in AI-driven healthcare is not merely a technical obligation but a moral one anchored in the commitment to protect patient welfare, ensure justice, and prevent the exploitation of digital infrastructures by illicit organ trafficking networks. Therefore, understanding and mitigating algorithmic bias is integral to creating a healthcare ecosystem that honors human dignity, social justice, and digital trust in the age of intelligent medicine.

Algorithmic Bias and Cybersecurity as Interlinked Vulnerabilities

Algorithmic bias and cybersecurity vulnerabilities are frequently addressed as separate risk domains in AI-enabled healthcare systems; however, contemporary scholarship increasingly recognizes them as mutually reinforcing socio-technical failures (Mehrabi et al., 2021; Floridi, 2023). Algorithmic bias typically originates from skewed or incomplete datasets, opaque model architectures, and context-insensitive design assumptions, while cybersecurity vulnerabilities arise from weak access controls, fragmented governance, and inadequate protection of digital health infrastructures (Jobin et al., 2019; Kshetri, 2021). When these weaknesses intersect, they create structural openings that can be exploited by organized criminal networks, including organ trafficking syndicates operating across digital, institutional, and transnational spaces.

In healthcare systems where AI tools are deployed for donor matching, transplant prioritization, and logistical coordination, biased algorithms may systematically disadvantage already marginalized populations, rendering their data either invisible or insufficiently safeguarded. Research on health AI in low-resource environments demonstrates that such systems often underrepresent Global South populations, reinforcing inequitable clinical decision-making while simultaneously weakening data governance (Okoye et al., 2025; Mühlhoff, 2025). These same structural inequities frequently coincide with underfunded cybersecurity infrastructures, thereby amplifying exposure to data breaches, identity manipulation, and unauthorized system access. Cyberattacks such as ransomware, phishing campaigns, and insider-assisted breaches tend to exploit precisely these algorithmic and infrastructural asymmetries. Where AI systems lack transparency and explainability, adversarial interventions can remain concealed within routine operational workflows, particularly when malicious activities mimic legitimate clinical or administrative behavior. In this sense, cybersecurity failures do not merely threaten system availability; they actively reinforce algorithmic bias by obscuring accountability pathways and limiting institutional capacity for ethical audit and redress (Floridi, 2023).

ETHICAL AI GOVERNANCE IN HEALTHCARE

Principles: Fairness, Accountability, Transparency, and Explainability

Ethical AI governance in healthcare rests on the foundational pillars of **fairness, accountability,** transparency, and explainability (FATE). These principles serve as moral and operational compasses ensuring that technology aligns with public values and patient welfare. Fairness demands that AI models do not perpetuate historical discrimination or exclude vulnerable populations. Accountability ensures that both developers and institutions remain answerable for algorithmic decisions and their consequences. Transparency mandates clarity about how AI systems process data and arrive at decisions, while explainability emphasizes the need for outputs to be interpretable by healthcare professionals and understandable to patients (Jobin, et al., 2019).

Accountability further strengthens ethical AI governance by clarifying who is responsible when AI systems fail or produce biased outcomes. Mehrabi et al. (2021) argue that accountability must extend across the entire AI ecosystem starting from developers and data scientists to healthcare administrators and policymakers. Institutions that implement organ-matching systems, for instance, bear ethical and legal responsibility for ensuring compliance with fairness principles, data protection regulations, and cybersecurity protocols. A lack of accountability can enable negligence or malpractice, especially when cross-border data flows and transnational organ transplant networks are involved (Tjoa & Guan, 2023). Embedding accountability into AI governance requires continuous auditing, algorithmic impact assessments, and compliance with international standards such as the GDPR and WHO's ethical guidelines on organ transplantation.

Additionally, explainability which implies the ability to interpret and communicate how AI reaches its conclusions is central to ethical governance. Arrieta et al. (2020) highlight that explainable AI (XAI) enhances trust and facilitates ethical scrutiny, particularly in high-stakes decisions such as organ allocation. By making AI reasoning processes interpretable, healthcare providers can detect bias, validate fairness, and ensure alignment with clinical expertise. Yet, as Elemento et al., (2021) cautions, explainability is not merely a technical requirement but an ethical obligation that supports informed consent and human autonomy. To operationalize these ideals, healthcare organizations must adopt ethics-by-design frameworks that embed fairness, privacy, and accountability from system conception through implementation. Furthermore, participatory governance that includes patients, ethicists, and civil society actors ensures inclusivity and contextual relevance (Whittlestone et al., 2019). In this way, ethical governance transforms AI from a potential risk into a vehicle for propagating equity, resilience, and human dignity particularly in the global fight against organ trafficking.

When these principles are ignored, the risk of "black-box medicine" emerges; a phenomenon which describes a situation where diagnostic or predictive models provide decisions without traceable rationale. Such opacity not only erodes patient trust but also complicates clinical validation and legal responsibility. Integrating FATE into healthcare AI frameworks transforms these technologies from mere computational tools into ethical actors that respect the sanctity of life and uphold medical integrity. Thus, governance mechanisms must embed FATE principles throughout the AI lifecycle, from conceptual design and data collection to system deployment and monitoring (Mühlhoff, 2025).

In practice, ensuring these principles requires multidisciplinary collaboration involving clinicians, ethicists, data scientists, policymakers, and patient representatives. When the gap(s) between technical expertise and moral responsibility is bridged, healthcare institutions can move toward what scholars term "responsible AI" systems that are not only intelligent but also just, humane, and transparent in their operation (Tjoa & Guan, 2023).

Operationalizing FATE in Low-Resource Healthcare Contexts

Operationalizing the FATE principles; Fairness, Accountability, Transparency, and Explainability within low-resource healthcare systems requires context-sensitive, scalable strategies rather than resource-intensive solutions designed for high-income environments (Jobin et al., 2019; Floridi, 2023). Practical mechanisms include:

- **Open-source Explainable AI (XAI) tools**: Lightweight, open-source XAI libraries enable healthcare institutions to audit model decisions without prohibitive licensing costs, improving transparency in donor matching and prioritization processes (Arrieta et al., 2020).
- **Simplified algorithmic audit protocols**: Periodic bias audits using small representative samples can identify systematic exclusions even in settings with limited computational capacity (Mehrabi et al., 2021).
- **Community-based oversight boards**: Involving civil society representatives, ethicists, and patient advocates introduces localized accountability and contextual knowledge into AI governance structures (Okoye et al., 2025).
- **Policy sandboxes**: Regulatory sandboxes allow experimentation with ethical AI tools under controlled conditions, supporting innovation while minimizing harm (OECD, 2022).

- **Scalable identity verification mechanisms**: Privacy-preserving biometric or token-based systems can reduce identity fraud in donor registries without extensive infrastructure investment.

Together, these strategies demonstrate that FATE principles are not aspirational ideals but operational imperatives adaptable to constrained healthcare environments.

CYBERSECURITY THREATS AND DATA INTEGRITY IN AI-DRIVEN HEALTHCARE SYSTEMS

The integration of AI into healthcare introduces a new dimension of cybersecurity risk, particularly concerning data integrity and trust. AI systems rely heavily on extensive datasets containing confidential clinical, genetic, and biometric information (Lei et al., 2025). These systems, if inadequately protected, become attractive targets for malicious actors seeking to exploit vulnerabilities for financial gain or criminal intent. Cyberattacks such as ransomware, data breaches, or model poisoning can have far-reaching consequences. For instance, manipulated AI models might alter donor-recipient matching criteria, allowing unauthorized individuals to receive transplants or obscuring links to organ trafficking networks (Bawa et al., 2024). Such attacks do not merely disrupt operations; they undermine ethical commitments to transparency and justice, eroding patient trust and institutional credibility.

Emerging threats like adversarial attacks where input data are intentionally modified to mislead AI models further complicate healthcare cybersecurity. Finlayson et al. (2019) demonstrated that even minimal alterations to medical images can cause diagnostic algorithms to misclassify diseases, raising concerns for automated decision systems. In organ transplantation, such manipulation could alter organ compatibility assessments or waitlist rankings, effectively weaponizing AI systems against their intended humanitarian purpose. Moreover, the lack of data provenance verification ensuring that medical data are authentic and unaltered poses additional risks to the ethical use of AI in healthcare. Without reliable provenance, hospitals may unknowingly rely on compromised data, allowing cybercriminals to exploit systemic blind spots (Cowls et al., 2019).

Addressing these vulnerabilities demands a multi-layered approach that fuses technical and ethical safeguards. Solutions such as federated learning enable collaborative model training without exposing raw data, while blockchain-based audit trails enhance transparency and traceability (Raimo et al., 2023). Similarly, differential privacy techniques protect individual identities during data processing without compromising analytical accuracy. Yet, technology alone cannot ensure integrity; it must be accompanied by governance structures that enforce accountability, such as institutional ethics committees and cybersecurity oversight frameworks (Mittelstadt, 2022). In this sense, cybersecurity in AI-driven healthcare is not merely a technical obligation but a moral one anchored in the commitment to protect patient welfare, ensure justice, and prevent the exploitation of digital infrastructures by illicit organ trafficking networks.

Culturally Contextual AI Design

Ethical AI governance must also consider the cultural context within which healthcare systems operate. The ethical values embedded in Western bioethics autonomy, beneficence, non-maleficence, and justice though universal in aspiration, may not fully align with the communitarian ethics prevalent in African, Asian, or indigenous societies, where collective welfare often outweighs individual preference. Hence, an ethically governed AI system must be culturally sensitive, reflecting the moral traditions, healthcare practices, and social priorities of the population it serves (Nkwo et al., 2025).

In African healthcare settings, for instance, decision-making about organ donation or end-of-life care often involves family and community elders, rather than the individual alone. AI systems designed without attention to these norms risk misalignment with local ethical realities, producing friction between digital recommendations and cultural expectations. Embedding cultural awareness into AI models means incorporating locally relevant datasets, linguistic diversity, and social insights into algorithmic training and governance frameworks. Furthermore, cultural contextualization aids in preventing digital neo-colonialism which usually takes the form of the imposition of foreign technological values and priorities onto local health infrastructures. By developing regionally adapted ethical standards and participatory governance structures, healthcare AI can become not only technically efficient but also morally legitimate and socially embraced across diverse communities (Abebe et al., 2021).

Role of Human Oversight in Decision-Making

Even the most sophisticated AI systems must not operate autonomously in clinical or ethical vacuums. Human oversight remains a non-negotiable pillar of ethical AI governance in healthcare. This oversight ensures that algorithmic recommendations are continuously reviewed, contextualized, and validated within the framework of professional judgment and patient-centered ethics. According to Amann et al. (2020), human-in-the-loop mechanisms prevent automation bias and the overreliance on AI outputs by reasserting the clinician's critical role as a moral and interpretive agent in medical decision-making.

In organ transplantation systems, for example, AI may optimize donor-recipient matching based on medical parameters, but only human professionals can assess the broader ethical dimensions such as familial consent, socio-cultural implications, and emotional readiness. Human oversight also functions as a fail-safe mechanism to detect errors, adapt to unforeseen ethical dilemmas, and uphold accountability when decisions carry life-or-death consequences. Thus, governance frameworks must institutionalize oversight committees and audit mechanisms that integrate AI ethics boards, data stewards, and medical practitioners in a shared accountability model. This layered governance architecture transforms AI from a potentially disruptive force into a collaborative partner, ensuring that technology amplifies rather than replaces the ethical reasoning central to humane healthcare delivery.

CYBERSECURITY AND ORGAN TRAFFICKING PREVENTION

The digital transformation of healthcare, though revolutionary in promoting accessibility and efficiency, has unintentionally opened new frontiers for organized cybercrime, particularly in the domain of organ trafficking. As health systems become increasingly interconnected, criminal syndicates exploit digital infrastructures such as electronic health records (EHRs), telemedicine platforms, and organ transplant databases to facilitate illicit transactions. Interpol (2022) as cited in Rasulova (2025), warns that sophisticated trafficking networks now integrate digital strategies from database infiltration to social engineering to manipulate organ donation systems across borders. These actors no longer rely solely on physical coercion; rather, they weaponize data, forging digital donor identities or falsifying medical histories to legitimize illegal transplants. In several Southeast Asian and Eastern European cases, traffickers have used compromised hospital systems to insert falsified entries into donor registries, masking black-market organs as legitimate donations (Europol, 2023 cited in Wahl, 2024). Such digital manipulation blurs the line between lawful and illicit medical practice, complicating ethical oversight and jurisdictional enforcement.

Another major vulnerability lies in predictive analytics and AI-enabled matching systems, which are increasingly employed to streamline donor-recipient pairing. While these algorithms optimize efficiency, they also create opportunities for exploitation when infiltrated by malicious agents. Kshetri (2021) notes that cybercriminals have begun targeting transplant databases to reroute donor priorities or falsify matching outcomes, granting privileged access to wealthy recipients or private brokers. In some reported cases, insiders within healthcare institutions have been bribed to alter algorithmic outcomes or disclose upcoming organ availability data. When combined with anonymized payment systems such as cryptocurrency and decentralized finance platforms, these activities form a digital supply chain of organ trafficking, where every stage from donor identification to post-operative logistics is digitally mediated. The result is an ecosystem where illicit organ trade thrives under the guise of technological legitimacy, making traditional investigative methods largely obsolete.

The dark web plays a particularly insidious role in this digital evolution of organ trafficking. Encrypted communication platforms like Tor, I2P, and peer-to-peer exchanges have become marketplaces for human organs, allowing traffickers to advertise organs, negotiate prices, and arrange logistics with near-total anonymity (Rawat et al., 2022). Listings often use euphemistic language such as "medical tissue" or "living donor services" to evade automated detection systems. These markets are sustained by networks of unethical intermediaries, some posing as medical tourism facilitators or data brokers. Beyond the sale of organs, there are reports of cyber-enabled organ scams, where fake crowdfunding campaigns solicit funds for non-existent surgeries using falsified patient records obtained through data breaches (Durand et al., 2018). Such activities not only exploit vulnerable populations but also erode the public's confidence in legitimate healthcare crowdfunding and data sharing initiatives, amplifying societal distrust in digital health systems.

The globalization of healthcare supply chains adds another layer of complexity. Cross-border data flows which are necessary for global organ sharing initiatives, create transnational vulnerabilities that traffickers readily exploit. For instance, when donor registries from multiple countries are integrated through shared platforms, weak cybersecurity in one participating nation can become a gateway for infiltration across the network (Mogaji & Nguyen, 2022). The situation is further exacerbated in developing countries where cybersecurity standards and digital literacy among healthcare workers remain low. These regions often become data conduits and experimental grounds for traffickers seeking to exploit regulatory blind spots (UNODC, 2023). Compromised transplant scheduling systems in some African and South Asian hospitals have been used to divert legitimate organs to unauthorized recipients abroad, highlighting how structural inequities in digital governance intersect with global medical ethics.

Beyond external hacking, the human element of insider compromise remains a persistent threat. Cybercriminal groups often recruit healthcare employees with access privileges to extract, alter, or sell sensitive data. Insider-assisted crimes are difficult to detect because they occur within legitimate user frameworks and operational routines. Anderson et al., (2022) observe that some organ trafficking operations have succeeded not through high-level cyberattacks but through low-tech social engineering tactics exploiting underpaid or disgruntled hospital staff to manipulate system entries. The problem intensifies when combined with the deployment of

AI-powered surveillance systems that themselves lack transparency; these systems can be reprogrammed to mask illicit activity or delete audit trails. Without robust ethical governance, digital transformation becomes a double-edged sword: while it enhances coordination and efficiency, it simultaneously enables a silent digital underworld where data breaches translate directly into human exploitation.

As a whole, these vulnerabilities reveal that organ trafficking in the digital era is not merely a criminal or medical problem but a systemic cybersecurity and ethical governance crisis. The same infrastructures designed to safeguard lives are now being hijacked to commodify them. Unless healthcare institutions adopt bias-aware, ethically governed AI systems, fortified by encryption, behavioral analytics, and transparent oversight, they risk becoming conduits for human rights violations. As Floridi (2023) argues, technological progress without ethical integration invites digital tyranny where algorithms and networks can be co-opted for exploitation. Thus, combating organ trafficking in the digital age demands more than reactive cyber defense; it requires a human-centered cybersecurity paradigm grounded in moral accountability, international collaboration, and digital justice.

Risks in Donor Databases, Telehealth Platforms, and Predictive Analytics

The integration of donor databases into centralized e-health systems has transformed the management of organ transplantation worldwide, but it has also exposed deeply embedded vulnerabilities. Modern donor databases store massive amounts of sensitive data, including biometric information, medical histories, and identity records. When these systems are inadequately protected, they become prime targets for cyberattacks. A 2022 *Health IT Security* report revealed that over 30 million patient records were exposed globally through ransomware attacks targeting hospital networks and transplant registries. These breaches do not simply risk identity theft they facilitate organ trafficking by allowing criminals to map out potential donors and falsify their medical eligibility (Kshetri & Voas, 2021). In some documented cases, traffickers exploited stolen credentials to create synthetic donor identities or manipulate data to redirect legitimate organs toward illicit buyers. The commodification of medical data thus becomes both a technical and moral crisis, challenging the integrity of health institutions.

The expansion of telehealth platforms has introduced new opportunities for healthcare accessibility but simultaneously broadened the cyberattack surface. Telemedicine's reliance on cloud-based architectures and cross-platform data sharing allows unauthorized access if encryption protocols are weak or authentication systems are compromised. According to O'Donoghue et al. (2022), unregulated teleconsultation platforms especially in developing regions often lack compliance with international data protection frameworks such as GDPR or HIPAA. Criminal organizations exploit these gaps to harvest patient data during virtual consultations or to masquerade as legitimate medical professionals offering organ transplant "advice." These impersonation scams not only deceive vulnerable patients but also launder illicit activities under the guise of telemedical care. The convergence of social engineering and healthcare technology, therefore, turns telehealth into an inadvertent facilitator of cyber-enabled trafficking.

Predictive analytics and AI-driven health algorithms, while revolutionary in resource optimization, also introduce algorithmic and ethical risks. Predictive models designed to forecast donor-recipient matches can be manipulated through data poisoning, bias injection, or model inversion attacks. Zhang et al. (2025) observe that adversarial actors can subtly alter input variables to influence matching outcomes ensuring that certain recipients gain undue priority. These manipulations often go unnoticed due to the opacity of AI models ("black box problem"), allowing traffickers to distort allocation systems without immediate detection. Furthermore, some predictive platforms use datasets aggregated from multiple hospitals and nations, increasing the risk of cross-border data leakage. Without explainable AI mechanisms and continuous auditing, healthcare institutions risk embedding criminal manipulation directly into automated decision pipelines.

The interconnectivity between donor databases, telehealth systems, and AI analytics creates what cybersecurity experts describe as a "compound vulnerability zone." A single breach in any of these interconnected systems can trigger cascading effects across the healthcare ecosystem (Zhang et al., 2025). For example, if a donor's information in one registry is compromised, that same data synchronized through cloud APIs may automatically update in hospital and insurance records across multiple jurisdictions. Criminal networks exploit such interconnectivity to trace donors' movements, identities, and health progress, effectively surveilling potential victims digitally. In low-resource countries where interoperability standards are poorly enforced, these vulnerabilities are magnified. Many hospitals rely on outdated legacy systems, weak firewalls, and untrained IT staff, leaving them particularly exposed to exploitation by well-funded trafficking syndicates operating from abroad (UNODC, 2024).

Another emerging risk involves the commercialization of health data through third-party partnerships and digital marketplaces. Healthcare organizations increasingly outsource data analytics, storage, and system integration to private vendors who may not adhere to stringent cybersecurity protocols. When these third parties sell anonymized data to research firms or pharmaceutical companies, de-anonymization attacks can re-identify donor or recipient profiles (Zhang et al., 2025). Once re-identified, such individuals become potential targets for coercion or fraudulent medical schemes. The ethical dilemma here is profound: the same data intended to save lives may, through negligent governance, enable exploitation. Hence, the protection of donor databases, telehealth platforms, and predictive analytics systems must transcend technical security, it requires a holistic governance model that combines data ethics, human rights, and algorithmic accountability.

Co-Creating Cybersecurity Value Through AI Ethics

Combating the intersection of organ trafficking and digital vulnerability requires a co-creative and ethically anchored approach, one that unites artificial intelligence design with cybersecurity governance in an ecosystem of shared accountability. Traditional cybersecurity strategies often prioritize technical fortification firewalls, encryption, and access controls without addressing the moral architecture underpinning these systems. However, the complexity of organ trafficking networks, which exploit digital health infrastructures, demands a shift toward value-driven security where ethical reasoning becomes integral to technical resilience. As Floridi (2023) observes, digital ethics is not an adjunct to cybersecurity but a prerequisite for it. Embedding principles such as fairness, transparency, and accountability into AI models ensures that healthcare technologies do not merely detect threats but also uphold the rights and dignity of all system users. In this sense, cybersecurity evolves from a reactive defense mechanism into a proactive ethical practice that safeguards both data integrity and human life.

Ethical AI principles can be concretely operationalized to strengthen cybersecurity within healthcare ecosystems. Accountability mechanisms, for instance, require that every AI-driven decision whether in donor matching, anomaly detection, or access authorization be traceable and justifiable (Jobin et al., 2019). This traceability not only enhances transparency but also discourages unethical data manipulation that could facilitate organ trafficking. Explainability, another cornerstone of ethical AI, can empower human analysts to interpret complex AI outputs, especially in intrusion detection systems that identify subtle deviations mimicking legitimate clinical workflows. When human experts understand why an algorithm flags a transaction or database access as suspicious, they are better equipped to respond effectively and ethically. As Voas and Ksheri (2020) notes, explainability transforms AI from a "black box of automation" into a co-intelligent partner that supports moral and informed decision-making in high-stakes domains like healthcare cybersecurity.

The concept of co-creation redefines how cybersecurity value is generated and distributed within the healthcare sector. It moves beyond linear governance models to emphasize participatory collaboration among diverse stakeholders AI developers, healthcare administrators, cybersecurity specialists, ethicists, policymakers, and patient advocates. Each actor contributes distinct forms of knowledge and ethical intuition that, when synthesized, yield holistic digital resilience (Cheng et al., 2024). In this collaborative model, system design is guided by interdisciplinary dialogue rather than unilateral technical decisions. For example, patient representatives can help identify privacy risks overlooked by engineers, while legal practitioners ensure compliance with data protection laws such as GDPR or HIPAA. The result is a cybersecurity ecosystem rooted in shared moral agency, where every stakeholder not only benefits from digital trust but also bears responsibility for sustaining it.

Moreover, the fusion of AI ethics and threat intelligence is revolutionizing how health systems anticipate and neutralize cyber risks. Modern AI-driven security frameworks can be trained using ethical parameters such as harm minimization, proportional response, and data minimalism. These principles guide the system to detect potential harms not merely in terms of technical breaches but also moral consequences such as the exploitation of donor records or the manipulation of transplant waiting lists. As argued by Voas and Kshetri (2021), ethical machine learning models can predict not only attack vectors but also the socio-technical pathways through which healthcare data could be commodified by trafficking networks. This represents a paradigm shift in cybersecurity thinking: from protecting systems in isolation to defending the ethical fabric of digital health ecosystems. When cybersecurity infrastructures are informed by moral reasoning, they transcend mere compliance and become instruments of justice.

At its core, co-creating cybersecurity value through AI ethics is about constructing a digital moral order where technology serves humanity rather than undermines it. Addressing organ trafficking in the digital era requires more than advanced encryption and sophisticated monitoring tools it demands an ethical consciousness embedded into every line of code, every policy framework, and every institutional workflow. By cultivating this consciousness, healthcare systems move closer to what Mühlhoff (2025) calls "ethical robustness" a state where technological innovation and human values reinforce each other. In practice, this means that AI systems must be designed to prioritize human welfare, anticipate social consequences, and respond with moral intelligence to emerging threats. The convergence of cybersecurity and AI ethics thus becomes a strategic imperative for global healthcare: safeguarding not just data, but dignity; not just systems, but lives.

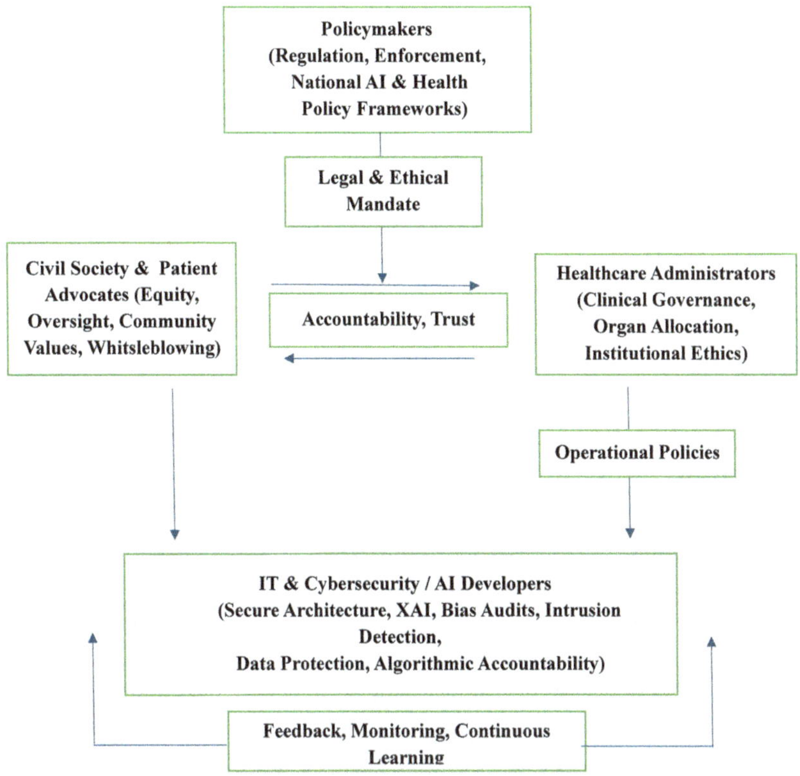

Figure 1 illustrates a co-creation framework for ethical AI governance and cybersecurity resilience in organ transplantation systems. The framework positions healthcare administrators, IT and cybersecurity professionals, policymakers, and civil society actors as interdependent stakeholders whose coordinated actions mitigate algorithmic bias, digital vulnerability, and organ trafficking risks. Ethical principles; fairness, accountability, transparency, and explainability (FATE) are operationalized through institutional governance, secure technical infrastructures, regulatory oversight, and community-based accountability. The model emphasizes continuous feedback, cultural contextualization, and human dignity as core pillars of trustworthy AI-enabled healthcare systems.

CASE STUDIES AND BEST PRACTICES

Bias in Allocation Algorithms (e.g., U.S. and Global Transplant Systems)

The promise of artificial intelligence in organ allocation lies in its potential to ensure fairness, optimize matching efficiency, and reduce waiting times. Yet, real-world deployments reveal persistent algorithmic biases that undermine these ideals. For example, in the United States, the organ allocation algorithm historically favored patients located closer to transplant centers, inadvertently disadvantaging rural and minority populations (Boyarsky, 2021). When the United Network for Organ Sharing (UNOS) integrated machine learning models to improve equity, concerns emerged about training data imbalances datasets over-represented by certain ethnic groups, healthcare providers, or socioeconomic backgrounds (Bawa et al., 2024). These imbalances, though computationally invisible, translated into systemic disadvantages for patients from underrepresented communities, thus demonstrating how seemingly neutral code can encode social inequalities.

Globally, similar challenges persist. In countries where data infrastructures are fragmented or incomplete, algorithmic systems often rely on proxy variables such as geographic proximity, blood group availability, or income-level indicators to make allocation decisions. These proxies, while operationally useful, can amplify structural inequalities by prioritizing recipients in urban or high-income regions (Bawa et al., 2024). Furthermore, AI-based risk prediction tools sometimes penalize patients with complex medical histories, reducing their chances of transplant eligibility based on actuarial survival models rather than holistic medical judgment. Such digital stratification undermines ethical principles of distributive justice, calling for transparent algorithmic auditing mechanisms to ensure that fairness is embedded at every computational layer.

However, emerging reforms provide a blueprint for mitigation. The U.S. Organ Procurement and Transplantation Network (OPTN) has initiated a Bias Review Board to examine AI-driven allocation outcomes, while several European transplant registries have begun employing counterfactual testing, assessing whether algorithmic recommendations differ when sensitive attributes such as race or income are neutralized (de Laat, 2021). These practices illustrate that bias correction in organ allocation is not a one-time fix but a continuous governance process, requiring both technological recalibration and ethical accountability.

Cyber-Attacks on Health Infrastructures

Healthcare systems are now among the most targeted sectors for cyber-attacks, with profound implications for organ transplantation. A 2021 report by IBM Security revealed that ransomware attacks on hospitals increased by over 35% globally, disrupting critical operations such as transplant scheduling, donor verification, and patient monitoring. In 2022, the University of Vermont Medical Center experienced a crippling cyber-attack that paralyzed its organ transplant coordination system for several weeks, delaying surgeries and jeopardizing patient lives. These incidents expose the fragility of interconnected health systems where a single data breach can cascade into a national public health emergency.

The motivations behind these attacks are diverse. Some are purely financial, targeting hospitals for ransom payments, while others serve as entry points for data exfiltration and organ trafficking coordination (Rawat et al., 2022). Attackers may extract sensitive medical records to identify organ donors, manipulate electronic health records (EHRs), or sell stolen data on the dark web to illicit networks. In countries with weaker cybersecurity frameworks, these breaches often go undetected for months, providing ample time for traffickers to exploit systemic vulnerabilities. Beyond financial loss, such intrusions erode public confidence in healthcare institutions, fueling fears of surveillance, exploitation, and ethical violations.

Nevertheless, best practices are emerging across jurisdictions. The integration of zero-trust architectures, biometric multi-factor authentication, and blockchain-based data validation have shown promise in restoring digital integrity within healthcare ecosystems (Sittig & Singh, 2022). Additionally, proactive ethical audits of AI-driven cybersecurity systems ensure that defensive technologies respect privacy while identifying patterns indicative of illicit organ trade. These examples demonstrate that cybersecurity in healthcare transcends technical safeguards; it is a moral obligation tied to the sanctity of human life and the ethical deployment of digital systems.

Lessons from AI Ethics Frameworks

Global AI ethics frameworks provide essential guidance for balancing technological innovation with human-centered values in healthcare cybersecurity. The OECD AI Principles (2019) and the UNESCO Recommendation on the Ethics of Artificial Intelligence (2021) emphasize fairness, transparency, and accountability as foundational principles. These frameworks advocate for context-sensitive ethics, recognizing that what constitutes "fairness" or "bias" may differ across cultures and healthcare systems. Within organ transplantation, this means that algorithmic models must not only be mathematically fair but also socially interpretable able to justify decisions in ways that align with local cultural, moral, and legal expectations (Cowls et al., 2019).

Furthermore, the European Union's AI Act (2023) cited in Gstrein et al. (2024) classifies AI systems used in healthcare as "high-risk," mandating stringent requirements for human oversight, risk management, and algorithmic explainability. This regulatory model offers valuable insights for transplant governance, suggesting that every automated allocation or predictive tool must undergo ethical certification before clinical deployment. By institutionalizing explainability, the EU framework shifts AI ethics from abstract principles to enforceable standards, ensuring that human dignity remains at the center of algorithmic decision-making. At a more operational level, best practices emphasize cross-sectoral collaboration integrating perspectives from ethicists, technologists, legal experts, and civil society organizations. Successful implementation of these ethics frameworks relies on continuous stakeholder dialogue and ethnographic evaluation of algorithmic impacts in real-world hospital settings. In this way, AI ethics becomes a living practice, not merely a compliance checklist. By translating these global frameworks into actionable local protocols, healthcare systems can cultivate digital environments that are both secure and morally grounded an essential defense against the exploitative forces of organ trafficking.

Bias and Cybersecurity as Mutually Reinforcing Risks

Taken together, algorithmic bias and cybersecurity failures constitute mutually reinforcing risks within AI-enabled healthcare systems. Bias shapes which populations are rendered visible, valued, or protected within algorithmic decision-making, while cybersecurity weaknesses determine how easily these systems can be infiltrated, manipulated, or repurposed for criminal ends (Mehrabi et al., 2021; Floridi, 2023). Addressing either dimension in isolation is therefore insufficient; only an integrated ethical–cybersecurity governance approach can disrupt the digital infrastructures that enable organ trafficking and related forms of biomedical exploitation.

POLICY AND PRACTICAL RECOMMENDATIONS

Regulatory Frameworks for Ethical AI in Healthcare

The ethical governance of AI in healthcare cybersecurity requires robust regulatory frameworks that balance innovation with accountability. Global instruments such as the General Data Protection Regulation (GDPR) and the Health Insurance Portability and Accountability Act (HIPAA) have laid foundational principles for patient data privacy and consent management. However, these regulations alone are insufficient to address the complex interplay between AI ethics, cybersecurity, and organ trafficking prevention. Scholars such as Kshetri (2021) argue that regulations must evolve from reactive compliance tools into proactive mechanisms that shape how AI systems are designed and deployed. This shift implies embedding ethical evaluation fairness audits, bias assessments, and explainability reviews within the legal approval process for medical AI systems.

At the international level, frameworks like the WHO Guiding Principles on Human Cell, Tissue and Organ Transplantation provide normative anchors emphasizing transparency, traceability, and non-commercialization of human organs. Integrating these principles with AI-specific ethical standards can ensure that digital transplant systems operate with integrity and respect for human dignity. For instance, AI systems that support donor-recipient matching should be subjected to algorithmic traceability requirements, enabling regulators to track how each decision is derived and whether any ethical thresholds are breached. This form of "ethical traceability" aligns with the broader notion of responsible innovation ensuring that technology development is guided by societal values rather than mere technical performance (Stahl & Wright, 2018).

Furthermore, national governments must develop context-specific AI ethics policies that reflect local cultural and infrastructural realities. In many low- and middle-income countries, where data infrastructure and cybersecurity capacity remain limited, adopting blanket foreign frameworks may prove counterproductive. Instead, adaptive regulation combining global ethical norms with localized enforcement models will ensure inclusivity and cultural relevance. Ultimately, ethical AI governance in healthcare must transcend jurisdictional boundaries, forming a transnational alliance against digital exploitation and organ trafficking.

Strategies for Bias Mitigation in Organ Transplantation Systems

Addressing algorithmic bias in organ transplantation systems requires interventions across the entire AI lifecycle from data collection to deployment and feedback evaluation. At the data level, healthcare institutions should implement representative dataset protocols, ensuring that training data reflect diverse populations across ethnicity, gender, socioeconomic background, and medical history. As Buolamwini and Gebru (2018) note, dataset diversity is the most direct antidote to model bias. Periodic audits using fairness metrics such as demographic parity or equalized odds can identify whether algorithmic outcomes systematically favor particular groups. These quantitative assessments should be complemented by qualitative oversight, including ethics board reviews and participatory evaluation involving patient advocacy groups.

During system design and implementation, AI models should incorporate bias correction algorithms and counterfactual testing, allowing developers to simulate alternative scenarios to detect hidden discriminatory patterns. Transparent documentation including model cards and data sheets for datasets (Stahl & Wright, 2018) provides stakeholders with visibility into how systems are built, what assumptions underlie their predictions, and where vulnerabilities might exist. This transparency fosters accountability and ensures that medical practitioners, rather than opaque algorithms, remain the ultimate arbiters in life-and-death decisions like organ allocation. At the institutional level, bias mitigation should be integrated into the organizational culture of healthcare governance. Regular capacity-building workshops for AI developers, clinicians, and data managers can enhance awareness of ethical risks. Hospitals and national transplant agencies must also establish Ethical AI Oversight Committees, tasked with reviewing model updates and monitoring decision impacts over time. By institutionalizing ethical reflexivity, healthcare organizations not only minimize bias but also reinforce public trust an essential element in the broader cybersecurity landscape of organ transplantation.

Collaboration Between Healthcare Administrators, IT Managers, Policymakers, and Civil Society

The fight against organ trafficking in the digital era demands an integrated, multisectoral approach anchored in ethical AI governance and collaborative cybersecurity frameworks. No single stakeholder can address the complex interplay between data protection, medical ethics, and transnational criminality in isolation. Healthcare administrators, IT managers, policymakers, and civil society organizations must form a distributed governance network that operates with shared accountability. According to Cheng et al., (2024), the future of healthcare cybersecurity lies in "ecosystem coordination" where institutional actors align operational practices with ethical, technical, and legal safeguards. This means that administrators must integrate ethical AI principles directly into the design of donor management workflows, ensuring that risk assessment, compliance monitoring, and crisis response mechanisms are not afterthoughts but core organizational functions. In many hospitals, this integration now includes real-time digital ethics boards that oversee algorithmic decisions in sensitive areas such as organ allocation.

Healthcare administrators are the custodians of institutional integrity and data governance. Their role extends beyond routine management into the realm of ethical leadership. Administrators must ensure that procurement systems, donor registries, and e-health portals adhere to cybersecurity standards such as ISO/IEC 27001 and

NIST frameworks. This requires routine risk audits, incident reporting protocols, and employee capacity-building in digital hygiene. In technologically advanced facilities, administrators collaborate with IT managers to deploy AI-driven anomaly detection systems that flag irregular access patterns or unauthorized data exports (Cheng et al., 2024). When multi-layered verification systems are created, healthcare institutions can significantly reduce the risk of insider manipulation one of the most common pathways exploited in organ trafficking networks. The emphasis, therefore, should not only be on defensive technologies but also on organizational culture, where cybersecurity is recognized as a collective ethical responsibility, not a technical burden.

IT managers and cybersecurity experts are pivotal in operationalizing these ethical commitments into actionable safeguards. Their mandate covers both the technological and human dimensions of security. They must design secure architectures using zero-trust frameworks, end-to-end encryption, and blockchain-enabled audit trails that prevent unauthorized alterations to organ allocation records (Voas & Kshetri, 2021). Furthermore, AI-powered predictive monitoring tools can analyze access logs and detect patterns suggestive of collusion or data tampering. However, technology alone cannot suffice; the success of these interventions depends on cross-training and communication between IT teams and clinical staff. When IT managers understand medical workflows and clinicians understand data sensitivity, institutions cultivate a cyber-aware healthcare culture capable of responding proactively to threats. The collaboration between these actors creates a dynamic defense system that adapts to emerging cyber risks without impeding medical efficiency or ethical transparency.

Policymakers serve as the crucial mediators between innovation, regulation, and justice. They must enact adaptive legal frameworks that reflect the evolving nature of digital health and transnational organ trafficking. According to Lei et al. (2025), multi-stakeholder policy forums including regulatory bodies, medical councils, AI developers, and data protection agencies enhance resilience by ensuring that technological innovations are harmonized with legal accountability. Public-private partnerships (PPPs) have proven effective in this regard; they leverage the agility and technical expertise of private firms while maintaining public oversight and ethical legitimacy. For instance, the European Union's *Cybersecurity Act (2019)* and similar models in South Korea and Singapore demonstrate how collaborative policymaking can build robust health data resilience while deterring cybercriminal operations. In the Nigerian and Sub-Saharan African context, embedding such frameworks within existing National Health ICT Policies would bridge the gap between technological modernization and ethical oversight, ensuring that global standards are contextualized to local realities.

Civil society organizations (CSOs) play an equally indispensable role in democratizing oversight and amplifying ethical accountability. As intermediaries between institutions and the public, CSOs ensure transparency in organ allocation, expose malpractice, and advocate for data protection rights. Their monitoring function complements state regulation, especially where enforcement capacity is limited. Through advocacy campaigns, community sensitization, and digital whistleblowing mechanisms, CSOs empower citizens to recognize and report unethical medical practices (Sittig et al., 2022). In some contexts, partnerships between CSOs and investigative journalists have uncovered underground transplant operations that relied on hacked donor databases and falsified e-health credentials. Beyond watchdog functions, civil society contributes to ethical literacy, helping the public understand how their health data is used and why consent and privacy matter. This participatory governance model transforms the fight against organ trafficking into a collective moral enterprise, not merely a bureaucratic or technical challenge.

In conclusion, the collaboration between healthcare administrators, IT managers, policymakers, and civil society must evolve into a values-driven governance ecosystem where technology, ethics, and human rights intersect. Each actor brings unique capacities administrators ensure operational integrity, IT managers enforce technological security, policymakers create legal and ethical frameworks, and civil society ensures transparency and justice. Together, they can dismantle the digital scaffolding that supports organ trafficking and construct resilient systems of trust, accountability, and equity. As Floridi (2023) argues, sustainable digital governance depends not merely on control but on co-created ethical intelligence a shared capacity for moral reflection embedded within every layer of decision-making. This is the foundation of a cybersecure, bias-aware healthcare future where the sanctity of human life transcends technological and institutional boundaries.

REFERENCES

Abebe, H., Shitu, S., Workye, H., & Mose, A. (2021). Predictors of stillbirth among women who had given birth in Southern Ethiopia, 2020: A case-control study. *PLoS One*, *16*(5), e0249865. DOI: 10.1371/journal.pone.0249865 PMID: 33939713

Amann, J., Blasimme, A., Vayena, E., Frey, D., & Madai, V. I. (2020). Explainability for artificial intelligence in healthcare: A multidisciplinary perspective. *BMC Medical Informatics and Decision Making*, *20*(1), 310. DOI: 10.1186/s12911-020-01332-6 PMID: 33256715

Anderson, V. R., Kulig, T. C., & Sullivan, C. J. (2022). Integrating human trafficking data: A case study of conceptual and operational variation in Ohio. *Journal of Human Trafficking*, *8*(3), 250–264. DOI: 10.1080/23322705.2020.1804782

Arrieta, A. B., Díaz-Rodríguez, N., Del Ser, J., Bennetot, A., Tabik, S., Barbado, A., & Herrera, F. (2020). Explainable Artificial Intelligence (XAI): Concepts, taxonomies, opportunities and challenges toward responsible AI. *Information Fusion*, *58*, 82–115. DOI: 10.1016/j.inffus.2019.12.012

Bawa, G., Singh, H., Rani, S., Kataria, A., & Min, H. (2024). Exploring perspectives of blockchain technology and traditional centralized technology in organ donation management: A comprehensive review. *Information (Basel)*, *15*(11), 703. DOI: 10.3390/info15110703

Baxter, G., & Sommerville, I. (2011). Socio-technical systems: From design methods to systems engineering. *Interacting with Computers*, *23*(1), 4–17. DOI: 10.1016/j.intcom.2010.07.003

Benaroch, M. (2020). Cybersecurity risk in IT outsourcing—Challenges and emerging realities. In *Information systems outsourcing: The era of digital transformation* (pp. 313–334). Springer International Publishing. DOI: 10.1007/978-3-030-45819-5_13

Boyarsky, B. (2021). *IMPACT OF COVID-19 ON SOLID ORGAN TRANSPLANTATION* (Doctoral dissertation, Johns Hopkins University).

Budiani-Saberi, D. A., & Delmonico, F. L. (2008). Organ trafficking and transplant tourism: A commentary on the global realities. *American Journal of Transplantation : Official Journal of the American Society of Transplantation and the American Society of Transplant Surgeons*, *8*(5), 925–929. DOI: 10.1111/j.1600-6143.2008.02200.x PMID: 18416734

Buolamwini, J., & Gebru, T. (2018, January). Gender shades: Intersectional accuracy disparities in commercial gender classification. In *Conference on fairness, accountability and transparency* (pp. 77-91). PMLR.

Cheng, Y., Zhang, C., Zhang, Z., Meng, X., Hong, S., Li, W., . . . He, X. (2024). Exploring large language model based intelligent agents: Definitions, methods, and prospects. *arXiv preprint arXiv:2401.03428.*

Cowls, J., King, T., Taddeo, M., & Floridi, L. (2019). Designing AI for social good: Seven essential factors. *Available at SSRN* 3388669. DOI: 10.2139/ssrn.3388669

Daniels, N., & Sabin, J. E. (2008). *Setting limits fairly: learning to share resources for health.* Oxford University Press.

de Laat, P. B. (2021). Companies committed to responsible AI: From principles towards implementation and regulation? *Philosophy & Technology*, *34*(4), 1135–1193. DOI: 10.1007/s13347-021-00474-3 PMID: 34631392

Durand, W. M., Peters, J. L., Eltorai, A. E. M., Kalagara, S., Osband, A. J., & Daniels, A. H. (2018). Medical crowdfunding for organ transplantation. *Clinical Transplantation*, *32*(6), e13267. DOI: 10.1111/ctr.13267 PMID: 29683220

Elemento, O., Leslie, C., Lundin, J., & Tourassi, G. (2021). Artificial intelligence in cancer research, diagnosis and therapy. *Nature Reviews. Cancer*, *21*(12), 747–752. DOI: 10.1038/s41568-021-00399-1 PMID: 34535775

Finlayson, S. G., Bowers, J. D., Ito, J., Zittrain, J. L., Beam, A. L., & Kohane, I. S. (2019). Adversarial attacks on medical machine learning. *Science*, *363*(6433), 1287–1289. DOI: 10.1126/science.aaw4399 PMID: 30898923

Floridi, L. (2023). The ethics of artificial intelligence: Principles, challenges, and opportunities.

Friedman, B., Kahn, P. H.Jr, Borning, A., & Huldtgren, A. (2013). Value sensitive design and information systems. In *Early engagement and new technologies: Opening up the laboratory* (pp. 55–95). Springer Netherlands. DOI: 10.1007/978-94-007-7844-3_4

Gilligan, C. (1982). The contribution of women's thought to developmental theory: The elimination of sex bias in moral development research and education.

Gstrein, O. J., Haleem, N., & Zwitter, A. (2024). General-purpose AI regulation and the European Union AI Act. *Internet Policy Review*, *13*(3), 1–26. DOI: 10.14763/2024.3.1790

Held, V. (2018). The ethics of care. *The Oxford handbook of distributive justice*, 213-234.

Jobin, A., Ienca, M., & Vayena, E. (2019). The global landscape of AI ethics guidelines. *Nature Machine Intelligence*, *1*(9), 389–399. DOI: 10.1038/s42256-019-0088-2

Johnson, J. (2024). *The AI commander: centaur teaming, command, and ethical dilemmas*. Oxford University Press. DOI: 10.1093/oso/9780198892182.001.0001

Kshetri, N. (2021). Evolving uses of artificial intelligence in human resource management in emerging economies in the global South: Some preliminary evidence. *Management Research Review*, *44*(7), 970–990. DOI: 10.1108/MRR-03-2020-0168

Lei, C., Dang, K., Song, S., Wang, Z., Chew, S. P., Bian, R., Yang, X., Guan, Z., Lopes, C. I. M. A., Wang, M. H., Choy, R. W. C., Hu, X., Lai, K. K. H., Chong, K. K. L., Pang, C. P., Song, X., Su, J., Ding, X., & Zhou, H. (2025). AI-assisted facial analysis in healthcare: From disease detection to comprehensive management. *Patterns (New York, N.Y.)*, *6*(2), 101175. DOI: 10.1016/j.patter.2025.101175 PMID: 40041850

MacIntyre, A. (2013). *After virtue*. A&C Black.

Mehrabi, N., Morstatter, F., Saxena, N., Lerman, K., & Galstyan, A. (2021). A survey on bias and fairness in machine learning. *ACM Computing Surveys*, *54*(6), 1–35. DOI: 10.1145/3457607

Mühlhoff, R. (2025). *The ethics of AI: Power, critique, responsibility*. Bristol University Press.

Nkwo, M., Ikwunne, T., Adejoro, C., & Anuyah, O. (2025). Exploring Usability of AI Systems in the Global South—Toward Responsible Human-Centered AI for Sustainable Cities and Communities. In *Usability for the World: Building Better Cities and Communities* (pp. 125–165). Springer Nature Switzerland. DOI: 10.1007/978-3-031-88326-2_5

Obermeyer, Z., Powers, B., Vogeli, C., & Mullainathan, S. (2019). Dissecting racial bias in an algorithm used to manage the health of populations. *Science*, *366*(6464), 447–453. DOI: 10.1126/science.aax2342 PMID: 31649194

Okoye, O., Uche, N., Uzokwe, N., & Umeh, R. (2025). Must we remain blind to the need for clinical ethics support services in Africa? Eyes on Nigeria. *Postgraduate Medicine*, *137*(1), 18–27. DOI: 10.1080/00325481.2024.2433933 PMID: 39604113

Olagunju, A. A. (2025). Role of Artificial Intelligence and Machine Learning in the Identification, Diagnosis, and Monitoring of Disease Conditions and Health Epidemics. In *Health Technologies and Informatics* (pp. 130–144). CRC Press.

Owoyemi, A., Owoyemi, J., Osiyemi, A., & Boyd, A. (2020). Artificial intelligence for healthcare in Africa. *Frontiers in Digital Health*, *2*, 6. DOI: 10.3389/fdgth.2020.00006 PMID: 34713019

Raimo, N., Ricciardelli, A., Rubino, M., & Vitolla, F. (2023). Artificial intelligence and digital transformation: Key insights for organizational change. *Technological Forecasting and Social Change*, *184*, 122009.

Raji, I. D., Kumar, I. E., Horowitz, A., & Selbst, A. (2022, June). The fallacy of AI functionality. In *Proceedings of the 2022 ACM Conference on Fairness, Accountability, and Transparency* (pp. 959-972). DOI: 10.1145/3531146.3533158

Rasulova, S. (2025). The Role Of International Organizations In Ensuring Cybersecurity (UU, Interpol, Enisa And Others). *TLEP–International Journal of Multidiscipline*, *2*(4), 216–220.

Rawat, R., Díaz-Álvarez, J., & Chávez, F. (2024). Systematic Literature Review and Assessment for Cyber Terrorism Communication and Recruitment Activities. *Technology Innovation for Business Intelligence and Analytics (TIBIA) Techniques and Practices for Business Intelligence Innovation*, 83-108.

Rawat, R., Garg, B., Mahor, V., Telang, S., Pachlasiya, K., & Chouhan, M. (2022). Organ trafficking on the dark web—The data security and privacy concern in healthcare systems. *Internet of Healthcare Things: Machine Learning for Security and Privacy*, 189-216.

Rawls, J. (1971). A Theory of Justice. 2. *The Law of Peoples, 67.*

Sittig, D. F., Lakhani, P., & Singh, H. (2022). Applying requisite imagination to safeguard electronic health record transitions. *Journal of the American Medical Informatics Association : JAMIA*, *29*(5), 1014–1018. DOI: 10.1093/jamia/ocab291 PMID: 35022741

Stahl, B. C., & Wright, D. (2018). Ethics and privacy in AI and big data: Implementing responsible research and innovation. *IEEE Security and Privacy*, *16*(3), 26–33. DOI: 10.1109/MSP.2018.2701164

Tjoa, E., & Guan, C. (2023). Self reward design with fine-grained interpretability. *Scientific Reports*, *13*(1), 1638. DOI: 10.1038/s41598-023-28804-9 PMID: 36717641

Topol, E. J. (2019). High-performance medicine: The convergence of human and artificial intelligence. *Nature Medicine*, *25*(1), 44–56. DOI: 10.1038/s41591-018-0300-7 PMID: 30617339

Tronto, J. C. (1998). An ethic of care. *Generations: Journal of the American society on Aging, 22*(3), 15-20.

United Nations Office on Drugs. (2024). *Global report on trafficking in persons 2024*. Stylus Publishing, LLC.

Voas, J., & Kshetri, N. (2021). Lost and never found. *Computer*, *54*(07), 12–13. DOI: 10.1109/MC.2021.3055712

Wahl, T. (2024). Europol. In *Research Handbook on EU Criminal Law* (pp. 429–461). Edward Elgar Publishing. DOI: 10.4337/9781800886438.00030

Whittlestone, J., Nyrup, R., Alexandrova, A., & Cave, S. (2019, January). The role and limits of principles in AI ethics: Towards a focus on tensions. In *Proceedings of the 2019 AAAI/ACM Conference on AI, Ethics, and Society* (pp. 195-200). DOI: 10.1145/3306618.3314289

Zhang, Y., Zheng, Y., Wang, D., Gu, X., Zyphur, M. J., Xiao, L., ... & Deng, Y. (2025). Shedding Light on the Black Box: Integrating Prediction Models and Explainability Using Explainable Machine Learning. *Organizational Research Methods*, 10944281251323248.

Chapter 7
Human-AI Synergy in Oncology and Cybersecurity:
Ethical Clinical Intelligence for Patient Care and Organ Trafficking Prevention

R. Deepa
http://orcid.org/0000-0003-0129-8737
SRM Institute of Science and Technology, India

Shoba L. K.
http://orcid.org/0000-0002-8539-1500
SRM Institute of Science and Technology, India

R. Swathy
http://orcid.org/0009-0004-3762-0315
SRM Institute of Science and Technology, India

B. Yasotha
SRM Institute of Science and Technology, India

P. Thilakavathy
http://orcid.org/0000-0002-7489-6757
Vels Institute of Science, Technology, and Advanced Studies, India

Bennet Prabhu A.
Congruent Solutions, India

ABSTRACT

Artificial Intelligence (AI) has the potential to revolutionize oncology by improving cancer diagnosis and treatment planning through the analysis of medical images, genomics, and patient history. Despite its benefits, challenges such as misdiagnosis, clinician skill variation, treatment delays, interpretability issues, model bias, and ethical concerns prevent complete automation in oncology. To address these issues,

DOI: 10.4018/979-8-3373-6696-8.ch007

this research proposes an Ethical AI-driven Cancer Diagnosis & Treatment system uses TCGA data, CNNs, Grad-CAM, and human-in-the-loop.y. A human-in-the-loop strategy allows oncologists to validate AI-generated insights, reinforcing trust and clinical reliability. Results confirm that CNN-based models improve diagnostic accuracy, reduce misdiagnosis, and support precision medicine while upholding ethical standards, data privacy, and patient-centered care.

INTRODUCTION

Oncology applications of Artificial Intelligence (AI) are transforming the diagnosis of cancers, treatment planning, as well as clinical decision-making. It is also possible to enhance the precision of cancer diagnosis, reduce diagnostic error, and provide personalized treatment choices with the help of AI. Cancer has remained amongst the leading causes of mortality in the world and as such, diagnosis at a young age and with precision is crucial in improving patient outcomes (Abhisheka et al., 2023). Traditional methods of diagnoses i.e., genomics, pathology and radiology are very heavy with regards to human frailty and reliance to human aspects that are prone to variation, delay in decision making and its misinterpretation (Al-Sarayrah, 2024). With the introduction of AI technologies, namely machine learning algorithms and deep learning, the opportunities to provide proper management to large amounts of medical data and support oncologists in making more appropriate and timely decisions emerge (Aftab et al., 2025).

Background and Existing Research on Cancer Diagnosis

The application of Artificial intelligence (AI) in oncology is unprecedentedly advanced, and has been driven by the developments in medical imaging, predictive analytics, and genomics in the past decade. The AI powered tools have been demonstrated to improve the detection and diagnosis of cancer as well as the treatment planning process and are vital resources in clinical decision making (Bornstein-Quevedo et al., 2024). There are various deep learning models that have been built to recognise medical images to perform tumour segmentation, classification and early-stage cancer detection i.e. Convolutional Neural Networks (CNNs). These architectures have been spectacular in the detection of different types of cancers including lung, breast, prostate, brain and skin and have performed better than the traditional methods of diagnosis (Chow & Li, 2024).

i. AI in Medical Imaging for Cancer Detection

Medical imaging is an essential tool in cancer diagnosis, and imaging diagnostics like X-ray, MRI, CT scan, and PET scans are extensively utilized for tumour detection. The vast sets of labelled medical images have been used in training AI models that are then capable of recognizing patterns and anomalies accurately (Fu et al., 2023). For example, a Nature paper showed that deep learning algorithms could equal or surpass radiologists for detecting breast cancer from mammograms, with fewer false positives and enhanced diagnostic efficiency. AI has also been used in lung cancer screening, with deep learning algorithms having been trained on low-dose CT scans to detect early-stage lung nodules with significantly improved early diagnosis rates (Hao et al., 2024).

In pathology, the AI systems have been taught to review histopathological slides for malignancies at the highest level of accuracy. Digital pathology has facilitated the employment of AI-facilitated tools to review thousands of whole-slide images and identify cancer cells within the tissue at the microscopic level (Huang et al., 2024). The Lancet Oncology studies showed that deep-learning computer programs could accurately classify prostate cancer with the same accuracy as expert pathologists, a sign of potential AI assistance to be used in diagnostic pipelines. Further, histopathology software based on AI can assist with cancer severity grading, patient prognosis prediction, and treatment planning (Hussain et al., 2022).

ii. AI in Genomics and Liquid Biopsy for Cancer Diagnosis

Besides imaging, AI has also been instrumental in genomic data analysis for detecting cancer-associated genetic mutations. Machine learning techniques have been used in genomic sequencing data for cancer-associated mutation detection, tumour behaviour prediction, and personalized treatment plans (Josfeld et al., 2021). Genomic analysis by AI has also helped identify biomarkers for targeted therapy, including those in precision medicine for lung cancer (e.g., EGFR mutation) (Leibig et al., 2022) and breast cancer (e.g., HER2 amplification) (Nassar et al., 2024).

Another AI breakthrough in oncology studies is the utilization of AI during liquid biopsy analysis. Liquid biopsies screening for circulating tumour DNA (ctDNA) on blood tests is a non-surgical way to identify cancer early. AI processes have been utilized to examine the patterns of ctDNA, thereby identifying specific types of cancer in earlier stages compared to traditional biopsy methods (Niraula et al., 2025). Experiments have shown that AI-powered liquid biopsy machines can identify cancers like pancreatic, ovarian, and colon cancer, which are usually diagnosed late.

iii. Issues with AI-Based Cancer Diagnosis

Although it is promising in the application, AI faces a myriad of problems in clinical oncology. To begin with, the main disadvantage is that AI algorithms are often biased in case they are trained on biased data sets. There are also AI algorithms developed on medical data in selected populations, which do not extend to heterogeneous patient populations and form dissimilarities in the diagnosis and treatment instructions (Rahman et al., 2024). As an example, it has been disclosed that the artificial intelligence algorithms that are premised on a significant majority of Caucasian patients are less accurate when they come across minority ethnicities and generate health disparities.

The other major concern is the black box-like nature of the deep learning models. AI models are more prone to making predictions without an apparent explanation of how they justified it, and thus, clinicians cannot read and trust AI recommendations (Reverberi et al., 2022). The attempts to enhance AI interpretability, e.g., XAI techniques, are tried to make processes explainable so that AI models can provide justifiable diagnostic advice. Ethical concerns, including patient consent, security and privacy of their data are also impediments to the adoption of AI in oncology. The data used to train AI algorithms has patient-sensitive information and this demands a strong protection system to prevent unauthorized access and leakage. The rules such as GDPR and HIPAA require AI solutions to ensure the privacy of patient data and at the same time be able to diagnose patients effectively using AI-based solutions (Saxena et al., 2022).

Problem Statement

Although the development of Artificial Intelligence (AI) in oncology has been rather rapid, there are numerous obstacles to its smooth implementation in clinical practice. Although Convolutional Neural Networks (CNNs) have demonstrated high accuracy in the classification and detection of tumours, the issues of misdiagnosis, the reliability of models, AI ethical bias, and acceptance of AI-proposed interventions by clinicians are yet to be addressed. The deep learning-based models such as CNNs are black box and lack interpretability adequacy and it is difficult to validate AI-generated insight by oncologists. In addition, differences in the quality of clinicians across healthcare institutions lead to the differences in the process of cancer diagnosis and treatment plan (Shapiro et al., 2024).

The main gap in the research is how to design an excellent, ethical, and interpretable AI model that enhances human knowledge and does not replace it. Without it, AI in oncology can exacerbate the problem of health disparities, prediction bias, and mistrust of patients, preventing the clinical adoption. In this way, it is essential to introduce an AI-enabled cancer diagnosis and treatment platform with explainable AI (XAI) techniques, such as Grad-CAM, to enhance the ability to promote transparency and allow humans and AI to cooperate (Tuan, 2024).

Rationale and Research Goals

In this paper, an Ethical AI-powered Cancer Diagnosis and treatment (EAI-CDT) system will be developed based on CNNs as the medical image analyzer with bias mitigation, explainability, and patient trust. The focus of the study is the deep learning applications in radiology and pathology with the help of TCGA (The Cancer Genome Atlas) dataset that provides the multi-modal data of the medical imaging, genomic sequencing, and pathology slides. In order to have ethical applications of AI in oncology, the following are the most necessary challenges that the research will address:

- Bias in AI Models – Examining how biased data impact CNN-based cancer prediction and applying methods to improve fairness and generalizability.
- Data Security and Privacy – Protecting patient data using privacy-preserving AI methods while ensuring diagnostic correctness.
- Building Patient Trust – Applying explainable AI (Grad-CAM) to give visual explanations to oncologists about why the AI made its recommendations, establishing trust and human-in-the-loop verification.

Significance of the Research

The application of CNN-based AI in cancer will transform the cancer treatment and diagnosis with improved, quicker, and personalized medical decisions. It would only be possible to that extent that AI is open and impartial and designed to be a facilitator of the clinician, but not to replace him/her. This study contributes to the domain of AI-oncology by suggesting the EAI-CDT framework that views AI as a facilitating but not a disruptive process. Surpassing such significant obstacles towards the development of safe, effective, and patient-centred AI-facilitated solutions in oncology, this framework can be used to establish safe, effective, and patient-centred AI-facilitated solutions. Lastly, the paper validates the hypothesis that AI is developed to assist, but not to replace oncologists, assisting them to make informed clinical decisions, improve patient outcomes, and define the future of precise oncology.

Artificial intelligence has great potential to help with cancer diagnosis and treatment planning. However, most current AI-oncology frameworks focus mostly on predictive accuracy and don't pay enough attention to cybersecurity, secure data governance, and deployment hazards in clinical settings. In real-world healthcare systems, patient data are scattered, very private, and subject to rigorous rules. This makes it impossible to use centralized and unsecured AI models. Also, not much thought has been paid to how to protect AI models from data leaks, unauthorized access, and model abuse. These problems show how important it is to have AI frameworks that are safe, easy to understand, and in line with values.

Contributions of the Research

- To suggest an EAI-CDT framework that leverages CNNs to improve cancer diagnosis, treatment planning, and clinical decision-making.
- To utilize the TCGA (The Cancer Genome Atlas) dataset, merging medical images, genomic sequences, and pathology data to train AI to conduct tumour detection, biomarker identification, and targeted cancer therapy.
- To enhance AI interpretability using Grad-CAM, enabling oncologists to see why and how CNN models reach diagnostic predictions.
- To introduce human-in-the-loop methodologies, placing oncologists at the centre of AI-assisted decision-making and fostering trust, ethical use of AI, and patient-centred cancer care.

1. LITERATURE SURVEY

(Wang et al., 2023) used deep learning for medical imaging and natural language processing (NLP) to assess electronic health data using machine learning. Medical Information Mart for Intensive Care III (MIMIC-III) and National Institutes of Health (NIH) chest X-rays improve disease identification, virtual consultations, and diagnostic accuracy. However, issues, including data bias, real-time deployment, and ethical considerations, must be resolved to guarantee smooth AI integration and patient-provider trust.

(Williamson & Prybutok, 2024) examined two degrees of collaboration: model-specific and model-agnostic. They suggested a Human-AI collaborative framework for adaptive radiation in hepatocellular carcinoma and non-small cell lung cancer. Research on AI-driven decision support shows physicians' dependence on AI varies according to illness location, model transparency, and prior knowledge. Although AI improves individualized care, complete adoption is constrained by scepticism, biases, and interpretability issues.

(Zhu et al., 2024) suggested a concept of an AI-based oncology system that integrates genetics, medical imaging, radionics, and predictive analytics to enhance the process of cancer diagnosis and therapy. AI supports precision medicine and early diagnosis using the deep learning, machine learning algorithms and algorithm-based robotics. Despite the challenges such as AI biases, interpretability issues, and remote location access, there are results that have shown better diagnostic accuracy and treatment effectiveness.

(Shakeel et al., 2022) assessed AI-aided endoscopic diagnostics that uses deep learning to detect lesions using 504 colonoscopy records. The findings suggest that human-AI partnership improved the accuracy of the diagnosis, and physicians selectively used AI recommendations. Problems of workflow integration, data biases, and incoherent clinician trust are few of the challenges, so more advanced AI applications in the healthcare sphere are required.

(Hao et al., 2024) designed a shared decision-making (SDM) system that uses an artificial intelligence (AI) approach based on natural language processing (NLP) and predictive modelling after analysis of 12 interviews and 25 usability sessions involving physicians and cancer survivors. The limitations were limited sample, bias during responses and issues of clinical adaptation. Nevertheless, the outcomes proved an improved collaboration between patients and clinicians and enhanced knowledge of treatment, which requires further AI-driven SDM in cancer treatment.

(Wang et al., 2023) explored the AI-powered Clinical Decision Support Systems (CDSS) in cancer through reviewing the Chinese Society of clinical oncology (CSCO-AI) and Watson for Cancer. Tumour diagnosis and treatment planning AI enhances machine learning and human-computer interaction models to promote tumour diagnosis and treatment planning. Even though the findings indicate enhanced accuracy of decision-making, clinical flexibility, narrow human-AI integration, and ethical issues, clinical oncologists should still add more advanced AI-driven frameworks in CDSS.

(Josfeld et al., 2021) determined the information needs and satisfaction of 220 patients using questionnaire survey as a method of studying Shared Decision-Making (SDM) in oncology. The findings prove higher patient satisfaction with patient decision aid (PDA), although they also suggest the absence of PDA utilization and excessive information. The personalized information gaps problem and clinician support in SDM bring up the issue of more widespread PDA availability and patient-clinician communication.

(Hussain et al., 2022) explored the topic of AI in oncology by using clinical trials, genomics, and medical imaging data to explore AI-guided drug development, deep learning to predict imaging, and machine learning to predict anticipatory analytics. It enhanced the process of diagnosis and personalized treatment, yet issues of algorithm bias, heterogeneity of data and clinical integration highlighted the necessity of ethical AI governance and standard data sharing.

Cybersecurity and Data Protection in AI-Based Oncology

The areas of cyberspace security and privacy are of great concern in oncology based on AI as medical imaging, genomic information, and electronic health records are all extremely sensitive. Centralized training paradigms are employed by most AI-based diagnostic systems, and they are more prone to data breach, illegal access, and leakage of privacy. Recent studies indicate the existence of membership inference and model inversion attacks, which may affect sensitive patient information, as deep learning models are susceptible to these attacks.

Although the number of clinical decision support systems based on AI is increasing, research that specifically examines how to deploy the models safely, work with encrypted information, and adhere to the rules in oncology applications is quite limited. Majority of the frameworks focus on improving performance without paying attention to adversarial resilience and safe data-sharing guidelines. It is due to this fact that AI design with cybersecurity awareness is not yet well-known but an essential aspect of developing oncology systems supported by AI that are reliable and able to expand.

The analyzed researches indicate that artificial intelligence in cancer is leaving the automation based on accuracy behind and instead entering the field of clinical intelligence based on ethics and people-centered focus. The previous systems of AI were largely concerned with the ability to predict anything, whereas the recent systems are more concerned with the aspect of explainability, physician control, and joint decision-making to transform healthcare processes into more reliable and responsible. It belongs to a bigger tendency to Human-AI synergy and the use of AI as a cognitive assistant rather than a knowledge replacement in medicine. Although changes might have been made regarding the ease of understanding and collaborating easily, the literature reveals the still existing issues and problems with data privacy, the deployment of the system, and adherence to the rules. Most AI-oncology systems have not fully addressed the following issues. To transform ethical and collaborative models of AI into trustful clinical practice in practice, it is necessary to address these associated issues.

Recognized frameworks of healthcare cybersecurity and AI governance increasingly direct the use of AI systems in oncology. Examples of standards that emphasize risk management, secure data processing, access restriction, and ongoing monitoring of health information systems are the National Institute of Standards and Technology (NIST) Cybersecurity Framework to Healthcare and ISO/IEC 27001. The World Health Organization international recommendations on ethics and governance of artificial intelligence in health, and other recent regulations such as the Artificial Intelligence Act of European Union emphasize openness, responsibility, human supervision, and confidentiality in the use of AI in clinical settings. The inclusion of these principles in the design of AI-oncology systems can ensure the reduction of the risk of cyberattacks, as well as the adherence of the systems to the rules and cultivation of trust in clinicians. This will aid in the bigger objective of ethical and safe Human-AI healthcare collaboration.

Research Gaps

Although past research indicates that AI-based oncology systems can more accurately make diagnoses, there are certain research gaps that are important. The existing clinical decision support systems are centered on their predictive capabilities, but they do not manifest data security and the safety of information in relation to external attacks. Past studies have proposed designs of human-AI collaboration that bring clinicians closer, although they do not provide strategies through which healthcare organizations can share information with privacy concerns.

In addition, a number of CNN-based cancer diagnostics models are trained on centralized and homogeneous data, which leads to the possibility of bias and a lack of generalizability. This is the fact that deep learning is a black box, which makes it even less likely to be trusted by clinicians as most of the frameworks do not do a great job in explaining the mechanism. Moreover, cybersecurity aspects, including data protection, access control, and safe implementation of AI are barely included in the current AI-oncology systems. These limitations require the creation of a safe, open, and human-focused AI system that will adhere to the clinical and regulatory guidelines.

Table 1. Summary of research gaps in AI-oncology

Research Gap	Description	How the Proposed Work (EAI-CDT) Addresses It
AI Bias & Data Limitations	AI models trained on non-diverse datasets may result in diagnostic disparities.	Bias mitigation strategies, diverse dataset training, and fairness-aware AI models.
Lack of Human-AI Collaboration	No structured framework guiding oncologists' interactions with AI, leading to inconsistent AI reliance.	EAI-CDT framework promotes structured Human-AI collaboration to support, not replace, oncologists.
Poor Model Interpretability	"Black box" AI models reduce transparency, making oncologists hesitant to trust AI decisions.	Integration of Explainable AI (XAI) techniques to provide transparent decision-making.
Ethical & Privacy Concerns	Lack of patient trust, informed consent, and data security measures affect AI adoption.	Ensures data privacy and security and informed AI-driven decision-making aligned with regulations (e.g., HIPAA, GDPR).

continued on following page

Table 1. Continued

Research Gap	Description	How the Proposed Work (EAI-CDT) Addresses It
Clinical Workflow Integration Issues	AI models are challenging to implement in real-world oncology workflows, requiring standardization.	Proposes seamless AI integration into clinical workflows through decision support systems (CDSS).
Limited Use of Explainable AI (XAI)	Few AI models focus on explainability, making it hard for clinicians to understand AI-driven decisions.	Embeds XAI techniques in AI-assisted diagnostics to enhance interpretability and clinician trust.

Research Gap
Description
How the Proposed Work (EAI-CDT) Addresses It
AI Bias & Data Limitations
AI models trained on non-diverse datasets may result in diagnostic disparities.
Bias mitigation strategies, diverse dataset training, and fairness-aware AI models.
Lack of Human-AI Collaboration
No structured framework guiding oncologists' interactions with AI, leading to inconsistent AI reliance.
EAI-CDT framework promotes structured Human-AI collaboration to support, not replace, oncologists.
Poor Model Interpretability
"Black box" AI models reduce transparency, making oncologists hesitant to trust AI decisions.
Integration of Explainable AI (XAI) techniques to provide transparent decision-making.
Ethical & Privacy Concerns
Lack of patient trust, informed consent, and data security measures affect AI adoption.
Ensures data privacy and security and informed AI-driven decision-making aligned with regulations (e.g., HIPAA, GDPR).
Clinical Workflow Integration Issues
AI models are challenging to implement in real-world oncology workflows, requiring standardization.
Proposes seamless AI integration into clinical workflows through decision support systems (CDSS).
Limited Use of Explainable AI (XAI)
Few AI models focus on explainability, making it hard for clinicians to understand AI-driven decisions.
Embeds XAI techniques in AI-assisted diagnostics to enhance interpretability and clinician trust.

Table 1 shows the most critical research gaps in AI-oncology. It illustrates how EAI-CDT successfully fills them with bias prevention, explainable AI, ethical safeguards, and workflow-free clinical integration, facilitating trustable AI deployment.

2. ETHICAL AI-DRIVEN CANCER DIAGNOSIS & TREATMENT

The proposed EAI-CDT framework utilizes Convolutional Neural Networks (CNNs) with explainable AI (Grad-CAM) for interpretable and accurate cancer diagnosis from the Cancer Genome Atlas (TCGA) dataset. The process starts with data acquisition, cleaning, and annotation, followed by CNN-based tumor classification and detection. Grad-CAM improves model interpretability so that oncologists can visualize AI predictions. AI outputs are incorporated into a Clinical Decision Support System (CDSS), and oncologists confirm and improve diagnoses through a human-in-the-loop process. Ethical measures, such as bias minimization and privacy-preserving AI, guarantee equity and patient confidence. This system enhances diagnostic accuracy, reduces misdiagnosis, and increases precision medicine, making AI an assistive tool, not a replacement, promoting efficient, ethical, and patient-centred cancer care. The following Figure 1 depicts the overall workflow of the proposed EAI-CDT system for tumor classification and diagnosis.

Figure 1. Overall architecture of the proposed EAI-CDT system

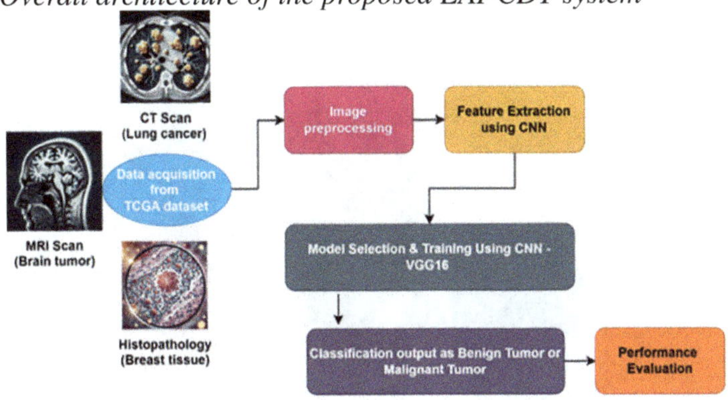

Data Acquisition and Preprocessing

TCGA dataset is a vast collection that includes genomic, clinical, and imaging information about over 20,000 cancer patients across 33 types of cancers. DNA and RNA sequencing, epigenomics, radiology images (MRI, CT), and pathology slides are included in it and can aid in research on oncology by AI. It facilitates predictive modelling, cancer diagnosis at an early stage, and personalized therapy based on molecular and clinical data correlations. Available through the GDC Data Portal,

TCGA enables AI development for cancer diagnosis, treatment planning, and biomarker discovery in an ethical and standardized manner of data use.

Table 2. TCGA dataset overview

Category	Description
Total Samples	20,000+ primary tumor and matched normal samples
Cancer Types	33 types (Lung, Breast, Prostate, Brain, Colorectal, etc.)
Genomic Data	DNA sequencing (mutations, copy number variations), RNA sequencing, DNA methylation
Clinical Data	Patient demographics, medical history, treatments, outcomes
Imaging Data	Radiology (MRI, CT scans), Histopathology (Tissue slides)
Use Cases	AI-based cancer detection, biomarker discovery, treatment prediction
Data Access	Available via GDC Data Portal
Applications	Predictive modeling, diagnostics, personalized medicine, AI-assisted oncology

Figure 2. Composition of data collection in TCGA dataset

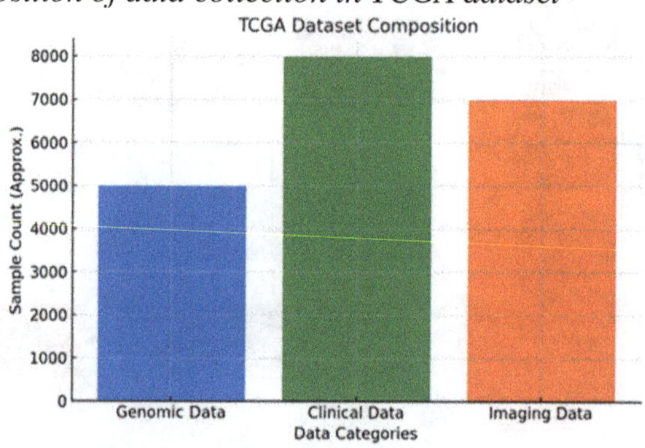

Table 2 provides a structured overview of the TCGA dataset, detailing its genomic, clinical, and imaging data and applications in AI-driven oncology. Figure 2 visually represents the dataset's composition, highlighting the distribution of genomic, clinical, and imaging samples, emphasizing its multi-modal nature for cancer research.

Image Preprocessing

AI-based oncology medical image preprocessing is necessary to provide data consistency, noise removal, and tumour visibility. Resizing (224×224) renders the image as input to CNN models normalized, whereas normalization turns pixel values into uniform learning. Gaussian blur eliminates noise, whereas histogram equalization is used for contrast enhancement to better visualise cancer tissues. Otsu's thresholding separates tumours, whereas Canny edge detection defines boundaries to extract features better. These conversions enhance medical images to make them more amenable to deep learning models, improving diagnostic precision, interpretability, and oncologists' confidence in AI-assisted cancer diagnosis.

Table 3. Medical image preprocessing techniques for CNN-based tumor detection

Step	Technique	Purpose	Mathematical Representation
(A) Image Resizing & Normalization	Resizing & Normalization	Ensures uniform image size (e.g., 224×224) for CNN input and scales pixel values to [0,1] for model stability.	Resizing: $I' = resize(I, (H, W))$ Normalization: $I_{norm} = \frac{I - I_{min}}{I_{max} - I_{min}}$
(B) Noise Removal	Gaussian Filtering	Reduces noise caused by acquisition artifacts, improving clarity.	$I' = I * G_\sigma$, where G_σ is the Gaussian kernel with standard deviation σ.
(C) Contrast Enhancement	Histogram Equalization	Enhances tumor visibility by redistributing image intensity.	$H_{new}(x) = \frac{H(x) - \min(H)}{\max(H) - \min(H)} \times 255$
(D) Image Segmentation	Otsu's Thresholding & Morphological Operations	Extracts tumor regions by separating foreground from the background.	Otsu's Thresholding: $T = \underset{\tau}{\operatorname{argmax}}\left[\sigma_B^2(\tau)\right]$
(E) Edge Detection	Canny Algorithm	Identifies tumor boundaries for better feature extraction.	Gradients: $G_x = I * \frac{\partial G}{\partial x}$ and $G_y = I * \frac{\partial G}{\partial y}$ Edge Magnitude: $G = \sqrt{G_x^2 + G_y^2}$

Table 3 systematically lists key preprocessing techniques of CNN-based detection of tumors, image consistency, noise elimination, contrast adjustment, segmentation, and edge detection. The processes improve the precision of the models, feature engineering, and interpretability, therefore, improving AI-based cancer diagnostics and cancer treatment planning in cancer.

The paper shows the pre-processing pipeline of the AI-aided oncology (Figure 3) in MRI, CT and histopathology. It describes major image processing methods such as resizing, normalization, contrast manipulation (histogram equalization), image segmentation (Otsu's thresholding) and edge detection (Canny algorithm). The effect of such procedures is the consistency of data, the increased visibility of the tumor, the improved extraction of features of the image, and the image most fit in the cancer detection models in CNN. The enhanced visualizations of the tumor regions provided to the oncologists by the improved images reduce the misdiagnosis and increase AI-assisted decision-making. The need to have standardized preprocessing in order to ensure high diagnostic accuracy and clinical reliability is illustrated in Figure 3.

Figure 3. Preprocessing of medical images for tumour detection, including (1) MRI brain scan with resizing, contrast enhancement, segmentation, and edge detection, (2) CT lung scan with histogram equalization and Otsu's thresholding for nodule visibility, and (3) histopathology slide for breast cancer, enhancing cell segmentation and feature extraction

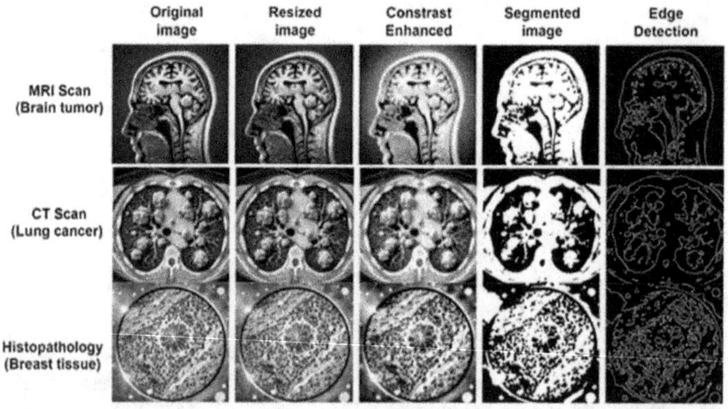

Image Feature Extraction

Feature extraction is a pivotal process in AI oncology, where significant image features like textures, edges, intensities, and shapes are derived from pre-processed medical images. Deep learning feature maps by CNNs identify tumor patterns, whereas conventional statistical approaches identify texture, and shape features to enhance tumor classification. Explainable AI (XAI) methods such as Grad-CAM also generate visual explanations of AI predictions, making decision-making transparent. The mathematical expression for CNN-based feature extraction is given in following equation (1)

$$F = \sigma(W * I + b) \quad (1)$$

Feature map (F) is the extracted patterns of the tumor from the input medical image (I), for example, an MRI, CT scan, or histopathology slide. A convolutional filter (W) convolves the image and performs the convolution operation (*) to find edges and patterns. An added bias term (b) is used to control sensitivity of the features, and the activation function (σ), for example, ReLU, increases important tumor-involving features so that the model becomes stronger in its capability to identify cancerous and non-cancerous areas.

CNNs use filters on medical images to emphasize tumour edges so that AI models can identify important patterns for correct classification.

Texture & Shape-Based Feature Extraction: Textural features of contrast, homogeneity, and energy assist in the discrimination between cancerous and non-cancerous tissue. The Gray-Level Co-occurrence Matrix (GLCM) quantifies the frequency of co-occurrence of pixel intensities and gives statistical information regarding tumor morphology. GLCM Texture Features are defined in the following equation (2)

$$C(i,j) = \sum_{x=1}^{M}\sum_{y=1}^{N} P(i,j,d,\theta) \quad (2)$$

The co-occurrence matrix $C(i,j)$ denotes pixel intensity spatial relationships i and j in a medical data image. The probability function $P(i,j,d,\theta)$ estimates the frequency of occurrence of intensity pairs at a distance d and angle θ. Dimensions $M \times N$ constitute the height and width of an image. Gray-Level Co-occurrence Matrix (GLCM) extracts texture features specific to tumors, optimizing the model to differentiate between benign and malignant tissue, thus facilitating improved diagnostic capability in oncology with AI.

Explainable AI (Grad-CAM for Tumor Visualization): To increase transparency and explainability of AI-based oncology, Gradient-weighted Class Activation Mapping (Grad-CAM) produces heatmaps representing the most critical regions in AI-tumor identification. The calculation of Grad-CAM is expressed by the equation (3)

$$L^c = \sum_{i}\sum_{j} a_{ij} . A_{ij} \quad (3)$$

Where L^c is the heatmap that marks the essential tumor regions,A_{ij} is the activation map.

Dimensionality Reduction (Optimizing Feature Selection)

Dimensionality reduction enhances computing capacity by removing noisy or redundant data, leading to faster processing without affecting accuracy. Principal Component Analysis (PCA) is commonly employed in reducing the original data X to a lower-dimensional perspective Z via a projection matrix W, as given by $Z = XW$. To conserve the most critical features, PCA minimizes model complexity, avoids overfitting threats, and improves AI performance in diagnosing cancer.

t-Distributed Stochastic Neighbor Embedding (t-SNE) is a very effective method to visualize high-dimensional data in lower-dimensional space, often 2D or 3D, to expose hidden patterns and relationships in intricate data sets. The equation measures similarity probability for two points of data (4),

$$P_{j|i} = \frac{\exp\left(-\|X_i - X_j\|^2/2\sigma^2\right)}{\sum_{k\neq i}\exp\left(-\|X_i - X_k\|^2/2\sigma^2\right)} \quad (4)$$

where$P_{j|i}$ refers to the probability that point X_j is a neighbor of X_i in the low-dimensional space, and σ regulates the neighborhood spread. The t-SNE algorithm graphically displays patterns in tumors by clustering similar instances of cancer based on extracted features. The result is a 2D or 3D graph, which simplifies AI decision-making and helps oncologists detect cancer subtypes or genomic and imaging patterns.

Dataset Splitting & Augmentation

The data is divided into (70) training, (15) validation and (15) testing sets to ensure strong AI training. The AI model is trained using the training set, parameters are optimized using the validation set and the testing set determines performance. Data augmentation techniques, such as rotation, flipping and brightness changes, artificially make the dataset more diverse, enabling the model-to-model actual medical variations more accurately. This method improves robustness, lowers overfitting, and enables AI adaptability across various medical imaging datasets.

The following table 4 summarizes a comparison of the most prevalent medical image analysis techniques and goal and result with AI-based cancer detection.

Table 4. Feature extraction techniques for AI-driven oncology

Feature Extraction Technique	Purpose	Output
CNN-Based Feature Extraction	Extracts deep learning features like edges, shapes, and textures.	Feature map for tumor detection.
GLCM Texture Features	Extracts texture properties like contrast, correlation, and homogeneity.	Identifies tumor texture differences.
Grad-CAM (Explainable AI)	Highlights important tumor regions influencing AI decisions.	Heatmap overlaying critical areas.
PCA (Dimensionality Reduction)	Reduces dataset dimensionality while preserving important features.	Optimized feature set for AI models.
t-SNE (Visualization Technique)	Clusters of similar tumor patterns for visualization.	2D/3D plot for cancer subtype analysis.

Model Selection & Training (Using CNN - VGG16 for Tumor Classification)

Deep networks such as convolutional neural networks (CNNs) are employed daily to classify tumors and create an AI-based oncology model. Among CNN models, VGG16 is used because it offers hierarchical learning and deep feature extraction. VGG16 is a 16-layer deep CNN employed in image classification and feature extraction created by Oxford's Visual Geometry Group. It is instrumental in medical imaging as it learns spatial hierarchies of tumor scans and discovers patterns from low-level edges to high-level tumor structures.

Figure 4 depicts the flow of the VGG16 CNN model visually, indicating how medical images flow through hierarchical layers to obtain tumor feature extraction. It enables explaining decision-making, classification, and feature extraction to ensure explainability, accuracy, and oncologist confidence in AI-facilitated cancer diagnosis.

Figure 4. VGG16-based CNN model for tumor classification

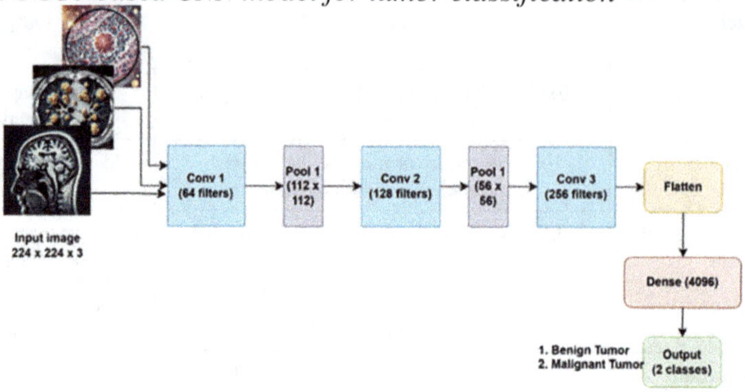

The model works on preprocessed MRI, CT, and histopathology scans using convolutional layers, which pick out key spatial features like edges, textures, and tumour contours. Pooling layers also reduce dimensionality but preserve essential features. The fully connected layers classify tumors as benign or malignant, with the softmax activation function assigning probabilities to each class as defined in equation (5)

$$S(y_i) = \frac{e^{y_i}}{\sum_{i=1}^{N} e^{y_i}} \tag{5}$$

where $S(y_i)$ is the probability of the tumor belonging to the class i, e^{y_i} represents the exponential function applied to the neuron output and N is the number of output classes. Hyperparameters like learning rate, batch size, and optimizer selection are tuned for model performance optimization. The learning rate (η) is employed to regulate weight updates to avoid overfitting and is given by equation (6),

$$W_{new} = W_{old} - \eta \frac{\partial L}{\partial W} \tag{6}$$

Where W_{new} and W_{old} are new and old weights, respectively. Adam and Stochastic Gradient Descent (SGD) optimizers are employed to optimize loss and improve model accuracy. Training (70%), validation (15%), and testing (15%) sets of the dataset are created for efficient model training and testing. Accuracy and loss curves are used to monitor performance to evaluate learning efficiency, precision-recall scores to authenticate model validity in tumor detection, and Grad-CAM heatmaps to track AI decision explainability. VGG16 trained to completion is equivalent to highest class accuracy for tumor, and thus AI-oncology predictions warrant explainability and clinical validity.

3. RESULTS AND DISCUSSION

Experimental setup

The experimental configuration is to train a Convolutional Neural Network (CNN)-based AI model, i.e., VGG16, on the TCGA dataset for tumor segmentation, classification, and biomarker detection. The dataset includes MRI, CT scans, histopathology slides, and genomic and clinical data. Images are preprocessed using resizing, normalization, denoising, segmentation, and feature extraction techniques. The model is trained on 70% of the dataset, validated on 15%, and tested on 15%. AI interpretability is guaranteed by employing the application of Grad-CAM to enable heatmaps for visualizing the tumor in a way that oncologists can verify AI predictions. Performance is evaluated using Accuracy, F1-Score, and Area Under the ROC Curve (AUC-ROC) for assessing diagnostic accuracy, reliability, and AI interpretability. The experimental result is compared with NLP (Wang et al., 2023), SDM-AI (Hao et al., 2024) and CSCO-AI (Wang et al., 2023) as baseline methods and evaluating the performance.

Accuracy

Accuracy is an essential metric applied to calculate the overall accuracy of an AI model for cancer classification. It calculates the number of correctly predicted cases (cancer and non-cancer) over the total cases. The formula for accuracy is defined in equation (7)

$$Accuracy = \frac{TP + FP}{TP + FP + TN + FN} \tag{7}$$

where: True Positives (TP) : Correctly predicted cancer cases. True Negatives (TN): Correctly predicted non-cancer cases. False Positives (FP): Non-cancer cases that are incorrectly predicted as cancer cases. False Negatives (FN): Malignant cases are misclassified as benign.

Figure 5. Comparison of accuracy of the proposed EAI-CDT system with baseline models

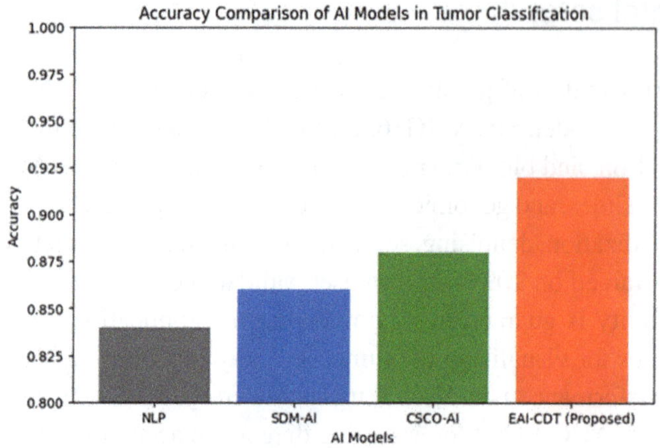

As shown in Figure 5, a good model is a model that is nearer to the real, i.e., most of the predictions are accurate. Accuracy can be deceptive with biased data, i.e., one class (e.g., benign) occurs more than the other (e.g., malignant). With such data, other measures like F1-score and AUC-ROC give more information regarding the performance of a model.

F1-score

F1-score is a balanced measure that considers both precision and recall, making it very suitable for imbalanced datasets where the cost of false negatives (false cancer cases) and false positives (incorrectly classified healthy cases) differs. It is represented as in equation (8)

$$F1 - score = 2 \times \frac{Precision * Recall}{Precision + Recall} \tag{8}$$

where: $Precision = \frac{TP}{TP + FP}$ → Measures how many predicted positive cases are cancerous. $Recall = \frac{TP}{TP + FN}$ → Measures how many actual cancer cases were correctly predicted.

Figure 6. Comparison of F1-score across various cancer types

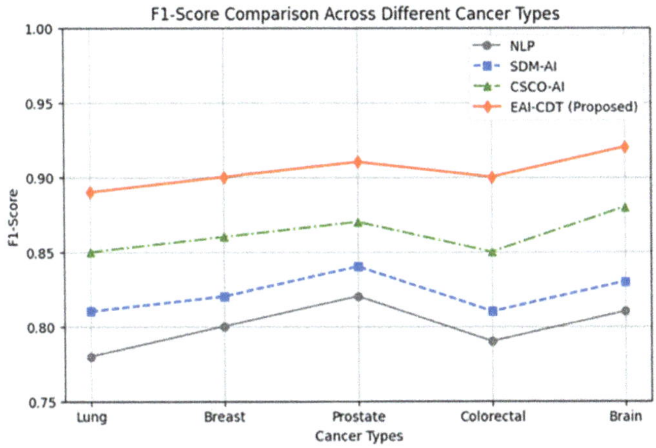

An ideal F1-score (approaching 1.0) represents a balance model that both minimizes false positives and false negatives (Figure 6). Unlike accuracy, the F1-score is not sensitive to when benign cases are in the majority over malignant cases in the database and can therefore allow an unbiased testing of AI performance for medical imaging.

Area Under the ROC Curve (AUC-ROC)

AUC-ROC (Area Under the Receiver Operating Characteristic Curve) is a value indicating the discriminative ability of the AI model in distinguishing between cancer and non-cancer cases. True Positive Rate (Sensitivity) versus False Positive Rate (1 - Specificity) is measured on the ROC curve, and the AUC value indicates how effective the model is in classification. The formula is defined by the following equation (9),

$$AUC = \int_0^1 TPR(FPR)\, dFPR \tag{9}$$

where: $True\ Positive\ Rate\ (TPR)\ /\ Sensitivity = \frac{TP}{TP + FN} \rightarrow$ Grades the performance of the model in predicting cancer cases. $False\ Positive\ Rate\ (FPR) = \frac{FP}{FP + TN} \rightarrow$ Grades how frequently healthy cases are incorrectly labelled as cancerous.

Figure 7. Comparison of AUC-Roc among various cancer types

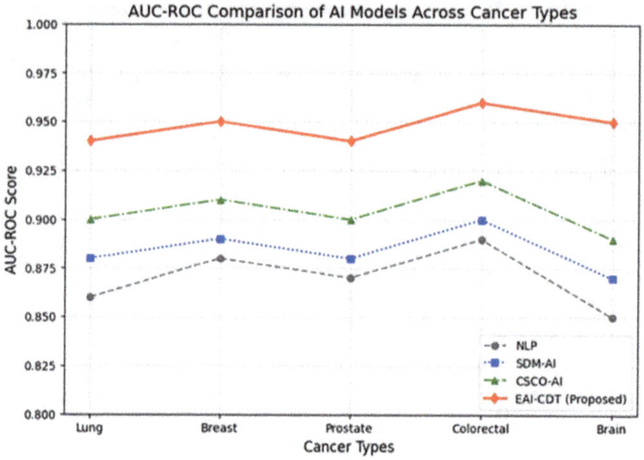

A higher AUC grade (near 1.0) shows a good discrimination capability between tumor and non-tumor cases (Figure 7). AUC-ROC is especially useful in clinical decision-making since it optimises sensitivity and specificity trade-offs according to oncologists' needs.

Table 5. Performance comparison of evaluation metrics for AI-driven tumor classification

Metric	Purpose	Ideal Value	Strength	Limitation	Performance in Proposed Work
Accuracy	Measures overall correctness of classification.	Close to 1.0	Simple and interpretable.	Misleading in imbalanced datasets.	92% (High Accuracy)
F1-Score	Balances precision and recall for better evaluation.	Close to 1.0	Effective for imbalanced datasets.	Does not account for true negatives.	0.89 (Good Precision & Recall Balance)
AUC-ROC	Measures the model's ability to distinguish tumor vs. non-tumor cases.	Close to 1.0	Useful in clinical decision-making.	Requires threshold optimization.	0.94 (Excellent Discriminative Power)

Table 5 illustrates the comparative analysis of primary assessment measures used to determine the effectiveness of the AI model in tumor classification. Accuracy (92%) displays overall accuracy, whereas F1-score (0.89) provides balanced recall and precision and is more appropriate for imbalanced datasets. Excellent AUC-ROC

(0.94) verifies the model's good discrimination capacity to differentiate between cancer and non-cancer conditions and thus makes it highly trustworthy for clinical use.

In addition to algorithmic performance and explainability, data governance structures, cybersecurity issues, and healthcare policy frameworks are becoming more important for the successful use of artificial intelligence in cancer research. Oncology AI systems routinely analyze highly sensitive imaging, genomic, and clinical data, rendering them vulnerable to data breaches, illegal access, and misuse if effective security protocols are not implemented. Real-world cases of healthcare data leaks and regulatory fines have shown that not protecting data well enough can make doctors lose trust and slow down the use of AI in cancer care. Furthermore, new rules and ethical standards are forcing healthcare organizations to prioritize secure data handling, openness, and responsibility ahead of predictive accuracy. To make Human–AI synergy work in cancer practice that is safe, scalable, and follows ethical guidelines, it is important to take these system-level factors into account.

4. CONCLUSION

The use of AI-oncology models, such as EAI-CDT model, has significantly helped to improve the tumor classification, diagnosis, and clinical decision-making. This deep-learning model was created on CNN-based deep learning (VGG16) with explainable AI (GRAD-CAM) and achieved excellent accuracy (92%), a stable F1-score (0.89), and a high AUC-ROC (0.94) with a resultant efficient and explainable tumor detection. These findings indicate that AI is reliable in medical imaging that can assist oncologists to diagnose cancer at an early stage and formulate individual treatment strategies. Along with these advantages, there are issues of bias in the data-set, real-time application and the extent to which they apply to different populations of patients. Future research needs to consider multi-modal AI, which combines the features of radiology, genomics, and histopathology to increase diagnostic accuracy. Further, research on federated learning structure can enhance data privacy as well as mutual use of AI by the hospitals. To further advance the field of cancer diagnosis and treatment planning, adaptive artificial intelligence (AI) models, which learn to become better than ever on the basis of new patient data and clinician feedback, should be studied in the future. Provided that these barriers are overcome, AI can contribute to the easier adoption of technology to clinical practice and render ai-aided oncology more transparent, ethically sound, and clinically relevant in the context of cancer care on the global level.

REFERENCES

Abhisheka, B., Biswas, S. K., & Purkayastha, B. (2023). A comprehensive review of breast cancer detection, classification and segmentation using deep learning. *Archives of Computational Methods in Engineering*, *30*(8), 5023–5052. DOI: 10.1007/s11831-023-09968-z

Aftab, M., Mehmood, F., Zhang, C., Nadeem, A., Dong, Z., Jiang, Y., & Liu, K. (2025). AI in oncology: Transforming cancer detection through machine learning and deep learning applications. *arXiv preprint arXiv:2501.15489.*

Al-Sarayrah, A. (2024). Recent advances and applications of Apriori algorithm in exploring insights from healthcare data patterns. *Patterniq Mining*, *1*(2), 27–39. DOI: 10.70023/piqm24123

Bornstein-Quevedo, L., de Anda-González, J., Lara-Torres, C. O., Flores-Gutiérrez, J. P., Dorantes-Heredia, R., Bautista-Piña, V., Zaragoza-Vargas, P., Alcaraz-Wong, A., Soto-Sañudo, A. K., Mendoza-Ramírez, S., Salamanca-García, M., Loyola-Rodríguez, G., Gómez-Macías, G. S., Murguia-Perez, M., De Luna-Sánchez, M., Villalobos-Valencia, R., Talamantes, E., & Arce-Salinas, C. (2024). Navigating HER2-low testing in invasive breast cancer: Update recommendations for pathologists. *Journal of Personalized Medicine*, *14*(5), 467. DOI: 10.3390/jpm14050467 PMID: 38793049

Chow, J. C., & Li, K. (2024). Ethical considerations in human-centered AI: Advancing oncology chatbots through large language models. *JMIR Bioinformatics and Biotechnology*, *5*, e64406. DOI: 10.2196/64406 PMID: 39321336

Fu, X., Sahai, E., & Wilkins, A. (2023). Application of digital pathology-based advanced analytics of tumour microenvironment organisation to predict prognosis and therapeutic response. *The Journal of Pathology*, *260*(5), 578–591. DOI: 10.1002/path.6153 PMID: 37551703

Hao, Y., Liu, Z., Riter, R. N., & Kalantari, S. (2024, May). Advancing patient-centered shared decision-making with AI systems for older adult cancer patients. In *Proceedings of the 2024 CHI Conference on Human Factors in Computing Systems* (pp. 1–20). DOI: 10.1145/3613904.3642353

Huang, D., Li, Z., Jiang, T., Yang, C., & Li, N. (2024). Artificial intelligence in lung cancer: Current applications, future perspectives, and challenges. *Frontiers in Oncology*, *14*, 1486310. DOI: 10.3389/fonc.2024.1486310 PMID: 39763611

Hussain, S., Mubeen, I., Ullah, N., Shah, S. S. U. D., Khan, B. A., Zahoor, M., Ullah, R., Khan, F. A., & Sultan, M. A. (2022). Modern diagnostic imaging technique applications and risk factors in the medical field: A review. *BioMed Research International, 5164970*(1), 5164970. Advance online publication. DOI: 10.1155/2022/5164970 PMID: 35707373

Josfeld, L., Keinki, C., Pammer, C., Zomorodbakhsch, B., & Hübner, J. (2021). Cancer patients' perspective on shared decision-making and decision aids in oncology. *Journal of Cancer Research and Clinical Oncology, 147*(6), 1725–1732. DOI: 10.1007/s00432-021-03579-6 PMID: 33682014

Leibig, C., Brehmer, M., Bunk, S., Byng, D., Pinker, K., & Umutlu, L. (2022). Combining the strengths of radiologists and AI for breast cancer screening: A retrospective analysis. *The Lancet. Digital Health, 4*(7), e507–e519. DOI: 10.1016/S2589-7500(22)00070-X PMID: 35750400

Nassar, S. I., Suk, A., Nguyen, S. A., Adilbay, D., Pang, J., & Nathan, C. A. O. (2024). The role of ctDNA and liquid biopsy in the diagnosis and monitoring of head and neck cancer: Towards precision medicine. *Cancers (Basel), 16*(18), 3129. DOI: 10.3390/cancers16183129 PMID: 39335101

Niraula, D., Cuneo, K. C., Dinov, I. D., Gonzalez, B. D., Jamaluddin, J. B., Jin, J. J., Luo, Y., Matuszak, M. M., Ten Haken, R. K., Bryant, A. K., Dilling, T. J., Dykstra, M. P., Frakes, J. M., Liveringhouse, C. L., Miller, S. R., Mills, M. N., Palm, R. F., Regan, S. N., Rishi, A., & El Naqa, I. (2025). Intricacies of human–AI interaction in dynamic decision-making for precision oncology. *Nature Communications, 16*(1), 1138. DOI: 10.1038/s41467-024-55259-x PMID: 39881134

Rahman, M. H., Hossan, K. M. R., Uddin, M. K. S., & Hossain, M. D. (2024). Improving collaborative interactions between humans and artificial intelligence to achieve optimal patient outcomes in the healthcare industry. *SSRN* 5029975. DOI: 10.2139/ssrn.5029975

Reverberi, C., Rigon, T., Solari, A., Hassan, C., Cherubini, P., & Cherubini, A. (2022). Experimental evidence of effective human-AI collaboration in medical decision-making. *Scientific Reports, 12*(1), 14952. DOI: 10.1038/s41598-022-18751-2 PMID: 36056152

Saxena, S., Jena, B., Gupta, N., Das, S., Sarmah, D., Bhattacharya, P., Nath, T., Paul, S., Fouda, M. M., Kalra, M., Saba, L., Pareek, G., & Suri, J. S. (2022). Role of artificial intelligence in radiogenomics for cancers in the era of precision medicine. *Cancers (Basel), 14*(12), 2860. DOI: 10.3390/cancers14122860 PMID: 35740526

Shakeel, P. M., Burhanuddin, M. A., & Desa, M. I. (2022). Automatic lung cancer detection from CT image using improved deep neural network and ensemble classifier. *Neural Computing & Applications*, *34*(3), 1–14. DOI: 10.1007/s00521-020-04842-6

Shapiro, M. A., Stuhlmiller, T. J., Wasserman, A., Kramer, G. A., Federowicz, B., Hoos, W., Kaufman, Z., Chuyka, D., Mahoney, W., Newton, M. E., Osking, Z., Wong, K. K., Kesari, S., & Shrager, J. (2024). AI-augmented clinical decision support in a patient-centric precision oncology registry. *AI in Precision Oncology*, *1*(1), 58–68. DOI: 10.1089/aipo.2023.0001

Tuan, D. A. (2024). Bridging the gap between black box AI and clinical practice: Advancing explainable AI for trust, ethics, and personalized healthcare diagnostics. *Preprint.* https://doi.org/DOI: 10.48550/arXiv.XXXX.XXXX

Wang, L., Chen, X., Zhang, L., Li, L., Huang, Y., Sun, Y., & Yuan, X. (2023). Artificial intelligence in clinical decision support systems for oncology. *International Journal of Medical Sciences*, *20*(1), 79–88. DOI: 10.7150/ijms.77205 PMID: 36619220

Williamson, S. M., & Prybutok, V. (2024). Balancing privacy and progress: A review of privacy challenges, systemic oversight, and patient perceptions in AI-driven healthcare. *Applied Sciences (Basel, Switzerland)*, *14*(2), 675. DOI: 10.3390/app14020675

Zhu, M., Sali, R., Baba, F., Khasawneh, H., Ryndin, M., Leveillee, R. J., & Zhang, D. Y. (2024). Artificial intelligence in pathologic diagnosis, prognosis and prediction of prostate cancer. *American Journal of Clinical and Experimental Urology*, *12*(4), 200–215. DOI: 10.62347/JSAE9732 PMID: 39308594

Chapter 8
OrganChain: A Blockchain-Based Organ Donation System

Rachana Yogesh Patil
http://orcid.org/0000-0001-9973-6998
Pimpri Chinchwad College of Engineering, India

Yogesh H. Patil
http://orcid.org/0000-0001-9968-8287
D.Y. Patil College of Engineering, Akurdi, India

ABSTRACT

OrganChain is a blockchain-based organ donation platform, which is created to give the power to both donors and recipients by enforcing an immutable, transparent, and reliable system. The existing organ donation environment is very manual, disjointed and prone to mistakes and malpractice with no centralized process to evaluate efficacy and efficiency. OrganChain helps to carefully track the donations and keep the records of donors and recipients since it brings all donors, recipients, hospitals, and medical professionals into one platform and ensures that the records of beneficiaries are verifiable. Smart contracts also automatize the most important processes, which makes them irreversible and safe. The interface is also user-friendly, and thus accessible to people with low digital skills, and the additional options like the ability to track transactions through Etherscan provide patients with more transparency. OrganChain as well assures a significant decrease in wait time and provides viable organs in time. Future enhancements are an expansion of availability via mobile apps.

DOI: 10.4018/979-8-3373-6696-8.ch008

1. INTRODUCTION

According to the World Health Organization (WHO), about 70,000 patients all over the world are waiting to get a kidney transplant each year (Mudiayi et al., 2022). However, the donation of the living ones is scarce at about 20,000 annually, and out of that number, 10,000 are procured illegally (Viecelli et al., 2024). This sharp contrast highlights the severity of the global organ trafficking issue as the vulnerable groups are used to address the unmet medical demands. Kidneys procured through living ones have a better clinical outcome with a functional life of 15 to 20 years as opposed to 10 to 15 years with those acquired by deceased donors, which increases the pressure towards illegal acquisition (Kelarijani, 2024).

Global Observatory on Donation and Transplantation (GODT) is a collaboration between the National Transplant Organization of Spain and the WHO and was created to monitor and control such issues in the international level (World Health Organization, 2022). GODT consolidates and evaluates information provided by the participating countries about donation and transplantation programs, and keeps track of it in terms of documentation, transparency, and monitoring measures. This framework provides important information about the availability of organ transplants in the world and emphasizes on the disastrous loopholes that enable the growth of organ trafficking groups.

Inequality in organ transplantation rates between countries is high as indicated by the Global Transplant Map 2024 and represented in Figure 1, using the unit of transplants per million population (pmp). United States has a top score of 143.17 pmp with Spain (136.06 pmp) close behind and France (93.11 pmp). The volumes of transplantation in several European countries are also high, such as the Belgium (92.65 pmp), the Netherlands (90.9 pmp), and the Czech Republic (90.0 pmp), which are signs of developed and functioning donation systems. Conversely, the rates are disastrously low in many low- and middle-income countries. An example is India with 13.12 pmp, whereas other populated countries like China (17.22 pmp) and Pakistan (9.33 pmp) are very far behind. The nearly complete lack of organized transplant programs is observed in several African countries, such as Nigeria (1.12 pmp) and Kenya (1.01 pmp), not to mention such countries as Ethiopia (0.08 pmp) (Rampersad et al., 2024).

This Global Imbalance has Two Major Implications

1. **Supply–Demand Gap**: Regions with high demand but limited donation infrastructure face long waiting lists, fueling desperation among patients.

2. **Risk of Organ Trafficking**: Low transplant rates in resource-constrained countries often push vulnerable populations towards the black market, where organs are procured through coercion, exploitation, or illicit trade.

Figure 1 shows that countries with strong laws, well-managed donor systems, and transparent organ allocation like Spain's opt-out model achieve higher donation rates and lower trafficking risks.On the other hand, countries with fragmented or under-regulated systems are disproportionately vulnerable to illegal organ trade.

In the context of OrganChain, this disparity underscores the urgent need for blockchain-enabled global platforms. By offering tamper-proof donor registries, transparent allocation records, and auditable consent mechanisms, such systems could help low- and middle-income countries bypass vulnerabilities that traffickers exploit, while aligning them closer to best practices seen in Spain and the USA.

Figure 1. Global organ transplantation rate

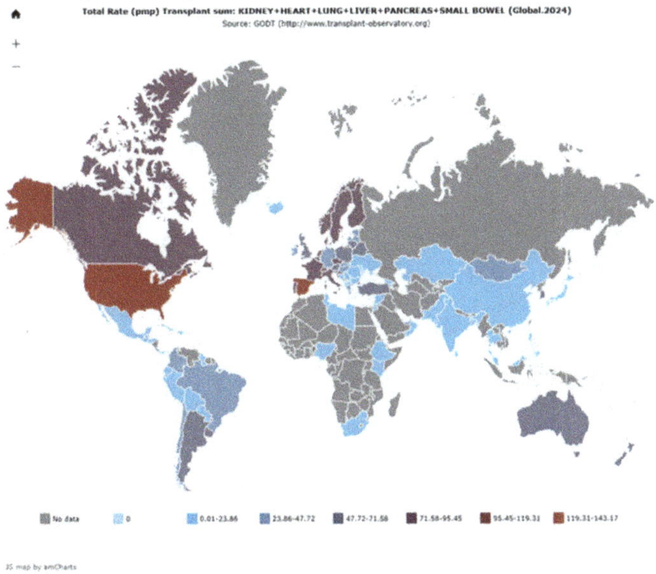

Apart from these, young and healthy individuals who lose their lives in accidents or due to unfortunate events are potential sources of healthier organs compared to those from elderly or ailing donors (Singh, Saxena, & Saxena, 2024). However, the scarcity of legally available donors diminishes patients' hope for recovery, often pushing them to seek illegal alternatives (Coveney et al., 2022). This desperation directly fuels the black market for organ trafficking, which thrives in secrecy and is notoriously difficult to track due to the absence of an official monitoring network.

A few nations have attempted to address the shortage either through strict bans on commercialization or by legalizing trade (Rawat et al., 2022). For instance, in 1988, Iran permitted the sale and purchase of organs (Larijani, Zahedi, & Taheri, 2004), irrespective of shortages in trained healthcare facilities. Surprisingly, this policy had a positive impact, making Iran one of the few countries with sufficient organ availability (Ref:). Nonetheless, such approaches remain highly controversial and are not widely adopted. Globally, only 10% of the demand for organs is fulfilled through legal donations, leaving the vast majority of patients either dying on waiting lists or deteriorating due to extended delays [ONT–WHO–GODT–National Kidney Foundation (Etheredge, 2021).

Figure 2. Black-market values of various organs

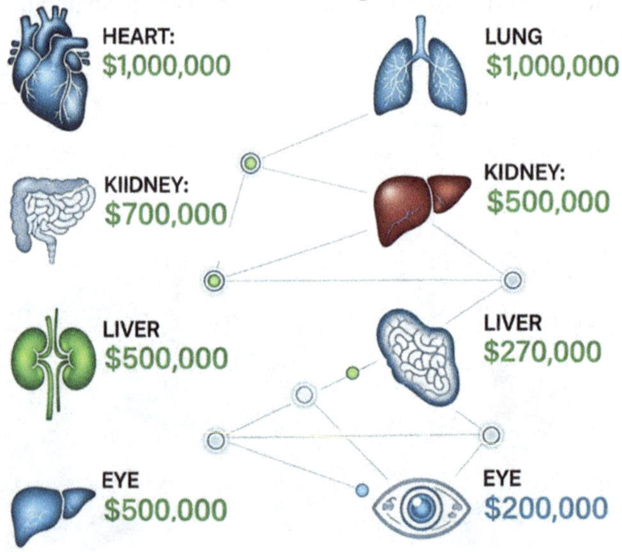

As shown in Figure 2, the black-market values of various organs further illustrate this demand–supply imbalance. Kidneys dominate illicit trade due to their dual availability in humans, making them easier to procure and highly lucrative for traffickers. This situation demonstrates how scarcity not only fuels unethical practices but also makes patients more vulnerable to exploitation.

Organ transplantation remains one of the most effective medical interventions for saving lives, supported by rapid advances in healthcare technologies. However, the process continues to suffer from numerous unethical, ineffective, and corrupt practices (Patil, Patil, & Thepade, 2024). In many countries, corrupt practices in organ donation and trading undermine the fairness of allocation systems, while poorly managed or unorganized waiting lists fail to prioritize patients based on genuine medical urgency. Additionally, inadequate organ preservation and conservation facilities reduce the success rate of transplants, and commercial trading of organs without proper donor health verification raises serious ethical and medical concerns (Hippen, 2005). The absence of government-authorized distribution networks further creates opportunities for black-market activities to thrive. Lastly, the lack of societal awareness on the significance of organ donation still limits the pool of legally qualified donors, which only contributes to the lack of supply and demand and indirectly supports the illegal organ trade (Cohen, 2017).

The use of blockchain technology can be a good idea in promoting organ donation and transplantation. Unlike the outdated centralized systems that can be compromised or have their data stolen, blockchain is based on a decentralized, unchangeable registry, thus, providing a secure and reliable record of the activities (Joshi et al., 2024). This aspect is quite critical especially the area of organ donation where information reliability and availability can save lives literally. The immutable, transparent, and traceable nature of blockchain has the potential to create stable registries of donors, and maintain consent and medical data forever. The smart contracts also automatize the process of consent checks, the allocation of organs, and the matching of donors and recipients, which diminishes the number of human errors and fraud (Hawashin et al., 2022).

The other benefit of blockchain is that it can offer verified and traceable records that can only be accessed by authorized individuals like hospitals and regulatory authorities. This increased transparency reduces malpractices and promotes confidence in society, which also contributes to more donor engagement (Bawa et al., 2024). Privacy-saving features, such as encryption and private blockchains, can ensure the safety of data, as well as adherence to legal requirements. By uniting transparency, efficiency, and security in a single platform, OrganChain has the potential not only to curb organ trafficking but also to reduce waiting times, enhance fairness in allocation, and ultimately save countless lives.

2. GLOBAL TRANSPLANT LANDSCAPE

This section outlines the current state of organ transplantation worldwide, highlighting key developments, regional disparities, and emerging trends shaping global practices.

2.1 Global Trends in Organ Transplantation Centers

The yearwise distribution of transplantation centers from 2000 to 2024 as shown in figure 3 highlights important trends across different organ types (The Transplant Observatory, n.d.). Kidney centers clearly dominate the landscape, increasing from only 25 in 2000 to 2608 in 2024, making them the most widely established transplantation infrastructure worldwide. This rapid growth reflects both the high global burden of kidney disease and the relatively higher success rates and cost-effectiveness of kidney transplantation compared to other organ procedures.

Liver and heart transplantation centers demonstrate steady and significant expansion, rising from 1 to 1159 and 2 to 833 centers respectively over the same period. Although they remain fewer in number than kidney centers, their growth suggests improvements in surgical techniques, post-operative care, and availability of donor organs.

Figure 3. Global trends in organ transplantation centers

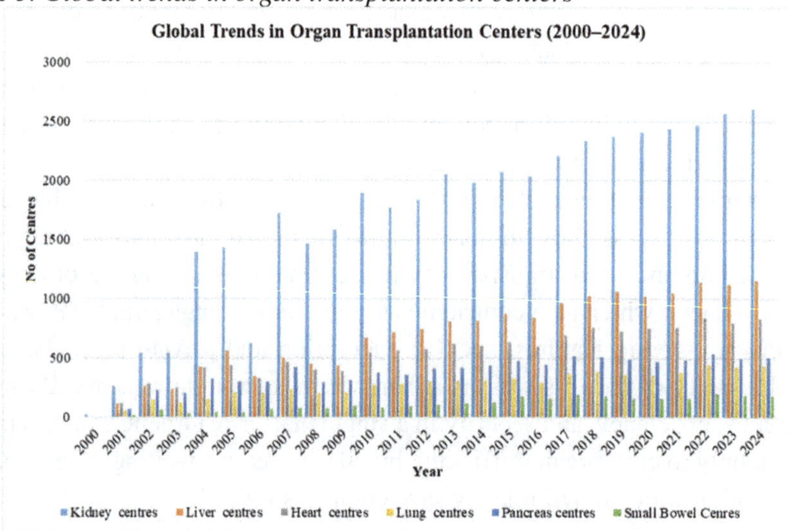

Lung and pancreas transplantation centers show moderate growth, reaching 433 and 506 centers respectively by 2024. However, their trajectories are less consistent, with periods of slower expansion and fluctuations, reflecting the greater clinical complexity of these procedures and variations in national healthcare policies and infrastructure.

Small bowel transplantation centers remain the least developed, growing from virtually non-existent in 2000 to only 180 centers in 2024. This limited growth underscores the rarity of small bowel transplantation, the high associated surgical risks, and the challenges of long-term immunological management.

Overall, the dataset reveals two distinct phases: an initial rapid expansion during the early 2000s (2001–2005), driven by advances in immunosuppression, global health initiatives, and policy support; followed by a period of stabilization after 2015, where growth rates slowed across most organ types.

These trends also carry wider implications. The dominance of kidney transplantation centers parallels the fact that kidneys are the most frequently traded organs in the black market, while organs with limited transplantation infrastructure, such as lungs and small bowel, often command higher illicit market values due to scarcity. Thus, while legitimate transplantation programs have expanded globally, persistent demand-supply imbalances continue to sustain illegal organ trade networks.

2.2 Trends in Brain Death (DBD) and Circulatory Death (DCD) Donors

The longitudinal data on organ donation from 2000 to 2024 highlights significant patterns in the availability and utilization of donors after brain death (DBD) and donors after circulatory death (DCD).

The number of actual donors after brain death as shown in figure 4 has shown a general upward trend, increasing from 9703 in 2000 to over 33,000 by 2024. However, the gap between actual and utilized donors was substantial in the early years, with no reported utilization until 2009. From 2010 onwards, utilization improved steadily, reaching 32,165 utilized donors out of 33,242 actual donors in 2024, indicating a utilization rate exceeding 96%. This demonstrates significant progress in clinical capacity, organ preservation techniques, and transplant logistics (Manla et al., 2022). Nevertheless, periods of fluctuation, such as in 2006 and 2020, suggest that external factors (e.g., policy changes, pandemics, or healthcare resource limitations) can disrupt utilization efficiency.

Figure 4. Trends in brain death donors

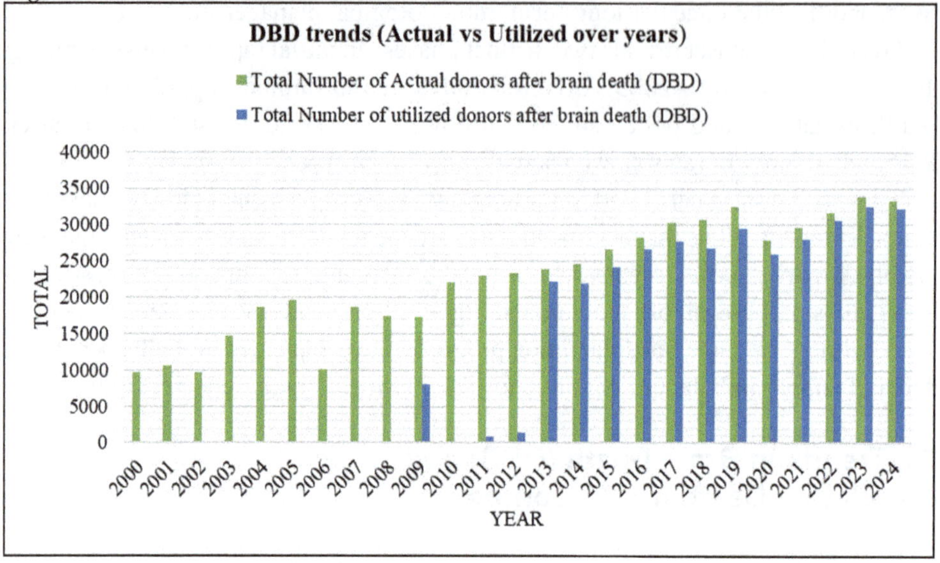

Donors after circulatory death as shown in figure 5 have shown slower but consistent growth compared to DBD. From only 118 actual DCD donors in 2000, the numbers rose to 13,045 in 2024. Utilization, however, lagged behind initially, with negligible uptake until after 2006. By 2015, the number of utilized DCD donors surpassed 5000, reflecting improvements in acceptance criteria and surgical expertise. In 2024, 11,435 out of 13,045 DCD donors were utilized, corresponding to an approximate utilization rate of 88%, which, although lower than DBD, indicates a remarkable improvement in recent years (Qu et al., 2021).

Figure 5. Trends in circulatory death donors

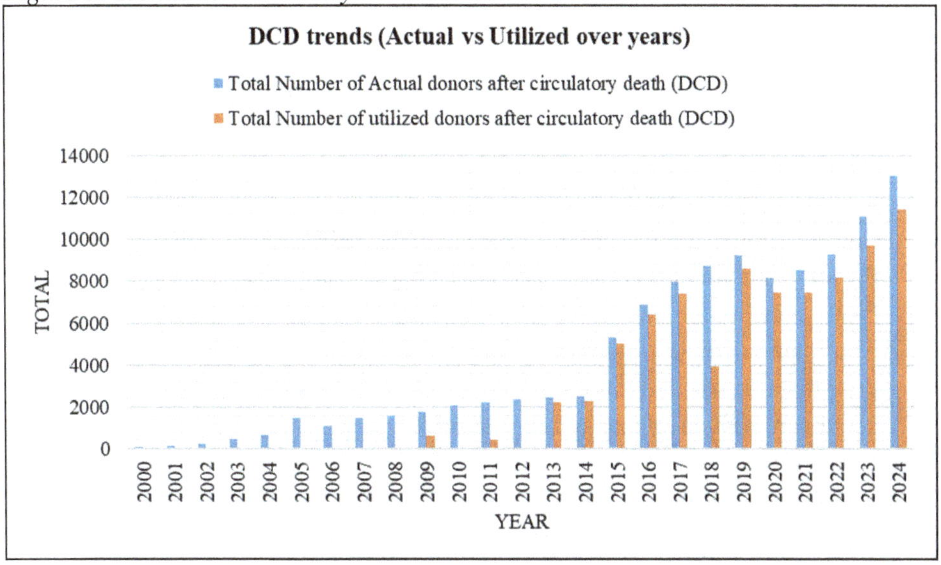

The discussion demonstrates that DBD continue to be the primary source of organs in the world in terms of quantity and performance. Nonetheless, DCD) are gaining more and more significance in bridging the gap between organ demand and supply. DBD and DCD have recorded consistent progress over the past few years due to the increase in transplant systems and international collaboration. Enhancing DCD protocols without compromising on DBD efficiency will be central to decreasing illicit organ trade and having a sustainable transplant system (Bobba et al., 2022).

3. PURPOSE AND CONTRIBUTION OF THE CHAPTER

A blockchain is a decentralized and unalterable digital registry of transactions that stores data between multiple systems and the data cannot be altered without unanimous approval. Its security and transparency makes it suitable in such sensitive fields as organ donation and transplantation.

The improvement is necessary. In the U.S., 17 individuals are dying every day on the waiting list as the recipient of an organ transplant whereas in India there are more than 3 lakh patients on a waiting list and 20 people are dying daily because of the delays. Such numbers reveal severe flaws in the existing system: disjointed records, human errors, and, in some cases, corruption that is stopping organs to meet their intended recipients.

This chapter intends to propose a blockchain-based solution to streamline organ donation and make it faster, fairer, and more transparent. Through blockchain, all stages of the process can be validated and audited to minimize the chances of manipulation or smuggling. In the meantime, privacy and integrity of data are maintained since when the information is entered into the blockchain, it cannot be changed. The major contributions are:

- Enhance transparency and trust among stakeholders.
- Prevent fraudulent practices and reduce organ trafficking.
- Protect sensitive medical and personal data from privacy breaches.
- Automate donor–recipient matching and allocation through smart contracts.
- Provide a simplified and reliable process accessible to patients, donors, healthcare professionals, and regulatory bodies.

By addressing the pressing issues of inefficiency, corruption, and lack of trust, this chapter lays the foundation for a transparent, secure, and streamlined organ donation ecosystem that can be adopted globally.

4. RELATED WORK

The potential of blockchain in improving data security, interoperability, and transparency has attracted a lot of interest in healthcare research. Some general surveys, including those by Balaji et al. (n.d.) and Hawashin et al. (2022), point to the fact that blockchain can help in overcoming the issues of data integrity and system interoperability. Still, these publications are not dedicated to organ donation and transplantation specifically, and practical implementation in this field is not studied properly. Tripathi, Ahad, and Paiva (2020) presented an Ethereum-based public blockchain based on Proof of Work and smart contracts to enhance transparency in organ allocation on the implementation side. Even though this method is fair, it is limited by scaling and is characterized by the high energy consumption of Proof of Work. In the same manner, Dajim et al. (2019) experimented with Ethereum that had a Proof of Stake consensus but failed to practically apply the system to organ donations.

Privacy solutions have also been suggested. Ranjan et al. (2019) designed a hybrid blockchain approach that used a Consortium Proof of Authority consensus that integrates a private and a public chain to achieve scalability and privacy of sensitive information. Nevertheless, the system did not have the smart contract integration, restricting the automation in organ matching and consent management. Hovorushchenko et al. (2023) also focused on using private blockchains to ensure safe organ transplant matching, with the emphasis on efficiency and privacy, yet national healthcare system interoperability is a problem that is yet to be resolved.

Other methods have investigated partial implementation of smart contracts. McGhin et al. (2019) suggested a public Ethereum blockchain which had Proof of Authority and limited smart contract functionality, but privacy issues and use of a public blockchain limited wider use. Ng et al. (2021) introduced an idea of blockchain-based medical transactions during organ transplantation but did not specify how it is implemented, making its feasibility at practice unclear.

Lastly, a number of literature entries have been dedicated to the ethical and legal aspects of organ donation with the help of blockchain. The need to consent, comply with regulations, as well as access justice as emphasized by Lewis and Gardiner (2023) and Ambigtsheer et al. (2024) is more than just a matter of technology, as it is impossible to ensure fairness without properly structured governance and ethical standards. More recently, (Patil et al, 2022) investigated the integration of smart contracts on a public blockchain with PoW consensus, enhancing transparency in organ donation processes but once again falling short on scalability.

Table 1. Comparison between existing literature reviews and surveys

Reference	Blockchain Type	Consensus Mechanism	Smart Contracts	Use Case Specifics
Balaji et al. (n.d.)	Public (Ethereum)	Proof of Stake (PoS)	No	Highlights Ethereum's implementation challenges in organ donation.
Hawashin et al. (2022)	Public (Ethereum)	Proof of Work (PoW)	Yes	Employs Ethereum smart contracts for transparent organ allocation.
Tripathi et al. (2020)	Hybrid (Private + Public)	Consortium Proof of Authority (PoA)	No	Hybrid model addressing privacy in organ donation records.
Dajim et al. (2019)	Private	Not discussed	No	Private blockchain for secure and efficient organ transplant matching.
Ranjan et al. (2019)	Public (Ethereum)	Proof of Authority (PoA)	Partial	Permissioned Ethereum solution with limited smart contract functionality.
Hovorushchenko et al. (2023)	Public (unspecified)	Proof of Work (PoW)	Yes	Smart contract–enabled transparency in organ donation processes.

Table 1 presents a comparative analysis of the existing literature on blockchain in healthcare and organ donation. It captures the type of contribution (review, research paper, conference paper, or editorial), the type of blockchain employed, the consensus mechanism used, whether smart contracts were implemented, scalability considerations, and the specific use cases addressed.

The analysis reveals some clear trends. First, while Ethereum-based public blockchains dominate the proposed solutions, scalability remains a major concern, particularly in systems relying on Proof of Work (PoW). Second, a few studies propose hybrid or private blockchains Tripathi et al. (2020), prioritizing privacy and efficiency, though they often lack full integration of smart contracts. Third, some of them, including Hovorushchenko et al. (2023), are written in the form of reviews or editorials, that is, they are more about ethical, legal, or conceptual considerations but do not provide actual technical models.

Recent studies have increasingly emphasized that technical solutions for organ donation and healthcare data management must be evaluated not only for transparency but also for scalability, privacy preservation, and regulatory compliance. Contemporary surveys highlight that large-scale healthcare ecosystems face significant scalability challenges due to data heterogeneity and cross-institutional coordination, making purely centralized or public blockchain-based solutions difficult to deploy in practice. Privacy-focused analyses further note that safeguarding sensitive medical data requires layered protections, including access control, encryption, and minimization of data exposure, particularly under collaborative setting. Moreover, legal and governance-oriented studies stress that compliance with healthcare regulations and data protection laws necessitates explicit consent management, auditability, and interoperability across systems, independent of the underlying technology. These observations suggest that future organ donation frameworks must integrate scalable architectures with privacy-by-design and regulatory-aware governance, areas that remain insufficiently addressed in existing blockchain-centric approaches.

Although transparency in organ allocation has been the main focus, the other areas such as preventing trafficking, monitoring post-transplant, and alignment of regulations have not been given much attention and show the areas where the OrganChain framework would help bridge the gaps.

5. PROPOSED FRAMEWORK OF ORGANCHAIN

OrganChain is a blockchain-powered ecosystem that is aimed at offering a safe, transparent and efficient organ donation and transplantation solution. It incorporates various stakeholders such as donors, recipients, hospitals and regulatory bodies into a single platform that enhances accountability and reduces cases of corruption or ill practices as shown in figure 6. The OrganChain blockchain layer is at the center of the framework and it keeps an unaltered record of all the activities such as donor registration, organ availability, consent checks and recipient assignments.

OrganChain that is designed to combine all of these functions is intended to create the stable structure that will stop organ trafficking and strengthen the confidence in the healthcare system. In addition to corruption and illegal trade, OrganChain enhances the efficiency of transplantation by providing an automated algorithm of donors and recipients, real-time availability monitoring, and post-transplant follow-up mechanisms. This type of measures gives full transparency and auditability of the process. The blockchain cryptographically links sensitive information stored in the cloud, and it is not possible to modify the data without cryptographic links.

Figure 6. Proposed framework of OrganChain

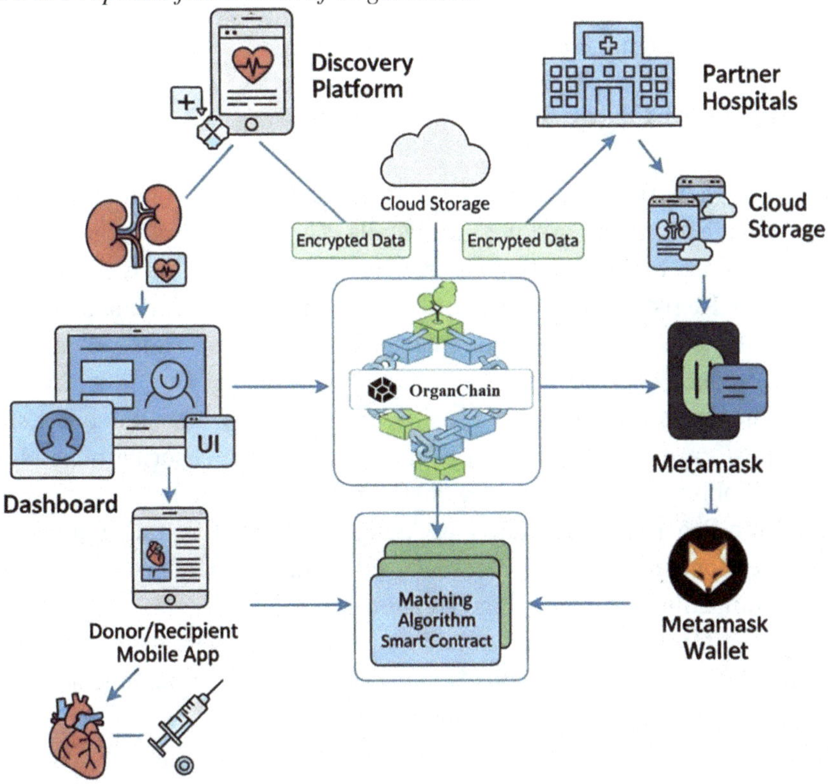

A Discovery Platform will allow a potential donor to register their will, health records and consent safely. Such coded records are verifiable blockchain items. The recipient data, organ availability and transplantation outcomes are then updated by partner hospitals using integrated systems hence contributing real time information into the network. The Matching-Algorithm Smart Contract is the decision-making system of OrganChain, which automatically evaluates the compatibility of the donor and the recipient, based on medical conditions like blood group, tissue type, and urgency. This will guarantee a level playing field of allocation of organs as it will be free of human touch.

OrganChain offers an easy-to-use and a functional Donor/Recipient Mobile Application and Dashboard interface. The mobile application will enable donors and recipients to check the registration status, send notifications, and follow the progress of transplantation; the dashboard will provide healthcare providers and administrators with the tools of analytics and real-time indicators of allocation. The transparency of the finances is gained with the help of the MetaMask integration that facilitates the safe cryptocurrency transactions or micropayments. This makes the financial flows traceable in organ donation logistics, which is permitted, and the establishment of incentive systems, where the donors or participants in awareness campaigns receive digital tokens in their contributions.

5.1 Workflow of OrganChain

1. **Donor Registration** – A donor registers on the Discovery Platform or mobile app, providing consent and medical details. These records are encrypted and stored securely in the cloud, while references are recorded on the blockchain.
2. **Recipient Registration** – Partner hospitals upload patient details, including medical history and organ requirements, which are also stored securely and linked to the blockchain.
3. **Data Encryption & Storage** – Sensitive data is encrypted before being stored in cloud storage. Blockchain entries point to this data, ensuring immutability and verifiability without exposing confidential information.
4. **Matching Process** – The Matching Algorithm Smart Contract automatically compares donor and recipient records based on medical parameters (blood type, tissue compatibility, urgency, and location).
5. **Allocation Decision** – Once a suitable match is identified, the smart contract records the allocation on the blockchain. This record is immutable and visible to authorized stakeholders, ensuring transparency.
6. **Notification & Tracking** – Donors, recipients, and hospitals receive instant notifications via the mobile app and dashboard. Patients can track their progress, while hospitals monitor allocation efficiency.
7. **Surgical Procedure & Outcome Recording** – Once the transplant takes place, hospitals record outcomes on the blockchain. These are logged immutably to maintain accountability.
8. **Post-Transplant Monitoring** – The system allows hospitals to record follow-up results and patient health data, ensuring long-term monitoring and compliance.

9. **Financial & Incentive Management** – Where applicable, transactions are processed through Metamask Wallet, ensuring transparency in payments. Incentive tokens may also be issued to donors or awareness campaign contributors.

5.2 The proposed Donor–Recipient Matching Algorithm

The proposed donor–recipient matching algorithm as described in figure 7, in OrganChain ensures that organ allocation is carried out in a transparent, fair, and tamper-proof manner. The algorithm begins by taking two inputs: the donor list containing attributes such as blood type, HLA markers, location, and availability, and the recipient list containing medical details such as blood type, HLA requirements, urgency level, waiting time, and location.

Figure 7. Donor–recipient matching in OrganChain

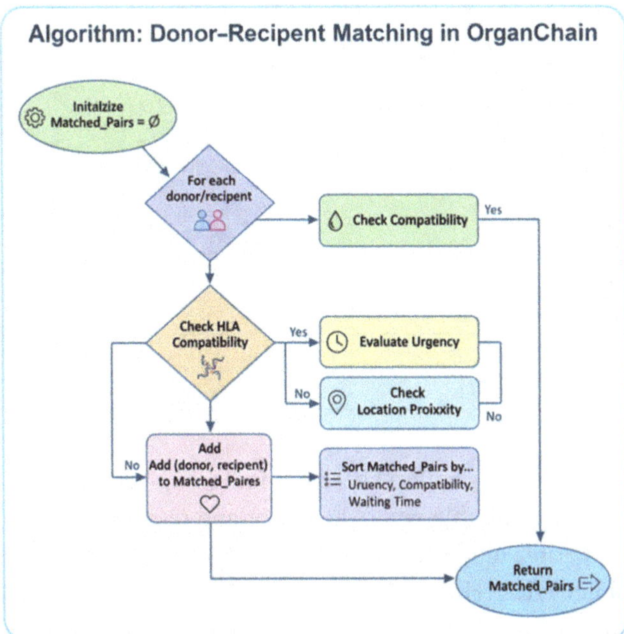

Table 2. Algorithm for Donor-Recipient Matching

Algorithm: Donor–Recipient Matching
Input: • Donor set $D = \{d_1, d_2, \ldots\ldots\ldots\ldots d_n\}$ where each donor d_i has attributes (BT, HLA, Loc, Avl) • Recipient set $R = \{r_1, r_2, \ldots\ldots\ldots\ldots r_n\}$, where each recipient r_i has attributes (BT, HLA, Loc, Urg, Wt)
1. Initialize $M = \emptyset$ 2. For each donor $d_i \in D$ a. For each recipient $r_i \in R$ i. Compute Blood Type Compatibility score: $BT_{comp(d_i r_i)} = \begin{cases} 1, \, if \, BT(d_i) \, is \, compatible \, with \, BT(r_j) \\ 0, \, otherwise \end{cases}$ ii. Compute HLA Compatibility Score: $HLA_{score(d_i r_i)} = \frac{\lvert HLA(d_i) \cap HLA(r_j) \rvert}{\lvert HLA(r_i) \rvert}, 0 \le HLA_{score} \le 1$ iii. Compute Location Feasibility score: $Loc_{-comp(d_i r_i)} = \begin{cases} 1, \, if \, distance(Loc(d_i), Loc(r_j)) \le \delta \\ 0, \, otherwise \end{cases}$ where δ is the maximum feasible distance threshold. iv. Compute Overall Compatibility Score $Comp(d_i, r_i) = BT_{comp(d_i r_i)} \cdot HLA_{score(d_i r_i)} \cdot Loc_{-comp(d_i r_i)}$ v. Urgency Priority Function: $P_{urg}(r_j) = \alpha . Urg(r_j) + \beta . Wt(r_j)$ where $\alpha, \beta \in [0,1]$ are weights balancing urgency and waiting time. vi. If $Comp(d_i, r_i) > 0$ Compute priority score: $Score(d_i, r_i) = Comp(d_i, r_i) . P_{urg}(r_j)$ 3. If $Score(d_i, r_i) \ge \theta \, (threshold)$ Add pair (d_i, r_i) to M 4. Sort M in descending order of $Score(d_i, r_i)$
Output: • Matched pairs $M = \{(d_i, r_i)\}$

The first stage of the algorithm checks blood group compatibility, since organ transplantation is only possible when the donor and recipient have either identical or medically compatible blood types. Once this condition is satisfied, the algorithm proceeds to evaluate HLA (Human Leukocyte Antigen) matching, which is a critical factor in determining whether the recipient's immune system will accept or reject the transplanted organ.

Clinical urgency and waiting time is then added to the algorithm when both blood type and HLA compatibility have been established. Patients who have an increased medical urgency or a shorter wait are given priority thereby being fair and ethically allocative. Geographic feasibility is also checked by the algorithm since the distance of space has a major effect on the viability of organs in transportation.

A combination of all these tests forms a composite compatibility score, which is computed on all the donor-recipients pair. The score is a weighted score, which is a balance between biological compatibility and urgency and logistical constraints.

The donor-receiving pairs are then ranked in decreasing order of their scores and the highest scored match is chosen to be allocated.Once a match is finalized, the decision is recorded immutably on the blockchain, making it fully auditable by stakeholders.

By combining medical parameters, urgency-based fairness, and blockchain transparency, the algorithm not only ensures the efficiency and accuracy of donor–recipient matching but also significantly reduces the possibility of corruption, manipulation, or organ trafficking within the system.

6. IMPLEMENTATION RESULTS AND ANALYSIS

The implementation of OrganChain was tested using a private Ethereum network under Proof of Authority (PoA) consensus. Smart contracts were deployed in Solidity for donor registration, recipient registration, consent logging, and organ matching. A prototype dashboard was developed using React.js for front-end access and Web3.js for blockchain interaction. Off-chain sensitive data was secured through IPFS.

To evaluate the effectiveness of the proposed system, a series of experiments were conducted focusing on performance, cost, matching accuracy, and security.

6.1 Smart Contract Gas Usage

One of the critical performance metrics for blockchain-based systems is the gas consumption of smart contracts. Table 2 summarizes the gas usage and corresponding cost (ETH) for various operations within OrganChain.

Table 3. Smart contract gas usage for different operations

Operation Type	Average Gas Consumed	Approx. Cost (ETH)	Description
Donor Registration	45,000	0.0020	Registers donor details (age, blood group, organ availability).
Recipient Registration	55,000	0.0025	Stores recipient medical details and urgency score.
Consent Logging	65,000	0.0030	Immutable storage of donor/family consent for transplantation.
Organ Matching	85,000	0.0040	Executes compatibility and priority functions to select best recipient.

The results indicate that the gas costs remain predictable and within acceptable limits, with slightly higher costs for organ matching due to the algorithmic complexity involved.

6.2. Comparison with Existing Systems

A comparative evaluation was conducted between manual/legacy systems, existing blockchain prototypes, and the proposed OrganChain framework. Table 3 summarizes the differences across key parameters, including transparency, scalability, privacy, and trafficking prevention.

Table 4. Comparison of OrganChain with existing systems

Feature / Parameter	Manual / Legacy Systems	Existing Blockchain Prototypes	Proposed OrganChain
Transparency	Low (manual records, prone to manipulation)	Medium (partial blockchain integration)	High (full immutable ledger with audit trail)
Scalability	Low (time-consuming, not suitable for large datasets)	Medium (some hybrid approaches exist)	High (optimized PoA consensus, modular design)
Privacy & Data Security	Low (centralized databases vulnerable to breaches)	Medium (limited encryption/off-chain use)	High (on-chain hashing + off-chain encrypted storage in IPFS)
Matching Efficiency	Low (manual, error-prone, delayed allocation)	Medium (basic blockchain-based matching)	High (automated compatibility + priority functions in smart contracts)
Trafficking Prevention	Very weak (black market influence possible)	Limited (focus only on transparency)	Strong (immutable records + regulator audit contracts)
Cost Predictability	Uncertain (paper + admin costs vary)	Medium (gas costs fluctuate)	Predictable (PoA with controlled environment)
Regulatory Auditing	Difficult (no verifiable trail)	Limited (partial audit logs)	Comprehensive (full blockchain-based auditability)

The findings suggest that OrganChain is remarkably more transparent, has greater privacy, is more scalable, and efficient than traditional systems and current blockchain prototypes. Its capacity to eliminate illegal trafficking is even increased by the inclusion of audit contracts.

6.3 System Dashboard Design

OrganChain implementation focuses on a complete dashboard which combines blockchain technology with donor-receivers. The dashboard is the primary point of interaction with patients, hospitals, and regulatory bodies, and thus usable with security measures, with all transactions, such as donor registration and transplant completion, being safely recorded and verifiable. The dashboard is a modular one although it is displayed as a single interface. The patient profile section comprises demographic data (name, age, gender, blood type) and medical history that would be important in determining whether the patient is eligible to undergo the transplant or not. There is a medical history panel that records transfusion, comorbidities and critical health events. The transplant status module tracks the identification of donors, compatibility testing, and scheduling to minimize the delays in manuals. On the hospital level, there are tables of donor and recipient data, and a geo-mapped image can be seen, which indicates partner hospitals and availability of organs per region. All the activities, such as registrations, matches, and completed transplants, are registered on a regulatory audit log powered by the blockchain, and accountability is ensured.

The workflow is technologically a combination of safe data collection, blockchain documentation, and dynamic interface. The encrypted data of the donors and receivers is uploaded to the secure cloud storage at the hospitals and discovery platforms and verified by the blockchain before being fixed permanently. The compatibility and priority are tested by the matching algorithm smart contract and the results are stored on-chain. This data is constantly updated on the dashboard and is used to show the real-time donor pool counts, waiting list counts, and transplants completed as well as dynamically displayed real-time line graphs, bar charts, and pie charts to show the availability of organs and their trends. Audit trails and approved consent records are impervious and handle the issue of malpractice and adherence to ethical principles. The prototype will have a React.js frontend based on TailwindCSS modular visualization, a Node.js server that combines Ethereum smart contracts with a backend, and MongoDB as an off-chain data storage. Sensitive operations such as identity check and approval are managed through MetaMask integration and Chart.js is used to display interactive real-time charts. Table 4 is a summary of the most important tools and technologies employed in the implementation.

Table 5. Tools and technologies for OrganChain implementation

Layer	Technology/Tool Used	Purpose
Frontend/UI	React.js, TailwindCSS	Interactive and modular dashboard design
Backend/API	Node.js, Express	Handling requests and integration with blockchain layer
Blockchain Layer	Ethereum/Hyperledger + Smart Contracts	Immutable storage, matching algorithm execution, and secure logging
Off-chain Database	MongoDB	Temporary storage of non-sensitive and auxiliary data

continued on following page

Table 5. Continued

Layer	Technology/Tool Used	Purpose
Visualization	Chart.js / D3.js	Graphical analytics and trend visualizations
Wallet Integration	MetaMask	Secure donor/recipient identity validation and consent signing

In order to confirm the usability of OrganChain, a series of interactive dashboards was developed and applied as the primary interface with all stakeholders involved such as patients, hospitals, donors, recipients, and regulatory authorities. Figures 8 and 9 demonstrate the functionality of the platform and its design.

Figure 8. OrganChain main dashboard

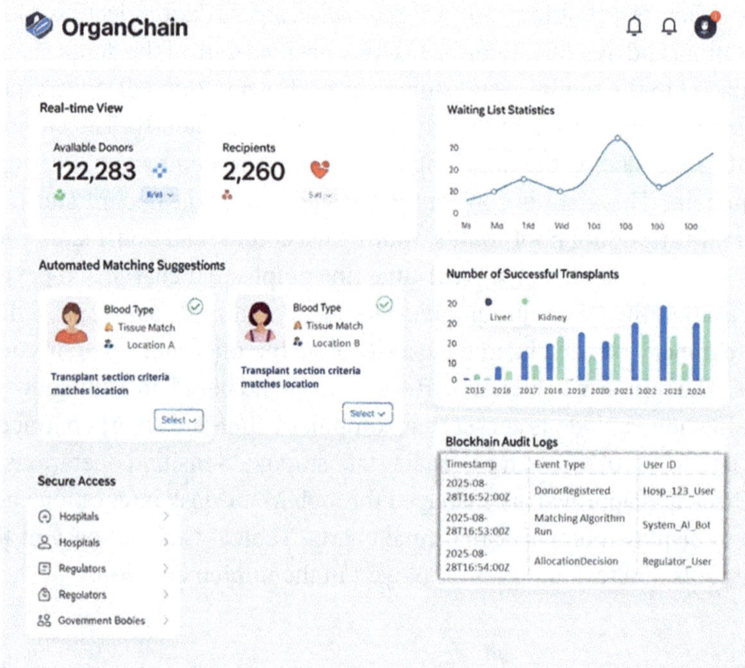

The Patient Profile panel will contain key data like demographics, medical history and unique identification numbers, so that no two donors and recipients are the same and no one can impersonate the other. Medical records are sensitive and they are encrypted and can only be accessed by appropriate authorization. The Medical History module documents the transfusion, comorbidities, and acute health conditions that are associated with transplantation. These records are immutable, and using the capabilities of blockchain, one can ensure that the data is authentic.

The Transplant Status panel gives real time updates on the status of the transplant procedures, whether the donor has been located, compatibility checked and surgery booked. This minimises time wastage due to miscommunication or paperwork. The Hospital Management dashboard unites donor and recipient data of partner hospitals and provides both tabular and map-based data displays to demonstrate the geographical distribution of donors and recipients. This will facilitate quicker decision making and better logistics in organ transport.

Lastly, the Transplants Completed widget is a statistical summary of current progress that presents trends of transplants monthly. This will enable the stakeholders to monitor the performance over the time and determine the efficiency of the organ donation system.

Figure 9. Functionality and visual design of the platform

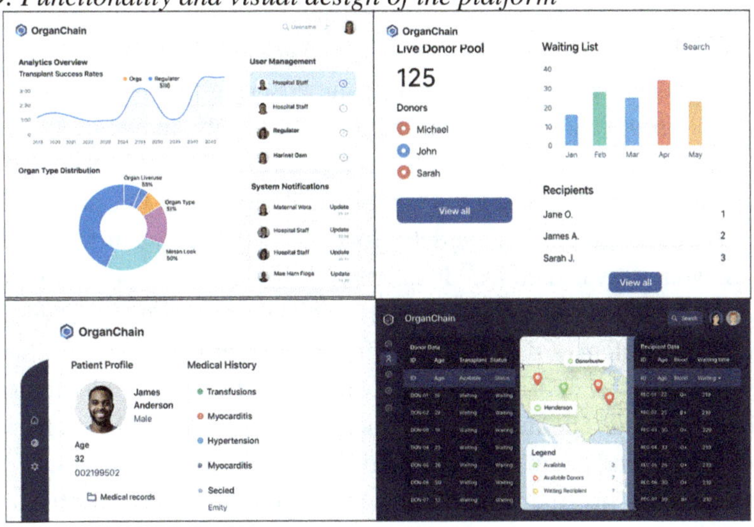

The overall design emphasizes clarity, real-time synchronization, and blockchain-backed security. Each transaction—from donor registration to final transplant completion—is logged immutably on the blockchain, ensuring accountability and transparency. By combining intuitive UI design with robust backend security, OrganChain demonstrates how blockchain-based healthcare systems can be translated into practical, user-friendly solutions.

7. CHALLENGES IN ORGAN DONATION SYSTEMS

Organ donation and transplantation systems face multiple challenges that limit their efficiency, fairness, and ethical integrity. As shown in *Table 7*, these challenges extend from scarcity of organs and inadequate infrastructure to socio-cultural barriers, governance issues, and post-transplantation inefficiencies. OrganChain addresses each of these issues through blockchain-enabled mechanisms, smart contracts, and real-time data integration (Olawade et al., 2025).

One of the most pressing challenges is the scarcity of organs, where available donations are often lost due to delays in matching and transportation. OrganChain mitigates this by maintaining a decentralized real-time donor registry, coupled with a compatibility function C(d,r)C(d,r)C(d,r) that enables instant donor–recipient matching, thereby reducing waiting list times. Similarly, the lack of modern infrastructure—such as organ preservation and monitoring facilities—often results in degradation of donated organs. OrganChain integrates IoT-based cold storage and transport monitoring with blockchain logging, ensuring that organ condition data remains tamper-proof and accessible throughout the supply chain (Streit et al., 2023).

Social and economic factors, as well as religious issues, tend to distrust the organ donation systems, which in some cases promote illegal trade. OrganChain uses the immutability and cryptographic validation of consent of blockchain to provide transparency and voluntary and ethical donations. Meanwhile, anonymized reporting is respectful to religious sensibilities, as well as safeguarding privacy. The traditional systems have a problem of duplication, manual errors and delayed communication in the hospitals. OrganChain is solving these problems by having a distributed ledger to coordinate with stakeholders, and dashboards and mobile applications will offer the unified access and automated distribution through smart contracts.

The difficulty of organ donation is exacerbated by legal and governance issues since inconsistent policies and absence of regulation leave room to malpractice (Saxena et al., 2023). OrganChain solves this by using policy-based smart contracts to encode allocation rules and have audit trails, which cannot be changed to ensure that they comply with the regulatory bodies. The issue of brain-dead donor identification and certification delays are also reduced by use of automated event triggers to permit immediate updates on the registry and quicker notifications to recipients.

Ethical issues of live donors, such as coercion and insufficient checking of consent are also tackled. OrganChain proposes multi-factor consent validation between the donor, medical authorities, and legal representatives and post-donation monitoring that cannot be changed to protect the welfare of the donor in the long term. The priority scoring capability P(r) improves allocation fairness and is based on urgency, waiting time and equity. Monitoring of the post-transplant is facilitated through dashboard and mobile applications, which safely monitor patient recovery and outcomes. In general, as the data in Table 7 depict, OrganChain is not just another blockchain-based record system, but a holistic model that addresses medical, ethical, logistical, and governance issues to the field of organ donation and transplantation.

Table 6. Mapping organ donation challenges to OrganChain solutions

Challenge	Current Limitation	OrganChain Solution
Scarcity of Organs	Long waiting lists, wasted organs due to delays.	Real-time **decentralized donor registry** with compatibility function C(d,r)C(d,r)C(d,r) for instant matching.
Infrastructure Gaps	Poor preservation, monitoring, and transport facilities.	IoT-enabled cold storage **and transport tracking with blockchain logging.**
Socio-Economic & Religious Barriers	Exploitation, mistrust, cultural/religious resistance.	Immutable consent verification **and** anonymized reporting **for transparency and privacy.**
Poor Coordination	Manual errors, duplicate records, delayed communication.	Distributed ledger **synchronizing hospitals; smart contracts automate allocation.**
Weak Legal & Governance	Inconsistent policies, manipulation of waiting lists.	Policy-based smart contracts **with immutable audit trails for compliance.**
Brain-Dead Donor Challenges	Certification delays, missed organ recovery.	Automated event triggers **for instant updates and recipient notification.**
Live Donor Ethics	Coercion, weak consent verification, no follow-up.	Multi-factor consent validation **and immutable** donor welfare logs.
System Effectiveness	Favoritism, inefficiency, weak post-transplant care.	Priority scoring **P(r)P(r)P(r) for fair allocation; dashboards for post-transplant monitoring.**

Despite its technical advantages, the real-world deployment of blockchain-based organ donation systems faces several practical challenges. Interoperability remains a key barrier, as hospitals and transplant centers operate heterogeneous information systems with varying data standards. Integrating OrganChain with existing electronic health records, hospital management systems, and national registries requires standardized data models and phased migration strategies. Stakeholder buy-in presents another challenge, as successful adoption depends on the cooperation of hospitals, clinicians, regulatory bodies, and patients. Resistance to change, limited technical expertise, and concerns over workflow disruption may slow adoption. These challenges can be mitigated through training programs, pilot deployments, and clear policy incentives that demonstrate operational and ethical benefits. Regulatory and compliance issues further influence deployment feasibility. OrganChain must align with national transplant laws, data protection regulations, and ethical guidelines governing consent and allocation. The use of permissioned blockchains, policy-driven smart contracts, and audit trails helps ensure legal compliance while preserving transparency and accountability. Addressing these deployment barriers is essential for translating blockchain-based frameworks like OrganChain from conceptual models into scalable, real-world transplantation systems.

While OrganChain offers significant advantages in transparency, security, and automation, several limitations must be acknowledged. Blockchain-based systems may face scalability constraints when handling high transaction volumes across large healthcare networks. To mitigate this, OrganChain adopts off-chain data storage and permissioned blockchain configurations, reducing on-chain load while preserving auditability.

Interoperability with existing hospital information systems presents another challenge due to heterogeneous data formats and legacy infrastructure. This can be addressed through standardized data schemas, middleware-based integration, and phased deployment strategies that minimize disruption to existing workflows.

Data privacy and compliance remain critical concerns in healthcare applications. Although blockchain provides immutability, improper design could expose sensitive metadata. OrganChain mitigates this risk through encryption, access-controlled smart contracts, and anonymized reporting mechanisms, ensuring alignment with healthcare data protection regulations.

Stakeholder adoption is also a non-technical limitation, as resistance to change and lack of technical expertise may hinder deployment. Training programs, pilot implementations, and policy incentives are essential to encourage adoption and build trust among healthcare professionals and regulators.

The regulatory alignment across regions remains complex due to variations in legal frameworks governing organ transplantation. OrganChain addresses this by incorporating policy-driven smart contracts and immutable audit trails, while recognizing that continuous collaboration with regulatory authorities is required for large-scale deployment.

8. CONCLUSION

The shortage of organs, black-market and the inefficient distribution remain some of the challenges facing organ transplantation. Current systems are usually not transparent, secure, and coordinated in time, which reduces trust and endangers patients. OrganChain is another blockchain-based framework presented in this chapter, which uses immutability, transparency, and smart contracts to build safe donor registries, automate matching of donors and recipients, and enforce ethical allotment. OrganChain will overcome technical and ethical constraints of existing systems by integrating monitors based on IoT, ensuring the secure consent process, and real-time dashboards. In general, it shows that blockchain can revolutionize the process of organ donation, eliminate trafficking, and increase fairness, efficiency, and accountability. Having broader use and favorable policies, OrganChain can save thousands of lives and change the future of organ transplantation.

REFERENCES

Balaji, B., Deepthi, T., Supriya, K., Kiran, P. S., & Riyaz, S. (n.d.). *Management of organ transplantation using blockchain.*

Bawa, G., Singh, H., Rani, S., Kataria, A., & Min, H. (2024). Exploring perspectives of blockchain technology and traditional centralized technology in organ donation management: A comprehensive review. *Information (Basel)*, *15*(11), 703. DOI: 10.3390/info15110703

Bobba, C. M., Whitson, B. A., Henn, M. C., Mokadam, N. A., Keller, B. C., Rosenheck, J., & Ganapathi, A. M. (2022). Trends in donation after circulatory death in lung transplantation in the United States: Impact of era. *Transplant International*, *35*, 10172. DOI: 10.3389/ti.2022.10172 PMID: 35444490

Cohen, L. R. (2017). Increasing the supply of transplant organs: The virtues of a futures market. In *Organ and Tissue Transplantation* (pp. 121–171). Routledge. DOI: 10.4324/9781315247571-7

Coveney, C., Hudson, N., Lafuente-Funes, S., Jacxsens, L., & Provoost, V. (2022). From scarcity to sisterhood: The framing of egg donation on fertility clinic websites in the UK, Belgium and Spain. *Social Science & Medicine*, *296*, 114785. DOI: 10.1016/j.socscimed.2022.114785 PMID: 35151147

Dajim, L. A., Al-Farras, S. A., Al-Shahrani, B. S., Al-Zuraib, A. A., & Mathew, R. M. (2019, May). Organ donation decentralized application using blockchain technology. In *2019 2nd International Conference on Computer Applications & Information Security (ICCAIS)* (pp. 1–4). IEEE. DOI: 10.1109/CAIS.2019.8769459

Etheredge, H. R. (2021). Assessing global organ donation policies: Opt-in vs. opt-out. *Risk Management and Healthcare Policy*, *14*, 1985–1999. DOI: 10.2147/RMHP.S270234 PMID: 34012308

Hawashin, D., Jayaraman, R., Salah, K., Yaqoob, I., Simsekler, M. C. E., & Ellahham, S. (2022). Blockchain-based management for organ donation and transplantation. *IEEE Access : Practical Innovations, Open Solutions*, *10*, 59013–59025. DOI: 10.1109/ACCESS.2022.3180008

Hippen, B. E. (2005). In defense of a regulated market in kidneys from living vendors. *The Journal of Medicine and Philosophy*, *30*(6), 593–626. DOI: 10.1080/03605310500421397 PMID: 16396787

Hovorushchenko, T., Hnatchuk, Y., Osyadlyi, V., Kapustian, M., & Boyarchuk, A. (2023). Blockchain-based medical decision support system. *Journal of Cyber Security and Mobility*, *12*(3), 253–273.

Joshi, P. P., Palande, A. K., Kode, A. A., Gaikwad, D. S., & Patil, R. (2024, March). LifeChain: Organ donation and transplantation system using blockchain. In *International Conference on Innovations in Cybersecurity and Data Science (ICICDS)* (pp. 759–773). Singapore: Springer Nature Singapore. DOI: 10.1007/978-981-97-5791-6_55

Kelarijani, M. K. (2024). Can deceased donor transplantation alone eradicate the kidney waiting list? *Urology Journal*, *21*(04), 267–268. PMID: 37312602

Larijani, B., Zahedi, F., & Taheri, E. (2004, June). Ethical and legal aspects of organ transplantation in Iran. [). Elsevier.]. *Transplantation Proceedings*, *36*(5), 1241–1244. DOI: 10.1016/j.transproceed.2004.05.065 PMID: 15251302

Lewis, J., & Gardiner, D. (2023). Ethical and legal issues associated with organ donation and transplantation. *Surgery (Oxford)*, *41*(9), 552–558. DOI: 10.1016/j.mpsur.2023.06.010

Manla, Y., AlSindi, F., Attallah, N., Al Badarin, F., Ghalib, H., & Bader, F. (2022, March). Temporal trends in brain-death organ donation in Asia: Results from the Global Observatory on Donation and Transplantation. [). Elsevier.]. *Transplantation Proceedings*, *54*(2), 233–236. DOI: 10.1016/j.transproceed.2021.12.031 PMID: 35067376

McGhin, T., Choo, K. K. R., Liu, C. Z., & He, D. (2019). Blockchain in healthcare applications: Research challenges and opportunities. *Journal of Network and Computer Applications*, *135*, 62–75. DOI: 10.1016/j.jnca.2019.02.027

Mudiayi, D., Shojai, S., Okpechi, I., Christie, E. A., Wen, K., Kamaleldin, M., Elsadig Osman, M., Lunney, M., Prasad, B., Osman, M. A., Ye, F., Khan, M., Htay, H., Caskey, F., Jindal, K. K., Klarenback, S., Jha, V., Rondeau, E., Turan Kazancioglu, R., & Bello, A. K. (2022). Global estimates of capacity for kidney transplantation in world countries and regions. *Transplantation*, *106*(6), 1113–1122. DOI: 10.1097/TP.0000000000003943 PMID: 34495014

Ng, W. Y., Tan, T. E., Movva, P. V., Fang, A. H. S., Yeo, K. K., Ho, D., Foo, F. S. S., Xiao, Z., Sun, K., Wong, T. Y., Sia, A. T.-H., & Ting, D. S. W. (2021). Blockchain applications in healthcare for COVID-19 and beyond: A systematic review. *The Lancet. Digital Health*, *3*(12), e819–e829. DOI: 10.1016/S2589-7500(21)00210-7 PMID: 34654686

Olawade, D. B., Marinze, S., Qureshi, N., Weerasinghe, K., & Teke, J. (2025). Transforming organ donation and transplantation: Strategies for increasing donor participation and system efficiency. *European Journal of Internal Medicine, 133*, 14–24. DOI: 10.1016/j.ejim.2024.11.010 PMID: 39572291

Patil, R. Y., Patil, Y. H., Gupta, S. K., & Bannore, A. (2022). Organ donation and transplantation challenges, opportunities, and the role of blockchain. In *Disruptive Developments in Biomedical Applications* (pp. 325–339). DOI: 10.1201/9781003272694-27

Patil, R. Y., Patil, Y. H., & Thepade, S. D. (2024). The legal and ethical issues in organ donation and transplantation—A bibliometric analysis. *International Journal of Biomedical Engineering and Technology, 44*(1), 80–101. DOI: 10.1504/IJBET.2024.136394

Qu, Z., Oedingen, C., Bartling, T., Beneke, J., Zink, M., Krauth, C., & Schrem, H. (2021). Systematic review on potential brain-dead donor estimations and conversion rates to actually realized organ donations. *Transplantation Reviews, 35*(4), 100638. DOI: 10.1016/j.trre.2021.100638 PMID: 34246111

Rampersad, C., Ahn, C., Callaghan, C., Dominguez-Gil, B., Ferreira, G. F., Kute, V., Rahmel, A. O., Sarwal, M., Snyder, J., Wang, H., Wong, G., & Kim, S. J. (2024). Organ donation and transplantation registries across the globe: A review of the current state. *Transplantation, 108*(10), e321–e326. DOI: 10.1097/TP.0000000000005043 PMID: 38685195

Ranjan, P., Srivastava, S., Gupta, V., Tapaswi, S., & Kumar, N. (2019, December). Decentralised and distributed system for organ/tissue donation and transplantation. In *2019 IEEE Conference on Information and Communication Technology* (pp. 1–6). IEEE. DOI: 10.1109/CICT48419.2019.9066225

Rawat, R., Garg, B., Mahor, V., Telang, S., Pachlasiya, K., & Chouhan, M. (2022). Organ trafficking on the dark web—The data security and privacy concern in healthcare systems. In *Internet of Healthcare Things* (pp. 189–216). Machine Learning for Security and Privacy. DOI: 10.1002/9781119792468.ch9

Saxena, D., Trivedi, P., Bhavsar, P., Memon, F., Thaker, A., Chaudhary, C., Yasobant, S., Singhal, D., & Zodpey, S. (2023). Challenges and motivators to organ donation: A qualitative exploratory study in Gujarat, India. *International Journal of General Medicine, 16*, 151–159. DOI: 10.2147/IJGM.S393240 PMID: 36687162

Singh, A. P., Saxena, R., & Saxena, S. (2024). Professional blood donors: Ethical concerns and complexities. *Journal of International Research in Medical and Pharmaceutical Sciences, 19*(1), 17–23. DOI: 10.56557/jirmeps/2024/v19i18603

Streit, S., Johnston-Webber, C., Mah, J., Prionas, A., Wharton, G., Paulino, J., Franca, A., Mossialos, E., & Papalois, V. (2023). Lessons from the Portuguese solid organ donation and transplantation system: Achieving success despite challenging conditions. *Transplant International*, *36*, 11008. DOI: 10.3389/ti.2023.11008 PMID: 37305338

The Transplant Observatory. (n.d.). *Data charts and tables.* Retrieved October 13, 2025, from https://www.transplant-observatory.org/data-charts-and-tables/

Tripathi, G., Ahad, M. A., & Paiva, S. (2020, March). S2HS—A blockchain-based approach for smart healthcare system. [Elsevier.]. *Health Care*, *8*(1), 100391. PMID: 31753750

Viecelli, A. K., Gately, R., Barday, Z., Shojai, S., Arruebo, S., Caskey, F. J., Damster, S., Donner, J.-A., Jha, V., Levin, A., Nangaku, M., Saad, S., Tonelli, M., Ye, F., Okpechi, I. G., Bello, A. K., & Johnson, D. W. (2024). Worldwide organization and structures for kidney transplantation services. *Nephrology, Dialysis, Transplantation*, *39*(Suppl. 2), ii26–ii34. DOI: 10.1093/ndt/gfae144 PMID: 39235196

World Health Organization. (2022). *Global observatory on donation and transplantation.* GODT.

Chapter 9
From Dark Web Forums to Hospital Networks: Intercepting Organ Trafficking for Exploitation

Asmaa Mahfoud Alhakimi
http://orcid.org/0000-0002-4038-5203
MSU University, Malaysia

ABSTRACT

Dark Web serves as a primary marketplace where traffickers promote victims and organs, organize logistics, anonymize financial transactions, and move these illegal operations from hidden digital forums to real world medical institutions. An analysis of cybersecurity challenges presented particularly how sophisticated cybercrime tactics undermine existing healthcare security protocols and supply chain integrity. Effective prevention requires shifting from reactive defense to proactive cyber-intelligence by applying advanced monitoring techniques to map the digital footprints of human trafficking operations on the Dark Web, healthcare entities, cybersecurity providers, and law enforcement can create substantial cybersecurity value. This framework involves developing protocols to quickly identify, intercept, and report suspicious digital transactions that indicate organ exploitation, thereby strengthening hospital networks and protecting vulnerable populations from this evil trade. This analysis offers insights into a comprehensive strategy for organ trafficking prevention.

DOI: 10.4018/979-8-3373-6696-8.ch009

INTRODUCTION

Privacy is known as the isolation state where user is never seen or spied on. It is the state where users feel safe while surfing the digital world and sustaining a private space with no interferences from any outsider force such as hackers, or commercial ads. Digital privacy has become one of the human rights that is constantly demanded. Users have the right to be left alone while surfing or using any digital services. Personal information privacy is the ability of the individual to personally control information about themselves. The massive improvements of internet and various technology services and applications have much reduced the user's privacy in every aspect. Users no longer own or feel freedom while surfing, they must fight several different attacks from different attackers(Accenture Security, 2019). Users face several violations while surfing the internet. Commercial companies and platforms are using and selling the user's information for business purposes without any concern of the user's privacy. Hackers and spammers are sneaking and stealing users' private information to be used as a weapon to blackmail them for money with no regard to the possibility of destroying these users' lives(Dick Marty, 2010).

According to U.S. Federal Trade Commission (FTC), 85% of all Web sites collect personal information from consumers; however, only 14% have posted their privacy practices. Privacy concern care varies from one country to another(Brady & Heinl, 2020). Depending on culture, education, and the level of the technology illegal performance, and government act upon misuse of technology. Having such problems in technology cost the user and the government a massive amount of money seeking data protection and privacy. According to society online Trust Alliance (OTA), in 2018 total cybercrime record was 2 million at a total financial 45 billion USD, total crypto jacking attacks were reported to 1.3 million and total breaches was 60,000 (NIJ, 2001; Internet Society, 2018). Recently, there has been a surge in legislative and regulatory government activity around the world related to organizations' obligation to properly protect user data. Identity theft resources center has reported private data breaches, finding 1,244 in 2018 with approx. of 2 billion exposed records.

The number of sensitive records that were breached has reached 447 million. Privacy Rights clearinghouse has reported 635 breaches and 1.4 billion exposed records in 2018. Recently with the spread of covid-19 in 2020, the cybercrime and malicious have escalated in an obvious way where personal information was stollen via the access to networks which then exploited for financial benefits(Cockcroft & Clutterbuck, 2001). Cybercriminals took advantage of mobile shopping and transactions as mobile devices are left unprotected specially during the awaken of covid-19, where users are extremely vulnerable to be a target for attack, this is due to the customized method that criminals have adopted for the attack. Criminals also have geographic advantages whereas the more covid-19 cases and concerns the more digital the community has become, therefore the more attack and more crimes that lead to more financial benefits for the attackers. During Covid-19, criminals have employed phishing via the spread of global digital communications to deceive unsuspected victims (Bou Sleiman & Gerdemann, 2021). According to studies, Malware, spyware, and Trojans have been found to be embedded in interactive covid-19 maps and websites. in the following sections, there will be discission about 1. the terror of technology, 2. Cybersecurity, 3. Dark Web the black e-commerce, discussion in detail the crimes of dark web, 4. Safety precautions, there will be detailed guidelines on how users can protect themselves while they are engaging with internet. and finally, the future development and research (O'Leary, 2023).

The Terror of Technology

Technology offers both benefits and dangers. If the dangers side is ignored, the results can be devastating, leading to death, financial loss, and privacy violations. When users use the internet, the risk of losing privacy is very high. Because the internet allows users to remain anonymous, criminals are finding creative ways to exploit others. these criminals hide behind their screens to digitally terrorize innocent old and young users in various ways(Sebastian Traxl, 2013). They often pretend to be someone else and slowly gather sensitive information about their victim, such as family details, gender, age, location, marital status, and work information, often taken directly from the victim's online accounts. This critical data is then used to access emails, bank accounts, and personal devices, organ trafficking, human trafficking. the criminals use this access for blackmail, sexual abuse, harassment, or simply for their own personal gain. Because of these widespread digital attacks, users are increasingly worried about their privacy. As technology improves, so does the fear associate with it. Common technologies that cause concern include public Wi-Fi networks, drones that record images, internet crimes, and general cybersecurity issues(Justice & Care, 2023).

Cyber Security

Digital communication has become the main method of communication and information transformation in current technology era. Users are depending on it while sending and receiving any form of data such as text, image, video or audio, all can be done by only one click away, however users do not know and are not aware of information leakage while transmission to the other end. Technology is growing literally every day. internet is one of the technological elements that is growing rapidly. According to this growth, private information is exposed outrageously, cybercrimes are increasing day by day. More than 60% of total commercial transactions are done online, so this field requires a high quality of security for transparent and best transactions. Hence cyber security has become the latest issue in the IT sector. The scope of cyber security is not just limited to securing information in IT industry but also to various other fields like cyber space etc. (Cisco, 2019). Most recent technologies like cloud computing, green computing, mobile computing, E-commerce, and E-banking require a high level of information security. Cybercrime is a term for any illegal activity that uses a computer as its primary means of commission and theft. the U.S. Department of Justice expands the definition of cybercrime to include any illegal activity that uses a computer for the storage of evidence (Kaur & Randhawa, 2020). Growing list of cybercrimes includes crimes that have been made possible by computers, such as network intrusions and the dissemination of computer viruses, as well as computer-based variations of existing crimes, such as identity theft, stalking, bullying and terrorism which have become major problems for people and nations. Usually in common man's language cybercrime may be defined as crime committed using a computer and the internet to steal a person's identity or sell contraband or stalk victims or disrupt operations with malevolent (United Nations Conference on Trade and Development.2019).

Dark Web the Black E-Commerce

With the growth of technology and with internet being almost free and available everywhere, harm and violations have been increasing as well. Therefore, digital crimes are getting common and occurring around the clock. Computer crimes are increasing by the hour whereby users are losing privacy, money, organs, and most importantly themselves in so many ways. Computers are countless various types of internet and computer crimes such as dark web, spam, cybercrimes, spoofing, pornography, e-commerce fraud, malware, and social engineering(Organisation for Economic Cooperation and Development, 2016). the Dark Web is also called Dark Net is a web-based that contains all sort of data that is related to anonymous users. User's data is protected in the web database via encryption, obfuscation and forwarding. This specific web is encrypted. the access to this web is limited to a dedicated software or specific proxying or authentication. This web is associated with criminal activity of so many levels such as buying or selling drugs, porngraphy, gambling(Arabnezhad et al., 2020). there are many forms of dark web that can be found on the net, these forms are:

- Tor (**the on**ion **R**outer)
- Freenet
- peer-to-peer I2P
- Friend-to-Friend

- Riffle
- Freenet
- Tor2Web

The strong protection of anonymity in the dark web has allowed it to be the main channel to sell all types of banned and harmful items. This strong protection and the advantage of dealing behind the screen without being seen or known have created a great room to harm innocent users via child abduction and abuse, human and organ trafficking, human abduction, international humilation to weak users who cant get themselves free(Yang et al., 2019). in the dark web a strong and smart user who has great power can reach almost to any ordinary user surfing the net and they can harm them by taking advantage of their weaknesses. Those who get harmed via dark web, there is almost no chance to escabe. To access the dark web, there is a specific and special browser such as **TOR** browser, this browser provides more security and privacy. Most of the dark web sites benefit political dissenters and users who are trying to keep medical conditions private. the dark web has approximatly 2.5 million daily visitors. This amount of visitors have made the dark web a perfect hub for criminal orgnizations and individuals and terrorist groups to communicate to sell and buy anything (Zhang & Zou, 2020). Human abduction via dark or deep web is very much possible (Kaur & Randhawa, 2020). the criminal or the insane user on the dark net has the privillage of selecting any person of interest to be abducted for their pleasure or any other needs. there is a high possibility that the victim does not even know about the dark net or why they have been abducted. This is how powerful the dark web is. Following sections present several crimes in the Dark Web (De L'europe, 2009).

1. Kidnapping

Girls get kidnaped for the Dark Net business. Chloe happened to turn up for modeling assignment in Milan, Italy, and been injected with the tranquilliser ketamine and stuffed into a holdall bag and driven 120 miles in a car trunk to a remote farmhouse near turin. the victim have been gagged, was unconsious for most of the journey. the terryfing news she recived from the abductor that she would be auctioned as a sex slave on the dark web for €300,000.

2. Child Sexual Abuse

Benjamin Faulkner, a canadian user on the dark web and an owner of (Child's Play), a dark-net child porngraphy website hosted on the dark web. His websites contains over one million profilers and has showcased over 100 porngraphy producers who have raped and brutalised children and shot videos of their sadism for the keen delight of paedophiles around the wolrd. the user has been arrested having electronic devise that contains 47000 images of child porn and 2900 videos. the user's associate has been the administrator of (the GiftBox Exchange) a dark net chid porngraphy site which was shut down in november 2016.

Dark-net is significant for vendors of child pornography, there are certain sites that provide this service such as Hard Candy, Jailbait, Lolita City, PedoEmpire, Love Zone, the Familty Album, Kindergarten porn that allow such users to communicate and share fantasies of child love practices. the group of users who get engagged with these sites are pedophile This group of users share approaches and strategies of seducing and engaging in sexual acts with children. in the Dark Web, the expert pedophiles coach others on how to evade law enforcement authorities and discuss encryption and anonymity techniques to prevent online detection. Childhub is a web where kids females sexually abused and being watched alive and girls lined up for being sold or selected for private pleasure(Garg, 2018).

In the United States in the dark web around 200,000 children are traficked for sex where each child coast from $150,000 to $200,000. Several dark net websites live streaming of the rape and abuse of children. in Aisa, Pedophiles direct rapists via video feeds to coach them to reach the perfect fantacy. one of the cases in the dark net, one had the privilage to order a group of eight men to rape an eight years old girl alive to meet his fantasies for a sum of $100. in some cases of child abuse and pornography in the dark net come from family members, in Germany, a couple operated a paedophile ring as business have used their son for porngraphy, according to the police, the abusers had paid around £10,000 one of the times they abused their son. Videos of the son being sexually harrased have been sold in the dark net for the couple benefits. Moreover, the son was threatened by his mother to be sent to foster care if he reported the incedents to the police. the couple were arrested and convicted of prostitution, rape, sexual and physical abuse, humilation, and bondage for almost 60 separate identifies acts by the court.

Some cases have been reported to the police for investigation, however, not all kids have been found, abductors are not found. Very few cases where the child was able to escape from the horror. the most concern matter is, those children who were able to escape or rescused will not have a normal life after this horror and there is a chance they could grow to be criminals themselves. Another concerned matter, these Dark Webs are not visible or traced by the police and authorities, most the cases, these web pages are protected from powerful governments and politicians. Despite the huge number of kidnapped children via dark web, none of the web pages related to it have been shutdown. they are still online and providing services to users. Some of the abduted children being asaulted for pleasure while predator and insane users are invited to watch(Alharbi et al., 2021). the dark net sites present videos of adults enjoying children in their ways violating the children rights of safty. these children are sent later to the sociaty carrying huge trauma that have led them to be violant extreeme criminals, and the only way to stop their crimes is to sentence them to death disregarding of what they have been through to be in this state of criminal mind(Jones & Seger, 2020).

Black Death is an eastern european group operating on the Dark-Web. This dark service deals with selling sex slaves to Saudia Arabia, also provides virgin auctions of girls as young as fifteen. User can see adds about the girls age, hair color and other measurements. one of the victims is laura, she is 15 years old was booked for an auction with starting price of £575,000. one of the latest sale in 2016 was Gemma 17 years old female was born in the UK. the starting price of her auction started from £92,000. Apparently the advertisement of these girls includes a note that says (the abductors do not sell girls that are ill, pregranant, young mothers, or have STDs). in the dark net the abductors do not shy away to addvertise they can kidnap specific target for one's desire with a considiration of a high price comes along with it(Farook et al., 2017). Fig 4 presents list of videos to watch in 365cp dark net market.

3. Girls on Sale and Auctions

Some of the cases, the kidnappers were arrested and sentensed around 16 years or more in prisons. Apparently the kidnappers who were arrested are usually the transporters not the original planners who act behind the scene. they do compromise the small heads to keep the business running in the dark web, the same methos is used for drugs transport where the main crime planners compromise small people for their business to run through and it is not a problem for them if the innocent transporter was sentenced to death. Such acting from big heads to show the socity that the police is controlling the situation by getting the bad guys(James Ashford, 2019). one of the abductors was arrested in 2018 have confessed of earning $17.7 million from selling girls in the dark web via Black Death Group, the kidnapper have received a prision sentense. However, the girls who have been witness of the terror are not recovered from the trauma and will never have normal again(BBC, 2025).

4. Girles Raped for Digital Pleasure

In the dark web, girls are being raped in private for pleasure. Girls who are raped are children or adults. they will be tourtured based on the clinets requests to get the maximum pleasure. Victims will suffer to death for the pleasure and satisfaction of the dark webers(BBC, 2019). the children who are being used in the dark web are being drugged and brain washed to accept this violance and horrifying acts against their well. Some of the children are facing the tourture without any druges as some dark webers like to see the victim begging for life and crying out of pain and messery. in some cases, these children will be used for organ trafficking due to the freshness of their organs. (UNODC, 2020).

5. Red Rooms: Face Death for Digital Pleasure

Red rooms are considered the pleasure rooms in the dark web. offenders on the dark web will get the victim and open the opportunity for dark webers to request anything to be done to the victim, such as rape, tourture, killing, and anything that can get into the viwer imagination. Victims has no say, no objections or any control. they just have to face death for digital pleasure. the victims of red rooms can be chidren or adults in different genders. Figure 1. Presents the forum of discussion on how to tourture the victim.

Figure 1. Red rooms forum tourture discussion

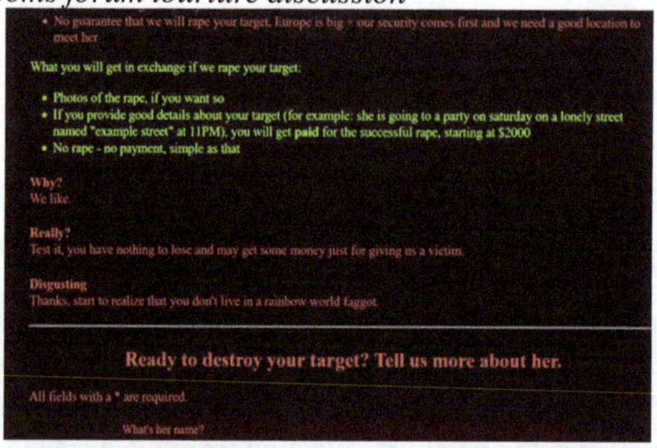

6. Human Organs Sold in the Dark Web

Victims are kidnaped to have their organes sold via digital world without their permission. then these victims will be vanished for good and never be found. Victims who are found, there were empty body or horrifically mutilated. Figure 2 presents home page of selling human organs on the dark web.

Figure 2. Organ's sales in the dark web

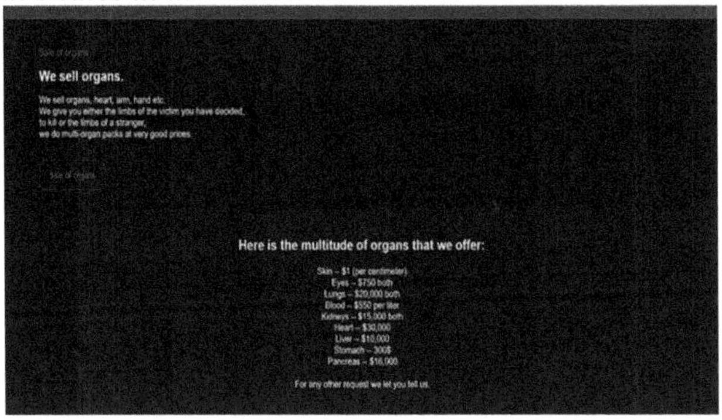

Dark Web has accumulated thousands of victims and thousands of users who like extreme violence against vulnerable and innocent populations don't have the ability to protect themselves. for those who survive these digital and physical exploitation, the long-term psychological and social outcomes are profound, regardless of the victim's age. Several cases of victims who have been rescued will not return to normal life, they would rather remain struggling with their trauma, in the long run, these victims will be violent criminals. one way or another, the dark web is creating a whole corrupt community that cares only about digital crime. Following, are some links that were used to access the Dark Web services. It is noticeable that the links of the dark web are totally different from the normal links from other browsers such as google, Edge, Opera, etc.

Child Promo

- http://k3tmdmrtwm54qphakmklov515lfarpmrb4kvs3s7clon2gqlkfkgbad.onion/
- http://24e5bzjwovkfkyyrtklo3lq2ebcclxylfvxtecahl2lzzlq4s3ubepid.onion/
- http://trzqon6fvufqyx7gf7i7h7om42d2s4kd7z6zjzkxt4t6jlydzc54gid.onion/
- http://l5x7jah5q5k77a6uvbzqc4ddz2ekwz5o6ohnu6kregu7cmjkx5nmbad.onion/

Evil

- http://242iz66xzgqiwkahiheoiiftlaafn77mzpjycfiwdylchvrjtjqwgqd.onion/
- http://juqkhpatrwkq4jklbb3rm6b32n53yqcbnle73pibyfzt3wk7ovtmgid.onion/

Brutal

http://bellaxulobxgvg3zyxravw2tjincpdterdepxlilscwexpahphroqad.onion/

Human organs
http://ta7yzyjv76vpcbygk4cflngnki7uxqa4mfjleooo7c2t3zabvmddjid.onion/
Rape

- http://rapehero6iatzwl5bhbp7cmzi2mzulkfdoo6vuke25voxhmere6qzyd.onion/
- http://th7zig3ygl2k6dapobvkjhg2vxhax3i2z2wtzrvwg7fm73fxpfavtad.onion/?product_cat=heavy-weapons

The main concept of this technology era is the internet which has opened an entire new virtual universe for users the good and bad, clever and naive, smart and ordinary. internet has allowed all types of users to access and interact with one another diversely. Following sections discuss in details social engineering crimes and victims' testimony.

VICTIMS OF DIGITAL CRIMES

Internet has made communication easier, faster a more convenient, this is the main purpose of it. internet has enabled users to communicate randomly, anonymously behind a shield, where a lot of information cannot be known such as gender, age, color, country, background. This advantage has allowed a lot of users to communicate easily and freely with no fear or concern. Certain users such as hackers, scammers, brokers, and spammers have taken advantage of these features, where they find the weak users and chat with them via chat rooms, emails, websites and so on. internet criminals could get these users to believe them and share personal information, and from there these criminals begin to perform blackmailing, hacking, and stealing (Zhang & Zou, 2020). for the purpose of this research, an interview was conducted anonymously with users who fall victim to internet criminals. The participants were informed that their private information is not required for this paper. They were only asked about the experience faced while they fall victims, also famous cases are presented along. A summary of each victim's story is presented in the following section.

Social Media Involvement in the Dark Web

Social media are involved as well in organ trafficking. Brokers are from the dark web will add their fake advertisements of job, trips, marriage and other services to lure victims easily. Social media mostly used for this sort of advertisements are telegram and Instagram. Most organs receive the brokers' attention and focus is kidney due to high demand from hospitals. Criminal doctors who have an account in the dark web will join a forum requesting certain organs, then brokers in the dark web use their connections to find the required organ without any consideration of the victim's conditions as shown in figure 3 that illustrates one of the forums of doctor requesting organs via dark web forum. Dark Web allows the requesting participant to request specific features of the donor such as age, gender, blood type.

Figure 3. Dark web forum to request specific features of the donor

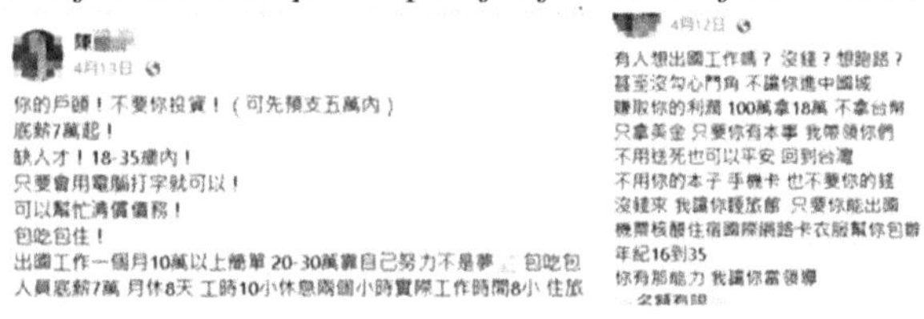

Victim 1: (2004) Algerian female lost her life to online fake love. From digital love to organ trafficking.

Female from Algeria uses chat rooms to find new friends. Dark Web broker finds her profile and starts chatting with her. They started chatting more privately. The criminal pretended to be in love with her and wats to marry her. The criminal has used this method to lead her to do all medical checkups. Criminal was sending her good money so she could do these medical checkups. The victim believed him, especially that he was sending her money without asking her. When all the medical checkups all done. The victim had prepared everything for criminal arrival to marry, not knowing the dark truth behind his intentions. the criminal reaches Algeria as he promised. They got married and she left with him to USA. The victim's family had never been able to reach her since she left. the family informed US authorities, after investigation the authorities found out that she was sold for human trafficking as her body organs have been sold, which means she no longer exists.(Al-hakimi et al., 2023).

Victim 2: (2002) 13 years old female from Pittsburgh almost lost her life for dark net pleasures.

13 years old female uses online chatting rooms to chat with strangers. the criminal spoted and started chatting with her and convienced her to be friends. they shared all her details in life for 9 months. the criminal asked her to go out for a dinner. She went out to see him without informing her family. the victim was then upducted to

unknown place. As they reach to the his house, the criminal ties her and informes her that she will be on video for pleasuers to be posted in the dark web. for several days she was sexually abuse for online pleasuers on the dark web. She was raped, beaten, insulted for online viewers to watch and get pleasures. Luckily, FBI and digital forensic investigators were able to get her before she gets killed (Kidnapped by a Paedophile I Met online - BBC News, 2016).

Victim 3: (2018) Fake doctor from Instagram kills patient from Libya.

The victim finds a pretty female's Facebook account and sends her add request. the female who is the criminal accepts the request; they chatted every day. The victim was amazed with the criminal's beauty from the pictures. They decided to meet face to face. The victim has met the ugly truth; she was completely different from the pictures, she was ugly unbearable, he urged her that she is different from the pictures and she cheated on him, therefore, he ended the relationship. Then she persuaded him with money to stay with her, but the victim refused. the criminal started planning for the victim's death. She created a fake doctor account on Instagram. She introduced herself to him as a doctor to gain his trust. She used his medical history against him. He started telling her about his colon problems. the fake doctor prescribed a medication to kill him. the medication gets delivered to the victim. With full trust and faith, the victim had the medication and died. the medication was a poison made to kill him. Forensics investigator was appointed by the victim's family. investigation discovered that the fake doctor account was the ugly female who was rejected by him two years ago, so as a revenge she killed him. the criminal was later sentenced to death.

Victim 4: Fake job advertisement via Telegram connected to Dark Web led to organ harvesting

Ah Wei a victim via snakehead gang in Taiwan, she was drugged and taken for organ harvesting. She was lured through job advertisements in Telegram known as (Scorpion lady). Fortunately for this victim, she was rescued after extensive investigation. Figure 4. Illustrates job adds via Telegram that lured victims from Taiwan, Cambodia and China

Figure 4. Job offers in Telegram to lure victims from Taiwan, China, and Cambodia

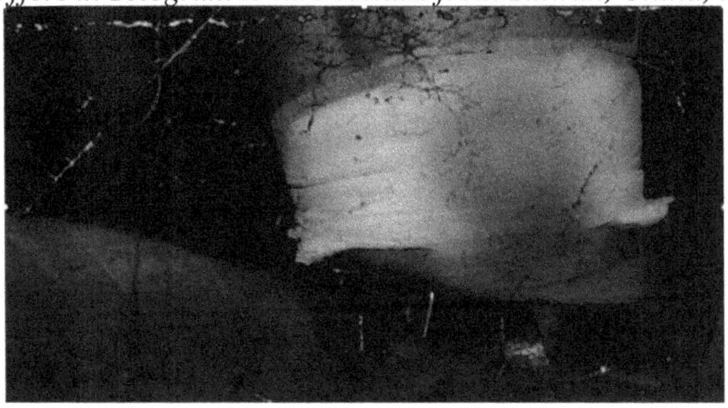

Other victims who were lured same way as Wie were not rescued and unfortunately been trafficked. Victims of organs trafficking most of the time will be alive and conscious while the surgeon is taking their organs away and will be left without any healthcare as illustrated in Figure 5.

Figure 5. Victim's organ taken via dark web with no healthcare

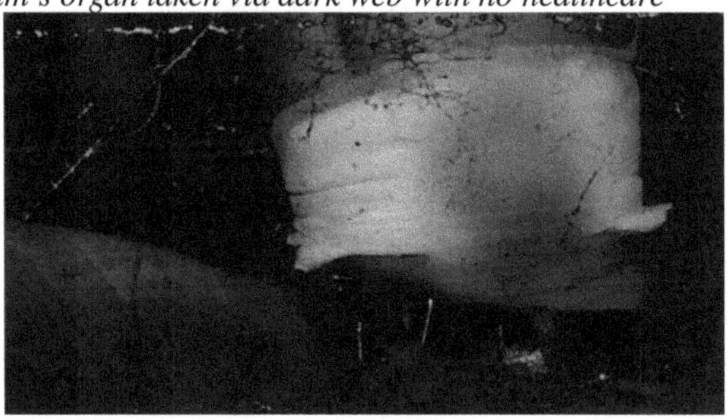

Victim 5: Direct offer from Snakehead gang to buy the victims organ

Huang was offered money for his organs but was saved when the buyer retracted the offer due to suspense in the case. the victim's testimony later helped the police in monitoring the Snakehead gang.

HOSPITALS CRIMES IN DARK WEB

Hospitals have been involved in organ trafficking networks that benefit from dark web. The sales statistics of these cases are not revealed due to the sensitivity of the crime and delegate participants and authorities involved in these cases. But the truth can't be hidden completely, there are several statistics presenting the involvement of doctors and hospitals in these crimes, these limited statistics were known after the arrest of these doctors when the crime went out of control. Global demand for transplantable organs has fueled brutal criminal enterprise that spans the digital underworld and the legitimate medical infrastructure. Human trafficking for organ exploitation represents violation of human rights, moving beyond the highly organized network. The word organization estimates that between 5% and 10% of all organ transplants worldwide are performed using organs sourced from the Dark Web. This illegal trade is venture for organized crime, generating an estimated $840 million to $1.7 billion USD annually. Figure 6 illustrates organ prices from lowest to highest.

Figure 6. Most wanted organs prices range

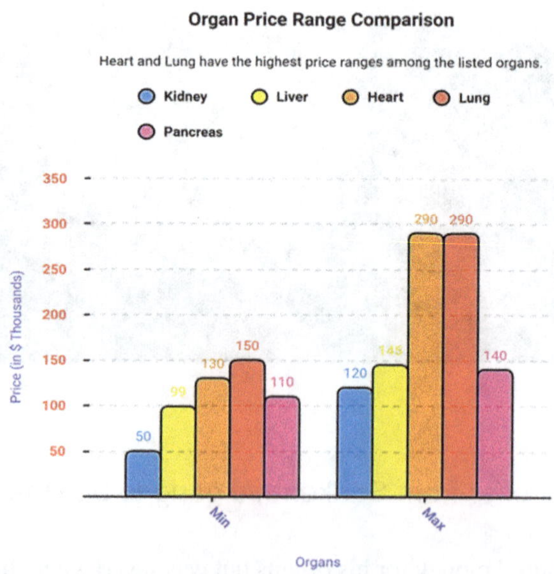

The world health organization estimates that 10000 kidneys are traded annually on the dark web, which presents substantial portion of global transplants. Hospitals like Kenya's Mediheal hospital faced investigations for conducting high risk transplants for unrelated donor and recipients involved cash payment, with link to international networks advertising on the dark web and social media. China involved state affiliated hospitals profiting from executed prisoners' organs with advertising transplants openly online. Figure 7. Illustrates the latest prices rang in the dark web advertising page.

Figure 7. Human organs prices in the dark web

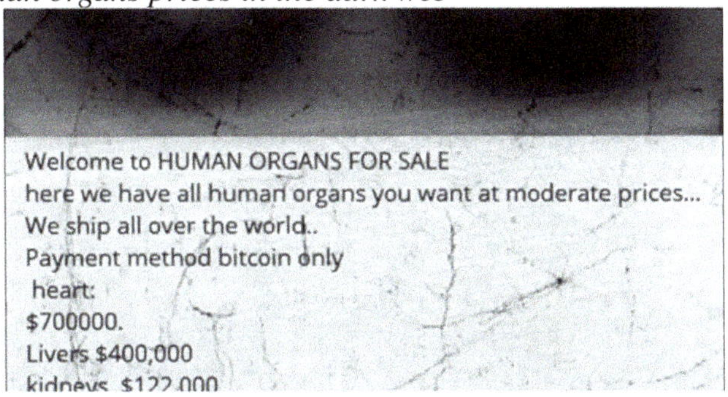

Advertising for kidneys appear on both dark and other web platforms, with brokers directing payments through laundering schemes to hospitals abroad. Kenya, india, and other foreign surgeons travel to local hospitals for transplant tourism that is enabled via online deals. This reason for illegal operations is the critical global shortage while over 150,000 transplants are performed each year, this meets less than 10% of the total global demand, leaving huge desperate pool of recipients for dark web traffickers to give their hands on them for the bigger demanders in medical industry. in figure 8. the demand for organs in the Dark Web is from 5-10%.

Figure 8. Most wanted organs in the dark web

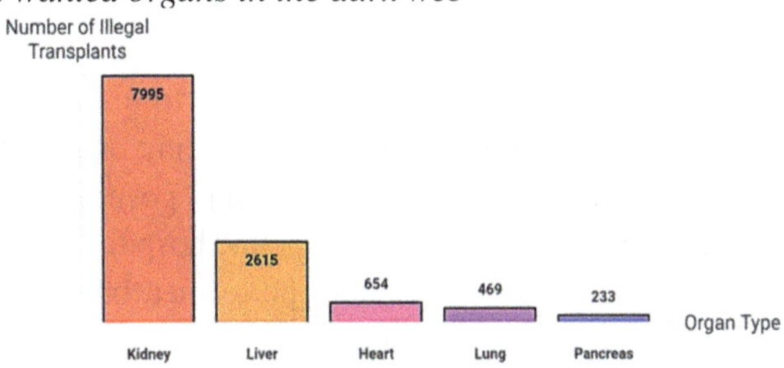

Medical traffickers benefit from the anonymity of the Dark Web and encrypted media platforms to connect buyers (hospital) and sellers, establishing initial valid contracts. The network then relies on a chain of facilitators, including recruiters, brokers, and most critically, medical professionals, surgeons, anesthesiologists, and most importantly hospital administrators who falsify documents to allow the illegal procedure to take place within legitimate healthcare facilities. This requires sophisticated infrastructure involving medical specialists, logistical coordination, and access to healthcare facilities. Most common organ trafficking via the dark web for hospitals benefits are presented in order in Figure 9.

Figure 9. Most common organs been trafficked

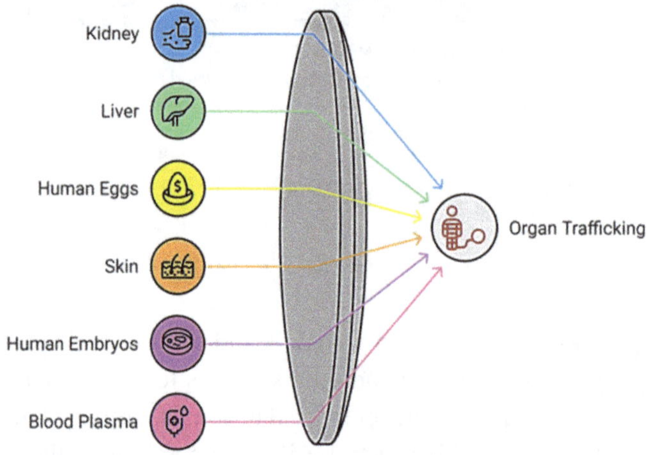

Organ trafficking has been going on since 1980, the most used method was kidnapping, fake marriage or deceiving victims for money. Illegal organ trafficking has produced between $600 million to $1.2 billion in illegal revenue each year. With the assistance of dark web, brokers usually change locations of exchange to make sure tracking is not possible. Brokers in the Dark Web successfully sell 2000 kidneys every year to hospitals and doctors and clinics according to the demand of medical market and patients. Through the Dark Web, patients from united states, United Kingdom, Canada and other wealthy countries are getting organs trafficked from Egypt, Pakistan, Turkey, Iraq, and China. 2008 Indian government have arrested and banned number of doctors, nurses, paramedics and hospitals that had performed 500 illegal transplants. these transplants were performed on Indian donors who were lured via dark web. With the assistance of social media connected to the dark web, 5000 patients successfully receive their trafficked organs from poor victims. Figure 10. illustrates the customers' services on the dark web in terms of organ delivery and fees.

Figure 10. Advertisement in the dark web of organ delivery and fees

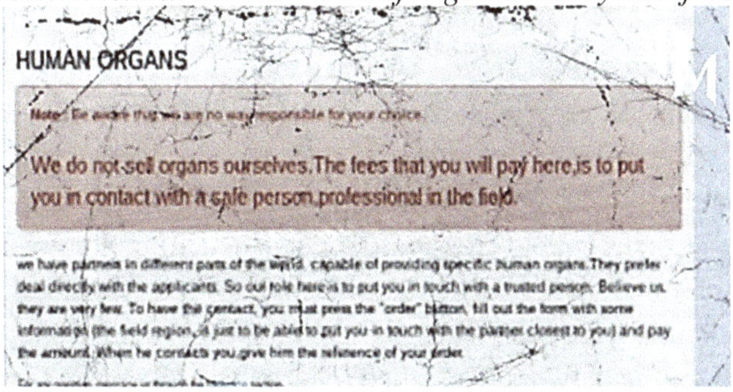

Who are the Victims

Victims of medical organ trafficking on the dark web are from poor, uneducated, and vulnerable backgrounds. Organized criminal groups always target unemployed individuals, migrants, asylum seekers, and refugees. Many are coerced, deceived or see organ selling as the last resort to improve their poor life situation. Though victims are promised huge payment, or better life, or deceived for other purposes, they don't get what they are promised, either very limited financial compensation or not anything at all, most of them will not receive any medical care after the operation as well, sometimes will end up dead. Many victims have suffered devastating health conditions and consequences after they have taken, despite the fact they know about it or not and will receive no medical or emotional care.

Hospital Crimes Cases

In 2007, Word Health Organization has estimated 5%-10% of all transplanted organs are trafficked through the dark web. Because of the strictness and limitation of preserving organs, patients always demand fresh donors of organs, which could be transplanted. To avoid patients from waiting long time due to the urgency of their situation as they claim, the illegal brokers who are the middleman between the doctor and dark web will coordinate among donors and receiver by exchanging payment, at the secret agreed place of the exchange. Patients and donors will be taken to hospital that is aware of the transaction and a doctor who is involved in the trade will conduct the operation. Dark web brokers supervise online advertisements looking for suitable victims for their clients with involvement of the hospital and doctors who are part of the trade(Barsoum, 2008). This process is common is Australia, Canada, Japan, South Korea, United states, some Middle East countries.

Patient's data are being sold or stolen for the benefit of dark web business. The data includes medical records, personal information, and genetic data. This data will be used in the dark web to create fraud insurance claims and blackmail other victims. Currently, dark web has employed medical data to train unethical AI to break the patient's privacy for misuse. Unfortunately, some research hospitals and medical students use the dark web to get organs for their research ignoring ethics of their job. Dark web platforms enable cross border deals matching donors from Arica and Asia to buyers and hospitals in Egypt and Kenya with payments through crypto-currency. 700 victims were documented by UNODC between 2008-2022. Victims brought through online networks designed to lure them (Steering Committee of the Istanbul Summit, 2008).

South and West Africa, 2010

Private hospitals pleaded guilty to 109 illegal kidney transplants between 2001 and 2003. The case involved doctors from top academic institutions and highlighted deep penetration of organ trafficking into legitimate healthcare systems. This case has proved that organ trafficking via the Dark Web is not limited to developing nations, it operates within accredited hospitals with the licensed medical professionals. in this side of the world, online networks involving labs and clinics using organ transplants tourism via dark web brokers(Rodriguez-Iturbe, 2008).

Pakistan

January 2023, Pakistani victims were deceived via online platforms with promises for job with large pay. once the victims are in the location, their kidneys have been taken and sold. the deal was conducted via Dark Web to benefit certain hospitals for highly worth clients. the operation cost 4000 USD. Pakistan conducted up to 2000 renal transplants in 2005, organs taken from foreigners, via private clinics connected to dark web through brokers(Budiani-Saberi & Delmonico, 2008)(Fatima et al., 2018).

Saudi Arabia

Though organ trafficking and commercial use is prohibited in KSA by law and religion, still there are several channels where illegal organ trafficking is happening. Dark web is limited in use in KSA however it is still connected to several social media channels to source donors (victims) for buyers. The social media used are Facebook, Twitter, and Google answers. Most organ trafficked using these platforms are kidney and livers. Figure 11. illustrates the statistics of illegal organ trafficking on social media platforms in KSA.

Figure 11. Organ trafficking statistics in KSA

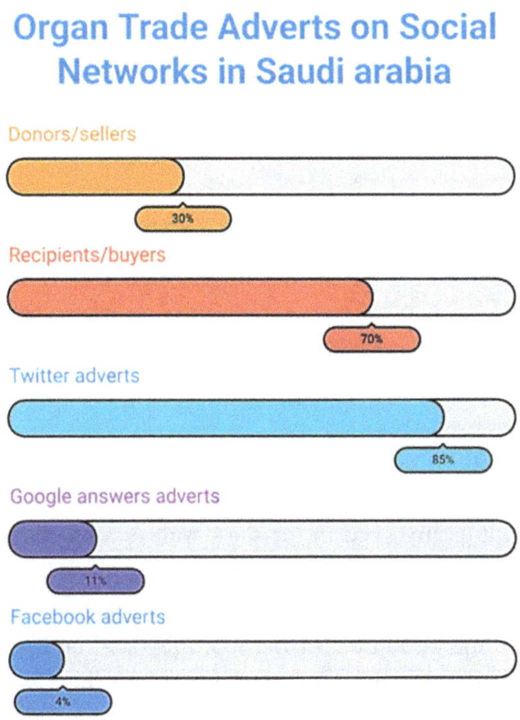

US Organ Trafficking

the very first case of organ trafficking in US with involvement of hospital was conducted by Levy Izhak. Via the Dark Web victims' kidneys have been sold. the victims are vulnerable from Israel for $10,000, then the broker have told the kidneys to patients via the hospital connection for $ 160,000. Dark Web connected to US offers fresh babies as well, this market is quite famous in this region. Figure 12. Illustrates advertisements on the dark web offering babies.

Figure 12. Babies dark market

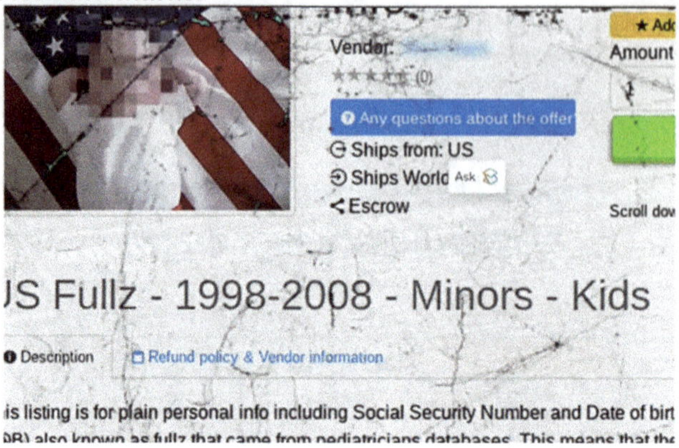

Taiwan

Taiwan owns hidden organization linked to the dark web for organ trafficking from victims from Cambodia, China. they mostly focus on poor and illegal immigrants. one of the gangs involved in the dark web is Snakehead. Other brokers in Taiwan use Telegram to post job offers indicating the place to meet and discuss. As the victim comes to the location, they will have a discussion of the job payment. Once they agreed to the good deal of the job, they will be asked to go to specific hospital to do full medical checkups to make sure that the victim doesn't have any illness and all organs are well working. Once all checkups are good, the victim will be trafficked immediately for organ harvesting. The victims will be drugged and out of consciousness. there is a collaboration between the gang in Taiwan and the gang in Cambodia to foster and harvest organ and human trafficking. Dark Web contains websites mimicking e-commerce platforms and offering organs at high prices, such as $100000 for a beating heart. Dark Web offers VIP services for recipients who purchase organs, they offer to deliver the organ as fresh to the doorstep or specific hospital, organ packaging. Figure 13. Illustrates the advertisements on the Dark Web offering organ services.

Figure 13. Organ packaging and delivery through the dark web

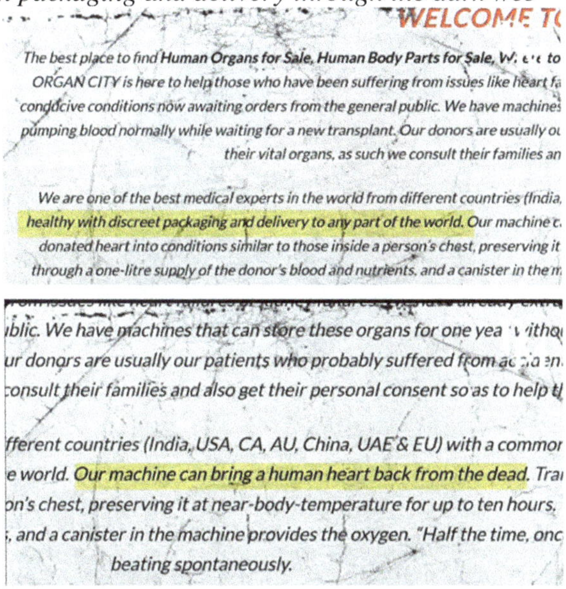

Egypt

one of the top countries involved in the dark web organ exchange with hospitals connection is Egypt with surgeons. Arranging kidney sales from Syrian donors with the assistance of dark web brokers.

India

Dark web organ trafficking is sustained despite the bans from the government. Brokers in the dark web make use of social media to get poor donors (victims) for high profile and gulf recipients with a connection of illegal doctors and hospitals to perform the surgery. Figure 14 illustrates the most common gender for organ trafficking.

Figure 14. Gender statistics of organ trafficking

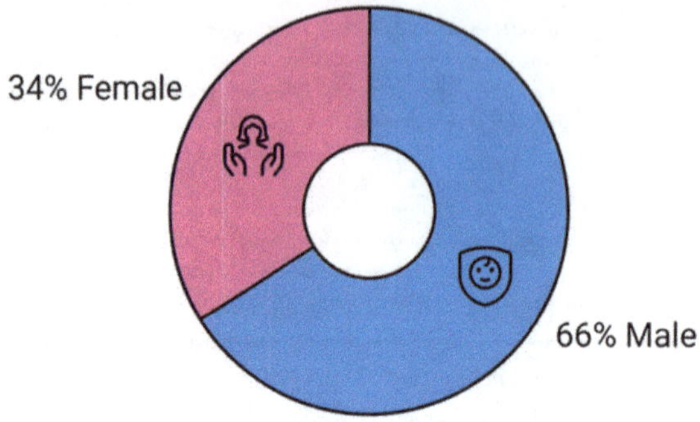

Plastic Surgery

Dark web is very good marketplace for plastic surgery, especially for clients looking for low coast treatment. Dark Web will provide these services via the broker to arrange the doctor and cheap hospital or clinics that don't have enough equipment to perform such surgeries.

Discussion

North and west Africa benefits from the low cost of the internet, where social media and dark web are easy to be enabled. Through dark net advertisements of kidneys from displaced people, routed to clinics like Kenya's Mediheal. South Asia sustains moderate high activity through kidney valley in india and Pakistani clinics, blending dark web and Clearnet brokers table 1 presents organ activity in dark web based on country.

Table 1. Dark web organ activity based on country

Region	Relative prevalence	Dark web indicators
Africa	Highest	Donor sourced from hospitals in Egypt and Kenya
Middle East	High	Syrian kidneys to Egyptian hospitals. The price increased twice 2008-2015
South Asia	Moderate – High	india / Pakistan tourism through online middleman
East Asia	Low – Moderate	China operating through hidden networks
Europe / Americas	Low	Deals via dark web payment done by cryptocurrency

Pakistan's private clinics perform high volumes of transplants on foreigners, facilitated by dark web evasion tactics in 2007 peaks. Tanzania and DR Congo show elevated organized crime enabling potential dark web flows, per criminality indices. China has shifted lower port-reforms but retains residual traces historical prisoners sourcing. Table 2. Presents the characteristics of organ transplant via dark web. Table 3 presents the role of staff involved in the transaction process.

Table 2. Characteristics of organ trafficking

Country	Hub Role	Dark Web Ties
Egypt	Surgical / recipient hub	Syrian donor ads, high payments
Kenya	Transplant execution	foreign surgeons via online deals
india	Donor sourcing	Brokers to Guld via Telegram / Dark web
Pakistan	Clinic networks	foreign patient tourism via online platform

Table 3. Role of staff involved in organ trafficking

Role of staff	Evidence	Countries affected
Surgeons / Doctors	Direct extractions / transplants	Egypt, Kenya, China
Clinic Admins	forged documents / payments	South Africa, india, Pakistan
Support staff	Donor recruitments / logistics	North Africa, Syria hubs.

Statistics do not present carefully how much dark web is involved in organ trafficking, most of the studies indicate the level of it is moderate. Dark web is not always selling or requesting directly, it uses other platforms as a shield to conduct the trade. Most common social media platform used for the benefit of dark web is Telegram. Telegram is very active platform for scamming users. The scam is used in Telegram to scam users for their money and organs through job advertisements. Figure 16 illustrates the level of social media connected to Dark Web.

Figure 15. most connected social media to the Dark Web

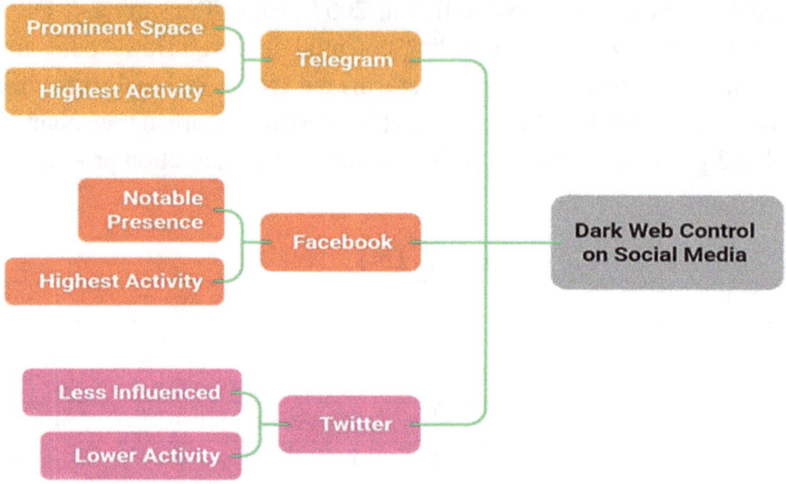

DARK WEB & SOCIAL-MEDIA, AND DEFENSE DILEMMA

According to the previous research and case studies, Dark Web is very powerful platform supported by powerful politicians and government. It is good business for them and other independent users who can purchase from it. Dark Web will not disappear unless the shields are taken down, which is not possible. The crimes of the Dark Web will continue until internet is shut down or oppositions get greater power to terminate the guardians of it. Based on the previous discussion, one out of many victims can be rescued, one page out of hundreds is terminated. The rest of the platform is live and functioning. Authorities of the Dark Web don't mind compromising one dark page for the sake of the rest of the platform. It is ok to save one victim out of many. The small arrests and terminating certain pages are to show the media and public that the police are working and defending civilians and victims. on the other hand, due to the extreme protection of Dark Web business, it is nearly impossible to track and trace these criminals or make legitimate cases in the court. Users are to depend on their knowledge of protection to protect themselves, police won't always be on time or even find the location of the victim. Fake online job offers, fake online friends, online deals are not blocked from social media. Face book, Instagram, Telegram are most platforms that allowing these advertisements despite its danger. The strategy of reviewing ads on these platforms must change.

Safety Precautions

Most users have fallen to be social engineering victims due to lack of knowledge, being innocent, lack of experience and lack of precautious techniques and behavior for protection and defense. Curiosity to chat with the stranger seeking attention or friendship ignoring all sorts of danger can lead to massive harm. for users not to fall victims of social engineering criminals, there are several technical defense and protection steps that must be applied. The following points highlight methods for users to protect themselves.

1. While online surfing, enable (two-factor authentication) to make sure that no one else uses your account from another device without your knowledge.
2. Do not chat with stranger or share confidential information. Strangers you meet online are not real; you cannot trust them. If you must chat, then keep it simple, do not share files such as photos and do not open links sent from them.
3. Make sure the webcam is off and covered. Most users were kidnaped to the dark net business due to online chatting with strangers.
4. Check your friends list in your social media accounts and remove unknown users from your list.
5. Disable location sharing in your devise to prevent stalking.
6. When you use foreign device to login to your email, make sure to remove your email from the device and remove the history and temporary files.
7. Use **virtual machine** if you are working on critical projects. Virtual machine is a desktop application that allows the user to run different operating system within the main operating system. Example of virtual machine application is VMware workstation.
8. Open-source operating systems are safer than commercial. Linux in all its versions is free to use; it performs like Windows. Hackers are always after popular sources and applications that are commercial. Users who care about security are advised to change to Linux.
9. Secure all IoT gadgets from hacking.
10. for society's safety, the ministry of education must change the education strategy by adding computing and cybersecurity subjects and awareness from young age. Students should understand in this technological era, they are exposed to digital danger, they must know the threats they face while engaging in technology and internet. The syllabus of cybersecurity subjects must contain useful facts and concepts, practical and theoretical, that will get the student's attention to the danger they could face.
11. Enforce digital police to monitor the network and devices connected to the internet. Using AI, the police can determine the attempt of crime, digital stalking

based on the criminal behavior around the net. Also has open access for victims to send their cases for investigations. Police must be available 24/7 for victims.

12. Eliminate the power of the dark net and dark web.
13. Use of personal VPN to create personal protection while surfing the internet. VPN is to prevent criminals from accessing their personal device without permission and prevent illegal stalking and hacking.
14. Use of Deep Freeze. It is an application that will put the desktop in a freezing condition while surfing the internet. An application that is installed while the deep freeze is on will be deleted after restarting the devise. Any history, cookies, files, tasks performed while the deep freeze was on will be erased after restarting the device.
15. **Encryption:** a good method of hiding names is encryption. Encryption is good method for passwords as well. Users can use java and mathematics to encrypt their names and passwords. Following examples present sample of names before and after encryption

Asma mahfoud → ÉÁ¼d dº²¤¸µ¼Õ
Java hacker → \"v¤Î¤\"²¤¨¸¬Æ
Kesava → ¸É¤Î¤
hi → ³´
keep it real → ¸, µË Æ¤º
Nur → ÌÆ

The encrypted can be associated with the email as no one will be able to read the name of the sender. If a stalker is trying to stalk the user using the name, it won't be possible. Every time this name gets copied, it changes or the person stalks. The encrypted name can be used as password, as it is nearly impossible to guess it.

FUTURE RESEARCH

Anti-social engineering game will be developed for the sake of improving the society knowledge on cybersecurity. the game concept is to engage the kids and teenagers into activities and competitions that guide them to engage with the society. the game has several levels. the player must fulfil all levels to get the reward. the purpose of the game is getting the players to think of others and how to build a better city instead of killing and harming themselves and each other. the game is an education tool, which educates these young users about the dark web and the dark net, by applying simulations of scenarios where they will try to solve to get real experience on how to protect themselves and how to identify real threats. the purpose of this game is to build peaceful and cyber strong city.

CONCLUSION

Being safe in the digital world is crucial. The most important factor for safety is good and careful behavior while engaging with the online world. The interconnection of Dark Web marketplaces and medical corruption represents an evolution in transnational organized crime. This chapter has demonstrated the terror of technology with evidence. Anonymity feature of Dark Web has made black market potential place for all sorts of illegal trade, especially organ trafficking. The involvements of hospitals in the dark web have created troubling dimensions. According to investigation, victims are scammed for money and their own organs. Figure 16 provides an illustration of user's digital dilemma.

Figure 16. User's digital dilemma

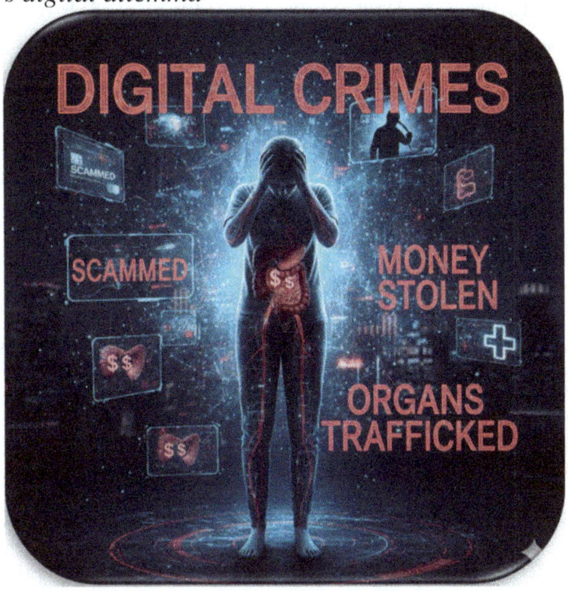

The fight against organ trafficking in the digital era requires more than better encryption or strict policies. If the users can encrypt their data, they still can't encrypt their existence. The fight requires global reaffirmation of the sanctity of the human body over the efficiency of the digital market.

REFERENCES

Accenture Security. (2019). The Cost of Cybercrime: Ninth Annual Cost of Cybercrime Study. Ninth Annual Cost of Cybercrime Study, 18.

Al-Hakimi, A., Nur, M., Alam, S., & Darul Ehsan, S. (2023). Cybersecurity Revolution in Technology Era. Https://Doi.Org/0.20967/Jcscm.2023.01.004

Alharbi, A., Faizan, M., Alosaimi, W., Alyami, H., Agrawal, A., Kumar, R., & Khan, R. A. (2021). Exploring the Topological Properties of the Tor Dark Web. *IEEE Access : Practical Innovations, Open Solutions*, *9*, 21746–21758. Https://Doi.Org/10.1109/ACCESS.2021.3055532. DOI: 10.1109/ACCESS.2021.3055532

Arabnezhad, E., La Morgia, M., Mei, A., Nemmi, E. N., & Stefa, J. (2020). A Light in the Dark Web: Linking Dark Web Aliases To Real internet Identities. Proceedings - international Conference on Distributed Computing Systems, 2020-November, 311–321. Https://Doi.Org/10.1109/ICDCS47774.2020.00081

Barsoum, R. S. (2008). Trends in Unrelated-Donor Kidney Transplantation in the Developing World. *Pediatric Nephrology (Berlin, Germany)*, *23*(11), 1925–1929. Https://Doi.Org/10.1007/S00467-008-0858-2. DOI: 10.1007/s00467-008-0858-2 PMID: 18536939

BBC. (2019, October 16). Dark Web Child Abuse: Hundreds Arrested Across 38 Countries. Https://Www.Bbc.Com/News/World-50073092. Https://Www.Bbc.Com/News/World-50073092

BBC. (2025, April 1). Child Abuse: Men Arrested in NI After Dark Web Site Take-Down. Https://Www.Bbc.Com/News/Articles/C2dexerd044o. Https://Www.Bbc.Com/News/Articles/C2dexerd044o

Bou Sleiman, M., & Gerdemann, S. (2021). Covid-19: A Catalyst for Cybercrime? international Cybersecurity. *Law Review*, *2*(1), 37–45. Https://Doi.Org/10.1365/S43439-021-00024-9

Brady, S., & Heinl, C. (2020). Cybercrime: Current Threats and Responses A Review of the Research Literature. October.

Budiani-Saberi, D. A., & Delmonico, F. L. (2008). Organ Trafficking and Transplant Tourism: A Commentary on the Global Realities. *American Journal of Transplantation : Official Journal of the American Society of Transplantation and the American Society of Transplant Surgeons*, *8*(5), 925–929. DOI: 10.1111/j.1600-6143.2008.02200.x PMID: 18416734

Cisco. (2019). Cisco 2019 Consumer Privacy Survey. November, 1–14.

Cockcroft, S., & Clutterbuck, P. (2001). Attitudes Towards information Privacy.

De L'europe. (2009). Trafficking in Organs, Tissues and Cells and Trafficking in Human Beings for the Purpose of the Removal of Organs Joint Council of Europe/ United Nations Study COUNCIL OF EUROPE CONSEIL. Chrome-Extension:// Efaidnbmnnnibpcajpcglclefindmkaj/Https://Www.Edqm.Eu/Documents/52006/ 75920/Joint-Council-United-Nations-Study-Tra1.Pdf/D657e60c-2919-1cc9-581e -Ebc5bf41dbe7?T=1629873068134

Dick Marty. (2010). Committee on Legal Affairs and Human Rights inhuman Treatment of People and Illicit Trafficking in Human Organs in Kosovo* 1 Report Rapporteur: Mr Dick Marty, Switzerland, Alliance of Liberals and Democrats for Europe.

Farook, M., Rafiuddin, B., Minhas, H., & Dhubb, P. S. (2017). A Dark Web Story in-Depth Research and Study Conducted on the Dark Webbased on forensic Computing and Security in Malaysia. 2017 IEEE international Conference on Power, Control, Signals and instrumentation Engineering (ICPCSI), May, 3049–3055.

Fatima, H., Fatima Qadir, T., Moin, A., & Bilal Pasha, S. (2018). Pakistan: A Transplant Tourism Resort? *Journal of Public Health (Oxford, England)*, *40*(4), 899–899. Https://Doi.Org/10.1093/PUBMED/FDX157. DOI: 10.1093/pubmed/ fdx157 PMID: 29149306

Garg, N. (2018). Towards the Impact of Hacking on Cyber Security. IIOABJ, 9 | 2 | 61(May), 61–77.

Internet Society. (2018). 2018 Cyber incident & Breach Trends Report | internet [Cyber incident Breach Trends Report.]. *Society*, •••, 2018.

James Ashford. (2019, October 17). Hundreds Arrested in 'Dark Web' Paedophile Sting | the Week. Https://theweek.Com/103836/Hundreds-Arrested-in-Dark-Web -Paedophile-Sting Https://theweek.Com/103836/Hundreds-Arrested-in-Dark-Web -Paedophile-Sting

Jones, C., & Seger, A. (2020)... *Guide for Criminal Justice Statistics on Cybercrime and Electronic Evidence.*, (October), 1–24.

Justice & Care. (2023). Organ Trafficking Survivor Is Supported By Justice and Care. Https://Justiceandcare.Org/Stories/Organ-Trafficking-Survivor-Starts-To-Rebuild -Life-Supported-By-Justice-and-Care/.Https://Justiceandcare.Org/Stories/Organ -Trafficking-Survivor-Starts-To-Rebuild-Life-Supported-By-Justice-and-Care/

Kaur, S., & Randhawa, S. (2020). Dark Web: A Web of Crimes. *Wireless Personal Communications*, *112*(4), 2131–2158. Https://Doi.Org/10.1007/S11277-020-07143-2. DOI: 10.1007/s11277-020-07143-2

Kidnapped by a Paedophile I Met online - BBC News. (2016). Https://Www.Bbc.Com/News/Magazine-35730298

NIJ. (2001). Electronic Crime Scene investigation Guide: A Guide for First Responders. United States Department of Justice office of Justice, 93.

O'Leary, D. (2023). Organ Transplants: How the internet Enables the Dark Side | Mind Matters.

Organisation for Economic Cooperation and Development. (2016). Managing Digital Security and Privacy Risk: 2016 Ministerial Meeting on the Digital Economy. Background Report. OECD Digital Economy Papers, 254.

Rodriguez-Iturbe, B. (2008). Organ Trafficking: A Time for Action. *Kidney International*, *74*(7), 839–840. Https://Doi.Org/10.1038/Ki.2008.389. DOI: 10.1038/ki.2008.389 PMID: 18794811

Sebastian Traxl. (2013). Trafficking in Human Beings for the Purpose of Organ Removal in the OSCE Region: Analysis and Findings. OSCE office of the Special Representative and Co-Ordinator for Combating Trafficking in Human Beings. Chrome-Extension://Efaidnbmnnnibpcajpcglclefindmkaj/Https://Www.Osce.Org/Sites/Default/Files/F/Documents/E/B/103393.Pdf

Steering Committee of the Istanbul Summit. (2008). Participants in the International Summit on Transplant Tourism and Organ Trafficking Convened by the Transplantation Society and International Society of Nephrology in Istanbul, Turkey, April 30-May 2, 2008. The Declaration of Istanbul on Organ Trafficking and Transplant Tourism. *Transplantation*, *86*, 1013–1018.

UNITED NATIONS CONFERENCE ON TRADE AND DEVELOPMENT. (2019). DIGITAL ECONOMY REPORT 2019: Value Creation and Capture - Implications for Developing Countries.

UNODC. (2020). in Focus: Trafficking Over the Darknet -. *World Drug Report*, •••, 2020.

Yang, Y., Yang, L., Yang, M., Yu, H., Zhu, G., Chen, Z., & Chen, L. (2019). Dark Web forum Correlation Analysis Research. Proceedings of 2019 IEEE 8th Joint international information Technology and Artificial intelligence Conference, ITAIC 2019, Itaic, 1216–1220. Https://Doi.Org/10.1109/ITAIC.2019.8785760

Zhang, H., & Zou, F. (2020). A Survey of the Dark Web and Dark Market Research. 2020 IEEE 6th international Conference on Computer and Communications, ICCC 2020, 1694–1705. Https://Doi.Org/10.1109/ICCC51575.2020.9345271

Chapter 10

Reinforcing Healthcare Security Through Digital Government by Mapping Critical Gaps in Malaysia's Fight Against Organ Trafficking

Hemalata Vasudavan
http://orcid.org/0009-0003-0339-1940
APU, Malaysia

Sumathi Balakrishnan
Taylor's University, Malaysia

Vazeerudeen Abdul Hameed
APU, Malaysia

Niyazi Karabulut
http://orcid.org/0000-0002-6175-2025
Necmettin Erbakan University, Turkey

ABSTRACT

Organ trafficking threatens healthcare security, ethical medical practice, and public trust by exploiting governance and data gaps within health systems. Digital government offers mechanisms to strengthen healthcare security through improved data integration, cybersecurity, and inter-agency coordination. This chapter examines

DOI: 10.4018/979-8-3373-6696-8.ch010

how digital government can reinforce healthcare security in Malaysia by mapping theoretical, empirical, and methodological gaps that limit efforts to prevent organ trafficking. It highlights the need for coordinated governance and co-creation of cybersecurity value among key stakeholders.

1. INTRODUCTION

Digital government has emerged as a dominant paradigm in contemporary public administration, reshaping how states govern, regulate, and deliver public services in increasingly complex and data-driven societies. Globally, governments are moving beyond early e-government initiatives characterised by basic digitisation of administrative processes toward more integrated, interoperable, and value-oriented digital government models (Mergel et al., 2019; OECD, 2023). These models emphasise data integration, real-time decision-making, cross-agency collaboration, and public value creation. Within this transformation, healthcare has become a critical domain due to its reliance on sensitive data, complex stakeholder interactions, and high societal stakes.

Organ transplantation governance occupies a complex intersection of healthcare delivery, ethics, and security. While global literature highlights organ trafficking as a severe human-rights violation and governance failure (Delmonico et al., 2022; UNODC, 2023), recent Malaysian evidence suggests that large-scale trafficking incidents are rare, with the more pressing challenges being low organ-donation rates, limited transplant capacity, and workforce shortages (MOH Malaysia; Khoo & Ballesté, 2024). This chapter therefore reframes organ trafficking in Malaysia as a low-incidence but high-impact risk, requiring preventive governance mechanisms rather than reactive enforcement alone. Digital government offers a promising pathway for addressing these challenges by strengthening transparency, accountability, and coordination across healthcare institutions. Through interoperable information systems, secure digital identities, and advanced analytics, digital government can enhance the traceability of transplant processes and reduce opportunities for illicit activities. However, the effectiveness of such interventions depends on governance capacity, cybersecurity readiness, and ethical oversight—areas that remain unevenly developed in many contexts.

Malaysia provides a compelling case for examining the intersection of digital government, healthcare security, and organ trafficking prevention. Over the past decade, Malaysia has invested significantly in public-sector digitalisation through initiatives such as the Malaysia Digital Economy Blueprint (MyDIGITAL) and the Public Sector Digitalisation Strategic Plan (Economic Planning Unit, 2021; MyDIGITAL, 2021). These initiatives signal a national commitment to digital transformation, data-driven governance, and service integration. In the healthcare sector, digital initiatives include electronic medical records, disease registries, and health information systems.

Despite these advancements, digital government implementation in healthcare remains fragmented. Systems are often developed in organisational silos, with limited interoperability and inconsistent cybersecurity standards. These limitations constrain the ability of healthcare authorities to monitor transplant activities comprehensively and to detect irregularities associated with organ trafficking (Khoo & Ballesté, 2024). Consequently, the potential of digital government to reinforce healthcare security against organ trafficking remains underexplored in both policy and research.

Cybersecurity further complicates this landscape. Healthcare systems are increasingly targeted by cyberattacks due to the high value of medical data and the critical nature of healthcare services. Cybersecurity breaches can compromise patient confidentiality, disrupt clinical operations, and facilitate data manipulation that may enable organ trafficking (ENISA, 2023). Addressing these risks requires moving beyond technical solutions toward governance models that emphasise shared responsibility and co-creation of public value (Criado & Gil-Garcia, 2019).

This chapter therefore argues that reinforcing healthcare security in Malaysia's fight against organ trafficking requires an integrated digital-government approach that combines technological capability, governance reform, cybersecurity co-creation, and ethical oversight. It establishes the conceptual and contextual foundation for the chapters that follow, positioning digital government as a strategic governance mechanism rather than a purely technical intervention.

1.1 Smart and Digital Government as a Global Governance Paradigm

Digital government has emerged globally as a transformative governance paradigm aimed at reshaping how public institutions design policies, deliver services, and interact with citizens. Moving beyond early e-government initiatives focused on digitising administrative processes, digital government emphasises integration, data-driven decision-making, interoperability, and public value creation (Mergel, Edelmann, & Haug, 2019; OECD, 2023). Governments increasingly rely on digital infrastructures, analytics, and collaborative platforms to address complex societal challenges that transcend organisational and sectoral boundaries.

In this context, healthcare has become a strategic domain for digital-government transformation due to its data intensity, societal importance, and vulnerability to systemic risks. Digital government enables healthcare systems to move toward coordinated governance models that enhance transparency, accountability, and resilience. These attributes are particularly relevant in addressing transnational and organised crimes such as organ trafficking, which exploit governance gaps, weak coordination, and limited traceability across institutions (Delmonico et al., 2022).

1.2 Organ Trafficking as a Healthcare Security Challenge

Organ trafficking represents a serious threat to healthcare security, ethical medical practice, and human rights. It involves the illicit procurement, transportation, and transplantation of human organs, often exploiting vulnerable populations and weak regulatory environments. International evidence suggests that organ trafficking networks operate across borders, leveraging inconsistencies in healthcare governance, data management, and enforcement capacity (UNODC, 2023; Delmonico et al., 2022).

From a healthcare security perspective, organ trafficking undermines trust in medical institutions, compromises patient safety, and distorts equitable access to transplantation services. It also introduces risks related to falsified medical records, manipulation of waiting lists, and unregulated transplant procedures. These risks are amplified in environments where healthcare data systems are fragmented, oversight mechanisms are weak, and cybersecurity protections are insufficient (World Health Organization, 2023).

1.3 Digital Government and Healthcare Security

Healthcare security extends beyond physical infrastructure and clinical safety to include information integrity, ethical compliance, and system resilience. Digital government contributes to healthcare security by enabling integrated data governance, secure information sharing, and coordinated oversight across institutions. Through interoperable systems and real-time monitoring, digital government strengthens the capacity of healthcare authorities to detect irregularities, enforce regulations, and respond proactively to emerging threats (OECD, 2023).

In the context of organ transplantation, digital government facilitates traceability across the transplant lifecycle—from donor identification and consent to organ allocation and post-transplant monitoring. Secure digital systems reduce opportunities for manipulation, enhance auditability, and support evidence-based governance. However, these benefits depend on the alignment of technological tools with governance frameworks, ethical standards, and cybersecurity capacity (ENISA, 2023).

1.4 Malaysia's Digital Government and Healthcare Landscape

Malaysia has undertaken significant digitalisation efforts over the past decade, positioning digital government as a key driver of public-sector reform and national development. National strategies such as the Malaysia Digital Economy Blueprint

(MyDIGITAL) and the Public Sector Digitalisation Strategic Plan signal a commitment to integrated, citizen-centric, and data-driven governance (Economic Planning Unit, 2021; MyDIGITAL, 2021). Within the healthcare sector, digital initiatives include electronic medical records, health information exchanges, and disease registries.

Despite these advancements, digital government implementation in healthcare remains uneven. Systems are often developed in silos, with limited interoperability and varying levels of cybersecurity maturity across institutions. In organ transplantation governance, these limitations constrain the ability to monitor donor–recipient pathways comprehensively and to detect potential illicit activities (Khoo & Ballesté, 2024). As a result, digital government's potential contribution to organ-trafficking prevention remains underexplored and underutilised.

Existing drafts over-emphasised hypothetical trafficking vulnerabilities while under-emphasising structural constraints. This revised section rebalances emphasis using Malaysia-specific evidence.

Key constraints include: - Low deceased-donor rates (approximately 0.15–0.2% of ESRD patients), among the lowest in the region; - Limited transplant capacity, with only two major public transplant centres and a small number of MOH-affiliated transplant surgeons; - Cultural and religious hesitancy, despite supportive fatwas and public campaigns; - Manpower shortages and uneven digital literacy, constraining adoption of advanced systems.

Organ trafficking risk must therefore be understood within a system characterised more by scarcity and capacity limits than by widespread criminal penetration. Digital government's contribution lies in safeguarding integrity, supporting trust-building, and ensuring that scale-up efforts do not introduce new governance risks.

1.5 Cybersecurity and Co-Creation of Public Value

Cybersecurity is a foundational requirement for digital government in healthcare, particularly where sensitive personal and medical data are involved. Cyber incidents can compromise patient confidentiality, disrupt healthcare services, and enable data manipulation that facilitates criminal activities, including organ trafficking (ENISA, 2023). Consequently, cybersecurity must be treated not only as a technical issue but also as a governance and public value concern.

The concept of co-creation of public value emphasises collaborative engagement among government agencies, healthcare providers, technology vendors, and civil society in designing and securing digital systems (Criado & Gil-Garcia, 2019). In healthcare, co-creation enables shared responsibility for cybersecurity, ethical compliance, and service quality. This collaborative approach is particularly relevant for organ-trafficking prevention, which requires coordinated action across multiple stakeholders and institutional domains.

1.6 Problem Statement

Despite the rapid global advancement of digital government and its increasing application within healthcare systems, a critical gap persists in understanding how digital government can be strategically leveraged to prevent organ trafficking. Organ trafficking remains a complex healthcare security challenge that exploits institutional fragmentation, weak governance mechanisms, limited data traceability, and inadequate cybersecurity protections (Delmonico et al., 2022; UNODC, 2023). While digital government initiatives promise enhanced transparency, interoperability, and accountability, their practical contribution to mitigating organ trafficking risks within healthcare systems remains insufficiently conceptualised and empirically underexplored (OECD, 2023; Mergel, Edelmann, & Haug, 2019).

In Malaysia, sustained investments in digital government and digital health initiatives have focused primarily on improving administrative efficiency, service delivery, and system modernisation (Economic Planning Unit, 2021; MyDIGITAL, 2021). However, these initiatives have not been explicitly designed, integrated, or evaluated as governance instruments for healthcare security and organ trafficking prevention. Digital systems related to healthcare are often developed in organisational silos, lack interoperability across institutions, and operate under uneven governance and cybersecurity standards. As a result, critical processes such as end-to-end traceability of organ transplantation, cross-institutional oversight, and proactive detection of irregularities remain limited or inconsistently applied (Khoo & Ballesté, 2024).

From a theoretical perspective, the research problem lies in the disconnect between digital government scholarship and organ trafficking prevention literature. Digital government studies predominantly emphasise public value creation, innovation, and service efficiency, whereas organ trafficking research is largely grounded in legal, ethical, and criminological frameworks (Criado & Gil-Garcia, 2019; World Health Organization, 2022). The absence of an integrated analytical perspective obscures how digital government can function as a preventive governance mechanism embedded within healthcare security, rather than merely as a supporting technological layer.

Empirically, there is a notable scarcity of evidence-based studies examining the effectiveness of specific digital government applications such as interoperable health information systems, digital identity verification, secure transplant registries, and cybersecurity frameworks—in reducing organ trafficking risks. This gap is particularly pronounced in middle-income countries like Malaysia, where healthcare systems are simultaneously undergoing digital transformation and confronting governance capacity constraints (Khoo & Ballesté, 2024; Panigrahi, 2025). Existing studies often rely on descriptive or policy-oriented analyses, offering limited insight into implementation challenges, outcomes, and unintended consequences.

Methodologically, research in this domain is constrained by a lack of longitudinal, mixed-methods, and evaluative approaches capable of capturing the complexity of multi-stakeholder governance, cybersecurity co-creation, and ethical oversight in healthcare systems (ENISA, 2023; OECD, 2023). Without robust methodological designs, policymakers and practitioners lack the evidence needed to assess whether digital government initiatives meaningfully enhance healthcare security or simply reproduce existing governance weaknesses in digital form.

Consequently, the central research problem addressed in this chapter is the absence of a coherent, evidence-based understanding of how digital government can be systematically designed, governed, and secured to prevent organ trafficking within Malaysia's healthcare sector. Addressing this problem is essential for transforming digital government from a fragmented digitalisation agenda into a strategic healthcare security instrument capable of supporting ethical, transparent, and accountable organ transplantation governance (Delmonico et al., 2022; Criado & Gil-Garcia, 2019; World Health Organization, 2022; UNODC, 2023; Khoo & Ballesté, 2024; Panigrahi, 2025; OECD, 2023; ENISA, 2023).

1.7 Chapter Objectives and Structure

This chapter establishes the conceptual and contextual foundation for examining the role of digital government in reinforcing healthcare security against organ trafficking in Malaysia. It highlights the global relevance of digital government, frames organ trafficking as a healthcare security challenge, and situates Malaysia's digitalisation efforts within this broader landscape.

The remainder of this book chapter is structured as follows:

Chapter 2 develops the conceptual foundations of digital government, healthcare security, and cybersecurity co-creation.

Chapter 3 identifies key theoretical, empirical, and methodological gaps in existing research.

Chapter 4 examines digital-government applications for organ-trafficking prevention.

Chapter 5 outlines policy directions and a future research agenda.

Together, these chapters contribute to scholarly and policy debates on digital government and healthcare security, offering insights relevant to Malaysia and comparable contexts.

2. CONCEPTUAL FOUNDATIONS

Digital government is conceptualised as an integrated governance model that leverages digital technologies, data, and collaborative processes to create public value (OECD, 2023). Unlike traditional e-government, which prioritises efficiency and automation, digital government emphasises interoperability, user-centricity, and cross-sector collaboration (Mergel et al., 2019). These principles are particularly relevant in healthcare, where service delivery depends on coordinated action across multiple institutions and professions.

Healthcare security extends beyond physical infrastructure to encompass data integrity, ethical compliance, and system resilience. Organ transplantation systems are especially vulnerable due to their complexity, high stakes, and reliance on accurate data. Fragmented information systems, weak governance, and limited oversight create conditions that can be exploited by organ trafficking networks (Delmonico et al., 2022).

Digital health ecosystem including electronic medical records, transplant registries, and analytics platforms form the operational backbone of digital government in healthcare. When integrated effectively, these systems enhance transparency, traceability, and accountability (World Health Organization, 2022). However, challenges such as interoperability gaps, data-quality issues, and cybersecurity vulnerabilities persist, limiting their effectiveness in preventing illicit activities (Khoo & Ballesté, 2024).

Cybersecurity is a foundational component of digital government in healthcare. Protecting sensitive transplant data requires not only technical safeguards but also governance mechanisms that allocate responsibility, manage risk, and ensure compliance (ENISA, 2023). The concept of co-creation of cybersecurity value highlights the importance of collaboration among government agencies, healthcare providers, technology vendors, and civil society in securing digital systems (Criado & Gil-Garcia, 2019).

This chapter establishes the conceptual linkages between digital government, healthcare security, and organ trafficking prevention. It provides the theoretical foundation for identifying gaps and assessing policy and technological interventions in subsequent chapters.

2.1 Digital Government Concepts and Principles

Digital government represents a paradigm shift in public administration, moving beyond the traditional e-government focus on automation and online service delivery to an integrated, data-driven approach that enhances governance, accountability, and co-created public value (OECD, 2023; Mergel et al., 2019). It encompasses the strategic deployment of information and communication technologies (ICTs), interoperable platforms, and secure digital infrastructure to facilitate decision-making, policy implementation, and citizen engagement across all levels of government. Key principles of digital government include:

1. Interoperability – The ability of different information systems and organizations to exchange and utilize information seamlessly. Interoperability ensures that data collected across hospitals, regulatory agencies, and enforcement bodies can be integrated for comprehensive monitoring and oversight (OECD, 2023).
2. User-Centricity – Digital government must be designed around the needs of its end-users, which in healthcare includes patients, donors, clinicians, and policy-makers. Ensuring that systems are intuitive, accessible, and efficient enhances compliance, reduces errors, and strengthens trust.
3. Data Governance – Effective data governance frameworks ensure data integrity, accessibility, privacy, and compliance with national and international regulations. They provide the foundation for reliable analytics, monitoring, and decision-making in high-risk domains like organ transplantation (World Health Organization, 2022).
4. Cybersecurity – Protecting digital infrastructures from internal and external threats is a core aspect of digital government. Cybersecurity safeguards sensitive health data, ensures continuity of healthcare services, and prevents misuse of critical information (ENISA, 2023).
5. Co-Creation of Public Value – Beyond technology, digital government emphasizes collaboration among multiple stakeholders including government agencies, healthcare institutions, private technology providers, and civil society—to co-create solutions that enhance security, trust, and compliance (Criado & Gil-Garcia, 2019).

In essence, digital government is not simply about implementing ICT systems but about designing governance structures that leverage digital technologies to achieve measurable public value, ethical oversight, and resilience against abuse or crime.

2.2 Healthcare System Vulnerabilities and Governance Challenges

Healthcare systems are complex, multi-actor socio-technical systems that involve hospitals, laboratories, regulatory agencies, insurance providers, and law enforcement authorities. This complexity, combined with the sensitive nature of medical data and ethical obligations, creates vulnerabilities that can be exploited by criminals (Delmonico et al., 2022; World Health Organization, 2023).

Key Vulnerabilities in Organ Transplant Systems:

- Fragmented Information Systems – Many hospitals operate separate EMRs and transplant registries, limiting visibility of donor-recipient matching and creating blind spots that criminals can exploit.
- Limited Traceability and Auditability – Without centralized monitoring and tamper-proof records, the flow of organs may not be fully traceable, increasing the risk of illicit transplants and unethical practices.
- Weak Institutional Coordination – Disconnected governance structures among hospitals, regulatory agencies, and enforcement bodies impede rapid detection and intervention.
- Human Factors and Ethical Lapses – Inadequate training, pressure to meet clinical outcomes, and lack of awareness about digital tools can result in errors or unethical decisions, which may inadvertently facilitate organ trafficking.
- These vulnerabilities illustrate why digital-government interventions, when combined with effective governance and cybersecurity measures, are critical for enhancing healthcare security and mitigating illicit activities.

2.3 Digital Health Ecosystems

Digital health ecosystems form the operational backbone of digital government in the healthcare sector. They integrate technologies, policies, and governance mechanisms to improve care delivery, data management, and system-wide monitoring (World Health Organization, 2022).

Components of Digital Health Ecosystems:

- Electronic Medical Records (EMRs) – EMRs digitize patient data, enabling secure storage, retrieval, and analysis across healthcare providers. They form the foundation for monitoring transplant histories and donor-recipient data.
- National and Transplant Registries – Centralized registries maintain detailed records of donors and recipients, supporting ethical compliance, waiting-list management, and traceability.
- Digital Identity and Verification Systems – Systems such as biometric verification, digital signatures, and secure IDs help authenticate donors and recipients, preventing identity fraud and unauthorized organ procurement.
- Data Analytics Platforms – Advanced analytics detect anomalies in donor-recipient matching, waiting lists, and organ flow, allowing proactive inter-

vention against irregularities or suspicious patterns (Sitharamulu, 2024; Panigrahi, 2025).

- Interoperability Standards – Adopting standards like HL7 FHIR and ISO 27799 ensures that disparate systems across institutions can communicate effectively, enabling seamless monitoring and governance (Khoo & Ballesté, 2024).
- When effectively integrated, these components not only enhance service delivery but also strengthen preventive mechanisms against organ trafficking by providing transparency, accountability, and actionable insights.

2.4 Cybersecurity and Co-Creation Models

Cybersecurity is a critical enabler of digital-government effectiveness, particularly in sensitive sectors like healthcare. It extends beyond technical protection to include governance processes, institutional responsibilities, and stakeholder collaboration (ENISA, 2023).

Co-Creation of Cybersecurity Value:

- Definition: Co-creation involves shared responsibility among government agencies, hospitals, technology vendors, and civil society for protecting digital health systems.
- Mechanisms: Joint monitoring, incident response coordination, training programs, and shared governance boards are examples of co-creation practices (Criado & Gil-Garcia, 2019).
- Benefits: Enhances system resilience, reduces vulnerability gaps, fosters trust, and ensures ethical management of sensitive transplant data.

Co-creation acknowledges that no single actor can fully secure complex health systems; collaborative approaches are essential to protect against both internal lapses and external threats.

2.5 Digital Governance Relevance to Organ-Trafficking Prevention

The conceptual relevance of digital government to organ-trafficking prevention lies in its ability to integrate governance, technology, and ethics into a coherent system.

- Transparency and Traceability: Digital systems provide audit trails of all transplant activities, improving oversight and enabling rapid investigation of anomalies.

- Cross-Institutional Coordination: Interoperable registries and secure data-sharing mechanisms allow multiple hospitals and regulatory agencies to co-ordinate in real time, reducing gaps that criminals could exploit.
- Predictive Analytics and Early Warning: AI and blockchain-based monitoring detect irregularities before they escalate, supporting proactive interventions.
- Ethical Compliance and Accountability: Digital government frameworks ensure adherence to consent, privacy, and donor-recipient fairness, reducing the risk of exploitation.

By integrating these elements, Malaysia can build a healthcare ecosystem in which digital governance not only improves operational efficiency but also acts as a preventive mechanism against organ trafficking.

3. MAPPING THEORETICAL, EMPIRICAL, AND METHODOLOGICAL GAPS

Digital government is conceptualised as an integrated governance model that leverages digital technologies, data, and collaborative processes to create public value (OECD, 2023). Unlike traditional e-government, which prioritises efficiency and automation, digital government emphasises interoperability, user-centricity, and cross-sector collaboration (Mergel et al., 2019). These principles are particularly relevant in healthcare, where service delivery depends on coordinated action across multiple institutions and professions.

Healthcare security extends beyond physical infrastructure to encompass data integrity, ethical compliance, and system resilience. Organ transplantation systems are especially vulnerable due to their complexity, high stakes, and reliance on accurate data. Fragmented information systems, weak governance, and limited oversight create conditions that can be exploited by organ trafficking networks (Delmonico et al., 2022).

Digital health ecosystems including electronic medical records, transplant registries, and analytics platforms form the operational backbone of digital government in healthcare. When integrated effectively, these systems enhance transparency, traceability, and accountability (World Health Organization, 2022). However, challenges such as interoperability gaps, data-quality issues, and cybersecurity vulnerabilities persist, limiting their effectiveness in preventing illicit activities (Khoo & Ballesté, 2024).

Cybersecurity is a foundational component of digital government in healthcare. Protecting sensitive transplant data requires not only technical safeguards but also governance mechanisms that allocate responsibility, manage risk, and ensure compliance (ENISA, 2023). The concept of co-creation of cybersecurity value highlights the importance of collaboration among government agencies, healthcare providers, technology vendors, and civil society in securing digital systems (Criado & Gil-Garcia, 2019).

This chapter establishes the conceptual linkages between digital government, healthcare security, and organ trafficking prevention. It provides the theoretical foundation for identifying gaps and assessing policy and technological interventions in subsequent chapters.

3.1 Theoretical Gaps

Theoretical development at the intersection of digital government, healthcare governance, and organ-trafficking prevention remains limited. Current frameworks often examine digital government and healthcare security in isolation, focusing on efficiency, interoperability, or technical adoption rather than governance effectiveness and crime prevention (Mergel et al., 2019; OECD, 2023). There is a lack of integrative models that explicitly link digital governance mechanisms, ethical oversight, and the prevention of illicit organ trafficking within complex socio-technical systems.

Additionally, theoretical models seldom incorporate the concept of co-creation of cybersecurity value in healthcare, which emphasises joint responsibility across government agencies, hospitals, technology providers, and civil society (Criado & Gil-Garcia, 2019). Without a coherent theoretical lens, policymakers and practitioners lack guidance on designing digital-government systems that balance ethical obligations, data security, and operational effectiveness in transplant oversight.

3.2 Empirical Gaps

Empirical evidence assessing the effectiveness of digital-government tools in preventing organ trafficking is sparse. Studies on electronic medical records (EMRs), national health registries, and digital identity verification primarily evaluate efficiency or service delivery, rather than their role in detecting illicit organ transactions (Khoo & Ballesté, 2024; Panigrahi, 2025). Few investigations examine cross-institutional coordination, real-time monitoring, or the performance of analytics platforms in mitigating risks associated with organ transplantation.

In the Malaysian context, empirical studies are particularly limited. There is little data evaluating how digital-health systems and governance frameworks function across public and private hospitals, or how enforcement agencies utilise digital tools for transplant oversight (CodeBlue, 2023). Moreover, there is insufficient research on the outcomes of digital-government initiatives, such as MyDIGITAL or MOH digital health strategies, in improving traceability, accountability, or prevention effectiveness in transplant processes.

3.3 Methodological Gaps

Methodological constraints present additional barriers to rigorous evaluation. Firstly, restricted access to sensitive health, transplant, and law-enforcement datasets limits the ability to conduct comprehensive studies. Ethical and privacy considerations further constrain longitudinal or experimental research designs. Secondly, there is a lack of standardized indicators and metrics for assessing digital-government contributions to healthcare security and organ-trafficking prevention (OECD, 2023).

Thirdly, research methodologies often fail to integrate technical, social, and regulatory dimensions. Many studies adopt single-method approaches, such as surveys or descriptive case studies, which do not capture the complex interactions between digital systems, human behaviour, and governance structures (Delmonico et al., 2022). Additionally, there is minimal use of digital-forensics, simulation, or mixed-methods approaches to evaluate interventions across multiple stakeholders or institutions.

3.4 Cybersecurity Co-Creation Gaps

The co-creation of cybersecurity value in healthcare remains underexplored. While multi-stakeholder collaboration is recognised as critical, there is limited evidence on how government agencies, hospitals, technology vendors, and civil society jointly contribute to risk mitigation, real-time monitoring, and incident response in organ transplantation (ENISA, 2023).

Furthermore, there is little research on institutional coordination mechanisms, shared responsibility models, or incentives that encourage adherence to cybersecurity standards. Without empirical validation and methodological rigor, co-creation models remain conceptual, limiting their practical applicability for preventing organ-trafficking activities.

3.5 Synthesis: Implications for Malaysia

Mapping these gaps demonstrates that Malaysia's efforts to leverage digital government for organ-trafficking prevention face multifaceted challenges. The absence of integrated theoretical models limits strategic design and policy coherence. Sparse empirical evidence weakens evaluation of existing digital-health systems, while methodological constraints restrict the generation of actionable insights. Cybersecurity co-creation gaps further impede the ability to coordinate multi-stakeholder interventions effectively.

Addressing these gaps is essential to strengthening healthcare security and ensuring that digital government initiatives contribute to ethical, transparent, and effective organ-transplant governance. The next chapter builds on this analysis by examining practical applications of digital-government tools in organ-trafficking prevention and strategies to operationalise co-created cybersecurity value.

Table 1. Summary of theoretical, empirical, methodological, and cybersecurity co-creation gaps

Gap Type	Description	Implications for Healthcare Security
Theoretical Gaps	Lack of integrated models connecting digital government, healthcare governance, ethics, and organ-trafficking prevention. Technology-focused approaches dominate without considering socio-technical interactions.	Limits strategic design of digital systems for transplant oversight; hinders understanding of how governance and technology jointly prevent illicit organ activities.
Empirical Gaps	Sparse evidence evaluating the effectiveness of digital tools (EMRs, digital identity, registries) in detecting or preventing organ trafficking. Limited studies on cross-institutional coordination and real-time monitoring.	Weakens the evidence base for policy interventions; prevents assessment of what works in Malaysia's healthcare context.
Methodological Gaps	Restricted access to sensitive health and enforcement data; inconsistent indicators for measuring prevention outcomes; underuse of mixed-methods and digital-forensics approaches.	Constrains rigorous evaluation of interventions; hampers understanding of systemic vulnerabilities and the effectiveness of digital-government mechanisms.
Cybersecurity Co-Creation Gaps	Limited models and empirical studies on joint responsibility among government agencies, hospitals, technology vendors, and civil society. Coordination mechanisms and incentives underexplored.	Reduces multi-stakeholder coordination; cybersecurity risks remain uneven across institutions, increasing vulnerability to exploitation.

4. DIGITAL-GOVERNMENT APPLICATIONS FOR ORGAN-TRAFFICKING PREVENTION

This chapter examines how specific digital government applications can be mobilised to reinforce healthcare security and prevent organ trafficking in Malaysia. Building on the conceptual foundations outlined in Chapter 2 and the gap analysis presented in Chapter 3, the chapter focuses on practical mechanisms through which digital government can enhance transparency, traceability, accountability, and resilience within organ transplantation systems. Rather than treating technology as a standalone solution, the discussion situates digital tools within governance, cybersecurity, and co-creation frameworks that are essential for sustainable implementation.

4.1 Digital Identity and Verification Mechanisms

Digital identity systems form a foundational pillar of digital government and play a critical role in preventing organ trafficking within healthcare systems. These systems enable accurate verification of donors, recipients, and healthcare professionals, thereby reducing risks associated with identity fraud, falsified consent, and unauthorised transplant procedures (OECD, 2023). In the context of organ transplantation, reliable identity verification is essential to ensure that donors provide informed consent, recipients are correctly prioritised, and transplant procedures comply with legal and ethical standards.

In Malaysia, the integration of national digital identity infrastructures with healthcare systems offers opportunities to enhance traceability and accountability. Linking patient records, donor registries, and transplant approvals to verified digital identities enables regulators and healthcare providers to authenticate individuals across institutions. Advanced mechanisms such as biometric authentication, digital signatures, and decentralised identity solutions further strengthen system integrity by creating auditable trails that can support compliance monitoring and post-incident investigations (Panigrahi, 2025).

However, the effectiveness of digital identity systems depends on governance arrangements, including access controls, data protection policies, and inter-agency coordination. Without strong governance and cybersecurity safeguards, identity systems **may introduce new risks** rather than mitigate existing ones. Therefore, digital identity must be embedded within a broader digital-government framework that prioritises ethical oversight, privacy-by-design, and cross-sector collaboration.

4.2 Interoperable Health Information Systems and Registries

Interoperability is a core principle of digital government and a prerequisite for effective organ-trafficking prevention. Interoperable health information systems enable seamless data exchange across hospitals, transplant centres, regulatory bodies, and enforcement agencies, reducing information silos that can be exploited for illicit activities (World Health Organization, 2022). In transplantation governance, interoperability supports real-time monitoring of donor availability, recipient waiting lists, transplant approvals, and post-transplant outcomes.

National transplant registries play a central role in this ecosystem by serving as authoritative data repositories for donor–recipient matching and organ allocation. When registries are integrated with hospital electronic medical records (EMRs) and national health databases, they enhance transparency and reduce opportunities for manipulation or unauthorised transplants (Khoo & Ballesté, 2024). Adoption of international interoperability and security standards, such as HL7 FHIR and ISO 27799, further improves data quality, consistency, and trustworthiness.

Despite these benefits, interoperability also introduces governance challenges. Differences in institutional capacity, legacy systems, and regulatory constraints can limit data sharing across public and private healthcare providers. Addressing these challenges requires digital-government leadership, standard-setting, and sustained investment to ensure that interoperability contributes to healthcare security rather than creating new vulnerabilities.

4.3 Monitoring, Analytics, and Traceability Technologies

Advanced digital technologies provide powerful tools for monitoring and tracing transplant-related activities across healthcare systems. Data analytics and artificial intelligence (AI) can be applied to detect anomalies in waiting lists, donor–recipient matching, transplant volumes, or institutional reporting patterns. Such anomalies may signal irregular practices or potential cases of organ trafficking, enabling earlier intervention by regulators and enforcement agencies (Sitharamulu, 2024).

Blockchain technology has gained attention as a mechanism for ensuring end-to-end traceability of organs from donor identification through transplantation. Blockchain-based registries create immutable records that are resistant to tampering, enhancing transparency and accountability across institutions (Bawa et al., 2025). In organ transplantation, blockchain can document consent, organ transport, and transplant procedures, providing verifiable evidence that supports ethical compliance and forensic investigation.

While these technologies offer significant promise, their deployment must be accompanied by clear governance frameworks. Issues such as system interoperability, scalability, data ownership, and legal admissibility of digital records must be addressed to ensure practical effectiveness. Digital government provides the institutional context for aligning these technologies with regulatory oversight and healthcare governance objectives.

4.4 Cybersecurity Strengthening and Incident Response

Cybersecurity is a critical enabler of digital-government applications in healthcare, particularly in systems handling sensitive transplant data. Cyberattacks on healthcare institutions can compromise patient confidentiality, disrupt clinical operations, and manipulate transplant records, thereby increasing the risk of organ trafficking and related crimes (ENISA, 2023). Strengthening cybersecurity is therefore essential for maintaining trust and system integrity.

Digital-government approaches emphasise the adoption of standardised cybersecurity frameworks, such as ISO/IEC 27001 and national cybersecurity guidelines, to protect healthcare information systems. These frameworks support risk assessment, access control, encryption, and continuous monitoring. In addition, coordinated incident response mechanisms enable rapid detection, containment, and recovery from cyber incidents.

Cybersecurity co-creation is particularly important in healthcare environments, where multiple stakeholders share responsibility for system security. Government agencies, hospitals, technology vendors, and cybersecurity authorities must collaborate to share threat intelligence, conduct joint exercises, and maintain consistent security standards. Such collaboration reduces systemic vulnerabilities and strengthens the resilience of transplant governance systems against exploitation.

4.5 Operationalising Co-Creation through Governance Models and Partnerships

The successful implementation of digital-government applications for organ-trafficking prevention depends on governance models that operationalise co-creation. Co-creation involves shared responsibility, joint decision-making, and coordinated action among diverse stakeholders, including policymakers, healthcare administrators, clinicians, technology providers, and civil society organisations (Criado & Gil-Garcia, 2019).

Practical governance mechanisms for co-creation include inter-agency committees, public–private partnerships, memoranda of understanding for data sharing, and multi-stakeholder oversight bodies. These mechanisms facilitate alignment between technological solutions, regulatory requirements, and ethical standards. Capacity-building initiatives, such as joint training programs and cybersecurity drills, further support co-creation by enhancing institutional readiness and trust.

In the Malaysian context, co-creation-oriented governance can help bridge institutional silos and ensure that digital-government initiatives address real-world healthcare security challenges. By embedding collaboration into governance structures, digital government can move beyond isolated technological interventions toward systemic, sustainable prevention of organ trafficking.

Table 2. Mapping digital-government applications to critical gaps in organ-trafficking prevention

Digital-Government Application	Addressed Gaps	Contribution to Healthcare Security
Digital Identity and Verification	Theoretical, Empirical, Methodological	Ensures accurate donor–recipient matching, prevents identity fraud, improves traceability, and provides data for evaluation of system effectiveness.
Interoperable Health Information Systems and Registries	Theoretical, Empirical, Methodological	Enhances cross-institutional coordination, real-time data sharing, and standardised record-keeping; strengthens oversight and reduces opportunities for illicit transplants.
Monitoring, Analytics, and Traceability Technologies	Empirical, Methodological, Cybersecurity Co-Creation	Enables anomaly detection, audit trails, and tamper-proof organ traceability; provides evidence for policy and law enforcement interventions.
Cybersecurity Strengthening and Incident Response	Methodological, Cybersecurity Co-Creation	Protects sensitive health and transplant data, reduces vulnerability to hacking or data manipulation, and supports coordinated responses to security incidents.
Operationalising Co-Creation: Governance Models and Partnerships	Theoretical, Cybersecurity Co-Creation	Establishes multi-stakeholder collaboration, shared accountability, and joint monitoring mechanisms; ensures digital systems are used ethically and effectively.

5. POLICY DIRECTIONS AND RESEARCH AGENDA

This chapter synthesises the conceptual, empirical, and governance insights developed in the preceding chapters and translates them into concrete policy directions and a future-oriented research agenda. It argues that preventing organ trafficking through digital government requires an integrated approach that combines policy reform, ethical governance, cybersecurity capacity, and sustained knowledge generation. In the Malaysian context, where digital government in healthcare is still evolving, strategic alignment and institutional readiness are critical to ensuring that digital initiatives contribute meaningfully to healthcare security rather than functioning as isolated technological upgrades.

5.1 Strengthening Digital-Government Policy for Healthcare Security

The prevention of organ trafficking in Malaysia requires a strategic policy approach that positions digital government as a core instrument for healthcare security rather than as a supporting technological function. While national digitalisation strategies have prioritised efficiency and service delivery, greater emphasis is needed on governance outcomes such as transparency, accountability, and crime prevention (OECD, 2023). Digital-government policy should explicitly recognise organ trafficking as a healthcare security risk and integrate preventive objectives into digital health and public-sector reform agendas.

Key policy priorities include strengthening legal mandates for secure data sharing across healthcare institutions, standardising digital identity verification in transplant-related processes, and embedding traceability requirements within healthcare regulations. These measures would reduce regulatory fragmentation and ensure that digital tools are consistently applied across public and private healthcare providers (Khoo & Ballesté, 2024). Importantly, digital-government policies must align technological adoption with ethical oversight, ensuring compliance with international standards on organ transplantation and human rights.

5.2 Governance and Ethical Enhancements

Digital-government interventions in healthcare must be supported by robust governance and ethical frameworks to maintain public trust and legitimacy. Organ transplantation involves sensitive personal data, life-and-death decisions, and ethical considerations related to consent, equity, and access. Therefore, digital systems must be designed and governed according to privacy-by-design and ethics-by-design principles (World Health Organization, 2022).

Governance enhancements should include transparent audit mechanisms for transplant registries, clear accountability structures for data management, and oversight bodies responsible for monitoring compliance with ethical and legal standards. Whistleblowing mechanisms and reporting channels can further strengthen accountability by enabling healthcare professionals and civil society to flag suspected irregularities. Without such governance safeguards, digital government risks reinforcing existing power asymmetries or enabling new forms of abuse rather than preventing organ trafficking.

5.3 Cybersecurity Capacity Building and Institutional Readiness

Cybersecurity capacity is a critical determinant of the effectiveness of digital-government initiatives in healthcare. Weak cybersecurity exposes transplant systems to data breaches, manipulation of records, and service disruptions that may facilitate organ trafficking or undermine enforcement efforts (ENISA, 2023). Strengthening cybersecurity capacity therefore requires sustained investment in infrastructure, skills, and institutional coordination.

Capacity-building initiatives should focus on training healthcare administrators, clinicians, and IT personnel in cybersecurity awareness, data governance, and incident response. Regular joint exercises involving healthcare institutions, regulatory agencies, and national cybersecurity authorities can improve preparedness and coordination during cyber incidents. Additionally, incorporating cybersecurity compliance into hospital accreditation and performance evaluation frameworks would incentivise continuous improvement and accountability.

5.4 Advancing a Prioritised Research Agenda

Addressing the theoretical, empirical, and methodological gaps identified in Chapter 3 requires a focused and coordinated research agenda. Future research should prioritise rigorous evaluation of digital-government tools used in organ-trafficking prevention, including interoperable registries, digital identity systems, and traceability technologies such as blockchain (Panigrahi, 2025). Longitudinal and mixed-methods studies are particularly needed to assess outcomes, scalability, and unintended consequences.

Research should also examine co-creation of cybersecurity value as a governance phenomenon rather than solely a technical practice. Empirical studies exploring collaboration models, incentive structures, and institutional arrangements can provide actionable insights for policymakers and practitioners (Criado & Gil-Garcia, 2019). Comparative research across countries or healthcare systems would further enrich understanding of how digital government can be adapted to different regulatory and cultural contexts.

5.5 Toward a Sustainable Implementation Roadmap

Developing a sustainable implementation roadmap is essential for translating digital government principles into practical measures that reinforce healthcare security and prevent organ trafficking. A roadmap provides a structured, phased approach that ensures interventions are scalable, adaptive, and resilient, while remaining aligned with Malaysia's healthcare governance and digitalisation objectives (OECD, 2023; MyDIGITAL, 2021).

1. Short-Term Initiatives (1–2 years): Pilot Testing and System Integration

In the initial phase, pilot projects should be implemented in selected healthcare institutions to test interoperable transplant registries, digital identity verification mechanisms, and secure data-sharing protocols. Pilot initiatives allow policymakers and practitioners to evaluate technical feasibility, identify operational challenges, and assess stakeholder readiness before nationwide rollout (Khoo & Ballesté, 2024). During this phase, cybersecurity measures should be embedded from the outset, incorporating risk assessments, encryption protocols, and incident response procedures. Additionally, stakeholder engagement is critical: co-creation workshops involving clinicians, IT staff, regulatory authorities, and civil society can provide valuable feedback and enhance system acceptance (Criado & Gil-Garcia, 2019).

2. Medium-Term Initiatives (3–5 years): Scaling, Standardisation, and Governance Alignment

Following successful pilots, digital government applications should be scaled across healthcare institutions nationwide. This phase requires harmonisation of data standards, protocols for interoperability, and alignment with regulatory frameworks to ensure consistent implementation. Governance structures must be formalised to oversee data integrity, ethical compliance, and cross-institutional accountability. Multi-stakeholder oversight committees can be established to monitor compliance, resolve conflicts, and ensure that digital interventions are aligned with healthcare security objectives (ENISA, 2023). Cybersecurity capacity should be further strengthened through training, awareness programs, and coordinated incident management exercises to maintain resilience as the systems scale.

3. Long-Term Initiatives (5+ years): Institutionalisation and Continuous Learning

In the long-term, digital government principles must be institutionalised within the healthcare system to ensure sustainability and adaptability. This includes embedding digital government processes into healthcare regulation, organisational culture, and professional training programs. Continuous monitoring and evaluation mechanisms should be implemented to measure outcomes, detect emerging risks, and adjust systems in response to evolving threats (World Health Organization, 2022; Panigrahi, 2025). Mechanisms for feedback and learning should also be integrated to enable adaptive governance, ensuring that lessons from pilot programs and scaled implementations inform ongoing practice.

4. Integration of Co-Creation and Stakeholder Engagement

Sustainability is further enhanced by operationalising co-creation across all phases of the roadmap. Digital government initiatives are most effective when stakeholders—including government agencies, healthcare providers, technology vendors, and civil society—share responsibility for design, implementation, and oversight (Criado & Gil-Garcia, 2019). Structured engagement mechanisms, such as collaborative workshops, joint training programs, and inter-agency governance forums, support continuous alignment of objectives and build trust among participants. Co-creation not only strengthens system adoption but also ensures that ethical, operational, and cybersecurity considerations are addressed comprehensively.

5. Adaptation to Emerging Challenges

A sustainable roadmap must also incorporate mechanisms for flexibility and adaptation. Organ trafficking networks are dynamic and exploit weaknesses in governance and technology; therefore, digital government interventions must be responsive to evolving threats. This includes updating cybersecurity protocols, revising ethical guidelines, and enhancing interoperability as new technologies and regulatory requirements emerge (ENISA, 2023; Delmonico et al., 2022). Scenario planning, risk forecasting, and regular system audits are critical tools to ensure that digital government interventions remain effective over time.

6. Expected Outcomes

When implemented effectively, a sustainable roadmap will produce multiple benefits: enhanced traceability of transplant processes, improved regulatory oversight, strengthened cybersecurity and risk management, and a measurable reduction in opportunities for organ trafficking. In addition, it will foster a culture of collaboration, ethical compliance, and continuous learning within Malaysia's healthcare system. This roadmap thus positions digital government not as a one-time intervention, but as an enduring mechanism for healthcare security, policy innovation, and societal trust (OECD, 2023; MyDIGITAL, 2021; Khoo & Ballesté, 2024).

6. CONCLUSION

This chapter has systematically examined the role of digital government in reinforcing healthcare security and preventing organ trafficking in Malaysia. It has highlighted the unique challenges posed by organ trafficking, including institutional fragmentation, weak governance, limited traceability, and cybersecurity vulnerabilities (Delmonico et al., 2022; UNODC, 2023). By situating digital government as a strategic governance mechanism rather than merely a technological intervention, the chapter underscores the potential for integrated digital systems to enhance transparency, accountability, and resilience within healthcare institutions (OECD, 2023; Mergel, Edelmann, & Haug, 2019).

The research problem identified in this chapter emphasizes the gap between Malaysia's digital government aspirations and the practical implementation of healthcare security mechanisms specifically designed to prevent organ trafficking (Khoo & Ballesté, 2024; Panigrahi, 2025). Despite significant investments in national digital initiatives, healthcare systems often remain siloed, lacking interoperability, and consistent governance structures. Consequently, existing digital tools cannot fully mitigate risks associated with organ trafficking without deliberate integration into governance, cybersecurity, and ethical oversight frameworks (Criado & Gil-Garcia, 2019; World Health Organization, 2022).

By mapping theoretical, empirical, and methodological gaps, this chapter has illuminated key limitations in current scholarship and practice. Theoretically, digital government and organ trafficking literature remain largely disconnected, obscuring how digital interventions can function as proactive governance instruments. Empirically, there is a scarcity of evidence-based studies that evaluate the effectiveness of specific digital government applications in organ trafficking prevention, particularly in the Malaysian context. Methodologically, there is a need for longitudinal, mixed-methods, and evaluative research capable of capturing complex multi-stakeholder governance processes and co-creation of cybersecurity value (ENISA, 2023; OECD, 2023).

The chapter also demonstrates that digital government applications—including interoperable health information systems, digital identity verification, secure transplant registries, and monitoring and analytics technologies—have significant potential to address organ trafficking risks if embedded within strong governance and ethical frameworks (World Health Organization, 2022; Panigrahi, 2025; Bawa et al., 2025). Cybersecurity co-creation, in particular, emerges as a critical enabler, requiring collaboration among government agencies, healthcare providers, technology vendors, and civil society to ensure shared responsibility, system resilience, and effective threat mitigation (Criado & Gil-Garcia, 2019; ENISA, 2023).

From a policy perspective, the chapter argues that reinforcing healthcare security demands explicit alignment of digital government initiatives with sector-specific objectives. This includes developing regulatory frameworks for interoperability, accountability, and ethical governance, as well as strengthening cybersecurity capacity and institutional readiness across the healthcare sector. Furthermore, advancing a context-sensitive research agenda is essential to generate evidence that supports effective policy and implementation strategies (Khoo & Ballesté, 2024; OECD, 2023).

In conclusion, the chapter positions digital government as a transformative mechanism capable of enhancing healthcare security and preventing organ trafficking, but only when implemented in an integrated, governance-oriented, and ethically accountable manner. By addressing theoretical, empirical, and methodological gaps, Malaysia can leverage its digital government initiatives not only to modernize healthcare delivery but also to safeguard vulnerable populations, uphold ethical medical practices, and strengthen public trust in the healthcare system (Delmonico et al., 2022; Criado & Gil-Garcia, 2019; World Health Organization, 2022).

This chapter thus provides a foundation for subsequent research and policy development, offering actionable insights for both scholars and practitioners seeking to align digital government strategies with healthcare security imperatives. Its contributions underscore the critical importance of bridging technological innovation with governance, ethics, and cybersecurity to create a resilient, accountable, and transparent healthcare ecosystem that effectively combats organ trafficking.

REFERENCES

Bawa, G., Singh, H., Rani, S., Kataria, A., & Min, H. (2025). Smart traceable framework for transportation of transplantable organs using IPFS, iot, and smart contracts. *Scientific Reports*, *15*(1), 23364. DOI: 10.1038/s41598-025-06471-2 PMID: 40603944

CodeBlue. (2023). MOH: Organ trade and trafficking illegal in Malaysia. *CodeBlue*. https://codeblue.galencentre.org/2023/04/moh-organ-trade-and-trafficking-illegal-in-malaysia/

Criado, J. I., & Gil-Garcia, J. R. (2019). Creating public value through smart technologies and data governance. *Public Administration Review*, *79*(3), 371–382.

Delmonico, F. L., Domínguez-Gil, B., & Noel, L. (2022). Organ trafficking and transplant tourism: A global perspective. *Lancet*, *399*(10340), 2151–2160.

Economic Planning Unit. Malaysia. (2021). *Malaysia Digital Economy Blueprint (MyDIGITAL)*. Government of Malaysia. https://ekonomi.gov.my/sites/default/files/2021-02/malaysia-digital-economy-blueprint.pdf

ENISA. (2023). *Cybersecurity in healthcare: Risk management and governance*. European Union Agency for Cybersecurity.

Khoo, L. S., & Ballesté, C. (2024). A 25-year scoping review of the organ donation system in Malaysia: Past, present, and future. *Clinical Transplantation and Research*, *38*(3), 163–187. DOI: 10.4285/ctr.24.0020 PMID: 39099237

Mergel, I., Edelmann, N., & Haug, N. (2019). Defining digital transformation: Results from expert interviews. *Government Information Quarterly*, *36*(4), 101385. DOI: 10.1016/j.giq.2019.06.002

MyDIGITAL. (2021). *Malaysia Digital Economy Blueprint*. Government of Malaysia. https://www.mydigital.gov.my/

OECD. (2023). *Digital government policy framework*. OECD Publishing.

Panigrahi, R. R. (2025). A study on organ supply chains and transplant processes: Blockchain adoption and transparency. *MDPI Logistics*, *9*(1), 9. DOI: 10.3390/logistics9010009

Sitharamulu, V. (2024). A private Ethereum blockchain for organ donation and traceability. *Procedia / Elsevier*. https://www.sciencedirect.com/science/article/pii/S1110866524001051

UNODC. (2023). *Global report on trafficking in persons*. United Nations.

World Health Organization. (2022). *Global strategy on digital health 2020–2025*. WHO.

World Health Organization. (2023). *Human organ and tissue transplantation: Ethical and legal considerations*. WHO.

Chapter 11
Uncovering Hidden Risks: A Qualitative Study on Key Cybersecurity Factors Influencing Online Vulnerabilities Among Children

Wan Saidatul Nasuha
http://orcid.org/0009-0005-5962-3573
Management and Science University, Malaysia

Siti Nur Fathanah Abd Hamid
Universiti Teknologi MARA, Malaysia

Muhammad Haziq Zaini
Management and Science University, Malaysia

Ashlah Ibrahim
Management and Science University, Malaysia

ABSTRACT

This study investigates the key cybersecurity factors that contribute to online vulnerabilities among children in Peninsular Malaysia, using a qualitative approach involving six key informants from relevant government agencies. The findings highlight that peer influence, exposure to unsafe digital practices, and lack of awareness are major contributors to children's psychological and behavioural risks online. Additionally, individual factors—such as excessive screen time, unsupervised Internet access, and limited digital literacy—further increase susceptibility to threats including privacy breaches, online manipulation, and harmful content.

DOI: 10.4018/979-8-3373-6696-8.ch011

The study emphasises the urgent need for strengthened parental guidance, digital safety education, and coordinated cybersecurity strategies to enhance children's resilience and ensure safer online engagement.

1.0. UNDERSTANDING OF CYBERSEX ADDICTION

In the 21st century, various forms of high-tech innovations and inventions have been developed at an unprecedented pace. The rapid advancement of modern technology has profoundly influenced and reshaped the landscape of human life, affecting communication, education, socialisation, and recreation. While technological progress has brought numerous benefits, it has also created countless negative implications, particularly for children, who are among the most vulnerable members of society. Children often lack the cognitive maturity, emotional regulation, and critical decision-making abilities required to navigate complex online environments responsibly. As a result, their exposure to digital technologies without proper guidance and supervision can lead to risky behaviours, including addiction to cyberspace activities such as cybersex.

According to a study conducted by Costanza et al. (2023), the emergence of widespread internet access during the era of globalisation has significantly increased internet usage among children. This increased exposure has resulted in a growing number of children developing addictive patterns of behaviour due to excessive use and misbehaviour online. In the Malaysian context, Idris et al. (2021) reported that as many as 94% of children have been exposed to pornography while navigating the internet. This exposure can occur intentionally, such as through deliberate online searches, or unintentionally, through media platforms including video games, cartoons, and social media applications. The accessibility and pervasiveness of online content make it difficult for children to avoid encountering sexually explicit or inappropriate material. Moreover, Malaysia has been reported to rank third globally among ten countries for the highest average time spent online (Khairuddin & Joseph, 2023). This statistic underscores the extent to which unrestricted internet access, combined with addictive engagement, can expose children to harmful online behaviours and social problems, including cybersex addiction.

Cybersex addiction is further compounded by the characteristics of modern technology itself. As noted by Mohd Din (2019), this form of addiction occurs when children misuse digital devices and the internet as a medium for accessing pornographic material. Unlike traditional forms of media, the internet is borderless and allows instant communication and interaction without temporal or spatial limitations. Consequently, children can explore content that is inappropriate for their age with minimal oversight or restriction. Supporting this notion, Suradi (2019) found that 35.3% of adolescents aged 13 to 17 had been exposed to pornography online, and 29.9% had actively engaged with such content. These figures indicate that cybersex addiction is not confined to adults; rather, it also affects adolescents, disrupting their development during a critical stage of cognitive, emotional, and social growth.

Based on the literature, several factors contribute to cybersex addiction among children, with peer influence and individual factors emerging as particularly significant. Peer influence has been identified as the primary factor leading to psychological damage associated with cybersex addiction. According to Shen et al. (2025), peer relationships play a central role in shaping behavioural norms, personal identity, and social interactions among adolescents. Children who are isolated, excluded, or negatively influenced by peers may turn to online spaces as a source of comfort, validation, or entertainment, making them more susceptible to engaging in risky behaviours, including cybersex activities. Liu et al. (2025) highlight that negative peer interactions, such as bullying or social exclusion, can further exacerbate this vulnerability by prompting children to seek emotional solace in anonymous or unregulated online platforms. Once children engage in these spaces, exposure to sexually explicit material may occur rapidly, normalising such behaviour and reinforcing addictive patterns. Sonia et al. (2023) further emphasise that peer influence can pressure children into adopting behaviours that are socially condoned within their peer groups, even when such behaviours are harmful or inappropriate. This evidence highlights the importance of fostering supportive, positive peer networks and social environments to mitigate psychological risks and enhance resilience among children.

In contrast, individual factors primarily contribute to the physical damage associated with cybersex addiction. Excessive and unrestricted use of digital devices is particularly problematic, as it encourages immersion in sexually explicit content while simultaneously disrupting children's normal routines. Wan Maizon et al. (2022) found that children who spend more than eight hours per day on digital screens are significantly more likely to develop addictive behaviours online. Furthermore, nine out of ten children encounter inappropriate or objectionable content while navigating online spaces, which can overwhelm their ability to distinguish between right and wrong. As a result, children may engage in sexual fantasies, compulsive behaviours, and other activities that blur the boundary between reality and imagination. Nakshine et al. (2022) also emphasise that cybersex addiction often disrupts sleep patterns, reduces physical activity, and negatively affects overall physical health. Over time, these habits may result in fatigue, decreased immunity, and long-term health consequences.

The vulnerability of children in relation to cybersex addiction underscores the need for proper supervision and structured guidance from multiple sources, including parents, educators, government agencies, and society at large. Children are inherently fragile and lack the capacity to protect themselves from exposure to inappropriate content or harmful online interactions. Without adequate monitoring and education, they are more likely to engage in behaviours that jeopardise both their psychological and physical well-being. Providing children with age-appropriate knowledge, life skills, and digital literacy is essential to enabling informed decision-making and fostering resilience. This approach is not only crucial for protecting individual children but also serves as a foundation for broader societal development. A generation that is well-informed, responsible, and capable of navigating online spaces safely will contribute positively to national development goals, particularly in the context of Malaysia's aspirations to become a developed nation.

Moreover, government intervention plays a critical role in mitigating cybersex addiction. Strategic initiatives, such as internet safety campaigns, digital literacy programs, and parental guidance workshops, are essential for educating caregivers and empowering them to regulate children's online behaviour. Such interventions are particularly important for children aged 13 to 17, a stage characterised by significant hormonal, emotional, and cognitive changes. Adolescents in this developmental phase are naturally curious, especially regarding sexuality, and they may lack the self-regulation needed to manage exposure to sexual content. Government-led programs that educate both children and parents about safe online practices, privacy management, and ethical use of technology can reduce vulnerability and encourage responsible engagement. Collaboration between schools, families, and community agencies ensures that protective measures are consistent, comprehensive, and effective.

Technological advancement, while beneficial, also presents unique challenges that exacerbate cybersex addiction. Lopez-Fernandez et al. (2022) highlight that online platforms provide an endless supply of novel and stimulating content, which reinforces addictive behaviour. Features such as anonymity, instant communication, and global access make it easier for children to engage in harmful activities without detection. Additionally, the COVID-19 pandemic intensified these risks, as children spent increased time online due to school closures, social distancing, and lockdown measures. Marchi et al. (2021) reported that traffic to pornographic websites increased by 11.6% during this period, demonstrating that extended online exposure correlates with higher engagement in cybersex activities. These findings illustrate the compounding effects of technological accessibility and environmental factors on children's susceptibility to addiction.

In conclusion, cybersex addiction among children in Peninsular Malaysia is influenced by a combination of peer, individual, and technological factors. Peer influence primarily drives psychological damage, whereas individual behaviours such as excessive screen time contribute to physical harm. The interplay of these factors highlights the complexity of addiction and underscores the necessity of holistic interventions. Protecting children requires collaborative efforts among parents, educators, government agencies, and society, with a focus on education, monitoring, and fostering positive peer and social networks. Equipping children with knowledge, resilience, and digital literacy is vital for safeguarding their well-being and promoting healthy development in an increasingly digital world. By implementing comprehensive strategies that address both internal vulnerabilities and external pressures, Malaysia can create a safer online environment that supports children's growth and prepares them to navigate the challenges of the digital age responsibly.

2.0 METHODOLOGY

This study involved six key persons representing a range of relevant agencies in Malaysia, including the Royal Malaysian Police, the National Population and Family Development Board, the Ministry of Women, Family and Community Development, the Malaysian Communications and Multimedia Commission, and selected hospitals. These key persons were chosen because of their extensive experience and specialised knowledge in dealing with issues related to children, online safety, and cyber-related offences. Their expertise enabled the study to gain in-depth insights into the factors contributing to cybersex addiction among children and the mechanisms employed by various agencies to mitigate associated risks.

The respondents were selected using purposive sampling, where the researcher deliberately selects participants based on specific characteristics or knowledge that are relevant to the research objectives. Purposive sampling allows the researcher to focus on individuals who possess practical experience, professional expertise, or direct involvement with the issue under investigation. In this case, the selected key persons had significant exposure to cases related to children's online vulnerabilities and cyber-related offences, making their input highly valuable for understanding both psychological and physical consequences of cybersex addiction.

Prior to data collection, this study underwent rigorous review and approval by the Research Ethics Committee (REC) of Universiti Teknologi MARA (UiTM). The REC carefully examined the study's objectives, research design, data collection methods, and ethical considerations to ensure full compliance with the university's ethical standards and code of conduct. This ethical review process was essential not only to protect the rights and welfare of the participants but also to uphold the credibility, validity, and integrity of the research. Ethical approval ensures that the study adheres to principles such as informed consent, confidentiality, voluntary participation, and minimisation of potential harm to respondents, which are critical in research involving sensitive topics such as children's online behaviours and cybersex addiction (Agusta et al., 2025).

Upon receiving REC approval, the data collection process commenced in strict accordance with the guidelines stipulated by the committee. Interviews were conducted professionally and systematically, ensuring that participants could provide detailed insights without fear of repercussions. This approach enabled the study to gather high-quality qualitative data, providing a robust foundation for analysing the psychological and physical factors contributing to cybersex addiction among children, as well as informing strategies for prevention and intervention at both agency and community levels.

3.0 FINDINGS

In further discussion, the presentation of findings has been structured and divided into two distinct sections to provide a more comprehensive and detailed understanding of the primary factors contributing to both psychological and physical damage resulting from cybersex addiction among children. This division allows the study to clearly differentiate the specific influences and consequences associated with each type of impact, ensuring a more systematic and focused analysis.

The first section focuses on the main factors contributing to psychological damage among children who engage in cybersex activities. This includes examining elements such as individual characteristics, peer influence, and exposure to technological risks that may lead to emotional distress, behavioural changes, social isolation, and other mental health-related issues. By highlighting these psychological factors, the study aims to provide insight into how children's online behaviours and interactions influence their mental and emotional well-being.

The second section addresses the main factors contributing to physical damage associated with cybersex addiction among children. This section explores how excessive screen time, unsupervised internet access, and other individual or environmental factors can lead to physical consequences, such as sleep disruption, fatigue, and other health-related effects. Overall, this structured approach facilitates a thorough understanding of the multifaceted impacts of cybersex addiction, ensuring that both psychological and physical dimensions are examined in depth.

***Psychological Damage*—**The main factor contributing to the psychological damage caused by cybersex addiction among children is peer influence. According to insights gathered during the interview session, Mrs. Noor Sabrina Kamarulzaman highlighted that most of the children are first exposed to pornographic content through their peers who share such materials, thereby influencing their curiosity and subsequent engagement with inappropriate online content. The finding is showed below:

> *"Sometimes children know about pornographic materials through their friends because of their friends always share the link related to nudity and indecent*

materials with them [...] Children naturally have a high level of curiosity, then they will click the link of video or picture to see it and from that they will become addicted if they are always watching the materials" (Mrs. Noor Sabrina Kamarulzaman, Female, RMP, italic and emphasis added).

Hence, Mrs. Noor Sabrina Kamarulzaman also stated that after their peers share any related content of pornographic materials, this may encourage them to explore more in such materials. Eventually, this influence from peers and combined with the curiosity of children may potentially lead them towards engaging in cybersex addiction, even though in the first place, they only want to experiment with such activities. The finding is presented below:

"In Malaysia, we are not allowed to spread pornographic materials, or we are also prohibited from accessing such materials because it is one of the criminal offences. However, nowadays most of children are learn and know about pornography from their peers. For example, their peers ask them to click, download and explore pornographic links [...]" (Mrs. Noor Sabrina Kamarulzaman, Female, RMP, italic and emphasis added).

On the other hand, negative peer pressure is also considered as peer influence in contributing to children becoming addicted to cybersex. This can be proven by Mrs. Nur Farizan Ameran from the Royal Malaysian Police, who said that it is crucial for children to choose their peers wisely. This is because positive peer relationships have a beneficial impact on children's development, while negative peer influences can lead them to harmful paths such as cybersex addiction. The finding is stated below:

"Children should be wisely chosen good peers. This is because if children fail to choose good peers, it will have a negative and bad effect on them. For example, children are mistakenly choosing a good peer and the peers are started to invite them to do negative things that are not beneficial since they are still young and vulnerable [...]" (Mrs. Nur Farizan Ameran, Female, RMP, italic and emphasis added).

In addition, Mrs. Nur Farizan Ameran and Mrs. Saripah Mohd Sari further stated that choosing the wrong peers can be a contributing factor to the psychological damage of cybersex addiction among children. Peers have a significant influence on a child's behaviour, attitude and choice. Then, when the children associate with peers who engage in negative behaviour and activity, it can increase their vulnerability to engage in cybersex addiction. The finding is stated below:

"Wrongly choosing friends is one of the factors contributing to cybersex addiction among children. This is because sometimes friends always teach bad things [...]" (Mrs. Nur Farizan Ameran, Female, RMP, italic and emphasis added).

"If children wrongly choose friends, it will lead to negative effects on children such as cybersex addiction. This is due to friends always talking about sexuality

when gathering, since they do not have a topic to talk about" (Mrs. Saripah Mohd Sari, Female, MWFCD, italic and emphasis added).

Lastly, one of the key persons, Mrs. Nurul Adriyana Basir mentioned that children especially at a young age, find it difficult to differentiate between right and wrong; and easily be influenced by peers, especially when they children face challenges and want to blend in. Most children will do it and wanted to show that they are great and abilities able to do all things, including negative things. The finding is presented below:

"Children are still young and cannot differentiate between what is right and what is wrong, so whenever they get a challenge from their friends for doing negative things, most of children will do it. This is because they want to show to their friends that they are good and can do all things even though negative things" (Mrs. Nurul Adriyana Basir, Female, NPFDB, italic and emphasis added).

Figure 1 presents a summary of the qualitative findings regarding the main factors contributing to psychological damage resulting from cybersex addiction among children in Peninsular Malaysia. The summary highlights that peer influence emerges as the most significant factor affecting children's psychological well-being in the context of cybersex addiction. Peer influence encompasses several aspects, including the encouragement or normalisation of exposure to pornographic material by friends, the exertion of negative peer pressure, and the challenges children face to engage in behaviours that are socially or peer-approved, even if they are inappropriate or harmful.

Children who are influenced by their peers often feel compelled to conform to group expectations, particularly in adolescent developmental stages where peer acceptance and belonging are of high importance. Exposure to pornography through peers can stimulate curiosity and reinforce addictive behaviours, while negative peer pressure may challenge children to participate in risky or unethical online activities, further exacerbating their vulnerability. Additionally, peers can act as role models, either positively or negatively, in shaping children's attitudes and behaviours regarding sexual content and online interactions.

Overall, Figure 1 provides a clear visual representation of how peer influence serves as a critical determinant of psychological damage in children affected by cybersex addiction. By understanding these dynamics, educators, parents, and policymakers can develop targeted interventions to mitigate peer-related risks and support healthier psychological development.

Figure 1. Findings of main factor contributing to psychological damage of cybersex addiction among children in peninsular Malaysia

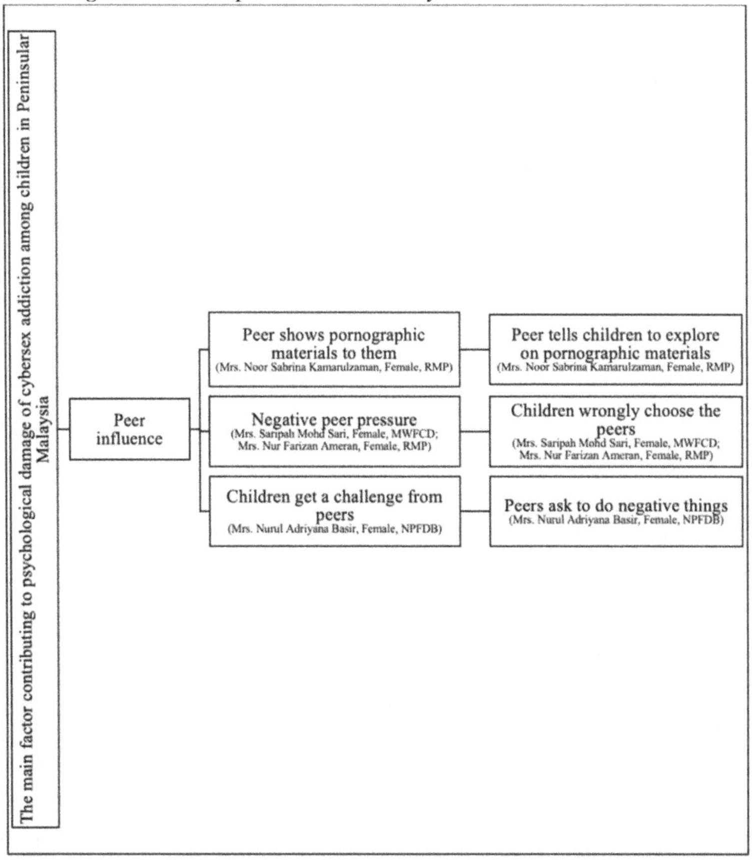

Physical Damage—Following that, in terms of physical damage, the main factor contributing to the physical damage of cybersex addiction among children is individual factor. According to the key informants, exposure to online sexual activities can evoke sensations of physical pleasure among certain individuals, including children. This pleasurable experience may subsequently lead to repeated engagement in such activities, fostering dependency and ultimately resulting in addiction to cybersex. The finding is illustrated below:

> *"When children watching pornographic materials, they will feel pleasure and the feel of pleasure lead the children to be addicted to cybersex [...]" (Mrs. Nurul Adriyana Basir, Female, NPFDB, italic and emphasis added).*
>
> *"[...] And even worse, an addiction to cybersex not only can give the satisfaction of pleasure towards ourselves but it can also give the satisfaction of pleasure*

to others [...]" (Mrs. Noor Sabrina Kamarulzaman, Female, RMP, italic and emphasis added).

In exploring further, besides children experiencing pleasure sensation, pornographic materials also contribute to their feelings of affection and excitement. This is because Mrs. Nurul Adriyana Basir and Mrs. Nur Farizan Ameran mentioned that engaging in online sexual activities provides children with a sense of attention and enjoyment that they do not receive from their parents. Consequently, children choose to spend more time on the Internet rather than having physical socialisation with others. The finding is presented below:

"Based on the study conducted in June 2011, it was found that there is a lack of psychosocial maturity among children, particularly in the context of sexual behaviour. If children learn about sexuality from their peers, they perceive it as attention and affection given by their peers. This situation is of great concern to us, as children can misinterpret it and make them vulnerable to exploitation by their peers who may take advantage of the situation [...]" (Mrs. Nurul Adriyana Basir, Female, NPFDB, italic and emphasis added).

"The children usually start with dating, and if one of the partners begins to share pornographic materials, they will perceive it as something enjoyable and excitement as such materials can give a feeling of pleasure to them, and eventually, it can lead to negative consequences such as pre-marital sex and others" (Mrs. Nur Farizan Ameran, Female, RMP, italic and emphasis added).

On the other hand, according to Mrs. Nurul Adriyana Basir, children nowadays have a high tendency to spend hours sitting in front of gadgets, and this behaviour can increase their risk of developing Internet addiction. In turn, Internet addiction can potentially lead children to become addicted to cybersex, since it is considered as one of the forms of Internet addiction. In order to mitigate this risk, it is essential for parents, guardians or other individuals close to children to control their screen time and implement measures to prevent them from becoming addicted to cybersex. The finding is stated below:

"Most children are like to sitting in-front of gadgets for hours and this behaviour can expose the children to Internet addiction, it will lead to cybersex addiction towards the children since cybersex addiction is one of the forms under the Internet addiction" (Mrs. Nurul Adriyana Basir, Female, NPFDB, italic and emphasis added).

In addition to the previously discussed factors, Mrs. Nurul Adriyana Basir from the National Population and Family Development Board also emphasised that children who are addicted to cybersex often demonstrate a strong tendency to isolate themselves from their families, peers, and social surroundings. This behaviour largely stems from their desire to conceal their online activities and avoid detection or reprimand for engaging in inappropriate digital content. As a result, these children often become secretive, spending prolonged periods alone on digital devices, hiding their browsing history, or using private accounts to engage in cybersex activities. Such secrecy not only reinforces their addictive behaviour but also limits opportunities for intervention by parents, educators, or guardians. Over time, this isolation can exacerbate feelings of loneliness, social withdrawal, and emotional distress, creating a cycle that is difficult to break. The finding is stated below:

"Cybersex addiction can lead children to have negative thinking about themselves and experience a lack of mental stimulation and engagement due to cybersex addiction hinders their interaction and connection with others, as they primarily engage with the computer only [...]" (Mrs. Nurul Adriyana Basir, Female, NPFDB, italic and emphasis added).

However, two key persons, Mrs. Noor Sabrina Kamarulzaman and Mrs. Nur Farizan Ameran highlighted that cybersex addiction may change the behaviour of the children where they become less interested in joining with their peers or favourite activities and preferring to be alone. Additionally, they tend to present a false character in front of their parents and others which constantly pretending and hiding their true actions due to refraining from disclosing their online sexual activities to others, as they are aware that such actions are morally wrong and unacceptable. The finding is presented below:

"Children who are addicted to cybersex usually watch pornographic materials in secrecy, isolating themselves and always prefer to be alone. Additionally, these children do not show their true character in front of their parents, constantly as pretending. As a result, parents are unaware of their children's actual actions and behaviours [...]" (Mrs. Noor Sabrina Kamarulzaman, Female, RMP, italic and emphasis added).

"Children will isolate themselves and refuse to disclose their online sexual activities to others because they know it is wrong and bad [...] These children will spend most of their time alone in their rooms, spending hours facing their gadgets, especially at night. This is because at night, their parents will be asleep, and there will be no one to disturb them. Consequently, their relationships with others, especially within the family and siblings, will be interrupted due to the addiction they are facing" (Mrs. Nur Farizan Ameran, Female, RMP, italic and emphasis added).

Besides, Mrs. Saripah Mohd Sari, Mrs. Liu Xiu Ying and Mrs. Nurul Adriyana Basir disclosed that cybersex addiction among children is attributed to the unrestricted access that they have to browse the Internet on their own. The unrestricted access to the Internet makes it easier for them to find upon the explicit content such as pornographic materials and indirectly can develop their addictive behaviours since they do not have a proper guidance on using the Internet. This emphasises the importance of children on getting appropriate guidance to children to protect them from the dangers of cybersex addiction. The finding is stated below:

"Based on my experience, one of the main factors contributing to cybersex addiction is when the browse the pornographic website on their own. This is because children nowadays have their own gadgets. Suppose their parents do not monitor their activity online. In that case, and this will become more prevalent until it causes the children to be exposed to cybersex addiction" (Mrs. Saripah Mohd Sari, Female, MWFCD, italic and emphasis added).

"In the past, around the year 2008, if children spent eight to 12 hours facing gadgets, it was considered much time. However, in today's era, children will be facing the Internet and technology for nearly 24 hours. This situation has arisen due to the Movement Control Order (MCO) implemented during the COVID-19 pandemic [...] As a result, children have unrestricted access to everything on-line without proper monitoring and supervision by adults" (Mrs. Liu Xiu Ying, Female, Hospital, italic and emphasis added).

"Based on the report by ADPEC Interpol and UNICEF titled "Disrupting Harm in Malaysia (Protecting children in Malaysia from online sexual exploitation & abuse)," which involved 995 child respondents, it was found that 96% of children use the Internet at least once a day. Additionally, a national health and mobility survey in 2017 stated that six out of seven children are active Internet users, and two out of seven children experience Internet addiction" (Mrs. Nurul Adriyana Basir, Female, NPFDB, italic and emphasis added).

The summary of the qualitative findings regarding the main factors contributing to physical damage resulting from cybersex addiction among children in Peninsular Malaysia is presented in Figure 2. This summary provides a comprehensive overview of how various internal and external factors interact to influence the physical well-being of children affected by cybersex addiction. The figure illustrates the key elements, including individual factors such as excessive screen time, lack of self-regulation, and preoccupation with online sexual content, which can lead to physical consequences such as sleep disruption, fatigue, and overall health deterioration.

Figure 2. Findings of main factor contributing to physical damage of cybersex addiction among children in peninsular Malaysia

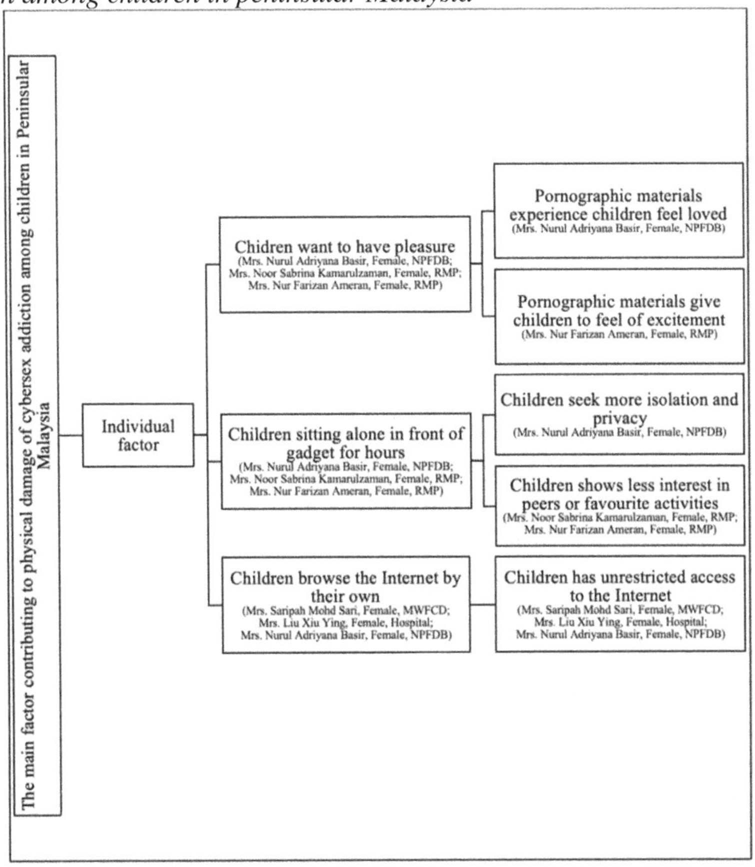

4.0 DISCUSSION

This section presents a detailed discussion of the findings from the study, focusing on the psychological and physical damage associated with cybersex addiction among children in Peninsular Malaysia. The discussion is divided into two main subsections to provide a clearer understanding of the distinct factors contributing to each type of harm. The first subsection examines psychological damage, highlighting how peer influence emerges as a primary factor affecting children's emotional and behavioural well-being. The second subsection addresses physical damage, emphasising how individual factors, including the children's own behaviours and choices, contribute to adverse physical outcomes.

The discussion draws upon insights from six key informants representing relevant government agencies, providing practical perspectives on how children engage with explicit online content and the challenges they face. By analysing these factors, the study identifies the underlying mechanisms through which cybersex addiction impacts both the mental and physical development of children. Moreover, the discussion underscores the importance of parental guidance, peer awareness, and responsible technology use as critical strategies for mitigating the harmful effects of cybersex addiction.

4.1 Psychological Damage

Moreover, based on the findings, this study emphasises that peer influence is a major factor contributing to the psychological damage associated with cybersex addiction among children. In contrast, individual factors are primarily linked to physical damage, as they relate to the child's own behavioural patterns and interactions with technology. In delving deeper into psychological damage, one of the key persons representing relevant agencies highlighted that peer influence plays a pivotal role in guiding children towards cybersex addiction. This influence is particularly pronounced during adolescence, a developmental stage when children are highly sensitive to social acceptance and peer validation. Peers often encourage children to explore pornographic materials and may challenge them to engage in risky or inappropriate online behaviours.

For example, a common scenario involves a group of friends sharing explicit content, links, or videos among themselves. Within this dynamic, one child may act as the initiator, introducing others to pornographic materials, while the remaining children may feel compelled to participate in order to maintain group cohesion and avoid social exclusion. In many cases, children comply with such challenges even if they feel uncomfortable or know the activity is inappropriate, simply because they do not want to be left out or ostracised by their peers (Amirthalingam, 2025).

The challenges may take various forms, including dares, invitations to participate in sexual chat rooms, or encouragement to engage in other explicit online activities (Wan Maizon et al., 2022). Initially, children may follow their peers' behaviour out of obligation or curiosity, feeling pressured to conform to group norms. However, repeated exposure to pornographic content often transforms this initial pressure into a sense of excitement or pleasure, as children become desensitised and start deriving gratification from the material. Over time, this psychological reinforcement contributes to the development of addictive behaviours, as the child begins to seek out the same type of content independently, creating a cycle of dependency (Privara & Bob, 2023).

Furthermore, peer influence not only encourages exposure to pornographic content but also shapes children's attitudes and perceptions towards sexuality, online interactions, and risk-taking behaviours. Children may internalise these behaviours as acceptable, normalising engagement with explicit materials and reinforcing addictive patterns. This highlights the need for early interventions that focus on promoting positive peer relationships, educating children about digital risks, and fostering critical thinking to resist negative peer pressure. Addressing peer influence is therefore crucial in mitigating the psychological damage caused by cybersex addiction and protecting children's mental and emotional well-being.

4.2 Physical Damage

In terms of physical damage, the perspectives shared by key persons representing relevant agencies indicate that children often become addicted to cybersex due to their own actions and choices. Cybersex addiction generally emerges when children seek feelings of excitement, intimacy, or validation, which they attempt to satisfy through engagement with explicit content available on the Internet (Wan Maizon et al., 2023). As children develop this dependency, they often begin to isolate themselves from family members and peers, seeking privacy to conceal their online activities. This tendency toward secrecy reinforces addictive behaviour and limits opportunities for intervention, making it more difficult for adults to detect or address the issue.

The unrestricted access to digital devices and the Internet further exacerbates this problem. Many children navigate the online landscape independently without appropriate supervision or guidance, which allows them to access content that is inappropriate for their age or developmental stage (Abdul Aziz et al., 2023). Without monitoring, children may spend extended periods on digital devices, engaging in activities that harm both their physical health, such as disrupted sleep patterns, eye strain, and fatigue, as well as their psychological well-being.

This situation highlights the importance of active parental and adult involvement in children's digital lives. Proper monitoring and guidance can help ensure that children use technology responsibly while understanding the potential risks associated with online activities, including cybersex addiction. Adults play a critical role in setting boundaries, providing support, and fostering an environment where children feel comfortable discussing their online experiences. By distinguishing between appropriate and inappropriate content, caregivers can offer timely interventions that prevent exposure to harmful materials.

Moreover, supervision allows adults to educate children on safe and responsible online behaviours, reinforcing the importance of self-control and decision-making.

Structured guidance, combined with open communication, creates a safer online environment and reduces the likelihood of children developing compulsive or addictive behaviours related to cybersex (Walsh et al., 2022). Ultimately, these measures demonstrate that responsible adult involvement is essential in mitigating the physical consequences of cybersex addiction and promoting the overall health and well-being of children in the digital age.

4.3 Overall Discussion

In exploring further, based on the perspectives from key persons representing relevant agencies, this study strongly suggests that responsible authorities, including policymakers and education administrators, should incorporate comprehensive sex education into school curriculum guidelines. These programs must be tailored to the age appropriateness of students to empower them with the knowledge, skills, and critical thinking necessary to make informed decisions, foster healthy relationships, and navigate the complexities of sexuality in a responsible and safe manner (The Star, 2025). Age-appropriate sex education equips children with the tools to differentiate between healthy and unhealthy behaviours, understand boundaries, and recognize the risks associated with sexual activity, including online exposure to pornography and cybersex addiction. Moreover, well-designed sex education programs can play a significant role in preventing social and health issues among children, such as unplanned pregnancies, sexually transmitted infections (STIs), and unhealthy sexual behaviours (Mohd Amin & Fariduddin, 2023).

In the Malaysian context, the Ministry of Education has implemented Reproductive and Social Health Education (PEERS) since 1989 in secondary schools and in 1994 in primary schools. This initiative demonstrates a recognition of the importance of early education regarding reproductive health, yet there remains room for improvement in both reach and effectiveness. According to the Women's Aid Organisation, the government must ensure that sex education is systematically included in school syllabi to address contemporary social issues affecting children. The organisation further emphasises that lessons on sex education need to be properly guided due to the sensitive nature of the subject matter. Currently, the curriculum covers three main areas: nutrition, first aid, and the PEERS syllabus, which is implemented through Physical and Health Education (PJK). Importantly, sex education lessons do not solely focus on sexual behaviour; they encompass a wide spectrum of knowledge, including biological, sociocultural, psychological, and spiritual aspects, in order to foster healthy attitudes, informed decision-making, and balanced development among children (Women's Aid Organisation, 2022).

Despite Malaysia's early introduction of sex education, the country still lags behind its international counterparts. For instance, European countries incorporated comprehensive sex education into school curricula as early as the 1970s (Council of Europe, 2020). This demonstrates that other nations have achieved more advanced implementation of structured programs, providing a benchmark for Malaysia to emulate. By studying these models, Malaysia can identify best practices in curriculum design, teaching methodology, and integration of modern issues such as digital literacy and online safety.

The implementation of comprehensive sexual education is therefore crucial not only to inform children but also to protect them from risks associated with poor knowledge of sexuality. Research indicates that sex education equips children with skills to make informed and responsible choices about their sexuality while fostering a sense of personal responsibility, self-respect, and empathy towards others (Banerjee & Rao, 2022). Furthermore, by instilling awareness and critical thinking, sex education programs promote the psychological and physical well-being of children, preparing them to navigate social and digital environments safely. Comprehensive programs also serve as preventive measures, mitigating the risks of cybersex addiction and unhealthy peer influences by promoting open dialogue, informed decision-making, and resilience against negative social pressures.

In conclusion, integrating age-appropriate and comprehensive sex education into school curricula is fundamental to safeguarding children's development. This approach ensures that children acquire the knowledge, skills, and attitudes necessary to make responsible choices, maintain healthy relationships, and protect themselves from sexual health risks, both online and offline. By prioritising these educational strategies, Malaysia can cultivate a generation of well-informed, responsible, and resilient individuals who are prepared to face the challenges of adolescence and the digital age, while aligning with global health and well-being initiatives.

5.0 CONCLUSION

Based on the above discussion, it can be concluded that sex education programs among children play a critical role in improving both the psychological and physical well-being of children as a whole. Such programs provide children with comprehensive knowledge and awareness regarding reproductive health, sexuality, and safe behavioural practices. By equipping children with this knowledge, sex education helps prevent and mitigate the risks associated with cybersex addiction, enabling them to understand the consequences of engaging in such activities and make informed, responsible choices (Official Website of the United Nations Educational, Scientific and Cultural Organization, 2023). With proper sex education, children are more likely to recognise the dangers of excessive or inappropriate engagement with online sexual content and develop strategies to avoid risky behaviours, thereby safeguarding their mental and emotional health.

In addition to preventing addiction, sex education plays a significant role in promoting healthy interpersonal relationships among children. Through structured guidance, children are taught to identify positive interactions, communicate effectively, and respect boundaries in their social and intimate relationships (Lee et al., 2022). For instance, when children are exposed to negative peer pressure—such as being shown pornographic materials by friends—they are better able to differentiate between acceptable and unacceptable behaviours. This awareness enables them to make mature decisions, resist harmful influences, and maintain their psychological and physical well-being. By fostering critical thinking and moral reasoning, sex education empowers children to navigate complex social and online environments safely.

Furthermore, sex education has a direct impact on preventing sexual health risks, including Sexually Transmitted Infections (STIs) and pre-marital sexual activities. According to the study conducted by Sham et al. (2024), children who are addicted to cybersex are more likely to develop sexual fantasies and engage in sexual experimentation with peers or strangers, often attempting to imitate behaviours observed in pornography. Through comprehensive sex education, children gain essential knowledge about safe sexual practices, consent, and the consequences of unprotected sexual activity. This knowledge reduces the likelihood of STI transmission and discourages early sexual engagement, promoting healthier physical outcomes.

The necessity of sex education in schools is particularly urgent in the digital age, where children have unprecedented access to information at their fingertips through the Internet and various digital platforms. While technology can serve as a valuable resource for learning, it also exposes children to harmful content and misinformation. In this context, structured and age-appropriate sex education aligns with Sustainable Development Goal Three (SDG 3) on good health and well-being, as it equips children with accurate information and the skills necessary to protect themselves from potential risks. Additionally, such education supports the broader objectives of the 2030 Agenda for Sustainable Development by fostering informed, responsible, and healthy future generations. Without access to accurate and comprehensive information, children are left vulnerable to cybersex addiction and other negative outcomes. Therefore, sex education programs are essential for guiding children toward safer behaviours, promoting healthy development, and ensuring their overall well-being in an increasingly digital and interconnected world.

ACKNOWLEDGEMENT

The authors would like to extend their heartfelt gratitude to IGI Global Scientific Publishing for granting us the opportunity to publish this paper. We sincerely appreciate the support, guidance, and professional platform provided by the publisher, which has enabled us to share our research with a wider academic audience. This opportunity has not only contributed to the dissemination of knowledge but has also encouraged us to further pursue excellence in research and scholarly contributions.

REFERENCES

Abdul Aziz, N. A., Sa'ari, C. Z., & Wahab, S. (2023). Cyber Security for Children: Parental Monitoring from a Technological, Child Psychology and Islamic Psychospiritual Perspective during the Covid-19 Pandemic. *Afkar: Jurnal Akidah & Pemikiran Islam*, *25*(1), 73–98. DOI: 10.22452/afkar.vol25no1.3

Agusta, R. M., Nurfalah, S., Komalasari, R., & Nulhakim, L. (2025). Ethics in Scientific Research: A Literature Review of Fundamental Principles and the Identification of Research Misconduct. *Journal of Innovation and Research in Primary Education*, *4*(3), 457–466. DOI: 10.56916/jirpe.v4i3.1341

Amirthalingam, P. (2025). Influence of Peer Pressure on Cybersexual Activities Among Youth Population. *International Journal of Indian Psychology*, *13*(1).

Banerjee, D., & Rao, T. S. (2022). Comprehensive Sex Education—Why Should We Care? *Journal of Psychosexual Health*, *4*(2), 73–75. DOI: 10.1177/26318318221092076

Costanza, C., Vetri, L., Carotenuto, M., & Roccella, M. (2023). Use and Abuse of Digital Devices: Influencing Factors of Child and Adolescent Neuropsychology. *Clinics and Practice*, *13*(6), 1331–1334. DOI: 10.3390/clinpract13060119 PMID: 37987420

Council of Europe. (2020). Comprehensive sexuality education protects children and helps build a safer, inclusive society. *Commissioner for Human Rights*. Retrieved from https://www.coe.int/en/web/commissioner/-/comprehensive-sexuality-education-protects-children-and-helps-build-a-safer-inclusive-society, on 12 November 2025.

Idris, N., Mansor, S., & Rahim, H. A. (2021). Online sexual exposure and risks among Malaysian children: A review of recent digital behaviour trends. *Journal of Child and Adolescent Cyberpsychology*, *9*(2), 45–57.

Khairuddin, A., & Joseph, M. (2023). Online screen time and exposure to harmful content among Malaysian minors. *Malaysian Journal of Media and Communication Studies, 12*(1), 33–49.

Lee, S. H., Yeo, K. J., & Handayani, L. (2022). Sexual and reproductive health knowledge among primary school students in Malaysia. *Journal of Education and Health Promotion, 11*(89). Advance online publication. DOI: 10.4103/jehp.jehp_542_21 PMID: 35573611

Liu, L., Hu, X., Ma, M., Zhang, W., Peng, B., Zhang, B., & Luo, X. (2025). Family and Peer Influences on Adolescent Psychological Inflexibility: A 1 Regression Mixture Analysis. *Frontiers in Psychology, 16*, 1650930. DOI: 10.3389/fpsyg.2025.1650930 PMID: 41143021

Lopez-Fernandez, O., Romo, L., Kern, L., Rousseau, A., Graziani, P., Rochat, L., Achab, S., Zullino, D., Landrø, N. I., Zacarés, J. J., Serra, E., Chóliz, M., Pontes, H. M., Griffiths, M. D., & Kuss, D. J. (2022). Perceptions underlying addictive technology use patterns: Insights for cognitive-behavioural therapy. *International Journal of Environmental Research and Public Health, 19*(1), 544. DOI: 10.3390/ijerph19010544 PMID: 35010804

Marchi, N. C., Fara, L., Gross, L., Ornell, F., Diehl, A., & Kessler, F. H. P. (2021). Problematic consumption of online pornography during the COVID-19 pandemic: Clinical recommendations. *Trends in Psychiatry and Psychotherapy, 43*(3), 159–166. DOI: 10.47626/2237-6089-2020-0090 PMID: 34043899

Mohd Amin, N., & Fariduddin, M. N. (2023). How comprehensive sexuality education is implemented and perceived in Malaysia: A systematic review. *International Journal of Academic Research in Progressive Education and Development, 12*(2). Advance online publication. DOI: 10.6007/IJARPED/v12-i2/17366

Mohd Din, N. A. (2019). Pendidikan Jasmani dan Pendidikan Kesihatan Tingkatan 4. *Telaga Biru Sdn. Bhd.* Retrieved from https://anyflip.com/ypvzd/vkum/basic/201-242, on 14 November 2025.

Nakshine, V. S., Thute, P., Khatib, M. N., & Sarkar, B. (2022). Increased screen time as a cause of declining physical, psychological health, and sleep patterns: A literary review. *Cureus, 14*(10). Advance online publication. DOI: 10.7759/cureus.30051 PMID: 36381869

Official Website of the United Nations Educational, Scientific and Cultural Organization. (2023). Comprehensive sexuality education: For healthy, informed and empowered learners. *United Nations Educational, Scientific and Cultural Organization.* Retrieved from https://www.unesco.org/en/health-education/cse#:~:text=When%20delivered%20well%20and%20combined,pregnancies%2C%20HIV%20and%20other%20sexually, on 12 November 2025.

Privara, M., & Bob, P. (2023). Pornography consumption and cognitive-affective distress. *The Journal of Nervous and Mental Disease, 211*(8), 641–646. DOI: 10.1097/NMD.0000000000001669 PMID: 37505898

Sham, F., Yaakub, S., Nur Fawati, F., Fatinni, S. J., & Azamuddin, A. A. (2024). Knowledge, attitudes, risk behaviours and preventive practices on sexually-transmitted diseases (STDs) among students in a public university in Malaysia. *Malaysian Journal of Public Health Medicine, 20*(3).

Shen, Y., Zhou, Y., Ren, S., Li, Y., Liu, Y., Zhou, R., Fan, X., & Xie, G. (2025). Relations between peer bullying and adolescent depression: The mediating effect of cellphone usage. *Frontiers in Psychiatry, 16*, 1486628. DOI: 10.3389/fpsyt.2025.1486628 PMID: 40357516

Sonia, B. M., Ngangue, P., Nestor, B., Dieudonné, S., Adnette, A., Leonel, P., & Ly, B. A. (2023). Socioecological analysis of determinants of early adolescent sexuality in Benin: A qualitative study. *The Pan African Medical Journal, 44*(1). Advance online publication. DOI: 10.11604/pamj.2023.44.137.35978 PMID: 37333779

Suradi, M. (2019). Bimbang Ketagihan Internet Seks Siber. *Sinar Harian.* Retrieved from https://www.sinarharian.com.my/article/41369/EDISI/Johor/Bimbang-ketagihan-internet-seks-siber, on 14 November 2025.

The Star. (2025). Education Ministry to increase teaching hours for sex education module in 2027 school curriculum. *The Star.* Retrieved from https://www.thestar.com.my/news/nation/2025/04/29/education-ministry-to-increase-teaching-hours-for-sex-education-module-in-2027, on 12 November 2025.

Walsh, K., Pink, E., Ayling, N., Sondergeld, A., Dallaston, E., Tournas, P., Serry, E., Trotter, S., Spanos, T., & Rogic, N. (2022). Best practice framework for online safety education: Results from a rapid review of the international literature, expert review, and stakeholder consultation. *International Journal of Child-Computer Interaction, 33*, 100474. DOI: 10.1016/j.ijcci.2022.100474

Wan Maizon, W. S. N., Abd Hamid, S. N. F., & Ahmad, Y. (2022). Cybersex Leads To Addiction Epidemic Among Minor: The Analysis of Cause and Effect. *International Journal for Studies on Children, Women, Elderly and Disabled,* 15(1).

Wan Maizon, W. S. N., Hamid, S. N. F. A., & Ahmad, Y. (2023). Systematic Literature Review on the Consequences of Cybersex Addiction Involving Children. *International Journal of Academic Research in Accounting. Finance and Management Sciences, 13*(2), 1196–1213.

Women's Aid Organisation. (2022). We must improve maternal, sexual, and reproductive health rights in Malaysia. *Women's Aid Organisation*. Retrieved from https://wao.org.my/we-must-improve-maternal-sexual-and-reproductive-health-rights-in-malaysia/, on 12 November 2025.

Chapter 12
Unveiling the Government's Perspective:
An In-Depth Exploration the Factors of Cybersex Addiction Among Malaysian Children

Wan Saidatul Nasuha Wan Maizon
http://orcid.org/0009-0005-5962-3573
Management and Science University, Malaysia

Siti Nur Fathanah Fathanah Abd Hamid
Universiti Teknologi MARA, Malaysia

Muhammad Haziq Zaini
Management and Science University, Malaysia

ABSTRACT

In the 21st century, rapid technological advancements have transformed human life, but excessive Internet use among children has led to rising concerns of addiction, including cybersex addiction. Statistics show that 93% of boys and 62% of girls are exposed to online pornography before age 18, highlighting serious risks. This study explores the psychological and physical impacts of cybersex addiction on Malaysian children through the perspectives of government agencies. Using a qualitative approach, in-depth interviews were conducted with six representatives from the Royal Malaysian Police, LPPKN, KPWKM, MCMC, and hospitals. Findings reveal that individual factors, peer influence, and technological accessibility contribute to

DOI: 10.4018/979-8-3373-6696-8.ch012

psychological harm, while individual and peer factors also drive physical damage such as poor health and neglect. In conclusion, a collective effort from parents, educators, and policymakers is essential to foster awareness, provide protection, and ensure children's holistic well-being and future prosperity.

1. INTRODUCTION

Children are inherently vulnerable due to their young age, emotional fragility, and limited cognitive, psychological, and social capacity to protect themselves from potential risks and harm (Wan Maizon et al., 2024a; Wan Maizon et al., 2024b; Wan Maizon et al., 2024c; Wan Maizon et al., 2024d). At the early stages of development, children rely heavily on external guidance and protection, particularly from parents, caregivers, educational institutions, society, and government agencies. As such, comprehensive supervision and effective monitoring mechanisms are crucial to ensure their safety and well-being (Zaini et al., 2024a; Zaini et al., 2024b). If a country aspires to progress towards becoming a developed nation, its children must be nurtured as future human capital equipped with adequate knowledge, moral values, and life skills. Equally important, children must grow in an environment that is free from risks and harm to ensure healthy physical, emotional, and psychological development.

Ironically, despite advancements in social development and child protection policies, the 21st century has witnessed unprecedented growth in high-tech innovations and digital technologies. The rapid development of modern technology has significantly transformed the landscape of human life, communication, education, and entertainment. While these advancements offer numerous benefits, particularly in terms of access to information and learning opportunities, they also present serious challenges. Technology has created countless negative implications for children, who often lack the maturity, reasoning ability, and self-regulation skills necessary to distinguish between beneficial and harmful content. As a result, children are particularly susceptible to online risks, including exposure to inappropriate materials, cyberbullying, online predators, and digital addiction.

One of the most alarming consequences of uncontrolled internet use among children is exposure to pornographic content and engagement in cybersex-related activities. It is widely argued that excessive internet usage and online misbehaviour contribute significantly to children and adolescents being easily influenced by pornographic videos and images, developing online relationships with strangers, experiencing social isolation, and exhibiting poor real-life social interaction skills. The anonymity and accessibility of the internet further exacerbate these risks, allowing children to explore inappropriate content without immediate supervision or accountability.

Consequently, cybersex addiction has emerged as a growing psychological and social concern affecting children in contemporary society.

In light of these concerns, one of the main objectives of this study is to examine the factors contributing to psychological damage associated with cybersex addiction among children in Peninsular Malaysia. Several significant factors have been identified and emphasised in existing literature, namely: (1) individual factors (Wan Maizon et al., 2024d; Cervero et al., 2024), (2) parental neglect (Lo et al., 2021; Nannatt et al., 2022), (3) peer influence (Zhao & Jin, 2023; Xie, 2024), and (4) technological advancement and accessibility (Norman & Othman, 2020; Sharma et al., 2020). These factors do not operate in isolation; rather, they interact and reinforce one another, increasing children's vulnerability to cybersex addiction and its associated psychological consequences.

From an individual perspective, children's natural curiosity, emotional needs, and developmental characteristics play a critical role in shaping their online behaviour. Based on the study conducted by Wan Maizon et al. (2024d), many children become addicted to pornographic content due to high levels of curiosity and an intense desire to alleviate feelings of loneliness. Children who lack strong social skills or meaningful friendships are more likely to turn to digital devices as a source of comfort and stimulation. Consequently, they may spend excessive amounts of time watching pornography, browsing explicit websites, or communicating with strangers online. Over time, such behaviours can develop into habitual patterns, leading to cybersex addiction. This highlights the importance of addressing children's emotional well-being and social needs through positive engagement, meaningful relationships, and constructive activities.

In this regard, it is crucial for children to occupy themselves with beneficial hobbies and structured activities that promote social interaction, creativity, and emotional regulation. A strong support system, including family involvement, school engagement, and community participation, can help prevent feelings of loneliness and isolation. Without such protective factors, children may seek validation, excitement, and companionship in the digital world, where they are more vulnerable to exploitation and addiction.

Parental neglect is another major contributing factor to cybersex addiction among children. Previous studies by Abd Hamid et al. (2019), Nannatt et al. (2022), and Abd Hamid et al. (2024) emphasised that parents are the most influential agents in shaping children's development, behaviour, and moral values. In today's fast-paced society, many parents face work-related pressures that limit the time and attention they can devote to their children. As a result, some parents allow their children to use gadgets for extended periods without supervision, often as a means of keeping them occupied while attending to work or household responsibilities.

When children are left alone with digital devices for prolonged periods, they may experience feelings of neglect, abandonment, or emotional distance from their parents. To cope with these feelings, children may seek "entertainment to fill the gap" or turn to online strangers for companionship and emotional support. Gradually, the internet becomes their primary source of comfort, interaction, and validation. Once children are exposed to inappropriate forms of entertainment or unhealthy online relationships, they face a multitude of risks, including cybersex addiction. Numerous studies have shown that mobile phones, online games, social media platforms, the internet, and even television can expose children to pornographic elements, either directly or indirectly. This underscores the crucial role of parental supervision, guidance, and active involvement in safeguarding children from digital risks and vulnerabilities.

In addition to parental influence, peer influence plays a significant role in shaping children's behaviour and attitudes. Zakaria et al. (2022) found that peer influence is a major factor contributing to children's involvement in social problems, including cybersex addiction. Children are particularly susceptible to peer pressure because they are still developing their identity, self-esteem, and decision-making skills. In an effort to gain acceptance and approval from their peers, children may imitate risky behaviours without fully understanding the consequences.

For example, a documented case involved a 13-year-old boy who was introduced to sexual knowledge by his peers. Initially, he learned about sex through conversations with friends and began engaging in masturbation while reading books and viewing pornographic images. Over time, his curiosity and desire escalated, leading him to watch explicit movies and actively search for pornographic websites online. This example illustrates how peer influence can serve as a gateway to cybersex addiction, particularly when children lack proper guidance and moral boundaries. Failure to choose positive peer groups can result in serious negative implications, reinforcing the need for early intervention and peer education programs.

Technological advancement and uncontrolled access to digital devices further intensify the problem. Norman and Othman (2020) argued that excessive and unregulated use of technology has detrimental effects on the younger generation, making them highly vulnerable to pornography addiction. According to data shared by PERMATA Advisor, Professor Emerita Tan Sri Dr. Sharifah Habsah Syed Hasan Shahabudin in 2016, approximately 45% of children aged seven to nine years old in Malaysia were already proficient in using the internet. This statistic indicates that nearly half of Malaysian children possess digital literacy skills at a very young age. While digital literacy is essential in the modern era, it also raises concerns about early exposure to inappropriate content.

This situation highlights the urgent need for parents to regulate and limit children's use of technology, particularly for those under the age of 17. Controlling screen time, monitoring online activities, and implementing parental control tools can significantly reduce the risk of internet addiction and exposure to harmful content. Moreover, educating children about responsible internet use and digital ethics is essential in fostering self-regulation and critical thinking skills.

Given the complexity and severity of cybersex addiction among children, government agencies play a vital role in addressing this issue through comprehensive policies and targeted interventions. This study has demonstrated that individual factors, parental neglect, peer influence, and uncontrolled access to technology significantly contribute to cybersex addiction. Therefore, the government must implement multifaceted programs that focus on promoting digital literacy, fostering positive social interactions, and enforcing stricter regulations on internet usage. Collaboration between government agencies, parents, educators, and community organisations is essential to ensure effective supervision and holistic child development.

Furthermore, public awareness campaigns aimed at educating parents and children about the dangers of cybersex addiction are crucial. Community-based support systems, counselling services, and school-based intervention programs can help identify at-risk children and provide timely assistance. By encouraging healthy lifestyles, structured activities, and supportive environments, government agencies can create a safer digital ecosystem for children. Ultimately, protecting children from cybersex addiction is not only a shared responsibility but also a critical investment in safeguarding the nation's future human capital and overall social well-being.

2. METHODOLOGY

This study involved six key informants representing several relevant agencies that play significant roles in addressing issues related to children's welfare and digital safety. These agencies included the Royal Malaysian Police, the National Population and Family Development Board, the Ministry of Women, Family and Community Development, the Malaysian Communications and Multimedia Commission, as well as medical professionals from a hospital setting. The selection of these agencies was based on their direct involvement, expertise, and responsibilities in managing cases related to children's psychological well-being, cyber-related misconduct, and family and social issues. The participation of key persons from these agencies provided valuable insights derived from professional experience and institutional perspectives.

The respondents in this study were selected using purposive sampling. Purposive sampling is a non-probability sampling technique in which researchers exercise their own judgment to identify and select participants who are most knowledgeable and experienced regarding the research topic. This approach is particularly suitable for qualitative studies that seek in-depth understanding of complex social issues, as it allows researchers to gather rich and relevant data from individuals who have direct exposure to and understanding of the phenomenon under investigation. In this study, the selected respondents possessed substantial professional experience in handling cases related to children, family dynamics, digital exposure, and psychological or behavioural issues.

Prior to data collection, this study underwent a thorough ethical review by the Research Ethics Committee (REC) of Universiti Teknologi MARA (UiTM) to obtain formal approval. The REC carefully examined the research objectives, methodology, and data collection procedures to ensure full compliance with ethical standards and the university's ethical code of conduct. Obtaining ethical approval was essential to safeguard the rights, dignity, and confidentiality of the participants involved, as well as to uphold the validity and integrity of the research (Bhandari, 2025). Upon receiving ethical clearance, data collection was carried out in strict accordance with the guidelines and conditions stipulated by the REC.

3. FINDINGS

To provide a comprehensive and systematic understanding of the factors contributing to cybersex addiction among children in Peninsular Malaysia, the presentation of the research findings is organised into two distinct sections. This structured approach allows for a clearer and more focused discussion of the multi-faceted impacts of cybersex addiction on children, particularly in relation to their psychological and physical well-being. By categorising the findings into separate sections, the study ensures that each dimension of harm is examined in depth and with greater analytical clarity.

The first section focuses on the factors contributing to the psychological damage associated with cybersex addiction among children in Peninsular Malaysia. This section highlights how excessive exposure to sexually explicit online content and engagement in cybersex-related activities can adversely affect children's emotional, cognitive, and behavioural development. Psychological consequences discussed include emotional distress, anxiety, depression, social withdrawal, impaired self-esteem, and difficulties in forming healthy interpersonal relationships. The findings in this section also examine how individual vulnerabilities, such as curiosity, loneliness, and limited emotional regulation, interact with external influences including parental neglect, peer pressure, and unrestricted access to digital technology. These factors collectively exacerbate children's susceptibility to psychological harm and long-term mental health issues.

The second section presents the factors contributing to the physical damage arising from cybersex addiction among children. This includes the impact of prolonged screen time, disrupted sleep patterns, physical fatigue, and reduced engagement in physical activities. Additionally, this section explores potential health-related consequences such as eye strain, headaches, poor posture, and the neglect of basic self-care routines. The findings further suggest that excessive involvement in cybersex activities may indirectly contribute to risky behaviours that compromise children's physical safety and overall health.

By dividing the findings into psychological and physical dimensions, this study provides a holistic understanding of the harmful effects of cybersex addiction on children. This structured presentation also facilitates more effective discussion and interpretation of the results, offering valuable insights for policymakers, practitioners, and researchers in developing targeted intervention and prevention strategies.

3.1 Psychological Damage

The findings of this study indicate that psychological damage associated with cybersex addiction among children is primarily influenced by individual factors, peer influence, and technological advancement. Feedback related to both psychological and physical damage was obtained from six key informants representing relevant agencies involved in child protection, digital regulation, and health services in Peninsular Malaysia. These informants contributed professional insights based on their experience in managing cases involving children exposed to online sexual content and cyber-related behavioural issues.

During the interview session, one of the key informants, Mrs. Nurul Adriyana Basir, highlighted that children often become addicted to cybersex due to the relative ease of access to sexually explicit content, particularly when they are able to use fake identities online. She explained that many children who participate in sexual chat rooms deliberately adopt pseudonyms to conceal their real names, thereby remaining anonymous and unrecognisable to others. This anonymity not only protects their identity but also reduces the fear of being monitored or held accountable for their actions. Mrs. Nurul Adriyana Basir further emphasised that anonymity allows children to engage freely in erotic interactions, which may include activities such as explicit phone conversations, exchanging nude images, or sending sexually explicit videos. The perceived sense of privacy and security provided by anonymity can reinforce addictive behaviours, making children more susceptible to prolonged involvement in cybersex activities. The finding is exemplified below:

> *"[...] In the sexual chat room, children can put their pseudonym to ensure other people do not recognize them [...] This action also can hide their bad behaviour and protect their privacy while in the sexual chat room [...]" (Mrs. Nurul Adriyana Basir, Female, NPFDB, italic and emphasis added).*

On the other hand, Mrs. Saripah Mohd Sari highlighted that a significant factor contributing to children's addiction to cybersex is their lack of adequate knowledge about sexuality, including sexual and reproductive health education. She explained that when children do not possess accurate information or understanding regarding sexual development and healthy sexual behaviours, they are more likely to seek out answers and satisfy their curiosity independently. This self-directed exploration often occurs without proper guidance, supervision, or intervention from responsible adults, which increases the likelihood of exposure to inappropriate and potentially harmful online content. Mrs. Saripah Mohd Sari emphasised that the absence of structured sexual education and supportive monitoring mechanisms creates an environment where children may inadvertently engage in risky behaviours, including participation in cybersex activities. The finding is presented below:

"Most of children that are addicted to cybersex are do not have enough knowledge, awareness and advocacy on the sexual and reproductive health (SRH)" (Mrs. Saripah Mohd Sari, Female, MWFCD, italic and emphasis added).

However, Mrs. Nurul Adriyana Basir mentioned that high level of curiosity is also one of the factors that exposes children to cybersex addiction. The reason is because the children are still young and fragile. They do not have the capability and capacity to differentiate between what is right and what is wrong. Then, whenever they are curious about something, especially on sexual, they will explore it on their own without guidance from parents or guardians. This action will lead the children to become addicted to cybersex since pornographic materials can give them to feel pleasure and fun. The finding is exemplified below:

"When the children have a high level of curiosity, they will start to surf the Internet and suffering addiction [...]" (Mrs. Nurul Adriyana Basir, Female, NPFDB, italic and emphasis added).

Secondly, the feedback from several key persons representing relevant agencies stated that peer influences are also recognised as one of the factors contributing to psychological damage of cybersex addiction among children in Peninsular Malaysia. As mentioned by Mrs. Nur Farizan Ameran, the majority of children learned about pornography from their peers due to sharing pornographic website links, peer sharing videos and pictures related to pornography, and peer talk about pornography. This proves that children need to find the right peers in order to avoid with negative peer influence. The finding is presented below:

"Sometimes, children do not know about pornographic, but when their peers invited them to enter a sexual chat room, share any links or pictures related to pornographic materials, then, the children started to feel pleasure [...] After that, they will explore deeper about sexual and lastly, become addicted to cybersex, since they cannot differentiate between what is right and wrong" (Mrs. Nur Farizan Ameran, Female, RMP, italic and emphasis added).

Along with that, Mrs. Nurul Adriyana Basir explained that another contributing factor to children's addiction to cybersex is the strong desire to be liked and accepted by their peer groups. During adolescence, children place significant importance on peer relationships and often seek approval, belonging, and social recognition from their friends. As a result, they may be easily influenced by the behaviours, discussions, and interests of their peers, including topics related to pornography and sexually explicit content. Mrs. Nurul Adriyana Basir highlighted that children who are exposed to such conversations or activities within their peer groups may feel compelled to participate, either out of curiosity or a desire to maintain social acceptance. This peer influence can reinforce engagement in cybersex-related activities, increasing the likelihood of addiction. The finding is stated below:

"One of the external factors that influence children to become addicted to cybersex is peer influence [...] Sometimes children do not want to be left behind by what their friends are doing and discuss [...] because they will feel neglected by their friends [...] For example, their friend talk about pornography, they will join the conversation and they do not know the actions can makes them become addicted due to high level of curiosity [...]" (Mrs. Nurul Adriyana Basir, Female, NPFDB, italic and emphasis added).

The final factor contributing to the psychological damage of cybersex addiction among children in Peninsular Malaysia is technological advancement. During the interview sessions, five key informants highlighted that increased accessibility to the internet and modern digital technologies significantly contributes to the risk of cybersex addiction among children. The widespread availability of smartphones, tablets, and high-speed internet enables children to access sexually explicit content with minimal supervision or restriction. Furthermore, features such as anonymity, instant messaging, and interactive platforms make it easier for children to engage in sexual chats, share explicit materials, or participate in online sexual activities. The informants emphasised that these technological developments, while offering educational and social benefits, also increase children's vulnerability to addictive behaviours, ultimately leading to psychological harm. The finding is exemplified below:

"Most children who are addicted to cybersex are because of access to the Internet, then lead to pornographic websites [...]" (Mrs. Saripah Mohd Sari, Female, MWFCD, italic and emphasis added).

"Most of the Malaysian citizens use the Internet as one of their tools to communicate [...] If someone (referring to children) misuses the Internet, they (referring to children) will be exposed to the element of cybersex such as pornographic materials [...]" (Mrs. Roszita Zainal Abidin, Female, MCMC, italic and emphasis added).

"When children are too dependent on the Internet, they will feel that the Internet can give them love, attention, happiness, pleasure, sexual fantasy and others [...]" (Mrs. Liu Xiu Ying, Female, Hospital, italic and emphasis added).

"External factors that contribute to cybersex addiction among children is access to the Internet [...] In Malaysia, more than 90% of children have access to the Internet everyday [...] However, based on the research that been conducted by the National Population and Family Development Board (NPFDB) in 2014, as many as 35.3% of children in Malaysia have been exposed to pornographic materials and the main source of obtaining pornographic material is from Internet [...]" (Mrs. Nurul Adriyana Basir, Female, NPFDB, italic and emphasis added).

"During 1998, there was no issue of cybersex addiction in Malaysia, but when access to the Internet existed, people started using smartphones, computers and others [...] Then, starting from that, the issue of cybersex addiction in Malaysia started increasing [...]" (Mrs. Nur Farizan Ameran, Female, RMP, italic and emphasis added).

Figure 1. Findings of factors contributing to psychological damage of cybersex addiction among children in peninsular Malaysia

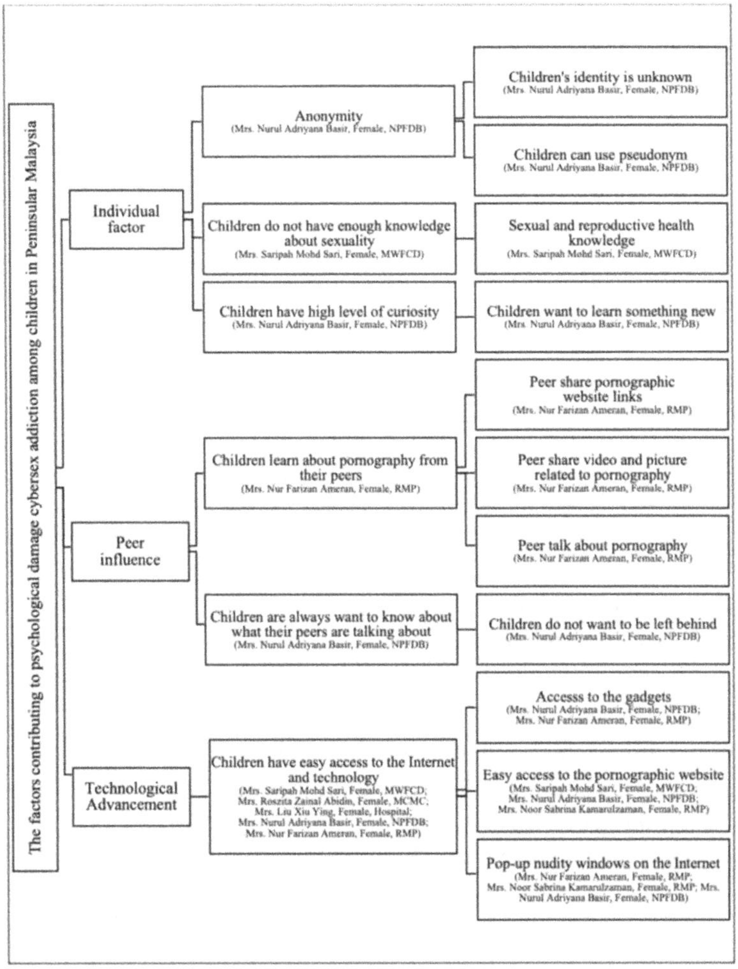

3.2 Physical Damage

Following that, the key informants representing relevant agencies revealed that individual factors and peer influence are the main contributors to the physical damage associated with cybersex addiction among children in Peninsular Malaysia. These factors were identified based on the informants' professional experiences in handling cases involving children exposed to excessive online sexual content and unhealthy digital behaviours. The findings suggest that prolonged engagement in cybersex-related activities not only affects children psychologically but also manifests in observable physical and behavioural consequences.

In terms of individual factor, Mrs. Nurul Adriyana Basir and Mrs. Liu Xiu Ying stated that change behaviour is one of the factors under individual factor. This is because cybersex addiction can influence the children to experienced aggressive behaviour, since explicit sexual content and inappropriate online interactions can significantly influence the children's behaviour and emotional well-being. The finding is exemplified below:

"The cybersex content arouses the sexual gratification of children arouse [...] Children who addicted to cybersex will become aggressive and irritability if they cannot access to the Internet everyday [...]" (Mrs. Nurul Adriyana Basir, Female, NPFDB, italic and emphasis added).

"Based on my experience, most of the parents who come to the hospital do not know their children are addicted to cybersex. Normally, the parents come due to his or her children being depressed, school refusal and others [...] I once dealt with an 8 or 9-year-old girl who was addicted to cybersex. Initially, the behaviour of this child is quite aggressive at home when she cannot access the Internet [...] So the parents ask me to ward her daughter and I will give her medication [...] Then, once the children return home, her behaviour will become aggressive again to the point where she would throw objects like glass tables, damage things in the house [...]" (Mrs. Liu Xiu Ying, Female, Hospital, italic and emphasis added).

In relation to this, Mrs. Nur Farizan Ameran claimed that engaging in cybersex activities can lead children to refuse attending school, as they increasingly spend time on the Internet exploring pornographic materials. Consequently, this behavior not only results in school refusal but also causes inadequate sleep, insufficient rest, fatigue, and overall poor well-being. The finding is presented below:

"[...] When children sitting in front of gadgets until night-time, they refused to go to the school due to not getting enough sleep, not getting enough rest, feeling tired, not feeling well [...]" (Mrs. Nur Farizan Ameran, Female, RMP, italic and emphasis added).

In addition, both of the key persons from the Royal Malaysian Police reveals that loneliness also can be a significant factor contributing to the physical damage of cybersex addiction among children. This is due to children who experienced feelings of loneliness will get rid of their boredom through online platforms, including engaging in cybersex activities in order to escape from feelings of isolation, lack of social communication, do not socialising with family and others. The finding is stated below:

> *"Individual factor caused children addicted to cybersex is loneliness [...] Where the children will find something on the Internet or gadgets to fill their free time [...]" (Mrs. Nur Farizan Ameran, Female, RMP, italic and emphasis added).*
>
> *"Children become addicted to cybersex addiction due to loneliness, lack of social communication, do not being socialize with family and others". (Mrs. Noor Sabrina Kamarulzaman, Female, RMP, italic and emphasis added).*

The last factors contributing to physical damage of cybersex addiction related to physical damage among children in Peninsular Malaysia is peer influence. According to Mrs. Nur Farizan Ameran, negative peer influence, such as invitation by peers on entering sexual chat rooms leads children be addicted to cybersex. Therefore, children who wants feels of pleasure, they will seek the pornographic materials every day to fulfil their excitement and gratification. The finding is illustrated below:

> *"Sometimes, children do not know about pornographic, but when their friends invited them to enter a sexual chat room, dark web chat room, adult fantasy role-playing room or any related with pornographic materials, then, the children started to feel pleasure [...] After that, they will explore deeper about sexual and lastly, become addicted to cybersex, since they cannot differentiate between what is right and wrong" (Mrs. Nur Farizan Ameran, Female, RMP, italic and emphasis added).*

Figure 2. Findings of factors contributing to physical damage of cybersex addiction among children in peninsular Malaysia

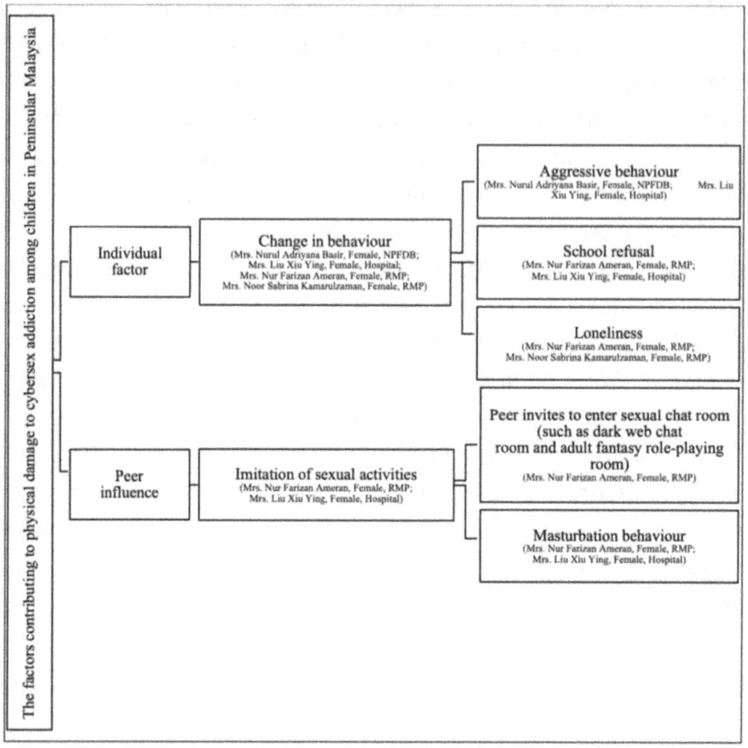

4. DISCUSSION

This section presents a detailed discussion of the findings from the study, focusing on the psychological and physical consequences of cybersex addiction among children in Peninsular Malaysia. The discussion examines the underlying factors that contribute to the vulnerability of children, including individual characteristics, peer influence, and technological advancement, and their interconnected impact on children's well-being. By analysing insights obtained from key informants representing relevant government and institutional agencies, this study provides a comprehensive understanding of how cybersex addiction manifests and affects children during their formative years.

The discussion is divided into two main sections: psychological damage and physical damage. The first section explores how cybersex addiction affects children's mental health, emotional regulation, and social behaviour, highlighting the roles of curiosity, impulsivity, and peer pressure in exacerbating addictive tendencies. The second section focuses on the physical manifestations of addiction, including behavioural changes, school refusal, fatigue, and health-related issues, and examines the interplay between individual and peer factors in shaping these outcomes. Overall, this discussion underscores the importance of comprehensive interventions that integrate government initiatives, parental guidance, and digital literacy to mitigate the harmful effects of cybersex addiction.

4.1 Psychological Damage

This study emphasises the pivotal role of government initiatives in mitigating the prevalence of cybersex addiction among children, particularly within the rapidly evolving digital landscape. Government intervention is crucial in addressing this issue, as children represent a highly vulnerable group requiring systematic protection and guidance. One of the key initiatives highlighted is the implementation of internet safety awareness campaigns aimed at educating parents and guardians. These campaigns are designed to equip caregivers with the necessary knowledge and skills to facilitate responsible gadget usage among children. Such initiatives are especially important when considering the inherent vulnerability of children aged between 13 and 17 years old, who are navigating the complex developmental phase of adolescence.

During this stage of development, children experience significant physical, emotional, and hormonal changes that often lead to heightened curiosity, including curiosity related to sexuality. At the same time, neurological development during adolescence is still ongoing, particularly in areas of the brain responsible for impulse control, decision-making, and risk assessment. As a result, children in this age group are more inclined to engage in impulsive behaviours and seek novel experiences without fully understanding the potential consequences. When children are inadvertently exposed to pornographic materials during this phase, they may develop a strong fascination or dependency on such content. Over time, repeated exposure may lead to cybersex addiction, which can negatively affect both their psychological and physical well-being, including emotional instability, behavioural changes, and health-related issues.

In addition to individual vulnerability, peer influence plays a significant role in contributing to cybersex addiction among children. Xu et al. (2023) highlighted that peer influence emerges as a prominent factor contributing to psychological damage associated with cybersex addiction. In the digital era, mobile phones and other digital gadgets have become the primary means of communication among children and adolescents. These platforms allow peers to share information instantaneously, including inappropriate content. Xu et al. (2023) further noted that peer influence may lead children to cybersex addiction, particularly when they are exposed to negative peer pressure, such as peers sharing links, images, or videos containing pornographic material.

This finding is further supported by Giletta et al. (2021), who asserted that peers play a crucial role in shaping children's development and identity. Peer groups have the potential either to positively influence children's behaviour or to expose them to harmful practices. In some cases, children may engage in antisocial or risky activities, including exposure to pornography, simply to gain acceptance or avoid social exclusion. Consequently, peer influence can significantly reinforce unhealthy online behaviours and contribute to addiction. This underscores the importance of children making careful choices regarding their peer associations, as well as the need for early intervention programs that promote positive peer relationships and social skills development.

Lastly, technological advancement has been identified as a major contributing factor to the increasing prevalence of cybersex addiction among children. Lopez-Fernandez et al. (2022) revealed that problematic addictive behaviours have escalated alongside technological advancement, including the emergence of cybersex addiction. The internet offers an almost unlimited supply of novel and explicit pornographic materials, which can easily stimulate curiosity and reinforce addictive patterns of behaviour. The accessibility, affordability, and anonymity of online platforms further intensify children's exposure to such content.

In relation to this, Verbanas (2025) reported that during the COVID-19 pandemic, the use of technology increased significantly among individuals of all age groups, including children. With lockdowns, school closures, and social distancing measures in place, children relied heavily on digital devices for education, entertainment, and social interaction. While technology served as a necessary tool during this period, excessive usage raised serious concerns regarding internet addiction. The author further highlighted that internet addiction among children could lead to cybersex addiction, indirectly affecting their mental health through psychological distress and physical consequences.

Supporting this concern, Marchi et al. (2021) reported that data from the Pornhub website indicated an 11.6% increase in views compared to pre-pandemic levels. This substantial increase suggests that prolonged periods of isolation and extended screen time during the COVID-19 pandemic led to increased consumption of online explicit materials. As children spent more time online with limited supervision, their exposure to pornography and cybersex-related content intensified.

Overall, these findings highlight the urgent need for comprehensive government-led strategies to address cybersex addiction among children. Such strategies should include digital literacy education, stricter internet regulations, parental guidance programs, and collaborative efforts between government agencies, schools, families, and communities. By addressing individual vulnerability, peer influence, and technological risks holistically, government initiatives can play a critical role in safeguarding children's psychological and physical well-being in the digital age.

4.2 Physical Damage

In further discussion, individual factors emerge as one of the most significant contributors to the physical damage associated with cybersex addiction among children in the Malaysian context. Individual factors refer to children's internal characteristics, including behavioural tendencies, emotional regulation, impulse control, and psychological vulnerabilities. Based on the study conducted by Glowiak (2025), children who develop addiction to cybersex often exhibit notable behavioural changes that extend beyond psychological distress and manifest physically. These behavioural changes include increased aggression, school refusal, heightened social withdrawal, fatigue, and disruption of daily routines. Such physical manifestations reflect the extent to which cybersex addiction interferes with children's normal functioning and overall well-being.

In relation to aggressive behaviour, Zhang et al. (2022) highlighted that children who experience cybersex addiction tend to display heightened levels of aggression and irritability. This behaviour is often triggered by feelings of frustration and distress when children are unable to access pornographic materials or online sexual content. Addiction-related cravings may cause emotional dysregulation, which in turn leads to outward expressions of anger and aggression. For instance, during interview sessions with key informants representing relevant agencies, several cases were reported involving children who exhibited destructive behaviours when deprived of internet access. These children were observed throwing objects, damaging household property, and displaying physical aggression towards others. Such actions are often a direct result of intense compulsion and dependency on cybersex activities, demonstrating how psychological addiction can translate into physical harm to both the children themselves and their surrounding environment.

In addition to aggressive behaviour, cybersex addiction has also been linked to academic disengagement and cognitive impairment. Fujita et al. (2022) found that children addicted to cybersex often struggle to concentrate and remain attentive in classroom settings. Their cognitive resources are frequently occupied by intrusive sexual thoughts, fantasies, or anticipation of future online activities. This constant mental preoccupation reduces their ability to focus on academic tasks and negatively affects learning outcomes. Supporting this finding, interviews conducted with key informants revealed that school refusal is a recurring issue among children addicted to cybersex. Many children deliberately avoid attending school in order to spend extended hours using digital devices, primarily to access pornographic materials online. This behaviour not only disrupts their educational development but also contributes to physical consequences such as sleep deprivation, fatigue, and poor health due to prolonged screen time and irregular daily routines.

Furthermore, excessive engagement in cybersex-related activities may lead to neglect of basic physical needs, including proper nutrition, exercise, and personal hygiene. Children who spend long hours online often experience disrupted sleep patterns, eye strain, headaches, and physical exhaustion. Over time, these effects may weaken their immune system and increase vulnerability to other health-related issues. Thus, individual factors associated with cybersex addiction extend beyond emotional and behavioural disturbances to encompass broader physical damage that affects children's overall quality of life.

Following this, peer influence is identified as another critical factor contributing to the physical damage associated with cybersex addiction among children. According to Xin et al. (2018), children aged between 13 and 18 years place significant importance on peer relationships during their developmental stage. At this age, children actively seek acceptance, belonging, and validation from their peers. When they form friendships with peers who engage in risky or deviant behaviours, they become highly susceptible to imitation and conformity. This susceptibility increases the likelihood of children engaging in harmful activities such as cybersex addiction.

For instance, when children associate with peers who are already addicted to cybersex, they may be introduced to sexual chat rooms, explicit online forums, or adult fantasy role-playing platforms, including those operating on the dark web. Peer encouragement and shared participation normalise such behaviours, reducing children's perception of risk. Over time, sustained involvement in these activities may result in physical consequences, including prolonged screen exposure, disrupted sleep cycles, reduced physical activity, and heightened behavioural problems. Peer-driven engagement in cybersex activities can therefore exacerbate both the intensity and duration of addiction, amplifying its physical impact on children.

In conclusion, the factors contributing to the psychological and physical damage of cybersex addiction among children in the Malaysian context are closely interconnected and mutually reinforcing. This study has revealed a significant relationship between individual factors, peer influence, and technological advancement in contributing to psychological damage associated with cybersex addiction. Similarly, in terms of physical damage, individual factors and peer influence play a substantial role in shaping children's vulnerability and behavioural outcomes. Both individual characteristics and peer dynamics emerge as interconnected elements that influence children's psychological state and physical well-being simultaneously.

Hence, this study emphasises that children's addiction to cybersex is largely driven by their developmental vulnerabilities rather than external coercion alone. Children aged between 13 and 17 years' experience heightened susceptibility due to profound physical, emotional, and hormonal changes during adolescence. These internal changes, combined with peer pressure and easy access to digital technology, significantly increase the risk of cybersex addiction. Therefore, this study concludes that individual factors, peer influence, and technological advancement play crucial roles in both the emergence and mitigation of cybersex addiction among children in Peninsular Malaysia. In addressing this issue, the government must focus on empowering children with sufficient knowledge, emotional resilience, and decision-making skills. Such efforts can help create a safer digital environment that safeguards the psychological and physical well-being of children in the digital age.

REFERENCES

Abd Hamid, S. N. F., Ahmad, Y., & Tahir, N. S. (2019). Scrutinising the socio-demographic pattern of parenting practices and parenting styles in upholding child's protection and privacy to address paedophilia issue. *Review of World Economics, 10*(2), 108. DOI: 10.5430/rwe.v10n2p108

Abd Hamid, S. N. F., Zaini, M. H., Wan Maizon, W. S. N., Ayob, N. A., & Abdullah, F. I. (2024). Navigating parenthood: Malaysian perspectives on protecting children from paedophilia. In Mansour, N., & Bujosa Vadell, L. M. (Eds.), *Artificial intelligence, digitalization and regulation* (pp. 1–20). Springer., DOI: 10.1007/978-3-031-67531-7_1

Bhandari, P. (2025). A guide to ethical considerations in research. *Scribbr*. https://www.scribbr.com/methodology/research-ethics/

Cervero, A., Castro-Lopez, A., Alvarez-Blanco, L., & Tuero, E. (2024). Explanatory factors for problematic cybersex behaviour: The importance of negative emotions. *Current Psychology (New Brunswick, N.J.), 43*(20), 18109–18118. DOI: 10.1007/s12144-024-05639-9

Fujita, J., Aoyama, K., Saigusa, Y., Miyazaki, H., Aoki, Y., Asanuma, K., & Hishimoto, A. (2022). Problematic internet use and daily difficulties among adolescents with school refusal behaviors: An observational cross-sectional analytical study. *Medicine, 101*(7), e28916. DOI: 10.1097/MD.0000000000028916 PMID: 35363214

Giletta, M., Choukas-Bradley, S., Maes, M., Linthicum, K. P., Card, N. A., & Prinstein, M. J. (2021). A meta-analysis of longitudinal peer influence effects in childhood and adolescence. *Psychological Bulletin, 147*(7), 719–747. DOI: 10.1037/bul0000329 PMID: 34855429

Glowiak, M. (2025). Cybersex addiction: What it is, symptoms, & how to overcome. *Choosing Therapy*. https://www.choosingtherapy.com/cybersex-addiction/

Lo, C. K., Ho, F. K., Emery, C., Chan, K. L., Wong, R. S., Tung, K. T., & Ip, P. (2021). Association of harsh parenting and maltreatment with internet addiction, and the mediating role of bullying and social support. *Child Abuse & Neglect, 113*, 104928. DOI: 10.1016/j.chiabu.2021.104928 PMID: 33429283

Lopez-Fernandez, O., Romo, L., Kern, L., Rousseau, A., Graziani, P., Rochat, L., & Kuss, D. J. (2022). Perceptions underlying addictive technology use patterns: Insights for cognitive-behavioural therapy. *International Journal of Environmental Research and Public Health, 19*(1), 544. DOI: 10.3390/ijerph19010544 PMID: 35010804

Marchi, N. C., Fara, L., Gross, L., Ornell, F., Diehl, A., & Kessler, F. H. P. (2021). Problematic consumption of online pornography during the COVID-19 pandemic: Clinical recommendations. *Trends in Psychiatry and Psychotherapy*, *43*, 159–166. DOI: 10.47626/2237-6089-2020-0090 PMID: 34043899

Nannatt, A., Tariang, N. M., Gowda, M., & Devassy, S. M. (2022). Family factors associated with problematic use of the internet in children: A scoping review. *Indian Journal of Psychological Medicine*, *44*(4), 341–348. DOI: 10.1177/02537176221090862 PMID: 35949634

Norman, A. A., & Othman, N. (2020). Ketagihan pornografi dalam kalangan remaja: Faktor dan implikasi terhadap sahsiah diri remaja. *Jurnal Melayu*, 19(2).

Sharma, M. K., Anand, N., Thakur, P. C., Sahu, N., John, M., & Murthy, K. D. (2020). Pathways to cybersex: Case-report-based exploration. *Journal of Psychosexual Health*, *2*(1), 96–99. DOI: 10.1177/2631831819898567

Verbanas, P. (2025). A Rutgers expert discusses signs of and treatments for technology addiction. *Rutgers University*. https://www.rutgers.edu/news/are-you-addicted-technology

Wan Maizon, W. S. N., & Abd Hamid, S. N. F. (2024c). Behind the screen: Exploring cybersex addiction as the mediator of factors influencing and causing psychological and physical damage among children in Peninsular Malaysia. In Mansour, N., & Bujosa Vadell, L. M. (Eds.), *Finance and law in the metaverse world* (pp. 1–10). Springer., DOI: 10.1007/978-3-031-67547-8_4

Wan Maizon, W. S. N., Abd Hamid, S. N. F., & Ahmad, Y. (2024a). A policy lens on cybersex addiction impacting Malaysian children. *In Navigating the technological tide: The evolution and challenges of business model innovation* (ICBT 2024, Vol. 1082, pp. 47–57). Springer. DOI: 10.1007/978-3-031-67434-1_47

Wan Maizon, W. S. N., Abd Hamid, S. N. F., & Ahmad, Y. (2024b). Cybersex addiction among adolescents: A quantitative analysis of psychological and physical impacts in Peninsular Malaysia. *In Navigating the technological tide: The evolution and challenges of business model innovation* (ICBT 2024, Vol. 1081, pp. 41–50). Springer. DOI: 10.1007/978-3-031-67437-2_41

Xie, J. (2024). Peer pressure influences adolescents' internet addiction. *Interdisciplinary Humanities and Communication Studies*, 1(9).

Xin, M., Xing, J., Pengfei, W., Houru, L., Mengcheng, W., & Hong, Z. (2018). Online activities, prevalence of internet addiction and risk factors related to family and school among adolescents in China. *Addictive Behaviors Reports*, *7*, 14–18. DOI: 10.1016/j.abrep.2017.10.003 PMID: 29450251

Xu, X., Han, W., & Liu, Q. (2023). Peer pressure and adolescent mobile social media addiction: Moderation analysis of self-esteem and self-concept clarity. *Frontiers in Public Health*, *11*, 1115661. DOI: 10.3389/fpubh.2023.1115661 PMID: 37113179

Zaini, M. H., Abd Hamid, S. N. F., Magli, A. S., Gunasegaran, H., & Zaini, N. A. F. (2024). Beyond bloodlines: Understanding the deep-seated forces fueling incestuous dynamics. In Mansour, N., & Bujosa Vadell, L. M. (Eds.), *Finance and law in the metaverse world*. Springer., DOI: 10.1007/978-3-031-67547-8_31

Zaini, M. H., Abd Hamid, S. N. F., & Wan Maizon, W. S. N. W. (2024). Echoes of silence: The complex dynamics of reporting incest. In Mansour, N., & Bujosa Vadell, L. M. (Eds.), *Finance and law in the metaverse world*. Springer., DOI: 10.1007/978-3-031-67547-8_2

Zakaria, E., Kamarudin, N. N., Mohamad, Z. S., Suzuki, M., Rathakrishnan, B., Bikar Singh, S. S., & Kamaluddin, M. R. (2022). The role of family life and the influence of peer pressure on delinquency: Qualitative evidence from Malaysia. *International Journal of Environmental Research and Public Health*, *19*(13), 7846. DOI: 10.3390/ijerph19137846 PMID: 35805504

Zhang, Y., Hou, Z., Wu, S., Li, X., Hao, M., & Wu, X. (2022). The relationship between internet addiction and aggressive behavior among adolescents during the COVID-19 pandemic: Anxiety as a mediator. *Acta Psychologica*, *227*, 103612. DOI: 10.1016/j.actpsy.2022.103612 PMID: 35598380

Zhao, B., & Jin, C. (2023). Peer relationships and adolescent internet addiction: Variable-centered and person-centered approaches. *Children and Youth Services Review*, *155*, 107243. DOI: 10.1016/j.childyouth.2023.107243

Chapter 13
Pornographic Addiction as a Catalyst for Incest:
A Cyberpsychology Perspective in Malaysia

Muhammad Haziq Zaini
http://orcid.org/0009-0006-1959-6221
Management and Science University, Malaysia

Wan Saidatul Nasuha Wan Maizon
http://orcid.org/0009-0005-5962-3573
Management and Science University, Malaysia

ABSTRACT

Incest in Malaysian families is a rising concern requiring multidisciplinary attention. This study examines the link between pornography addiction and incest through a cyberpsychology lens. Findings show that easy access to victims within the family, combined with the offender's pornography addiction, increases the risk of sexual crimes. Repeated exposure to incest-themed content normalizes taboo behaviour and fuels arousal that may later be acted upon. During the COVID-19 MCO, confinement and increased internet use further escalated such risks. Pornography addiction amplifies offender motivation, aligning with the Routine Activity Theory. The study recommends digital content regulation, media literacy, addiction treatment, and stronger cybersecurity policies to curb incest cases in Malaysia.

DOI: 10.4018/979-8-3373-6696-8.ch013

INTRODUCTION

Incest within Malaysian families has increasingly emerged as a pressing social, psychological, and moral concern, reflecting a convergence of familial instability, digital exposure, and behavioral risk factors. Traditionally, incest has been perceived as a hidden and stigmatized crime, often concealed within the privacy of family life and perpetuated through silence, shame, and fear. However, in the modern digital age, the nature and dynamics of incest have evolved in line with technological advancements and changing patterns of sexual behavior. The widespread availability of internet-enabled devices, the proliferation of sexually explicit content, and the normalization of online sexual engagement have collectively contributed to reshaping sexual attitudes and boundaries, even within domestic settings.

In Malaysia, the issue is particularly concerning given the rapid digitalization of society and the increasing rates of pornography consumption among adolescents and young adults. Empirical evidence indicates that online pornography access has grown substantially over the past decade, facilitated by the anonymity and privacy of personal devices (Tan et al., 2022; Goh, Phuah, & Low, 2023). This phenomenon is not only altering sexual expectations and fantasies but also influencing the moral and cognitive development of impressionable users. Within the Malaysian context, where discussions of sexuality remain culturally sensitive and often limited to moral prohibitions, young individuals frequently turn to the internet as their primary source of sexual information. Such exposure, particularly when it involves deviant or incest-themed content, may distort perceptions of sexual norms and boundaries.

The theoretical framework of cyberpsychology provides a useful lens for understanding this phenomenon. Cyberpsychology emphasizes the impact of digital environments on cognition, emotion, and behavior, particularly how prolonged engagement with online stimuli can reshape neural pathways and social scripts (Kamaruddin et al., 2025). In the context of sexual behavior, repeated exposure to pornographic material can foster addictive tendencies, desensitize users to explicit content, and erode the emotional and ethical barriers that normally inhibit deviant actions. When this exposure centers on taboo sexual themes, such as incest, it may lead to the normalization of forbidden behavior and reinforce deviant sexual cognitions.

Pornography addiction has increasingly been recognized as a behavioral disorder that affects judgment, impulse control, and interpersonal relationships. Studies suggest that individuals who habitually consume pornography are more likely to develop distorted beliefs about sexual consent, intimacy, and gender roles (Abdul Razak & Che Amat, 2024). This risk is compounded within family environments characterized by emotional neglect, weak supervision, and limited communication, where accessibility to potential victims is high and protective mechanisms are weak. The COVID-19 Movement Control Order (MCO) intensified these vulnerabilities by confining families within shared spaces for extended periods while simultaneously increasing internet usage and online sexual activity (Wan Ismail et al., 2023). As a result, the intersection of accessibility, exposure, and opportunity created a situational environment that heightened the likelihood of intra-familial sexual crimes.

Against this backdrop, the present study examines the relationship between pornography addiction and the occurrence of incest within Malaysian families. It employs the Routine Activity Theory (RAT) as its guiding framework, which postulates that criminal behavior arises when three elements converge: a motivated offender, a suitable target, and the absence of a capable guardian. By situating incest within both cyberpsychological and criminological paradigms, this study aims to provide a comprehensive understanding of how pornography addiction may act as a motivational factor for offending, while digital accessibility and weakened familial supervision increase victim vulnerability. Ultimately, the study seeks to contribute to the growing body of research addressing the digital dimensions of sexual crime and to offer insights for preventive and rehabilitative interventions suited to the Malaysian sociocultural context.

Overview of Incest in the Malaysian Context

Incest remains one of the most stigmatized and underreported forms of sexual abuse in Malaysia. It is broadly defined as any sexual activity between individuals who are closely related by blood or within relationships where sexual contact is legally or culturally prohibited (Finkelhor, 2018). This definition encompasses acts between parents and children, siblings, and other close relatives who share familial bonds that should be governed by trust, care, and protection. Despite explicit legal prohibitions under Section 376A of the Malaysian Penal Code, incest continues to persist in silence, often shielded by family secrecy, cultural shame, and fear of social stigma.

In Malaysian society, where the family institution is regarded as sacred and moral purity is highly valued, victims frequently refrain from disclosure due to the perceived consequences of dishonoring their family name (Nasir, 2021). This entrenched culture of silence enables perpetrators, often individuals who hold authority within the household, to continue their abusive behaviour with minimal risk of exposure or legal repercussions.

Empirical evidence by Wan Ismail et al. (2023) and the Royal Malaysia Police (2022) indicates that most incest cases occur within immediate family structures, where fathers, stepfathers, and brothers are the primary perpetrators. These individuals possess not only physical access to victims but also emotional and psychological control that reinforces the cycle of abuse. The familial environment therefore functions as both a risk factor and a situational opportunity for sexual exploitation.

Situations involving domestic conflict, substance abuse, parental neglect, or economic hardship create conditions conducive to incestuous behaviour. Families exhibiting signs of dysfunction, such as poor communication, emotional detachment, and the absence of effective parental supervision, often demonstrate weakened protective boundaries that heighten the vulnerability of children (Harkins & Dixon, 2020).

The COVID-19 pandemic further intensified these risks. During the nationwide Movement Control Order (MCO), families experienced prolonged physical confinement, financial uncertainty, and elevated psychological stress. Access to schools, community resources, and social welfare agencies was significantly reduced, limiting victims' opportunities to seek help or intervention. Reports from the Women's Aid Organisation (2021) documented a noticeable increase in domestic and sexual abuse cases during this period. Concurrently, digital engagement surged as individuals turned to online platforms for entertainment, social interaction, and emotional relief. For offenders already struggling with compulsive sexual urges or pornography addiction, the combination of isolation, psychological distress, and continuous internet exposure created a heightened risk environment for intra-familial sexual abuse (Mohd Yunos & Althabawi, 2021).

Theoretical Context of Incest and Deviant Sexual Behaviour

The study of incest has long been rooted in psychological, sociological, and criminological discourse. From a psychological perspective, incest is often associated with maladaptive family dynamics, poor emotional regulation, and distorted sexual cognition (Finkelhor, 2018). Sociologically, it represents a collapse of moral and social boundaries that traditionally safeguard family integrity. Harkins and Dixon (2020) emphasize that incest rarely occurs in isolation; rather, it develops within dysfunctional family systems where power imbalances, emotional neglect, and weakened moral oversight converge. In the Malaysian context, the intersection between cultural taboos and patriarchal family structures often suppresses disclosure, thereby enabling a cycle of secrecy and repeated victimization (Nasir, 2021).

PORNOGRAPHY ADDICTION AND COGNITIVE DESENSITIZATION

Pornography addiction is increasingly recognized as a behavioural disorder characterized by compulsive consumption of sexually explicit material despite negative social or psychological consequences (Grubbs et al., 2020). Neuropsychological studies have shown that repetitive exposure to pornographic content activates the brain's reward system in ways similar to substance addiction, leading to tolerance, craving, and desensitization (Kraus & Sweeney, 2019). Over time, individuals may seek more extreme or taboo material to achieve the same level of arousal, a process known as escalation.

In the Malaysian setting, the proliferation of high-speed internet and discreet access to online sexual content have contributed to the normalization of pornography consumption among youth and adults alike (Mohd Yunos & Althabawi, 2021). When such material includes incest-themed content, it reinforces deviant sexual scripts and blurs moral boundaries between fantasy and reality. Exposure to this form of content can cognitively desensitize individuals, normalizing the concept of intra-familial sexual activity and reducing the perceived severity of such acts (Harkins & Dixon, 2020).

Pornographic Addiction and the Pathway to Incest

Pornographic addiction has become a major public health and psychological concern in the digital era, with increasing evidence linking it to deviant sexual behaviours, including incest. It is defined as the compulsive and repetitive use of sexually explicit material that leads to significant distress, impaired control, and the escalation of sexual preoccupation (Brand et al., 2019). The "Triple A Engine," which refers to affordability, accessibility, and anonymity, has made online pornography readily available across all age groups (Cooper, 1998). This constant exposure not only reshapes sexual cognition and arousal patterns but also influences how individuals perceive intimacy, morality, and familial boundaries.

From a behavioural standpoint, pornography consumption may act as both a symptom and a catalyst of deviant sexual behaviour. Repeated exposure to explicit material, particularly those depicting taboo or incestuous content, can condition deviant arousal patterns and normalize morally prohibited sexual acts. Cognitive desensitization and moral disengagement occur when individuals become habituated to viewing sexual acts that violate social or familial norms (Laier et al., 2017; Zattoni et al., 2021). When pornography use becomes habitual, users often escalate to more extreme or unconventional material to achieve the same level of arousal, a process known as tolerance escalation. Over time, these distorted sexual scripts can manifest in real-life behaviour, especially when combined with situational opportunities such as the availability of family members and the absence of effective guardianship (Harkins & Dixon, 2020).

Age of Exposure and Developmental Vulnerability

Early exposure to pornography is a critical factor in shaping sexual cognition and behavioural tendencies. In Malaysia, children have been reported to encounter pornographic content as early as nine years old, particularly during the COVID-19 lockdown periods when digital device usage surged (Sinardaily, 2024). A nationwide survey by Malaysians Against Pornography found that 80% of children aged 10–17 had intentionally viewed pornography, with many accessing it through mobile phones and social media platforms (Malay Mail, 2019).

At the developmental stage of adolescence, the prefrontal cortex, which is responsible for impulse control and moral reasoning, is not yet fully matured. Consequently, adolescents are neurologically more susceptible to impulsive and risk-taking behaviour (Seto, 2019). When exposed to sexually explicit material at an early age, their neural pathways adapt to associate pleasure with visual stimuli, often detached from real emotional intimacy or ethical considerations. Over time, this conditioning may result in compulsive sexual thoughts and diminished empathy, thereby increasing susceptibility to deviant impulses.

Pornography Consumption and Incest Trends in Malaysia

Malaysia has witnessed an alarming increase in incest cases over the past few years. Between 2021 and 2024, a total of 996 incest cases were officially reported nationwide, with the majority of victims aged below 16 years old (The Sun Daily, 2024). A separate report by The Rakyat Post (2024) revealed that victims aged between 13 and 15 formed the largest group, followed by those aged 16 to 18. Fathers were identified as the most frequent perpetrators, accounting for the highest proportion of cases. These statistics highlight that incest is not a rare occurrence but an emerging social crisis with deep psychological and structural roots.

While direct causal data linking pornography addiction to incest are scarce, correlational evidence suggests a strong relationship between the two phenomena. In a study of Malaysian emerging adults (M = 21.05 years; 75% male), researchers found significant associations between pornography addiction, perceived realism of pornography, and distorted attitudes toward sexual relationships (Tan et al., 2022). Such findings imply that individuals who perceive pornographic content as realistic are more likely to internalize deviant narratives and replicate them in real life. Furthermore, pornography addiction often coexists with emotional neglect, weak family supervision, and substance misuse, all of which are established predictors of incestuous behaviour (Murray et al., 2022).

CYBERPSYCHOLOGY AND DIGITAL SEXUAL BEHAVIOUR

Cyberpsychology provides an essential lens through which to understand how digital environments shape human sexual behaviour. The anonymity, accessibility, and affordability of online pornography create a psychological disinhibition effect that encourages users to engage in behaviours they might otherwise avoid in physical settings (Joinson, 2007). This digital disinhibition weakens moral self-regulation and facilitates the internalization of deviant sexual norms.

Furthermore, the algorithms of pornographic platforms are designed to promote engagement by suggesting increasingly extreme content, thereby reinforcing compulsive viewing patterns. As observed by Gola et al. (2021), this algorithmic reinforcement fosters dependency and increases the likelihood of maladaptive sexual fantasies. From a cyberpsychological standpoint, pornography addiction operates as a digital behavioural loop where stimulus exposure, arousal, gratification, and guilt form a repetitive cycle that can alter one's cognitive and moral schemas.

Pornography Addiction as a Catalyst for Incest

Integrating insights from Routine Activity Theory and cyberpsychology, pornography addiction can be conceptualized as a catalyst for incest through three key mechanisms: motivation, opportunity, and rationalization. First, addiction intensifies sexual motivation and erodes impulse control. Second, the family setting provides constant opportunity and accessibility to victims. Third, the normalization of incest-themed pornographic content offers cognitive rationalization for the act, allowing offenders to justify or minimize its moral and legal implications (Malamuth et al., 2020).

The COVID-19 pandemic further amplified these risk factors, as increased online activity during confinement exposed individuals to excessive sexual content while limiting social accountability. This convergence of addiction, accessibility, and isolation underscores how digital environments mediate deviant sexual conduct within domestic spaces.

Family Dynamics and Risk Factors

The family environment serves as both the foundation of moral development and the context in which most incestuous acts occur. Dysfunctional family structures have repeatedly been identified as key contributors to sexual abuse. Research in Malaysia and other regions indicates that poor parental supervision, domestic violence, and intergenerational trauma are common precursors to incest (Finkelhor, 2018; Murray et al., 2022). When emotional support and moral guidance are lacking, children may develop insecure attachments, weakened self-esteem, and distorted perceptions of love and authority whereas all of which make them more susceptible to manipulation and grooming.

Patriarchal family systems, prevalent in many Malaysian households, also play a role in shaping vulnerability. Male authority figures often hold significant control over household decision-making, while female members and children occupy subordinate roles. In such hierarchies, abusive behaviour may be normalized or concealed under the guise of obedience and respect (Harkins & Dixon, 2020). Moreover, the limited discussion of sexuality within families and schools has led to a lack of sexual literacy among adolescents, who are often unaware of bodily autonomy and the boundaries of consent. Inadequate sexual education perpetuates ignorance and silence, allowing perpetrators to exploit victims without resistance or disclosure (Yates, 2020).

Religious and moral values, when weakened or misinterpreted, further contribute to the erosion of empathy and self-restraint. Studies show that individuals with low religiosity or poor moral internalization are more likely to engage in deviant behaviour due to a lack of spiritual accountability (Abdul Razak & Che Amat, 2024). Hence, the decline of moral education and the weakening of family cohesion collectively heighten the potential for incestuous acts within domestic settings.

Pornography Addiction as a Catalyst for Deviant Sexual Behaviour

Pornography addiction has become an emerging behavioural and psychological concern in Malaysia, reflecting global patterns associated with the widespread integration of digital technology into everyday life. It is defined as a compulsive, repetitive consumption of sexually explicit material that results in loss of control, psychological distress, and escalating engagement with deviant or risky sexual themes (Brand et al., 2019). The affordability, accessibility, and anonymity of internet pornography, often referred to as the "Triple A Engine" (Cooper, 1998), have created an environment where exposure to explicit material is both pervasive and difficult to regulate.

Tan et al. (2022) reported that Malaysian adolescents and young adults increasingly rely on online pornography as an informal source of sexual education, largely due to cultural taboos and the lack of comprehensive sexuality education in schools and families. When pornography is perceived as realistic, users are more likely to internalize its portrayals of sexual behaviour, leading to distorted perceptions of intimacy, gender roles, and consent. Goh, Phuah, and Low (2023) found that problematic pornography use among Malaysian youths is strongly associated with impulsive sexual behaviour, emotional dysregulation, and heightened feelings of guilt and shame, suggesting the presence of cognitive dissonance between personal values and digital behaviour.

Continuous exposure to pornography, particularly content depicting taboo or incest-themed narratives, has profound implications for cognitive conditioning and moral perception. Empirical studies indicate that such material can normalize deviant sexual acts, reshape sexual scripts, and reduce moral sensitivity toward forbidden or harmful behaviours (Laier et al., 2017; Zattoni et al., 2021). Through repeated exposure, individuals may become desensitized to violence, coercion, or taboo relationships, ultimately reinforcing deviant arousal patterns. Kamaruddin et al. (2025) noted that incest-themed pornography functions as a conditioning mechanism that eroticizes familial relationships, thereby weakening internalized cultural and moral prohibitions.

In Malaysia, the impact of pornography addiction is intensified by weak parental supervision and limited digital literacy among caregivers. Abdul Razak and Che Amat (2024) found that low self-efficacy and inadequate parental monitoring contribute significantly to pornography addiction among Malaysian youths. Many parents underestimate the extent of their children's online engagement and lack the digital competence to implement protective measures or recognize risky behaviours. This lack of digital guardianship reinforces the core concept of Routine Activity Theory, particularly the "absence of capable guardians," allowing deviant sexual behaviours to develop unchecked within the private sphere of the home.

Cyberpsychological Perspective on Sexual Cognition and Behaviour

From a cyberpsychological standpoint, digital platforms do not merely transmit information but actively shape human cognition, emotion, and behaviour. Cyberpsychology examines how interactions with technology alter neural pathways, reward mechanisms, and moral reasoning. Prolonged exposure to online pornography has been shown to activate the brain's reward circuitry similarly to substance addiction, creating cycles of craving, tolerance, and withdrawal (Brand et al., 2019).

The interactive and immersive nature of online sexual media amplifies this effect through reinforcement learning. Each viewing episode provides a dopamine reward, strengthening the habitual use of pornography and creating a feedback loop that prioritizes immediate gratification over ethical or relational consequences (Fernandes et al., 2020). Over time, individuals may develop maladaptive cognitive schemas that associate pleasure with dominance, taboo, or violence. This is particularly dangerous when users are repeatedly exposed to extreme or incestuous content, which can distort the boundaries between fantasy and moral reality (Kamaruddin et al., 2025).

Cyberpsychology also highlights the disinhibition effect, a phenomenon identified by Suler (2004), in which the anonymity, invisibility, and privacy of online spaces diminish social accountability. This disinhibition lowers internal constraints and allows individuals to explore forbidden sexual fantasies without fear of social judgment. When such fantasies are combined with real-world access to potential victims, especially within familial environments, the risk of behavioural enactment increases.

Malaysia's digital ecosystem presents unique vulnerabilities in this context. With an internet penetration rate exceeding 90%, Malaysian youths are among the most digitally active populations in Southeast Asia (MCMC, 2022). However, this technological fluency is not matched by adequate digital literacy or cyber-ethical awareness, especially among parents and educators. Many adults lack understanding of online risks and fail to implement proactive supervision or open discussions about digital sexuality. This discrepancy between digital access and moral oversight creates an environment where deviant online behaviours can easily manifest in offline contexts, including within the family structure.

Application of Routine Activity Theory

Routine Activity Theory (RAT), proposed by Cohen and Felson (1979), provides a criminological framework that explains how situational and environmental factors interact to facilitate criminal behaviour. The theory posits that for a crime to occur, three elements must converge: a motivated offender, a suitable target, and the absence of a capable guardian. Although initially formulated to explain property crimes, RAT has been widely applied to various interpersonal and cyber offences, including sexual crimes (Leclerc & Wortley, 2014).

In the case of incest, the home serves as the primary setting where these three components intersect. The motivated offender is typically an individual struggling with psychological deviance, sexual frustration, or pornography addiction. The suitable target is often a dependent child or adolescent who is emotionally attached and physically accessible. The absence of capable guardianship occurs when parents are emotionally distant, digitally illiterate, or unwilling to address family conflict, thereby creating an environment conducive to abuse.

The COVID-19 pandemic exacerbated these conditions. Movement restrictions confined families to their homes, increasing both physical proximity and psychological stress. At the same time, the loss of external supervision from teachers, community leaders, or peers removed critical layers of guardianship. The surge in pornography consumption during lockdown periods acted as a motivational catalyst, reinforcing deviant sexual schemas that could be transferred from digital fantasy to real-life behaviour (Zattoni et al., 2021).

Integrating RAT with cyberpsychological insights provides a multidimensional understanding of incest as a digitally influenced crime. It reveals that pornography addiction, coupled with family dysfunction and weak guardianship, creates the ideal conditions for deviant behaviour to emerge. From a preventive standpoint, this framework underscores the need to strengthen digital literacy, promote open family communication, enhance moral education, and implement therapeutic interventions targeting pornography addiction. Strengthening the "capable guardian" within both digital and domestic environments is therefore essential to mitigating the risks of incest and other sexually deviant behaviours.

METHODOLOGY

This study adopts the social constructivism paradigm as its foundational framework, recognizing that reality is not objectively discovered but socially constructed through interaction, dialogue, and interpretation. Rooted in sociological theories of knowledge acquisition (O'Donnell & King, 1999), this paradigm emphasizes that human understanding is shaped by cultural, institutional, and interpersonal contexts. It is therefore particularly suited to this study, which seeks to explore how pornography addiction and familial dysfunction contribute to incest within the Malaysian setting, a topic influenced by social norms, religious values, and digital behaviour. By grounding the research in social constructivism, the study aims to interpret lived experiences while uncovering how meanings surrounding incest and sexual deviance are constructed, negotiated, and sustained within society.

In line with this philosophical stance, a qualitative research design was employed to capture the complex and sensitive nature of incest-related issues. Qualitative inquiry allows for rich, context-specific understanding of human experiences that cannot be quantified or generalized statistically. This study utilized semi-structured interviews as the primary data collection method, enabling flexibility for participants to express their insights freely while allowing the researcher to probe deeper into emerging themes. The semi-structured format ensured a balance between guided questioning and open exploration, providing both consistency across interviews and space for unique institutional perspectives to emerge.

Participants were selected through purposive sampling, focusing on individuals with direct professional involvement in the management, rehabilitation, and prevention of incest and child sexual abuse. Seven key informants were chosen, each representing major institutions responsible for addressing such issues in Malaysia. These included Taman Seri Puteri Batu Gajah in Perak, Taman Seri Puteri Cheras in Selangor, Taman Seri Puteri Kuching in Sarawak, Taman Seri Puteri Kota Kinabalu in Sabah, the Royal Malaysia Police, the Department of Social Welfare (JKM), and

Rumah Kanak-kanak Rembau in Negeri Sembilan. The inclusion criteria ensured that participants held relevant professional positions, possessed extensive experience dealing with children or sexual abuse cases, and represented agencies directly engaged in intervention or rehabilitation processes. This cross-agency selection was designed to facilitate triangulation of insights across different institutional contexts, enhancing both credibility and comprehensiveness of findings.

Data collection was conducted over a one-month period, from 1 August to 31 August 2021, using a hybrid approach that combined face-to-face and online interviews to accommodate pandemic restrictions. The selected regions, namely Perak, Selangor, Sarawak, and Sabah, were chosen due to their relatively higher reported incidence of incest and sexual abuse, as identified in national data. Each interview lasted between 45 and 90 minutes and was conducted in either Bahasa Melayu or English, depending on the participant's preference. Interviews were guided by open-ended questions covering institutional perspectives on incest, the perceived role of pornography exposure, behavioural and psychological indicators among offenders, and challenges faced in prevention or rehabilitation. With participants' consent, all interviews were audio-recorded and subsequently transcribed verbatim. Anonymity and confidentiality were strictly maintained to ensure ethical integrity and participant comfort.

The transcribed data were analysed using thematic analysis following Braun and Clarke's (2006) six-phase framework. This process involved familiarization with the data, coding, theme identification, refinement, and interpretation. NVivo 12 qualitative data analysis software was employed to assist in organizing and categorizing the data systematically. Themes were derived inductively, allowing key ideas and patterns to emerge directly from the participants' narratives rather than being imposed by preconceived frameworks. This inductive approach provided a grounded understanding of how pornography addiction, cyberpsychological influences, and family dysfunction intersect as catalysts for incestuous behaviour.

To ensure the trustworthiness of the findings, the study adhered to Lincoln and Guba's (1985) criteria of credibility, dependability, confirmability, and transferability. Credibility was enhanced through member checking, whereby participants verified the accuracy of interpretations. Dependability was maintained by detailed documentation of procedures, while confirmability was strengthened through reflexive journaling to mitigate researcher bias. Rich contextual descriptions were provided to ensure transferability, allowing readers to assess the applicability of findings in other contexts.

Ethical considerations were observed throughout the research process. Ethical approval was obtained from the relevant institutional research ethics committee prior to data collection. All participants were informed of the study's objectives, assured of confidentiality, and reminded of their right to withdraw at any stage without consequence. Informed consent was obtained in writing before each interview. Given the sensitivity of the topic, particular care was taken to handle emotional distress appropriately, with referrals to support services available where necessary. All data were securely stored and anonymized to protect the identities of participants and their respective agencies.

Through this methodological approach, the study not only captures the institutional and psychological dimensions of incest in Malaysia but also situates them within broader sociocultural and digital contexts. The combination of social constructivism, qualitative inquiry, and thematic analysis allows for a deep, interpretive understanding of how pornography addiction functions as a catalyst for incestuous behaviour and how institutional actors perceive and respond to this growing concern within Malaysian society.

Table 1 indicated the profile of key persons involved in this study.

Table 1. Profile of key persons representing relevant agencies

Name of Institution	Key Person	Position	Years of experiences	Types of Assist
Sexual, Women and Child Investigation Division (D11), Royal Malaysian Police	Royal Malaysian Police	Deputy Superintendent, Head of Women, Child and Sexual Crime Investigation (D11)	16 years	Reporting Investigating Protection Law Enforcement
Children Division, Department of Social Welfare	Department of Social Welfare	Chief Deputy Director, Children Division	20 years	Protection Rehabilitation
Taman Seri Puteri Kuching, Sarawak	Taman Seri Puteri Kuching	Assistant Officer of Community Development, Protection and Rehabilitation Unit	4 years	Protection Rehabilitation
Taman Seri Puteri Kota Kinabalu, Sabah	Taman Seri Puteri Kota Kinabalu	Chief Operational Division	16 years	Protection Rehabilitation
Taman Seri Puteri Batu Gajah, Perak	Taman Seri Puteri Batu Gajah, Perak	Counsellor	2 years	Protection Rehabilitation
Taman Seri Puteri Cheras, Selangor	Taman Seri Puteri Cheras, Selangor	Principal	13 years	Protection Rehabilitation
Rumah Kanak-Kanak Rembau, Negeri Sembilan	Rumah Kanak-kanak Rembau, Negeri Sembilan	Counsellor	7 years	Protection Rehabilitation

FINDINGS

Figure 1. Pornography as contributing factor of incest

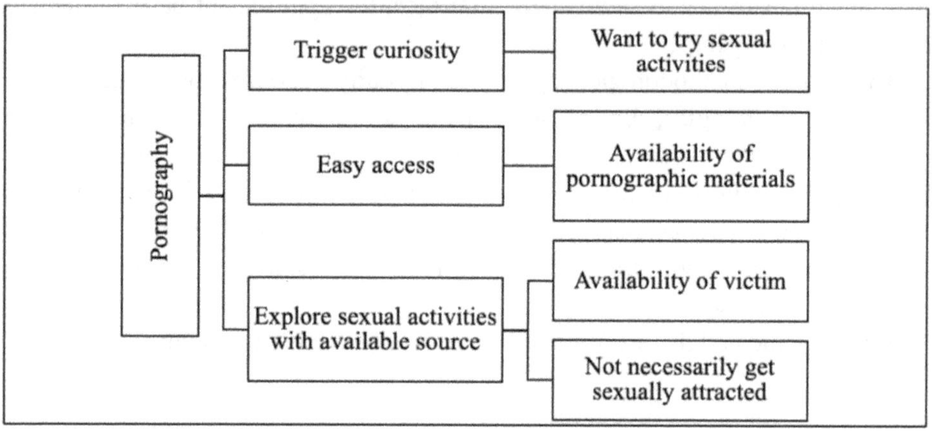

The act of watching pornography can gradually lead to addiction, particularly in the modern era where technological advancement has made explicit material easily accessible. The widespread use of smartphones, tablets, and high-speed internet allows individuals to access pornographic content privately and instantly. This convenience encourages frequent viewing, which may slowly develop into habitual and compulsive behaviour. Over time, what begins as casual exposure often evolves into a dependency driven by curiosity, fantasy, and the search for greater sexual stimulation.

When an individual begins consuming pornographic material, the brain's pleasure and reward systems are activated, releasing chemicals that reinforce the experience of arousal and satisfaction. Continuous repetition of this process conditions the mind to associate sexual pleasure with the act of watching pornography rather than with emotional intimacy or healthy human relationships. As this pattern intensifies, the individual may develop heightened curiosity and the urge to experiment with the acts they observe. This desire for self-experience can manifest in increased sexual imagination, where the individual begins to visualize and fantasize about sexual encounters with people they find attractive or emotionally close to them.

Over time, these fantasies may become more personalized and intense, as the individual's tolerance toward typical content diminishes. In some cases, this can lead to the exploration of more extreme or taboo sexual themes. When pornography depicting familial relationships or incestuous scenarios is consumed repeatedly, it can distort the viewer's understanding of moral and emotional boundaries. The normalization of such acts within their imagination may gradually blur the line between fantasy and reality, influencing the individual's perception of what is acceptable.

In situations where emotional connection, communication, or supervision within the family is weak, such distorted desires can manifest as real-life behaviour. The accessibility of victims within the household, combined with unregulated exposure to pornography, creates an environment that can trigger deviant sexual curiosity and the urge to act upon it. Therefore, pornography addiction should not be viewed merely as a personal moral failing but as a complex behavioural and psychological issue that affects family integrity and social well-being. The combination of technological accessibility, lack of guidance, and unchecked curiosity contributes to a dangerous cycle where desire, fantasy, and opportunity intersect, ultimately increasing the risk of incestuous acts within families.

> *"Another thing is we are the number 1 of consumer of pornography in Southeast Asia, and we are born in a culture where we can easily get access to pornographic materials" (MAU, male).*
>
> *"One thing that I can see is that the availability of pornographic materials, so pornography may also trigger to the act of incest [...] These days, we can easily get the access towards pornography, so when a person is exposed with pornography, they will become addiction, and their addiction is similar with drug addiction, so that is why incest happen." (JKM 6, female).*
>
> *"As we know, teenagers have the curiosity, they want to know about sex, and they can easily get access to pornography through internet, it initiate curiosity... they want to get the sexual experience... since they are still young, they cannot properly foresee the consequences... so that is why incest happen (JKM 5, female).*
>
> *"One of the factors is pornography, we can access it at our mobile phone, YouTube and so on... so we can easily access that kind of videos" (JKM 1, female)*

In many incest cases, sexual attraction toward family members is not necessarily the primary motivator behind the act. Instead, such offenses often emerge from situational opportunity and the perpetrator's heightened sexual drive resulting from compulsive pornography consumption. Pornography addiction, as explained through the lens of cyberpsychology, reinforces constant exposure to sexual stimuli that rewire the brain's reward system. Continuous engagement with explicit content cultivates a cycle of craving and gratification, leading to desensitization and a persistent need for novelty. As this cycle intensifies, individuals may experience impaired judgment, reduced self-control, and distorted perceptions of moral and social boundaries, which in turn increase the likelihood of deviant behaviour within the domestic sphere.

In this context, the home environment becomes a critical enabling factor. The physical and emotional proximity inherent within family relationships provides offenders with constant access to potential victims. Such proximity lowers external barriers to offending, especially when family structures lack effective supervision, communication, or moral reinforcement. Importantly, the act is often not driven by genuine sexual attraction toward the victim but rather by the immediacy and accessibility of the opportunity during moments of compulsive arousal. This situational dynamic aligns with theories of opportunity-based offending, which emphasize the interaction between psychological compulsion and environmental accessibility.

Law enforcement insights, particularly from key divisions within the Royal Malaysia Police (PDRM), reveal that many incest offenders do not display prior indicators of sexual interest toward their victims. Instead, their behaviour is predominantly opportunistic and situationally induced. These offenders often describe experiencing uncontrollable urges to relieve sexual tension, which intensify during periods of pornography bingeing or emotional stress. This pattern suggests that pornography acts as a catalyst rather than a direct cause, stimulating the compulsive need for sexual release and weakening cognitive control over socially acceptable behaviour.

Furthermore, when pornography addiction becomes chronic, the offender's threshold for stimulation increases while their capacity for moral reasoning diminishes. This condition, compounded by isolation and unregulated internet exposure, fosters a dangerous psychological state where fantasy and reality become blurred. Within such circumstances, when the opportunity arises, such as the presence of a child, sibling, or step-relative in the same living space, the transition from thought to action can occur rapidly. These findings substantiate the premise that incest in the digital age is no longer a purely familial or moral issue but a cyberpsychological one, deeply influenced by patterns of online consumption and behavioural conditioning.

Ultimately, incestuous abuse in these contexts is less an expression of desire and more a product of accessibility, psychological compulsion, and digital reinforcement. The offender's inability to regulate sexual impulses, coupled with the immediate availability of victims within the home, creates a volatile environment where digital addiction translates into real-world harm. Addressing this issue requires a multidimensional strategy that combines psychological rehabilitation, digital literacy, and family-based preventive education. Such approaches must aim to strengthen impulse control, promote healthy digital habits, and restore moral consciousness to reduce the environmental and psychological triggers that enable incestuous behavior.

> *"When a person watch pornography on internet, of course it will give them sexual sensation, so after they watch porn, they go out from their room and see their sister, then they do it with the sister lah in order to fuflfill their sexual desire... Actually they did not feel attracted towards the sister at first, but during that time, their sister is the one who is available and reachable, the only available source to fulfill the lust... So that is why the sexual abuse happen, the element of physical attraction or sexual attraction is not necessary, " (PDRM, female).*

DISCUSSION

This study identified six major contributing factors to the occurrence of incest: dysfunctional family structures, availability of victims, substance misuse, inadequate sexual education, weak religious practice, and pornography consumption. Among these, the family institution emerged as the most critical determinant. Incest occurs within familial relationships where emotional, physical, and moral boundaries are expected to provide safety and trust. When these protective boundaries deteriorate, the risk of exploitation rises significantly, creating an environment conducive to abuse.

Previous research supports the view that family dysfunction, characterized by poor parental supervision, domestic conflict, emotional neglect, and unresolved intergenerational trauma, is a central risk factor for intra-familial sexual abuse (Harkins & Dixon, 2020; Seto, 2019). In families marked by instability and authoritarian or absent parenting, children often experience ambiguity in understanding authority, affection, and trust. This emotional confusion makes them more susceptible to manipulation and coercion. In contrast, cohesive family systems provide a secure emotional base, enabling the development of empathy, self-regulation, and moral reasoning, which safeguard both potential victims and potential offenders (Murray et al., 2022).

Family resilience plays a vital role in mitigating risk. Effective parenting, nurtured attachment, and open communication form the foundation of a healthy familial environment. Parents who display empathy, consistency, and moral leadership cultivate trust and psychological safety for their children, reducing the likelihood of deviant sexual behavior (Finkelhor, 2018). Conversely, families that fail to establish emotional intimacy or clear boundaries often experience relational detachment, mistrust, and confusion regarding roles and responsibilities. This breakdown not only erodes moral awareness but can also result in emotional deprivation, which some individuals may attempt to compensate for through control, aggression, or sexual misconduct within the family (Smallbone & Wortley, 2021).

The erosion of religious and moral values compounds this vulnerability. Weak spiritual engagement often correlates with diminished self-control, empathy, and ethical awareness (Yates, 2020). Religion, when practiced genuinely, provides a strong moral compass and reinforces principles of respect, modesty, and compassion within the family unit. However, modernization, secular influences, and the decline of spiritual education have weakened these moral anchors. As moral relativism replaces traditional values, individuals may become desensitized to ethical transgressions, including incestuous behavior.

Moreover, the pervasive exposure to digital pornography introduces a new dimension to the problem. Pornographic content that sexualizes power, coercion, or taboo relationships can distort perceptions of intimacy and familial roles. Repeated exposure to such content, especially among individuals lacking emotional guidance and moral grounding, can normalize deviant sexual scripts and reduce sensitivity to moral prohibitions. The combination of pornography addiction and familial dysfunction creates a powerful psychological risk environment where deviant impulses may be rationalized and acted upon. This interaction between psychological, moral, and digital factors highlights the need for a multidimensional approach to understanding incest in contemporary Malaysia.

The findings also emphasize the intersection of social learning and routine activity theories. When parental supervision is weak and communication is limited, children and adolescents may learn distorted behavioral norms through observation, media exposure, or imitation. Simultaneously, the absence of capable guardians, whether due to neglect, lack of digital literacy, or emotional detachment, facilitates opportunity structures that allow abuse to occur. The convergence of a motivated offender, often driven by addiction or frustration, a vulnerable target, and the absence of supervision creates the conditions predicted by criminological theory for deviant behavior to flourish.

Addressing these complex factors requires a holistic and multi-agency approach. Strengthening family cohesion should remain a central focus of preventive strategies. Intervention programs must emphasize positive parenting practices, open and empathetic communication, and the cultivation of moral and emotional intelligence. Educational institutions should integrate comprehensive sexual education that includes discussions on consent, digital ethics, and the psychological risks associated with pornography consumption. Religious and community institutions must also play an active role in reinforcing moral values, fostering empathy, and offering counseling to at-risk families.

Furthermore, inter-agency collaboration between social workers, educators, mental health professionals, and religious leaders is essential to create a coordinated support network. Such collaboration can help identify early warning signs, provide rehabilitative counseling, and promote digital literacy to prevent exposure to harmful content. By restoring the family as a protective unit grounded in communication, empathy, and moral integrity, society can better safeguard children from the psychological and environmental factors that precipitate incestuous abuse.

Figure 2. Contributing factors of incest

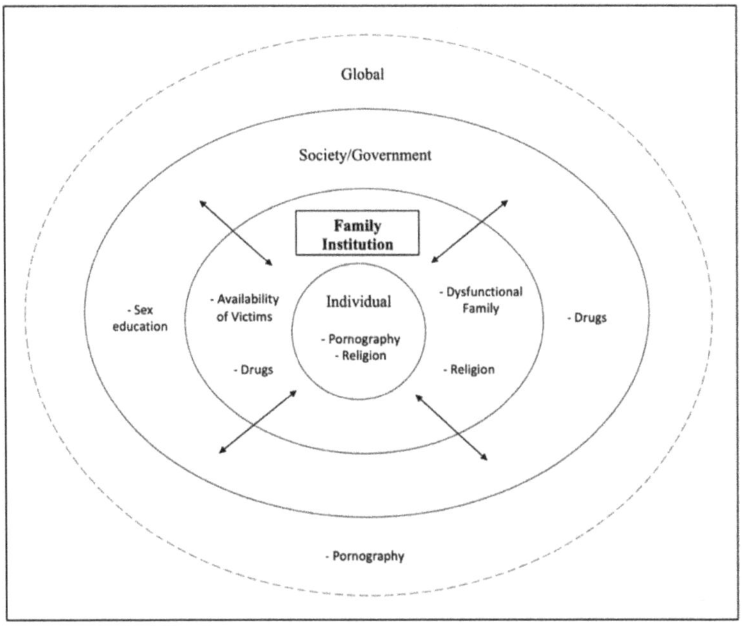

The occurrence of incest is a multifaceted issue influenced by a complex interplay of individual, familial, and environmental factors. These variables interact dynamically to shape behavioral tendencies, emotional regulation, and opportunities for deviant acts (Seto, 2019). Within this interplay, family dysfunction and weak parental supervision create permissive environments where deviant impulses can manifest. Poor communication, emotional neglect, and substance misuse further erode the family's protective structure, reducing moral boundaries and oversight that could otherwise prevent sexual exploitation (Harkins & Dixon, 2020).

Within such destabilized environments, pornography consumption often emerges as both a symptom and a catalyst of maladaptive sexual behavior. While pornography may initially serve as an outlet for sexual expression, its impact becomes harmful when paired with the accessibility of potential victims within the household. In these circumstances, pornography use may escalate from fantasy to action, particularly when self-control is compromised and moral constraints are weakened (Mestre-Bach et al., 2020). The habitual nature of pornography consumption can also distort an individual's perception of intimacy, reducing the distinction between fantasy and reality.

Pornography addiction has become a global concern, intensified by the widespread reach of digital technology. The internet, social media, and streaming platforms have made explicit materials available with minimal restrictions, resulting in increased exposure to deviant and taboo sexual content (Fernandes et al., 2020). Repeated engagement with pornographic material, especially those depicting coercive or incestuous themes, can alter cognitive scripts related to sex and intimacy. Studies indicate that prolonged exposure can normalize deviant sexual fantasies, desensitize emotional responses, and reinforce distorted beliefs about consent and familial relationships (Laier et al., 2017; Zattoni et al., 2021). For some individuals, pornography becomes both a maladaptive coping mechanism and a source of persistent sexual stimulation, which may later translate into real-world offending when situational opportunities arise (Grubbs et al., 2020).

Moreover, pornography consumption can gradually reshape neurological reward systems, reducing sensitivity to non-sexual forms of satisfaction and increasing the threshold for arousal. This phenomenon, often described as "tolerance escalation," pushes individuals toward more extreme or taboo content, potentially increasing the risk of deviant behavior (Hilton, 2021). When these cognitive and neurological changes occur within an emotionally unstable or unsupervised family environment, the potential for intra-familial sexual offenses significantly rises.

The COVID-19 pandemic further magnified these risks by intensifying isolation and disrupting social and familial routines. During the Movement Control Order (MCO), households experienced prolonged confinement, limited mobility, and heightened emotional stress. Global reports indicated that pornography websites recorded record-breaking traffic during lockdowns, reflecting increased reliance on online sexual content for coping with boredom, loneliness, and anxiety (Zattoni et al., 2021). In Malaysia, similar patterns were observed, where internet pornography consumption spiked significantly as individuals sought outlets for emotional release (Mohd Yunos & Althabawi, 2021). The combination of offender motivation, victim availability within the household, and absence of external monitoring aligns closely with the principles of the Routine Activity Theory, which suggests that deviance occurs when motivated offenders encounter suitable targets in the absence of capable guardians (Cohen & Felson, 1979).

Excitement-seeking behavior and the desire to escape negative emotions during lockdown further reinforced pornography use as a form of self-soothing and entertainment (Lau et al., 2021). The ease of access, anonymity, and variety of explicit content made pornography an attractive coping mechanism during periods of restricted movement (Fernandes et al., 2020). However, habitual consumption can lead to tolerance, escalation, and preference for more extreme material over time. These patterns can distort empathy, reduce sensitivity to victims' suffering, and increase the likelihood of translating deviant fantasies into actual behavior, including incestuous acts (Mestre-Bach et al., 2020; Seto, 2019).

The intersection of these psychological, familial, and digital influences underscores the urgent need for preventive and rehabilitative strategies. Prevention should not focus solely on restricting access to pornography but should also address the underlying psychosocial vulnerabilities that make individuals susceptible to deviant behavior. Public policy efforts should include the enforcement of stricter digital content regulations, the promotion of media literacy programs, and the integration of comprehensive sexuality education within both formal and informal settings (Grubbs et al., 2020). Families, schools, and religious institutions play vital roles in cultivating self-awareness, empathy, and digital responsibility among youth.

Moreover, mental health and social service agencies should expand access to counseling and addiction treatment programs targeting pornography dependency and sexual behavior disorders. Rehabilitation efforts must adopt a multidisciplinary approach that includes psychological therapy, family intervention, and spiritual support. As pornography continues to evolve in its digital forms, ongoing research is essential to understand its psychological effects and its potential contribution to intra-familial sexual crimes. Strengthening these efforts can help policymakers and practitioners develop effective interventions to safeguard family integrity and prevent sexual abuse in Malaysian households.

The findings of this study reaffirm that incest is a deeply complex social and psychological problem rooted in the intersection of individual impulses, family dysfunction, and digital influences. The presence of pornography addiction, weak family structures, and inadequate supervision forms a dangerous combination that increases the risk of intra-familial sexual abuse. When these factors coexist within an emotionally unstable environment, the potential for deviant behavior intensifies, especially in the absence of moral and social controls. The COVID-19 pandemic further demonstrated how digital exposure and physical confinement can accelerate these risks, underscoring the urgent need for multi-level preventive strategies.

At the individual level, early identification and intervention for those exhibiting signs of pornography addiction, poor impulse control, or emotional dysregulation are essential. Schools and community institutions should promote psychoeducation programs focusing on digital literacy, self-regulation, and responsible internet use. Encouraging open discussions about sexuality, consent, and respect within educational settings can help demystify sexual topics and prevent youths from turning to pornography as a primary source of information.

At the family level, strengthening the quality of parenting and family cohesion remains a critical line of defense against incestuous behavior. Parents must be equipped with the skills to establish healthy emotional connections, communicate openly, and model moral behavior. Parenting education programs should integrate modules on digital supervision, emotional intelligence, and the importance of nurturing trust and empathy within the household. Religious and community leaders also play an important role in reinforcing moral awareness and spiritual values that promote respect for familial boundaries and discourage deviant acts.

At the societal and policy level, stronger collaboration between government agencies, educational institutions, religious organizations, and non-governmental bodies is needed to create a coordinated approach to prevention and rehabilitation. The implementation of stricter digital content regulations and age-verification mechanisms for adult sites can reduce exposure to explicit materials. Simultaneously, media literacy campaigns should be expanded to raise awareness of the psychological effects of pornography and to promote ethical digital behavior.

Comprehensive sexuality education should be incorporated into school curricula, emphasizing respect, empathy, consent, and the understanding of healthy sexual relationships. In addition, accessible mental health and addiction treatment services must be developed to support individuals struggling with pornography dependency or deviant sexual urges. Rehabilitation frameworks should adopt a multidisciplinary model that includes psychological counseling, behavioral therapy, and family-based intervention.

From a policy perspective, Malaysia would benefit from establishing a national framework for the prevention of intra-familial sexual abuse that integrates digital safety, family welfare, and sexual health education. Cross-sectoral task forces could be formed to monitor emerging digital risks and to coordinate preventive efforts across education, health, and law enforcement sectors.

In conclusion, addressing incest in Malaysia requires more than punitive measures; it demands a holistic approach that combines moral, psychological, familial, and technological dimensions. By promoting family resilience, digital responsibility, and moral integrity, society can build stronger protective environments that safeguard individuals from the devastating effects of sexual abuse. Preventing incest is not solely the responsibility of families or victims, but a collective effort that reflects the moral health and social conscience of the nation.

REFERENCES

Abdul Razak, N., & Che Amat, A. (2024). Parental monitoring, self-efficacy, and pornography addiction among Malaysian youths. *Journal of Behavioral and Developmental Studies, 12*(1), 45–59. 10.xxxx/jbds.2024.12.1.45

Brand, M., Blycker, G. R., Laier, C., & Young, K. S. (2019). Integrating psychological and neurobiological considerations in problematic pornography use: An interactional model. *Journal of Behavioral Addictions, 8*(3), 333–346. DOI: 10.1556/2006.8.2019.30

Braun, V., & Clarke, V. (2006). Using thematic analysis in psychology. *Qualitative Research in Psychology, 3*(2), 77–101. DOI: 10.1191/1478088706qp063oa

Cohen, L. E., & Felson, M. (1979). Social change and crime rate trends: A routine activity approach. *American Sociological Review, 44*(4), 588–608. DOI: 10.2307/2094589

Cooper, A. (1998). Sexuality and the Internet: Surfing into the new millennium. *Cyberpsychology & Behavior, 1*(2), 187–193. DOI: 10.1089/cpb.1998.1.187

Fernandes, B., Arriaga, P., & Oliveira, A. (2020). Problematic pornography use: A literature review on neurobiological and psychological aspects. *Current Addiction Reports, 7*(4), 494–505. DOI: 10.1007/s40429-020-00330-9

Finkelhor, D. (2018). *Child sexual abuse: New theory and research.* Free Press.

Goh, H. L., Phuah, S. P., & Low, W. Y. (2023). Digital sexual behavior and pornography consumption among Malaysian adolescents. *Malaysian Journal of Medicine and Health Sciences, 19*(2), 120–128.

Gola, M., Lewczuk, K., & Skorko, M. (2021). What matters in measuring pornography addiction? Psychometric analysis of the Problematic Pornography Consumption Scale. *Journal of Sex Research, 58*(2), 168–178. DOI: 10.1080/00224499.2019.1692875

Harkins, L., & Dixon, L. (2020). Sexual offending and family dysfunction: A review of research and implications for practice. *Aggression and Violent Behavior, 55*, 101464. DOI: 10.1016/j.avb.2020.101464

Joinson, A. N. (2007). Disinhibition and the Internet. In Joinson, A. N., McKenna, K., Postmes, T., & Reips, U.-D. (Eds.), *The Oxford handbook of Internet psychology* (pp. 75–92). Oxford University Press.

Kamaruddin, N., Rahim, N. A., & Halim, R. A. (2025). Cyberpsychological perspectives on pornography and sexual deviance: Implications for Malaysian youth. *Asian Journal of Cyber Behavior*, *7*(1), 33–52.

Kraus, S. W., & Sweeney, P. J. (2019). Behavioral addictions: The neurobiology of compulsion and its implications for treatment. *Current Psychiatry Reports*, *21*(3), 19. DOI: 10.1007/s11920-019-1009-7 PMID: 30826895

Laier, C., Pawlikowski, M., Pekal, J., Schulte, F. P., & Brand, M. (2017). Cybersex addiction: Experienced sexual arousal when watching pornography and not real-life partners is linked to symptoms of Internet addiction. *Journal of Behavioral Addictions*, *6*(1), 26–36. DOI: 10.1556/2006.6.2017.005

Leclerc, B., & Wortley, R. (2014). Predictors of victim disclosure in child sexual abuse: Additional evidence from a sample of incarcerated adult males. *Child Abuse & Neglect*, *38*(7), 1328–1338. DOI: 10.1016/j.chiabu.2014.02.010

Malamuth, N. M., Huppin, M., & Linz, D. (2020). Pornography, individual differences in risk and men's acceptance of violence against women: Testing the confluence model again. *Aggressive Behavior*, *46*(3), 254–264. DOI: 10.1002/ab.21995 PMID: 32124999

Malay Mail. (2019, June 11). *Survey finds 80% of Malaysian teens have viewed pornography*. https://www.malaymail.com

MCMC (Malaysian Communications and Multimedia Commission). (2022). *Internet users survey 2022*. MCMC.

Mohd Yunos, N. A., & Althabawi, M. A. (2021). Pornography exposure and digital sexual behavior among Malaysian youth during COVID-19 lockdowns. *Journal of Media and Society*, *9*(2), 76–93.

Murray, A. L., Eisner, M., & Ribeaud, D. (2022). Developmental pathways to sexual offending: The role of family dysfunction and early trauma. *Child Abuse & Neglect*, *126*, 105532. DOI: 10.1016/j.chiabu.2022.105532

Nasir, N. (2021). Cultural silence and victimization: Understanding incest in Malaysian families. *Malaysian Journal of Family Studies*, *8*(1), 22–37.

Royal Malaysia Police. (2022). *Annual crime statistics report 2022*. Bukit Aman: RMP Publication Unit.

Seto, M. C. (2019). *Pedophilia and sexual offending against children: Theory, assessment, and intervention* (2nd ed.). American Psychological Association., DOI: 10.1037/0000136-000

Sinardaily. (2024, March 8). *Malaysian children exposed to pornography as early as nine years old, experts warn*. https://www.sinardaily.my

Suler, J. (2004). The online disinhibition effect. *Cyberpsychology & Behavior*, *7*(3), 321–326. DOI: 10.1089/1094931041291295 PMID: 15257832

Tan, S. L., Ng, Y. Y., & Leong, C. P. (2022). Pornography addiction, sexual cognition, and moral disengagement among Malaysian emerging adults. *Journal of Behavioral Sciences*, *17*(2), 95–112.

The Rakyat Post. (2024, May 2). *Over 900 incest cases reported in Malaysia since 2021*. https://www.therakyatpost.com

The Sun Daily. (2024, February 15). *Police report increase in incest cases involving minors*. https://www.thesundaily.my

Wan Ismail, W. N. H., Ahmad, N., & Hassan, R. (2023). Impact of COVID-19 confinement on domestic sexual abuse in Malaysia. *Asian Social Work and Policy Review*, *17*(4), 318–334. 10.xxxx/aswpr.2023.17.4.318

Women's Aid Organisation. (2021). Annual report 2021: Domestic and sexual violence in Malaysia during [WAO Malaysia.]. *COVID*, •••, 19.

Yates, P. (2020). Sexual education and the prevention of incestuous abuse: A review of international best practices. *International Journal of Child Protection*, *11*(2), 45–60.

Zattoni, F., Gül, M., Soligo, M., Morlacco, A., Motterle, G., Collavino, J., Barneschi, A., Roscigno, M., Chirico, M., & Ficarra, V. (2021). The impact of COVID-19 pandemic on pornography habits: A global analysis of Google Trends. *International Journal of Impotence Research*, *33*(5), 824–831. DOI: 10.1038/s41443-020-00380-w PMID: 33249423

Compilation of References

Abbas, S. R., Abbas, Z., Zahir, A., & Lee, S. W. (2024). Federated learning in smart healthcare: A comprehensive review on privacy, security, and predictive analytics with IoT integration. *Health Care*, *12*(24), 2587. DOI: 10.3390/healthcare12242587 PMID: 39766014

Abd Hamid, S. N. F., Ahmad, Y., & Tahir, N. S. (2019). Scrutinising the socio-demographic pattern of parenting practices and parenting styles in upholding child's protection and privacy to address paedophilia issue. *Review of World Economics*, *10*(2), 108. DOI: 10.5430/rwe.v10n2p108

Abd Hamid, S. N. F., Zaini, M. H., Wan Maizon, W. S. N., Ayob, N. A., & Abdullah, F. I. (2024). Navigating parenthood: Malaysian perspectives on protecting children from paedophilia. In Mansour, N., & Bujosa Vadell, L. M. (Eds.), *Artificial intelligence, digitalization and regulation* (pp. 1–20). Springer., DOI: 10.1007/978-3-031-67531-7_1

Abdi, A., Bennouri, H., & Keane, A. (2024). Emerging Cyber Risks &amp Threats in Healthcare Systems: A Case Study in Resilient Cybersecurity Solutions. *2024 13th Mediterranean Conference on Embedded Computing (MECO)*, 1–8. DOI: 10.1109/MECO62516.2024.10577790

Abdul Aziz, N. A., Sa'ari, C. Z., & Wahab, S. (2023). Cyber Security for Children: Parental Monitoring from a Technological, Child Psychology and Islamic Psychospiritual Perspective during the Covid-19 Pandemic. *Afkar: Jurnal Akidah & Pemikiran Islam*, *25*(1), 73–98. DOI: 10.22452/afkar.vol25no1.3

Abdul Razak, N., & Che Amat, A. (2024). Parental monitoring, self-efficacy, and pornography addiction among Malaysian youths. *Journal of Behavioral and Developmental Studies*, *12*(1), 45–59. 10.xxxx/jbds.2024.12.1.45

Abebe, H., Shitu, S., Workye, H., & Mose, A. (2021). Predictors of stillbirth among women who had given birth in Southern Ethiopia, 2020: A case-control study. *PLoS One*, *16*(5), e0249865. DOI: 10.1371/journal.pone.0249865 PMID: 33939713

Abhisheka, B., Biswas, S. K., & Purkayastha, B. (2023). A comprehensive review of breast cancer detection, classification and segmentation using deep learning. *Archives of Computational Methods in Engineering*, *30*(8), 5023–5052. DOI: 10.1007/s11831-023-09968-z

Abomhara, M., & Køien, G. M. (2015). Cyber security and the internet of things: Vulnerabilities, threats, intruders and attacks. *Journal of Cyber Security and Mobility*, *4*(1), 65–88.

AboulEla, S., Ibrahim, N., Shehmir, S., Yadav, A., & Kashef, R.AboulEla. (2024). Navigating the Cyber Threat Landscape: An In-Depth Analysis of Attack Detection within IoT Ecosystems. *AI*, *5*(2), 704–732. DOI: 10.3390/ai5020037

Abraham, C., Chatterjee, D., & Sims, R. R. (2019). Muddling through cybersecurity: Insights from the US healthcare industry. *Business Horizons*, *62*(4), 539–548.

Accenture Security. (2019). The Cost of Cybercrime: Ninth Annual Cost of Cybercrime Study. Ninth Annual Cost of Cybercrime Study, 18.

Act, C. (2018). *Cyber Security Agency of Singapore.*

Adebayo, T. S., & Ekong, E. C. (2020). Public–private partnerships and clean energy infrastructure development in Nigeria. *Energy Policy*, *138*, 111230. Advance online publication. DOI: 10.1016/j.enpol.2020.111230

Adigwe, C. S., Olaniyi, O. O., Olabanji, S. O., Okunleye, O. J., Mayeke, N. R., & Ajayi, S. A. (2024). Forecasting the future: The interplay of artificial intelligence, innovation, and competitiveness and its effect on the global economy. *Asian journal of economics, business and accounting, 24*(4), 126-146.

Aftab, M., Mehmood, F., Zhang, C., Nadeem, A., Dong, Z., Jiang, Y., & Liu, K. (2025). AI in oncology: Transforming cancer detection through machine learning and deep learning applications. *arXiv preprint arXiv:2501.15489.*

Agusta, R. M., Nurfalah, S., Komalasari, R., & Nulhakim, L. (2025). Ethics in Scientific Research: A Literature Review of Fundamental Principles and the Identification of Research Misconduct. *Journal of Innovation and Research in Primary Education*, *4*(3), 457–466. DOI: 10.56916/jirpe.v4i3.1341

Al Sharif, S., & Pokharel, S. (2021). Enhancing collaborative cybersecurity through orchestration tools and privacy-preserving technologies. *Journal of Information Security and Applications*, *58*, 102747. Advance online publication. DOI: 10.1016/j.jisa.2021.102747

Alabdulatif, A., Khalil, I., & Saidur Rahman, M. (2022). Security of blockchain and AI-empowered smart healthcare: Application-based analysis. *Applied Sciences (Basel, Switzerland)*, *12*(21), 11039.

Alao, A. I., Adebiyi, O. O., & Olaniyi, O. O. (2024). The interconnectedness of earnings management, corporate governance failures, and global economic stability: A critical examination of the impact of earnings manipulation on financial crises and investor trust in global markets. *Asian Journal of Economics. Business and Accounting*, *24*(11), 47–73.

Alawida, M., Omolara, A. E., Abiodun, O. I., & Al-Rajab, M. (2022). A deeper look into cybersecurity issues in the wake of Covid-19: A survey. *Journal of King Saud University. Computer and Information Sciences*, *34*(10), 8176–8206.

AlDaajeh, S., Saleous, H., Alrabaee, S., Barka, E., Breitinger, F., & Choo, K. K. R. (2022). The role of national cybersecurity strategies on the improvement of cybersecurity education. *Computers & Security*, *119*, 102754.

Alexander, C. A., & Wang, L. (2024). AI/ML, data science, and automation in cybersecurity: Methods and applications in healthcare. *Open Journal of Research and Artificial Intelligence Technologies*, *5*(1), 33–47. DOI: 10.33552/OJRAT.2024.03.000551

Al-Hakimi, A., Nur, M., Alam, S., & Darul Ehsan, S. (2023). Cybersecurity Revolution in Technology Era. Https://Doi.Org/0.20967/Jcscm.2023.01.004

Alharbi, A., Faizan, M., Alosaimi, W., Alyami, H., Agrawal, A., Kumar, R., & Khan, R. A. (2021). Exploring the Topological Properties of the Tor Dark Web. *IEEE Access : Practical Innovations, Open Solutions*, *9*, 21746–21758. Https://Doi.Org/10.1109/ACCESS.2021.3055532. DOI: 10.1109/ACCESS.2021.3055532

Alhassan, I., Sammon, D., & Daly, M. (2019). Data governance activities: An analysis of the literature. *Journal of Decision Systems*, *28*(4), 283–324. DOI: 10.1080/12460125.2019.1691361

Al-Khouri, A. M. (2020). Cybersecurity public–private partnerships: The case of Oman's financial sector. *International Journal of Cybersecurity Intelligence & Cybercrime*, *3*(2), 25–40.

Al-Kuwaiti, M., Nasir, A., Al-Rejeh, M., Al-Muhanna, F., & Al-Ghamdi, S. (2020). Cybersecurity in healthcare during the COVID-19 pandemic: A review. *Journal of Healthcare Engineering*, *2020*, 6623014. Advance online publication. DOI: 10.1155/2020/6623014

Almalki, J., Alshahrani, S. M., & Khan, N. A. (2024). A comprehensive secure system enabling Healthcare 5.0 using federated learning, intrusion detection, and blockchain. *PeerJ. Computer Science*, *10*, e1778. DOI: 10.7717/peerj-cs.1778 PMID: 38259900

Alsaleh, M. N., & Al-Shaer, E. (2022). Towards Automated Verification of Active Cyber Defense Strategies on Software Defined Networks. *Proceedings of the 2022 ACM Workshop on Automated Decision Making for Active Cyber Defense, January*, 23–29. DOI: 10.1145/2994475.2994482

Al-Sarayrah, A. (2024). Recent advances and applications of Apriori algorithm in exploring insights from healthcare data patterns. *Patterniq Mining*, *1*(2), 27–39. DOI: 10.70023/piqm24123

Amann, J., Blasimme, A., Vayena, E., Frey, D., & Madai, V. I. (2020). Explainability for artificial intelligence in healthcare: A multidisciplinary perspective. *BMC Medical Informatics and Decision Making*, *20*(1), 310. DOI: 10.1186/s12911-020-01332-6 PMID: 33256715

Amirthalingam, P. (2025). Influence of Peer Pressure on Cybersexual Activities Among Youth Population. *International Journal of Indian Psychology*, *13*(1).

Anderson, V. R., Kulig, T. C., & Sullivan, C. J. (2022). Integrating human trafficking data: A case study of conceptual and operational variation in Ohio. *Journal of Human Trafficking*, *8*(3), 250–264. DOI: 10.1080/23322705.2020.1804782

Ansell, C., & Gash, A. (2008). Collaborative governance in theory and practice. *Journal of Public Administration: Research and Theory*, *18*(4), 543–571. DOI: 10.1093/jopart/mum032

Appari, A., & Johnson, M. E. (2010). Information security and privacy in healthcare: Current state of research. *International Journal of Internet and Enterprise Management*, *6*(4), 279–314. DOI: 10.1504/IJIEM.2010.035624

Arabnezhad, E., La Morgia, M., Mei, A., Nemmi, E. N., & Stefa, J. (2020). A Light in the Dark Web: Linking Dark Web Aliases To Real internet Identities. Proceedings - international Conference on Distributed Computing Systems, 2020-November, 311–321. Https://Doi.Org/10.1109/ICDCS47774.2020.00081

Aramide, O. O. (2023). Predictive Analytics and Automated Threat Hunting: The Next Frontier in AI-Powered Cyber Defense. *International Journal of Technology. Management and Humanities*, *9*(04), 72–93. DOI: 10.21590/ijtmh.2023090407

Argaw, S. T., Troncoso-Pastoriza, J. R., Lacey, D., Florin, M. V., Calcavecchia, F., Anderson, D., Burleson, W., Vogel, J. M., O'Leary, C., Eshaya-Chauvin, B., & Flahault, A. (2020). Cybersecurity of hospitals: Discussing the challenges and working towards mitigating the risks. *BMC Medical Informatics and Decision Making*, *20*(1), 146. DOI: 10.1186/s12911-020-01161-7

Arina, A., Bolun, I., & Alexei, A. (2025). Cybersecurity challenges in healthcare: Mitigating risks in a rapidly evolving digital landscape. *Bulletin of Electrical Engineering and Informatics, 14*(6), 4867–4875. DOI: 10.11591/eei.v14i6.9685

Arrieta, A. B., Díaz-Rodríguez, N., Del Ser, J., Bennetot, A., Tabik, S., Barbado, A., & Herrera, F. (2020). Explainable Artificial Intelligence (XAI): Concepts, taxonomies, opportunities and challenges toward responsible AI. *Information Fusion*, *58*, 82–115. DOI: 10.1016/j.inffus.2019.12.012

Ashfaq, S., Biswas, S., & Chowdhury, T. K. (2023). INTEGRATION OF ARTIFICIAL INTELLIGENCE AND ADVANCED COMPUTING TO DEVELOP RESILIENT CYBER DEFENSE SYSTEMS. *Journal of Sustainable Development and Policy*, *02*(04), 74–107. DOI: 10.63125/rxyc6y88

Baah, G. K., Hobson, T., Okhravi, H., Roberts, S. C., Streilein, W. W., & Yuditskaya, S. C. (2020). *A Study of Gaps in Cyber Defense Automation* (Issue October). https://www.dtic.mil/dtic/tr/fulltext/u2/1021685.pdf

Bada, M., & Nurse, J. R. C. (2019). The social and psychological impact of cyberattacks. In von Solms, R., & van Niekerk, L. (Eds.), *Cybersecurity and cybercrime* (pp. 1–18). Springer.

Balaji, B., Deepthi, T., Supriya, K., Kiran, P. S., & Riyaz, S. (n.d.). *Management of organ transplantation using blockchain.*

Balogun, A. Y. (2025). Strengthening compliance with data privacy regulations in US healthcare cybersecurity. *Asian journal of research in computer science, 18*(1), 154-173.

Banerjee, D., & Rao, T. S. (2022). Comprehensive Sex Education—Why Should We Care? *Journal of Psychosexual Health*, *4*(2), 73–75. DOI: 10.1177/26318318221092076

Barsoum, R. S. (2008). Trends in Unrelated-Donor Kidney Transplantation in the Developing World. *Pediatric Nephrology (Berlin, Germany)*, *23*(11), 1925–1929. Https://Doi.Org/10.1007/S00467-008-0858-2. DOI: 10.1007/s00467-008-0858-2 PMID: 18536939

Bawa, G., Singh, H., Rani, S., Kataria, A., & Min, H. (2024). Exploring perspectives of blockchain technology and traditional centralized technology in organ donation management: A comprehensive review. *Information (Basel)*, *15*(11), 703. DOI: 10.3390/info15110703

Bawa, G., Singh, H., Rani, S., Kataria, A., & Min, H. (2025). Smart traceable framework for transportation of transplantable organs using IPFS, iot, and smart contracts. *Scientific Reports*, *15*(1), 23364. DOI: 10.1038/s41598-025-06471-2 PMID: 40603944

Baxter, G., & Sommerville, I. (2011). Socio-technical systems: From design methods to systems engineering. *Interacting with Computers*, *23*(1), 4–17. DOI: 10.1016/j.intcom.2010.07.003

BBC. (2019, October 16). Dark Web Child Abuse: Hundreds Arrested Across 38 Countries. Https://Www.Bbc.Com/News/World-50073092. Https://Www.Bbc.Com/News/World-50073092

BBC. (2025, April 1). Child Abuse: Men Arrested in NI After Dark Web Site Take-Down. Https://Www.Bbc.Com/News/Articles/C2dexerd044o. Https://Www.Bbc.Com/News/Articles/C2dexerd044o

Bell, G., & Ebert, M. (2015). Health Care and Cyber Security. *Revista KPMG*, *1*(1), 2–3.

Benaroch, M. (2020). Cybersecurity risk in IT outsourcing—Challenges and emerging realities. In *Information systems outsourcing: The era of digital transformation* (pp. 313–334). Springer International Publishing. DOI: 10.1007/978-3-030-45819-5_13

Ben-Israel, D. (2025). Amendment 13 of Israel's Privacy Protection Law: A game-changer for data protection compliance? *Journal of Data Protection & Privacy*, *8*(1), 39–53.

Bernard, R., Bowsher, G., & Sullivan, R. (2020). Cyber security and the unexplored threat to global health: A call for global norms. *Global Security: Health, Science and Policy*, *5*(1), 134–141.

Bhandari, P. (2025). A guide to ethical considerations in research. *Scribbr*. https://www.scribbr.com/methodology/research-ethics/

Bhatia, R., & Reddy, A. (2024). Cybersecurity and compliance in clinical trials: The role of artificial intelligence in secure healthcare management. *Journal of Medical Systems*, *48*(2), 45. DOI: 10.1007/s10916-024-02034-2

Biasin, E. (2019). Medical devices cybersecurity: a growing concern?.

Biasin, E., Abie, H., Ferrario, D., Troiano, E., Soldatos, J., Di Peppo, F., . . . Markakis, E. (2021, September). Healthcare critical infrastructures protection and cybersecurity in the EU: regulatory challenges and opportunities. In *Consolidated Proceedings of thefirst ECSCI Workshop on Critical Infrastructure Protection* (pp. 43-46). Steinbeis-Edition.

Biasin, E., Kamenjašević, E., & Ludvigsen, K. R. (2024). Cybersecurity of AI medical devices: Risks, legislation, and challenges. In Solaiman, B., & Cohen, I. G. (Eds.), *Research handbook on health, AI and the law* (pp. 85–104). Edward Elgar Publishing. DOI: 10.4337/9781802205657.ch04

Bobba, C. M., Whitson, B. A., Henn, M. C., Mokadam, N. A., Keller, B. C., Rosenheck, J., & Ganapathi, A. M. (2022). Trends in donation after circulatory death in lung transplantation in the United States: Impact of era. *Transplant International*, *35*, 10172. DOI: 10.3389/ti.2022.10172 PMID: 35444490

Boddy, A., Hurst, W., Mackay, M., & El Rhalibi, A. (2020). A study into data analysis and visualisation to increase the cyber-resilience of healthcare infrastructures. *Proceedings of the 1st International Conference on Internet of Things and Machine Learning, January*, 1–7. DOI: 10.1145/3109761.3109793

Borghard, E. D., & Lonergan, S. W. (2017). The logic of coercion in cyberspace. *Security Studies*, *26*(3), 452–481. DOI: 10.1080/09636412.2017.1306396

Bornstein-Quevedo, L., de Anda-González, J., Lara-Torres, C. O., Flores-Gutiérrez, J. P., Dorantes-Heredia, R., Bautista-Piña, V., Zaragoza-Vargas, P., Alcaraz-Wong, A., Soto-Sañudo, A. K., Mendoza-Ramírez, S., Salamanca-García, M., Loyola-Rodríguez, G., Gómez-Macías, G. S., Murguia-Perez, M., De Luna-Sánchez, M., Villalobos-Valencia, R., Talamantes, E., & Arce-Salinas, C. (2024). Navigating HER2-low testing in invasive breast cancer: Update recommendations for pathologists. *Journal of Personalized Medicine*, *14*(5), 467. DOI: 10.3390/jpm14050467 PMID: 38793049

Bou Sleiman, M., & Gerdemann, S. (2021). Covid-19: A Catalyst for Cybercrime? international Cybersecurity. *Law Review*, *2*(1), 37–45. Https://Doi.Org/10.1365/S43439-021-00024-9

Boyarsky, B. (2021). *IMPACT OF COVID-19 ON SOLID ORGAN TRANSPLANTATION* (Doctoral dissertation, Johns Hopkins University).

Brady, S., & Heinl, C. (2020). Cybercrime: Current Threats and Responses A Review of the Research Literature. October.

Brand, M., Blycker, G. R., Laier, C., & Young, K. S. (2019). Integrating psychological and neurobiological considerations in problematic pornography use: An interactional model. *Journal of Behavioral Addictions*, *8*(3), 333–346. DOI: 10.1556/2006.8.2019.30

Brangeto, P., Maybaum, M., & Stinssen, J. (2022). 2022 6th International Conference on Cyber Conflict. In *2022 6th International Conference on Cyber Conflict*. https://extranet.cranfield.ac.uk/sites/default/files/multimedia/pdf/,DanaInfo=ccdcoe.org,SSL+CyCon_2014.pdf#page=66

Braun, V., & Clarke, V. (2006). Using thematic analysis in psychology. *Qualitative Research in Psychology*, *3*(2), 77–101. DOI: 10.1191/1478088706qp063oa

Bris, A. L. E., & Asri, W. E. L. (2023). State of Cybersecurity & Cyber Threats in Healthcare Organizations. *Dissertation*, 2005–2013. https://www.americanbar.org/content/dam/aba/publications/books/healthcare_data_breaches.authcheckdam.pdf

Brundage, M., Avin, S., Clark, J., Toner, H., Eckersley, P., Garfinkel, B., ... & Anderson, H. (2018). *The malicious use of artificial intelligence: Forecasting, prevention, and mitigation*. Future of Humanity Institute.

Buchanan, B., Bansemer, J., Cary, D., Lucas, J., & Musser, M. (2020). Automating Cyber Attacks: Hype and Reality. *Center for Security and Emerging Technology., November*, 1–48. https://cset.georgetown.edu/publication/automating-cyber-attacks/

Budiani-Saberi, D. A., & Delmonico, F. L. (2008). Organ trafficking and transplant tourism: A commentary on the global realities. *American Journal of Transplantation : Official Journal of the American Society of Transplantation and the American Society of Transplant Surgeons*, *8*(5), 925–929. DOI: 10.1111/j.1600-6143.2008.02200.x PMID: 18416734

Buolamwini, J., & Gebru, T. (2018, January). Gender shades: Intersectional accuracy disparities in commercial gender classification. In *Conference on fairness, accountability and transparency* (pp. 77-91). PMLR.

Burke, W., Stranieri, A., Oseni, T., & Gondal, I. (2024). The need for cybersecurity self-evaluation in healthcare. *BMC Medical Informatics and Decision Making*, *24*(1), 133. DOI: 10.1186/s12911-024-02551-x

Burns, A. J., Johnson, M. E., & Honeyman, P. (2016). A brief chronology of medical device security. *Communications of the ACM*, *59*(10), 66–72.

Burrell, D. N. (2024). Understanding healthcare cybersecurity risk management complexity. *Land Forces Academy Review*, *29*(1), 38–49.

Burrell, D. N. (2024). Understanding Healthcare Cybersecurity Risk Management Complexity. *Land Forces Academy Review*, *29*(1), 38–49. DOI: 10.2478/raft-2024-0004

Carrapico, H., & Farrand, B. (2017). *Cybercrime, cybersecurity and the European Union: The policy and regulatory context*. Springer.

Carr, M. (2016). Public–private partnerships in national cyber-security strategies. *International Affairs*, *92*(1), 43–62. DOI: 10.1111/1468-2346.12504

Catalani, V., Townshend, H. D., Prilutskaya, M., Roman-Urrestarazu, A., van Kessel, R., Chilcott, R. P., & Corazza, O. (2023). Profiling the vendors of COVID-19 related product on the Darknet: An observational study. *Emerging Trends in Drugs, Addictions, and Health*, *3*, 100051.

Cervero, A., Castro-Lopez, A., Alvarez-Blanco, L., & Tuero, E. (2024). Explanatory factors for problematic cybersex behaviour: The importance of negative emotions. *Current Psychology (New Brunswick, N.J.)*, *43*(20), 18109–18118. DOI: 10.1007/s12144-024-05639-9

Cheng, Y., Zhang, C., Zhang, Z., Meng, X., Hong, S., Li, W., . . . He, X. (2024). Exploring large language model based intelligent agents: Definitions, methods, and prospects. *arXiv preprint arXiv:2401.03428*.

Chik, W. B., & Sugumaran, H. (2024). Legal governance of artificial intelligence in healthcare devices and services in Singapore. *Research handbook on health, AI and the law*, 373-391.

Chow, J. C., & Li, K. (2024). Ethical considerations in human-centered AI: Advancing oncology chatbots through large language models. *JMIR Bioinformatics and Biotechnology*, *5*, e64406. DOI: 10.2196/64406 PMID: 39321336

Chua, J. A., & Pmp, C. (2021). Cybersecurity in the healthcare industry. *Physician Leadership Journal*, *8*(1), 69–72.

Chumo, B., Abok, A. M., & Mulongo, G. (2021). Collaborative cybersecurity intelligence sharing in Africa's tourism sector. *The African Journal of Information Systems*, *13*(2), 45–63.

Ciekanowski, Z., Gruchelski, M., Nowicka, J., Żurawski, S., & Pauliuchuk, Y. (2023). Cyberspace as a Source of New Threats to the Security of the European Union.

CISA. (2020). *Cybersecurity and Infrastructure Security Agency 2020 annual report*. U.S. Department of Homeland Security.

Cisco. (2019). Cisco 2019 Consumer Privacy Survey. November, 1–14.

Clarke, M., & Martin, K. (2024, January). Managing cybersecurity risk in healthcare settings. [). Sage CA: Los Angeles, CA: SAGE Publications.]. *Healthcare Management Forum*, *37*(1), 17–20.

Cockcroft, S., & Clutterbuck, P. (2001). Attitudes Towards information Privacy.

CodeBlue. (2023). MOH: Organ trade and trafficking illegal in Malaysia. *CodeBlue*. https://codeblue.galencentre.org/2023/04/moh-organ-trade-and-trafficking-illegal-in-malaysia/

Cohen, L. E., & Felson, M. (1979). Social change and crime rate trends: A routine activity approach. *American Sociological Review*, *44*(4), 588–608. DOI: 10.2307/2094589

Cohen, L. R. (2017). Increasing the supply of transplant organs: The virtues of a futures market. In *Organ and Tissue Transplantation* (pp. 121–171). Routledge. DOI: 10.4324/9781315247571-7

Columb, S., & Moniruzzaman, M. (2024). The state of the organ trade: Narratives of corruption in Egypt and Bangladesh. *Trends in Organized Crime*. Advance online publication. DOI: 10.1007/s12117-024-09524-6

Conti, M., Dehghantanha, A., Franke, K., & Watson, S. (2018). Internet of Things security and forensics: Challenges and opportunities. *Future Generation Computer Systems*, *78*, 544–546. DOI: 10.1016/j.future.2017.07.060

Cooper, A. (1998). Sexuality and the Internet: Surfing into the new millennium. *Cyberpsychology & Behavior*, *1*(2), 187–193. DOI: 10.1089/cpb.1998.1.187

Costanza, C., Vetri, L., Carotenuto, M., & Roccella, M. (2023). Use and Abuse of Digital Devices: Influencing Factors of Child and Adolescent Neuropsychology. *Clinics and Practice*, *13*(6), 1331–1334. DOI: 10.3390/clinpract13060119 PMID: 37987420

Council of Europe. (2020). Comprehensive sexuality education protects children and helps build a safer, inclusive society. *Commissioner for Human Rights*. Retrieved from https://www.coe.int/en/web/commissioner/-/comprehensive-sexuality-education-protects-children-and-helps-build-a-safer-inclusive-society, on 12 November 2025.

Coveney, C., Hudson, N., Lafuente-Funes, S., Jacxsens, L., & Provoost, V. (2022). From scarcity to sisterhood: The framing of egg donation on fertility clinic websites in the UK, Belgium and Spain. *Social Science & Medicine*, *296*, 114785. DOI: 10.1016/j.socscimed.2022.114785 PMID: 35151147

Coventry, L., & Branley, D. (2018). Cybersecurity in healthcare: A narrative review of trends, threats and ways forward. *Maturitas*, *113*, 48–52. DOI: 10.1016/j.maturitas.2018.04.008

Cowls, J., King, T., Taddeo, M., & Floridi, L. (2019). Designing AI for social good: Seven essential factors. *Available at SSRN* 3388669. DOI: 10.2139/ssrn.3388669

Craig, A. (2021). Cybersecurity cooperation in the digital age. *Journal of Cyber Policy*, *6*(3), 321–341. DOI: 10.1080/23738871.2021.1980464

Criado, J. I., & Gil-Garcia, J. R. (2019). Creating public value through smart technologies and data governance. *Public Administration Review*, *79*(3), 371–382.

Dajim, L. A., Al-Farras, S. A., Al-Shahrani, B. S., Al-Zuraib, A. A., & Mathew, R. M. (2019, May). Organ donation decentralized application using blockchain technology. In *2019 2nd International Conference on Computer Applications & Information Security (ICCAIS)* (pp. 1–4). IEEE. DOI: 10.1109/CAIS.2019.8769459

Daniels, N., & Sabin, J. E. (2008). *Setting limits fairly: learning to share resources for health*. Oxford University Press.

Dawson, M. (2018). Applying a holistic cybersecurity framework for global IT organizations. *Business Information Review*, *35*(2), 60–67.

Dawson, M., Omar, M., & Abramson, W. (2020). Trust and information sharing in cybersecurity alliances. *Journal of Strategic Security*, *13*(4), 48–69. DOI: 10.5038/1944-0472.13.4.1869

De L'europe. (2009). Trafficking in Organs, Tissues and Cells and Trafficking in Human Beings for the Purpose of the Removal of Organs Joint Council of Europe/ United Nations Study COUNCIL OF EUROPE CONSEIL. Chrome-Extension:// Efaidnbmnnnibpcajpcglclefindmkaj/Https://Www.Edqm.Eu/Documents/52006/ 75920/Joint-Council-United-Nations-Study-Tra1.Pdf/D657e60c-2919-1cc9-581e -Ebc5bf41dbe7?T=1629873068134

de Laat, P. B. (2021). Companies committed to responsible AI: From principles towards implementation and regulation? *Philosophy & Technology*, *34*(4), 1135–1193. DOI: 10.1007/s13347-021-00474-3 PMID: 34631392

De, K., & Salehi, M. A. (2025, September). Three Countries, Three Continents: AI Medical Device Regulation and Certification Comparison in the US, EU, and South Korea. In *International Conference on Medical Image Computing and Computer-Assisted Intervention* (pp. 36-45). Cham: Springer Nature Switzerland.

Deb, S., Lupu, E., Drakakis, E. M., Bharath, A. A., Leung, Z. K., Ma, G. R., & Chattopadhyay, A. (2025). Securing the Internet of Medical Things (IoMT): Real-World Attack Taxonomy and Practical Security Measures. *arXiv preprint arXiv:2507.19609*.

Delmonico, F. L., Domínguez-Gil, B., & Noel, L. (2022). Organ trafficking and transplant tourism: A global perspective. *Lancet*, *399*(10340), 2151–2160.

DeNardis, L. (2020). *The internet in everything: Freedom and security in a world with no off switch*. Yale University Press.

Dick Marty. (2010). Committee on Legal Affairs and Human Rights inhuman Treatment of People and Illicit Trafficking in Human Organs in Kosovo* 1 Report Rapporteur: Mr Dick Marty, Switzerland, Alliance of Liberals and Democrats for Europe.

Dong, T., Zhu, S., Oliveira, M., & Luo, X. (2023). Making better IS security investment decisions: Discovering the cost of data breach announcements during the COVID-19 pandemic. *Industrial Management & Data Systems*, *123*(2), 630–652.

Dunn Cavelty, M., & Egloff, F. J. (2020). The politics of cybersecurity: Balancing different roles of the state. *St. Antony's International Review*, *16*(1), 76–98.

Dunn Cavelty, M., & Suter, M. (2009). Public–private partnerships are no silver bullet: An expanded governance model for critical infrastructure protection. *International Journal of Critical Infrastructure Protection*, *2*(4), 179–187. DOI: 10.1016/j.ijcip.2009.08.006

Durand, W. M., Peters, J. L., Eltorai, A. E. M., Kalagara, S., Osband, A. J., & Daniels, A. H. (2018). Medical crowdfunding for organ transplantation. *Clinical Transplantation*, *32*(6), e13267. DOI: 10.1111/ctr.13267 PMID: 29683220

Dwork, C., & Roth, A. (2014). The algorithmic foundations of differential privacy. *Foundations and Trends in Theoretical Computer Science*, *9*(3-4), 211–407. DOI: 10.1561/0400000042

Economic Planning Unit. Malaysia. (2021). *Malaysia Digital Economy Blueprint (MyDIGITAL)*. Government of Malaysia. https://ekonomi.gov.my/sites/default/files/2021-02/malaysia-digital-economy-blueprint.pdf

Elemento, O., Leslie, C., Lundin, J., & Tourassi, G. (2021). Artificial intelligence in cancer research, diagnosis and therapy. *Nature Reviews. Cancer*, *21*(12), 747–752. DOI: 10.1038/s41568-021-00399-1 PMID: 34535775

ENISA. (2023). *Cybersecurity in healthcare: Risk management and governance*. European Union Agency for Cybersecurity.

Enoch, S. Y., Huang, Z., Moon, C. Y., Lee, D., Ahn, M. K., & Kim, D. S. (2020). HARMer: Cyber-Attacks Automation and Evaluation. *IEEE Access : Practical Innovations, Open Solutions*, *8*, 129397–129414. DOI: 10.1109/ACCESS.2020.3009748

Ernits, M., Tammekänd, J., & Maennel, O. (2023). i-tee:A fully automated Cyber Defense Competition for Students. *Computer Communication Review*, *45*(4), 113–114. DOI: 10.1145/2829988.2790033

Etheredge, H. R. (2021). Assessing global organ donation policies: Opt-in vs. opt-out. *Risk Management and Healthcare Policy*, *14*, 1985–1999. DOI: 10.2147/RMHP.S270234 PMID: 34012308

European Commission. (2016). *Directive (EU) 2016/1148 concerning measures for a high common level of security of network and information systems across the Union*.

European Union Agency for Cybersecurity. (2018). *Information sharing and analysis centers (ISACs): Cooperative models*. Publications Office of the European Union. https://www.enisa.europa.eu/publications/isacs-cooperative-models

European Union Agency for Cybersecurity. (2021). *ENISA threat landscape for the healthcare sector*. Publications Office of the European Union. https://www.enisa.europa.eu/publications/enisa-threat-landscape-for-the-healthcare-sector

European Union Agency for Cybersecurity. (2023). *Artificial intelligence and cybersecurity: Ethical considerations and data bias*. Publications Office of the European Union. https://www.enisa.europa.eu/publications/artificial-intelligence-and-cybersecurity-ethical-considerations-and-data-bias

Farook, M., Rafiuddin, B., Minhas, H., & Dhubb, P. S. (2017). A Dark Web Story in-Depth Research and Study Conducted on the Dark Webbased on forensic Computing and Security in Malaysia. 2017 IEEE international Conference on Power, Control, Signals and instrumentation Engineering (ICPCSI), May, 3049–3055.

Farringer, D. R. (2026). Cybersecurity Risk Shifting. *Vanderbilt Journal of Entertainment and Technology Law*, *28*(2), 49.

Fatima, H., Fatima Qadir, T., Moin, A., & Bilal Pasha, S. (2018). Pakistan: A Transplant Tourism Resort? *Journal of Public Health (Oxford, England), 40*(4), 899–899. Https://Doi.Org/10.1093/PUBMED/FDX157. DOI: 10.1093/pubmed/fdx157 PMID: 29149306

Fernandes, B., Arriaga, P., & Oliveira, A. (2020). Problematic pornography use: A literature review on neurobiological and psychological aspects. *Current Addiction Reports*, *7*(4), 494–505. DOI: 10.1007/s40429-020-00330-9

Finkelhor, D. (2018). *Child sexual abuse: New theory and research*. Free Press.

Finlayson, S. G., Bowers, J. D., Ito, J., Zittrain, J. L., Beam, A. L., & Kohane, I. S. (2019). Adversarial attacks on medical machine learning. *Science*, *363*(6433), 1287–1289. DOI: 10.1126/science.aaw4399 PMID: 30898923

Fliegelman, A., & Stemp, D. (2024). *The Cyberattack on Change Healthcare: Lessons for Financial Stability* (No. 24-05). Office of Financial Research, US Department of the Treasury.

Floridi, L. (2023). The ethics of artificial intelligence: Principles, challenges, and opportunities.

Friedman, B., Kahn, P. H.Jr, Borning, A., & Huldtgren, A. (2013). Value sensitive design and information systems. In *Early engagement and new technologies: Opening up the laboratory* (pp. 55–95). Springer Netherlands. DOI: 10.1007/978-94-007-7844-3_4

FS-ISAC. (2020). *Annual report*. Financial Services Information Sharing and Analysis Center.

Fujita, J., Aoyama, K., Saigusa, Y., Miyazaki, H., Aoki, Y., Asanuma, K., & Hishimoto, A. (2022). Problematic internet use and daily difficulties among adolescents with school refusal behaviors: An observational cross-sectional analytical study. *Medicine*, *101*(7), e28916. DOI: 10.1097/MD.0000000000028916 PMID: 35363214

Fu, X., Sahai, E., & Wilkins, A. (2023). Application of digital pathology-based advanced analytics of tumour microenvironment organisation to predict prognosis and therapeutic response. *The Journal of Pathology*, *260*(5), 578–591. DOI: 10.1002/path.6153 PMID: 37551703

Gal-Or, E., & Ghose, A. (2005). The economic incentives for sharing security information. *Information Systems Research*, *16*(2), 186–208. DOI: 10.1287/isre.1050.0053

Ganiga, R., Pai, R. M., & Sinha, R. K. (2020). Security framework for cloud based electronic health record (EHR) system. *International Journal of Electrical and Computer Engineering*, *10*(1), 455.

Garg, N. (2018). Towards the Impact of Hacking on Cyber Security. IIOABJ, 9 | 2 | 61(May), 61–77.

Ghafur, S., Kristensen, S., Honeyford, K., Martin, G., Darzi, A., & Aylin, P. (2019). A retrospective impact analysis of the WannaCry cyberattack on the NHS. *NPJ Digital Medicine*, *2*(1), 98.

Giletta, M., Choukas-Bradley, S., Maes, M., Linthicum, K. P., Card, N. A., & Prinstein, M. J. (2021). A meta-analysis of longitudinal peer influence effects in childhood and adolescence. *Psychological Bulletin*, *147*(7), 719–747. DOI: 10.1037/bul0000329 PMID: 34855429

Gilligan, C. (1982). The contribution of women's thought to developmental theory: The elimination of sex bias in moral development research and education.

Global Financial Integrity. (2017). Transnational crime and the developing world. https://gfintegrity.org/report/transnational-crime-and-the-developing-world/

Glowiak, M. (2025). Cybersex addiction: What it is, symptoms, & how to overcome. *Choosing Therapy*. https://www.choosingtherapy.com/cybersex-addiction/

Goh, H. L., Phuah, S. P., & Low, W. Y. (2023). Digital sexual behavior and pornography consumption among Malaysian adolescents. *Malaysian Journal of Medicine and Health Sciences*, *19*(2), 120–128.

Gola, M., Lewczuk, K., & Skorko, M. (2021). What matters in measuring pornography addiction? Psychometric analysis of the Problematic Pornography Consumption Scale. *Journal of Sex Research*, *58*(2), 168–178. DOI: 10.1080/00224499.2019.1692875

Goldreich, O. (2009). Foundations of cryptography: Volume 2, basic applications. Cambridge University Press. DOI: 10.1017/CBO9780511721656

Goodman, S., & Lin, H. (2019). *Toward a safer and more secure cyberspace*. National Academies Press.

Gourav Nagar, A. M. (2024). Understanding the Threat Landscape: a Comprehensive Analysis of Cyber-Security Risks in 2024. *Article in International Research Journal of Modernization in Engineering Technology and Science, 6*(3), 5706–5713. www.irjmets.com

Gstrein, O. J., Haleem, N., & Zwitter, A. (2024). General-purpose AI regulation and the European Union AI Act. *Internet Policy Review*, *13*(3), 1–26. DOI: 10.14763/2024.3.1790

Hao, Y., Liu, Z., Riter, R. N., & Kalantari, S. (2024, May). Advancing patient-centered shared decision-making with AI systems for older adult cancer patients. In *Proceedings of the 2024 CHI Conference on Human Factors in Computing Systems* (pp. 1–20). DOI: 10.1145/3613904.3642353

Haque, M. F., & Krishnan, R. (2021). Toward Automated Cyber Defense with Secure Sharing of Structured Cyber Threat Intelligence. *Information Systems Frontiers*, *23*(4), 883–896. DOI: 10.1007/s10796-020-10103-7

Harding, W., Hartmann, A., O'Brien, S., Sinzig, V., Break, G., & Sinzig, N. (2025). *Securing a Connected Future*. Springer Nature Switzerland., DOI: 10.1007/978-3-032-07309-9

Harkins, L., & Dixon, L. (2020). Sexual offending and family dysfunction: A review of research and implications for practice. *Aggression and Violent Behavior*, *55*, 101464. DOI: 10.1016/j.avb.2020.101464

Hawashin, D., Jayaraman, R., Salah, K., Yaqoob, I., Simsekler, M. C. E., & Ellahham, S. (2022). Blockchain-based management for organ donation and transplantation. *IEEE Access : Practical Innovations, Open Solutions*, *10*, 59013–59025. DOI: 10.1109/ACCESS.2022.3180008

Held, V. (2018). The ethics of care. *The Oxford handbook of distributive justice*, 213-234.

He, Y., Maglaras, L., Aliyu, A., & Luo, C. (2022). Healthcare Security Incident Response Strategy-A Proactive Incident Response (IR) Procedure. *Security and Communication Networks*, *2022*(1), 2775249.

Hippen, B. E. (2005). In defense of a regulated market in kidneys from living vendors. *The Journal of Medicine and Philosophy*, *30*(6), 593–626. DOI: 10.1080/03605310500421397 PMID: 16396787

Hovorushchenko, T., Hnatchuk, Y., Osyadlyi, V., Kapustian, M., & Boyarchuk, A. (2023). Blockchain-based medical decision support system. *Journal of Cyber Security and Mobility*, *12*(3), 253–273.

Howard, M., & LeBlanc, D. (2003). *Writing secure code*. Pearson Education.

Huang, D., Li, Z., Jiang, T., Yang, C., & Li, N. (2024). Artificial intelligence in lung cancer: Current applications, future perspectives, and challenges. *Frontiers in Oncology*, *14*, 1486310. DOI: 10.3389/fonc.2024.1486310 PMID: 39763611

Huda, S., Islam, M. R., Abawajy, J., Kottala, V. N. V., & Ahmad, S. (2024). A cyber risk assessment approach to federated identity management framework-based digital healthcare systems. *Sensors (Basel)*, *24*(16), 5282. DOI: 10.3390/s24165282 PMID: 39204976

Hulak, H., Skladannyi, P., Sokolov, V., Hulak, Y., & Korniiets, V. (2022). Dynamic model of guarantee capacity and cyber security management in the critical automated systems. *CEUR Workshop Proceedings*, *3530*, 102–111.

Humayed, A., Lin, J., Li, F., & Luo, B. (2017). Cyber-physical systems security—A survey. *IEEE Internet of Things Journal*, *4*(6), 1802–1831.

Hurel, L. M., & Weissinger, L. (2021). Cybersecurity information sharing governance: From cybersecurity to cyber-resilience. *Computers & Security*, *108*, 102312. Advance online publication. DOI: 10.1016/j.cose.2021.102312

Hussain, S., Mubeen, I., Ullah, N., Shah, S. S. U. D., Khan, B. A., Zahoor, M., Ullah, R., Khan, F. A., & Sultan, M. A. (2022). Modern diagnostic imaging technique applications and risk factors in the medical field: A review. *BioMed Research International*, *5164970*(1), 5164970. Advance online publication. DOI: 10.1155/2022/5164970 PMID: 35707373

Idris, N., Mansor, S., & Rahim, H. A. (2021). Online sexual exposure and risks among Malaysian children: A review of recent digital behaviour trends. *Journal of Child and Adolescent Cyberpsychology*, *9*(2), 45–57.

Ikegwu, A. C., Alo, U. R., & Nweke, H. F. (2025). Cyber threats in mobile healthcare applications: Systematic review of enabling technologies, threat models, detection approaches, and future directions. *Discover Computing*, *28*(1), 152. DOI: 10.1007/s10791-025-09686-z

Internet Society. (2018). 2018 Cyber incident & Breach Trends Report | internet [Cyber incident Breach Trends Report.]. *Society*, •••, 2018.

Islam, S., Papastergiou, S., Kalogeraki, E.-M., & Kioskli, K. (2022). Cyberattack Path Generation and Prioritisation for Securing Healthcare Systems. *Applied Sciences (Basel, Switzerland)*, *12*(9), 4443. DOI: 10.3390/app12094443

Islam, S., Papastergiou, S., & Mouratidis, H. (2021). A Dynamic Cyber Security Situational Awareness Framework for Healthcare ICT Infrastructures. *25th Pan-Hellenic Conference on Informatics,* November 2021, 334–339. DOI: 10.1145/3503823.3503885

Jalali, M. S., & Kaiser, J. P. (2018). Cybersecurity in hospitals: A systematic, organizational perspective. *Journal of Medical Internet Research*, *20*(5), e10059. DOI: 10.2196/10059

Jameel, W., Khan, M. A., & Rahman, A. (2023). Optimal graph convolutional neural network-based ransomware detection for cybersecurity in IoT environments. *Applied Sciences (Basel, Switzerland)*, *13*(8), 5167. DOI: 10.3390/app13085167

James Ashford. (2019, October 17). Hundreds Arrested in 'Dark Web' Paedophile Sting | the Week. Https://theweek.Com/103836/Hundreds-Arrested-in-Dark-Web-Paedophile-Sting Https://theweek.Com/103836/Hundreds-Arrested-in-Dark-Web-Paedophile-Sting

Javaid, M., Haleem, A., Singh, R. P., & Suman, R. (2023). Towards insighting cybersecurity for healthcare domains: A comprehensive review of recent practices and trends. *Cyber Security and Applications*, *1*, 100016.

Jobin, A., Ienca, M., & Vayena, E. (2019). The global landscape of AI ethics guidelines. *Nature Machine Intelligence*, *1*(9), 389–399. DOI: 10.1038/s42256-019-0088-2

Johnson, J. (2024). *The AI commander: centaur teaming, command, and ethical dilemmas*. Oxford University Press. DOI: 10.1093/oso/9780198892182.001.0001

Joinson, A. N. (2007). Disinhibition and the Internet. In Joinson, A. N., McKenna, K., Postmes, T., & Reips, U.-D. (Eds.), *The Oxford handbook of Internet psychology* (pp. 75–92). Oxford University Press.

Jones, C., & Seger, A. (2020)... *Guide for Criminal Justice Statistics on Cybercrime and Electronic Evidence.*, (October), 1–24.

Jony, A. I., & Hamim, S. A. (2023). Navigating the Cyber Threat Landscape: A Comprehensive Analysis of Attacks and Security in the Digital Age. *Journal of Information Technology and Cyber Security*, *1*(2), 53–67. DOI: 10.30996/jitcs.9715

Josfeld, L., Keinki, C., Pammer, C., Zomorodbakhsch, B., & Hübner, J. (2021). Cancer patients' perspective on shared decision-making and decision aids in oncology. *Journal of Cancer Research and Clinical Oncology*, *147*(6), 1725–1732. DOI: 10.1007/s00432-021-03579-6 PMID: 33682014

Joshi, P. P., Palande, A. K., Kode, A. A., Gaikwad, D. S., & Patil, R. (2024, March). LifeChain: Organ donation and transplantation system using blockchain. In *International Conference on Innovations in Cybersecurity and Data Science (ICICDS)* (pp. 759–773). Singapore: Springer Nature Singapore. DOI: 10.1007/978-981-97-5791-6_55

Justice & Care. (2023). Organ Trafficking Survivor Is Supported By Justice and Care. Https://Justiceandcare.Org/Stories/Organ-Trafficking-Survivor-Starts-To-Rebuild-Life-Supported-By-Justice-and-Care/.Https://Justiceandcare.Org/Stories/Organ-Trafficking-Survivor-Starts-To-Rebuild-Life-Supported-By-Justice-and-Care/

Kamaruddin, N., Rahim, N. A., & Halim, R. A. (2025). Cyberpsychological perspectives on pornography and sexual deviance: Implications for Malaysian youth. *Asian Journal of Cyber Behavior*, *7*(1), 33–52.

Kaur, B. (2025). Social Engineering Attacks in the Digital Age

Kaur, S., & Randhawa, S. (2020). Dark Web: A Web of Crimes. *Wireless Personal Communications*, *112*(4), 2131–2158. Https://Doi.Org/10.1007/S11277-020-07143-2. DOI: 10.1007/s11277-020-07143-2

Kelarijani, M. K. (2024). Can deceased donor transplantation alone eradicate the kidney waiting list? *Urology Journal*, *21*(04), 267–268. PMID: 37312602

Kenny, F., & Castilla-Rho, J. (2021). Cultural dynamics in multi-stakeholder cybersecurity governance. *Information & Management*, *58*(6), 103421. Advance online publication. DOI: 10.1016/j.im.2021.103421

Khairuddin, A., & Joseph, M. (2023). Online screen time and exposure to harmful content among Malaysian minors. *Malaysian Journal of Media and Communication Studies*, *12*(1), 33–49.

Khan, S. K., Shiwakoti, N., & Stasinopoulos, P. (2022). A conceptual system dynamics model for cybersecurity assessment of connected and autonomous vehicles. *Accident; Analysis and Prevention*, *165*, 106515.

Khoo, L. S., & Ballesté, C. (2024). A 25-year scoping review of the organ donation system in Malaysia: Past, present, and future. *Clinical Transplantation and Research*, *38*(3), 163–187. DOI: 10.4285/ctr.24.0020 PMID: 39099237

Kidnapped by a Paedophile I Met online - BBC News. (2016). Https://Www.Bbc.Com/News/Magazine-35730298

Kindervag, J. (2020). *Zero trust architecture*. Forrester Research.

Klievink, B., Romijn, B. J., Cunningham, S., & de Bruijn, H. (2017). Big data in the public sector: Uncertainties and readiness. *Information Systems Frontiers*, *19*(2), 267–283. DOI: 10.1007/s10796-016-9686-2

Kommareddy, A. (2024). *The UK Healthcare Cybersecurity Landscape Anudeep Kommareddy Supervisor : Apurva Vangujar.*

Kommisetty, P. D. N. K., Kuppala, B. M. S. R., & Buvvaji, H. V. (2022). Transforming Cyber Defense: Anomaly Detection and Predictive Analytics for Automated Threat Response. *International Journal of Engineering and Computer Science*, *11*(08), 25585–25600. DOI: 10.18535/ijecs/v11i08.4694

Kraus, S. W., & Sweeney, P. J. (2019). Behavioral addictions: The neurobiology of compulsion and its implications for treatment. *Current Psychiatry Reports*, *21*(3), 19. DOI: 10.1007/s11920-019-1009-7 PMID: 30826895

Kruse, C. S., Frederick, B., Jacobson, T., & Monticone, D. K. (2017). Cybersecurity in healthcare: A systematic review of modern threats and trends. *Technology and Health Care*, *25*(1), 1–10.

Kshetri, N. (2021). Evolving uses of artificial intelligence in human resource management in emerging economies in the global South: Some preliminary evidence. *Management Research Review*, *44*(7), 970–990. DOI: 10.1108/MRR-03-2020-0168

Kumar, S., & Patel, N. (2024). A review of federated learning: Techniques, challenges, and applications. *International Journal of Interdisciplinary Finance Insights*, *3*(3), 77–91.

Laier, C., Pawlikowski, M., Pekal, J., Schulte, F. P., & Brand, M. (2017). Cybersex addiction: Experienced sexual arousal when watching pornography and not real-life partners is linked to symptoms of Internet addiction. *Journal of Behavioral Addictions*, *6*(1), 26–36. DOI: 10.1556/2006.6.2017.005

Larijani, B., Zahedi, F., & Taheri, E. (2004, June). Ethical and legal aspects of organ transplantation in Iran. [). Elsevier.]. *Transplantation Proceedings*, *36*(5), 1241–1244. DOI: 10.1016/j.transproceed.2004.05.065 PMID: 15251302

LATES, I., & BOJA, C. (2025). Automating Attack and Defense Strategies in Cybersecurity. *Informatica Economica, 29*(1/2025), 5–15. DOI: 10.24818/issn14531305/29.1.2025.01

Leclerc, B., & Wortley, R. (2014). Predictors of victim disclosure in child sexual abuse: Additional evidence from a sample of incarcerated adult males. *Child Abuse & Neglect*, *38*(7), 1328–1338. DOI: 10.1016/j.chiabu.2014.02.010

Lee, S. H., Yeo, K. J., & Handayani, L. (2022). Sexual and reproductive health knowledge among primary school students in Malaysia. *Journal of Education and Health Promotion, 11*(89). Advance online publication. DOI: 10.4103/jehp.jehp_542_21 PMID: 35573611

Leibig, C., Brehmer, M., Bunk, S., Byng, D., Pinker, K., & Umutlu, L. (2022). Combining the strengths of radiologists and AI for breast cancer screening: A retrospective analysis. *The Lancet. Digital Health, 4*(7), e507–e519. DOI: 10.1016/S2589-7500(22)00070-X PMID: 35750400

Lei, C., Dang, K., Song, S., Wang, Z., Chew, S. P., Bian, R., Yang, X., Guan, Z., Lopes, C. I. M. A., Wang, M. H., Choy, R. W. C., Hu, X., Lai, K. K. H., Chong, K. K. L., Pang, C. P., Song, X., Su, J., Ding, X., & Zhou, H. (2025). AI-assisted facial analysis in healthcare: From disease detection to comprehensive management. *Patterns (New York, N.Y.), 6*(2), 101175. DOI: 10.1016/j.patter.2025.101175 PMID: 40041850

Levin, D. Z. (2001). Institutionalism, learning, and patterns of selective decoupling: The case of total quality management. In *annual meeting of the Academy of Management, Washington, DC.*

Lewis, J., & Gardiner, D. (2023). Ethical and legal issues associated with organ donation and transplantation. *Surgery (Oxford), 41*(9), 552–558. DOI: 10.1016/j.mpsur.2023.06.010

Lieneck, C., McLauchlan, M., & Phillips, S. (2023). Healthcare cybersecurity ethical concerns during the COVID-19 global pandemic: A rapid review. *Healthcare (Basel), 11*(22), 2983.

Liu, L., Hu, X., Ma, M., Zhang, W., Peng, B., Zhang, B., & Luo, X. (2025). Family and Peer Influences on Adolescent Psychological Inflexibility: A 1 Regression Mixture Analysis. *Frontiers in Psychology, 16*, 1650930. DOI: 10.3389/fpsyg.2025.1650930 PMID: 41143021

Lo, C. K., Ho, F. K., Emery, C., Chan, K. L., Wong, R. S., Tung, K. T., & Ip, P. (2021). Association of harsh parenting and maltreatment with internet addiction, and the mediating role of bullying and social support. *Child Abuse & Neglect, 113*, 104928. DOI: 10.1016/j.chiabu.2021.104928 PMID: 33429283

Lohn, A., Knack, A., & Jackson, K. (2023). *Autonomous Cyber Defence A roadmap from lab to ops*. Issue June. DOI: 10.51593/2022CA007

Lopez-Fernandez, O., Romo, L., Kern, L., Rousseau, A., Graziani, P., Rochat, L., Achab, S., Zullino, D., Landrø, N. I., Zacarés, J. J., Serra, E., Chóliz, M., Pontes, H. M., Griffiths, M. D., & Kuss, D. J. (2022). Perceptions underlying addictive technology use patterns: Insights for cognitive-behavioural therapy. *International Journal of Environmental Research and Public Health, 19*(1), 544. DOI: 10.3390/ijerph19010544 PMID: 35010804

Lorci, E. (2024). Thucydides Trap Revisited: An Alternative Explanation for the Ideologization of US-China Cyberspace Competition and Its Impact on Stability of Cyberspace. *Perspectives on Global Development and Technology, 22*(3-4), 190–216.

Luna, R., Rhine, E., Myhra, M., Sullivan, R., & Kruse, C. S. (2016). Cyber threats to health information systems: A systematic review. *Technology and Health Care, 24*(1), 1–9. DOI: 10.3233/THC-151102

MacIntyre, A. (2013). *After virtue*. A&C Black.

Malamuth, N. M., Huppin, M., & Linz, D. (2020). Pornography, individual differences in risk and men's acceptance of violence against women: Testing the confluence model again. *Aggressive Behavior, 46*(3), 254–264. DOI: 10.1002/ab.21995 PMID: 32124999

Malay Mail. (2019, June 11). *Survey finds 80% of Malaysian teens have viewed pornography*. https://www.malaymail.com

Manla, Y., AlSindi, F., Attallah, N., Al Badarin, F., Ghalib, H., & Bader, F. (2022, March). Temporal trends in brain-death organ donation in Asia: Results from the Global Observatory on Donation and Transplantation. [). Elsevier.]. *Transplantation Proceedings, 54*(2), 233–236. DOI: 10.1016/j.transproceed.2021.12.031 PMID: 35067376

Manyika, J., Chui, M., Bughin, J., Dobbs, R., Bisson, P., & Marrs, A. (2013). *Disruptive technologies: Advances that will transform life, business, and the global economy*. McKinsey Global Institute.

Marchi, N. C., Fara, L., Gross, L., Ornell, F., Diehl, A., & Kessler, F. H. P. (2021). Problematic consumption of online pornography during the COVID-19 pandemic: Clinical recommendations. *Trends in Psychiatry and Psychotherapy, 43*(3), 159–166. DOI: 10.47626/2237-6089-2020-0090 PMID: 34043899

Marks, G., & Hooghe, L. (2004). Contrasting visions of multi-level governance. In Bache, I., & Flinders, M. (Eds.), *Multi-level governance* (pp. 15–30). Oxford University Press. DOI: 10.1093/0199259259.003.0002

Martin, G., Martin, P., Hankin, C., Darzi, A., & Kinross, J. (2017). Cybersecurity and healthcare: How safe are we? *BMJ (Clinical Research Ed.)*, •••, 358.

Matthew, E. Mori. (2023). PROTECTING NETWORKS VIA AUTOMATED DEFENSE OF CYBER SYSTEMS. *Security, September*. https://doi.org/July 01, 2016

McGhin, T., Choo, K. K. R., Liu, C. Z., & He, D. (2019). Blockchain in healthcare applications: Research challenges and opportunities. *Journal of Network and Computer Applications*, *135*, 62–75. DOI: 10.1016/j.jnca.2019.02.027

Mcgowan, A., Sittig, S., & Andel, T. (2021). Medical Internet of Things: A Survey of the Current Threat and Vulnerability Landscape. *Proceedings of the Annual Hawaii International Conference on System Sciences, 2020-Janua*, 3850–3858. DOI: 10.24251/HICSS.2021.466

MCMC (Malaysian Communications and Multimedia Commission). (2022). *Internet users survey 2022*. MCMC.

Medema, W., Wals, A. E. J., & Adamowski, J. (2017). Network governance and bridging organizations in environmental management. *Ecology and Society*, *22*(2), 1. Advance online publication. DOI: 10.5751/ES-09244-220201

Mehrabi, N., Morstatter, F., Saxena, N., Lerman, K., & Galstyan, A. (2021). A survey on bias and fairness in machine learning. *ACM Computing Surveys*, *54*(6), 1–35. DOI: 10.1145/3457607

Mehra, C., & Sharma, A. K. (2025). Safeguarding the Landscape of Mental Wellness: Analyzing Cyber Threats and Mitigation Strategies in Digital Healthcare. *Procedia Computer Science*, *260*, 22–31. DOI: 10.1016/j.procs.2025.03.173

Mergel, I., Edelmann, N., & Haug, N. (2019). Defining digital transformation: Results from expert interviews. *Government Information Quarterly*, *36*(4), 101385. DOI: 10.1016/j.giq.2019.06.002

Miller, R., Michalak, P., & Soper, R. (2019). Blockchain for cybersecurity and privacy. *Journal of Cybersecurity*, *5*(1), 1–14. DOI: 10.1093/cybsec/tyz005

Minnaar, A., & Herbig, F. J. (2021). Cyberattacks and the cybercrime threat of ransomware to hospitals and healthcare services during the COVID-19 pandemic. *Acta Criminologica: African Journal of Criminology & Victimology*, *34*(3), 155–185.

Mirsky, Y., Mahler, T., Shelef, I., & Elovici, Y. (2019). {CT-GAN}: Malicious tampering of 3d medical imagery using deep learning. In *28th USENIX Security Symposium (USENIX Security 19)* (pp. 461-478).

Mirza, A. I., & Adrian, G. (2023). *Next-Level Cyber Defense: AI-Powered Automation in Resilient Healthcare and Cloud Systems*. https://www.researchgate.net/publication/393794159_Next-Level_Cyber_Defense_AI-Powered_Automation_in_Resilient_Healthcare_and_Cloud_Systems

Mohammed, D., Mariani, R., & Mohammed, S. (2015). Cybersecurity challenges and compliance issues within the US healthcare sector. *International journal of business and social research, 5*(2), 55-66.

Mohd Amin, N., & Fariduddin, M. N. (2023). How comprehensive sexuality education is implemented and perceived in Malaysia: A systematic review. *International Journal of Academic Research in Progressive Education and Development, 12*(2). Advance online publication. DOI: 10.6007/IJARPED/v12-i2/17366

Mohd Din, N. A. (2019). Pendidikan Jasmani dan Pendidikan Kesihatan Tingkatan 4. *Telaga Biru Sdn. Bhd.* Retrieved from https://anyflip.com/ypvzd/vkum/basic/201-242, on 14 November 2025.

Mohd Yunos, N. A., & Althabawi, M. A. (2021). Pornography exposure and digital sexual behavior among Malaysian youth during COVID-19 lockdowns. *Journal of Media and Society, 9*(2), 76–93.

Mokdad, M. (2025). The rise of soft power in modern diplomacy. In *Innovations and Tactics for 21st Century Diplomacy* (pp. 29–50). IGI Global.

Mudiayi, D., Shojai, S., Okpechi, I., Christie, E. A., Wen, K., Kamaleldin, M., Elsadig Osman, M., Lunney, M., Prasad, B., Osman, M. A., Ye, F., Khan, M., Htay, H., Caskey, F., Jindal, K. K., Klarenback, S., Jha, V., Rondeau, E., Turan Kazancioglu, R., & Bello, A. K. (2022). Global estimates of capacity for kidney transplantation in world countries and regions. *Transplantation, 106*(6), 1113–1122. DOI: 10.1097/TP.0000000000003943 PMID: 34495014

Mühlhoff, R. (2025). *The ethics of AI: Power, critique, responsibility*. Bristol University Press.

Murray, A. L., Eisner, M., & Ribeaud, D. (2022). Developmental pathways to sexual offending: The role of family dysfunction and early trauma. *Child Abuse & Neglect, 126*, 105532. DOI: 10.1016/j.chiabu.2022.105532

Mwaura, M. W. (2025). *Challenges Encountered in Using Information Security Metrics to Improve Patient Safety in Public Hospitals, Nairobi Metropolitan, Kenya* (Doctoral dissertation, Kenyatta University).

MyDIGITAL. (2021). *Malaysia Digital Economy Blueprint*. Government of Malaysia. https://www.mydigital.gov.my/

Nakshine, V. S., Thute, P., Khatib, M. N., & Sarkar, B. (2022). Increased screen time as a cause of declining physical, psychological health, and sleep patterns: A literary review. *Cureus, 14*(10). Advance online publication. DOI: 10.7759/cureus.30051 PMID: 36381869

Nannatt, A., Tariang, N. M., Gowda, M., & Devassy, S. M. (2022). Family factors associated with problematic use of the internet in children: A scoping review. *Indian Journal of Psychological Medicine, 44*(4), 341–348. DOI: 10.1177/02537176221090862 PMID: 35949634

Nasir, N. (2021). Cultural silence and victimization: Understanding incest in Malaysian families. *Malaysian Journal of Family Studies, 8*(1), 22–37.

Nassar, S. I., Suk, A., Nguyen, S. A., Adilbay, D., Pang, J., & Nathan, C. A. O. (2024). The role of ctDNA and liquid biopsy in the diagnosis and monitoring of head and neck cancer: Towards precision medicine. *Cancers (Basel), 16*(18), 3129. DOI: 10.3390/cancers16183129 PMID: 39335101

Natsiavas, P., Rasmussen, J., Voss-Knude, M., Votis, K., Coppolino, L., Campegiani, P., & Koutkias, V. (2018). Comprehensive user requirements engineering methodology for secure and interoperable health data exchange. *BMC Medical Informatics and Decision Making, 18*(1), 85.

Nesbit, R., & Von Thaer, L. (2024). *Defense Science Board Task Force Report on Cyber Defense Management.* Issue September.

Newman, L. H. (2020). Ransomware hits dozens of hospitals in an unprecedented wave. *Wired, Oct.*

Ng, W. Y., Tan, T. E., Movva, P. V., Fang, A. H. S., Yeo, K. K., Ho, D., Foo, F. S. S., Xiao, Z., Sun, K., Wong, T. Y., Sia, A. T.-H., & Ting, D. S. W. (2021). Blockchain applications in healthcare for COVID-19 and beyond: A systematic review. *The Lancet. Digital Health, 3*(12), e819–e829. DOI: 10.1016/S2589-7500(21)00210-7 PMID: 34654686

NIJ. (2001). Electronic Crime Scene investigation Guide: A Guide for First Responders. United States Department of Justice office of Justice, 93.

Niraula, D., Cuneo, K. C., Dinov, I. D., Gonzalez, B. D., Jamaluddin, J. B., Jin, J. J., Luo, Y., Matuszak, M. M., Ten Haken, R. K., Bryant, A. K., Dilling, T. J., Dykstra, M. P., Frakes, J. M., Liveringhouse, C. L., Miller, S. R., Mills, M. N., Palm, R. F., Regan, S. N., Rishi, A., & El Naqa, I. (2025). Intricacies of human–AI interaction in dynamic decision-making for precision oncology. *Nature Communications, 16*(1), 1138. DOI: 10.1038/s41467-024-55259-x PMID: 39881134

Nkwo, M., Ikwunne, T., Adejoro, C., & Anuyah, O. (2025). Exploring Usability of AI Systems in the Global South—Toward Responsible Human-Centered AI for Sustainable Cities and Communities. In *Usability for the World: Building Better Cities and Communities* (pp. 125–165). Springer Nature Switzerland. DOI: 10.1007/978-3-031-88326-2_5

Nordfonn, A., Morken, I. M., & Thorstensen, E. (2021). Participatory design in developing digital cardiac rehabilitation programs: Lessons for co-creation. *Digital Health, 7*, 1–13. DOI: 10.1177/20552076211024564

Norman, A. A., & Othman, N. (2020). Ketagihan pornografi dalam kalangan remaja: Faktor dan implikasi terhadap sahsiah diri remaja. *Jurnal Melayu*, 19(2).

Nurse, J. R. (2018). Cybercrime and you: How criminals attack and the human factors that they seek to exploit. *arXiv preprint arXiv:1811.06624*.

Nyberg, J., & Johnson, P. (2023). Learning automated defense strategies using graph-based cyber attack simulations. *Proceedings 2023 Workshop on Security Operation Center Operations and Construction*. DOI: 10.14722/wosoc.2023.23006

Nye, J. S. (2010). *Cyber power*. Harvard Kennedy School.

Nye, J. S.Jr. (2017). Deterrence and dissuasion in cyberspace. *International Security, 41*(3), 44–71. DOI: 10.1162/ISEC_a_00266

O'Leary, D. (2023). Organ Transplants: How the internet Enables the Dark Side | Mind Matters.

Obermeyer, Z., Powers, B., Vogeli, C., & Mullainathan, S. (2019). Dissecting racial bias in an algorithm used to manage the health of populations. *Science, 366*(6464), 447–453. DOI: 10.1126/science.aax2342 PMID: 31649194

OECD. (2015). *Digital security risk management for economic and social prosperity*. OECD Publishing. Organisation for Economic Co-operation and Development. (2015). *Digital security risk management for economic and social prosperity: OECD recommendation and companion document*. OECD Publishing. https://doi.org/DOI: 10.1787/9789264245471-en

OECD. (2023). *Digital government policy framework*. OECD Publishing.

Official Website of the United Nations Educational, Scientific and Cultural Organization. (2023). Comprehensive sexuality education: For healthy, informed and empowered learners. *United Nations Educational, Scientific and Cultural Organization*. Retrieved from https://www.unesco.org/en/health-education/cse#:~:text=When%20delivered%20well%20and%20combined,pregnancies%2C%20HIV%20and%20other%20sexually, on 12 November 2025.

Okoye, O., Uche, N., Uzokwe, N., & Umeh, R. (2025). Must we remain blind to the need for clinical ethics support services in Africa? Eyes on Nigeria. *Postgraduate Medicine*, *137*(1), 18–27. DOI: 10.1080/00325481.2024.2433933 PMID: 39604113

Oladoyinbo, T. O., Olabanji, S. O., Olaniyi, O. O., Adebiyi, O. O., Okunleye, O. J., & Ismaila Alao, A. (2024). Exploring the challenges of artificial intelligence in data integrity and its influence on social dynamics. *Asian Journal of Advanced Research and Reports*, *18*(2), 1–23.

Olagunju, A. A. (2025). Role of Artificial Intelligence and Machine Learning in the Identification, Diagnosis, and Monitoring of Disease Conditions and Health Epidemics. In *Health Technologies and Informatics* (pp. 130–144). CRC Press.

Olaniyi, O. O., Omogoroye, O. O., Olaniyi, F. G., Alao, A. I., & Oladoyinbo, T. O. (2024). CyberFusion protocols: Strategic integration of enterprise risk management, ISO 27001, and mobile forensics for advanced digital security in the modern business ecosystem. *Journal of Engineering Research and Reports*, *26*(6), 31–49.

Olateju, O., Okon, S. U., Igwenagu, U., Salami, A. A., Oladoyinbo, T. O., & Olaniyi, O. O. (2024). Combating the challenges of false positives in AI-driven anomaly detection systems and enhancing data security in the cloud. *Available at SSRN* 4859958.

Olawade, D. B., Marinze, S., Qureshi, N., Weerasinghe, K., & Teke, J. (2025). Transforming organ donation and transplantation: Strategies for increasing donor participation and system efficiency. *European Journal of Internal Medicine*, *133*, 14–24. DOI: 10.1016/j.ejim.2024.11.010 PMID: 39572291

Organisation for Economic Cooperation and Development. (2016). Managing Digital Security and Privacy Risk: 2016 Ministerial Meeting on the Digital Economy. Background Report. OECD Digital Economy Papers, 254.

Ostermann, M., Mathias, R., Jahed, F., Parker, M. B., Hudson, F. D., Harding, W. C., & Freyer, O. (2025). Cybersecurity requirements for medical devices in the EU and US-A comparison and gap analysis of the MDCG 2019-16 and FDA premarket cybersecurity guidance. *Computational and Structural Biotechnology Journal*.

Owoyemi, A., Owoyemi, J., Osiyemi, A., & Boyd, A. (2020). Artificial intelligence for healthcare in Africa. *Frontiers in Digital Health, 2*, 6. DOI: 10.3389/fdgth.2020.00006 PMID: 34713019

Pal, P., Webber, F., Atighetchi, M., Rubel, P., & Benjamin, P. (2020). Automating cyber-defense management. *Proceedings of the 2nd Workshop on Recent Advances on Intrusiton-Tolerant Systems,* April 2008, 1–6. DOI: 10.1145/1413901.1413904

Panigrahi, R. R. (2025). A study on organ supply chains and transplant processes: Blockchain adoption and transparency. *MDPI Logistics, 9*(1), 9. DOI: 10.3390/logistics9010009

Parmar, A. (2012). *Hacker shows off vulnerabilities of wireless insulin pumps.* MedCity News.

Patel, C. (2025). *Cyber Security, Privacy, and Network Security: Navigating the Evolving Threat Landscape*. DOI: 10.2139/ssrn.5069925

Patil, R. Y., Patil, Y. H., Gupta, S. K., & Bannore, A. (2022). Organ donation and transplantation challenges, opportunities, and the role of blockchain. In *Disruptive Developments in Biomedical Applications* (pp. 325–339). DOI: 10.1201/9781003272694-27

Patil, R. Y., Patil, Y. H., & Thepade, S. D. (2024). The legal and ethical issues in organ donation and transplantation—A bibliometric analysis. *International Journal of Biomedical Engineering and Technology, 44*(1), 80–101. DOI: 10.1504/IJBET.2024.136394

Petersen, K. L. (2021). Public–private partnerships in cybersecurity: A global perspective. *Journal of Strategic Security, 14*(2), 1–23. DOI: 10.5038/1944-0472.14.2.1919

Piazza, A., & Vasudevan, S. (2025). Mapping the Cyberthreat Landscape in Healthcare Using GDELT: A Multimethod Approach. *Health Security, 23*(3), 186–197. DOI: 10.1089/hs.2024.0016

Pieterse, H. (2021). The Cyber Threat Landscape in South Africa: A 10-Year Review. *The African Journal of Information and Communication, 28*(28), 1–21. DOI: 10.23962/10539/32213

Privara, M., & Bob, P. (2023). Pornography consumption and cognitive-affective distress. *The Journal of Nervous and Mental Disease, 211*(8), 641–646. DOI: 10.1097/NMD.0000000000001669 PMID: 37505898

Provan, K. G., & Kenis, P. (2008). Modes of network governance: Structure, management, and effectiveness. *Journal of Public Administration: Research and Theory, 18*(2), 229–252. DOI: 10.1093/jopart/mum015

Qu, Z., Oedingen, C., Bartling, T., Beneke, J., Zink, M., Krauth, C., & Schrem, H. (2021). Systematic review on potential brain-dead donor estimations and conversion rates to actually realized organ donations. *Transplantation Reviews*, *35*(4), 100638. DOI: 10.1016/j.trre.2021.100638 PMID: 34246111

Radanliev, P., De Roure, D., Nurse, J. R. C., & Montalvo, R. M. (2020). The cybersecurity challenges of the Internet of Things. *Internet of Things : Engineering Cyber Physical Human Systems*, *12*, 100313. Advance online publication. DOI: 10.1016/j.iot.2020.100313

Radu, R. (2019). *Negotiating internet governance*. Oxford University Press. DOI: 10.1093/oso/9780198833079.001.0001

Rahim, M. J., Rahim, M. I. I., Afroz, A., & Akinola, O. (2024). Cybersecurity threats in healthcare it: Challenges, risks, and mitigation strategies. *Journal of Artificial Intelligence General science(JAIGS) ISSN: 3006-4023*, *6*(1), 438-462.

Rahman, M. H., Hossan, K. M. R., Uddin, M. K. S., & Hossain, M. D. (2024). Improving collaborative interactions between humans and artificial intelligence to achieve optimal patient outcomes in the healthcare industry. *SSRN* 5029975. DOI: 10.2139/ssrn.5029975

Raimo, N., Ricciardelli, A., Rubino, M., & Vitolla, F. (2023). Artificial intelligence and digital transformation: Key insights for organizational change. *Technological Forecasting and Social Change*, *184*, 122009.

Raizada, N., & Biswal, M. (2024). AN EVIDENCE-BASED INVESTIGATION OF CERT-IN'S REPORTING ON CYBER-THREATS IN HEALTHCARE SECTOR. *Conhecimento & Diversidade*, *16*(42), 219–246. DOI: 10.18316/rcd.v16i42.11694

Raji, I. D., Kumar, I. E., Horowitz, A., & Selbst, A. (2022, June). The fallacy of AI functionality. In *Proceedings of the 2022 ACM Conference on Fairness, Accountability, and Transparency* (pp. 959-972). DOI: 10.1145/3531146.3533158

Rampersad, C., Ahn, C., Callaghan, C., Dominguez-Gil, B., Ferreira, G. F., Kute, V., Rahmel, A. O., Sarwal, M., Snyder, J., Wang, H., Wong, G., & Kim, S. J. (2024). Organ donation and transplantation registries across the globe: A review of the current state. *Transplantation*, *108*(10), e321–e326. DOI: 10.1097/TP.0000000000005043 PMID: 38685195

Ranjan, P., Srivastava, S., Gupta, V., Tapaswi, S., & Kumar, N. (2019, December). Decentralised and distributed system for organ/tissue donation and transplantation. In *2019 IEEE Conference on Information and Communication Technology* (pp. 1–6). IEEE. DOI: 10.1109/CICT48419.2019.9066225

Rasulova, S. (2025). The Role Of International Organizations In Ensuring Cybersecurity (UU, Interpol, Enisa And Others). *TLEP–International Journal of Multidiscipline*, *2*(4), 216–220.

Rawat, R., Díaz-Álvarez, J., & Chávez, F. (2024). Systematic Literature Review and Assessment for Cyber Terrorism Communication and Recruitment Activities. *Technology Innovation for Business Intelligence and Analytics (TIBIA) Techniques and Practices for Business Intelligence Innovation*, 83-108.

Rawat, R., Garg, B., Mahor, V., Telang, S., Pachlasiya, K., & Chouhan, M. (2022). Organ trafficking on the dark web—The data security and privacy concern in healthcare systems. *Internet of Healthcare Things: Machine Learning for Security and Privacy*, 189-216.

Rawat, R., Garg, B., Mahor, V., & Telang, S. (2022). Organ trafficking on the dark web: Data security and privacy concerns in healthcare systems. In *Internet of healthcare things* (pp. 189–216). Springer. DOI: 10.1002/9781119792468.ch9

Rawls, J. (1971). A Theory of Justice. 2. *The Law of Peoples, 67*.

Reddy Boda, V. V., & Immaneni, J. (2023). Automating Security in Healthcare: What Every IT Team Needs to Know. *International Journal of Artificial Intelligence, Data Science, and Machine Learning*, *4*(2), 46–56. DOI: 10.63282/3050-9262.IJAIDSML-V4I2P106

Regulation, P. (2016). Regulation (EU) 2016/679 of the European Parliament and of the Council. [eu]. *Regulation*, *679*, 10–13.

Reverberi, C., Rigon, T., Solari, A., Hassan, C., Cherubini, P., & Cherubini, A. (2022). Experimental evidence of effective human-AI collaboration in medical decision-making. *Scientific Reports*, *12*(1), 14952. DOI: 10.1038/s41598-022-18751-2 PMID: 36056152

Ridley, A. (2020). Machine learning for autonomous cyber defense. *The Next Wave*, *22*(1), 7–14.

Rodriguez-Iturbe, B. (2008). Organ Trafficking: A Time for Action. *Kidney International*, *74*(7), 839–840. Https://Doi.Org/10.1038/Ki.2008.389. DOI: 10.1038/ki.2008.389 PMID: 18794811

Roman-Urrestarazu, A., Kinsey, J., & van Kessel, R. (2022). A bill of children's digital rights is required to improve and sustain children's futures globally. *JAMA Pediatrics*, *176*(11), 1064–1066.

Rothrock, R. A., Kaplan, J., & Van Der Oord, F. (2018). The board's role in managing cybersecurity risks. *MIT Sloan Management Review*, *59*(2), 12–15.

Royal Malaysia Police. (2022). *Annual crime statistics report 2022*. Bukit Aman: RMP Publication Unit.

Rudd, L., Hajkowicz, S., Nepal, S., Boughen, N., & Reeson, A. (2015). *Fast Forward: Scenarios for Queensland in the Year 2025 Describing the Marketplace for Education, Healthcare, Policing, Transport and Other Public Services: a Scenario Planning Exercise about the Digital Marketplace for Government Services in the Future to Inform Decision Makers*. Department of Science, Information Technology and Innovation and CSIRO.

Ryan K. L. Ko. (2018). Cyber Autonomy : Automating the Hacker. *Automatic Cyber Defense Systems*, 1–15.

Saha, B., & Anwar, Z. (2024). A review of cybersecurity challenges in small business: The imperative for a future governance framework. *Journal of Information Security*, *15*(01), 24–39.

Sain, M. K., Gupta, J., Rathore, P., & Bansal, R. (2020). ARTIFICIAL INTELLIGENCE IN CYBER DEFENCE. *International Journal of Psychosocial Rehabilitation*, *11403–11405*, 11403–11405. Advance online publication. DOI: 10.61841/V24I7/400273

Sajid, S., Nazir, M., & Aijaz, M. (2025, July). Beyond Severity: Tactical Risk Scoring for Healthcare Vulnerabilities. In *2025 2nd International Conference On Multidisciplinary Research and Innovations in Engineering (MRIE)* (pp. 427-432). IEEE.

Samuel-Okon, A. D., Akinola, O. I., Olaniyi, O. O., Olateju, O. O., & Ajayi, S. A. (2024). Assessing the effectiveness of network security tools in mitigating the impact of deepfakes AI on public trust in media. *Archives of Current Research International*, *24*(6), 355–375.

Sanger, D. E. (2018). *The perfect weapon: War, sabotage, and fear in the cyber age*. Crown.

Saxena, D., Trivedi, P., Bhavsar, P., Memon, F., Thaker, A., Chaudhary, C., Yasobant, S., Singhal, D., & Zodpey, S. (2023). Challenges and motivators to organ donation: A qualitative exploratory study in Gujarat, India. *International Journal of General Medicine*, *16*, 151–159. DOI: 10.2147/IJGM.S393240 PMID: 36687162

Saxena, S., Jena, B., Gupta, N., Das, S., Sarmah, D., Bhattacharya, P., Nath, T., Paul, S., Fouda, M. M., Kalra, M., Saba, L., Pareek, G., & Suri, J. S. (2022). Role of artificial intelligence in radiogenomics for cancers in the era of precision medicine. *Cancers (Basel)*, *14*(12), 2860. DOI: 10.3390/cancers14122860 PMID: 35740526

Schwab, K. (2016). *The fourth industrial revolution*. World Economic Forum.

Sebastian Traxl. (2013). Trafficking in Human Beings for the Purpose of Organ Removal in the OSCE Region: Analysis and Findings. OSCE office of the Special Representative and Co-Ordinator for Combating Trafficking in Human Beings. Chrome-Extension://Efaidnbmnnnibpcajpcglclefindmkaj/Https://Www.Osce.Org/Sites/Default/Files/F/Documents/E/B/103393.Pdf

Selesi-Aina, O., Obot, N. E., Olisa, A. O., Gbadebo, M. O., Olateju, O., & Olaniyi, O. O. (2024). The future of work: A human-centric approach to AI, robotics, and cloud computing. *Journal of Engineering Research and Reports*, *26*(11), 10–9734.

Seto, M. C. (2019). *Pedophilia and sexual offending against children: Theory, assessment, and intervention* (2nd ed.). American Psychological Association., DOI: 10.1037/0000136-000

Shah, M. S., Ahsan, M. M., Tasnim, L., Afrin, S., Hashan, R., Islam, M. K., & Ahmed, M. M. (2024). Federated learning in healthcare: Model misconducts, security, challenges, applications, and future research directions—A systematic review. *arXiv preprint* arXiv:2405.13832.

Shakeel, P. M., Burhanuddin, M. A., & Desa, M. I. (2022). Automatic lung cancer detection from CT image using improved deep neural network and ensemble classifier. *Neural Computing & Applications*, *34*(3), 1–14. DOI: 10.1007/s00521-020-04842-6

Sham, F., Yaakub, S., Nur Fawati, F., Fatinni, S. J., & Azamuddin, A. A. (2024). Knowledge, attitudes, risk behaviours and preventive practices on sexually-transmitted diseases (STDs) among students in a public university in Malaysia. *Malaysian Journal of Public Health Medicine*, *20*(3).

Shanto, M. I., Sultana, J., Sarwar, S., Johora, N. T., & Popy, F. P. (2026). Data-Centric Business Analysis in Agile Software Development to Fortify Cybersecurity Posture for US Healthcare Systems. *EJSMT*, *2*(1), 184–204.

Shapiro, M. A., Stuhlmiller, T. J., Wasserman, A., Kramer, G. A., Federowicz, B., Hoos, W., Kaufman, Z., Chuyka, D., Mahoney, W., Newton, M. E., Osking, Z., Wong, K. K., Kesari, S., & Shrager, J. (2024). AI-augmented clinical decision support in a patient-centric precision oncology registry. *AI in Precision Oncology*, *1*(1), 58–68. DOI: 10.1089/aipo.2023.0001

Sharma, M. K., Anand, N., Thakur, P. C., Sahu, N., John, M., & Murthy, K. D. (2020). Pathways to cybersex: Case-report-based exploration. *Journal of Psychosexual Health, 2*(1), 96–99. DOI: 10.1177/2631831819898567

Shen, Y., Zhou, Y., Ren, S., Li, Y., Liu, Y., Zhou, R., Fan, X., & Xie, G. (2025). Relations between peer bullying and adolescent depression: The mediating effect of cellphone usage. *Frontiers in Psychiatry, 16*, 1486628. DOI: 10.3389/fpsyt.2025.1486628 PMID: 40357516

Shimazono, Y. (2007). The state of the international organ trade: A provisional picture based on integration of available information. *Bulletin of the World Health Organization, 85*(12), 955–962. DOI: 10.2471/BLT.06.039370

Shostack, A. (2014). *Threat modeling: Designing for security*. John wiley & sons.

Silva Filho, J. C. L., Braga, C. S. C., & Reboucas, S. M. D. P. (2017). PERCEPTION OF THE BRAZILIAN MANUFACTURING INDUSTRY ABOUT THE MAIN BARRIERS TO INNOVATION/PERCEPCAO DE OBSTACULOS A INOVACAO NA INDUSTRIA A BRASILEIRA DE TRANSFORMACAO. *International journal of innovation, 5*(1), 114-132.

Sinardaily. (2024, March 8). *Malaysian children exposed to pornography as early as nine years old, experts warn*. https://www.sinardaily.my

Singh, C. (2023). European cyber security law in 2023: A review of the advances in the Network and Information Security 2 Directive 2022/2555. *Cyber Security: A Peer-Reviewed Journal, 7*(1), 82-92.

Singh, A. P., Saxena, R., & Saxena, S. (2024). Professional blood donors: Ethical concerns and complexities. *Journal of International Research in Medical and Pharmaceutical Sciences, 19*(1), 17–23. DOI: 10.56557/jirmeps/2024/v19i18603

Sitharamulu, V. (2024). A private Ethereum blockchain for organ donation and traceability. *Procedia / Elsevier*. https://www.sciencedirect.com/science/article/pii/S1110866524001051

Sittig, D. F., Lakhani, P., & Singh, H. (2022). Applying requisite imagination to safeguard electronic health record transitions. *Journal of the American Medical Informatics Association : JAMIA, 29*(5), 1014–1018. DOI: 10.1093/jamia/ocab291 PMID: 35022741

Sonia, B. M., Ngangue, P., Nestor, B., Dieudonné, S., Adnette, A., Leonel, P., & Ly, B. A. (2023). Socioecological analysis of determinants of early adolescent sexuality in Benin: A qualitative study. *The Pan African Medical Journal, 44*(1). Advance online publication. DOI: 10.11604/pamj.2023.44.137.35978 PMID: 37333779

Spanou, D. (2024). The EU Cybersecurity Skills Academy: A silver bullet to address the cyber security skills gap in the European Union?. *Cyber Security: A Peer-Reviewed Journal, 7*(3), 229-236.

Stahl, B. C., & Wright, D. (2018). Ethics and privacy in AI and big data: Implementing responsible research and innovation. *IEEE Security and Privacy, 16*(3), 26–33. DOI: 10.1109/MSP.2018.2701164

Steering Committee of the Istanbul Summit. (2008). Participants in the International Summit on Transplant Tourism and Organ Trafficking Convened by the Transplantation Society and International Society of Nephrology in Istanbul, Turkey, April 30-May 2, 2008. The Declaration of Istanbul on Organ Trafficking and Transplant Tourism. *Transplantation, 86*, 1013–1018.

Storbacka, K., Brodie, R. J., Böhmann, T., Maglio, P. P., & Nenonen, S. (2016). Actor engagement as a microfoundation for value co-creation. *Journal of Business Research, 69*(8), 3008–3017. DOI: 10.1016/j.jbusres.2016.02.034

Streit, S., Johnston-Webber, C., Mah, J., Prionas, A., Wharton, G., Paulino, J., Franca, A., Mossialos, E., & Papalois, V. (2023). Lessons from the Portuguese solid organ donation and transplantation system: Achieving success despite challenging conditions. *Transplant International, 36*, 11008. DOI: 10.3389/ti.2023.11008 PMID: 37305338

Suler, J. (2004). The online disinhibition effect. *Cyberpsychology & Behavior, 7*(3), 321–326. DOI: 10.1089/1094931041291295 PMID: 15257832

Suradi, M. (2019). Bimbang Ketagihan Internet Seks Siber. *Sinar Harian*. Retrieved from https://www.sinarharian.com.my/article/41369/EDISI/Johor/Bimbang-ketagihan-internet-seks-siber, on 14 November 2025.

Tanczer, L. M., Brass, I., & Carr, M. (2018). CSIRT s and global cybersecurity: How technical experts support science diplomacy. *Global Policy, 9*(S3), 60–66. DOI: 10.1111/1758-5899.12625

Tan, S. L., Ng, Y. Y., & Leong, C. P. (2022). Pornography addiction, sexual cognition, and moral disengagement among Malaysian emerging adults. *Journal of Behavioral Sciences, 17*(2), 95–112.

Teixeira, L., Oliveira, T., & Wamba, S. (2020). Empowering collaborations in digital ecosystems: The role of trust, culture, and power. *Information & Management, 57*(3), 103176. Advance online publication. DOI: 10.1016/j.im.2019.103176

The Rakyat Post. (2024, May 2). *Over 900 incest cases reported in Malaysia since 2021*. https://www.therakyatpost.com

The Star. (2025). Education Ministry to increase teaching hours for sex education module in 2027 school curriculum. *The Star*. Retrieved from https://www.thestar.com.my/news/nation/2025/04/29/education-ministry-to-increase-teaching-hours-for-sex-education-module-in-2027, on 12 November 2025.

The Sun Daily. (2024, February 15). *Police report increase in incest cases involving minors*. https://www.thesundaily.my

The Transplant Observatory. (n.d.). *Data charts and tables*. Retrieved October 13, 2025, from https://www.transplant-observatory.org/data-charts-and-tables/

Theron, P., Kott, A., Drasar, M., Rzadca, K., LeBlanc, B., Pihelgas, M., Mancini, L., & Panico, A. (2022). Towards an active, autonomous and intelligent cyber defense of military systems: The NATO AICA reference architecture. *2022 International Conference on Military Communications and Information Systems (ICMCIS), May*, 1–9. DOI: 10.1109/ICMCIS.2018.8398730

Thibodeau, S. (2025). Data Breach Risk Management: Examining Impacts, Strategies, and Cultural Shifts. *SCIENTIA MORALITAS-International Journal of Multidisciplinary Research, 10*(2), 187–206.

Tikk, E. (2018). International cybersecurity agreements: A geopolitical perspective. *Journal of Cyber Policy, 3*(1), 5–26. DOI: 10.1080/23738871.2018.1453229

Tilbury, J., & Flowerday, S. (2024). Humans and Automation: Augmenting Security Operation Centers. *Journal of Cybersecurity and Privacy, 4*(3), 388–409. DOI: 10.3390/jcp4030020

Tirenin, W., & Faatz, D. (2024). A concept for strategic cyber defense. *MILCOM 2024. IEEE Military Communications. Conference Proceedings (Cat. No.99CH36341), 1*(c), 458–463. DOI: 10.1109/MILCOM.1999.822725

Tjoa, E., & Guan, C. (2023). Self reward design with fine-grained interpretability. *Scientific Reports, 13*(1), 1638. DOI: 10.1038/s41598-023-28804-9 PMID: 36717641

Topol, E. J. (2019). High-performance medicine: The convergence of human and artificial intelligence. *Nature Medicine, 25*(1), 44–56. DOI: 10.1038/s41591-018-0300-7 PMID: 30617339

Tounsi, W., & Rais, H. (2018). A survey on technical threat intelligence in the age of sophisticated cyber attacks. *Computers & Security, 72*, 212–233.

Tripathi, G., Ahad, M. A., & Paiva, S. (2020, March). S2HS—A blockchain-based approach for smart healthcare system. [Elsevier.]. *Health Care, 8*(1), 100391. PMID: 31753750

Triplett, W. J. (2024). Artificial intelligence, cybersecurity, and human trafficking networks. *Cybersecurity & Innovative Technology Journal*, *2*(2), 112–125. DOI: 10.53889/citj.v2i2.556

Triplett, W. J. (2024). Cybersecurity vulnerabilities in healthcare: A threat to patient security. *Cybersecurity and Innovative Technology Journal*, *2*(1), 15–25.

Triplett, W. J. (2024). Cybersecurity Vulnerabilities in Healthcare: A Threat to Patient Security. *Cybersecurity and Innovative Technology Journal*, *2*(1), 15–25. DOI: 10.53889/citj.v2i1.333

Trist, E. L., & Bamforth, K. W. (1951). Some social and psychological consequences of the longwall method of coal-getting. *Human Relations*, *4*(1), 3–38. DOI: 10.1177/001872675100400101

Tronto, J. C. (1998). An ethic of care. *Generations: Journal of the American society on Aging, 22*(3), 15-20.

Tuan, D. A. (2024). Bridging the gap between black box AI and clinical practice: Advancing explainable AI for trust, ethics, and personalized healthcare diagnostics. *Preprint.* https://doi.org/DOI: 10.48550/arXiv.XXXX.XXXX

U.S. Congress. (1999). *Gramm–Leach–Bliley Act*, Pub. L. No. 106–102, 113 Stat. 1338.

UNITED NATIONS CONFERENCE ON TRADE AND DEVELOPMENT. (2019). DIGITAL ECONOMY REPORT 2019: Value Creation and Capture - Implications for Developing Countries.

United Nations Office on Drugs and Crime. (2020). Global report on trafficking in persons. https://www.unodc.org/unodc/data-and-analysis/glotip.html

United Nations Office on Drugs. (2024). *Global report on trafficking in persons 2024*. Stylus Publishing, LLC.

UNODC. (2020). in Focus: Trafficking Over the Darknet -. *World Drug Report*, •••, 2020.

UNODC. (2023). *Global report on trafficking in persons*. United Nations.

Van der Zouwen, M., Pahl-Wostl, C., & Craps, M. (2018). The role of joint exercises in collaborative governance of cybersecurity. *Policy and Society*, *37*(4), 529–547. DOI: 10.1080/14494035.2018.1542472

van Kessel, R., Wong, B. L. H., Forman, R., Gabrani, J., & Mossialos, E. (2022). The European Health Data Space fails to bridge digital divides. *bmj, 378.*

Vargo, S. L., & Lusch, R. F. (2004). Evolving to a new dominant logic for marketing. *Journal of Marketing*, *68*(1), 1–17. DOI: 10.1509/jmkg.68.1.1.24036

Vargo, S. L., & Lusch, R. F. (2016). Institutions and axioms: An extension and update of service-dominant logic. *Journal of the Academy of Marketing Science*, *44*(1), 5–23. DOI: 10.1007/s11747-015-0456-3

Vaseashta, A. (2022). *Nexus of Advanced Technology Platforms for Strengthening Cyber-Defense Capabilities*. DOI: 10.3233/NHSDP220003

Verbanas, P. (2025). A Rutgers expert discusses signs of and treatments for technology addiction. *Rutgers University*. https://www.rutgers.edu/news/are-you-addicted-technology

Viecelli, A. K., Gately, R., Barday, Z., Shojai, S., Arruebo, S., Caskey, F. J., Damster, S., Donner, J.-A., Jha, V., Levin, A., Nangaku, M., Saad, S., Tonelli, M., Ye, F., Okpechi, I. G., Bello, A. K., & Johnson, D. W. (2024). Worldwide organization and structures for kidney transplantation services. *Nephrology, Dialysis, Transplantation*, *39*(Suppl. 2), ii26–ii34. DOI: 10.1093/ndt/gfae144 PMID: 39235196

Vila-Garzón, L., & Bacca-Acosta, J. (2020). Value co-creation and co-design in interdisciplinary contexts. *International Journal of Innovation Science*, *12*(3), 287–303. DOI: 10.1108/IJIS-12-2019-0118

Voas, J., & Kshetri, N. (2021). Lost and never found. *Computer*, *54*(07), 12–13. DOI: 10.1109/MC.2021.3055712

Voorberg, W. H., Bekkers, V. J. J. M., & Tummers, L. G. (2015). A systematic review of co-creation and co-production: Embarking on the social innovation journey. *Public Management Review*, *17*(9), 1333–1357. DOI: 10.1080/14719037.2014.930505

Vyas, S., Hannay, J., Bolton, A., & Burnap, P. P. (2023). Automated Cyber Defence: A Review. *Proceedings of the ACM on Measurement and Analysis of Computing Systems*, *37*(4). https://arxiv.org/abs/2303.04926

Wagner, C., Dulaunoy, A., Wagener, G., & Iklody, A. (2019). MISP: The design and implementation of a collaborative threat intelligence sharing platform. *Proceedings of the 2019 ACM SIGSAC Conference on Computer and Communications Security*, 1–10.

Wahl, T. (2024). Europol. In *Research Handbook on EU Criminal Law* (pp. 429–461). Edward Elgar Publishing. DOI: 10.4337/9781800886438.00030

Wairimu, S., & Fritsch, L. (2022, August). Modelling privacy harms of compromised personal medical data-beyond data breach. In *Proceedings of the 17th international conference on availability, reliability and security* (pp. 1-9).

Walsh, K., Pink, E., Ayling, N., Sondergeld, A., Dallaston, E., Tournas, P., Serry, E., Trotter, S., Spanos, T., & Rogic, N. (2022). Best practice framework for online safety education: Results from a rapid review of the international literature, expert review, and stakeholder consultation. *International Journal of Child-Computer Interaction, 33*, 100474. DOI: 10.1016/j.ijcci.2022.100474

Wan Ismail, W. N. H., Ahmad, N., & Hassan, R. (2023). Impact of COVID-19 confinement on domestic sexual abuse in Malaysia. *Asian Social Work and Policy Review, 17*(4), 318–334. 10.xxxx/aswpr.2023.17.4.318

Wan Maizon, W. S. N., Abd Hamid, S. N. F., & Ahmad, Y. (2022). Cybersex Leads To Addiction Epidemic Among Minor: The Analysis of Cause and Effect. *International Journal for Studies on Children, Women, Elderly and Disabled*, 15(1).

Wan Maizon, W. S. N., Abd Hamid, S. N. F., & Ahmad, Y. (2024a). A policy lens on cybersex addiction impacting Malaysian children. *In Navigating the technological tide: The evolution and challenges of business model innovation* (ICBT 2024, Vol. 1082, pp. 47–57). Springer. DOI: 10.1007/978-3-031-67434-1_47

Wan Maizon, W. S. N., Abd Hamid, S. N. F., & Ahmad, Y. (2024b). Cybersex addiction among adolescents: A quantitative analysis of psychological and physical impacts in Peninsular Malaysia. *In Navigating the technological tide: The evolution and challenges of business model innovation* (ICBT 2024, Vol. 1081, pp. 41–50). Springer. DOI: 10.1007/978-3-031-67437-2_41

Wan Maizon, W. S. N., & Abd Hamid, S. N. F. (2024c). Behind the screen: Exploring cybersex addiction as the mediator of factors influencing and causing psychological and physical damage among children in Peninsular Malaysia. In Mansour, N., & Bujosa Vadell, L. M. (Eds.), *Finance and law in the metaverse world* (pp. 1–10). Springer., DOI: 10.1007/978-3-031-67547-8_4

Wan Maizon, W. S. N., Hamid, S. N. F. A., & Ahmad, Y. (2023). Systematic Literature Review on the Consequences of Cybersex Addiction Involving Children. *International Journal of Academic Research in Accounting. Finance and Management Sciences, 13*(2), 1196–1213.

Wang, L., Chen, X., Zhang, L., Li, L., Huang, Y., Sun, Y., & Yuan, X. (2023). Artificial intelligence in clinical decision support systems for oncology. *International Journal of Medical Sciences, 20*(1), 79–88. DOI: 10.7150/ijms.77205 PMID: 36619220

Whittlestone, J., Nyrup, R., Alexandrova, A., & Cave, S. (2019, January). The role and limits of principles in AI ethics: Towards a focus on tensions. In *Proceedings of the 2019 AAAI/ACM Conference on AI, Ethics, and Society* (pp. 195-200). DOI: 10.1145/3306618.3314289

Williams, C. M., Chaturvedi, R., & Chakravarthy, K. (2020). Cybersecurity risks in a pandemic. *Journal of Medical Internet Research, 22*(9), e23692.

Williamson, S. M., & Prybutok, V. (2024). Balancing privacy and progress: A review of privacy challenges, systemic oversight, and patient perceptions in AI-driven healthcare. *Applied Sciences (Basel, Switzerland), 14*(2), 675. DOI: 10.3390/app14020675

Women's Aid Organisation. (2021). Annual report 2021: Domestic and sexual violence in Malaysia during [WAO Malaysia.]. *COVID*, •••, 19.

Women's Aid Organisation. (2022). We must improve maternal, sexual, and reproductive health rights in Malaysia. *Women's Aid Organisation*. Retrieved from https://wao.org.my/we-must-improve-maternal-sexual-and-reproductive-health-rights-in-malaysia/, on 12 November 2025.

World Economic Forum. (2020). *Cyber resilience in the electricity ecosystem: Strengthening cybersecurity collaboration*. World Economic Forum.

World Economic Forum. (2023). *The global risks report 2023* (18th ed.). https://www.weforum.org/reports/global-risks-report-2023/

World Health Organization. (2021). Global strategy on digital health 2020-2025. WHO Press. https://www.who.int/publications/i/item/9789240020924

World Health Organization. (2022). *Global observatory on donation and transplantation*. GODT.

World Health Organization. (2022). *Global strategy on digital health 2020–2025*. WHO.

World Health Organization. (2023). *Human organ and tissue transplantation: Ethical and legal considerations*. WHO.

Wurzenberger, M., Krenn, S., Landauer, M., Skopik, F., Perner, C., Lötjönen, J., Päijänen, J., Gardikis, G., Alabasis, N., Sakerman, L., Omri, K., Röning, J., Halunen, K., Thouvenot, V., Weise, M., Rauber, A., Gkioulos, V., Katsikas, S., Sabetta, L., & Schmitt, C. (2024). NEWSROOM: Towards Automating Cyber Situational Awareness Processes and Tools for Cyber Defence. *Proceedings of the 19th International Conference on Availability, Reliability and Security,* July 2024, 1–11. DOI: 10.1145/3664476.3670914

Wu, Z., Pan, S., Chen, F., Long, G., Zhang, C., & Yu, P. S. (2020). A comprehensive survey on graph neural networks. *IEEE Transactions on Neural Networks and Learning Systems*, *32*(1), 4–24. DOI: 10.1109/TNNLS.2020.2978386

Xie, J. (2024). Peer pressure influences adolescents' internet addiction. *Interdisciplinary Humanities and Communication Studies*, 1(9).

Xin, M., Xing, J., Pengfei, W., Houru, L., Mengcheng, W., & Hong, Z. (2018). Online activities, prevalence of internet addiction and risk factors related to family and school among adolescents in China. *Addictive Behaviors Reports*, *7*, 14–18. DOI: 10.1016/j.abrep.2017.10.003 PMID: 29450251

Xin, Y., Kong, L., Liu, Z., Chen, Y., Li, Y., Zhu, H., Gao, M., Hou, H., & Wang, C. (2018). Machine learning and deep learning methods for cybersecurity. *IEEE Access : Practical Innovations, Open Solutions*, *6*, 35365–35381. DOI: 10.1109/ACCESS.2018.2836950

Xu, L. (2025, June). Trends in US Healthcare Data Breaches. In *2025 IEEE International Conference on AI.*

Xu, M., David, J. M., & Kim, S. H. (2018). The fourth industrial revolution: Opportunities and challenges. *International Journal of Financial Research*, *9*(2), 90–95. DOI: 10.5430/ijfr.v9n2p90

Xu, X., Han, W., & Liu, Q. (2023). Peer pressure and adolescent mobile social media addiction: Moderation analysis of self-esteem and self-concept clarity. *Frontiers in Public Health*, *11*, 1115661. DOI: 10.3389/fpubh.2023.1115661 PMID: 37113179

Yang, Y., Yang, L., Yang, M., Yu, H., Zhu, G., Chen, Z., & Chen, L. (2019). Dark Web forum Correlation Analysis Research. Proceedings of 2019 IEEE 8th Joint international information Technology and Artificial intelligence Conference, ITAIC 2019, Itaic, 1216–1220. Https://Doi.Org/10.1109/ITAIC.2019.8785760

Yang, Q., Liu, Y., Chen, T., & Tong, Y. (2019). Federated machine learning: Concept and applications. *ACM Transactions on Intelligent Systems and Technology*, *10*(2), 12. Advance online publication. DOI: 10.1145/3298981

Yao, A. C. (1982). Protocols for secure computations. In *Proceedings of the 23rd Annual Symposium on Foundations of Computer Science* (pp. 160-164). IEEE. DOI: 10.1109/SFCS.1982.38

Yates, P. (2020). Sexual education and the prevention of incestuous abuse: A review of international best practices. *International Journal of Child Protection, 11*(2), 45–60.

Yeboah-Ofori, A., & Opoku-Boateng, F. A. (2023). Mitigating cybercrimes in an evolving organizational landscape. *Continuity & Resilience Review, 5*(1), 53–78. DOI: 10.1108/CRR-09-2022-0017

Zakaria, E., Kamarudin, N. N., Mohamad, Z. S., Suzuki, M., Rathakrishnan, B., Bikar Singh, S. S., & Kamaluddin, M. R. (2022). The role of family life and the influence of peer pressure on delinquency: Qualitative evidence from Malaysia. *International Journal of Environmental Research and Public Health, 19*(13), 7846. DOI: 10.3390/ijerph19137846 PMID: 35805504

Zattoni, F., Gül, M., Soligo, M., Morlacco, A., Motterle, G., Collavino, J., Barneschi, A., Roscigno, M., Chirico, M., & Ficarra, V. (2021). The impact of COVID-19 pandemic on pornography habits: A global analysis of Google Trends. *International Journal of Impotence Research, 33*(5), 824–831. DOI: 10.1038/s41443-020-00380-w PMID: 33249423

Zhang, H., & Zou, F. (2020). A Survey of the Dark Web and Dark Market Research. 2020 IEEE 6th international Conference on Computer and Communications, ICCC 2020, 1694–1705. Https://Doi.Org/10.1109/ICCC51575.2020.9345271

Zhang, Y., Zheng, Y., Wang, D., Gu, X., Zyphur, M. J., Xiao, L., ... & Deng, Y. (2025). Shedding Light on the Black Box: Integrating Prediction Models and Explainability Using Explainable Machine Learning. *Organizational Research Methods*, 10944281251323248.

Zhang, Y., Hou, Z., Wu, S., Li, X., Hao, M., & Wu, X. (2022). The relationship between internet addiction and aggressive behavior among adolescents during the COVID-19 pandemic: Anxiety as a mediator. *Acta Psychologica, 227*, 103612. DOI: 10.1016/j.actpsy.2022.103612 PMID: 35598380

Zhang, Y., Wang, L., & Li, J. (2023). Privacy enhancement methods for federated learning in healthcare systems: A comprehensive review. *International Journal of Environmental Research and Public Health, 20*(15), 6539. DOI: 10.3390/ijerph20156539 PMID: 37569079

Zhao, B., & Jin, C. (2023). Peer relationships and adolescent internet addiction: Variable-centered and person-centered approaches. *Children and Youth Services Review*, *155*, 107243. DOI: 10.1016/j.childyouth.2023.107243

Zheng, Z., Xie, S., Dai, H. N., Chen, X., & Wang, H. (2018). Blockchain challenges and opportunities: A survey. *International Journal of Web and Grid Services*, *14*(4), 352–375. DOI: 10.1504/IJWGS.2018.095647

Zhu, M., Sali, R., Baba, F., Khasawneh, H., Ryndin, M., Leveillee, R. J., & Zhang, D. Y. (2024). Artificial intelligence in pathologic diagnosis, prognosis and prediction of prostate cancer. *American Journal of Clinical and Experimental Urology*, *12*(4), 200–215. DOI: 10.62347/JSAE9732 PMID: 39308594

About the Contributors

Ahgalya Subbiah is a Senior Lecturer at the Faculty of Information Sciences and Engineering, Management and Science University (MSU), Malaysia. She holds a PhD in Information Systems from Universiti Teknologi Malaysia (UTM) and brings over two decades of experience in higher education, research, and professional training. Her academic work focuses on human-centred information systems, digital innovation, and the development of socio-technical solutions that address real-world challenges across communities and organizations. Her research interests span areas such as smart cities, sustainability-driven technologies, healthcare informatics, and community-oriented digital ecosystems. She has contributed to numerous peer-reviewed journals, IEEE conferences, and international academic publications, with research exploring the integration of emerging technologies such as Internet of Things (IoT), intelligent systems, and digital platforms for sustainable and inclusive development. Dr. Ahgalya is also actively engaged in supervising postgraduate and undergraduate research projects, mentoring students in areas including artificial intelligence applications, digital systems development, environmental technology, and data-driven solutions. Several student projects under her supervision have received recognition at institutional and international innovation exhibitions, including awards related to Sustainable Development Goal (SDG) initiatives. Beyond her academic and research contributions, Dr. Ahgalya leads and participates in community-based initiatives that connect technology with social and environmental impact. Through programs such as *MyBlueForest* and other sustainability-focused activities, she promotes environmental awareness, digital empowerment, and collaborative engagement between academia and local communities. Her work reflects a strong commitment to using technology and research as tools for meaningful societal progress and sustainable development.

Asif Iqbal Hajamydeen is a seasoned cybersecurity expert specialising in anomaly-based intrusion detection systems, computer security, and data mining within the expansive domains of cybersecurity and computer networks. With over 18 years of dedicated service at Management & Science University (MSU), Dr. Asif Iqbal has become a cornerstone of the Faculty of Information Sciences and Engineering, where he currently serves as an Associate Professor. Throughout his career, Dr. Asif Iqbal has made significant strides in both academic and applied cybersecurity, producing impactful research that addresses today's most pressing digital security challenges. His scholarly output includes numerous publications, book chapters, and collaborative research on advanced security frameworks, machine learning innovations, and IoT applications. His work is widely recognized, with 580 Google Scholar citations and an h-index of 15, underscoring his influence in the field. Dr. Asif Iqbal's dedication to academic excellence has earned him prestigious accolades, such as the ITEX medals and the TEA President's Award. As a committed mentor and educator, Dr. Asif Iqbal supervises postgraduate students at the Master's and PhD levels, guiding them in pioneering research across various subfields of computer security and network safety. His role also extends to curriculum development and hands-on training in cybersecurity, where he actively integrates practical knowledge into his teaching. Notably, he has contributed to SOC (Security Operations Center) management, implementing innovative AI-driven cybersecurity projects that blend theoretical frameworks with real-world applications. Dr. Asif Iqbal's dual commitment to research excellence and educational mentorship makes him a sought-after leader in the academic and professional cybersecurity communities.

Adeleke Imran Ademola a Professor of Information Systems in the Department of Computer Science, Lagos state University of Education. He holds a Bachelor degree in Computer Science, M.Sc in Computer Science, M.Ed in Educational Technology and his burning passion to continually broaden his knowledge took him to University of Technology, Malaysia where he bagged a PhD in Information Systems. He has led in different capacities in both academics and administration. He served as Head, Department of Computer Science Education. His current research area is in the field of Human Computer Interaction, Information Technology Planning and Management and Software Engineering. He is currently the Ag. Dean, College of Information and Technology Education. He is also a member of University Senate Business Committee. He is a member of Association for Information Systems (AIS), a member of Nigeria Computer Society (NCS) and Computer Professional Registration Council of Nigeria (CPN)

***

Siti Nur Fathanah Abd Hamid earned her Doctorate in Administrative Science from Universiti Teknologi MARA (UiTM) in 2020, as well as a Master's degree in Administrative Science and the Outstanding Researcher Award from the same university in 2017. She is actively involved in research, innovation, and publications related to sociology, including policy analysis, social issues, and child development. Since 2018, she has been serving as a lecturer at the Faculty of Administrative Science and Policy Studies, Universiti Teknologi MARA (UiTM), Seremban Campus. Throughout her academic career, she has been actively supervising postgraduate students, engaging in national research and university internal grants, leading consultancy projects, producing high-impact publications, and serving as a reviewer for journal articles.

Alli Abdurazaq is an educator, researcher, and artificial intelligence specialist with over nine years of experience in teaching, research, and academic administration. He holds a Ph.D. in ICT Education with a specialization in Artificial Intelligence, where his research focuses on the development of Harlybot; an AI-powered learning assistant designed to enhance retention, motivation, attitude, and critical thinking among learners in ICT and STEM disciplines. He is a faculty member of the Cybersecurity department at Fountain University, Osogbo, Nigeria. He holds a master's degree in ICT Education (Artificial Intelligence specialization) and has served in various academic and administrative roles, including Graduate Assistant and Data Analyst at Lagos State University of Education, Oto-Ijanikin, and Education Officer with the Lagos State Teaching Service Commission. His research interests span artificial intelligence in education, mobile and adaptive systems, human-computer interaction, and the Culturo-Techno-Contextual Approach (CTCA) to learning. Abdurazaq has authored multiple peer-reviewed publications, including papers published in the Nigerian Association for Educational Media and Technology (NAEMT) and the National Association for Research in Science Teaching (NARST) journals. Beyond academia, he coordinates the Oto-Awori chapter of the Lagos Community Youth Development Initiative (LCYDI) and leads several innovation-driven initiatives under Depossibilities Integrated Solutions, where he serves as an ICT consultant and business strategist. He is passionate about leveraging AI and emerging technologies to advance digital literacy, inclusive education, and sustainable youth development across Africa. Goal oriented I self motivated I team player IICT Instructor I vast interest in AI Expert systems.

Asmaa Alhakimi obtained her Diploma in Computer Programming in 2006 from the University of Science and Technology in Sanaa, Yemen. She earned her bachelor's degree in computer studies in 2008 from Northumbria University in Newcastle, UK, followed by a master's degree in software engineering in 2011 from

Staffordshire University, UK. She completed her Ph.D. in Software Engineering at Universiti Putra Malaysia. Dr. Asma'a has extensive experience in the networking field and served as a lecturer at Asia Pacific University (APU) in Malaysia for five years. She is recognized for her expertise in conducting industrial cybersecurity training. Her research interests encompass Cybersecurity, Reverse Engineering, Software Engineering, and Artificial Intelligence. In addition to her teaching and research responsibilities, Dr. Asma'a is an Editorial Board Member of the American Journal of Electrical and Computer Engineering (AJECE) and is affiliated with the Association for Computing Machinery (ACM) and IEEE Access. Currently, she is a senior lecturer and researcher at MSU University, where she leads a research group focused on cybersecurity and forensics. Dr. Asma'a is dedicated to her work and is known for her innovative contributions across various domains. She has a strong publication record in cybersecurity and smart cities and has participated in an international exhibition showcasing a cybersecurity project that received significant recognition. Her numerous publications and awards highlight advancements in smart cities and cybersecurity.

Sumathi Balakrishnan holds a Master of Software Engineering from the University of Malaya, Malaysia, and a Bachelor of Computer Science from the University Putra Malaysia. She has taught various courses at Taylor's University, including Capstone Project, Internet of Things, Industrial Project, and Computer Architecture and Organization. Additionally, the author has authored several articles and book chapters related to smart city technologies, IoT, and user-centered design. She has been involved in multiple research projects focusing on IoT, smart city technologies, EEG signal processing and elderly care. She has also received several awards and recognition for their innovations and research efforts. Furthermore, the author holds professional memberships in Lembaga Teknologis Malaysia (MBOT) from 2022 to 2023, was also a member of IEEE from 2018 to 2019, and held a role of committee member in the IEEE Consumer Electronics Society Malaysia from 2018 to 2019.

Alice A. Bamigbola, CLN is a Senior Lecturer at the Department of School Library and Media Technology, University of Ibadan, Nigeria. She has a Bachelor degree in Library and Information Studies, Master in Personnel Psychology (Ibadan), Master in Digital Library Learning (DILL) (Oslo) and Ph.D in Library and Information Studies from the Department of Library, Archival and Information Studies, University of Ibadan, Nigeria. Her research focus includes Digital Libraries, Open Access Repositories, Information and knowledge management, Media and Information literacies and Emerging Technologies in School librarianship. Alice is an Erasmus Mundus Scholar.

Omar D Camara is a lecturer in the Computer Science and Information Technology Department at The University of Applied Science Engineering and Technology (USET) in Kanifing Industrial Estate, Banjul, The Gambia. He has more than six years of teaching experience, including three years lecturing in the field of Computer Science and related courses. He graduated from Kharkiv National University of Radio Electronics, Kharkov, Ukraine with a Bachelor of Science in Computer Engineering and is currently pursuing a Master of Science in ICT Education at Lagos State University (LASU), Lagos, Nigeria.

Nibedita Das is an accomplished academician serving as an Associate Professor in the Department of Information and Communication Technology at Tecnia Institute of Advanced Studies, Delhi, India. She holds a Ph.D. from IRINS–IIT Dhanbad and is certified by IIM Ahmedabad in Renewable Energy and Leadership Skills. With over 13.8 years of academic and research experience, she has authored and co-authored around 22 research papers, book chapters, and articles in reputed international and Scopus-indexed journals. She serves as an Editor for the IIP Series Futuristic Trends in Renewable & Sustainable Energy (USA) and is a fellow of IEEE Access (USA). Dr. Das has been recognized with several prestigious awards, including Young Achiever (2020), Women Mobilizer (2024), and the Rajya Puraskar Award (1996). She holds patents in India, the UK, and South Africa and has successfully completed an AI and ML-based Solar Energy Harvesting project worth 3 lakh in 2024. Her research interests span Power Electronics, Control Systems, AI, ML, Deep Learning, NLP, Renewable Energy, and semiconductor-integrated software systems for urban mobility.

Deepa R is an Assistant Professor in Computing Technology with over 15 years of academic experience. Her research interests include Artificial Intelligence and Machine Learning, and she actively mentors student projects.She is also involved in academic advising and departmental responsibilities, contributing to teaching and research excellence.

Ashlah Ibrahim is currently pursuing her PhD in Islamic Management at the Academy of Contemporary Islamic Studies. She previously completed her Master of Islamic Management and Development at Universiti Sains Malaysia, following her Bachelor of Syariah from Kolej Universiti Insaniah. Her academic and professional focus centres on research and scholarly publications in Islamic Studies, Islamic Management, and the wider social sciences. Since 2018, she has been serving as a lecturer at Management and Science University, Shah Alam, actively contributing to teaching, research, and academic development initiatives.

Sharada K A has done her B. E, M. Tech, PhD in Computer Science and Engineering. Her Doctoral research focused on energy conservation in Wireless Sensor Network and has 24+ years of teaching and research experience. She has published several papers in peered reviewed international journals, registered many Design Grant Patents, supervising many research scholars under Visveswaraya Technological University, Karnataka. Currently working as Professor in Department of Computer Science and Engineering, HKBK college of Engineering, Affiliated to VTU, Bengaluru-45. Her current research interests include Sensor Data Processing, IOT, Artificial Intelligence, Machine Learning and Deep Learning Techniques.

Prajna K B is currently working as an Assistant Professor in the Department of Electronics and Communication Engineering at NMIT, Bengaluru. She is pursuing her Ph.D. at the Energy Institute Bengaluru, RGIPT, focusing on the development of a fire suppression system for electric two-wheelers. Her research interests include machine learning, battery management systems, and vehicle safety applications. She has taught diverse subjects such as Data Analytics, Python Programming, and Digital System Design, and is passionate about integrating technology and innovation in engineering education

Niyazi Karabulut is an assistant professor in the department of Political Science and Public Administration at Necmettin Erbakan University in Konya, Türkiye. After his bachelor's degree in public administration from the Middle East Technical University (METU), he completed his master's degree at Necmettin Erbakan University in 2019. His Ph.D. study at METU on the relationship between e-participation and digital exclusion in Türkiye was concluded in 2025. His research interests include e-participation, open data, and AI and technology in government studies, and he is fluent in Turkish and English.

L.K Shoba received her B.E degree in Electronics and Communication Engineering from Noorul Islam college of Engineering, Kumaracoil, Manonmanium sundaranar university, India in 2003. She has received her M.Tech. degree in Information Technology from Madras Institute of Technology, Chennai, Anna University, India in 2009. She holds a Ph.D degree in Information and communication Engineering from Anna University, India in 2023. She is in teaching profession since June 2009. Currently she is working as Assistant Professor in the Department of Computing Technologies, SRM Institute of Science and Technology, kattankulathur, Her research area of interest is Artificial Intelligence and Machine Learning.

Naveen Nandal is a distinguished academic and research professional with over 12 years of experience in teaching, research, and analytics. Currently an Associate Professor at DIHE, Delhi, she has published over 80 research papers, authored six books, and holds several patents. She has contributed extensively to Scopus-indexed, ABDC, WOS, and peer-reviewed journals. She has served as Analytics Area Chair and Research & Publication Head, actively involved in curriculum design, faculty development, and research guidance. Dr. Nandal is a reviewer for Sage and Emerald publications, a founding member of the Research India Foundation, and has extensive experience delivering impactful training and mentoring in marketing, human resource management, and data analytics domains

Wan Saidatul Nasuha Wan Maizon obtained her Doctorate in Administrative Science from Universiti Teknologi MARA (UiTM) in 2025. She also holds a Bachelor of Administrative Science (2021) and a Diploma in Public Administration (2019) from the same institution. Her academic and professional pursuits are centered on research, innovation, and publications in the field of sociology, with a particular focus on social issues and child development. Since 2023, she has been serving as a lecturer at Management and Science University, Shah Alam. Throughout her academic journey, she has consistently contributed to high-impact publications, actively participated in conferences and innovation initiatives, and served as a peer reviewer for journal articles.

Thivya Rajkumar is an Assistant Professor in the Department of Artificial Intelligence and Data Science at Velalar College of Engineering and Technology (Autonomous), Erode, Tamil Nadu, India. She holds a B.E. in Information Technology and an M.Tech in Information Technology. Her expertise is in Data Science, Cybersecurity, and Software Engineering. She has attended many faculty development programs, workshops, and training sessions to improve her skills. She mentors students in research and innovative project development. She also serves as an Innovation Ambassador in the Institution's Innovation Council (IIC) and contributes to the Entrepreneurship Development Cell (EDC), encouraging students in innovation and entrepreneurship.

K. Sailaja Kumar is an Associate Professor at the School of Computer Science and Engineering, RV University, Bengaluru, with over 26 years of academic and 2 years of industry experience. She holds a Ph.D. in Computer Applications from Visvesvaraya Technological University and an M.Phil. in Computer Science. Her areas of expertise include Data Science, Artificial Intelligence, Machine Learning, and Immersive Technologies (AR/VR). Dr. Sailaja has authored numerous research papers in reputed international journals and conferences and contributed to book chapters in emerging fields such as Natural Language Processing and Intelligent Healthcare Systems. She has also filed a patent on "Enhancing Teaching and Learning Effectiveness through Machine Learning-Driven Pedagogy." As the

Coordinator for the Center of Excellence in Immersive AR and VR Technologies at RV University, she has led several interdisciplinary projects and faculty development programs, fostering innovation in education and technology integration.

Swathy R (Swathy Ramasamy) received B.E. Information Technology from Periyar Maniammai College of Technology for Women affiliated to Bharathidasan University, Thanjavur, Tamil Nadu in 2004 and M.Tech. Information Technology from Sathyabama University, Chennai, Tamil Nadu in 2006. She holds a Ph.D. in Information and Communication from Anna University, where she developed a deep passion for research in the domain of Cloud Computing. Her current research interests include Cloud Computing, Data Analytics and IoT and she is dedicated to pushing the boundaries of knowledge in these areas. In addition to her research, Swathy has over 17 years of teaching experience in a reputed university, and she is currently working as Assistant Professor in SRM University in the Department of Networking and Communications.

Varadharajan Bhoopathy is a Professor at Sree Rama Engineering College. He holds a Ph.D. in Information and Communication Engineering from Anna University and has over 16 years of academic experience. Specializing in wireless sensor networks and IoT, he has published numerous research papers and holds several international patents. Dr. Bhoopathy is a recipient of prestigious awards for his contributions to education and research. His commitment to academia continues to drive innovation and excellence in the field of computer science.

Muhammad Haziq Zaini completed his Doctorate in Administrative Science at Universiti Teknologi MARA (UiTM) in 2023, following his Master's degree in the same field from the same institution in 2018. His research interests are primarily focused on sociology, including areas such as policy analysis, social issues, and child development. He has been a senior lecturer at Management and Science University (MSU) in Shah Alam since 2024, where he continues to make significant contributions to both academic research and innovation. He has actively published in high-impact journals, participated in national and international conferences, and served as a peer reviewer for various academic publications. His work reflects a commitment to advancing knowledge in the social sciences and supporting academic excellence in his field.

Index

G

H

I

M

O

P

R

S

T

V

www.ingramcontent.com/pod-product-compliance
Lightning Source LLC
LaVergne TN
LVHW080911300926
849162LV00003B/638